*What They Said
in 1989*

What They Said
In 1989

The Yearbook Of World Opinion

Compiled and Edited by

ALAN F. PATER

and

JASON R. PATER

MONITOR BOOK COMPANY

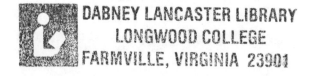

To

The Newsmakers of the World . . .

May they never be at a loss for words

Preface to the First Edition (1969)

Words can be powerful or subtle, humorous or maddening. They can be vigorous or feeble, lucid or obscure, inspiring or despairing, wise or foolish, hopeful or pessimistic . . . they can be fearful or confident, timid or articulate, persuasive or perverse, honest or deceitful. As tools at a speaker's command, words can be used to reason, argue, discuss, cajole, plead, debate, declaim, threaten, infuriate, or appease; they can harangue, flourish, recite, preach, discourse, stab to the quick, or gently sermonize.

When casually spoken by a stage or film star, words can go beyond the press-agentry and make-up facade and reveal the inner man or woman. When purposefully uttered in the considered phrasing of a head of state, words can determine the destiny of millions of people, resolve peace or war, or chart the course of a nation on whose direction the fate of the entire world may depend.

Until now, the *copia verborum* of well-known and renowned public figures—the doctors and diplomats, the governors and generals, the potentates and presidents, the entertainers and educators, the bishops and baseball players, the jurists and journalists, the authors and attorneys, the congressmen and chairmen-of-the-board—whether enunciated in speeches, lectures, interviews, radio and television addresses, news conferences, forums, symposiums, town meetings, committee hearings, random remarks to the press, or delivered on the floors of the United States Senate and House of Representatives or in the parliaments and palaces of the world—have been dutifully reported in the media, then filed away and, for the most part, forgotten.

The editors of *WHAT THEY SAID* believe that consigning such a wealth of thoughts, ideas, doctrines, opinions and philosophies to interment in the morgues and archives of the Fourth Estate is lamentable and unnecessary. Yet the media, in all their forms, are constantly engulfing us in a profusion of endless and increasingly voluminous news reports. One is easily disposed to disregard or forget the stimulating discussion of critical issues embodied in so many of the utterances of those who make the news and, in their respective fields, shape the events throughout the world. The conclusion is therefore a natural and compelling one: the educator, the public official, the business executive, the statesman, the philosopher—everyone who has a stake in the complex, often confusing trends of our times—should have material of this kind readily available.

These, then, are the circumstances under which *WHAT THEY SAID* was conceived. It is the culmination of a year of listening to the people in the public eye; a year of scrutinizing, monitoring, reviewing, judging, deciding—a year during which the editors resurrected from almost certain oblivion those quintessential elements of the year's *spoken* opinion which, in their judgment, demanded preservation in book form.

WHAT THEY SAID is a pioneer in its field. Its *raison d'etre* is the firm conviction that presenting, each year, the highlights of vital and interesting views from the lips of prominent people on virtually every aspect of contemporary civilization fulfills the need to give the *spoken* word the permanence and lasting value of the *written* word. For, if it is true that a picture is worth 10,000 words, it is equally true that a verbal conclusion, an apt quote or a candid comment by a person of fame or influence can have more significance and can provide more understanding than an entire page of summary in a standard work of reference.

The editors of *WHAT THEY SAID* did not, however, design their book for researchers and scholars alone. One of the failings of the conventional reference work is that it is blandly written and referred to primarily for facts and figures, lacking inherent "interest value." *WHAT THEY SAID*, on the other hand, was planned for sheer enjoyment and pleasure, for searching glimpses into the lives and thoughts of the world's celebrities, as well as for serious study, intellectual reflection and the philosophical contemplation of our multifaceted life and mores. Furthermore, those pressed for time, yet anxious to know what the newsmakers have been saying, will welcome the short excerpts which will make for quick, intermittent reading—and rereading. And, of course, the topical classifications, the speakers' index, the subject index, the place and date information—documented and authenticated and easily located—will supply a rich fund of hitherto not readily obtainable reference and statistical material.

Finally, the reader will find that the editors have eschewed trite comments and cliches, tedious and boring. The selected quotations, each standing on its own, are pertinent, significant, stimulating—above all, relevant to today's world, expressed in the speakers' own words. And they will, the editors feel, be even more relevant tomorrow. They will be re-examined and reflected upon in the future by men and women eager to learn from the past. The prophecies, the promises, the "golden dreams," the boastings and rantings, the bluster, the bravado, the pleadings and representations of those whose voices echo in these pages (and in those to come) should provide a rare and unique history lesson. The positions held by these luminaries, in their respective callings, are such that what they say today may profoundly affect the future as well as the present, and so will be of lasting importance and meaning.

ALAN F. PATER
JASON R. PATER

Beverly Hills, California

Table of Contents

PART THREE: GENERAL

Editorial Treatment

ORGANIZATION OF MATERIAL

Special attention has been given to the arrangement of the book—from the major divisions down to the individual categories and speakers—the objective being a logical progression of related material, as follows:

(A) The categories are arranged alphabetically within each of three major sections:

Part One:	"National Affairs"
Part Two:	"International"
Part Three:	"General"

In this manner, the reader can quickly locate quotations pertaining to particular fields of interest (see also *Indexing*). It should be noted that some quotations contain a number of thoughts or ideas—sometimes on different subjects—while some are vague as to exact subject matter and thus do not fit clearly into a specific topic classification. In such cases, the judgment of the Editors has determined the most appropriate category.

(B) Within each category the speakers are in alphabetical order by surname, following alphabetization practices used in the speaker's country of origin.

(C) Where there are two or more quotations by one speaker within the same category, they appear chronologically by date spoken or date of source.

SPEAKER IDENTIFICATION

(A) The occupation, profession, rank, position or title of the speaker is given as it was *at the time the statement was made* (except when the speaker's relevant identification is in the past, in which case he is shown as "former"). Thus, due to possible changes in status during the year, a speaker may be shown with different identifications in various parts of the book, or even within the same category.

(B) In the case of a speaker who holds more than one position simultaneously, the judgment of the Editors has determined the most appropriate identification to use with a specific quotation.

(C) The nationality of a speaker is given when it will help in identifying the speaker or when it is relevant to the quotation.

THE QUOTATIONS

The quoted material selected for inclusion in this book is shown as it appeared in the source, except as follows:

(A) *Ellipses* have been inserted wherever the Editors have deleted extraneous words or overly long passages within the quoted material used. In no way has the meaning or intention of the quotations been altered. *Ellipses* are also used where they appeared in the source.

(B) *Punctuation and spelling* have been altered by the Editors where they were obviously incorrect in the source, or to make the quotations more intelligible, or to conform to the general style used throughout this book. Again, meaning and intention of the quotations have not been changed.

(C) *Brackets* ([ ]) indicate material inserted by the Editors or by the source to either correct obvious errors or to explain or clarify what the speaker is saying. In some instances, bracketed material may replace quoted material for sake of clarity.

(D) *Italics* either appeared in the original source or were added by the Editors where emphasis is clearly desirable.

Except for the above instances, the quoted material used has been printed verbatim, as reported by the source (even if the speaker made factual errors or was awkward in his choice of words).

Special care has been exercised to make certain that each quotation stands on its own and is not taken "out of context." The Editors, however, cannot be responsible for errors made by the original source, i.e., incorrect reporting, mis-quotations, or errors in interpretation.

DOCUMENTATION AND SOURCES

Documentation (circumstance, place, date) of each quotation is provided as fully as could be obtained, and the sources are furnished for all quotations. In some instances, no documentation details were available; in those cases, only the source is given. Following are the sequence and style used for this information:

Circumstance of quotation, place, date/Name of source, date:section (if applicable), page number.

Example: *Before the Senate, Washington, Dec. 4/The Washington Post, 12-5:(A)13.*

The above example indicates that the quotation was delivered before the Senate in Washington on December 4. It was taken for *WHAT THEY SAID* from *The Washington Post*, issue of December 5, section A, page 13. (When a newspaper publishes more than one edition on the same date, it should be noted that page numbers may vary from edition to edition.)

(A) When the source is a television or radio broadcast, the name of the network or local station is indicated, along with the date of the broadcast (obviously, page and section information does not apply).

(B) An asterisk (*) before the (/) in the documentation indicates that the quoted material was written rather than spoken. Although the basic policy of *WHAT THEY SAID* is to use only *spoken* statements, there are occasions when written statements are considered by the Editors to be important enough to be included. These occasions are rare and usually involve Presidential messages and statements released to the press and other such documents attributed to persons in high government office.

INDEXING

(A) The *Index to Speakers* is keyed to the page number. (For alphabetization practices, see *Organization of Material*, paragraph B.)

(B) The *Index to Subjects* is keyed to both the page number and the quotation number on the page (thus, 210:3 indicates quotation number 3 on page 210); the quotation number appears at the right corner of each quotation.

(C) To locate quotations on a particular subject, regardless of the speaker, turn to the appropriate category (see *Table of Contents*) or use the detailed *Index to Subjects*.

(D) To locate all quotations by a particular speaker, regardless of subject, use the *Index to Speakers*.

(E) To locate quotations by a particular speaker on a particular subject, turn to the appropriate category and then to that person's quotations within the category.

(F) The reader will find that the basic categorization format of *WHAT THEY SAID* is itself a useful subject index, inasmuch as related quotations are grouped together by their respective categories. All aspects of journalism, for example, are relevant to each other; thus, the section *Journalism* embraces all phases of the news media. Similarly, quotations pertaining to the U.S. President, Congress, etc., are in the section *Government*.

MISCELLANEOUS

(A) Except where otherwise indicated or obviously to the contrary, all universities, organizations and business firms mentioned in this book are in the United States; similarly, references made to "national," "Federal," "this country," "the nation," etc., refer to the United States.

(B) In most cases, organizations whose names end with "of the United States" are Federal government agencies.

SELECTION OF CATEGORIES

The selected categories reflect, in the Editors' opinion, the most widely discussed public-interest subjects, those which readily fall into the over-all sphere of "current events." They represent topics continuously covered by the mass media because of their inherent importance to the changing world scene. Most of the categories are permanent; they appear in each annual edition of *WHAT THEY SAID*. However, because of the transient character of some subjects, there may be categories which appear one year and may not be repeated the next.

SELECTION OF SPEAKERS

The following persons are always considered eligible for inclusion in *WHAT THEY SAID*: top-level officials of all branches of national, state and local governments (both U.S. and foreign), including all United States Senators and Representatives; top-echelon military officers; college and university presidents, chancellors and professors; chairmen and presidents of major corporations; heads of national public-oriented organizations and associations; national and internationally known diplomats; recognized celebrities from the entertainment and literary spheres and the arts generally; sports figures of national stature; commentators on the world scene who are recognized as such and who command the attention of the mass media.

The determination of what and who are "major" and "recognized" must, necessarily, be made by the Editors of *WHAT THEY SAID* based on objective personal judgment.

Also, some persons, while not generally recognized as prominent or newsworthy, may have neverthe-less attracted an unusual amount of attention in connection with an important issue or event. These people, too, are considered for inclusion, depending upon the specific circumstance.

SELECTION OF QUOTATIONS

The quotations selected for inclusion in *WHAT THEY SAID* obviously represent a decided minority of the seemingly endless volume of quoted material appearing in the media each year. The process of selecting is scrupulously objective insofar as the partisan views of the Editors are concerned (see *About Fairness*, below). However, it is clear that the Editors must decide which quotations *per se* are suitable for inclusion, and in doing so look for comments that are aptly stated, offer insight into the subject being discussed, or into the speaker, and provide—for today as well as for future reference—a thought which readers will find useful for understanding the issues and the personalities that make up a year on this planet.

ABOUT FAIRNESS

The Editors of *WHAT THEY SAID* understand the necessity of being impartial when compiling a book of this kind. As a result, there has been no bias in the selection of the quotations, the choice of speakers or the manner of editing. Relevance of the statements and the status of the speakers are the exclusive criteria for inclusion, without any regard whatsoever to the personal beliefs and views of the Editors. Furthermore, every effort has been made to include a multiplicity of opinions and ideas from a wide cross-section of speakers on each topic. Nevertheless, should there appear to be, on some contro-versial issues, a majority of material favoring one point of view over another, it is simply the result of there having been more of those views expressed during the year, reported by the media and objectively con-sidered suitable by the Editors of *WHAT THEY SAID* (see *Selection of Quotations*, above). Also, since persons in politics and government account for a large percentage of the speakers in *WHAT THEY SAID*, there may exist a heavier weight of opinion favoring the philosophy of those in office at the time, whether in the United States Congress, the Administration, or in foreign capitals. This is natural and to be expected and should not be construed as a reflection of agreement or disagreement with that philosophy on the part of the Editors of *WHAT THEY SAID*.

Abbreviations

The following are abbreviations used by the speakers in this volume. Rather than defining them each time they appear in the quotations, this list will facilitate reading and avoid unnecessary repetition.

ABM:	anti-ballistic missile
ABT:	American Ballet Theatre
ACT:	American College Test
AIDS:	acquired immune deficiency syndrome
ANC:	African National Congress
AP:	Associated Press
APR:	*The American Poetry Review*
ASW:	anti-submarine warfare
CEO:	chief executive officer
CIA:	Central Intelligence Agency
CPSU:	Communist Party of the Soviet Union
D.C.:	District of Columbia
DH:	designated hitter
DOD:	Department of Defense
EC:	European Community
EMS:	European Monetary System
FAA:	Federal Aviation Administration
FBI:	Federal Bureau of Investigation
MFLN:	Farabundo Marti National Liberation Front (El Salvador)
GDR:	German Democratic Republic (East Germany)
GE:	General Electric Company
GM:	General Motors Corporation
HUD:	Department of Housing and Urban Development
ICBM:	intercontinental ballistic missile
ICU:	intensive-care unit
INF:	intermediate-range nuclear forces
IOC:	International Olympic Committee
IRA:	individual retirement arrangement
KGB:	Soviet secret police
KKK:	Ku Klux Klan
LBO:	leverage buyout

MBA:	Master of Business Administration
MFA:	Master of Fine Arts
MIT:	Massachusetts Institute of Technology
MPAA:	Motion Picture Association of America
m.p.h.	miles per hour
NAACP:	National Association for the Advancement of Colored People
NASA:	National Aeronautics and Space Administration
NATO:	North Atlantic Treaty Organization
NBA:	National Basketball Association
NCAA:	National Collegiate Athletic Association
NEA:	National Endowment for the Arts
NFL:	National Football League
NRA:	National Rifle Association
NYU:	New York University
OAS:	Organization of American States
OPEC:	Organization of Petroleum Exporting Countries
PAC:	political action committee
PDF:	Panama Defense Forces
PLO:	Palestine Liberation Organization
p.r.:	public relations
PRI:	Institutional Revolutionary Party (Mexico)
R&B:	rhythm & blues
SAC:	Strategic Air Command
SAT:	Scholastic Aptitude Test
SDI:	Strategic Defense Initiative
S&L:	savings & loan
START:	strategic arms reduction talks
TV:	television
UN:	United Nations
UNITA:	National Union for the Total Independence of Angola
UNO:	National Opposition Union (Nicaragua)
UPI:	United Press International
U.S.:	United States
U.S.A.:	United States of America
U.S.S.R.:	Union of Soviet Socialist Republics
VCR:	videocassette recorder
WGA:	Writers Guild of America

The Quote of the Year

East and west, north and south, on every continent, we can see the outlines of a new world of freedom. Of course, freedom's work remains unfinished. The trend we see is not yet universal. Some regimes still stand against the tide. Some rulers still deny the right of the people to govern themselves. But now the power of prejudice and despotism is challenged. Never before have these regimes stood so isolated and alone, so out of step with the steady advance of freedom. Today we are witnessing an ideological collapse—the demise of the totalitarian idea of the omniscient, all-powerful state. There are many reasons for this collapse. But in the end, one fact alone explains what we see today. Advocates of the totalitarian idea saw its triumph written in the laws of history. They failed to see the love of freedom that was written in the human heart.

—GEORGE BUSH
President of the United States.
At United Nations,
New York, Sept. 25.

PART ONE

National Affairs

Presidential Inaugural Address

Delivered by George Bush, President of the United States, at the Capitol, Washington, January 20, 1989.

Mr. Chief Justice, Mr. President, Vice President Quayle, Senator Mitchell, Speaker Wright, Senator Dole, Congressman Michel and fellow citizens, neighbors and friends.

There is a man here who has earned a lasting place in our hearts and in our history. President Reagan, on behalf of our nation I thank you for the wonderful things that you have done for America.

I've just repeated, word for word, the oath taken by George Washington 200 years ago, and the Bible on which I placed my hand is the Bible on which he placed his. It is right that the memory of Washington be with us today, not only because this is our Bicentennial Inauguration but because Washington remains the father of our country. And he would, I think, be gladdened by this day. For today is the concrete expression of a stunning fact: our continuity these 200 years since our Government began.

We meet on democracy's front porch, a good place to talk as neighbors and as friends. For this is a day when our nation is made whole, when our differences for a moment are suspended. And my first act as President is a prayer—I ask you to bow your heads.

"Heavenly Father, we bow our heads and thank You for Your love. Accept our thanks for the peace that yields this day and the shared faith that makes its continuance likely. Make us strong to do Your work, willing to heed and hear Your will, and write on our hearts these words: 'Use power to help people.' For we are given power not to advance our own purposes nor to make a great show in the world, nor a name. There is but one just use of power and it is to serve people. Help us remember, Lord. Amen."

Breeze of Freedom

I come before you and assume the Presidency at a moment rich with promise. We live in a peaceful, prosperous time but we can make it better. For a new breeze is blowing and a world refreshed by freedom seems reborn; for in man's heart, if not in fact, the day of the dictator is over. The totalitarian era is passing, its old ideas blown away like leaves from an ancient, lifeless tree.

A new breeze is blowing—and a nation refreshed by freedom stands ready to push on. There's new ground to be broken and new action to be taken. There are times when the future seems thick as a fog; you sit and wait, hoping the mist will lift and reveal the right path.

But this is a time when the future seems a door you can walk right through—into a room called Tomorrow. Great nations of the world are moving toward democracy—through the door to freedom. Men and women of the world move toward free markets—through the door to prosperity. The people of the world agitate for free expression and free thought—through the door to the moral and intellectual satisfactions that only liberty allows.

We know what works: Freedom works. We know what's right: Freedom is right. We know how to secure a more just and prosperous life for man on earth: through free markets, free speech, free elections and the exercise of free will unhampered by the state.

For the first time in this century—for the first time in perhaps all history—man does not have to invent a system by which to live. We don't have to talk late into the night about which form of government is better. We don't have to wrest justice from the kings—we only have to summon it from within ourselves.

We must act on what we know. I take as my guide the hope of a saint: In crucial things, unity—in important things, diversity—in all things, generosity.

Meaning of America

America today is a proud, free nation, decent and civil—a place we cannot help but love. We know in our hearts, not loudly and proudly but as a simple fact, that this country has meaning beyond what we see and that our strength is a force for good.

Have we changed as a nation even in our time? Are we enthralled with material things, less appreciative of the nobility of work and sacrifice? My friends, we are not the sum of our possessions. They are not the measure of our lives. In our hearts we know what matters. We cannot hope only to leave our children a bigger car, a bigger bank account. We must hope to give them a sense of what it means to be a loyal friend, a loving parent, a citizen who leaves his home, his neighborhood and town better than he found it.

And what do we want the men and women who work with us to say when we're no longer there? That we were more driven to succeed than anyone around us? Or do we stop to ask if a sick child had gotten better, and stayed a moment there to trade a word of friendship.

No President, no government can teach us to remember what is best in what we are. But if the man you have chosen to lead this Government can help make a difference, if he can celebrate the quieter, deeper successes that are made not of gold and silk but of better hearts and finer souls; if he can do these things, then he must.

America is never wholly herself unless she is engaged in high moral principle. We as a people have such a purpose today. It is to make kinder the face of the nation and gentler the face of the world.

Social Problems

My friends, we have work to do. There are the homeless, lost and roaming. There are the children who have nothing—no love, no normalcy. There are those who cannot free themselves of enslavement to whatever addiction—drugs, welfare, the demoralization that rules the slums. There is crime to be conquered, the rough crime of the streets. There are young women to be helped who are about to become mothers of children they can't care for and might not love. They need our care, our guidance and our education, though we bless them for choosing life.

The old solution, the old way, was to think that public money alone could end these problems. But we have learned that that is not so. And in any case, our funds are low. We have a deficit to bring down. We have more will than wallet; but will is what we need.

We will make the hard choices, looking at what we have, perhaps allocating it differently, making our decisions based on honest need and prudent safety. And then we will do the wisest thing of all: We will turn to the only resource we have that in times of need always grows: the goodness and the courage of the American people.

And I am speaking of a new engagement in the lives of others—a new activism, hands-on and involved, that gets the job done. We must bring in the generations, harnessing the unused talent of the elderly and the unfocused energy of the young. For not only leadership is passed from generation to generation, but so is stewardship. And the generation born after the Second World War has come of age.

I've spoken of a thousand points of light—of all the community organizations that are spread like stars throughout the nation doing good. We will work hand in hand, encouraging, sometimes leading, sometimes being led, rewarding. We will work on this in the White House, in the Cabinet agencies. I will go to the people and the programs that are the brighter points of light, and I'll ask every member of my Government to become involved. The old ideas are new again because they're not old, they are timeless: duty, sacrifice, commitment, and a patriotism that finds its expression in taking part and pitching in.

Bipartisanship

And we need a new engagement, too, between the Executive and the Congress. The challenges before us will be thrashed out with the House and the Senate. And we must bring the Federal budget into balance. And we must insure that America stands before the world united: strong, at peace and fiscally sound. But, of course, things may be difficult.

We need compromise; we've had dissension. We need harmony; we've had a chorus of discordant voices. For Congress, too, has changed in our time. There's grown a certain divisiveness. We've seen the hard looks and heard the statements in which not each other's ideas are challenged, but each other's motives. And our great parties have too often been far apart and untrusting of each other.

It's been this way since Vietnam. That war cleaves us still. *But, friends, that war began in earnest a quarter of a century ago; and surely the statute of limitations has been reached.* This is a fact: The final lesson of Vietnam is that no great nation can long afford to be sundered by a memory.

A new breeze is blowing—and the old bipartisanship must be made new again.

To my friends—and yes, I do mean friends—in the loyal opposition—and yes, I mean loyal—I put out my hand. I'm putting out my hand to you, Mr. Speaker. I'm putting out my hand to you, Mr Majority Leader. For this is the thing: This is the age of the offered hand. And we can't turn back clocks, and I don't want to. But when our fathers were young, Mr. Speaker, our differences ended at the water's edge. And we don't wish to turn back time, but when our mothers were young, Mr. Majority Leader, the Congress and the Executive were capable of working together to produce a budget on which this nation could live. Let us negotiate soon and hard, but in the end let us produce.

The American people await action. They didn't send us here to bicker. They asked us to rise above the merely partisan. In crucial things, unity—and this, my friends, is crucial.

Foreign Affairs

To the world, too, we offer new engagement and a renewed vow: We will stay strong to protect the peace. *The "offered hand" is a reluctant fist; but the fist, once made, is strong and can be used with great effect.*

There are today Americans who are held against their will in foreign lands, and Americans who are unaccounted for. Assistance can be shown here and will be long remembered. Good will begets good will. Good faith can be a spiral that endlessly moves on.

"Great nations like great men must keep their word." When America says something, America means it, whether a treaty or an agreement or a vow made on marble steps. We will always try to speak clearly, for candor is a compliment. But subtlety, too, is good and has its place.

While keeping our alliances and friendships around the world strong, ever strong, we will continue the new closeness with the Soviet Union, consistent both with our security and with progress. One might say that our new relationship in part reflects the triumph of hope and strength over experience. But hope is good. And so is strength. And vigilance.

Democracy

Here today are tens of thousands of our citizens who feel the understandable satisfaction of those who have taken part in democracy and seen their hopes fulfilled. But my thoughts have been turning the past few days to those who would be watching at home—to an older fellow who will throw a salute by himself when the flag goes by, and the woman who will tell her sons the words of the battle hymns. I don't mean this to be sentimental. I mean that on days like this we remember that we are all part of a continuum, inescapably connected by the ties that bind.

Our children are watching in schools throughout our great land. And to them I say, thank you for watching democracy's big day. For democracy belongs to us all and freedom is like a beautiful kite that can go higher and higher with the breeze. And to all I say: No matter what your circumstances or where you are, you are part of this day. You are part of the life of our great nation.

A President is neither prince nor pope, and I don't seek "a window on men's souls." In fact, I yearn for a greater tolerance, and easy-goingness about each other's attitudes and way of life.

The Drug Problem

There are few clear areas in which we as a society must rise up united and express our intolerance and the most obvious now is drugs. And when that first cocaine was smuggled in on a ship, it may as well have been a deadly bacteria, so much has it hurt the body, the soul of our country. And there is much to be done and to be said, but take my word for it: This scourge will stop.

Much to Do

And so, there is much to do; and tomorrow the work begins. And I do not mistrust the future; I do not fear what is ahead. For our problems are large, but our heart is larger. Our challenges are great, but our will is greater. And if our flaws are endless, God's love is truly boundless.

Some see leadership as high drama, and the sound of trumpets calling. And sometimes it is that. But I see history as a book with many pages—and each day we fill a page with acts of hopefulness and meaning.

The new breeze blows, a page turns, the story unfolds—and so today a chapter begins: a small and stately story of unity, diversity and generosity—shared and written together.

Thank you. God bless you and God bless the United States of America.

The State of the Union Address

Delivered by George Bush, President of the United States, at the Capitol, Washington, February 9, 1989.

Mr. Speaker, Mr. President, distinguished members of the House and Senate, honored guests, fellow citizens:

Less than three weeks ago, I joined you on the West Front of this very building and, looking over the monuments to our proud past, offered you my hand in filling the next page of American history with a story of extended prosperity and continued peace. Tonight, I am back, to offer you my plans as well. The hand remains extended, the sleeves are rolled up, America is waiting, and now we must produce.

Together, we can build a better America.

It is comforting to return to this historic chamber. Here, 22 years ago, I first raised my hand to be sworn into public life. So tonight, I feel as if I am returning home to friends. And I intend, in the months and years to come, to give you what friends deserve: frankness, respect, and my best judgment about ways to improve America's future.

In return, I ask for an honest commitment to our common mission of progress. If we seize the opportunities on the road before us, there will be praise enough for all.

The people didn't send us here to bicker. It's time to govern.

Our Challenge

Many presidents have come to this chamber in times of great crisis. War. Depression. Loss of national spirit. Eight years ago, I sat in that very chair as President Reagan spoke of punishing inflation and devastatingly high interest rates and people out of work, American confidence on the wane.

Our challenge is different. We are fortunate. A much changed landscape lies before us tonight.

So I don't propose to reverse direction. We are headed the right way. But we cannot rest. We are a people whose energy and drive have fueled our rise to greatness. We are a forward-looking nation: generous, yes, but ambitious as well—not for ourselves, but for the world.

Complacency is not in our character—not before, not now, not ever. And so tonight, we must take a strong America and make it even better. We must address some very real problems. We must establish some very clear priorities. And we must make a very substantial cut in the federal budget deficit.

Some people find that agenda impossible. But I am presenting to you tonight a realistic plan for tackling it. My plan has four broad features: attention to urgent priorities, investment in the future, an attack on the deficit, and no new taxes.

Budget Deficit

This budget represents my best judgment of how we can address our priorities. There are many areas in which we would all like to spend more than I propose. I understand that, but we cannot until we get our fiscal house in order.

Next year alone, thanks to economic growth, without any change in the law, the federal government will take in over $80 billion more than it does this year. That's right: over $80 billion in new revenues, with no increase in taxes. Our job is to allocate those new resources wisely.

We can afford to increase spending by a modest amount but enough to invest in key priorities and still cut the deficit by almost 40 percent in one year. That will allow us to meet the targets set forth in the Gramm-Rudman-Hollings law. But to do that, we must recognize that growth above inflation in federal programs is not preordained, that not all spending initiatives were designed to be immortal.

I make this pledge tonight: My team and I are ready to work with the Congress, to form a special leadership group, to negotiate in good faith, to work day and night—if that's what it takes—to meet the budget targets and to produce a budget on time.

We cannot settle for business as usual. Government by continuing resolution or government by crisis will not do. I ask the Congress tonight to approve several measures which will make budgeting more sensible.

We could save time and improve efficiency by enacting two-year budgets. Forty-three governors have the line-item veto. Presidents should have it too. At the very least, at the very least, when a president proposes to rescind federal spending, the Congress should be required to vote on that proposal, instead of killing it by inaction. And I ask for Congress to honor the public's wishes by passing a constitutional amendment to require a balanced budget. Such an amendment, once phased in, will discipline both Congress and the executive branch.

Several principles describe the kind of America I hope to build with your help in the years ahead. We will not have the luxury of taking the easy, spendthrift approach to solving problems because higher spending and higher taxes put economic growth at risk. Economic growth provides jobs and hope. Economic growth enables us to pay for social programs. Economic growth enhances the security of the nation. And low tax rates create economic growth.

Goals for Society

I believe in giving Americans greater freedom and greater choice, and I will work for choice for American families—whether in the housing in which they live, the schools to which they send their children, or the child care they select for their young.

You see, I believe that we have an obligation to those in need, but that government should not be the provider of first resort for things that the private sector can produce better.

I believe in a society that is free from discrimination and bigotry of any kind. I will work to knock down the barriers left by past discrimination and to build a more tolerant society that will stop such barriers from ever being built again.

I believe that family and faith represent the moral compass of the nation, and I will work to make them strong, for as Benjamin Franklin said: "If a sparrow cannot fall to the ground without His notice, [can] a great [nation] rise without His aid?"

And I believe in giving people the power to make their own lives better through growth and opportunity. Together, let's put power in the hands of the people.

Three weeks ago, we celebrated the bicentennial Inaugural, the 200th anniversary of the first presidency. And if you look back, one thing is so striking about the way the Founding Fathers looked at America: They didn't talk about themselves. They talked about posterity. They talked about the future.

American Leadership

We, too, must think in terms bigger than ourselves. We must take actions today that will ensure a better tomorrow. We must extend American leadership in technology, increase long-term investment, improve our educational system and boost productivity. These are the keys to building a better future.

Here are some of my recommendations:

■ I propose almost $2.2 billion for the National Science Foundation to promote basic research and keep us on track to double its budget by 1993.

■ I propose to make permanent the tax credit for research and development.

■ I have asked Vice President Quayle to chair a new Task Force on Competitiveness.

■ I request funding for NASA and a strong space program: an increase of almost $2.4 billion over the current fiscal year. We must have a manned space station; a vigorous, safe space shuttle program; and more commercial development in space. The space program should always go "full throttle up." That's not just our ambition, it's our destiny.

■ I propose that we cut the maximum tax rate on capital gains to increase long-term investment. History on this is clear: this will increase revenues, help savings and create new jobs.

We won't be competitive if we leave whole sectors of America behind. This is the year we should finally enact urban enterprise zones, and bring hope to the inner cities.

Education

But the most important competitiveness program of all is one which improves education in America. When some of our students actually have trouble locating America on a map of the world, it is time for us to map a new approach to education.

We must reward excellence, and cut through bureaucracy. We must help schools that need help most. We must give choice to parents, students, teachers and principals. And we must hold all concerned accountable. In education, we cannot tolerate mediocrity.

I want to cut that dropout rate and make America a more literate nation. Because what it really comes down to is this: the longer our graduation lines are today, the shorter our unemployment lines will be tomorrow.

So tonight I am proposing the following initiatives:

■ The beginning of a $500 million program to reward America's best schools: "merit schools."

■ The creation of special presidential awards for the best teachers in every state, because excellence should be rewarded.

■ The establishment of a new program of National Science Scholars, one each year for every member of the House and Senate, to give this generation of students a special incentive to excel in science and mathematics.

■ The expanded use of magnet schools which give families and students greater choice.

■ And a new program to encourage "alternative certification" which will let talented people from all fields teach in our classrooms.

I have said I'd like to be "the Education President." Tonight I ask you to join me by becoming "the Education Congress."

War Against Drugs

Just last week, as I settled into this new office, I received a letter from a mother in Pennsylvania who had been struck by my message in the Inaugural address. "Not 12 hours before," she wrote, "my husband and I received word that our son was addicted to cocaine. He had the world at his feet. Bright, gifted, personable, he could have done anything with his life. And now he has chosen cocaine."

"Please," she wrote, "find a way to curb the supply of cocaine. Get tough with the pushers. Our son needs your help."

My friends, that voice crying out for help could be the voice of your own neighbor. Your own friend. Your own son. Over 23 million Americans used illegal drugs last year, at a staggering cost to our nation's well-being.

Let this be recorded as the time when America rose up and said "no" to drugs. The scourge of drugs must be stopped, and I am asking tonight for an increase of almost a billion dollars in budget outlays to escalate the war against drugs. The war must be waged on all fronts.

Our new drug czar, Bill Bennett, and I will be shoulder to shoulder in the executive branch, leading the charge.

Some money will be used to expand treatment to the poor and to young mothers. This will offer the helping hand to the many innocent victims of drugs, like the thousands of babies born addicted or with AIDS because of the mother's addiction.

Some will be used to cut the waiting time for treatment. Some money will be devoted to those urban schools where the emergency is now the worst. And much of it will be used to protect our borders, with help from the Coast Guard, the Customs Service, the departments of state and justice and, yes, the U.S. military.

I mean to get tough on the drug criminals, and let me be clear: This president will back up those who put their lives on the line every single day: our local police officers.

My budget asks for beefed-up prosecution, for a new attack on organized crime and for enforcement of tough sentences. And for the worst kingpins, that means the death penalty.

I also want to make sure that, when a drug dealer is convicted, there is a cell waiting for him. He should not go free because prisons are too full. So let the word go out: If you are caught and convicted, you will do time.

But, for all we do in law enforcement, in interdiction and treatment, we will never win this war on drugs unless we stop demand for drugs. So some of this increase will be used to educate the young about the dangers of drugs. We must involve the parents. We must involve the teachers. We must involve communities. And, my friends, we must involve ourselves, each and every one of us, in this campaign.

One problem related to drug use demands our urgent attention and our continuing compassion. That is the terrible tragedy of AIDS. I am asking for $1.6 billion for education to prevent the disease and for research to find a cure.

Environment

If we're to protect our future, we need a new attitude about the environment. We must protect the air we breathe. I will send to you shortly legislation for a new, more effective Clean Air Act. It will include a plan to reduce by date certain the emissions which cause acid rain, because the time for study alone has passed and the time for action is now.

We must make use of clean coal. My budget contains full funding, on schedule, for the clean-coal technology agreement we have made with Canada. We made that agreement with Canada, and we intend to honor the agreement.

I believe we should expand our parks. So I am asking to fund new acquisitions under the land and water conservation fund.

We must protect our oceans. I support new penalties against those who would dump medical waste and other trash into our oceans. The age of the needle on the beaches must end.

In some cases, the gulfs and oceans off our shores hold the promise of oil and gas reserves which can make our nation more secure and less dependent on foreign oil. When those with the most promise can be tapped safely, as with much of the Alaska National Wildlife Refuge, we should proceed. But we must use caution. We must respect the environment.

So tonight I am calling for the indefinite postponement of three lease sales which have raised troubling questions: two off the coast of California and one which could threaten the Everglades in Florida. Action on these three lease sales will await the conclusions of a special task force set up to measure the potential for environmental damage.

I am directing the attorney general and the administrator of the Environmental Protection Agency to use every tool at their disposal to speed and toughen the enforcement of our laws against toxic waste dumpers. I want faster clean-ups and tougher enforcement of penalties against polluters.

Social Welfare

In addition to caring for our future, we must care for those around us. A decent society shows compassion for the young, the elderly, the vulnerable and the poor. Our first obligation is to the most vulnerable—infants, poor mothers, children living in poverty—and my proposed budget recognizes this. I ask for full funding of Medicaid—an increase of over $3 billion—and an expansion of the program to include coverage of pregnant women who are near the poverty line.

I believe we should help working families cope with the burden of child care. Our help should be aimed at those who need it most: low-income families with young children. I support a new child-care tax credit that will aim our efforts at exactly those families without discriminating against mothers who choose to stay at home.

Now, I know there are competing proposals. But remember this: the overwhelming majority of all preschool child care is now provided by relatives and neighbors, churches and community groups. Families who choose these options should remain eligible for help. Parents should have choice.

And for those children who are unwanted or abused, whose parents are deceased, I believe we should encourage adoption. I propose to reenact the tax deduction for adoption expenses, and to double it to $3,000. Let's make it easier for these kids to have parents who love them.

We have a moral contract with our senior citizens. In this budget, Social Security is fully funded, including a full cost-of-living adjustment. We must honor our contract. We must care about those in "the shadows of life," and I, like many Americans, am deeply troubled by the plight of the homeless. The causes of homelessness are many, the history is long, but the moral imperative to act is clear.

Thanks to the deep well of generosity in this great land, many organizations already contribute. But we in government cannot stand on the sidelines. In my budget, I ask for greater support for emergency food and shelter, for health services and measures to prevent substance abuse, and for clinics for the mentally ill—and I propose a new initiative involving the full range of government agencies. We must confront this national shame.

There is another issue that I have decided to mention here tonight. I have long believed that the people of Puerto Rico should have the right to determine their own political future. Personally, I strongly favor statehood. But I ask the Congress to take the necessary steps to let the people decide in a referendum.

Certain problems, the result of decades of unwise practices, threaten the health and security of our people. Left unattended, they will only get worse, but we can act now to put them behind us.

Savings Deposits

Certainly, the savings of Americans must remain secure. Let me be clear: Insured depositors will continue to be fully protected. But any plan to refinance the system must be accompanied by major reform. Our proposals will prevent such a crisis from recurring. The best answer is to make sure that a mess like this will never happen again.

The majority of thrifts in communities across this nation have been honest; they have played a major role in helping families achieve the dream of home ownership. But make no mistake: those who are corrupt, those who break the law, must be kicked out of the business and they should go to jail.

Nuclear Plants

We face a massive task in cleaning up the waste left from decades of environmental neglect at our nuclear weapons plants. Clearly, we must modernize these plants and operate them safely. That is not at issue. Our national security depends on it.

But beyond that, we must clean up the old mess that's been left behind, and I propose in this budget to more than double our current effort to do so. This will allow us to identify the exact nature of the various problems so we can clean them up—and clean them up we will.

Defense Spending

We have been fortunate during these past eight years. America is a stronger nation today than it was in 1980.

Morale in our armed forces has been restored. Our resolve has been shown. Our readiness has been improved. We are at peace. There can no longer be any doubt that peace has been made more secure through strength. When America is stronger, the world is safer.

Most people don't realize that after the successful restoration of our strength, the Pentagon budget has actually been reduced in real terms for each of the last four years. We cannot tolerate continued real reductions in defense.

In light of the compelling need to reduce the deficit, however, I propose a one-year freeze in the military budget—something I proposed last fall in my flexible freeze plan. This freeze will apply for only one year and, after that, increases above inflation will be required. I will not sacrifice American preparedness, and I will not compromise American strength.

I should be clear on the conditions attached to my recommendation for the coming year:
■ The savings must be allocated to those priorities for investing in our future that I have spoken about tonight;
■ This defense freeze must be a part of a comprehensive budget agreement which meets the targets spelled out in the Gramm-Rudman-Hollings law without raising taxes, and which incorporates reforms in the budget process.

I have directed the National Security Council to review our national security and defense policies and report back to me within 90 days to ensure that our capabilities and resources meet our commitments and strategies.

I am also charging the Department of Defense with the task of developing a plan to improve the defense procurement process and management of the Pentagon—one which will fully implement the Packard Commission report. Many of the changes can only be made with the participation of the Congress, so I ask for your help.

We need fewer regulations. We need less bureaucracy. We need multi-year procurement and two-year budgeting. And frankly—and don't take this wrong—we need less Congressional

11

micromanagement of our nation's military policy.

Foreign Affairs

Securing a more peaceful world is perhaps the most important priority I'd like to address tonight. We meet at a time of extraordinary hope. Never before in this century have our values of freedom, democracy and economic opportunity been such a powerful and intellectual force around the globe.

Never before has our leadership been so crucial, because while America has its eyes on the future, the world has its eyes on America. It is a time of great change in the world, and especially in the Soviet Union. Prudence and common sense dictate that we try to understand the full meaning of the change going on there, review our policies, and then proceed with caution. But I have personally assured General Secretary [Mikhail] Gorbachev that at the conclusion of such a review, we will be ready to move forward. We will not miss any opportunity to work for peace.

The fundamental fact remains that the Soviets retain a very powerful military machine, in the service of objectives which are still too often in conflict with ours. So let us take the new openness seriously. But let's also be realistic. And let us always be strong.

There are some pressing issues we must address:

I will vigorously pursue the Strategic Defense Initiative.

The spread and even use of sophisticated weaponry threatens global security as never before.

Chemical weapons must be banned from the face of the earth, never to be used again. Look, this won't be easy. Verification will be extraordinarily difficult. But civilization and human decency demand that we try.

The spread of nuclear weapons must be stopped. I will work to strengthen the hand of the International Atomic Energy Agency. Our diplomacy must work every day against the proliferation of nuclear weapons.

And, around the globe, we must continue to be freedom's best friend.

We must stand firm for self-determination and democracy in Central America, including in Nicaragua. It is my strongly held conviction that when people are given the chance, they inevitably will choose a free press, freedom of worship, certifiably free and fair elections.

We must strengthen the alliance of industrial democracies—as solid a force for peace as the world has ever known. This is an alliance forged by the power of our ideals, not the pettiness of our differences. So let us lift our sights—to rise above fighting about beef hormones to building a better future, to move from protectionism to progress.

I have asked the Secretary of State to visit Europe next week and to consult with our allies on the wide range of challenges and opportunities we face together, including East-West relations. And I look forward to meeting with our NATO partners in the near future.

I, too, shall begin a trip shortly—to the far reaches of the Pacific Basin, where the winds of democracy are creating new hope, and the power of free markets is unleashing a new force.

When I served as our representative in China just 14 or 15 years ago, few would have predicted the scope of the changes we've witnessed since then.

But in preparing for this trip, I was struck by something I came across from a Chinese writer [Lin Yutang]. He was speaking of his country, decades ago, but his words speak to each of us, in America, tonight.

"Today," he said, "we are afraid of the simple words like goodness and mercy and kindness." My friends, if we're to succeed as a nation, we must rediscover those words.

An Appeal to Americans

In just three days, we mark the birthday of Abraham Lincoln—the man who saved our union, and gave new meaning to the word opportunity. Lincoln once said: "I hold that while man exists, it is his duty to improve not only his own condition, but to assist in ameliorating [that of] mankind."

It is this broader mission to which I call all Americans, because the definition of a successful life must include serving others.

To the young people of America, who sometimes feel left out: I ask you tonight to give us the benefit of your talent and energy through a new program called YES, for Youth Entering Service to America.

To those men and women in business: remember the ultimate end of your work—to make a better product, to create better lives. I ask you to plan for the longer term and avoid that temptation of quick and easy paper profits.

To the brave men and women who wear the uniform of the United States of America: thank you. Your calling is a high one—to be the defenders of freedom and the guarantors of liberty. And I want you to know that this nation is grateful for your service.

To the farmers of America: We appreciate the bounty you provide. I want you to know we will work with you to open foreign markets to American agricultural products.

To the parents of America: I ask you to get involved in your child's schooling, meet the teachers, care about what is happening there. It is not only your child's future on the line, it is America's.

To kids in our cities: don't give up hope. Say no to drugs. Stay in school. And yes, "keep hope alive."

To those 37 million Americans with some form of disability: you belong in the economic mainstream. We need your talents in America's workforce. Disabled Americans must become full partners in America's opportunity society.

To the families of America, watching tonight in your living rooms: hold fast to your dreams, because ultimately America's future rests in your hands.

And to my friends in this chamber: I ask your cooperation to keep America growing while cutting the deficit. It's only fair to those who now have no vote—the generations to come.

Let them look back and say that we had the foresight to understand that a time of peace and prosperity is not the time to rest, but a time to press forward. A time to invest in the future.

And let all Americans remember that no problem of human making is too great to be overcome by human ingenuity, human energy and the untiring hope of the human spirit. I believe this. I would not have asked to be your president if I didn't.

Need for Fortitude

Tomorrow, debate on the plan I have put forward begins. I ask Congress to come forward with your proposals. Let us not question each other's motives. Let us debate. Let us negotiate. But let us solve the problem.

Recalling anniversaries may not be my specialty in speeches, but tonight is one of some note. On February 9, 1941, just 48 years ago tonight, Sir Winston Churchill took to the airwaves during Britain's hour of peril.

He had received from President Roosevelt a hand-carried letter quoting Longfellow's famous poem: "Sail on, oh ship of state. Sail on, oh union, strong and great! Humanity with all its fears, with all the hopes of future years; Is hanging breathless on thy fate!"

Churchill responded on this night by radio broadcast to a nation at war, but directed his words to Roosevelt. "We shall not fail or falter," he said. "We shall not weaken or tire. Give us the tools, and we will finish the job."

Tonight, almost a half century later, our peril may be less immediate, but the need for perseverance and clear-sighted fortitude is just as great.

Now, as then, there are those who say it can't be done. There are voices who say that America's best days have passed. That we are bound by constraints, threatened by problems, surrounded by troubles which limit our ability to hope.

Well, tonight I remain full of hope. We Americans have only begun on our mission of goodness and greatness. And to those timid souls, I repeat the plea—give us the tools and we will do the job.

Thank you, and God bless you, and God bless America.

The American Scene

Douglas Applegate
United States Representative,
D-Ohio

1

[Criticizing the Supreme Court's recent ruling which permits dissenters to desecrate the American flag]: I am mad as hell. What in God's name is going on? This is an outrage. What will they allow next? Allow fornication in Times Square at high noon?

June 22/
Los Angeles Times, 6-23:(I)1.

Robert H. Bork
Former Judge,
United States Court of Appeals
for the District of Columbia

2

[Criticizing the Supreme Court's decision allowing the desecration of the American flag as a means of social expression]: The flag is a unique kind of national symbol, one of the few symbols of our community. Preventing its desecration does not prevent you from expressing an idea . . . I think there's no way of curing this by statute. I think the only way of curing this decision would be by Constitutional amendment, which would really not be an amendment to the Constitution so much as it would be an amendment to some judges.

Broadcast interview/
"This Week with David Brinkley,"
ABC-TV, 6-25.

Horace Busby
Democratic Party consultant

3

[At his recent inaugural, President] Bush was picking up on a broad and great theme of the middle and latter half of the 20th century—"unity, diversity, generosity." Unity is the most important thing an American President has to be concerned about because the country has so many groupings, and you don't have a country worth having without unity. He must find ways to let diversity express itself—to be respectful and to be respected.

The Christian Science Monitor,
1-23:1.

George Bush
President of the United States

4

America today is a proud, free nation, decent and civil, a place we cannot help but love. We know in our hearts, not loudly and proudly, but as a simple fact, that this country has meaning beyond what we see, and that our strength is a force for good . . . America is never wholly herself unless she is engaged in high moral principle. We as a people have such a purpose today. It is to make kinder the face of the nation and gentler the face of the world.

Inaugural address,
Washington, Jan. 20/
The Washington Post, 1-21:(A)10.

5

[Criticizing the Supreme Court's recent ruling which permits dissenters to desecrate the American flag]: I understand the legal basis for that decision, and I respect the Supreme Court and, as President of the United States, I will see that the law of the land is fully supported. But I have to give you my personal, emotional response. Flag-burning is wrong—dead wrong—and the flag of the United States is very, very special.

June 22/
Los Angeles Times, 6-23:(I)23.

6

On Wednesday morning, the Supreme Court issued a decision which held that a person could not be convicted for desecration of our flag, the American flag, and because to do so would infringe upon the right to political protest. Now, we've got to be very careful in our society to

(GEORGE BUSH)

preserve the right to protest government action. However, I believe that the flag of the United States should never be the object of desecration. Flag-burning is wrong. Protection of the flag, a unique national symbol, will in no way limit the opportunity nor the breadth of protest available in the exercise of free-speech rights. And I have the greatest respect for the Supreme Court, and indeed for the Justices who interpreted the Constitution as they saw fit. But I believe the importance of this issue compels me to call for a Constitutional amendment [prohibiting flag desecration]. Support for the First Amendment need not extend to desecration of the American flag. And we are reviewing proposed language for a Constitutional amendment. We are beginning consultation with members of the United States Congress who hold similar views. And as President, I will uphold our precious right to dissent; but burning the flag goes too far, and I want to see that matter remedied.

News conference,
Washington, June 27/
The Washington Post, 6-28:(A)4.

John C. Danforth
United States Senator,
R-Missouri

1

[Arguing against a Constitutional amendment that would prohibit desecration of the American flag]: The flag has been altered any number of times. But in the 200-year-plus history of our Constitution, the Bill of Rights [guaranteeing the right to dissent] has never been altered . . . Every country has a flag. But America has the Bill of Rights, and it is the crowning glory of our country.

Before the Senate,
Washington, Oct. 17/
The Washington Post, 10-18:(A)1.

Robert J. Dole
United States Senator, R-Kansas

2

[Supporting legislation to outlaw desecration of the American flag, after the U.S. Supreme

Court ruled that such desecration is permitted as a form of dissent]: Some critics say we're wrong on this one, that this is a freedom-of-speech issue. Americans are speaking out in every corner of the country. And what they are saying is, "Keep your hands off Old Glory." Americans may not know every nuance of Constitutional law. But they know desecration when they see it. They're demanding action. So today I say to America: "We hear you loud and clear."

At rally, Iwo Jima Memorial,
Arlington, Va./
The Christian Science Monitor,
7-6:8.

Robert K. Dornan
United States Representative,
R-California

3

[Criticizing the Supreme Court's recent ruling which permits dissenters to desecrate the American flag]: [Flag-burning] is no more a form of protest than the KKK's cross-burning. The act of flag-burning is not meant to convey any political idea. It is an act that is solely meant to provoke and offend . . . It is simply an act of cultural and patriotic destruction.

June 22/
Los Angeles Times, 6-23:(I)23.

Don Edwards
United States Representative,
D-California

4

[Arguing against a Constitutional amendment that would outlaw desecration of the American flag, after the U.S. Supreme Court's recent ruling allowing such desecration as a form of dissent]: Remember that the flag is sturdy, flying proudly through every fierce battle of every war and through times of social upheaval. The Constitution, however, is fragile and can be amended by the votes of legislators caught up in the emotional whirlwinds of the moment.

At House Subcommittee on Civil
and Constitutional Rights hearing,
Washington, July 13/
The New York Times, 7-14:(A)8.

Michael D. Eisner
Chairman,
Walt Disney Company

1

What the world sees in American entertainment is the portrayal of a people living in a system of political and economic freedom. Freedom of expression, the freedom to succeed, the freedom to fail and try again.

At Denison University
commencement/
The Christian Science Monitor,
6-12:12.

Jack Fields
United States Representative,
R-Texas

2

[Criticizing a recent U.S. Supreme Court ruling allowing desecration of the American flag as a form of dissent]: [The man who desecrates the flag] has the right to say what he likes. [But] he goes too far when he desecrates everything we believe in and everything that we stand for. He is not desecrating a piece of cloth. He is desecrating everything that America is and lives for and fights and dies for.

Before the House, Washington/
The Christian Science Monitor,
7-6:8.

Charles Fried
Former Solicitor General
of the United States

3

[Approving of the Supreme Court's decision allowing desecration of the American flag as a means of social expression]: I think that's a wonderful decision. When I think of what's happened in Red China and what happens in Iran, I'm glad we've got no doctrine of civil blasphemy . . . It makes me prouder of the flag, rather than the opposite.

Broadcast interview/
"Face the Nation,"
CBS-TV, 6-25.

Lee A. Iacocca
Chairman,
Chrysler Corporation

4

We're [the U.S.] not going to dominate the 21st century like we have the 20th. In fact, we're going to have to compete for most of what we now take for granted, including our standard of living.

At Fairleigh Dickinson University
commencement/
USA Today, 5-24:(A)9.

Jesse L. Jackson
Civil-rights leader

5

[On calls for a Constitutional amendment that would outlaw the burning of the American flag]: The fact is we all find burning the flag repugnant. We find burning crosses repugnant. But they have been burning crosses longer than they have been burning flags and there has been no rush for a Constitutional amendment to stop the burning of crosses.

Washington, June 30/
The New York Times, 7-1:7.

David Johnson
Co-director, Cooperative
Learning Center,
University of Minnesota

6

Americans have been able to cooperate better than anyone else in the world. We have a history of cooperative work. In the frontier, Americans cooperated to build barns, build houses, harvest crops. In World War I and World War II, we could pull together to get the job done. Pulling together to get the job done, strong individuality, creativity and entrepreneurship—that's the heart of capitalism.

The New York Times, 1-4:(B)7.

Edward M. Kennedy
United States Senator,
D-Massachusetts

7

[Supporting the Supreme Court's ruling that allows desecration of the American flag as a form

(EDWARD M. KENNEDY)

of dissent]: Those who have given their lives in battle under our hallowed flag did so to preserve the liberties guaranteed to all Americans by our Constitution. First among those is the right to freedom of expression. If that right is to be meaningful, it must extend to views that are unpopular, that are mean-spirited, that are wrong. The American flag is the most venerable symbol of all that is great and good about America. To cast contempt upon it is to reject all that we hold dear as a free and civilized people. Anyone who burns an American flag deserves the contempt of every American citizen. But if the First Amendment stands for anything, it means that the government cannot punish someone for criticizing our society—even if that criticism is as nasty and obnoxious as [desecrating the flag].

The Washington Post, 6-27:(A)22.

Joel Kotkin
Journalist; West Coast editor,
"Inc." magazine

1

When civilizations are on the ascendant it's because they have a belief and an idea. The miracle that Japan had in the last 30 years is a miracle of will ... People felt they had a mission, they were going to fulfill it, work really hard. We [in the U.S.] need to have a sense that we have a future, that we can still be a leader, *the* leader. And if we indulge and accept decline, then it's all over.

Interview, Los Angeles/
The Christian Science Monitor,
2-3:14.

William M. Kunstler
Lawyer

2

[Saying desecration of the American flag should not be prohibited by law]: I understand that this flag has serious, important meanings, real meaning to real people out there. But that does not mean that it may [not] have different

meanings to others and that they may not—under the First Amendment—show their feelings.

Before U.S. Supreme Court,
March/Newsweek, 7-3:20.

Jim Lehrer
Co-anchorman,
"MacNeil/Lehrer NewsHour,"
PBS-TV

3

I happen to believe we Americans are becoming a nation of liars. I, for one, think it's awful. All kinds of people lie ... [but] it is the lying at the top levels of our society that concerns me the most, because morality, like water and unlike money, really does trickle down.

At Southern Methodist University
commencement/
USA Today, 5-24:(A)9.

Ron Marlene
United States Representative,
R-Montana

4

[Criticizing the Supreme Court decision allowing desecration of the American flag as a form of dissent]: Yesterday these six brave soldiers [depicted raising the flag on the Iwo Jima Memorial] were symbolically shot in the back by five men in black robes ... Six brave men raised the flag; five Supreme Court Justices tore it down. Perhaps another monument with the names of the black-robed Justices cut in stone should be laid like a tombstone at the foot of the Iwo Jima Memorial.

June 22/The Washington Post,
6-23:(A)1.

Howard M. Metzenbaum
United States Senator,
D-Ohio

5

[Arguing against a Constitutional Amendment that would prohibit desecration of the American flag as a method of dissent, in the wake of a Supreme Court ruling that such desecration was Constitutional]: [Future generations would]

17

(HOWARD M. METZENBAUM)

cringe with embarrassment [if Congress passes such an amendment to restrict people's rights]. They will look back and say, "How foolish, how shameful that the nation weakened the Bill of Rights for the first and only time in our history on the basis of an offensive act [flag-burning] committed only by an outrageous few." [The issue has degenerated into] shameful and crass demagoguery with a cold eye toward the next election.

Before House Subcommittee
on Civil and Constitutional Law,
Washington, July 13/
The Washington Post, 7-14:(A)7.

Robert H. Michel
United States Representative,
R-Illinois

1

[Calling for a Constitutional amendment prohibiting the desecration of the American flag]: We are taking this step because it is the only way to protect the flag, given the recent Supreme Court decision [allowing flag-desecration as a form of dissent]. The flag already is consecrated through 200 years of love and sacrifice and reverence of a special, almost sacred, kind. We seek only to protect it, just as you'd protect any loved one under attack.

Washington, June 29/
Los Angeles Times, 6-30:(I)16.

George J. Mitchell
United States Senator,
D-Maine

2

[Criticizing the Supreme Court decision allowing desecration of the American flag as a form of dissent]: I do not believe that Americans have to see the flag that symbolizes their freedom to speak devalued and cheapened in the cause of preserving that freedom. Every American has the right to speak freely and to dissent from the policies of the government or from the orthodox and accepted views of the day. It is precisely that vast freedom that renders so unnecessary the

condoning of the desecration of the flag as a means of expressing dissent.

June 22/
The Washington Post, 6-23:(A)8.

3

[Criticizing President Bush's support for a Constitutional amendment prohibiting desecration of the American flag as a form of dissent]: To me, the most distressing aspect of this matter has been the eagerness with which the President sought to exploit the flag for political purposes. Such eager support for amending the Bill of Rights based on public-opinion polls and short-term political gains is inappropriate. The flag and the Constitution should be unifying values in American life. They ought not to be used to divide Americans.

Washington, Oct. 19/
The New York Times, 10-20:(A)1.

Bill Moyers
Broadcast journalist

4

There's a vague sense of unease in the country, a suspicion that democratic politics—choosing our leaders—no longer controls the nation's destiny. Voter participation in 1988 was the second lowest in the 20th century; and in the non-Southern states, where three-fourths of all Americans live, the turnout rate was the lowest in 164 years.

Interview, New York/
Los Angeles Times, 11-12:(Calendar)4.

Rupert Murdoch
Media entrepreneur

5

It is the American way of organizing society that is prevailing in the world. The U.S. has been extremely lucky in its continental size, its natural resources, its hard-working population, its diversity. But the ultimate American resource is more intangible. *The Economist* magazine put it very well last year, in a long survey of Japan: "Many Japanese think that the [pro-Japan] gap in economic performance between their country and

(RUPERT MURDOCH)

America will continue to widen for a while, but will then narrow, as Japan's natural disadvantages—especially its aging population—and America's inherent advantages—the suppleness of its society, its ability to attract the best people from all over the globe—reassert themselves." *The Economist* concluded by quoting an aide to former Japanese Prime Minister Nakasone: "The 20th century was the American century. The 21st century will be the American century." And I think he was right. Whatever the human race is going to achieve will probably be achieved here first . . . In the 18th century, Voltaire said that every man had two countries: his own, and France. In the 20th century, that has become true of the U.S. And it is particularly true for the English-speaking world.

Lecture at Manhattan Institute,
New York, November/
The Wall Street Journal, 12-5:(A)22.

Muammar el-Qaddafi
Chief of State of Libya

1

With regard to the American people, they are completely ignorant of the world, completely, and they know nothing about the outside world. And unfortunately, during the recent years, the American Administration has become more interested with the outside world than with the internal problems . . . Thus, so many ills prevailed within the American society—like drugs, diseases, poverty and AIDS, cancer. All of these are the result of the American Administration's non-interest in the internal affairs of the American people.

Broadcast interview,
Tripoli, Libya/
"Barbara Walters Interview,"
ABC-TV, 1-27.

Ronald Reagan
President of the United States

2

Those of us who are over 35 or so years of age grew up in a different America. We were taught, very directly, what it means to be an American, and we absorbed almost in the air a love of country and an appreciation of its institutions. If you didn't get these things from your family, you got them from the neighborhood, from the father down the street who fought in Korea or the family who lost someone at Anzio. Or you could get a sense of patriotism from school. And if all else failed, you could get a sense of patriotism from the popular culture. The movies celebrated democratic values and implicitly reinforced the idea that America was special. TV was like that, too, through the mid-'60s. But now we're about to enter the '90s, and some things have changed. Younger parents aren't sure that an unambivalent appreciation of America is the right thing to teach modern children. And as for those who create the popular culture, well-grounded patriotism is no longer in style . . . If we forget what we did, we won't know who we are. I am warning of an eradication of the American memory that could result, ultimately, in an erosion of the American spirit.

Broadcast address to the nation,
Washington, Jan. 11/
The Washington Post, 1-12:(A)8.

Patricia Schroeder
United States Representative,
D-Colorado

3

This has been a decade where the trilogy was me, myself and I. We've got to start thinking about *us,* our community, our country and how we are going to compete. There's never been a time when our country needs you more.

At Simmons College commencement/
USA Today, 5-24:(A)9.

John Sears
Executive director,
Franklin D. Roosevelt
Four Freedoms Foundation

4

While many 19th-century [tourist] attractions embodied the power and grandeur of nature or some new achievement in art, technology or social organization, many 20th-century attrac-

(JOHN SEARS)

tions represent mythologized versions of the American past. We now visit places that re-create the past, such as Williamsburg [Va.] and Sturbridge Village [Mass.]. The fact that we go to such great lengths to re-create an earlier time probably reflects both our insecurity about our own history—we're still a very new country— and our fascination with technology; we like the magic of re-creating a whole village or way of life. Today, we also mythologize the lives of indi-viduals, be they Presidents or performers such as Dolly Parton, whose Dollywood in her home-town of Pigeon Forge, Tennessee, is both a shrine to a public figure revered by many and a theme park. The popularity of these places is closely connected to our obsession with the American success story—the idea that someone from humble origins can become President or a famous and wealthy singer. People of all classes and backgrounds visit these places. They provide a common experience that appears both mythic and trivial, provoking both awe and irreverence.

Interview/
U.S. News & World Report, 8-14:52.

Saeki Shoichi
Professor, Chuo University
(Japan)

1

Japanese media all too easily convey the impression of an America helplessly watching its own decay with an irritation bordering on hysteria. Yet the frank, open-minded and dispas-sionate attitudes of the younger generation, the bottomless crucible of a society that day after day, month after month absorbs countless new immigrants, and the presence of an extraordinary religious hunger and moralistic impulse, are forces to be reckoned with.

The Atlantic Monthly,
February:(A)12.

George P. Shultz
Secretary of State
of the United States

2

Great nations have suffered decline but they were imperial, or absolutist, or dominated by tradition-bound classes. Our nation is none of these. Our democracy holds the potential for resilience and rejuvenation in the face of any challenge. So ours is a winning hand.

Before Citizens Network
for Foreign Policy,
Washington, Jan. 9/
The Washington Post, 1-10:(A)4.

Robert Theobold
Futurist

3

We've got a system that isn't working, and not working much more seriously than we think. The evidence: the $200-billion cost of bailing out the savings-and-loan industry, demonstrating the failure of our regulatory system and the collapse of political integrity; the drug problem, which Washington hasn't a clue as to solving; the schooling issue, which is clearly out of con-trol . . . We say we have not only a successful economic system but also a decision-making system that works. It seems to me that's exactly what we don't have. This decision-making sys-tem that we think works so well is in fact dying. And yet we cling to the belief that whoever is in charge of the systems can understand them and fine tune them, and everything will work out. That's naive. The fact is, we haven't won the Cold War. Both we and the Communists are losing the industrial era. The difference is, we see the problem with their system but fail to see, because we are too close, the problems with our own.

Interview/
The Washington Post, 12-1:(A)27.

Dennis Thompson
Professor, and head of
the ethics program,
Harvard University

4

The fact that we get concerned that ethics is on the agenda and that we disagree a lot is one of the healthiest signs in American public life that I've seen in a long time.

Interview, Cambridge, Mass./
The Christian Science Monitor,
1-12:12.

Ted Weiss
United States Representative,
D-New York
1

[Criticizing those who want a Constitutional amendment prohibiting the desecration of the American flag after the Supreme Court ruled that such desecration is allowable as a form of dissent]: What makes America such a great democracy is that we do not silence the political expression even of those with whose views we most fundamentally disagree. In the 200 years since the adoption of the Bill of Rights, the Constitution has been amended only 16 times, mostly to expand our rights. It would be tragically ironic if in this year of its celebration, we were to adopt an amendment weakening the Bill of Rights. We have nothing to fear from the flag-burners. We have a great deal to fear from those who have lost faith in the Constitution.

June 27/
Los Angeles Times, 6-28:(I)13.

Tom Wolfe
Author, Journalist
2

Since the 1960s we have had extraordinary freedom in this country, and we are seeing the good and the bad sides of the same coin. We've had tremendous prosperity. In many ways we have fulfilled the dream of the old utopian societies of the mid-19th century. But the other side of the coin of prosperity is money fever and [vanity] . . . But I for one would not want to change this country. When you think about conditions across the long panorama, the poverty—there's never been anything like this country, no parallel for what money and freedom have brought to America.

Interview/Time,
2-13:90.

Boris N. Yeltsin
Member,
Congress of Peoples Deputies
of the Soviet Union
3

[On his visit to the U.S.]: I was always told that Americans are crude, rude and malicious. I have found them to be industrious, benevolent and well-intentioned.

USA Today,
9-15:(A)4.

21

Civil Rights • Women's Rights

Marcus Alexis
Dean, School of Business,
University of Illinois

1

There has been considerable progress [for blacks in the corporate world]. In businesses, blacks are no longer confined to administrative tasks, personnel management or public relations. They now have access to decision-making jobs, to the jobs where you really learn to be a manager. [But] you don't become the boss just because you are the most competent but also because you are part of the "network." You have to live in the right neighborhoods and socialize with the right people. One of my friends, a very high-ranking black executive, much to his chagrin, has never managed to get accepted at the golf club where his white underlings play.

Interview/World Press Review,
May:35.

Norman Amaker
Professor of law,
Loyola University,
Chicago

2

[On President Reagan's civil-rights record]: [He has done] a disservice to the American people. He has sent signals to the community at large that the civil-rights laws will not be taken seriously.

Interview/
Los Angeles Times, 1-20:(I)1.

Lee Atwater
Chairman, Republican
National Committee

3

One of the things I'm most proud of about President Bush is that he has had, for over eight months now, a sustained approval rating in the black community of 60 per cent. That's unprecedented for a Republican President. And I think that is because virtually every black leader in this country knows George Bush personally and because George Bush has a solid record on civil rights.

Interview/
USA Today, 12-14:(A)13.

Margaret Atwood
Author

4

[Saying her views on the women's movement may surprise some people]: Particularly in view of the kind of stuff [one hears] from certain elements of the women's movement, which is that women are egalitarian and they want a world of peace and friendliness and everybody interacting with one another. Anybody who has been in not just the women's movement but any kind of movement that involves women knows that there are power plays, power struggles. The—what word shall we use here?—the *approach* is different [from men], but that doesn't mean that those elements are not present. They are present.

Interview, Toronto/
Mother Jones, April:44.

Myrna Blyth
Editor-in-chief,
"Ladies' Home Journal"

5

Ten years ago, we talked about women working as a possibility, not a probability. Now, working is a reality for most women. In other words, we change our attitudes very quickly as we get accustomed to them. The work-force will change dramatically in the '90s. We will see more women middle managers, more minority middle managers. Hopefully, by the end of the '90s, we'll see more women CEOs. It will happen. It doesn't happen as dramatically as people imagine. And it doesn't happen in a way that everything is terrific once it happens.

Interview/USA Today, 5-9:(A)11.

George Bush
Vice President,
and President-elect,
of the United States

1

What becomes of [the late civil-rights leader] Martin Luther King's dreams is up to us. We must not fail him. We must not fail ourselves. And we must not fail the nation he loved so much and gave his life for. I understand that . . . We resolve today . . . that our nation, our America, will indeed remember Martin Luther King, Jr.; that his fight for equality, justice, freedom and peace will indeed be still pursued in the years to come and forevermore; that bigotry and indifference to disadvantage will find no safe home on our shores, in our public life, in our neighborhoods or in our home. Reverend King's dream for his children and for ours will be fulfilled. This must be our mission together. It will, I promise, be my mission as President of the United States.

At prayer breakfast,
Washington, Jan. 16/
Los Angeles Times, 1-17:(I)1,14.

2

I've always felt the need to stand for fair play and against bigotry, and I certainly would like to have an Administration that projects that. I'm not sure that that means some [far-] reaching legislative agenda. I will find ways to speak out in terms of the need to eliminate the last vestiges of bigotry . . . The problem is some people are going to measure compassion . . . by whether you can triple the budget for this account . . . or this service program. I won't be able to do that.

Interview/Newsweek, 1-30:32.

George Bush
President of the United States

3

[Saying he is against abortion]: There are people of good-will who will disagree, [but] after years of somber and serious reflection on the issue, this is what I think: America needs a human-life amendment. And I think that when it

comes to abortion, there's a better way—the way of adoption, the way of life.

To anti-abortion demonstrators,
Washington, Jan.23/
Los Angeles Times, 1-24:(I)19.

4

The law cannot tolerate any discrimination and my Administration will not tolerate abuse of that principle. The hard lesson of the passing years is that it has not been enough to wage a war against the old forms of bigotry and inequality. The lives of the disadvantaged in this country are affected by economic barriers at least as much as by the remnants of legal discrimination.

At ceremony marking
25th anniversary of
1964 Civil Rights Act,
Washington, June 30/
Los Angeles Times, 7-1:(I)2.

John C. Danforth
United States Senator,
R-Missouri

5

When you hear a racist slur or a bigoted joke, you have the power to encourage it, to laugh at it, to spread it. No law will be able to stop you. No law will even slow you down. But if you want to stop it, you can. You can stop it absolutely cold. You can be alert to meanness, and you can let it be known that you don't approve of it. When you hear the racist slur or the sexist slur, you can stare down the person who spoke it. You can shake your head and turn away. You can make it clear that in your presence, meanness will not be tolerated. Laws have been passed against discrimination. But no law is stronger than your own moral statement. Truly, each one of you is a universal lawgiver.

At Rockhurst College commencement,
May 14/The Washington Post, 6-6:(A)22.

Dennis DeConcini
United States Senator,
D-Arizona

6

I cannot think of any area where the Federal government has so completely abdicated its

(DENNIS DeCONCINI)

responsibility as it has in the Indian affairs . . . The Federal agencies entrusted with administering Indian programs have clearly failed in their responsibility. Moreover, they have failed to even recognize their own inadequacies.

Washington, June 8/
The New York Times, 6-10:(A)10.

Ramona Edelin
President,
National Urban Coalition

1

African-Americans [blacks] are doing everything anybody else is doing, but we're not doing it for ourselves. We're not doing it together. There's a reason why we don't have African-American Nintendos and African-American Nikes and other products that we spend billions on at Christmas time. We're always too busy to do whatever it is we need to do for ourselves, because someone else's culture dictates how we even spend our time.

Interview/USA Today, 4-20:(A)9.

Harry Edwards
Professor of sports sociology,
University of California,
Berkeley

2

. . . affirmative action is not a universal panacea. It's a tool, and no area indicates that more than sports. The NBA, for example, is 75 per cent black, and there was no affirmative action involved in it. But if you had an affirmative-action plan in the NBA based on society at large, you'd have 10 per cent black players and 90 per cent white players. As a tool, affirmative action would be counter-productive. The front-office situation in baseball, in sports in general, is not amenable to traditional civil-rights remedies.

Interview/Time, 3-6:62.

Bruce Fein
Legal scholar

3

In the United States it is very, very difficult to get a sensible discussion of free speech because the words themselves carry such an emotional overtone . . . In the United States there is an almost religious reverence for anything that travels under the banner of free speech. In any argument that's labeled "free speech" people become hysterical about any possible restrictions.

The Washington Post, 7-29:(C)5.

Arthur S. Flemming
Chairman, Citizens'
Commission on Civil Rights;
Former Chairman,
United States Commission
on Civil Rights

4

[On the prospects for President-elect Bush pushing ahead on the civil-rights front]: I've been around here long enough to know that when people move into new positions with challenging responsibilities, that they sometimes respond. I'm not going to get into evaluating [Bush's] past as far as civil rights. All I'm interested in is his future in the field of civil rights. I feel that as far as the future is concerned, there is real reason for hope that he will look with favor on the kinds of recommendations that are included in our report.

Washington, Jan.17/
The Washington Post, 1-18:(A)3.

Mary Hatwood Futrell
President, National
Education Association

5

The designation "African-American" [instead of "black"] can be very positive. It has a more positive connotation than simply calling ourselves black. African-American talks about our culture, our history as well as our present standing. It means that I not only am an American and not only have ties here, but I also have roots and ties in Africa, which is our base of origin. It is very positive for young people. It helps them to understand who they are and that they do indeed have a foundation that goes way back. The term will help give young people a sense of pride, a sense of heritage, and a sense of identity with our past, present and future.

Ebony, July:78.

William Gibson
*Chairman, National
Association for the
Advancement of Colored People*
1

Unlike in the '60s, many people no longer consider it a crisis circumstance [for blacks today]. During the '60s, if you were black in America it didn't matter how much money you had. When it came to social status, your skin color determined what hotel you could stay in, what restaurant you could eat in, what form of public transportation you could ride. Today, because such blatant forms of racism are no longer legally permitted, many people think the crisis in America is over, and that is unequivocally untrue.

Ebony, July:130.

Roberta Hestenes
President, Eastern College
2

I regret that our culture has shifted to the place where it does not seem to affirm the value of the mother who chooses to remain at home with her children [rather than working]. There's nothing particularly praiseworthy about selling necklaces at Penney's or writing memos in an office, over against the opportunity to shape a life, to build values, to show love. I did what I did because God called me, not because I had a career track. But if a woman has gifts that are to be used for a broader family, she's sinful if she doesn't use them. They're given for the common good. They should not be used at the expense of her children. But I found I had energy left over after caring for my children—plenty of it. It wasn't "either/or."

Christianity Today, 3-3:18.

Benjamin L. Hooks
*Executive director,
National Association for
the Advancement of Colored People*
3

[President] Bush has brought civility to Pennsylvania Avenue. There is no question that [he] has done much to raise the iron curtain that has

separated the White House from black Americans over the past several years. [But] this present Supreme Court is more dangerous to the legitimate hopes and aspirations of black people . . . than [former Alabama Governor] George Wallace crying, "Segregation today, segregation tomorrow, segregation forever."

*At NAACP convention, Detroit,
July 9/USA Today, 7-10:(A)1.*

4

[On President Bush's civil-rights record so far]: The President has commemorated the 25th anniversary of the Civil Rights Act. He has spoken with black South African leaders. Vice President Dan Quayle said the right things [at the NAACP convention]. But, I must add, the future of blacks and civil rights will not rise and fall on what Bush may say or do. No President ever makes or breaks a black initiative. But a President can be an awfully great help . . . Right now we are waiting for him to translate his promises into action. We plan to promote legislation to counter four recent Supreme Court decisions. We would like for him to support this legislation. We want him to live up to his dream of becoming the education President. We certainly want his Administration to support programs that bring economic progress to the average black American. We want him to support affirmative action, business set-asides for black entrepreneurs, and more educational opportunities for black youth.

*Interview, Detroit/
The Christian Science Monitor,
7-20:8.*

5

[Criticizing the current U.S. Supreme Court for allegedly handing down rulings to the detriment of civil rights]: I wouldn't mind if the Justices were stand-patters, but they're go-backers. If they'd stood pat, we'd at least have had the victories of the past . . . They have with relish been tearing up the fabric of what has brought America together over the last 20 years.

*The Christian Science Monitor,
9-26:2.*

Jesse L. Jackson
Civil-rights leader

1

If we were going to teach history, Western civilization, we must tell the truth. In our history books, there is a tremendous denial of the tragic truth of the slave trade. People tend not to know, to wipe it off. We [blacks] are the living descendants of this massive dislocation of people. There is a grand deletion of our history as Americans, a gaping hole in our culture. Others came [to the U.S.] to drop their chains; we were issued chains on arrival.

At African-American Institute Conference,
Lusaka, Zambia/
The New York Times, 1-11:(A)19.

John E. Jacob
President,
National Urban League

2

In 1988, blacks were three times as likely as whites to be poor. [Blacks were] 2½ times as likely to be jobless. Housing segregation increased. For the second straight year, black life expectancy declined. [Improvement was limited to] those most ready, most educated and most trained. But clearly, over-all, black America is not doing well.

News conference, Jan. 24/
The Washington Post, 1-25:(A)3.

3

Today, the term "African-American" is coming into broader usage [as an alternative to using the word "black"], and I'm all for it. It suggests a new maturity in our community and a healthy attitude toward our past. African-American, like other ethnic descriptions, is an accurate identification that places black Americans firmly within an ethnic, cultural and historical context. It links us to the history and experience of our forebears in Africa and our brothers and sisters in the world-wide black diaspora. Some polls indicate a majority of African-Americans already favor the term over black. But we should avoid an intra-community conflict over nomenclature, or campaigns designed to pressure people into using African-American instead of black. Our immediate concern is to focus on poverty, unemployment, housing, health and other key issues. However, to the extent that "African-American" evolves into our generally used name, it might help our young people rekindle the pride and maturity necessary to reach our goals.

Ebony, July:78.

4

[Criticizing Supreme Court Justice Sandra Day O'Connor for tipping the Court against civil-rights legislation]: Her role is ironic. She graduated from one of the nation's top law schools, but leading law firms wouldn't even interview her because they didn't hire women . . . She is on the bench today not simply because of her brilliance or her outstanding achievements, but because [former] President Reagan wanted a woman on the Supreme Court for political reasons. So the victim of discrimination today votes against other victims of discrimination. The beneficiary of affirmative action today votes against affirmative action for others.

At National Urban League conference,
Washington, Aug. 6/
The Washington Post, 8-7:(A)18.

5

The [U.S. Supreme] Court we once looked to as the protector of minority rights has itself become a threat to our rights. When the Court goes on the warpath against reasonable affirmative-action decrees that remedy past discrimination, it says that African-Americans [blacks], women and minorities won't be allowed to play catch-up.

At National Urban League conference,
Washington, Aug. 6/
The New York Times, 8-7:(A)6.

Gerald D. Jaynes
Professor of economics,
Yale University;
Director, National Research Council
study on trends in the black community

6

We have really two major findings, one positive, the other negative. By any calibration other

(GERALD D. JAYNES)

than that of an unrepentant segregationist, race relations and blacks' status are remarkably improved since the World War II era. However, the major fraction of this improvement was in place by 1970. Since then, material measures of status relative to whites have not improved and many have deteriorated.

July 27/The New York Times,
7-28:(A)8.

John Paul II
Pope

1

Respect for minority groups should be considered, in some way, the touchstone for harmonious social coexistence and as an index of the civil maturity achieved by a country and its institutions. Guaranteeing the participation of minorities in public life is a sign of elevated civil progress, and this turns to the honor of those nations in which all citizens are guaranteed such participation in a climate of true liberty.

Speech on "World Day of Peace,"
Vatican City,
Jan. 1/
Los Angeles Times, 1-2:(I)4.

2

[Arguing against abortion]: The dignity of the person can only be protected if the person is considered as inviolable from the moment of conception until natural death. A person cannot be reduced to the status of a means or a tool of others. Society exists to promote the security and dignity of the person. Therefore, the primary right which society must defend is the right to life. Whether in the womb or in the final phase of life, a person may never be disposed of in order to make life easier for others. Every person must be treated as an end to himself.

At Uppsala University,
Sweden, June 9/
Los Angeles Times,
6-10:(I)3.

Nancy L. Johnson
United States Representative,
R-Connecticut

3

[Arguing against government prohibition of abortion]: People must make the point that there is no other medical procedure that the government simply declares illegal and that the idea of denying women information is deeply contradictory to the concept of women's autonomy.

Ms., April:94.

Jack Kemp
Secretary of Housing and
Urban Development of
the United States

4

Phase 2 of the civil-rights struggle in America is for decent and affordable housing, homes and home-ownership and jobs and economic development and fair housing and education and giving people those tools that everyone needs in order to advance up that ladder of opportunity. The Constitution of the United States was written for every single one of us . . . Those [words] were not written just for white people. They were written for all people.

Interview/
Los Angeles Times, 4-9:(I)20.

5

[Saying he is prepared, and the Republican Party should be prepared, to take a more active role in promoting civil rights]: I wasn't there when Rosa Parks integrated transportation in Montgomery, Alabama. I wasn't there when the students integrated the lunch counters. I wasn't there when the schools were integrated in the '50s and '60s. I wasn't there at the Lincoln Memorial when Martin Luther King talked about "the dream." But ladies and gentlemen, I'm here today.

Before National Association for the
Advancement of Colored People,
Detroit, July 10/
The Washington Post, 7-11:(A)7.

27

C. Everett Koop
Surgeon General
of the United States

1

[On the possibility that the Supreme Court will reverse the *Roe vs. Wade* decision that legalized abortion, and turn over legalization authority to the states]: In order to get *Roe vs. Wade* passed, the number of back-alley abortion deaths had to be exaggerated by a hundredfold. The greatest number of deaths ever in one year was 373. That's a terrible number, but it wasn't 10,000. And I think that with the techniques that are being used by abortionists now, those same techniques will be used in the future, and they are safer. That doesn't mean that there's not going to be a black market and we [won't] have problems [if *Roe vs. Wade* is reversed]. It will open Pandora's box because we'll have 50 problems [each state acting individually] instead of one.

Broadcast interview/
"CBS This Morning,"
CBS-TV, 1-19.

Madeleine M. Kunin
Governor of Vermont (D)

2

As we look closely at the '80s, we can all pretty happily conclude that women have come a great distance. I think all of us are leading lives that we hadn't quite dared to imagine a few years ago in business, science, the arts, the government. So, why, then, are our numbers so small in positions of leadership at the highest level? The class portrait of the power structure in this country is still indisputably male. We've made progress in that we've taken responsibility for our own lives. But we also need to see *ourselves* as individuals capable of creating change. That is what political and economic power is all about: having a voice, being able to shape the future. Not that women's presence alone will bring these changes about. But women's absence from decision-making positions has deprived the country of this necessary perspective.

At symposium on
women in the 1990s,
New York, May/
Ladies' Home Journal, November:62.

Ann F. Lewis
Former political director,
Democratic National Committee

3

The women's movement has hit the mainstream. [It] clearly reflects middle America, culturally and socially, and there is no debate about the agenda. We no longer argue where the issue is child care or reproductive rights, political action or economic equity. We have arrived at a state where the agenda is understood and agreed on, even though we may have different strategies.

Kansas City/The New York Times,
1-9:(A)8.

Joseph E. Lowery
President, Southern Christian
Leadership Conference

4

[Attributing a recent rash of letter bombs to racial hatred]: We've cried out that domestic terrorism is just as perilous and threatening to our national security as international terrorism. The hate mail has continued, the telephone threats have continued, and occasional outbursts such as the one at Howard Beach [N.Y.] are still with us.

USA Today, 12-20:(A)3.

William Lucas
Assistant Secretary-designate,
Civil Rights Division,
Department of Justice
of the United States

5

[On those who criticize his nomination]: I resent being treated as if I was a potted plant along the way of advancement of civil rights . . . If a case is brought to me involving a cross burning on the lawn of a citizen, believe me, this is not just cold facts to me. I have been there. I have smelled the smoke. I have smelled the fear.

At Senate Judiciary Committee
hearing on his confirmation,
Washington, July 19/
The Washington Post, 7-20:(A)4.

Manuel Lujan, Jr.
Secretary of the Interior
of the United States

1

[On the American Indian]: The first word that comes to mind is integration, but it's more than that . . . Begin with youngsters and give them a superb education, and they will become part of society as a whole . . . As long as you have that division, you will always have your same reservation system. Probably the Number 1 thing that we need to address in the whole Bureau of Indian Affairs is education. Maybe that sounds too pat an answer, but I just don't think anybody can progress without being a part of the main society.

Interview/USA Today, 4-26:(A)11.

Wilma Mankiller
Chief of the Cherokee
(Indian) nation

2

Asking the meaning of [Indian] sovereignty is like asking an Indian what is the meaning of life.

USA Today, 2-9:(A)8.

Bob Martinez
Governor of Florida (R)

3

[Addressing anti-abortion demonstrators]: I stand with you. I stand with you because you are the voice of the unheard, those who have rights but no one has listened to. We're talking about an unborn baby who's seeking life. It's a heartbeat, a heartbeat that must be heard and seen.

Tallahassee, Fla., Oct. 9/
The New York Times, 10-11:(A)1.

Douglas S. Massey
Professor of sociology, and
director of Population
Research Center,
University of Chicago

4

[On racial segregation]: Where you live determines the chances you get in this world. It determines the school your children go to, the crime you're exposed to, the peer influences on your children. If you're isolated from the mainstream, it's not a fair world, it's not a fair contest. Segregation is structural underpinning of the underclass . . . Whites' irrational fear of blacks will never break down until people are brought into contact with each other. A lot of richness of life is lost by whites by not being in contact with blacks.

The New York Times, 8-5:6.

Kate Michelman
Executive director, National
Abortion Rights Action League

5

[Criticizing anti-abortionists]: These people seem to support life only from conception to birth. Once the child is born, they vote against support—such as school-lunch programs—for women and children in times of need. I would also think people who are so adamantly opposed to abortion would do everything to help prevent unwanted pregnancies. Yet these same people oppose family-planning programs and contraceptive research and advertising. They also oppose sex education in the schools. The quality-of-life issues don't seem to concern them.

Interview/
Cosmopolitan, July:132.

Charles Moody, Sr.
Vice provost for minority affairs,
University of Michigan,
Ann Arbor

6

You run into racism in the workplace. You run into racism in housing. You run into racism in trying to get mortgages and loans. You run into racism when people watch when you go into stores and [they] ask for extra kinds of identification. They don't care if you're an assistant provost at a major university—they see you as a black person. I think people as individuals can do something about it by looking at themselves and trying to change that part of the institution or community that they have control over. All of us have control over some part of it, even if it is just ourselves.

Interview/USA Today, 9-11:(A)6.

Eleanor Holmes Norton
Professor of law,
Georgetown University;
Former Chairman, Equal
Employment Opportunity
Commission of the United States

1

Sheer numbers of [black] people mean nothing if they have no political consciousness and no direction. We must find a way to call up the inner strength and discipline that have characterized us [blacks] for 300 years. The ability to do that will enhance us in the next century and help change the course of race relations.

Ebony, April:88.

2

There is an inherent decency in the white community that was brought out by the civil-rights movement of the '60s, but that can only be sustained if they have more frequent contact with average blacks . . . There needs to be a continuing public, conciliatory dialogue between racial and cultural groups so that those who continue to harbor a racial prejudice feel isolated. We need to talk these things out, not act on them. Black-white relations between average Americans are not hostile—they simply are not close enough. The kind of integrated society that has been hypothesized simply has not yet been achieved.

Interview/USA Today, 9-11:(A)6.

Reza Pahlavi
Exiled son of the
late Shah of Iran

3

In today's world we have seen that the role of women is fundamental to the progress of nations. Why should we live with 50 per cent of our potential when we can have 100 per cent? Women have a tremendous role to play. The amount of what they have had to put up with, having been made the lowest of Iranians by the present regime [in Iran] and still being the strongest activists, proves their importance. I see them as equals and have said so to my countrymen.

Interview/People, 4-3:51.

Sally Parr
Executive director,
National Women's Hall of Fame

4

We are the only institution that honors women nationally—women who have made a difference, not just locally and not just to a small region, but to the whole country . . . The Eleanor Roosevelts and the Marian Andersons and the Gwendolyn Brookses and the Helen Hayeses of the world, and the women who started the suffrage movement in 1848. It is a historical institution that writes women back into history . . . Whatever we write into or out of history shows what matters to us. We're writing women into history and, to most people, that matters. It matters to the women who have been honored. It matters that our daughters have an opportunity to develop their potential. And as long as we provide role models, interpretations and explanations, we help make the country better for all people.

Interview/USA Today, 6-14:(A)11.

Daniel J. Popeo
General counsel,
Washington Legal Foundation

5

[On civil-rights leaders who criticize blacks and other minorities who are nominated for key Federal posts by conservative Republican Presidents]: My feeling is we've come full circle in America. We've got civil-rights activists that are so radical that they are opposing minorities who are nominated, saying they are unqualified when in reality they just don't like anyone who would be nominated by a conservative Republican President.

July 11/The New York Times,
7-12:(A)10.

Dan Quayle
Vice President
of the United States

6

Affirmative action is a social policy that has in fact worked. Affirmative action is right, and affirmative action is going to be maintained as the

(DAN QUAYLE)

policy of the Bush Administration. What we have been in opposition to is absolute [racial] quotas. We are committed to fairness, and black Americans ought to understand that.

Interview, Detroit, July 12/
The New York Times, 7-13:(A)14.

1

[Saying the Bush Administration is committed to civil rights]: I feel confident we can work together and build an America we all envision. There is no place for the [Ku Klux] Klan, neo-Nazis, skinheads or any other racist group in our country . . . This is not rhetoric. This is not politics. This, my friends, is the right thing to do. We may differ from time to time on the course this nation must travel, but we agree on the ultimate destination.

Before board members of
Southern Christian Leadership Conference,
Atlanta, Aug. 15/
The New York Times, 8-16:(A)12.

Ronald Reagan
President of the United States

2

[On his opposition to abortion]: Our critics call themselves pro-choice. But have they ever stopped to think that the unborn never have a choice? When *Roe vs. Wade* [the Supreme Court decision legalizing abortion] goes, as I have faith it must, the way of Dred Scott and "separate but equal," a new debate will rise in the statehouses of our land. And the voice that I believe must be heard and, in the end shall be heard, over all the others, is the voice of life.

Before Knights of Malta of America,
New York, Jan. 13/
The New York Times, 1-14:7.

3

One of the great things that I have suffered in this job is this feeling and this editorializing comment that somehow I'm on the other side [of the civil-rights struggle]. As a sports announcer, when blacks were denied the right to play major-league baseball, I was one of the little group in the

nation that editorialized constantly that they shouldn't be, that they should be allowed to participate in sports. [As Governor of California,] I appointed more blacks to executive and policy-making positions in government than all the previous Governors of California put together.

Broadcast interview, Washington/
"60 Minutes," CBS-TV, 1-15.

4

[On today's civil-rights leaders]: Sometimes I wonder if they really want what they say they want, because some of those leaders are doing very well leading organizations based on keeping alive the feeling that they're victims of prejudice.

Broadcast interview, Washington/
"60 Minutes," CBS-TV, 1-15.

Patricia Schroeder
United States Representative,
D-Colorado

5

One of the problems with being a working mother, whether you're a Congresswoman or a stenographer or whatever, is that everybody feels perfectly free to come and tell you what they think: "I think what you're doing to your children is terrible." "I think you should be home." They don't do that to men.

Interview, Boston/
The Christian Science Monitor,
3-15:14.

6

It is tragic that our history got rewritten so we didn't put in the role women really played. Women came to this country, not on cruise ships; they came here on the same ships men did . . . You've got a long, proud tradition of women who helped build this country, and so don't feel at all bad about wanting to walk shoulder to shoulder with the men. That's what we've got to do. We need all the brainpower this country can have if we're going to compete in the new, global village.

At Simmons College commencement/
The Christian Science Monitor,
6-12:13.

Joanne Simpson
President, American
Meteorological Society

1

Any comparison between the way it was [for women] when I started and the way it is now is like comparing the covered wagon with a jet plane. But this doesn't mean that women don't still have obstacles to overcome. American women just assume things are going to keep getting better. But I tell them, "Don't ever take progress and freedom for granted." Sometimes you have to fight just to keep the opportunities you have.

Interview/
The Christian Science Monitor,
10-30:14.

Eleanor Smeal
President, Fund for
the Feminist Majority;
Former president, National
Organization for Women

2

[On her support for keeping abortions legal]: Every three minutes, world-wide, a woman is dying from a botched illegal abortion. We show how these women's lives could be saved. We have the technology. It would cost 18 cents a woman. How much is a woman's life worth? But [the] moralizing, hypocritical discussion—and that's how I feel about it—[by anti-abortionists] is not dealing with the living and dying of real women—[they're] talking about saving embryos. [They're] talking about when life begins, and these women are dying.

Interview/USA Today, 7-20:(A)9.

Anne Smith
Editor-in-chief,
"Working Woman" magazine

3

If corporations think that any woman who has a child should automatically plateau in her job or be viewed as on a "mommy track" that won't take her to the top, then that will be very unfortunate indeed. It already happens, and would happen much more, if there were a formal

process to let women hold back. It also means that in many cases they would be overlooked by their corporation, whether the women wanted it or not. They would be on a slower track and not viewed as promotable.

Interview/USA Today, 3-13:(A)7.

Susan Smith
Associate legislative director,
National Right to Life Committee

4

[On her organization's stand against abortion]: None of us would be in this if we were talking about a woman's right to get her ears pierced, or to get a hysterectomy, or to have a tumor removed or a hangnail taken care of. The reason that all of us come together on this— liberals, conservatives, black, white, young, old—is because of the profound conviction that abortion kills the life of a unique, defenseless individual. The reason we're involved is the very fact that it's not just a woman's body.

Interview/USA Today, 7-20:(A)9.

Rodney Strong
Director, Office of Contract Compliance
of Atlanta

5

The affirmative-action effort is not simply about building jobs and income among blacks. We're trying also for some significant capital formation in the black community among people who will take the risk of investing in black areas when white firms won't. We're concerned with seeing this happen just as much as we are with seeing jobs and income, but I think it will take at least 10 more years of affirmative-action efforts before we see significant progress.

The New York Times, 1-27:(A)7.

Louis W. Sullivan
Secretary-designate of
Health and Human Services
of the United States

6

I am opposed to abortion, excepting in the case where the life of the mother is threatened, or in

(LOUIS W. SULLIVAN)

cases of rape or incest. I support a human-life amendment, embracing the exceptions just noted. Like President Bush, I would welcome a Supreme Court decision overturning *Roe vs. Wade* [the 1973 Court ruling legalizing abortion].

At Senate Finance Committee hearing
on his confirmation,
Washington, Feb. 23/Los Angeles Times, 2-24:(I)6.

Dick Thornburgh
Attorney General
of the United States

1

The pursuit and promotion of civil rights in America is more than a legal obligation, it is a moral imperative embodied in our national sense of fairness and justice.

At Operation PUSH convention,
Chicago, June 27/
The Christian Science Monitor,
6-29:8.

2

I know how I feel about civil rights, what my record is in civil rights. Civil-rights laws will be vigorously enforced and we will attack every barrier to equal opportunity that we can find, using appropriate tools; and if those tools aren't enough, then we will seek new tools.

Interview/USA Today, 7-25:(A)9.

Faye Wattleton
President, Planned Parenthood Federation
of America

3

I have always seen [abortion rights] as an issue of choice and an issue of self-determination. Make no mistake—the double standard is alive and well in our society. The imposition of male values, the exploitation, the statistics on rape, and date rape in particular, all point to the perception that women are there to be used, that women's choices and desires are not to be honored and respected. You simply cannot get away from the fundamental diminution of women's integrity when it comes to issues of sexual morality and behavior. We're out of the kitchen and it is unlikely that we're going to go

back. So how do you maintain control over a major segment of the community that has always been controlled? The strong, overarching message is that the best way is by maintaining sexual control. Reproductive freedom is critical to a whole range of issues. If we can't take charge of this most personal aspect of our lives, we can't take care of anything. It should not be seen as a privilege or as a benefit, but a fundamental human right.

Interview/Ms., October:50.

William L. Webster
Attorney General of Missouri

4

[On the U.S. Supreme Court's recent decision which expands states' rights on abortion issues]: We don't believe it will have any short-term impact on abortion, but I think you have to go to the longer-term significance of the ruling. Essentially, [the older] *Roe vs. Wade* [Court ruling] said that in the first trimester, almost no state regulation limiting abortion could withstand scrutiny, and in the second trimester, the issue would be viability. Now the Court has sent a strong signal that the trimester framework is flawed, that states have a substantial interest in regulating abortion, and that it would entertain additional state regulations. The Court seemed to invite it in the text of its opinion. The long-term result is that substantial responsibility to regulate abortion is returned to the states.

Interview/
Christianity Today, 8-18:37.

Pete Wilson
United States Senator,
R-California

5

[On abortion]: The decision to terminate a pregnancy is so intensely personal that no one but the woman can be permitted to make it. Government does nothing wise or good if it enacts laws that force this decision underground [by outlawing abortion] and compel otherwise law-abiding citizens to resort to illegal and dangerous back-alley medical treatment or self-performed abortions.

Los Angeles Times, 11-17:(A)46.

Commerce • Industry • Finance

Michael H. Armacost
United States Ambassador
to Japan

1

[On concern about foreign companies buying U.S. firms]: Some Americans worry that for a substantial, perhaps a technologically critical, part of the U.S. economy, a measure of control over decisions affecting our national interest could be lost. There is a natural concern that foreign managers may not be sensitive to American traditions and unwritten rules . . . Some Americans worry that our social harmony may be disrupted.

To U.S. and Japanese business leaders,
Tokyo, Oct. 19/
Los Angeles Times, 10-20:(D)2.

Ben Bagdikian
Professor, Graduate School
of Journalism,
University of California,
Berkeley

2

[On the current "merger mania" among larger entertainment companies]: [The result of mergers is] going to be a loss for the public in a number of ways. The most important loss is a loss of diversity. There's a loss of diversity of ownership, but there's also a loss in diversity in the content—there will be fewer choices. [Diversity] is important in the entertainment business because it socializes whole generations on what social values are, what a desirable personality and social being is. And what it does is narrow down those choices to those kinds of depictions . . . that make the most money the fastest for the biggest operators.

Interview/
Los Angeles Times, 6-25:(IV)3.

Gerald L. Baliles
Governor of Virginia (D)

3

Too often in the past, exports have been seen [in the U.S.] as something that is done when the market is down here and there is a need to unload unsold inventory. While you may be able to find markets for that stored inventory, when the market picks up here at home and they don't continue to supply the foreign markets, then we get a bad image of not being reliable suppliers of quality goods. So the challenge is to persuade businesses that there is money to be made overseas and that filling those market needs keeps them operating, citizens employed and revenues being generated for state and local governments. It all fits together.

Interview/
USA Today, 7-27:(A)9.

George Ball
Chairman,
Prudential-Bache
Securities

4

The collective lust for immediate financial gratification—by individuals, institutions, arbitrageurs and companies alike—has fostered an unhealthy promiscuous approach to investing.

USA Today, 2-7:(B)4.

Max Baucus
United States Senator,
D-Montana

5

[Criticizing Japan's barriers to foreign products]: For years, Japan has told the rest of the world that Japan is different. Snow-ski exporters were told that they could not export skis to Japan because Japanese snow was different. U.S. ranchers were told that they could not export beef to Japan because Japanese intestines were different . . . I have always taken Japan's claims of uniqueness with a grain of salt. Usually, they were simply excuses for protectionism.

The Christian Science Monitor,
11-6:2.

Karl D. Bays
Chairman,
Whitman Corporation

1

Business has a legal and moral responsibility to its owners—the shareholders—when it supports worthwhile causes. Managers don't have the right to arbitrarily reduce profits in the name of sweet charity. An individual may be motivated by a sense of pure kindness in giving money away. But shareholders have the right to expect some reasonable relationship to a corporation's goals, whether building good-will, promoting the product, enhancing the company's reputation, or improving the quality of life in cities where employees live and work. And they have a right to expect that any contribution the corporation makes will help solve a problem. Otherwise, a manager should hold on to the shareholders' money. We get literally thousands of requests for cash support each year. But we'd rather give $25,000 to one group that one of our executives is working with, than $500 to 50 organizations where we have no direct involvement. We like to know that our contribution will make a difference.

Speech, June/
The Wall Street Journal,
10-2:(A)14.

Lloyd Bentsen
United States Senator,
D-Texas

2

Today our great industrial heartland is under attack. Not from foreign military forces. From new technology. From foreign competition— often from our allies. You see the evidence everywhere. You see it in ships pulling up to American docks loaded not with immigrants but with Volkswagens. You see it in the living-rooms of America—in those VCRs so many of you tonight have sitting by the TV set. None of those VCRs are made in America—not one. It's all very well to say [as President Bush has said]: Read my lips. Japanese computer companies tell customers: Read my chips.

Broadcast address to the nation,
Washington, Feb. 9/
USA Today, 2-10:(A)6.

C. Fred Bergsten
Director, Institute for
International Economics

3

The Reagan Administration talked a wonderful free-trade game, but their macroeconomic policy made it impossible to carry out a free-trade policy. By avoiding government intervention on the foreign-exchange market [to slow the strong dollar, which increased imports], they forced themselves into a situation where they had to go protectionist.

The Wall Street Journal,
9-22:(R)27.

Robert C. Bonner
United States Attorney
for Los Angeles

4

In a lot of business crime or corruption, we are talking about individuals who are viewed as pillars of the community. High-level executives are cheating because they are not happy with a million-dollar income. The greed factor enters in, which has the effect of lowering the moral tone of society in general. Very frequently, we've seen the reaction of lower-level employees, who are otherwise good citizens in the community, look at what's going on and they see the greed, corruption and deceit. There is a tendency to think that if the big guys are getting away with it, why shouldn't I be getting my share?

Interview/
Los Angeles Times, 1-29:(IV)3.

Tom Bradley
Mayor of Los Angeles

5

Some politicians find it fashionable to rail against foreign investment [in the U.S.]—to conjure up images of foreign takeovers. At its best, this is nothing but political grandstanding. But at its worst, this is a dangerous strain of racism that must be rebutted. Make no mistake about it. Some who criticize foreign investment are really expressing outright prejudice against non-Anglo participants [in the U.S. economy].

Before Los Angeles World Affairs
Council, Feb. 16/
Los Angeles Times, 2-17:(I)18.

Nicholas F. Brady
Secretary of the Treasury
of the United States

1

[On the phenomenon of leveraged buyouts of corporations]: . . . I admit that I have a growing feeling that we are headed in the wrong direction when so much of our young talent and the nation's financial resources are aimed at financial engineering, while the rest of the world is laying the foundation for the future. At this point we are at a crossroads on LBOs. We ought to watch a little longer. We have a habit in this country of correcting things just as they are about to correct themselves.

Before Senate Finance Committee,
Washington/
The New York Times, 2-1:(C)2.

Richard C. Breeden
Chairman-designate,
Securities and Exchange
Commission of the
United States

2

Free markets don't work if investors believe markets are dominated by fraud and corruption . . . I am a strong believer in the free market . . . but that does not need to connote tolerance of fraud. To achieve the result of a clean market, [you need] an element of predictability in the law and the understanding that it will be vigorously enforced.

At Senate Banking Committee hearing
on his confirmation,
Washington, Sept. 14/
Los Angeles Times, 9-15:(IV)3.

Andrew F. Brimmer
Former Member,
Federal Reserve Board

3

[I] would like to see more done for education by business. The kind of education I'm talking about is at the elementary and secondary level. Businesses are already contributing to colleges. Businesses should do likewise for elementary and secondary schools. Business people can play

a role as counselors and teachers. A firm might make available an engineer or mathematician to go into schools and teach. Business should do more to offer on-the-job training for unskilled, or limited-skills, people, perhaps through a [lower] learning wage. We would give business tax credits to do this.

Interview/
Los Angeles Times, 1-1:(IV)3.

Alan Bromberg
Authority on securities law;
Professor,
Southern Methodist University

4

I would like to see a national consensus developed, preferably in the form of Federal legislation, on corporate take-overs and buyouts that would recognize the efficiencies and benefits they bring as well as the dislocations and hardships they can cause. This would involve tax policies and labor policies and limitations on the ability of states to Balkanize corporate law by different anti-takeover statutes everywhere. [There also should be] some kind of limitation on management self-entrenchment and self-enrichment.

Interview/
Los Angeles Times, 1-1:(IV)3.

George Bush
President of the United States

5

[South] Korea's economy has benefited greatly from the free flow of trade. Yet today in many countries there is a call for greater protectionism. I am asking you to join the United States in rejecting these shortsighted pleas. Protectionism may seem to be the easy way out, but it is really the quickest way down.

Before South Korean National Assembly,
Seoul, Feb. 27/
The Washington Post, 2-27:(A)11.

6

The power of commerce is a force for progress. Open markets are the key to continued growth in

(GEORGE BUSH)

the developing world. Today the United States buys over one half of the manufactured exports that all developing nations combined sell to the industrialized world. It's time for the other advanced economies to follow suit, to create expanded opportunities for trade. I believe we'll learn, in the century ahead, that many nations of the world have barely begun to tap their true potential for development. The free market and its fruits are not the special preserve of a few. They are a harvest that everyone can share.

At United Nations,
New York, Sept. 25/
The New York Times, 9-26:(A)8.

Robert C. Byrd
United States Senator,
D-West Virginia

1

The United States has plenty of leverage to use in any [trade] negotiation, but we tippy-toe when it comes to Japan. Our United States Treasury turns to Japan with knees trembling when we go out to sell our bonds. We have not yet come to realize that our economic strength is our national security and that trade is a major pillar of our economic well-being.

Before the Senate, Washington/
The New York Times, 5-27:19.

Tom Campbell
United States Representative,
R-California

2

As we extend into world trade and into the higher-technology aspects of world trade, it is essential that we unleash the genius of the American economic system, and to that end particularly to allow the U.S. companies who wish to pool their research, to pool their capital and to pool risk to do so. In 1984, we passed the National Cooperative Research Act. This allowed American companies who wished to pool their research and development to do so. But it had a critical shortage: It did not allow American companies who wished to take their thoughts,

the product of their innovation, and make the product to do so. It did not allow American companies to collaborate and to develop its commercialization of those products. This is critical to allow. The reason is that so much is learned not only from the research and development, but from the manufacturing of the good itself, and so much is learned from talking with the customers and learning from them what problems they have, particularly in high technology.

Before the House, Washington,
Feb. 22/
The Washington Post, 3-2:(A)22.

Colby Chandler
Chairman,
Eastman Kodak Company

3

[On the difficulty of U.S. companies competing against Japanese firms]: All of us [in the U.S.]—government, business—have built little fortresses, and we shoot darts across, and we hurt each other. And Japan, Inc., is what we are competing against. We're not competing against Company A, B or C. We are competing with products introduced in the market by [Japanese] Company A and produced in collaboration with several other companies that supply the components, produced as a result of a combined research of [the Japanese] government, academia and other companies. Produced in an environment in which the cost of capital is a couple of per cent. Produced in an environment in which the tax system favors exports, gives them great incentive to export, great incentive to run at a loss for several years if the long-term gain is there. Produced in an environment in which the share owners are willing to forgo dividends indefinitely.

Interview/
USA Today, 4-4:(A)7.

Tetsuo Chino
President,
Honda Motor Company
(North America)

4

The bottom line of our company is to respect people. You have to respect the local community

37

(TETSUO CHINO)

or you can't grow and, to do so, you [Honda, a Japanese company] have to become more American. We are trying to localize everywhere we operate. In Europe we are trying to be more European, in Brazil more Brazilian. This is a natural step for increasing business in the host country.

Interview/
The New York Times, 2-14:(C)2.

John Cleese
Actor, Humorist

1

Flippancy [on the job] is almost never right, except perhaps between very good friends who understand what the score is. But humor, if it is the right type, is absolutely splendid. It relaxes people and makes them more spontaneous and creative. But a lot of executives are scared of humor, and I think it's because their personality type finds humor fundamentally unappealing. A lot of them are a bit pompous, and pompous people don't like to be around humor because they know a humorous atmosphere will puncture their act. While some of the most splendid people I've met are top executives—they are funny, wry, highly intelligent and very insightful—some of the most awful people I've encountered have also been executives. You meet one or two of them and think to yourself: "What are they supposed to be, the mouthpieces for the clever ones?"

Interview/
U.S. News & World Report,
10-16:105.

John L. Clendenin
Chairman, United States
Chamber of Commerce;
Chairman, BellSouth Corporation

2

We haven't quite accommodated some of the dramatic shifts in the working population, such as the impact on children when both parents work. But the question is whether we can saddle American business with additional economic burdens and expect them to remain competitive. What do we gain by driving several hundred thousand workers into unemployment because the small and medium-sized businesses that had employed them were unable to absorb the costs of these new [social] mandates? Does that put us ahead as a nation? Clearly, it does not.

Interview/
Nation's Business, June:62.

Mary Congdon
Chief executive officer,
U.S. West Communications

3

Most good managers today don't give orders. They ask advice of the people who are actually going to be out there doing the job. It's a more consultative style. Ultimately, of course, the manager makes the decision and takes responsibility for it . . . Managers who don't recognize that and who manage in the old militaristic way will not be as successful.

Interview/
Nation's Business,
April:12.

Gerald Curtis
Director,
East Asian Institute,
Columbia University

4

[On criticism by some Americans of large Japanese investments in the U.S.]: There was a lot of intense European concern about the dominance of American money. Now there's American concern about the power of Japanese money. Well, in retrospect, American investments in Europe helped revitalize the European economy, and Japanese investments in this country are going to help revitalize the American economy . . . The Japanese may buy a big building or part of Rockefeller Center, but they can't bring it back to Tokyo. It's still there—it means that Japanese money is in the U.S. economy. It's one way to recycle Japanese [trade] surpluses.

The New York Times, 12-18:(A)17.

John D. Dingell
United States Representative,
D-Michigan

1

[Criticizing a Federal Reserve ruling permitting certain banks to buy and sell corporate bonds]: The Fed is on its way to giving banks an invitation to shoot craps with the taxpayers' money.

Time, 1-30:51.

Christopher J. Dodd
United States Senator,
D-Connecticut

2

[Criticizing a Bush Administration proposal to impose a fee on bank and savings-and-loan accounts to help pay for a bail-out of ailing S&Ls]: I fail to see why the Administration would continue to push a tax on deposits. As a class, depositors are the party least responsible for the thrift industry's problems. The proposal would not only be unfair, it would be a dangerous disincentive to savings at precisely the time when we should be doing all we can to increase the savings rate.

Jan. 29/
The New York Times,
1-30:(C)2.

Anthony Downs
Economist;
Senior fellow,
Brookings Institution

3

I'm against limiting the flow of Japanese capital into the United States. We are doing a lot of investment overseas, and we don't want our outflows limited. Second, foreign investment benefits both owners and sellers. If we want to stop the Japanese from buying property, we should lower our Federal deficits. Without a big surplus, the Japanese won't have the money to purchase a lot of overseas real estate. That's the way to do it.

Interview/
U.S. News & World Report,
1-30:59.

Thomas F. Eagleton
Former United States Senator,
D-Missouri

4

[On his just-announced resignation as a director of the Chicago Mercantile Exchange]: From the time of the FBI sting early this year to the most recent handling of the Monieson [commodities fraud] case, I have grown increasingly dissatisfied with the way the Chicago Mercantile Exchange handles decisions relating to the public interest, confidence and well-being. Whether the decision relates to open outcry or verbal orders or index arbitrage or floor surveillance or discipline of members or penalties for thievery or eduction/training of members or, more recently, the Brian Monieson matter, the Merc decision is usually a non-Lincolnian decision of insiders by insiders for insiders.

Resignation letter, Nov. 7/*
The Washington Post, 11-8:(B)1.

Stuart B. Ewen
Associate professor,
Department of Communication,
Hunter College

5

Advertising has become the primary mode of public address . . . The term "consumer" has become a substitute for the term citizen . . . The truth is that which sells . . . If people buy it, it's right.

Broadcast interview/
The Wall Street Journal,
11-6:(A)14.

George Fisher
Chief executive officer,
Motorola, Inc.

6

Earlier in this century, the British tended to win Nobel Prizes, and the U.S. brought the products to market. In the last few decades, the Americans have been winning the prizes, but others are marketing the products. Tracing these historical trends invites us to speculate about how various regions of the world will be classified in the 21st century. If you believe in a circu-

(GEORGE FISHER)

lar view of history, it might be time to start thinking about Europe again.

Speech at Japan Society,
New York, October/
The Wall Street Journal,
11-28:(A)14.

Karl Flemke
President, Junior Achievement

1

[For success in business,] there's no real substitute for formal education through high school and college and taking some business courses. But the key is to involve young people as early as possible in an entrepreneurial environment. That's what we do with Junior Achievement. We have young people actually running companies at an early age. The new jobs are being created by small business ventures—new company start-ups. And the work force is really contracting in the bigger companies. So the opportunity is in these young companies.

Interview/
USA Today, 8-7:(A)11.

Milton Friedman
Economist

2

[On the Oct. 13, 1989, stock-market crash]: This is a particularly big fluctuation, a very substantial decline in percentage terms. But the market will recover from it, just as it recovered from the one-day, 508-point decline in 1987. There is nothing about the decline in the market, in and of itself, that need give any concern about the economy.

Time, 10-23:67.

Richard J. Fruehan
Director, Center for Iron and
Steelmaking Research,
Carnegie-Mellon University

3

The Japanese [steel] companies look to the future and realize that in the long term, an industrial nation cannot look at steel as a growth industry. American companies do little if any work in alternative materials that could replace steel . . . The biggest problem the steel industry will face in five years will be having enough good technical people to carry on. The age group of 25 to 45 hardly exists in research centers in the United States steel industry.

The New York Times, 8-7:(C)7.

John Kenneth Galbraith
Professor emeritus of economics,
Harvard University

4

The institutional truth of the financial world holds that association with money implies intelligence. And it holds broadly that the greater the amount of money, the greater the intelligence. And that the pursuit of money by whatever design within the law is always benign . . . In truth, the larger the amount of money commanded, the greater very often the error, on occasion even the stupidity. So it was with the men—and in the manner of the great banks, the few women—who made those [bad] loans to Latin America . . .

At Smith College commencement/
The Christian Science Monitor,
6-12:13.

James Goldsmith
British financier

5

[On so-called "hostile" takeovers of failing companies]: Hostile to whom? Not to shareholders. They were offered a premium for shares in a declining business and they could reinvest their cash elsewhere. Not to the employees of the underlying businesses. They were suffering from the conglomerate structure. Deconglomeration would lead their business to renewed independence or alternatively to joining a group which could help their future development. Not to suppliers, customers or local communities, and not to the economy as a whole, because the dismantling of a faulty structure leads to positive improvement and a more productive deployment of resources. So, in reality, hostile in this

(JAMES GOLDSMITH)

context means hostile to head-office staff... Following a hostile takeover, management is changed.

At International Mergers and Acquisitions Conference, London, Nov. 16/ The Wall Street Journal, 11-24:(A)6.

Mikhail S. Gorbachev
General Secretary, Communist Party of the Soviet Union; President of the Soviet Union

1

[Speaking to U.S. businessmen about investing and doing business in the Soviet Union]: If you get a foothold in the Soviet market, the opportunities will be endless. Right now, we are rethinking everything, rearranging everything... Invest, do a deal, don't be afraid—the profits are there. Do you want to do just more than come and sell? If you are interested in joint manufacturing ventures, come and invest. The profits will be there, the profits will be there ... Provided you are not greedy and that you work openly with us, provided you just don't want to come in, sell quick and then leave, your opportunities will be great here. Patience pays.

At U.S. trade show, Moscow, Oct. 17/ Los Angeles Times, 10-18:(D)3.

Craig Gordon
Director, Grassroots Research

2

The consumer is getting more active. I don't know if it's a revolt yet ... Manufacturers have become real sensitive to it. Almost every consumer product now has an "800" complaint line. A lot of manufacturers have discovered they'd rather have the person vent the frustration at them instead of going to other avenues, whether it's government or boycotting the product, or whatever. There's a lot more choices and a lot less brand loyalty than there was before ... I

think businesses are becoming more aware of how important it is to get the consumer in the decision-making process.

Interview/ Los Angeles Times, 5-14:(IV)3.

Katharine Graham
Chairman, Washington Post Company

3

Labor-intensive industries, such as communications, are almost always disadvantaged to some degree as they get larger. Still, just because being big doesn't necessarily make sense, it doesn't mean that companies are not going to get even larger. The competitive urge to grow has never been stronger. The adrenaline is really pumping. Human nature has taken over: People want to be big because they want to be big. No evidence has ever surfaced that the dinosaurs, even on the brink of extinction, wanted to trade places with the cockroaches, who would endure for a billion years.

Before San Francisco Advertising Club/ Los Angeles Times, 6-25:(IV)3.

Robert Guccione
Founder, "Penthouse" magazine

4

New money is really represented by the entrepreneurs who create it. I am proud to represent new money. It's a great mistake that my children and grandchildren will be given, somehow, more credibility because they will represent old money. They will have lost all of the excitement of the game, the wonderful memories I had in getting there in the first place.

Interview/ USA Today, 2-2:(A)9.

Greg Harris
Lecturer in marketing, London Business School (Britain)

5

Twenty-five years ago, when TV was introduced, you had some bright spark saying it would

41

(GREG HARRIS)

create the global consumer. Five years ago, when satellite was introduced, you had the same thing. Basically, nobody's ever found this "global consumer."

The Wall Street Journal,
9-22:(R)12.

Raymond Hay
Chief executive officer,
LTV Corporation

1

I believe the trade deficit is a bigger part of the problem than the financial [Federal budget] deficit. The trade deficit is the major reason why we have the [budget] deficit that we have today, and if we could solve the trade deficit and get ourselves even in trade, the rest of the problems would be substantially easier to deal with.

Interview/
USA Today, 6-7:(A)11.

Samuel L. Hayes III
Professor of
investment banking,
Harvard Business School

2

[On bond dealer Michael Milken's $550-million 1987 compensation from his employer, Drexel Burnham Lambert]: It's embarrassing to our financial system. It portrays the image of an industry that has gotten totally out of control in terms of its greed for money.

The New York Times, 4-3:(C)2.

Richard Heckert
Chairman, E. I. du Pont de Nemours
& Company

3

What is good for business broadly may not be good for the country. We'll build our plants where they belong, and that isn't always in the United States.

The Washington Post, 3-20:(A)24.

Jesse Helms
United States Senator,
R-North Carolina

4

[On the huge Japanese trade surplus with the United States]: This coddling of the Japanese is not the attitude that made our nation great. It is not an attitude that will preserve this nation as one after the other of our fine industries are destroyed. If we are to survive as a nation, we must take a stand.

Los Angeles Times,
8-7:(I)15.

Theodore M. Hesburgh
President emeritus,
University of Notre Dame

5

In general, I find the level of ethical conduct quite high in American business. I wish I could say the same for European business. I find that foreign businesses are very much more prone to pay bribes and do all kinds of things to get orders. I think some of our toughest competitors overseas are the worst—the Europeans and Japanese.

Interview/
Los Angeles Times, 1-29:(IV)3.

Carla A. Hills
United States Trade
Representative-designate

6

[If we want to reduce our trade imbalance,] the United States must save more and consume less. Retaliation [against foreign countries] cannot be the goal of our policy . . . Our strategic goal is to open markets, not close them. [But] I will not hesitate to act [by using retaliatory measures] to fight unfair trade practices . . . The credible threat of retaliation provides essential leverage in our market-opening efforts.

At Senate Finance Committee
hearing on her confirmation,
Washington, Jan. 27/
Los Angeles Times,
1-28:(I)17.

Carla A. Hills
United States Trade
Representative

1

[Saying Japan must open its markets more to foreign imports]: I see us at a crossroads—a crossroads where we can eliminate barriers to trade and have world-wide competition and a vibrant world system . . . or, alternatively, the peril that the anxieties will grow so large that individual markets turn inward [decreasing both world trade and prosperity]. The global trading system . . . cannot function when the second-largest market of the world [Japan] does not fully participate.

News conference, Tokyo, Oct. 13/
Los Angeles Times, 10-14:(D)4.

Shirley Hufstedler
Former Secretary of
Education of the United States;
Former U.S. Circuit Court
of Appeals Judge

2

Dishonesty [in business] worries me and the more powerful the person or entity that is dishonest, the more it worries me. Persons very high up, indeed, were manipulating securities markets for their own benefit and for very great profits, and they were not underlings. The very conspicuous defections from the path of honesty by some highly prominent figures should not be taken as a view that business over-all is corrupt or dishonest, because that is just not true. Most businesses are run faithfully with a great deal of very hard work and with considerable concern about the public weal as well as the success of the business.

Interview/
Los Angeles Times, 1-29:(IV)3.

Lee A. Iacocca
Chairman,
Chrysler Corporation

3

I grew up believing protectionism was pretty dumb, and I still do. But somewhere along the line we [in the U.S.] stopped being idealists and started being patsies.

Time, 6-5:52.

Shintaro Ishihara
Japanese politician

4

[American business] is in decline because of American managers who only care about their short-term gains so that they can boast about them at the next shareholders' meeting. Japanese managers use shareholders' meetings to explain their long-term plans and ask shareholders to bear with limited dividends. Japan has succeeded in rebuilding its economy because it has kept its ideosyncrasies, that is to say, management philosophy, labor-management relations and company-shareholders relations based on human feelings.

Interview/
Time, 11-20:82.

Jesse L. Jackson
Civil-rights leader

5

[Saying the general public should not have to pay to save the ailing savings-and-loan industry, as is proposed in legislation that would have the Federal government bail-out the S&Ls]: Those who never were invited to the party shouldn't be asked to pay to clean up the mess—and only the wealthy were invited.

USA Today,
5-8:(A)8.

Gregg Jarrell
Former Chief Economist,
Securities and Exchange Commission
of the United States

6

[On a Supreme Court ruling allowing states to block hostile takeovers of corporations]: This will have a tremendous deterrent effect on hostile takeovers. When you combine this with the difficulties in the junk-bond market, we may be witnessing the death knell of financial acquisitions.

Nov. 6/
Los Angeles Times,
11-7:(A)1.

43

Vernon Jordan, Jr.
Former president,
National Urban League

1

Foreign-based multinationals must ensure that their American subsidiaries are seen as . . . conforming to the highest standards of corporate social responsibility as defined by the practices and politics of leading American corporations . . . The philosophy of corporate social responsibility, as it has evolved in America, is rooted in the belief that such behavior is an essential precondition for the continued existence of the free-enterprise system. It was also recognized that, in a free society, image is important—and that a good corporate image is both a defense against attacks on corporations and a policy supportive of business success. Those beliefs were supported by surveys that showed that companies with strong social-responsibility programs enjoyed greater financial success than others. Put bluntly, in America, corporate social responsibility is good business.

To businessmen, Tokyo, Jan. 11/
The Washington Post,
1-24:(A)22.

David T. Kearns
Chairman, Xerox Corporation

2

At Xerox, we define quality as meeting customer requirements. It's an axiom as old as business itself. Yet much of American business lost sight of that. Xerox was one of these companies. But by focusing on quality, we have turned that around . . . We realize that we are in a race without a finish line. As we improve, so does our competition. Five years ago, we would have found that disheartening. Today, we find it invigorating.

Time, 11-13:78,81.

Jack Kemp
Secretary of Housing and
Urban Development
of the United States

3

Enterprise zones will be of little help . . . if there is no capital available to invest in new businesses in the zones. The people who cannot afford high capital-gains taxes are not the rich. Publisher John Johnson, a true entrepreneur, just wrote a deeply inspiring book called *Succeeding Against the Odds*. The seed capital he needed to begin publishing in 1942 amounted to just $500—so near, yet so far. Unable to get a loan from Chicago's biggest bank, his only solution came from his mom, who put up her new furniture as collateral for a $500 loan from a small thrift . . . Not every potential entrepreneur is lucky enough to have a mom with even $500 worth of furniture to put up. But somebody has to invest the seed corn when an idea-rich but money-poor man or woman in a ghetto or barrio wants to imitate the John Johnsons . . . by putting their dreams to work. And that somebody should not be stopped because the capital-gains tax is too high to make the risk worth taking . . . If we are serious about unlocking the door to opportunity, we have to unlock the seed capital for black and Hispanic and minority and women's enterprises. We must convince Congress to cut the capital-gains tax to 15 per cent nation-wide and to eliminate it in our rural and urban enterprise zones.

Before National Association for the
Advancement of Colored People,
July 10/
The Wall Street Journal,
8-8:(A)10.

Robert Kirby
Chief executive,
Capital Guardian Trust;
Member, Presidential
commission that investigated
the 1987 stock-market crash

4

[On stock-market price gyrations caused by index arbitrage, a form of computerized trading]: They are destroying the public's confidence in our stock market. If this velocity caused by index arbitrage makes the public feel that the insiders are running it up and down to make billions, they are going to get disenchanted with the whole bloody system.

The New York Times,
11-2:(A)1.

Shigeru Kobayashi
President,
Shuwa Corporation
(Japan)

1

No matter how hard America tries, there are a lot of old commercial practices among the causes of the trade imbalance. It's the same in the securities industry, the construction industry and the distribution industry. There are many things Americans cannot understand . . . Go to an American company after noon on a Friday, and there's hardly anybody around—they go to lunch and don't come back. You can't win when you do that sort of thing. The Americans of old have disappeared. They've stopped working and lost their fighting spirit.

Interview,
Tokyo/
Los Angeles Times,
8-20:(IV)1,6.

Andrew Kohut
President,
Gallup Organization

2

The most important thing to recognize is that a populist attitude toward American business is a fundamental American value. Americans consistently believe that companies have profits that are way too large, and feel that large companies have too much power . . . Whether consumerism will become once again a very focused, crystallized movement in the way it was in the early '70s, I don't know . . . What our studies show is that the feeling is greater among women than it is among men, that women tend to be consumerist to a far greater degree than men, and that older people are much more suspicious of the motives and power of American business than younger people. So if you're going to find a rebirth of consumerism, it is probably not going to be among young people. It is going to be among middle-aged and older people, and it's probably going to be among women.

Interview/
Los Angeles Times,
5-14:(IV)3.

Richard D. Lamm
Director, Center for Public
Policy and Contemporary Issues,
University of Denver;
Former Governor of Colorado (D)

3

There are lots of problems in the American business community, but outright corruption is certainly not at the top of the list. In Mexico and South America and a number of other countries, corruption is a way of business. In the United States, corruption is the exception, not the rule. The recent scandals have made me believe that it is more prevalent than I thought it was. In other societies, this would be just shrugged off. The fact that it is such big news [in the U.S.] shows that it is a breach of the overwhelming business ethic. I think that we have to keep it in perspective. As we get to be a more materialistic or self-serving culture, I suspect we are going to have more and more scandals. What bothers me is that the trend is toward more and more corruption. The current amount of corruption as a way of doing business in America does not bother me, but the trend very much bothers me.

Interview/
Los Angeles Times, 1-29:(IV)3.

Jim Leach
United States Representative,
R-Iowa

4

[Criticizing the way the Federal Home Loan Bank Board handled deals involving those who took over ailing savings-and-loan institutions last year]: Bank Board deals which privatize profit, while socializing risk, amount to nothing less than a societal decision to allow those with potentially large tax liabilities—that is, the rich—to get richer.

At House Banking Committee hearing,
Washington, Jan. 10/
The New York Times, 1-11:(C)4.

5

[On the Federal bail-out of ailing savings-and-loan institutions]: The public is being asked to foot the major burden of the savings-and-loan

(JIM LEACH)

reform. That burden is likely to exceed $100-billion, and it stems from loose laws which led to loose regulation. In my judgment, there is a triad of governmental responsibility—Congress, which is the handmaiden of the thrifts, regulators, who listened too closely to thrifts, and states like Texas and California, which passed even more egregious laws impelling growth and poor practices in the thrift industry. The public ought to be outraged.

The Christian Science Monitor,
2-22:7.

Frank Lorenzo
Chairman,
Texas Air Corporation
(parent company of
Eastern Airlines)

1

[On his reputation for being a tough boss who is feared by his employees]: I'm not paid to be a candy ass. I'm paid to go and get a job done. I could have ended up with another job, but the job I ended up with was piecing together a bunch of companies that were all headed for the junk heap. You know, everything's wonderful when you've got $600-million a year cash flow. That wasn't our lot. I had to draw charts that said, "This is when the cash runs out, fellows, and unless we do something we're going to have to make changes pretty quickly." I've got to be the bastard who sits around Eastern Airlines and says, "Hey, we're losing $3-million a day or whatever the number is and bang, bang, bang, bang, what do you do?" So, some jobs are easier than others.

Interview/
USA Today, 5-23:(A)11.

Akio Morita
Chairman,
Sony Corporation (Japan)

2

Instead of seeking to buy key components from Japan, American industries should produce those components by themselves. The strength of my company is we have a policy of producing all

key components ourselves. Service industries [which are more and more prevalent in the U.S.] do not add value. It's production that adds value. American industry may be behind today, but I'm not saying they have no chance to catch up. If it's necessary, we can help you by making our technology available. Technology should be borderless.

Interview, New York/
Newsweek, 10-9:66.

Robert A. Mosbacher
Secretary of Commerce of the
United States

3

I am a total free-trader. I believe in free and fair trade. But I do not believe in unilateral free trade any more than I believe in unilateral disarmament.

Interview/
The Washington Post, 4-28:(A)23.

4

We've [the U.S.] got to realize that it's a shrinking world, and if we want to do more than flip the hamburgers for the world, we've got to come out with quality products . . . We need a strategy to innovate, produce, market and sell world-class products in each and every industry.

Before Economic Club of Detroit
and at prior news conference,
May 8/
The Washington Post, 5-9:(B)1.

Victor Navasky
Editor, "The Nation"
magazine

5

[On the current "merger mania" among large media companies]: The bigger they are, the harder they fall. They're just getting in more and more trouble, as illustrated by the tragic comedy that's going on right now. It's a combination of good, old-fashioned American greed and losing sight of why they went into the media business in the first place. [*Time* magazine's founder] Henry Luce didn't go into that business to acquire other

COMMERCE / INDUSTRY / FINANCE

(VICTOR NAVASKY)

businesses. He went into it because he had a way of putting out a magazine that could tell the truth in short form every week. Of course, it was his version of the truth. The people who came after lost sight of all that. I suspect that's true in every business. In Hollywood, they thought they had a way of entertaining and making some money for doing that, but the vision of the founders and occupation of the successors are very different things.

Interview/
Los Angeles Times, 6-25:(IV)3.

Al Neuharth
Former chairman,
Gannett Company;
Founder, "USA Today"

1

To me, an s.o.b. is someone who uses whatever tactics it takes to get the job done, to rise to the top. And in truth, I think that more CEOs or bosses would use my tactics in some degree than will admit it . . . I'm going to kick you in the butt if you screw up and pat you on the back when you do well. I treat everyone alike. Sometimes I get complimented and sometimes I get criticism.

Interview, New York/USA Today
Los Angeles Times, 10-4:(V)1.

2

. . . in most major corporations I've seen too damn many [older] people—mostly guys, not women—hanging on [to their executive positions] by the fingernails, to their own detriment and to that of their company. My predecessor did that, and we had to wrestle the title away from him when he was 72. So when I became CEO at the age of 49, I made a deal with the board that my contract said I'd retire as chairman no later than my 65th birthday. It forced me to make damn sure that the next generation of management was in place, and it permitted me to concentrate on the years from 50 to 60, which I think are the years of leadership. In your 20s you play, in your 30s you take risks and tempt failures, and in your 40s you have to start earning. And in your

50s you ought to lead. In your 60s you ought to figure out how and when to leave, and then go do something else.

Interview/
Lear's, December:20.

Edward O'Brien
President, Securities Industry
Association

3

[Criticizing a Federal Reserve ruling allowing certain banks to buy and sell corporate bonds, something heretofore reserved for securities firms]: It represents piecemeal dismantling of the appropriate separation that exists in the financial-services industry—a system that has worked exceedingly well for more than 50 years.

Time, 1-30:51.

Donald G. Ogilvie
Executive vice president,
American Bankers Association

4

[On a Treasury Department proposal to charge a fee on bank and savings-and-loan deposits to aid ailing S&Ls]: Taxing bank customers to bail out the savings-and-loan industry would be a gross injustice. Ford wasn't asked to bail out Chrysler, Newark [N.J.] wasn't asked to bail out New York, nor should every American consumer with a bank account be asked to bail out the Federal Savings and Loan Insurance Corporation.

Los Angeles Times, 1-26:(I)16.

Kenneth H. Olsen
President, Digital Equipment
Corporation

5

Capital investment in Japan is 18 to 20 per cent of their gross national product. In this country it's almost half that. And the thing that is terrifying for the future is the trade balance is going to mushroom in the wrong direction because we're investing less and less, and they're investing more and more . . . I'm not bashing the Japanese when I say this, but we're having a con-

(KENNETH H. OLSEN)

test with them in which they're generating low interest rates to support their business and we're taxing exports, keeping our interest rates high.

Interview/
The New York Times, 11-14:(C)2.

Joseph Perella
Principal,
Wasserstein, Perella & Co.,
investment bankers

1

Congress is saying "maybe we should limit the interest deductibility on acquisitions and LBO debt" because they simplistically think that will slow [the corporate merger and take-over momentum] down. But it wouldn't slow it down. It just changes the way you value companies. Stocks would trade lower, which would help foreigners take over American assets even cheaper. They ought to make equity more attractive by encouraging long-term investing. For example, if an investor owns stock for five years and sells it at a gain, he doesn't pay tax. Do you realize how much money would be invested for the long term under those circumstances?

Interview/
USA Today, 1-3:(B)2.

John J. Phelan, Jr.
Chairman, New York
Stock Exchange

2

[On volatility in the stock market]: I think there are two kinds of volatility. [First there is] the volatility that is normal to the marketplace, which on a day-to-day basis shouldn't bother anybody. Then there is what some of our friends like to call "synthetic volatility"—man-made volatility [such as caused by program trading]. That's the volatility people really object to. Anyone who thought [I said] you have to get used to the market being down 190 points in an hour and a half is crazy. What I'm trying to say is from time to time in all markets around the world, natural volatility seems to be increasing. I didn't

ever have index arbitrage [program trading] in mind when I talked about that.

Interview/
USA Today, 11-10:(B)10.

T. Boone Pickens
Entrepreneur

3

[On his being denied seats on the board of a Japanese company of which he owns more than 20 per cent]: I'm beginning to wonder if the reasons I'm denied this right is because I'm not Japanese . . . You [Japanese] invest freely in my country, the United States, yet I invest in Japan and am excluded. Trade and investment opportunities between our countries are simply not a two-way street. Japan should not be surprised at the frustration much of the world has with its cloistered system.

To board of directors
of Koito Manufacturing Co.,
Tokyo, June 29/
Los Angeles Times, 6-30:(IV)1.

4

In view of how the current business cycle has matured, you'll probably have some of these junk-bond deals fail. But that's part of the [securities] market. It's part of the free-enterprise system. I don't see that a great number of them are going to fail. I think the junk-bond market is pretty well distributed over a lot of big players.

Time, 10-23:69.

Sol Price
Chairman emeritus,
Price Club

5

[On ethics in business]: I suspect that the basic rule is that bad behavior drives good behavior out of the marketplace . . . The problem that the businessman has is that if everybody is doing it, how does he compete and survive if he doesn't do it? We have a public and government that doesn't get very excited at cheating. Society doesn't get very outraged about things that go on. We tolerate and accept corruption. If anything,

(SOL PRICE)

people are becoming more and more numb about it. It worries me as a businessman, and it worries me more as a citizen. It worries me about my kids and grandkids. The only way we keep score in our society, unfortunately, is by how much money you acquire and not how you've acquired it or what else you've done.

Interview/
Los Angeles Times, 1-29:(IV)3.

Philip J. Purcell
Chairman,
Dean Witter Reynolds, Inc.,
securities

1

. . . Americans are losing confidence in the markets, and most people think it's because of volatility. The market is not moving in ways that clients understand. That creates a totally unacceptable situation where the American investing public does not have faith in our capital-raising system. So we decided to look at what to do about it. We started looking for causes of volatility, and one of them in our judgment is index arbitrage and other forms of program trading. There is no doubt that index arbitrage creates volatility. There are some academics who are not so sure, but they look at long-time horizons, and trading isn't done in long-time horizons. You trade in an instant.

Interview/
The New York Times, 11-28:(C)2.

Ronald Reagan
Former President of the
United States

2

[Defending the purchase of U.S. companies and real estate by foreign investors]: The United States still is the widest investor in other countries, owning properties that are an investment and so forth, so how can we complain if someone wants to invest in us? As a matter of fact, I think they want to invest in us because we're a good investment.

Japanese broadcast interview,
Oct. 25/
The Washington Post, 10-26:(A)1.

3

[Americans] don't believe U.S. products are being given fair access over here [in Japan]. Fairness is a very strong strain in the American people. It all started in 1773 when we thought the British weren't being fair, so we threw their tea into the Boston Harbor. That episode in our history is called the Boston Tea Party. We don't want a Japanese Tea Party.

Speech to business leaders,
Osaka, Japan, Oct. 28/
The Washington Post, 10-28:(A)17.

Robert Reich
Economic analyst,
Kennedy School of Government,
Harvard University

4

Today, it's becoming all but impossible to determine the difference between "us" [U.S. companies] and "them" [foreign companies]. Increasingly, there is no such thing as a pure "American" company or a pure "foreign" company. In many ways, they behave the same.

Los Angeles Times, 8-8:(IV)1.

David Rockefeller
Former chairman,
Chase Manhattan Bank,
New York

5

[On bond dealer Michael Milken's $550-million 1987 compensation from his employer, Drexel Burnham Lambert]: Such an extraordinary income inevitably raises questions as to whether there isn't something unbalanced in the way our financial system is working. One has to be concerned when the norms that have been accepted over the years suddenly become so distorted.

The New York Times, 4-3:(C)1.

Jim Sanders
President, Beer Institute

6

[Criticizing the Surgeon General's call for less glamorous advertising of alcoholic beverages]:

(JIM SANDERS)

Studies have often shown that there is no way to prove a causal relationship between advertising and alcohol consumption. It also seems rather naive to try and prevent glamorous people from selling something. To be successful in a competitive market, you show attractive people doing attractive things.

The Washington Post, 6-1:(A)4.

Charles E. Schumer
United States Representative,
D-New York

1

[On the House's decision to impose tighter regulations on the financial system in exchange for a government bailout of the ailing savings-and-loan industry]: There is a strong populist wind sweeping across the House. Members are just ticked off at the thrifts, the industry that created the problems, the industry that wasn't even contrite about it, and that to the very end was fighting the kind of changes that were necessary. There is a feeling that *laissez-faire* is over. Leaving it up to the thrifts and regulators doesn't work any more.

Washington, June 16/
The New York Times,
6-17:17.

Charles R. Schwab
Chairman, Charles Schwab
Corporation,
securities brokers

2

The major challenge in successful investing, I think, has always been understanding the emotions of the environment. Right now, the apathetic emotional level is the reverse of the buoyancy of the middle of 1987. But if you go back over history, one should always do major investing in those periods of apathy, because those gains will show up in very robust numbers when the next period of buoyancy comes.

Interview/
The New York Times, 1-3:(C)2.

Richard Schwartz
President,
Rocketdyne Division,
Rockwell International

3

In the scientific or technical world, engineers are sometimes thought of as being brilliant in technical skills, but having people-skills that could use a fair amount of work. The higher up you go, the more people-skills mean—picking the right people, motivating them, making them a part of a team . . . If you can somehow put together the sum total of technical, business and people-management knowledge, you'll be a party to successful ventures.

Interview/
Los Angeles Times, 1-29:(IV)4.

L. William Seidman
Chairman, Federal Deposit
Insurance Corporation

4

[On the Bush Administration's proposal of a customer fee on bank and S&L accounts to help pay for bailing out the ailing S&L industry]: It's the "reverse toaster" theory. Instead of the bank giving you a toaster when you make a deposit, you give *them* one.

Los Angeles Times, 1-25:(IV)1.

5

[On the problems involved in liquidating failed banks that are taken over by the FDIC]: In our experience, liquidation is a very difficult job. It involves closing institutions down, suing people, selling property into depressed markets, closing locations, firing people—all the kinds of jobs that can create a lot of unhappiness.

Interview/
The Washington Post, 5-5:(B)1.

6

[Criticizing the savings-and-loan industry for balking at minimum capital standards required as part of a government bailout plan for ailing savings institutions]: You are talking about an industry that has fought supervision since day

(L. WILLIAM SEIDMAN)

one, an industry that has been under-capitalized and a regulatory system that has done a lot of imprudent things. Now they want us to chisel those into stone. You have the industry once again lobbying for a condition that caused the problem in the first place.

The New York Times, 5-29:24.

Harley Shaiken
Associate professor,
Department of Communication,
University of California,
San Diego

1

The [corporate] merger is judged simply by the bottom line, not the social consequences. One of the widely touted benefits of mergers is that you can produce more with fewer people . . . There is no legal, moral or economic pressure to consider what happens to those who are affected.

Los Angeles Times, 10-2:(I)1.

George P. Shultz
Secretary of State
of the United States

2

Within an office, or department, or any organization, putting trust in people will produce trustworthy people. That's the foremost of the many reasons against the widespread and routine use of lie-detector tests. Management through fear and intimidation is not the way to promote honesty and protect security.

Before Citizens Network for
Foreign Affairs,
Washington, Jan. 9/
The Washington Post, 1-11:(A)19.

Alfred C. Sikes
Chairman, Federal
Communications Commission
of the United States

3

I think over all we need freer markets and consequently that would suggest less regulation, and

yet there is need for more regulation in some areas. As markets are freed, lethargic enterprises can no longer be lethargic. They have to look carefully at their costs, service, prices and at innovation. As a result, the consumer gets lower prices and better products.

Interview/
The New York Times, 10-3:(C)2.

Harold C. Simmons
Industrialist

4

[On people like himself who buy large amounts of company stocks in order to influence them]: I think that term [corporate] "raider" is very misleading because it implies that somebody is taking something by force without paying for it. Basically, corporate raiders are willing to pay a price for a stock higher than anyone else is willing to pay, or else they don't buy it.

Interview/
The Washington Post, 4-5:(F)1.

Allen Sinai
Chief economist,
The Boston Company

5

The [U.S.] trade deficit continues to look sticky, and last year's improvement has stalled out. So long as we keep importing, the trade deficit can't improve very much, and that has been the pattern for some time. For it to get better, we'll need either a slower economy with fewer imports, or a lower dollar and some other improvement in our competitiveness abroad to get higher market share and exports. But that can be long in coming.

April 14/Los Angeles Times, 4-15:(I)22.

Stanley Sporkin
Judge, United States District Court
for the District of Columbia,
Former Director,
Division of Enforcement,
Securities and Exchange Commission
of the United States

6

Some of the business fraud is the price we have to pay for the free-market system that we have. It

(STANLEY SPORKIN)

is a deregulation environment, a free-market environment which has tremendous positives and benefits about it. Our system is the best in the world, but there is a price that we are paying. Hopefully, we are not going to get to the point where the price we pay for it is going to be in terms of life and death. And that is a real possible problem.

Interview/
Los Angeles Times, 1-29:(IV)3.

C. Eugene Steuerle
Former Deputy Assistant Secretary
for Tax Policy,
Department of the Treasury
of the United States

1

[On the corporate-tax system which taxes corporate profits twice, once to the corporation and then to its shareholders]: While there is debate among economists as to whether the corporate tax deters ventures by existing corporations who already have assets tied up within the corporation, there is no doubt that the corporate tax serves as a barrier to new, risky business. [Since] it is the threat of entry by new firms that forces established firms to be competitive . . . , when the deck is stacked against new firms, it affects the competitiveness, and hence the productivity, of all firms.

The Washington Post,
11-6:(Business)6.

Robert Tamarkin
Futures-market historian;
President, Intermarket
Publishing Corporation

2

[On revelations of fraud in the commodities exchanges]: Problems like these have been with the exchanges from the very beginning. These markets can only be regulated by having a policeman in each pit. This is an example of the failure of self-policing and shows the weakness of the Commodities Futures Trading Commission in regulating the pits.

Los Angeles Times, 1-20:(I)1.

Lester C. Thurow
Dean, Sloan School of
Management, Massachusetts
Institute of Technology

3

[On the increase in foreign, especially Japanese, buying of and investing in U.S. business, real estate and other assets]: We should worry more about Americans selling America than the Japanese buying America. We shouldn't worry about who is buying it, but that we're selling it. It doesn't make any difference whether or not it's Great Britain or Canada who buys it. If we keep selling, in the long run we're slowly going to be selling off our capitalistic inheritance. That would mean that, in the future, fewer Americans will be capitalists and more of the capitalists in America will be foreigners. But you can't blame that on the foreigners; you've got to blame that on us.

Interview/
USA Today, 11-1:(A)11.

Donald Trump
Entrepreneur

4

My style of deal-making is quite simple and straightforward. I just keep pushing and pushing and pushing to get what I'm after.

Time, 1-16:48.

5

One of the sad facts [about the investment industry] I have seen in the last six, seven years is that you used to be smart if you bought low and sold high. Today, you only seem to get credit if you go out and get [take over] the company.

Interview/
Newsweek, 10-16:56.

Ted Turner
Chairman, Turner
Broadcasting System

6

One thing that people don't understand is that money never has been what motivates me. If it had've been, I never would have been where I

(TED TURNER)

was. I was willing to take chances because I didn't think the money was that important. The challenge and the adventure were the main things with me and the sense of achievement and accomplishment, and wanting to do something in my life that would really be spectacular. I've always had grandiose schemes—I would have loved to have been with Christopher Columbus or Magellan or Sir Francis Drake; I'm an adventurer more than I am a businessman. I didn't want to go broke, but making money wasn't the thing. I didn't do this to make money.

Interview/
Daily Variety,
3-1:(F)18.

Makoto Utsumi
Director-General,
International Finance Bureau,
Ministry of Finance of Japan

1

I see the danger that American industry has become too comfortable with profits, rather than making efforts for exports. So a further decline of the dollar, rather than making more American products for sale, I fear, would make America more for sale [to foreign investors] . . . The problem is not the price-competitiveness of U.S. industry, but the willingness and capacity to export. Many of them are eager for profits rather than quantitative improvements.

At Foreign Correspondents Club
of Japan, Tokyo, Jan. 17/
The Washington Post,
1-18:(A)11.

Jack Valenti
President, Motion Picture Association
of America

2

In a world growing smaller each day . . . trade barriers are as old-fashioned and as dangerous as armed conflict.

Speech to business executives,
Brussels, Oct. 31/
Los Angeles Times, 11-1:(F)1.

Gore Vidal
Author

3

Multinationals are going to inherit the earth. They already run everything anyway . . . They are literally beyond any country's power to regulate. Why not go backwards? Eliminate the countries and just keep the multinationals. They don't want war. All they want to do is make ghastly gadgets at the cheapest price possible and sell them at the most expensive price. We can live with that. If they become wicked monopolies, the people will have redress: You can just not buy their products.

Interview/
Mother Jones, May:13.

Lawrence J. White
Former member, Federal
Home Loan Bank Board

4

[On the recent bailout legislation to help the ailing savings-and-loan industry]: It really addresses only one of the four important reforms that are needed, and that's the tougher capital standards, meaning that institutions will have to have higher net worth to operate. It nods in the direction of a second one—strengthening the regulators' powers of early intervention in an institution that's going down the tubes. But it ignores entirely the two most important reforms—changing the accounting system so an institution's balance sheet accurately reflects its true market value, and improvements in the deposit-insurance system.

Interview, Washington/
The New York Times, 8-17:(A)13.

Donald E. Wildmon
Media critic

5

[On his call to boycott certain products because of their sponsorship of what he considers objectionable material, such as PepsiCo's sponsoring the singer Madonna]: Pepsi said to our young people in the country, "Here is the role model we think worthy of $10-million in support." Here is a pop singer who makes a video

(DONALD E. WILDMON)

that's sacrilegious to the core. Here's a pop star that made a low-budget porn film. Here's a pop star who goes around in her concerts with sex oozing out, wearing a cross. Now Pepsi is saying to all the young people of the new generation, "Here is the person we want you to emulate and imitate." They can do that. They've got every right to give Madonna $10-million, put it on television every night if they want to. All I'm saying is, "Don't ask me to buy Pepsi if you do it. You've got the right to spend your money where you want to; I've got the right to spend my money where I want to . . ."

Interview/
Time, 6-19:55.

Clayton K. Yeutter
Secretary of Agriculture
of the United States

1

[Calling for a slow end to Federal farm subsidies]: Farming is a business and ought to be handled in a business-like way by everyone, including the Federal government. And we ought not to be running long-term, welfare-like programs in agriculture.

News conference,
Washington, Feb. 24/
The Washington Post,
2-25:(A)4.

2

When governments get involved in agriculture, it is usually the consumer who pays the price. A lot of consumers throughout the world today pay much more for food than would be necessary if we had a more free and open marketplace in agriculture. Taxpayers are picking up the tab for all of these subsidy programs. The taxpayer burden for these trade distortions is immense. Whether one's interest is that of producer, consumer or taxpayer, in all three cases we badly need agricultural trade reform.

Interview/
USA Today, 4-4:(A)7.

Crime • Law Enforcement

Virgilio Barco Vargas
President of Colombia

1

[Addressing illegal-drug users around the world on how their habit has adversely affected life in his country, home of international drug traffickers, and elsewhere]: Those of you who depend on cocaine have created the largest, most vicious criminal enterprise the world has ever known. What might seem to be a matter of a purely personal habit has had explosive public consequences. Colombia's survival as the oldest democracy in Latin America is now at risk, but so is the safety of your streets. Enough is enough.

International broadcast address,
Bogota, Colombia,
Aug. 28/Los Angeles Times, 8-29:(I)13.

Jim Barko
Fraud instructor,
FBI Academy

2

When you say "white-collar crime," it sounds narrow but it's not. How many ways can you cheat someone? Hundreds of thousands of ways. There is so much money out there in so many different shapes and forms—commodities, securities, Medicare and MediCal benefits, Social Security—that the temptations are there.

Los Angeles Times, 8-27:(IV)5.

Marion Barry
Mayor of Washington

3

[On the importation of illegal drugs into the U.S.]: The national government needs to go to these five or six countries in South and Central America, send the Army, the Navy, the Air Force, the Marines and the Coast Guard, burn up those fields, eradicate those cocoa leaves, blow up those labs, stop it at its source. If we had a foreign ideology that was invading this country like drugs are, killing families, we'd have declared war immediately. When low-income

people are killed and shot [in the U.S. because of drugs], it does not necessarily matter as much as when moderate- to upper-income people are shot.

Broadcast interview/
"This Week With David Brinkley,"
ABC-TV, 3-19.

Neil J. Behan
Chief of Police of
Baltimore County, Md.

4

I tell my officers that they are not to leave a neighborhood after a hate crime until that victim and neighborhood are made whole again. A cross-burning is not a simple arson, and a swastika painted on a temple is not mere vandalism.

The New York Times, 5-12:(A)8.

William J. Bennett
Director, White House Office
of Drug Abuse Policy

5

[On the movement to end private ownership of assault weapons]: From the numbers I've seen, the majority of the NRA's members do not like to think of themselves as associated with assault weapons. The people I know take their kids out and teach them how to hunt, go after ducks and deer. They do not like to think of themselves as bearers of assault weapons. They don't think of themselves as soldiers, and they sure as hell don't think of themselves as terrorists or assassins. That message has to get through to the leadership of the NRA [which opposes banning private ownership of assault weapons].

Interview/USA Today, 3-20:(A)11.

6

How do we reduce the demand for [illegal] drugs? . . . Taking an aggressive line toward drugs—forbidding their use altogether and using

55

(WILLIAM J. BENNETT)

real authority to back up this absolute proscription—is the key to all prevention strategies.

Before Washington Hebrew Congregation,
May/
The Washington Post,
5-15:(A)9.

1

There are those who say the problems of the inner city and the affluent suburb are so varied that anti-drug efforts with similar approaches cannot work. There are those who say that the cultural differences between affluent and poor, between Hispanic and Anglo are so profound that each "culture" must come up with its own approach. I say that's wrong. It is obviously the case that someone who speaks Spanish as a first language will be more receptive to a message in Spanish. But the necessary message for rich and poor, black and white and Hispanic and Indian alike, is the same: Drug use is intolerable, use and the potential for use will be confronted on all fronts, and those who use and those who sell will face certain consequences.

Before Washington Hebrew Congregation,
May/
The Wall Street Journal,
6-19:(A)10.

2

[Saying special military-style "boot camps" may be one way to discourage drug use]: We are looking into this boot-camp thing, which we've seen in several states, which looks to be a very productive kind of thing. You take the first offender, particularly a young person, and he goes to boot camp—that's a lot less expensive than jail; he gets up at 4:30 in the morning, he does push-ups, he runs a good bit . . . It's inexpensive, it teaches good lessons and the recidivism rate is very, very low because it is so unpleasant; people don't want to go back to it.

Broadcast interview/
"Face the Nation,"
CBS-TV, 5-7.

3

When you take drugs or sell drugs, you're killing people. You helped inject the needle in that vein. You helped him inhale crack. You helped pull the trigger of the gun that shoots somebody . . . You start by buying the drug; but in the end, the drug will buy you. I'm not telling you these things just to scare you. But drugs are a plenty scary business, and it's good to be scared of something that can really hurt you.

To students at
W. R. Thomas Middle School,
Miami, May 18/
Los Angeles Times, 5-19:(I)17.

4

A lot of money and a lot of the work is going to have to be done by states [in the fight against drugs]. It won't do us very much good at all if all we do is pass good Federal laws and build Federal prisons and have Federal treatment programs if the states don't come in to play. I think we'll probably propose spending more Federal money, but there's not a way in the world we can pick up everybody's bill. You can't have the Federal government paying for local law enforcement.

Interview/USA Today, 6-12:(A)11.

5

[On whether drug dealers should be beheaded in the U.S. as is done in Saudi Arabia]: Morally, I don't have any problem with that at all. One of the things that I think is a problem is that we are not doing enough that is morally proportional to the nature of the offense. What we need to do is find some Constitutional and legally permissible way to do what [is suggested]—not literally to behead, but to make the punishment fit the crime—and the crime is horrible.

TV broadcast/"Larry King Live,"
CNN-TV, 6-15.

6

[On Colombian President Virgilio Barco's recent internationally televised speech condemning his country's drug cartels and world-wide

(WILLIAM J. BENNETT)

drug users]: Barco has done two very important things for us. One, he has reminded the world how bad the bad guys are. Remember a few days ago when you . . . would talk about Colombia as if it were run by the narcos? Now what Americans are seeing is this brave old man [Barco], this young woman [Colombian Justice Minister Monica de Greiff] and her child, fighting these criminals. The other point [Barco] made in his televised speech—that . . . the casual user is partially responsible for the violence—is the focus of the [U.S.] drug strategy.

Interview/Newsweek, 9-11:32.

1

[Arguing against legalization of now-illegal drugs]: If drugs were legalized, there would be more cocaine babies, more wrecked lives. There would be more wrecked trains, buses and airplanes. And, by legalizing drugs, you would also be legitimating their use. And that would increase the number of abusers . . . Every time you make something that is illegal legal, you increase its use. Look at the experience of other countries. When they legalized drugs, use increased. After Prohibition, liquor consumption increased by an enormous amount.

Interview/
USA Today, 10-30:(A)11.

2

America's intellectuals—and here I think particularly of liberal intellectuals—have spent much of the last nine years decrying the social programs of the two Republican Administrations in the name of the defenseless poor. But today, on the one outstanding issue that disproportionately hurts the poor—that is wiping out many of the poor—where are the liberal intellectuals to be found? They are on the editorial and op-ed pages, and in magazines like this month's *Harper's,* telling us with an ignorant sneer that our [anti-] drug policy won't work. Many universities, too, which have been quick to take on the challenges of sexism, racism and ethnocentrism, seem content on the drug issue to

wag a finger at us, or to point it mindlessly at American society in general. In public-policy schools, there is no shortage of arms-control scholars. Isn't it time we had more drug-control scholars? . . . I would remind you that not all crusades led by the United States government, enjoying broad, popular support, are brutish, corrupt and sinister. What is brutish, corrupt and sinister is the murder and mayhem being committed in our cities' streets. One would think that a little more concern and serious thought would come from those who claim to care so deeply about America's problems.

Speech, Harvard University,
Dec. 11/
The Washington Post, 12-13:(A)24.

Joseph R. Biden, Jr.
United States Senator,
D-Delaware

3

[On President Bush's announced plan to fight drug trafficking]: Quite frankly, the President's plan is not tough enough, bold enough or imaginative enough to meet the crisis at hand . . . What we need is another D-day, not another Vietnam—not a limited war, fought on the cheap, and destined for stalemate and human tragedy . . . In a nutshell, the President's plan does not include: enough police officers to catch the violent thugs; enough prosecutors to convict them; enough judges to sentence them; or enough prison cells to put them away.

Broadcast address to the nation,
Washington,
Sept. 5/USA Today, 9-6:(A)5.

James MacGregor Burns
Historian

4

[Criticizing President Bush's speech outlining his plan to fight the illegal-drug problem]: The failure to mention taxes in the drug speech is a clue to the fiscal and I would say intellectual bankruptcy of his proposals. It's obvious that when you're concentrating people's attention on the problem and fail to ask people generally to be responsible for financing that problem, it raises

(JAMES MAC GREGOR BURNS)

questions of how sincere the President is about the program. I don't take seriously a speech that would not raise the question of mobilizing fiscal resources.

The New York Times, 9-12:(A)12.

George Bush
President of the United States

1

[On private ownership of assault weapons]: I'd like to find some way to do something about these automated weapons. I'd like to see some way to enforce the laws that are already on the books about automated AK-47s [rifles] coming into this country. And I'd like to find a way to be supportive of the police who are out there on the line all the time. And maybe there is some answer to it. But I also want to be the President that protects the rights of people to have arms, so you don't go so far that the legitimate rights on some [gun-ownership] legislation are impinged on.

News conference, Washington,
Feb.21/
The New York Times, 2-22:(A)10.

2

It used to be unthinkable to shoot a cop. [But] no longer ... Today, narcotics agents are sometimes the first ones shot, targeted by criminals armed with a staggering array of battlefield weaponry ... Well, we've got to deliver some news to the bad guys. The hunting season is over ... Drug dealers need to understand a simple fact: You shoot a cop and you're going to be severely punished—fast. And if I had my way, I'd say with your life.

At New York field office of
Drug Enforcement Administration,
March 9/
The Washington Post, 3-10:(A)4.

3

No one—not parents, not churches, not bankers, and certainly not chemical-makers—can afford to be AWOL in the war on drugs. [I

would like to see] U.S. chemical manufacturers demonstrate their courage and civic responsibility by entering into a true partnership with our government as we try to stop narcotics at the source. These companies can make an important contribution to our nation's fight against illegal drugs. They should make it their job to join in ... Few Americans are aware that illegally diverted barrels of dangerous chemicals—clearly marked with corporate logos—are routinely seized [by drug traffickers] in the jungles of Colombia.

At drug-enforcement conference,
Miami, April 27/
The Washington Post,
4-28:(A)16.

4

We're going to up the stakes for those who calculate that our criminal-justice system is a crapshoot where the risks are worth the rewards. And when criminals think about reaching for a gun, they're going to know—and they're going to learn—that they will do time. Hard time.

To visiting U.S. attorneys,
Washington, June 16/
Los Angeles Times, 6-17:(I)25.

5

Our message to the drug cartels is this: The rules have changed. We will help any government that wants our help. When requested, we will for the first time make available the appropriate resources of America's armed forces. We will intensify our efforts against drug smugglers on the high seas, in international airspace and at our borders. We will stop the flow of chemicals from the United States used to process drugs. We will pursue and enforce international agreements to track drug money to the front men and financiers. And then we will handcuff these money-lenders and jail them—just like any street dealers. And for drug kingpins, the death penalty.

Broadcast address to the nation,
Washington, Sept. 5/
Los Angeles Times, 9-6:(I)11.

(GEORGE BUSH)

1

[On the drug-abuse problem]: Drugs have strained our faith in our system of justice. Our courts, our prisons, our legal system are stretched to the breaking point. The social costs of drugs are mounting . . . Who's responsible? . . . Everyone who uses drugs. Everyone who sells drugs. And everyone who looks the other way . . . And we need your help. If people you know are users, help them get off drugs. If you are a parent, talk to your children about drugs . . . If we fight this war as a divided nation, then the war is lost. But if we face this evil as a nation united, this will be nothing but a handful of useless chemicals.

Broadcast address to the nation,
Washington, Sept. 5/
Los Angeles Times, 9-6:(I)11.

2

[On his new plan to fight illegal drugs]: We can pay for this fight against drugs without raising taxes or adding to the budget deficit. We have submitted our plan to Congress that shows just how to fund it within the limits of our bipartisan budget agreement. Now, I know some will still say that we are not spending enough money. But those who judge our strategy only by its price tag simply don't understand the problem. Let's face it, we've all seen in the past that money alone won't solve our toughest problems. To be strong and efficient, our strategy needs these funds. But there is no match for a united America, a determined America, an angry America.

Broadcast address to the nation,
Washington, Sept. 5/
The Washington Post, 9-6:(A)18.

3

Over the last few days there's been a lot of talk about our new [anti-drug-trafficking] strategy. Some, incredibly, say, "Well, it's not enough." This from the very people who oppose the death penalty. It's that kind of thinking that's lost too many battles already. So let's not let these critics lose the war . . . [We] will require the bravery and sacrifice that Americans have shown before and must again. As veterans, you know how battles are often fought—house by house, block by block. Well, we'll win this battle [against drugs] the same way. We're going to win it kid by kid, neighborhood by neighborhood.

Before American Legion,
Baltimore, Sept. 7/
The New York Times, 9-8:(A)10.

4

Every dollar that goes to [illegal] drugs fuels the killing. As long as there are Americans willing to buy drugs, there will be people willing to sell drugs—and people willing to kill as a cost of doing business. There is a connection between the suppliers and even "occasional" or "weekend" users that can never be forgotten. Casual drug use is responsible for the casualties of the drug war. From the city streets of America to the street bombings of Colombia, even dabblers in drugs bear responsibility for the blood being spilled.

Broadcast address, Washington,
Sept. 12/
Los Angeles Times, 9-13:(I)18.

5

[Saying recent incidents in which assault rifles were used to commit massacres in the U.S. does not change his mind about not banning private ownership of those kinds of weapons]: I have seen no evidence that a law banning a specific weapon is going to guard against [such rampages]. We must do everything we can to enforce laws that are already on the books . . . If you have somebody who is deranged . . . I'm afraid you're going to have incidents like this.

To reporters,
Washington, Sept. 15/
The Washington Post,
9-16:(A)1.

6

Republicans believe that, when asked what kind of society Americans deserve, our answer must be a nation in which the people are safe and feel safe. Republicans want tougher enforce-

(GEORGE BUSH)

ment—more prisons, more courts, more prosecutors and tougher sentences.

At fund-raiser for New Jersey
Republican gubernatorial nominee
Jim Courter, East Brunswick, N.J.,
Sept. 22/
The Washington Post, 9-23:(A)5.

Joe Casey
Chief of Police
of Nashville, Tenn.;
Former president,
International Association
of Chiefs of Police

1

[Being a policeman] always has been a tough
job. But I do think that the stress and the frustration have intensified in recent years. It takes a
very special man or woman to enter law enforcement today . . . They know they are going to live
in constant public scrutiny. Their code of conduct
is stricter than almost anybody else's in town—
even a Sunday-school teacher. They know that
their human errors are going to be judged by the
entire citizenry. They know that they aren't going
to ever get rich in the job—thankfully, salaries are
getting better. They know that they have to worry
about their safety in ways that nobody else in the
community has to worry. There is that additional stress of worrying about what happens to
their families if something happens to them.

Interview/USA Today, 8-24:(A)9.

Dick Cheney
Secretary of Defense
of the United States

2

[On an increased role for the military in
fighting the drug-trafficking problem]: The Defense Department is not a law-enforcement
agency. We do not enforce domestic criminal
laws, nor can we solve society's [drug] demand
problem. But there is much that we can do
without usurping the police role. We will work on
the drug program at every phase—at the source,
in the delivery pipeline and to further support

Federal, state and local law-enforcement agencies . . . There is no quick, easy answer to the
drug problem. It is a problem that's been with us
for a long time, and it's gotten much worse lately.
If we're going to be successful in dealing with the
drug problem in the country, it will be because we
have a broad-gauge strategy that addresses the
production in the host countries, the problem of
transiting the drugs into the United States and
then the problems of consumption within the
United States itself.

Press briefing,
Washington, Sept 18/
Los Angeles Times, 9-19:(I)6.

Mario M. Cuomo
Governor of New York (D)

3

[On crime in New York City]: [Crime has]
changed life in the city dramatically. The wealthy
and the business community are guarded by the
largest army of unofficial security agents in the
history of the nation. Parks and other public
places are declared off-limits to the prudent, and
surrendered to marauders. [The situation is so
bad] that large numbers of our people throw their
fists in the air and shout for "death" [capital
punishment] as a solution, despairing of a more
intelligent answer.

Before City Bar Association,
New York, May 8/
The New York Times,
5-9:(A)21.

4

The death penalty is debasing. If we were to
bring it back, it would return us to the company of
South Africa, the Soviet Union, Iran, Saudi
Arabia and others—none of the nations we
normally point to as our peers in civilization . . .
A very important part of the argument for the
death penalty has been that the people manifestly
want it. Poll after poll has been shown, one newspaper tumbling over the other to be first with their
poll that shows the large number of people who
want it. For six years, I have been saying I don't
believe people want it, and if legislators were
really honest about it, they would put two
propositions on the ballot—the death penalty,
and life imprisonment without parole; no pos-

(MARIO M. CUOMO)

sibility of clemency. And life imprisonment without parole would win.

Interview/USA Today, 5-31:(A)9.

Samuel Del Villar
Mexican authority on narcotics

1

Trying to get rid of drugs is like Sisyphus pushing the rock up the mountain. We can arrive at the top, but the "rock" [the drug problem] will keep falling back as long as there is a huge illicit market in the U.S., and the focus is on eradicating crops instead of organizations.

The Christian Science Monitor,
4-13:2.

George Deukmejian
Governor of California (R)

2

I don't think the public should get lulled into thinking that even if you have a law that bans the sale of assault-type semi-automatic weapons that this will solve the problem ... Nobody should be under this illusion. I'm just trying to be realistic and make the point that there are so many guns out there and available. For the criminal element who wants to get these guns, they are going to get them one way or another.

News conference,
Washington, Feb. 27/
Los Angeles Times, 2-28:(I)3.

Barry Feld
Professor of law,
University of Minnesota

3

Rehabilitation [of violent criminals] is not very effective. The conventional wisdom is that most of those who commit serious crimes are going to be reinvolved.

USA Today, 5-3:(A)10.

Raymond L. Flynn
Mayor of Boston

4

This has been a wasted year, a wasted year in the war on drugs. The Federal government has not backed up its rhetoric with real dollars, and that's what this is all about. I'm not going to be party to some sort of hypocrisy, where everybody talks about this concerted plan dealing with drugs, unless they're willing to come to the table with money. I think it's a hypocrisy. It's really not a war on drugs at all. It's something that is deceiving the cities of this country.

News conference,
Washington, July 24/
The New York Times, 7-25:(A)8.

Steven Freeman
Director of legal affairs,
New York office,
Anti-Defamation League of
B'nai B'rith

5

There is a special dimension to hate crimes that sets them apart from your garden-variety assaults. A victim of an ordinary crime knows it was random chance, but hate-crime victims know they were singled out because of who they are.

The New York Times, 5-12:(A)8.

Daryl F. Gates
Chief of Police of Los Angeles

6

[Calling for a ban on private ownership of assault weapons]: I get sick of [gun-owners] waving their flags and their guns in my face. I'm just as much of a patriot as anybody. In my judgement, [gun-control opponents] have not been responsible and they have not been reasonable. I want to get rid of those assault weapons. They have no place on the streets of Los Angeles. My police officers are tired of hearing my conservative friends voice their rights under the Second Amendment.

To reporters, Los Angeles, Feb.8/
Los Angeles Times, 2-9:(II)10.

Joe Gerwens
Chief of Police
of Fort Lauderdale, Fla.

7

[On drug-related violent crime]: Maybe you displace it for a week, but it pops up somewhere

(JOE GERWENS)

else. The whole system is just backlogged and stopped-up and, while it may look great in the newspapers that the police made so many arrests, it's just a Band-Aid. Everyone is absolutely overwhelmed by the problem. And when they look at what any meaningful solution would cost, it just scares the hell out of them.

The Washington Post,
4-4:(A)14.

W. Wilson Goode
Mayor of Philadelphia

1

Political will translates, in any language, into political courage. That's what it's going to take for all of us to push for strong, comprehensive crime-prevention politics . . . Calling for bits and pieces will not be hard; calling for interim measures that will not upset our national budget planners will not be hard. But calling for what we know is really needed if we are to keep crime problems from getting worse will be hard indeed. I believe that kind of political will exists at the local level; I would like to think that, together, we can instill it at the national level.

At European and North American
Conference on Urban Safety and
Crime Prevention, Montreal/
The Washington Post,
10-24:(A)24.

2

We waited until 1986 for Congress to pass our first national drug-control law, and we didn't put any teeth in it, and we didn't put much money in it. In 1988, Congress passed the law again, and we still didn't put any teeth in it, or much money in it. Now we are getting ready for a new national anti-drug strategy promoted by President Bush and cheered by the Congress, and it may have some teeth in it, and some more money, but likely not enough of either.

At European and North American
Conference on Urban Safety and
Crime Prevention, Montreal/
The Washington Post, 10-24:(A)24.

Douglas Hogg
Minister of State,
Department of Trade and
Industry of the United Kingdom

3

[On the introduction of crack cocaine into Britain]: I conclude that enforcement measures are very important, but that demand reduction is even more important. I think there are distinguishing factors between the situation here [in Britain] and in the United States. The murders in Washington at the moment would not be replicated here because of the difficulty of access to firepower here. In terms of enforcement, the authorities in the United States didn't respond sufficiently quickly to the development of crack. I'm not going to say they got it wrong, but the lesson includes the necessity of effective drug education measures as well.

Interview, London/
The New York Times, 7-27:(A)4.

Jesse L. Jackson
Civil-rights leader

4

[On the illegal-drug problem]: The Federal government cannot solve a national and international problem with a local solution. [U.S.] drug czar William Bennett's emergency plan for the District of Columbia gives us the first indication of the [Bush] Administration's approach to the drug war. The proposed solutions focus on the distributors, but not on the suppliers or the demanders. To announce a plan that excludes the input of local government, local police and the community crosses the line from needed Federal assistance to unwanted Federal intervention. With this announcement, the Administration seems more intent on embarrassing local officials than on waging a serious war on drugs.

Interview/Ebony, August:156.

5

If the [drug] cartel in Colombia [which supplies cocaine to users in the U.S.] was selling poisoned fish or poisoned grapes, we would not consume them, and they would starve to death. Fighting the drug war starts at the level of the

(JESSE L. JACKSON)

appetite for drugs in *our* capital, not just the growth of it in *theirs*.

At University of the District of Columbia, Washington, Sept. 6/ The Washington Post, 9-7:(A)28.

1

This drug war is a peculiar war. Treason abounds. Pushers and consumers have allied with the drug cartel against themselves, their religion and their country. This is a war where the enemy is exploiting the soft underbelly of our national character. For the greedy, drugs represent excess; for the poverty-stricken, money; for the pusher, a flash of power. Drug pushers are terrorists, and those who consume drugs are engaged in treason.

At University of the District of Columbia/ Washington, Sept. 6/ The Washington Post, 9-8:(A)23.

2

[On President Bush's new plan to fight the drug cartels in Colombia which supply much of the U.S. cocaine market]: President Bush announced a drug plan for Bogota, Colombia. Where is his plan for the District of Columbia and cities across the [U.S.]? . . . Mr. Bush's plan does not match the breadth of this social crisis. It greatly underestimates the military arsenals and viciousness of the drug lords and pushers. They not only have deadly firepower, from AK-47s to Uzis, superior to the weapons of police; they have a reckless attitude and no respect for human life.

Before House Select Committee on Narcotics Abuse and Control, Washington, Sept. 15/ The New York Times, 9-16:6.

John E. Jacob
*President,
National Urban League*

3

We [blacks] must be tough and unforgiving on [illegal] drugs. We intend to rid our community of

drug pushers. We will be unsympathetic to them. We believe there ought to be drug treatment, but that is not the issue for us at this juncture other than to try to make sure that treatment is available on demand. The issue has to be that drug users have to stop using in our community; drug dealers have to stop dealing in our community. We want them out.

Interview/USA Today, 8-10:(A)13.

Don Kates
Lawyer, Criminologist

4

[Criticizing those who favor banning private ownership of guns]: Much of the gun-control controversy derives from cultural intolerance—a kind of liberal bigotry. Liberals would be appalled at any idea of banning homosexuality because a tiny minority of homosexuals was spreading AIDS irresponsibly; but that's what they say to gun owners. Elitists want to ban guns for everybody else but themselves. Even though they favor such bans, *New York Times* publisher Arthur Sulzberger and former San Francisco Mayor Dianne Feinstein obtained permits, based on their public prominence, to carry concealed guns.

Interview/ U.S. News & World Report, 5-8:28.

Edward M. Kennedy
*United States Senator,
D-Massachusetts*

5

[On President Bush's newly announced plan for fighting drug trafficking]: The phony war of the past eight years is over. For the first time in this decade, we have an Administration pledged to do what it takes to rid the nation and its communities of the scourge of drug abuse. Obviously, there will be disagreements and divisions in the months ahead over the most effective priorities . . . and for allocating scarce resources. But I am optimistic that, with the President and Congress working together at last, the worst is over.

Sept. 5/ Los Angeles Times, 9-6:(I)10.

Edward I. Koch
Mayor of New York

1

In the 1920s, we had a lot of police officers killed in the line of duty. Now, in the 1980s, we have a lot of police officers who were shot down in the line of duty. And you say to yourself, what happened? What happened to our society? We know about the '20s: we had a lawless society. And I regret to say that it appears in the '80s that we have a lawless society.

At ceremony for slain police officers,
New York, May 19/
The New York Times, 5-20:10.

2

There are only two things certain in life if you are dealing with criminals—speedy trials and certain punishment. And we don't have either.
The New York Times, 7-19:(A)16.

George Latimer
Mayor of St. Paul, Minn.

3

[On the fight against illegal drugs]: You have to fight the demand side. Education, change of behavior and values are finally going to be more important than interdiction, drug busts and foreign policy.

USA Today, 2-3:(A)3.

Joseph McNamara
Chief of Police
of San Jose, Calif.

4

We've been sold a bill of goods by a powerful gun lobby. "Buy a gun and you're safe," they say. But a gun is a lethal weapon. Even pros can get killed. Do you feel safer on the street knowing every other person owns a gun?
The New York Times, 4-17:(A)1.

Robert M. Morgenthau
District Attorney
of Manhattan (New York City)

5

Anybody who goes out into the streets of New York and sees what's going on there will under-

stand that we are facing a major crisis, not just in drugs but all of the crimes that go with it—murder, child abuse, robbery, all of it. But nobody, at the national or the state or the city level, seems prepared to make the sort of commitment of resources that is necessary.
The New York Times, 4-4:(A)16.

Patrick Murphy
Director, police policy board,
National Conference of Mayors

6

People don't understand that it isn't the police who prevent crime. It is the community. The primary mission of the police is to help people control and protect their communities. But for that to happen, people in the community have to believe that they have some power and that the police are their agents. They don't believe that now ... People don't know what crimes are happening in their own neighborhoods. In the old days, you would know that the guy around the corner just did time for burglary or rape because the cop on the beat would tell you. And you would tell him of any suspicious activity that you happened to hear about. Now the cop doesn't know you, and you don't know him ... People need to feel they have some power. When a community embraces the responsibility of protecting itself, it creates and strengthens the bonds that hold it together. Strong communities are our best weapons against crime.

Interview/
The Washington Post, 3-6:(A)15.

George Napper
Commissioner of
Public Safety of Atlanta

7

[Criticizing the proliferation of private ownership of guns]: America the beautiful is increasingly becoming America the violent. Handguns, recently joined by assault weapons, are part of an ugly picture that is surfacing all over the country ... all the carnage now going on is the best reason to continue doing whatever we can to keep guns out of everyone's hands.
Interview/
U.S. News & World Report, 5-8:28.

Dave Nolan
Founder, Libertarian Party

1

[Calling for the legalization of illicit drugs]: At this moment in time, the Drug Enforcement Administration is the greatest threat to the liberties of the American people. The war on drugs is a war on the Constitution and a war on the American people. It must be stopped.

Panel discussion,
Philadelphia, Aug. 31/
The New York Times, 9-2:7.

Javier Perez de Cuellar
Secretary General
of the United Nations

2

[On the fight against drug-trafficking]: The drug business is a billionaire's business. You need billions if you want to fight billions . . . What is needed is a tremendous financial effort, not only a military effort or a technical effort.

News conference, United Nations,
New York, Sept. 19/
Los Angeles Times, 9-20:(I)7.

Robert Philobosian
Chairman, California State
Task Force on Gangs and Drugs

3

Today's [teen-age] gangs are urban terrorists. Heavily armed and more violent than before, they are quick to use terror and intimidation to seize and protect their share of the lucrative crack cocaine market as well as markets for other drugs.

News conference,
Sacramento, Calif., Jan. 11/
The New York Times, 1-12:(A)13.

Charles B. Rangel
United States Representative,
D-New York

4

[On the drug-abuse problem]: When you see what is happening to American youth, when you see what is happening to America, when you see

the type of contamination that corrupts our police departments and criminal-justice system, one might suspect that this would be enough to alert us that this thing can get worse—and it will get worse before it gets better. Yet the folly of not doing anything is something I will never, never, ever understand. We need outrage! I don't know what is behind the lackadaisical attitudes toward drugs, but I do know that the American people have made it abundantly clear: They are outraged by the indifference of the U.S. government to this problem. Not only is there a lack of commitment, but a feeling that we are not even supposed to talk about it.

Ebony, March:130.

5

We haven't even fired the first shot in the war on drugs. Illicit narcotics coming into our country have tripled in the last decade, as have drug-related crimes and hospital emergency-room overdoses and deaths. But you cannot say we're "losing" the war because we have not even fought it yet. There has not been a policy or strategy. It would seem to me that if the [Presidential] Cabinet members recognized the serious threat to our way of life posed by drugs, then we should have heard some signal from them by now. But we haven't. You name the area— domestic, foreign—and we don't have the slightest idea what we have going for us.

Interview/Ebony, August:156.

Robert Raven
Lawyer; President,
American Bar Association

6

I divide the [criminal-justice] system into three parts: law enforcement in the front end, courts in the middle, and prisons, probation and correction on the other end. You can state the problem very simply: None of the parts work. Only one out of 10 crimes—about 3 million crimes of 34 million committed every year—even get exposed to arrest. We have no certainty of punishment . . . [And] the country has been sold on the point that if you can't have certainty and swiftness of punishment, at least you ought to have

(ROBERT RAVEN)

severity for the few you catch. The idea is to throw them all in jail, no matter what kind of crime they've committed, and keep them there for a long time. It's horrendous the money we're spending. We're building 100 new jails in the states, 10 more on the Federal side.

Interview/USA Today, 8-2:(A)9.

Ellis Rubin
Lawyer

1

[On why he supports capital punishment]: Because I think it is society's wish to extract revenge. There is a need for that. I don't know if it's a deterrent, but I know that I've looked into the eyes of hundreds of people accused of a capital crime, and they're deathly afraid of capital punishment. At the very least, capital punishment is valuable in that it brings about plea bargains so that there doesn't have to be an expensive trial.

*Interview/
USA Today, 11-27:(A)11.*

Thomas Reppetto
*Chairman,
Citizens Crime Commission
(New York City)*

2

I don't think we have the capacity in the criminal-justice system to imprison all the street-level drug dealers. On the other hand, if we just run them through the front door and out the back, where's the deterrent? They take being arrested as a cost of doing business. Hell, they take being killed as a cost of doing business.

The Washington Post, 4-4:(A)1.

Charles "Buddy" Roemer
Governor of Louisiana (D)

3

In an execution in this country, the test ought not to be reasonable doubt. The test ought to be is there any doubt.

Newsweek, 8-28:15.

Aaron H. Rosenthal
*Chief of detectives
of Manhattan
(New York City Police Dept.)*

4

[On today's drug-related violent crimes]: Every day, someone redefines the word heinous. All these crimes of the century you once read about, today they wouldn't even get three lines in the newspaper.

The Washington Post, 4-4:(A)14.

Kurt L. Schmoke
Mayor of Baltimore

5

[Advocating the decriminalization of certain illegal drugs]: The biggest misconception is that people think I favor people using drugs, which is not true at all. Alcohol is legal, but we don't favor kids drinking scotch. What I am saying is that the drug issue is two-fold. It's the problem of abuse and the problem of crime associated with drug trafficking. The criminal-justice system might be good dealing with one, but it's sure not good dealing with the abuse problem. If addicts had access to drugs through the public health system and not through criminals, they would not have to steal and break into houses and shoot people in order to get to the substance.

Los Angeles Times, 1-1:(I)4.

6

... our current drug laws not only are not helping us win the war on drugs, they're helping us *lose* the war on drugs. This is true for at least three reasons. First, we are wasting billions of dollars on law enforcement, money that could be more effectively used for education, treatment and prevention. Second, a law-enforcement approach to drugs simply raises the black-market price of drugs, making drug trafficking a progressively more attractive business for criminals. And third, because the money to be made from selling drugs is a lure to poor children, we are at risk of losing a large share of an entire generation of young people, many of whom are African-American [black], to drug abuse, incarceration and poverty.

Interview/Ebony, August:158.

(KURT L. SCHMOKE)

1

[On his suggestion to legalize certain now-illegal drugs as a way of dealing with the narcotics problem]: When I talk to groups, I usually ask three questions: Do you think we're winning the war against drugs? Do you think we've won the war? Do you think that doing more of the same in the next decade will win? And usually people say no. And then I ask: Do you think we ought to have a strategy that takes the profits out of drug dealing? Do you think we ought to have a strategy that allows 90 per cent of our addicts to be treated, rather than 90 per cent to be excluded from drug treatment? Do you think we ought to have a strategy that allows us to reduce the spread of AIDS among intravenous drug users? And, of course, they agree. Now, if I say, "Do you think we should decriminalize drugs?", they say, "Oh no, you're crazy, that's a horrible thing." So when I am allowed to talk to people about substance, and not about labels, I really get a very strong and positive response.

Interview/
USA Today, 10-30:(A)11.

William S. Sessions
Director, Federal Bureau
of Investigation

2

I do not agree that we should decriminalize narcotics and controlled substances. We have no idea and we can only speculate as to what the increase in drug usage would be. We all know that drug treatment costs are tremendous. We've taken a leadership role in signing international drug agreements under which a number of countries will begin to enact laws and provisions that will allow for everything from drug exportation, to actively pursuing traffickers, to allowing for extradition. We really haven't yet begun to fight. We must build a will among the American people that we will not be conquered by the scourge of drugs.

Interview/USA Today, 1-24:(A)9.

3

[On assault rifles being sold legally to the general public]: Every law-enforcement officer knows that guns are very much on the minds of all of us. We've had some tragic incidents where our own agents have been killed because of a lack of hitting power or killing power of our own weapons and our own ammunition. Where there seems to be no rationale for having those types of weapons for any purpose other than making war and killing people, it would seem to me that there is some rationale for limitation on that type of weapon.

Interview/
USA Today, 1-24:(A)9.

George P. Shultz
Former Secretary of State
of the United States

4

It seems to me we're not really going to get anywhere [in the fight against illegal drugs] until we can take the criminality out of the drug business and the incentives for criminality out of it. Frankly, the only way I can think of to accomplish this is to make it possible for addicts to buy drugs at some regulated place at a price that approximates their cost. When you do that, you wipe out the criminal incentives, including, I might say, the incentive that the drug pushers have to go around and get kids addicted, so that they create a market for themselves. They won't have that incentive because they won't have that market ... We need at least to consider and examine forms of controlled legalization of drugs. I find it very difficult to say that. Sometimes, at a reception or cocktail party, I advance these views and people head for somebody else. They don't even want to talk to you. I know that I'm shouting into the breeze here, as far as what we're doing now. But I feel that if somebody doesn't get up and start talking about this now, the next time around, when we have the next iteration of these programs, it will still be true that everyone is scared to talk about it. No politician wants to say what I just said, not for a minute.

Before Stanford
Business School alumni,
Oct. 7/
The Wall Street Journal,
10-27:(A)18.

Michael Clay Smith
*Associate professor
of criminal justice and higher
education administration,
University of Southern Mississippi*

1

[On crime on college campuses]: All crime statistics are unreliable. Crime studies show only about 50 per cent of all felonies are ever reported to the police. There is a lot of politics that goes into reporting crime statistics, and that's more true on campuses. It may not be that an order came down from a vice president to hide crime statistics, but rather that the police chief, or someone, sensed what would happen if figures got out that were rather high.

Interview/USA Today, 1-23:(A)15.

Dewey R. Stokes
*President,
Fraternal Order of Police*

2

If we pass a seven-day waiting period for the purchase of handguns, that's not going to stop all crime. It's dumb to think that. But why can't we, as a society, take an intelligent, common-sense look at it and say that a waiting period is going to stop some people from committing crimes of passion by providing a cooling-off period? And a lot of weapons out there are not needed for home protection or for sporting purposes. You don't shoot rabbits with an AK-47 [assault rifle] or a "street sweeper."

*Interview/
USA Today, 12-12:(A)13.*

Maurice T. Turner, Jr.
*Chief of Police
of the District of Columbia*

3

[On the high rate of violent crime in Washington]: If I thought that 1,000 more [police] officers would immediately solve this problem, I would vehemently request them. But no number of police is going to quickly abate the lawlessness in this city without immediate, well-coordinated increases in prosecutors, judges, extended court hours to hear cases, court staff,

more jail and prison space and, most of all, a changing of the morals and values of persons in our society. Two years from now, unless something is done about the public's unquenchable thirst and demand to snort and inject drugs, the then Chief of Police will have no other choice than to ask for 1,000 more officers.

*Before D.C. Council,
Feb.24/
The Washington Post,
2-25:(A)1.*

Ernest van den Haag
*Former professor
of jurisprudence,
Fordham University*

4

Crimes are committed not just against a victim, but against society. There must be appropriate punishment for misbehavior. The punishment for heinous murder, not all murder, death. The murderer has forfeited his right to live among us.

*Interview/
The New York Times,
5-3:(A)9.*

Dale Volcker
New York State Senator (R)

5

[Arguing in favor of capital punishment]: The opponents of the death penalty say that somehow it takes away from the civilization. But would anyone say that our streets are more civilized today [in the State of New York, which has no death penalty]? I don't claim that we can deter every murder, but I do claim we can deter some murders. We're at a point where we have to send a dramatic message out to the streets. The turning point in the murder rate was when the death penalty was abolished [in the 1960s]. My father, Julius Volcker, who was in the [state] Assembly at the time . . . said violent crimes would reach record proportions. He was like a prophet.

*The Washington Post,
3-10:(A)3.*

William von Raab
Commissioner, United States
Customs Service

1

[Criticizing government anti-drug programs]: There is a latent passivism that exists with respect to the drug war, a fear of getting into a battle that we cannot win because we won't make the kinds of serious sacrifices necessary to win. And that includes political sacrifices. There are too many people in some of the departments who are fainthearted, and a faint heart is not going to win this war.

Interview,
Washington, July 27/
Los Angeles Times, 7-28:(I)20.

2

[Criticizing the war on drugs]: We are fighting an uninspired war of attrition. A war of words. The drug issue is *not* a priority right now. I don't think our government, either in Congress or the Administration, has the stomach necessary to win this battle . . . Since the election [of President Bush in 1988], I've heard virtually nothing from the powers that be about the war on drugs. On occasion there is a ceremonial session in which some official talks to us for 10 minutes, but as a practical matter, we have been becalmed for a year now. No initiatives, no bold strokes.

Time, 8-7:18.

Sol Wachtler
Chief Judge, New York State
Court of Appeals

3

What we've done, by having these massive [drug] arrests, without thinking in terms of the courts, the Probation Department, Legal Aid, the district attorneys and the jails, is to encourage a disrespect for the system that is very dangerous. If you put people into the system and then you can't properly process them and punish them, then the word on the street is, "It doesn't matter if you're arrested, because you can always plead to a lesser charge."

The New York Times,
4-4:(A)16.

Benjamin Ward
Commissioner of Police
of New York City

4

[At a ceremony for slain police officers]: I'm never comfortable at this ceremony, and I've attended many of them. I am never comfortable with that which I cannot understand, and I always find it so difficult to understand how anyone could kill a policeman.

New York, May 19/
The New York Times,
5-20:10.

Franklin Zimring
Criminologist, University of California,
Berkeley

5

There's an enormous ambivalence afoot in America today. We want to have the death penalty as a statement, as the ultimate weapon, like the [nuclear] missiles in the silo. But we really don't want to use it.

The New York Times,
6-19:(A)11.

Defense • The Military

James Abrahamson
Lieutenant General,
United States Air Force (Ret.);
Former Director,
Strategic Defense Initiative
(Space Defense System)

1

[Supporting the proposed "Brilliant Pebbles" defense system employing small missiles orbiting in space]: It's a natural and reasonable thing for human beings to be looking for a way to defend themselves. And if you can defend yourself without threatening terrible destruction on all of mankind, then that seems to me a much better approach. But, in the long run, there is no supreme weapon. The only hope is human understanding. But we are not yet at a point where we can rely on human understanding. We should always work toward that, however.

Interview/USA Today, 5-11:(A)11.

Gordon Adams
Director,
Defense Budget Project

2

[Saying both Congress and the Administration are reluctant to take the initiative in defense and arms-control matters]: In a dance, you have a leader and a follower. The problem here is that both the Congress and the Administration want to follow. The Administration is not leading because it has not defined its strategic priorities or its treaty position, and the Congress can't, because of differences within the House and Senate among the Democrats. Nobody wants to put their foot down first and waltz.

The New York Times, 9-18:(A)10.

Kenneth L. Adelman
Former Director,
Arms Control and
Disarmament Agency
of the United States

3

[On the controversy over whether John Tower should be confirmed as Defense Secretary in light of his alleged drinking and womanizing]: A defense Secretary has no private life. In the military chain of command just below the President, he must be of sound and clear mind by day and by night.

Interview, Feb. 15/
Los Angeles Times, 2-16:(I)20.

Sergei F. Akhromeyev
Chief, Soviet Armed Forces
General Staff

4

As a Soviet military man, I am concerned by some actions of the U.S. I am saying this not to offend anyone but so that the American public will know. First, the U.S. and NATO are still pursuing a position-of-strength policy toward the Soviet Union and the Warsaw Pact. We have elaborated a new defensive doctrine and put it into practice. We are unilaterally reducing our armed forces by 500,000 and have reduced them by 220,000 already. But the U.S. and NATO have not introduced a new doctrine. They are still guided by flexible response and nuclear deterrence. Why aren't they changing their doctrine? That causes mistrust here.

Interview/Time, 11-13:58.

Les Aspin
United States Representative
D-Wisconsin

5

[Soviet leader Mikhail] Gorbachev is talking about dramatic revisions [reductions] in the Soviet military. Here in the United States, we're so used to managing responses to an increasing Soviet threat that we have little idea how to cope with a decreasing threat.

May 1/
The Washington Post, 5-2:(A)4.

6

The defense budget is not going up, it is falling. The lean days are coming, the flush days are

(LES ASPIN)

gone. We can't pay for everything we would like to have in the budgets that are coming down the pike.

At House Armed Services
Committee hearing,
Washington, June 28/
The New York Times, 6-29:(A)10.

James A. Baker III
Secretary of State-designate
of the United States

1

There has been recently concluded in Paris an international conference on chemical weapons. I think we need to continue to move that process forward. Some people say, well, you can never get a chemical-weapons agreement because it's so difficult to verify, or you can't expect to stop the proliferation of chemical weapons because it's just going to happen. And I suppose my answer to those folks would be that our non-proliferation efforts sometimes work better than we think they might.

At Senate Foreign Relations
Committee hearing on his confirmation,
Washington, Jan. 17/
The New York Times, 1-18:(A)10.

McGeorge Bundy
Former Assistant
to the President
of the United States
(John F. Kennedy and
Lyndon B. Johnson)
for National Security Affairs

2

Some broad conclusions can be drawn from the nuclear experience. Maintaining the tradition of non-use has to be the first objective. [Dwight] Eisenhower did a marvelous job for nuclear peace as the first NATO commander. He kept saying, "The Russians aren't coming, and we can defend ourselves." That still applies, but there are several basic rules. The first is that since you're stuck with the bomb, the fundamental requirement for your own force is that it be genuinely survivable. You must keep second-strike capability; you must never tempt the other side to think it could win. Unfortunately, both sides, especially their military, are trained to think in terms of victory. It is very important not to let special interests, including the interests of individual services, govern the big decisions. No Administration so far has made sure that we have a national assessment and national choices rather than service assessment and service choices. I complain about [President] Ronald Reagan a lot . . . But he was the first President to say sharply and clearly that nuclear war cannot be won and must never be fought. He's absolutely right. Explaining it straight is very important.

Interview/
U.S. News and World Report,
1-9:44.

Arleigh Burke
Admiral,
United States Navy (Ret.);
Former Chief of Naval Operations

3

Genuine knowledge of combat at sea is very limited because it's hard to describe. The ability to handle the extraordinary or the unexpected is much more important than people realize. The only way you can train for it is to tell people it's going to happen, that there will be surprises and they better be ready. But nobody really believes it until it happens.

The Washington Post, 9-15:(C)8.

4

The difference between a good officer and an excellent one is about 10 seconds. A fine rule is to get going sooner than anticipated, travel faster than expected and arrive before you're due.

The Washington Post, 9-15:(C)8.

George Bush
President of the United States

5

In the Middle East, in South Asia, in our own hemisphere, a growing number of nations are acquiring advanced and highly destructive [mili-

71

(GEORGE BUSH)

tary] capabilities, in some cases weapons of mass destruction and the means to deliver them. And it is an unfortunate fact that the world faces increasing threat from armed insurgencies, terrorists and . . . narcotics traffickers; and in some regions, an unholy alliance of all three. Our task is clear: we must curb the proliferation of advanced weaponry. We must check the aggressive ambitions of renegade regimes. And we must enhance the ability of our friends to defend themselves . . . Let me just mention two points in particular: First, the need for an effective deterrent, one that demonstrates, to our allies and adversaries alike, American strength, American resolve; and second, the need to maintain an approach to arms reduction that promotes stability at the lowest feasible level of armaments.

At U.S. Coast Guard Academy
commencement, May 24/
The New York Times, 5-25:(A)4.

1

As I reflect on this scene . . . I think of generations of young people on both sides of the Atlantic who have grown up in peace and prosperity . . . It may be difficult for them to understand why we need to keep a strong military deterrent to prevent war and to preserve freedom and democracy. The answer is here, among the quiet of the graves.

At cemetery for World War II
American war dead,
Nettuno, Italy, May 28/
The Washington Post,
5-29:(A)19.

2

More than 20 nations now possess chemical weapons or the capability to produce them, and these horrible weapons are now finding their way into regional conflict. This is simply unacceptable. For the sake of mankind, we must halt and reverse this threat. Today I want to announce steps that the United States is ready to take, steps to rid the world of these truly terrible weapons, toward a treaty that will ban, eliminate, all

chemical weapons from the earth in 10 years from the day it is signed.

At United Nations,
New York, Sept. 25/
USA Today, 9-26:(A)13.

3

[On calls in the U.S. to cut military expenditures in light of current pro-democracy reforms in Eastern Europe and the Soviet Union]: There has been such a euphoric feeling on Capitol Hill about this change that they think they can just cut the heart out of the defense program. And that I will resist. I don't want to encourage the thought that we always have to operate at these substantial levels [of defense spending]. But, on the other hand, I don't want to encourage reckless cuts.

Interview, Washington/
U.S. News & World Report,
12-25:34.

Frank C. Carlucci
Secretary of Defense
of the United States

4

[Addressing President Reagan, who is leaving office after two terms]: Our military stands taller, its members are more respected in their communities, better qualified, better educated and better trained because of our leadership. You have restored not only our national strength but also our sense of purpose. This has come through clearly to every member of the armed forces, whatever their rank and wherever stationed. We pay you the highest compliment when we say to you, sir, that your command has been a success. We will all miss you.

At Andrews Air Force Base, Md.,
Jan. 12/
The New York Times, 1-13:(A)9.

Dick Cheney
Secretary of Defense
of the United States

5

However real the reform rhetoric coming out of the Kremlin, Moscow's armaments compel

(DICK CHENEY)

caution on our part. To date there has been no reduction in their strategic systems targeted against the United States. Until we see a significantly lessened military capability on the part of the Soviets, we cannot possibly justify major reductions in our own.

At swearing-in celebration for him,
Washington, March 21/
The Washington Post, 3-22:(A)8.

1

[On the proposed U.S. space defense system]: You can argue that SDI will become more important in the future than it has in the past because the possibility exists that you'll have other nations with ballistic missiles—with nuclear weapons or chemical warfare capabilities—that could be used against the United States. If you had a number of nations that had the capacity to do serious damage to the United States because they had ballistic-missile capability, then the old "mutually assured destruction" concept doesn't work nearly as well. You might well then want to move to a defense regime like SDI. So I think SDI is a very important concept . . . I expect at some point the United States will deploy SDI.

Broadcast interview/
"Daybreak," CNN-TV, 3-28.

2

[On the proposed SDI space defense system]: Oftentimes during the Reagan Administration, it was described in terms that, frankly, I think oversold the concept. We have this notion that occasionally was mentioned, the idea of a total, complete shield that would be absolutely leakproof and block all incoming missiles. If you think about it in those terms, it's going to be an extremely remote proposition. If, on the other hand, you look at it as a system that could interfere with a Soviet first strike on the United States, that would be able to knock out a lot of incoming warheads and thereby increase deterrence, then it becomes a very different proposition.

Broadcast interview/
"Today," NBC-TV, 3-28.

3

[Saying more military bases in the U.S. may be closed in an effort to save money]: While I understand the problems that some of my former colleagues [in Congress] face—individual situations in their districts—I just have to believe that there are opportunities for economies in reviewing a base structure that has been basically unchanged for 50 or 60 years.

Interview, Washington, March 30/
Los Angeles Times, 3-31:(I)4.

4

[Criticizing the House for cutting the defense budget]: My former colleagues voted as they did not because they had a better idea about how to deter the Soviet threat, but because many of them seemed to think there is no real threat any more [because of recent reforms in the Soviet Union]. It is as if they had decided to give away their overcoats on the first sunny day in January . . . The Soviet Union has been making major improvements to every leg of its strategic arsenal. In systems ranging from intercontinental missiles and bombers to submarines and strategic defense, the Soviet Union is getting stronger while our Congress debates and our country treads water.

Before Veterans of Foreign Wars,
Las Vegas, Nev., Aug. 23/
The New York Times,
8-24:(A)12.

5

[Saying the U.S. should not fundamentally reduce its military strength despite reforms being undertaken by the Soviet Union]: There has been no change in the strategic military posture of the Soviet Union. If anything, their strategic military capabilities are more robust today than they were four years ago, when [Soviet leader Mikhail Gorbachev] came to power . . . Now is not the time for us to dismantle our alliances . . . nor is it time to think that there's sufficient change in the Soviet Union or in the East Bloc for us to fundamentally alter . . . the heart of our policies and strategies of the last 40 years.

Interview, Los Angeles, Sept. 20/
Los Angeles Times,
9-21:(I)11.

(DICK CHENEY)

1

[Supporting the proposed SDI space defense system]: An effective strategic defense could be the single most important military bequest this generation could make to the future . . . I call on the critics to cease their attempts to make perfection the enemy of the good, and let's get down to the real debate about how defenses fit into our strategy for nuclear stability, deterrence and arms reductions.

Speech, Washington, Oct. 12/
Los Angeles Times, 10-13:(A)4.

2

[On proposed cuts in U.S. defense spending spurred by an apparently more passive and reform-minded Soviet Union]: There is an irreducible minimum of defense capability that the United States is going to require, no matter what happens in the Soviet Union. We are a superpower, and we're always going to want to have the capacity to deploy military force to safeguard American interests and to preserve our capacity to influence events in the world.

Interview, Washington, Nov. 24/
Los Angeles Times, 11-25:(A)30.

William J. Crowe, Jr.
Admiral, United States Navy;
Chairman, Joint Chiefs of Staff

3

We could be at the dawn of a new era in East-West relations which will offer genuine opportunities to reduce strategic and conventional arms. We should move in this direction, however, as tangible evidence of change [in the Soviet Union] mounts and our confidence grows, not as a result of rhetorical hopes and [Soviet] promises.

At Senate hearing, Washington/
The Washington Post, 5-8:(A)22.

George Deukmejian
Governor of California (R)

4

Many have suggested that we further limit defense spending. That can be done if our allies,

who want us to reduce the [Federal budget] deficit, agree to a greater sharing of the burden of maintaining our defenses around the world.

At World Economic Forum conference,
Davos, Switzerland, Jan. 29/
Los Angeles Times, 1-30:(I)15.

J. William Fulbright
Former United States Senator
D-Arkansas

5

[On whether the U.S. could be duped into a threatening situation if it reduces its military forces too much in negotiating with the Soviets]: I'm assuming we're not absolute idiots. I can remember when the official spokesman of the United States said 400 nuclear weapons was all we needed to deter aggression. And [now] we have, I guess, 10,000 or 15,000. We've gone all out in the stupid thing. That doesn't mean we don't want to have any at all. There's a great difference in 400 and 4,000 or 15,000. We've overdone it, and we've ruined our economy and fueled an extraordinary expenditure of money for military bases around the world . . . We ought to respond to every opportunity to de-escalate the arms race. It's foolish for us to sit here and see both countries ruin their economy on this silly arms race. [Soviet leader Mikhail] Gorbachev's arms proposals are sensible and, certainly, the least we can do is respond. I'd like to see us take the initiative and go a little farther to keep it going.

Interview/
USA Today, 6-5:(A)11.

Roger G. Harrison
Deputy Assistant
Secretary of State
of the United States

6

There has been a gradual erosion of the moral, as well as the legal, barriers against use of chemical weapons. We are in danger of chemical weapons becoming just another weapon of choice. We seek to raise the political costs of their use, and we hope that even countries accused of using chemical weapons will join in

(ROGER G. HARRISON)

affirming support for the 1925 protocol [banning use of chemical weapons].

Washington, Jan. 2/
The New York Times, 1-3:(A)1.

Richard C. Holbrooke
Former Under Secretary of State
of the United States

1

We spend $304-billion a year on defense. That defense budget, which was probably always too high, was justified by its proponents for one reason only. All the other reasons were secondary. The reason was the Soviet threat. That threat's changing [with the reforms in the Soviet Union]. It would be insanity not to go after that defense budget, but we can't do it in a single year. And we can't do it unilaterally. It should be a long-term objective, articulated publicly by the President, the way [Harry] Truman articulated the Truman Doctrine in 1947.

Interview/USAToday, 11-16:(A)7.

Jeanne Holm
Major General,
United States Air Force (Ret.);
Former Director,
Women in the Air Force

2

[Criticizing arguments that women do not belong in the armed forces because of a lack of required physical strength]: The vast majority of jobs in the military don't require any unusual strength at all. The notion that strength should be the basis for people's effectiveness in the military is just a fraudulent claim. If you're talking about the infantry, which has a great deal of physically demanding work, then [yes] it is a criterion and everybody who does it should be physically capable of doing it.

Interview/USA Today, 8-16:(A)9.

Edward M. Kennedy
United States Senator,
D-Massachusetts

3

[Saying he will not vote for the confirmation of John Tower as Defense Secretary because of his involvement with defense contractors in the private sector]: Perhaps in spite of his extraordinarily lucrative financial ties to the country's largest defense contractors involving hundreds of thousands of dollars, Senator Tower could still bring an open mind to the awesome decisions that lie ahead on our national defense. But America should not be forced to take that chance.

The New York Times, 2-24:(A)11.

Oskar Lafontaine
Governor of Saarland
(West Germany)

4

We live in an over-armed world. Politicians do not even understand what it means to have thousands of nuclear warheads. This is why they talk about "peas" or "pebbles' in these discussions. We have thousands of nuclear systems in [West] Germany already, and we want them away. The discussion of "balance" in weapons is a crazy discussion in a situation of overkill capacity. Therefore, it is not a matter of an abstract concept of "balance" but of human necessity to start such negotiations . . . The motto of today is disarmament, not the opposite.

Interview/The Wall Street Journal,
5-15:(A)13.

Carl M. Levin
United States Senator,
D-Michigan

5

[Arguing against the confirmation of John Tower as Defense Secretary]: By hiring himself out as a consultant to defense contractors to advise them on matters relating to the ongoing, confidential START talks, [former] Senator Tower created an inherent conflict [of interest]. The large sums paid to him for his services created a duty to give his clients his best advice. At the same time, he had a public duty to safeguard the confidential information to which he was privy. Inevitably, there is a great prospect for conflict [of interest] in those duties . . . Senator Tower does not see a problem here, that moving immediately from the government's confidential negotiator on a treaty to a defense con-

(CARL M. LEVIN)

tractor's consultant on that same treaty creates an appearance of using inside information for personal gain. Are appearances important in this area? They are. Yet, Senator Tower said he hadn't thought of it and doesn't see a problem in that situation. And that's very disturbing to me.

Before the Senate,
Washington, March 2/
The New York Times, 3-3:(A)10.

Richard G. Lugar
United States Senator,
R-Indiana

1

There may be a possibility of conventional-arms reductions [before the START talks]. But I would think that most of this [kind of talk] is simply mere chatter by people who are unaware of what has occurred in international arms negotiations for many years. For example, from the standpoint of NATO—even our friendly governments don't have a unified position on the subject [of conventional arms]. I'm not sure we have a negotiating position within our own government as to what would be desirable. So among those with no responsibility, the thought is that somehow or other we've got to get at this. But finding out how to do it—that is a more complex issue than any other arms-control issue, and we really don't have a framework for thinking it through.

The Atlantic Monthly, February:65.

Edward J. Markey
United States Representative,
D-Massachusetts

2

[Saying the nuclear-freeze movement in the U.S. did much to contribute to the current U.S.-Soviet arms-reduction progress]: What the freeze movement did in the United States, like the Greens in Europe, was to bring nuclear strategy out of the elite foreign-policy salons and move it to the grass roots. Public education led to public activism, and public activism has seriously constrained decision-makers' options over the last six or seven years.

The New York Times, 6-5:(A)14.

Edward C. Meyer
General (Ret.) and
former Chief of Staff,
United States Army

3

The Army as an entity has to reassess in the next year its 21st-century role. And that's going to be based on two major factors: what its real contribution is going to be in Central Europe, assuming there will be 21 days' warning of an attack, [and the implications of] structural disarmament [fewer weapons purchased because of rising costs].

Interview, June 2/
The Washington Post, 6-3:(A)11.

Mikhail Milshtein
Military analyst,
Soviet Institute for the Study
of the U.S.A. and Canada

4

The United States, to justify anything in their military policy, has always presented the Soviet Union as the reason . . . It's obvious the United States needs a *perestroika* [reform] in its political and military thinking and it goes to people in the Pentagon especially. It's about time for them to look at these problems from a different angle.

Interview/Los Angeles Times, 5-4:(I)17.

John Newhouse
Former Assistant Director,
Arms Control and
Disarmament Agency
of the United States

5

We feel that our [U.S.] weapons have an edge [over the Soviets]. We operate from a broader and deeper technological base. We deploy our weapons at sea, where the Soviets are most vulnerable. We have a larger and much better bomber force. The Soviets have the advantage in land-based missiles, but the land is their natural strategic environment, just as the sea is our natural environment. We have long coastlines and easy access to the open sea . . . The real point is that the sides are basically equivalent, which is why neither side is going to launch a nuclear attack.

Interview/USA Today, 1-30:(A)11.

Paul H. Nitze
Former Special Adviser
to the President of the
United States (Ronald Reagan)
for Arms-Control Negotiations

1

[On fears that, if nuclear weapons were eliminated from military arsenals, the world would be vulnerable to those who would detonate nuclear devices in suitcases, etc.]: Nothing is wholly risk-free. One must compare the alternative. It seems to me that the risks posed by cheating or suitcase bombs in a world from which nuclear arms had been eliminated from military arsenals would be orders of magnitude less than the risks and potential costs posed by a possible breakdown in the present deterrence regime based upon the ultimate threat of massive nuclear retaliation.

Before Philadelphia World Affairs
Council/The Atlantic Monthly,
February:66.

Sam Nunn
United States Senator,
D-Georgia

2

[On conflict-of-interest charges against John Tower, who is nominated to be Secretary of Defense]: John Tower was the head negotiator at our START negotiations. He knew the information, he knew the confidential negotiating positions, he knew the fall-back positions of the Administration on key weapons systems, like the MAX and *Midgetman.* Right after he got through, he immediately went to work for defense contractors . . . I don't know whether he crossed the line in giving those contractors confidential information. I'm not saying that. What I'm saying is it's the appearance that is so bad . . . and what kind of example does that set with all these other people in the Department of Defense? We're trying to close the revolving door. We're trying to clean up the procurement scandal . . . Can he set an example and restore confidence in the Pentagon procurement system? I think that will be very difficult.

Broadcast interview/
"Meet the Press." NBC-TV,
2-26.

John Piotrowski
General,
United States Air Force;
Commander-in-Chief,
North American Aerospace
Defense Command

3

[On the reform program in the Soviet Union and the resultant less hostile policy toward the West]: The Soviets, for a number of years—no matter how you look at negotiations and building down weapons—will have the ability to wreak unthinkable damage on the United States. And if their [now-friendly] attitude changes, they will have the forces to do that. What we're looking at is a leadership and an attitude within the Soviet Union which is less hostile. Their forces, however, are not less capable . . . I hope we never forget how we got [to that less-hostile attitude]. It wasn't unilateral build-down [of forces by the U.S.], it wasn't appeasement. It wasn't "setting a good example" by destroying missiles. In fact, we got here by building ground-launch cruise missiles and *Pershing*-2s and B-1s and pushing the Soviets to the recognition that they couldn't blackmail us.

Interview/
USA Today, 12-13:(A)13.

Dan Quayle
Vice President
of the United States

4

Future developments in technology areas . . . could cause, over the next 10 to 15 years, a revolution in military affairs. This will require us to develop new operational concepts, new military organizations, and new methods of warfare. The Defense Department has initiated a new strategic-planning tool called "Competitive Strategies" to help identify, develop and field the weapons systems we need to be competitive with our major adversary, and to understand how those weapons might be used operationally.

At U.S. Military Academy-
West Point commencement/
The Christian Science Monitor,
6-12:13.

(DAN QUAYLE)

1

[On the proposed U.S. space defense system]: We have redefined [SDI and] put it into missions, requirements, doctrine and strategy much differently than we did in the early 1980s ... [Former President Ronald Reagan] talked about this impenetrable shield that was going to be completely leak-proof ... I believe that, in the semantics of, let's say, political jargon, that that was acceptable. But it clearly was stretching the capability of a strategic defense system.

To reporters, Washington,
Sept. 6/
Los Angeles Times, 9-7:(I)1.

Ronald Reagan
President of the United States

2

Common sense told us that to preserve the peace we'd have to become strong again after years of weakness and confusion. So we rebuilt our defenses, and this New Year we toasted the new peacefulness around the globe. Not only have the superpowers actually begun to reduce their stockpiles of nuclear weapons—and hope for even more progress is bright—but the regional conflicts that wrack the globe are also beginning to cease.

Broadcast address to the nation,
Washington, Jan. 11/
The Washington Post, 1-12:(A)8.

3

The luster has been restored to the reputation of our fighting forces after a time during which it was shamefully fashionable to deride and even condemn service such as yours. Those days will never come again ... You [in the armed forces] have made yourselves a shining example of how men and women confine within themselves qualities of self-sacrifice, bravery, camaraderie and true courage. These are many of the noblest virtues to which humankind can aspire. They are martial virtues.

At Andrews Air Force Base, Md.,
Jan. 12/
Los Angeles Times, 1-13:(I)4.

4

[On the 595 Americans in the armed forces who were killed during his eight years in office]: In the air and on the seas, in battle or as victims of terrorism, they gave their lives while in the service of their country, while representing us and defending what we hold dear. They volunteered; they chose to serve. They gave their lives. They are our heroes.

At Andrews Air Force Base, Md.,
Jan. 12/
The New York Times, 1-13:(A)9.

5

[On the proposed SDI space defense system]: Yes, we have to go forward with SDI ... It was my idea. The very beginning when I first came here, I had a meeting with the Joint Chiefs [of Staff], and asked if they believed it was possible to conceive of a weapon, a defensive weapon—there's always been a defensive weapon for every other weapon invented—that could start eliminating these [nuclear missile] weapons if they were ever used as they came out of their silos. And they asked for a few days, and they came back in a few days and said, yes, they believed that such a thing could be considered. And I said, well, start.

Interview, Washington, Jan. 18/
The New York Times,
1-19:(A)14.

6

[On the arms-reduction agreements he arrived at with Soviet leader Mikhail Gorbachev]: Have I embraced him too quickly? What harm has been done? He's reduced his forces. We have the first treaty that the Soviets have ever signed in which they agreed to destroy weapons they already had ... I'm motivated by deeds, not just words. And the deeds have been there. We have the verification to an extent that I don't think anyone had ever dreamed would have been possible.

Interview, Washington,
Jan. 18/
The New York Times,
1-19:(A)14.

(RONALD REAGAN)

1

When I became President, on any given day half our military planes couldn't fly because of a lack of spare parts. We had to rebuild our military. And now we are closer to peace with the Soviet Union than any time [in] the last 40 years.

At Covenant House, New York,
Nov. 14/USA Today, 11-15:(A)3.

Stanley R. Resor
Former Secretary of the Army
and former Under Secretary of Defense
of the United States

2

We are getting close enough to these major, present-day arms-control goals that we should think quite seriously about what comes next. Goals for the future should give some political impetus to complete in the next year the negotiations that are now under way—a feeling of momentum—and they should provide both sides with the conceptual framework of how to continue the process of arms reduction over the next decade, the next two or even three decades.

At conference of Association of
Soviet Lawyers and U.S.-based
Lawyers Alliance for Nuclear
Arms Control, Moscow, Oct. 16/
Los Angeles Times, 10-17:(A)12.

Brent Scowcroft
Assistant to President
of the United States
George Bush for
National Security Affairs

3

[On the proliferation of chemical and biological weapons]: It is a problem akin in its scope to that of nuclear proliferation because these weapons, especially in city attacks and in antipopulation attacks, can be every bit as devastating as nuclear weapons, and they are much harder to control because the plants to produce them are, in many cases, like pharmaceutical plants, like insecticide plants. It's a terrible problem.

Broadcast interview/
"This Week With David Brinkley,"
ABC-TV, 1-22.

Eduard A. Shevardnadze
Foreign Minister
of the Soviet Union

4

Over the past two years, our [Soviet] position has evolved in a radical way—from manufacturing chemical weapons to abandoning their production altogether, from hushing up data on the existing stockpiles to publishing such data, from seeking to protect chemical production and storage facilities from the eyes of others to recognizing the concept of comprehensive verification and inviting foreign observers to watch the elimination of chemical weapons . . . We call upon all countries—those which produce chemical weapons as well as those which have resumed their production or intend to manufacture them—to demonstrate their responsibility to the world community and stop doing that and thus make a contribution toward concluding a convention on the elimination of chemical weapons.

At conference on chemical weapons,
Paris, Jan. 8/
The Washington Post, 1-9:(A)1,16.

5

We [Soviets] have absolutely no intention of trying to drive a wedge between the NATO allies. But we do have a position of principle. We must begin negotiating the reduction and eventual elimination of tactical nuclear missiles. We shall in the future be even more aggressive in pursuing this goal because it is in the interest of all European nations, the Soviet Union and the U.S. Why can't we negotiate along parallel tracks on strategic weapons, conventional arms, chemical weapons and also tactical nuclear weapons? And then, later on, we shall discuss the naval forces, which is a topic the West does not like.

Interview, Moscow/Time, 5-15:32.

6

Why are [nuclear weapons] dangerous? Not only because of their sheer destructive power. They're unacceptable because they widen the chasm between national and universal interests. The equality of nations and the unity of the world become empty talk when someone's national

(EDUARD A. SHEVARDNADZE)

selfishness is driven by the idea of nuclear supremacy over the world camouflaged as national-security interests ... We believe that reliance on nuclear weapons serves the national interests of no one. It is also an obstacle to more democratic international relations. Only the elimination of nuclear capabilities would help us to attain real security.

At United Nations,
New York, Sept. 26/
The New York Times, 9-27:(A)6.

1

[Saying his country's large radar complex in Siberia is a violation of the ABM treaty with the U.S.]: All these years, we have been fighting for the preservation of the anti-ballistic missile treaty as the basis for strategic stability. Yet, at the same time, the construction of this station, as big as an Egyptian pyramid, directly and openly violated the ABM treaty.

Before Supreme Soviet, Moscow,
Oct.23/
Los Angeles Times, 10-24:(A)1.

2

[Acknowledging that the Soviet radar station at Krasnoyarsk is a violation of the ABM treaty]: We were charged with violation of the ABM Treaty because of the station. It took the government quite a while to learn all the truth of the project. Finally, we saw it clearly: The station had been built on the wrong site, not where it should have been. All these years, we have been working hard to keep up the ABM Treaty as a foundation for strategic stability. We have been looking for options and having very complicated debates on the interpretation of each article of the Treaty and its supplements' contents. And all the while, there stood the station, the size of an Egyptian pyramid, representing, to put it bluntly, a violation of the ABM Treaty. At last we resolved this issue and announced we would dismantle the station. This has brought some discontent in the country, as if we were forgoing our own interests. In fact, we are saving the ABM

Treaty and opening the way to the conclusion of the treaty on strategic weapons, and we're gaining the legal and moral right to demand clarity on the question of American installations in Greenland and England, which were modernized, we understand, in violation of the Treaty.

Before Supreme Soviet, Moscow,
Oct. 23/
The New York Times, 10-25:(A)6.

George P. Shultz
Secretary of State
of the United States

3

I personally think that the idea of nuclear deterrence, as we have thought about it, as something that's just going to last in perpetuity, that's not likely. Among the changes that are taking place is the emergence of other kinds of weapons that are threatening [such as chemical and biological weapons] and a growing sense of unease about nuclear weapons.

Interview, Washington, Jan. 4/
The Washington Post, 1-6:(A)26.

Lawrence Skantze
General, United States Air Force
(Ret.)

4

There's a vast majority of the American people who want to feel that the defense budget is reasonable and will maintain an adequate and strong defense. I don't think you'd have that same consensus to say "well now, let's now spend that on solving pollution or homelessness" ... You will never get the breadth of a consensus for that sort of thing that you can for defense, because the average person who is a taxpayer, middle income, doing their thing, working hard, recognizes they need a [national] defense and will support that.

Interview/Los Angeles Times, 6-11:(IV)3.

Mark Sommer
Research director,
Alternative Defense Project

5

Qualitative disarmament reasserts a distinction that has been lost for years between the

(MARK SOMMER)

capacity to attack and the capacity to protect. Nuclear deterrence has dominated our thinking about defense in general. In that theory, it's true, it is only through the capacity to attack, or to threaten attack, that you have the capacity to protect. But it's possible to think of conventional deterrence in a less punitive way. Look at the standoff in Europe. Each alliance says it's configured only for defense, yet both armies are prepared to take the battle over into the other's territory. They don't understand that they could relinquish that capacity to attack without weakening their capacity to protect.

Interview/
The Atlantic Monthly, June:46.

Fortney H. (Pete) Stark
United States Representative,
D-California

1

On February 18, 1988, Admiral Ronald J. Hays, Commander-in-Chief of the U.S. Pacific Command, testified before the House Armed Services Committee: "We have worked hard to maintain an adequate number of steaming days, flying hours and vehicle miles so that equipment are exercised and the people are trained . . . With fewer exercises . . . force readiness will deteriorate." This year, Rear Admiral Thomas Brooks, Director of Naval Intelligence, testified before the House Armed Services Committee that the Soviet Navy has had a decline in its steaming hours, and an increase in its time at anchor, and he said, "increased the number of ships in port ready to respond to an enemy attack, thus improving the ability of the Soviet Navy to transition rapidly to war." When the enemy spends less money on its Navy, it is good [for them] and a sign of their war-like preparations. When we do it, it is dangerous and bad. No matter what the enemy says, we should do more. One does not know whether to laugh or cry at these positions. I come down on the side of it being very, very sad.

Before the House, Washington,
March 8/
The Washington Post, 3-24:(A)22.

Margaret Thatcher
Prime Minister
of the United Kingdom

2

I know some of the media in the West accuse us [the U.S. and Britain] of failing to measure up to [Soviet leader Mikhail] Gorbachev's constant stream of initiatives [on arms control]. Of course, initiatives make a much better story than constancy and sticking to your principles, but in the real world it has been constancy and steadiness, particularly in defense, which has served us well for 40 years.

At dinner for visiting U.S. President Bush,
London, June 1/
Los Angeles Times, 6-2:(I)10.

John G. Tower
Secretary of Defense-designate
of the United States

3

[A] majority of Americans believe that we have wasted an enormous amount of money on defense, that there has been this mismanagement, there has been fraud, there's been waste and abuse. And I think that if we are to maintain a strong defense establishment in this country, we must restore public confidence, not just in the Pentagon but in the national-security process.

At Senate Armed Services
Committee hearing on his
confirmation, Washington, Jan. 25/
Los Angeles Times, 1-26:(I)12.

4

[On criticism of his drinking habits and possible conflicts-of-interest]: I have never been dependent on alcohol. Twelve years ago, I gave up spirits. I used to be a pretty good Scotch drinker. I haven't tasted Scotch in 12 years. After that, I had only wine; had perhaps an occasional martini, occasionally a little vodka with smoked salmon, caviar or something like that. I hereby swear that, if confirmed, during the course of my tenure as Secretary of Defense I will not consume alcohol of any type or form, including wine, beer or spirits of any kind. I think I'd be obliged to resign if I broke a pledge. I've never broken a

(JOHN G. TOWER)

pledge in my life. And I will live in a goldfish bowl. So there will be plenty of enforcers out there on me . . . [As for conflict-of-interest,] I reject the charge totally. When I came out [of government as arms-control negotiator], I went into the private sector [to work for defense contractors]. I used my experience and my knowledge. But I always did it ethically, legally, and I never told anything that wasn't already in the public domain. When I completed my work in the private sector, and tried to return to government, I gave up that income to come back and perform a public service for a much, much reduced annual income.

Broadcast interview/
"This Week With David Brinkley."
ABC-TV, 2-26.

Paul Walker
Co-director, Institute for Peace
and International Security

1

Frankly, the best way of telling offensive from defensive weapons is to ask the other side what weapons of yours *they* perceive as offensive.

Interview/
The Atlantic Monthly, June:46.

Paul C. Warnke
Former Director,
Arms Control and
Disarmament Agency
of the United States

2

Just because of geography, mobile missiles are a better bet for [the Soviets] than for us. We'd find a hell of a lot of difficulty having a genuinely road-mobile system . . . We could probably deploy missiles only on military bases, where they'd be inherently more vulnerable, while the Soviets have lots more room for mobiles to roam. And you're not going to have peace groups demonstrating against them, either . . . [On the other hand,] submarines are not as good an option for the Soviets as they are for us, because they just don't have the ready access to the open

sea that we do. So it doesn't bother me that they are going to mobile missiles.

Interview/The Atlantic Monthly.
February:60.

James H. Webb, Jr.
Former Secretary of the Navy
of the United States

3

[On the concern about safety in Navy operations in the wake of several recent accidents]: I would say there are three problems here. One is the continuous operating environment where you can get careless. The second is the technical nature of the equipment, but I would say by and large the people are very good right now. The third is the training environment, teaching people how to anticipate problems and to make sure . . . junior leaders are supervising when the people under them are in a dangerous environment.

Broadcast interview/
"CBS This Morning,"
CBS-TV, 11-15.

William H. Webster
Director of Central Intelligence
of the United States

4

There are a number of serious dangers inherent in nuclear proliferation. First is the obvious danger that nuclear weapons might be used in regional conflicts . . . The sheer quantity and distribution of nuclear weapons and nuclear material across the globe could increase the risk of theft, sabotage and terrorism . . . More than 20 countries may be developing chemical weapons and at least 10 countries are working to produce biological weapons.

At Town Hall,
Los Angeles, March 30/
Los Angeles Times, 3-31:(I)15.

5

[Saying Soviet proposals for verification procedures in arms-control agreements may not be acceptable to the U.S.]: [There are concerns in the defense community] that this may in fact be

(WILLIAM H. WEBSTER)

difficult if not dangerous for us to go whole hog on. It has to do with emerging defense strategies and other considerations, [especially] locations of some of our more sensitive operations . . . To give them [the Soviets] unrestricted access to our most sensitive areas is a very heavy price to pay [for reciprocal U.S. inspections rights in the Soviet Union]. So it's a tough trade-off.

To reporters, Washington, April
6/
The Washington Post, 4-7:(A)17.

Larry D. Welch
General and Chief of Staff,
United States Air Force

1

[Saying a U.S. decision to stop the B-2 *Stealth* bomber program would negatively affect the U.S. negotiating position at the START talks]: [It is] largely inconceivable that we could continue with current negotiating positions without the B-2. In my view, we would simply have to go back to the drawing board and virtually start over in crafting some new negotiating position . . . As we evaluated the sufficiency of the START positions that we have advanced in these negotiations . . . we have particularly counted heavily on the contribution of the manned penetrating bomber. I simply cannot believe that we could proceed with negotiations on that basis were we

to have a drastically different expectation about the contribution of the manned penetrating bomber.

Before Senate Armed Services Committee,
Washington, July 21/
Los Angeles Times, 7-22:(I)25.

Paul Wolfowitz
Assistant Secretary for Policy,
Department of Defense
of the United States

2

[On the Soviet Union's plans to reduce its armed forces]: After the announced unilateral reductions, the Warsaw Pact will still outnumber the North Atlantic Treaty Organization in tanks, artillery and divisions by 2 to 1. The planned reduction of 500,000 troops will still leave the Soviets with approximately 5 million men in their armed forces, including internal-security forces, KGB border guards and military railroad and construction units. [Soviet leader Mikhail] Gorbachev's recent announcement that he will cut nuclear forces by 500 [warheads] is remarkable compared to the reductions the United States has made in its own forces. What is remarkable is that the Soviets will retain 9,500 weapons after the reduction is implemented.

Before House Armed Services Committee,
Washington, May 17/
The Washington Post, 5-18:(A)39.

The Economy • Labor

Thomas Bailey
Senior research associate,
Columbia University

1

Well-educated people are not only the most likely to find employment, but also are the most likely to receive training from their employers. Once trained, their greater productivity earns them more. They switch jobs less frequently and are rarely unemployed. If they change jobs, they find another easily and are more likely to receive further training from new employers.

The New York Times, 9-25:(A)12.

Gerald L. Baliles
Governor of Virginia (D)

2

We have to have a trained work-force and flexible capital so that we can meet the needs, the shifts, the changes that go on in world markets almost on a daily basis. A competitive country must invest in its roads, bridges, airports. How do you compete in world markets if you can't move your people and products across town or across the country? And a competitive nation invests in its children because they represent the work-force.

Interview/USA Today, 7-27:(A)9.

Anthony C. Beilenson
United States Representative,
D-California

3

[Criticizing the $1.17-trillion Federal budget passed by the House]: The agreement . . . falls so far short of what is demanded of us that it does not deserve our support. This resolution is yet another attempt to slip by, for just one year, by using phony economic assumptions, moving spending off-budget, advancing next year's payments to this year, assuming better tax compliance, extending existing reforms about to expire, assuming asset sales that almost certainly won't occur, and using other gimmicks

to comply with the Gramm-Rudman-Hollings [budget] targets.

Before the House, Washington/
The Washington Post, 5-5:(A)4.

Owen Bieber
President, United Automobile Workers
of America

4

There will always be a basic conflict between the interest of workers and the interest of employers. But there needs to be something better than only conflict and only raw antagonism . . . Are we smart enough and strong enough as trade-unionists to understand that we don't have to embrace the employer, that we only have to care about our own members, in order to want to be involved in programs that make the work-place function better?

At United Automobile Workers
convention, Anaheim, Calif.,
June 18/Los Angeles Times, 6-9:(IV)2.

Barry Bluestone
Professor of political economy,
University of Massachusetts

5

I went to a public high school in Detroit, and graduated in 1962. About half my class went on to college, half didn't. At my 10th and 20th class reunions, those who went on to college were making somewhat more than those who had not, but the gap wasn't enormous—we were in Detroit, remember. But when the class of 1980 meets for its anniversary, I predict the gap will have grown enormously. In goods production, college graduates earned 2.1 times as much as high-school drop-outs in 1963. Today they earn 2.4 times as much. But the service economy is putting more and more of a premium on advanced education. So while college graduates in services earned 2.2 times as much as high-school drop-outs in 1963, today they earn 3.5 times as much. There certainly is a relationship between

(BARRY BLUESTONE)

the decline in manufacturing employment and the growth in inequality. But even more powerful, there has been a restructuring within industries.

Interview/The Wall Street Journal,
7-26:(A)14.

Frank Borman
Former chairman,
Eastern Airlines

1

We should begin to move toward taxing consumption—a value-added tax . . . It would certainly help our exports. Almost all of Europe is under the value-added taxing system. Also, it may encourage saving instead of consumption. One of the ways you discourage consumption is to tax it.

Interview/
Los Angeles Times, 1-1:(IV)3.

Michael J. Boskin
Chairman, Council of
Economic Advisors to
President of the United States
George Bush

2

While I start from a firm set of [economic] principles, I've always considered myself pragmatic and eclectic, trying to understand and appreciate different points of view. In the end, the decisions are political decisions made by elected officials, and that's as it should be. Economic analysis and advice is only one input—sometimes quite important, other times less so.

Interview/
The New York Times, 9-5:(A)10.

Bill Bradley
United States Senator,
D-New Jersey

3

Personally, what do I think we should do [to help the economy]? I think we should cut spending. I think we should pass a gasoline tax and have an increase in cigarette taxes, in the neigh-

borhood of $25 [-billion] to $30-billion. I, however, would not advocate that in the United States publicly, because I am a Democrat.

At World Economic Forum
conference, Davos, Switzerland,
Jan. 29/Los Angeles Times, 1-30:(I)3.

Nicholas F. Brady
Secretary of the Treasury
of the United States

4

It is important that we do not make a mockery of the Gramm-Rudman [balanced-budget spending guidelines]. It is not only the law of the land, it is the wheel horse of the fiscal discipline that will drive our deficit down. Meeting its deficit-reducing targets is very important to the continued vitality of our economy.

To business executives,
Dallas, March 28/
The New York Times, 3-29:(C)2.

George Bush
President of the United States

5

I'm not thinking beyond anything other than to say I will not raise taxes, and I've got to stay with that approach . . . And the fundamental reason for that is, I want to keep the economy going, I want to keep the recovery—not recovery, but the growth—going in this economy. I do not want to kill off investment or employment opportunity. And the higher the taxes, the more you do that.

Interview, Washington/
The New York Times, 1-26:(A)10.

6

[On whether the minimum wage should be raised]: I've always said that my position on minimum wage is that I would want it linked to a training wage, to a differential of sorts, so that you don't throw people out of work by raising the minimum wage. And I'm not one who has felt that the minimum wage is the key to economic prosperity for people in the lowest end of the economic spectrum. [But] I have a certain flexibility on that question.

News conference,
Washington, Jan. 27/
The New York Times, 1-28:6.

(GEORGE BUSH)

1

[Saying he opposes raising the minimum wage to $4.55 an hour]: My difference with the majority in Congress is not about 30 cents an hour on the minimum-wage legislation; it's about hundreds of thousands of people, largely unskilled people, who won't have a job to go to if the minimum-wage legislation before the Congress now becomes law.

Before American Retail Federation,
Washington, May 17/
The Washington Post, 5-18:(A)1.

2

I mean to live by what I've said: no new taxes . . . We don't have to raise taxes. We have to release the energies of free enterprise. In a growing economy, tax revenues will take care of themselves. In fiscal 1990 alone, thanks to expanding economic activity, the Treasury will take in more than $80-billion in increased revenues, not through higher taxes but under the existing tax structure—$80-billion more in one year. So let's not be hunting for ways to wring another dollar in taxes out of our economy. Let's concentrate on creating conditions for continued growth.

Before United States Chamber of
Commerce/Nation's Business,
June:92.

3

We're used to thinking of unemployment as a case of too many people and too few jobs. [But in the 1990s, it] will be just the opposite: more than enough jobs and too few people qualified to fill them.

Before National Urban League,
Washington, Aug. 8/
The Washington Post, 8-9:(A)4.

4

The Peruvian economist, Hernando de Soto, has helped us understand a world-wide economic phenomenon. By walking the streets of Lima, not analyzing economic statistics, he found that the poor of Latin America—who have never read Jefferson or Adam Smith—ran their affairs democratically, outside the formal economy, organizing their private, parallel economy in a free and unregulated manner. De Soto's great contribution has been to point out what, in retrospect, may seem obvious: People everywhere want the same things. And when left alone by government, people everywhere organize their lives in remarkably similar ways. De Soto's prescription offers a clear and promising alternative to economic stagnation in Latin America and other parts of the world. Governments must bring the "informal" workers into the regular economy—and then get out of the way and let the individual enterprise flourish.

At World Bank/International
Monetary Fund meeting,
Washington, September/
The Wall Street Journal, 10-4:(A)30.

Stuart M. Butler
Director, domestic-policy
studies, Heritage Foundation

5

There had been a rapid increase, prior to [former President Ronald] Reagan, of both spending and taxing. What Reagan has essentially done has been to top out or slow down the rising taxes. You had two runaway elements of public finance: spending and taxes. We've got control of one of them, taxes, and the deficit is the symptom of the fact that we haven't got control of the other. So the solution is to get rid of that other runaway item, which is the spending side.

Interview/The Atlantic Monthly,
February:40.

David Calleo
Professor of European studies,
School of Advanced
International Studies,
Johns Hopkins University

6

It is hard to overestimate the degree of contempt people around the world have for U.S. economic policy. Foreigners are appalled, even disgusted, by our inability to come to terms with

(DAVID CALLEO)

the [Federal] budget [as well as] the incredible braggadocio that substituted for disciplined policy [during the Reagan Administration].

The Washington Post, 5-31:(F)3.

Otis Chandler
Chairman, executive
committee of the board of
directors, Times Mirror Company

1

I think the best of all possible worlds is to hire a person who's already been out in the work-place and has practical experience. I would rather have a person with an undergraduate degree who's worked five years, gone back and earned an MBA, and then come back to us. You know that person is dedicated to the company and the industry, and is better equipped after earning an MBA. An MBA is certainly one of the first things we look at in a person's background. Now an MBA is not just the exception, it's the rule.

Interview/
Los Angeles Times, 8-13:(IV)5.

Bill Clinton
Governor of Arkansas (D)

2

You can't blame the Germans or the Japanese for the fact that we [the U.S.] are under-educated. You can't blame them for the money we waste in the draining effect of the Federal deficit—or the fact that we'd rather spend money bailing out the savings-and-loan industry or promoting mergers and acquisitions [of companies] than investing in emerging technologies.

Los Angeles Times, 8-7:(I)14.

Edith Cresson
Minister for European Affairs
of France

3

[Saying the Japanese are taking advantage of the U.S. in economic and trade matters]: [You] Americans don't see what's going on with the Japanese. They are like ants, eating you up. You

just don't notice it. You don't feel it. You don't see it.

Los Angeles Times, 3-27:(I)13.

Mario M. Cuomo
Governor of New York (D)

4

The simplistic approach that says to be a liberal, you must constantly give money—even if you don't have it, even [if] you're going to go bankrupt—is stupid. All of my fight was for a liberal agenda. [But] it would have so debilitated our economic base, it would have cost us so much credibility in the investment community that, in the long run, poor people would suffer. We are the state, not the Federal government. The Federal government can create money. It can run deficits. In the state, there is no source of wealth other than the wealth we generate out of our own tax system. That's where we get the money for wheelchairs.

Interview/The Washington Post,
5-8:(A)3.

5

Unfortunately, we live in the 24-second television world. But if you have the time to tell the people the truth, you can sell revenue increases [taxes] to people. But these revenue increases must not be burdensome and must be spent wisely. You have to tell them how you plan to spend it. If you say it is for [fighting] drugs, 100 per cent will be in favor of the revenue increase. For education, 90 per cent. For housing, 50 per cent. For a vague social agenda, zero. It's a question of selling it.

Interview, New York/
Los Angeles Times, 7-22:(I)16.

6

[On President Bush's statements that he will not raise taxes]: You can't say, "I don't believe in tax increases," when you ask for $5-billion in revenue increases, and raise the Federal-government interest costs by $100-million a year by borrowing money to bail out the savings-and-loans. You can't send Transportation Secretary

(MARIO M. CUOMO)

Samuel K. Skinner to the National Governors' Association to say, "We agree with you, we need infrastructure rebuilding; that's why I have traveled to three states to help you pass local taxes," and then not seek the passage of new Federal taxes. And you can't send Budget Director Richard G. Darman to Congress to tell members if they try to salvage social programs this year they must bear the onus for raising taxes next year. At some point you have to be realistic and say, "Look, what we need here is revenues. I'm on the line, we're raising taxes." If you don't say that—and yes, I am willing to—you can't get away with the "kinder-and-gentler" rhetoric [that Bush prescribes for the nation].

Interview/
Los Angeles Times, 9-10:(V)3.

George Deukmejian
Governor of California (R)

1

Make no mistake, there was indeed a mandate in the vote for President [last year. Americans] voted for the candidate [Bush] who told them without hesitation that taxes should not be increased . . . I know the conventional wisdom says that a tax increase is the answer. [But the] deficit can and must be reduced by controlling spending. We cannot risk triggering a world-wide recession through a major tax increase.

At World Economic Forum
conference, Davos, Switzerland,
Jan. 29/Los Angeles Times, 1-30:(I)15.

Michel Deville
Economist,
Banque Paribas, Paris

2

The rate of growth of the world economy in 1989 is still threatened by radical change in American economic policy next spring. Too virtuous a stance would lead to recession, while too relaxed an approach would make for renewed inflation.

The Christian Science Monitor,
1-4:2.

Elizabeth Hanford Dole
Secretary of Labor
of the United States

3

We're looking at a very serious situation in which we have a skills gap. We're moving from an industrial economy to a service-oriented economy. And that means that jobs now and in the future are going to require higher skill levels. In other words, people are going to have to read well, to write effectively, to utilize mathematics and to be really articulate.

Interview/USA Today, 9-5:(A)11.

Byron L. Dorgan
United States Representative,
D-North Dakota

4

[Criticizing proposed changes in the tax law]: We're going to end up with capital gains [tax reduction] and [expanded] IRAs. It's an awful plan. George Bush wants to give tax breaks to the rich, and we [Democrats] want to give tax breaks to the near rich . . . Why are we considering tax breaks for the rich when we're up to our necks in debt?

The Washington Post, 9-22:(A)10.

William Dunkelberg
Dean, School of Business
and Management,
Temple University

5

[On increasing the minimum wage]: It sounds great to say, "Let's help the working poor," but where does that money come from? People think, "Let's take money away from big, bad business, which has pools of money lying around." Well, there are no pools of money.

USA Today, 11-10:(B)4.

Richard J. Durbin
United States Representative,
D-Illinois

6

The minimum wage is not welfare. The minimum wage is not a social-welfare program. It is

(RICHARD J. DURBIN)

not a vehicle to compensate persons in financial need. It is not a subsidy to families. It is not a stipend. But the beginning wage is, in fact, the basic compensation for the lowest-paid workers in America who get up every morning, put on their work clothes and go to work. It is a wage paid for work done, not to aid the poor nor to relieve the pressures of family life. It is an important mechanism to raise the standard of living for people in America, to avoid the sort of economic exploitation which these folks and their families would inevitably face if the Congress of the United States of America is unresponsive.

Before the House,
Washington, Oct. 10/
The Washington Post, 10-12:(A)22.

Susan Engeleiter
Administrator, Small
Business Administration
of the United States

1

We in Wisconsin kept a low capital-gains tax rate when the Federal rate went up, and we find the lower rate has really stimulated economic growth in that state. I've philosophically always believed that the number of state or Federal mandates on businesses of all sizes should be kept as low as possible.

Interview/Nation's Business, June:66

Jeff Faux
President,
Economic Policy Institute

2

I think [Federal budget] deficits do matter. But I think that other things matter as well. The problem with the debate is that it has become dangerously over-simplified, as if all our problems could be resolved by simply erasing the fiscal deficit. I think that's wrong economically, and I think it risks what could be a very, very disastrous outcome—that is, a recession . . . We're talking about a long economic bath for America, the likes of which we haven't seen since the 1930s.

The Atlantic Monthly,
February:40.

3

[On what to do with the anticipated "peace dividend," monies saved from a decreased U.S. military budget in light of pro-democracy reforms and a friendlier foreign policy now sweeping through Eastern Europe and the Soviet Union]: It's a whole new world when there's no Berlin Wall. The peace dividend is just a buzzword for the issue of where we should put our nation's resources. The public believes that our national security now depends on our economic strength, not our military power. So it's time to start a debate about what new directions we should go.

Los Angeles Times, 12-26:(A)29.

William Friday
Former president,
University of North Carolina

4

It's abundantly clear today that if you're going to develop a career in business, industry and in the professions, you have to be able to use your mind. You have to be fully aware of computation skills. You have to be able to deal with communications. If you do not do these things, if you do not possess these competencies, you're going to be left out.

Interview/USA Today, 8-23:(A)9.

Paul Gann
President, People's Advocate

5

I don't think that the Tax Reform Act [of 1986] has been that valuable to the tax-paying public. I have certified public accountants that work for my organization, and they are still puzzled about tax reform, and they wonder what is it really going to turn out to be. We should have the courage to increase taxes for the things that are necessary because I resent the fact that we are borrowing money for generations that haven't even been born yet. The cost of government should go down. We have too much government. We have government running out of our ears, and our eyes and our nose, and every day they increase our costs. Either let's pay our way or let's cut budgets. We need an honest reform, not a

(PAUL GANN)

gobbledygook like we have had up to this point. What we have to do is reduce the size of the cost of government or we are going to have to increase taxes—one of the two.

Interview/Los Angeles Times,
3-5:(Your Taxes)22.

George Gilder
Author, Economist

1

We need a new economic model because the computer has become the most important fundamental economic force. We have got to recognize this. In the past, economics was a study and science of scarcity and the physical notions and properties that governed its technology: friction, entropy, land, labor, etc. But all of a sudden the world broke away from this into an entirely new arena.

Interview/
Los Angeles Times, 9-10:(IV)3.

Felipe Gonzalez
Prime Minister of Spain

2

Socialism is the deepening of democracy. Public power must try to prevent the worst consequences of a society that lives off free competition and savage confrontation in the marketplace. A mixed economy on a world scale is inescapable. The great error of Communism is that of the dinosaurs. They did not adapt, so they died. You can't be socially effective if, at the same time, you're not economically efficient.

Interview, Madrid/
Time, 10-23:54.

William F. Goodling
United States Representative,
R-Pennsylvania

3

When the minimum wage goes up, the very people we say we want to help—the young, the unskilled, the disadvantaged—are the first people to get laid off.

USA Today, 6-14:(A)10.

Phil Gramm
United States Senator,
R-Texas

4

[On the Tax Reform Act of 1986]: I don't think that we are truly going to get a measure of the full impact of the reform package for some time to come. But overall, I believe that it is an improvement in the tax system, even though during the transition it has been very unfair to some individuals and to some industries. It represented a change in the rules of the game on a retroactive basis, and that's always difficult. I think that, to some extent, our problems were the sort of problems that a family would have moving into a new house. The house may be bigger and better, but you've got to get over the pain of moving. I don't doubt that the new tax system is superior to the old one in both efficiency and equity. I think that the change made in 1986 was so substantial that other than simply correcting obvious and unintended inequities, that we ought to leave the tax code alone.

Interview/Los Angeles Times,
3-5:(Your Taxes)22.

Thomas A. Gray
Chief Economist,
Small Business Administration
of the United States

5

From the perspective of 20/20 hindsight, it appears almost certain that the October, 1987, crash in the [stock] market did the economy a favor by slowing the rate of growth of consumption expenditures and providing some time for businesses to increase output capability to meet escalating domestic and foreign demands. As a consequence, we are now in the 73rd month of continuous growth. This is the longest peacetime expansion since reasonably accurate record-keeping began in the 1850s.

Interview/Nation's Business, January:18.

William H. Gray III
United States Representative,
D-Pennsylvania

6

[Arguing against reinstatement of the capital-gains tax preference]: In 1986, we made a com-

(WILLIAM H. GRAY III)

mitment that we were going to simplify the [tax] code; we were going to get shelters out of the code and make it fairer. The capital-gains proposal goes against the grain of tax reform by, once again, putting back special breaks for a very narrow group of people.

Interview/USA Today, 9-27:(A)7.

1

[Criticizing Republicans who want a capital-gains tax cut and reductions in social spending to pay for it]: If they want to cut education aid, farm aid and housing aid . . . to provide tax breaks to [entrepreneur] Donald Trump, I'll fight that any time. I'll be glad to debate that from the corn fields of Iowa to the bayous of Louisiana.

The Washington Post, 11-2:(A)16.

Alan Greenspan
Chairman,
Federal Reserve Board

2

Our strategy continues to be centered on moving toward, and ultimately reaching, stable prices—that is, price levels sufficiently stable so that expectations of change do not become major factors in key economic decisions. Current inflation rates, by that criterion, clearly are too high and must be brought down.

Before House Banking Committee,
Washington, Jan. 24/
The New York Times, 1-25:(A)1.

3

[Criticizing the idea that the large Federal budget deficit doesn't matter and is not worth worrying about]: It is beguiling to contemplate the strong economy of recent years in the context of very large deficits, and to conclude that the concerns about the adverse effects of the deficit on the economy have been misplaced. But this argument is fanciful. The deficit already has begun to eat away at the foundations of our economic strength. And the need to deal with it is becoming more urgent.

Before House Ways and Means
Committee, Washington,
Feb. 2/The Washington Post, 2-3:(G)1.

Robert Greenstein
Director, Center on Budget
and Policy Priorities

4

The Bush [Federal] budget appears to provide a kinder, gentler nation, with more for education, the environment and child care. [But in reality,] the budget camouflages many cuts in domestic programs and exaggerates a few small increases. A number of the new initiatives are smaller than the budget rhetoric would indicate, turn out not truly to represent increases when the budget numbers are carefully examined or are actually cuts, skillfully packaged to appear as increases.

The New York Times, 2-11:7.

Robert Hormats
Vice chairman, Goldman,
Sachs International

5

Even though we're still the strongest economy in the world, we just can't take the '90s for granted. Our economy is no more unsinkable than the *Titanic*. It needs to be managed carefully.

U.S. News & World Report,
12-25:36.

Steny H. Hoyer
United States Representative,
D-Maryland

6

[On the possible veto of a $4.55 an hour minimum-wage bill by President Bush, who favors no higher than $4.25]: What this all comes down to is three thin dimes: that's the difference between us and the President. We're talking about helping the millions of people who work but live in poverty and giving them a living wage.

Washington, May 11/
Los Angeles Times, 5-12:(I)4.

Lane Kirkland
President, American Federation
of Labor-Congress of
Industrial Organizations

7

I do not see Armageddon for the labor movement every other day. This trade-union move-

(LANE KIRKLAND)

ment has been through a lot of struggles. We were born to trouble . . . If there were no troubles, if there were no need for working people to be aggressively and effectively represented, we wouldn't exist.

Bal Harbour, Fla./
Los Angeles Times, 2-27:(I)20.

1

Today, more than ever, the solidarity of labor is the instrument of history and the lever that moves the world. The central theme of this convention is the oldest and the most modern bedrock principle of trade unionism—solidarity . . . Today, history is moving before your eyes. In every quarter of the globe, events are in the saddle and are driving the reluctant leaders they have overtaken. We are proud and inspired that trade-unionism is an element of this dynamic trend.

At AFL-CIO convention,
Washington, Nov. 13/
The Washington Post, 11-14:(A)18.

Edward I. Koch
Mayor of New York

2

Since 1981, we've had Presidents who said "make my day" and "read my lips." We made President Reagan's day by keeping our eyes on his "shining city on the hill." But while our eyes were on the hill, his hands were in our pockets. President Bush told us to read his lips. Well, I have read those lips. I can tell you that although the President's mouth says, "No new taxes," his lips say, "Plenty of new taxes, all passed by state and local governments."

State of the City Message,
New York, Dec. 5/
The New York Times, 12-6:(A)21.

Andrew Kohut
President,
Gallup Organization

3

Looking at trends in public-opinion polls over the years, we show consistently smaller numbers of Americans saying they are members of [labor] unions and consistently smaller numbers of Americans saying positive things about labor unions. The American public gives pretty low ratings to unions and the people who run them. We asked the public not too long ago to rate the honesty and ethical standards of various occupations, and the percentage who rated the honesty and ethical standards of labor-union leaders as "high" was only 14 per cent . . . It's clear to me that the American public doesn't see the typical American labor leader as altruistic. A lot of people blame labor unions for our competitiveness problem. Secondly, people see labor unions as acting in their own self-interest and not in the broader public interest. These two elements are cutting against labor at this point in time.

Interview/
Los Angeles Times, 8-13:(IV)3.

Bruce Lee
Western regional director,
United Automobile Workers
of America

4

On social legislation, [organized labor] has always been in the forefront and will continue to be. The fight is on a different front today. Now labor has to be in front on how the shop floor is run, how the employees are treated when they go to the workplace. You have to do more than just negotiate wages and benefits. You have to really get into the decision-making process and how the employees work in that system.

Interview/
Los Angeles Times, 8-13:(IV)3.

Richard L. Lesher
President, United States
Chamber of Commerce

5

I think the White House will put on the table soon a very plausible scenario for . . . balancing the [Federal] budget by 1993 without more taxes. Despite all the people [in Congress] still calling for increased taxes, I think reasonable people soon will be able to see that none are necessary.

To Washington press corps/
Nation's Business, February:50.

Frank S. Levy
Professor, School of
Public Affairs,
University of Maryland

1

In the '70s, corporations had workers coming out of their ears, so they didn't have to worry about the quality of the work-force. They could just discard what they couldn't use. But once you have the labor force growing slowly and you start bumping into scarcity, then you have to assess the quality of the whole work-force, because you can't just throw away the bottom quarter or 20 per cent. Then you realize that we're all in this together.

The Atlantic Monthly, August:59.

Alan Magazine
President, Council
on Competitiveness

2

[On the poor education received by many students in the U.S. and its effects on business hiring]: We have, in a sense, a ticking time bomb that can't be ignored any more. Some people have been saying that for 10 years, but now people in the corporations are really seeing it. They're seeing it in the kinds of people they're hiring, the amount of money they have to spend for basic training to get people up to a level that they can do even menial jobs; they're seeing it in the results of the tests that they give hundreds of people for minimum-wage jobs, and the number of people who actually pass those tests.

Interview/
The Atlantic Monthly, August:59.

Mike Mansfield
United States Ambassador
to Japan

3

[Japan wants] the United States to be the Number 1 economic power in the world. They want to be able to continue to penetrate into our markets. They wish that we would do something about the national debt and the foreign debt, and those are of our making, of our responsibility. Under [Prime Minister] Takeshita they're bring-ing about a restructuring of the domestic economy and doing a good job. They have opened up their markets much more ... It's not a case of pity, because basically the Japanese like us. It's one of concern, because they think that if we fail in retaining the Number 1 spot they could well fall also.

Interview, Washington/
The Washington Post, 1-16:(A)19.

Douglas McCabe
Associate professor
of labor relations,
Georgetown University

4

The existence of [labor] unions tends to help non-union workers in terms of wages and benefits. If we move to a totally union-free society, I pity the poor non-union worker.

Interview/USA Today, 3-7:(A)7.

Jim Michaels
Editor, "Forbes" magazine

5

[On the Tax Reform Act of 1986]: One of the beneficial side effects is that it has killed the tax-shelter business, which is a misuse of scarce capital. I think it has helped as far as the average American is concerned. It has put something extra in their take-home pay, which helps counter the continued toll that inflation takes on the household budget. To that extent, it has also somewhat moderated the pressure for inflationary wage increases. That is very healthy. What's harder to measure, but it's certainly there, is that it has been a boost to incentive in that higher-paid people, creative people, can keep a larger part of what they earn.

Interview/Los Angeles Times,
3-5:(Your Taxes)22.

Daniel J. B. Mitchell
Director, Institute of
Industrial Relations,
University of California,
Los Angeles

6

The place where [labor unions] are most important, when we're talking at the Federal

(DANIEL J. B. MITCHELL)

level, are in coalitions. It's very difficult now for unions to get legislation that is specifically union-sector oriented... But when you talk about things such as adjustments to the Social Security Act, then labor is very influential because they then build coalitions with other groups that have common interests. Even in absolute numbers, if you have an organization or a group of organizations that represent millions of people and can mobilize funds and mobilize people to knock on doors and ring doorbells and drive people to the polls, they matter in the political setting for that reason.

Interview/
Los Angeles Times, 8-13:(IV)3.

George J. Mitchell
United States Senator,
D-Maine

1

After eight years in office, President Reagan has proposed, endorsed and signed into law 13 tax increases, and in the process has convinced everybody in America that he's against taxes.

Broadcast interview/
"This Week with David Brinkley,"
ABC-TV, 1-1.

2

The President's [Bush] own capital-gains-tax proposal would give the top 1.1 per cent of all taxpayers, those with incomes in excess of $200,000, an average tax cut of almost $31,000 a year. How can anyone justify wanting to give a $30,000-a-year tax cut to the richest Americans and at the same time opposing 30 cents an hour more [in the minimum wage] for the poorest Americans?

Before the Senate,
Washington, April 11/
The New York Times, 4-12:(A)9.

3

[Saying President Bush shouldn't veto a bill to increase the minimum wage to $4.55 an hour]:

The President has a perceived political need to look tough, to veto a bill. If he wants to prove how tough he is, let him choose a bill other than one in which a veto will harm millions of the poorest Americans.

Washington Post, 5-18:(A)1.

4

[Criticizing a proposed reduction in the capital-gains tax rate]: It is so bad, so wrong for the economy. It will do for the deficit what crack [cocaine] does for the user: a quick, short high followed by a long, painful depression.

Broadcast interview/
"Meet the Press," NBC-TV, 10-1.

5

[Criticizing President Bush's pursuit of a cut in the capital-gains tax]: Capital gains has become the Holy Grail of this Administration. It has cast aside any concern for the [Federal budget] deficit. It has cast aside any concern for the budget process. It has cast aside any concern for fairness. It has now cast aside any concern for relations with this Congress.

Before the Senate,
Washington, Oct. 24/
The Washington Post, 10-25:(A)5.

Akio Morita
Chairman,
Sony Corporation (Japan)

6

I'm worrying for America seriously, seriously. I'm worrying about why America has changed, has lost industrial power and just is making money by moving money around. Unless you produce something, you cannot have basic power in an economy.

To foreign journalists,
Tokyo, Oct. 3/
The Washington Post, 10-4:(F)3.

7

Maybe I sound arrogant to the American people. Some people say I'm an America-basher.

(AKIO MORITA)

But since I came to this country, I learned from American friends to speak frankly. Unless American industry changes its attitude, that will be a problem for all of us. The United States is the center of our free economic system, which I believe in. So for our whole free world, we need strong American leadership, and a strong American industry.

Interview, New York/
Newsweek, 10-9:66.

Robert A. Mosbacher
Secretary of Commerce
of the United States

1

The private sector can make mistakes on [economic] winners and losers, and it doesn't impinge on the whole nation. But when the public sector does, it's very liable to impinge. The public sector doesn't live in the day-to-day market, and I think too much government involvement hurts the whole country. And that's one of the reasons we don't want to do it. Besides that, it is anathema to us as Americans to have the government tell us what we should be in. It doesn't make economic sense. It doesn't allow basic choices in freedom. I'm against it.

Interview/USA Today, 5-24:(A)9.

2

The world economy is being integrated primarily by the aggressive force of private enterprise, by the multinational corporation and by the small domestic firm seeking its first export market. The East [-ern countries] will be fully integrated into the world economy only when its own enterprises do likewise and when their enterprises and ours are fully and freely working together ... There is no single, immutable blueprint guiding the path from state control to a compatible, market economy. Yet all of us know the elements which are needed for a market economy to operate. And we know there is no half-way house ... The leaders of the East can waste decades pretending that the body is not a corpse and looking for timid measures that can some-

how be accommodated ideologically to the past. Or they can proceed to the real business—the very difficult business—of transition to the market economies ... As a businessman myself, my advice to them is: Take the plunge! The water is fine.

At conference sponsored by Institute
for East-West Security Studies,
Frankfurt/
The Washington Post, 10-26:(A)30.

Vance Packard
Author

3

... we are rapidly getting into a situation where vast wealth is not creating any social usefulness. And it's not helping ultra-rich people themselves. They don't need it. Most live relatively simple lives. We should think of stimulating them to undertake more socially useful activities ... They could put it in venture-capital enterprises where there's a risk or enterprises that contribute to social well-being. Our system really needs rapid social and economic growth. But the ultra-rich are just storing it away for personal consumption ... When you get people who have wealth they couldn't possibly consume in 2,000 years, you have a situation that doesn't make sense for any economy. We've got 34 per cent of all the wealth in the country controlled by 1 per cent of the people. That is a very high figure and in the past, such as in 1929, it did create great economic troubles.

Interview/USA Today, 2-2:(A)9.

John Palmer
Dean, Maxwell School
of Citizenship,
Syracuse (N.Y.) University

4

[President-elect] Bush could put together $10-billion to $15-billion [in deficit cuts] without a gas tax, and by cutting defense a bit he could have $40-billion. Putting forward a credible and effective plan for continued decreases in the deficit are absolutely essential ... His best bet is to put forward a bold deficit-reduction package that would include tax increases, defense cuts, and

(JOHN PALMER)

cuts in the domestic area where cuttable—and show how the deficits will be on a downward path. Then there would be room for new initiatives.

The Christian Science Monitor,
1-6:2.

Leon E. Panetta
United States Representative,
D-California

1

[On the political maneuvering involved in Congress' work on the Federal budget]: We pretend we're running a legitimate operation, but we've got a gambling establishment in the back room. We spend as much as we need to cover our political rear ends.

Newsweek, 10-23:29.

Joseph Perella
Principal,
Wasserstein, Perella & Co.,
investment bankers

2

[On arguments against corporate take-overs, because they frequently result in employees losing jobs]: Some do. But that is the biggest crock of bleeding-heart bull. No one was sitting around crying when all the GM, Chrysler and Ford workers were being let go because of poor management for years in Detroit. Those were blue-collar workers. Right now, it's the layers of corporate fat where jobs are lost. Not the people making Oreo cookies.

Interview/USA Today, 1-3:(B)2.

Donald E. Petersen
Chairman,
Ford Motor Company

3

I have a deep concern, shared with every CEO with whom I talk, about an adequate flow of well-educated Americans into our society to fulfill the needs we have if we are going to remain a big force in the world economy. It's critically impor-

tant, especially in the technical areas and in subjects such as math and science.

Interview/USA Today, 8-14:(A)9.

Richard Rahn
Vice president and
chief economist,
United States Chamber
of Commerce

4

All those economists have been saying for years that the economy couldn't grow as fast as it has. My colleagues in this profession simply don't understand entrepreneurship. As a result, they're consistently wrong in their forecasts.

Nation's Business, January:11.

5

The message of today's dismal employment report [for May] should be unambiguously clear to Fed [-eral Reserve Board] policy-makers: It is time to lower interest rates. Employment in manufacturing has come to a standstill in the past few months, while over-all employment growth is way below the pace of 1988. Clearly, the economy has slowed far more than the Fed intended, and continuation of its high-interest-rate policy threatens to throw us into a recession.

June 2/
Los Angeles Times, 6-3:(I)24.

Ronald Reagan
President of the United States

6

Common sense told us that when you put a big tax on something, the people will produce less of it. So we cut the people's tax rates, and the people produced more than ever before. The economy bloomed like a plant that had been cut back and could now grow quicker and stronger. Our economic program brought about the longest peacetime expansion in our history: real family income up, the poverty rate down, entrepreneurship booming and an explosion in research and new technology.

Broadcast address to the nation,
Washington, Jan. 11/
The Washington Post, 1-12:(A)8.

Ronald Reagan
Former President
of the United States

1

Today, I start stumping to help future Presidents—Republican or Democrat—get the tools they need to bring the [Federal] budget under control. One of my biggest disappointments as President was that I wasn't able to balance the budget. After all, I'd made a pledge to the American people that I wasn't able to fulfill—at least not yet.

Speech, University of Southern
California, Feb. 6/
Los Angeles Times, 2-7:(I)1.

Jerome M. Rosow
President,
Work in America Institute

2

One thing to keep in mind about the future of American [labor] unions . . . is the demand of workers for the right to unionize. Which is the *sine qua non* of whether a political system has any democratic features. And those who believe that the unions are *passe* or that unions can disappear and managers can manage their workers best without union representation are talking about an autocratic totalitarian state. This country will never survive as a democracy without free trade unions.

Interview/
Los Angeles Times, 8-13:(IV)3.

Dan Rostenkowski
United States Representative,
D-Illinois

3

I personally will strongly resist any efforts to undo tax reform, including a return to preferential rates for capital gains. I'm not about to tell the wage earners in Chicago that they should pay a higher rate than the stockbrokers. [If the loophole door is ajar,] it will open wide for every preference mankind can devise in the next tax bill . . . I honestly believe that for at least a period of time we ought to leave the [tax] code alone.

Before National Press Club,
Washington, Feb. 9/
The Washington Post, 2-10:(A)18.

Jeffrey Sachs
Economist,
Harvard University

4

Ten years ago, there weren't that many people we [the U.S.] could borrow money from. We were reluctant to run deficits out of fear of creating sky-high inflation. Now there is a global bank-teller window that is open 24 hours a day, and we've been one of the most frequent customers. [But] we're faking it. Our living standard isn't being maintained by higher productivity or wages. It's maintained by foreign capital.

Time, 1-30:47.

Carlos Salinas de Gortari
President of Mexico

5

[On American criticism of Mexican immigrants who work in the U.S.]: Let's get rid of the myths: Mexican workers do not push anyone out of a job; they work efficiently and with dignity for wages, in many cases, below the market wage, doing jobs that are not done by American citizens . . . We fail to understand why the "American dream" must be harsh for the Mexican immigrants who have decided to share it.

Before Joint Session of
U.S. Congress, Washington,
Oct. 4/The Washington Post,
10-5:(A)43.

Terry Sanford
United States Senator,
D-North Carolina

6

If we are to have a balanced [Federal] budget, it should be understood that Congress cannot balance a budget that comes from the President, as it has for the past eight years, almost one-quarter of a trillion dollars in the red. [Former] President Reagan was a smoothie. He pretended he didn't have much to do with the budget. He said he just took what Congress gave him . . . The truth of the matter is that the President has even more to do with the budget than he has to do with foreign policy. He is the director—the real director—of the budget. Congress can shift a few

(TERRY SANFORD)

percentage points here or there, but it remains the President's budget.

Before the Senate,
Washington, Nov. 14/
The Washington Post,
11-17:(A)22.

James R. Sasser
United States Senator,
D-Tennessee

1

[Criticizing President Bush's proposal for a cut in capital-gains taxes]: At a time when virtually every segment of our country is being asked to sustain a sacrifice of one form or another, it is simply unacceptable to be considering tax breaks for the very wealthiest segment of the American population.

Los Angeles Times, 2-9:(I)19.

Edward L. Schneider
Executive director,
Andrus Gerontology Center,
University of Southern California

2

[Saying the elderly are not affected as much as younger people by current economic problems]: Housing prices are skyrocketing, high-paying jobs are becoming scarce, college tuitions are going out of sight and the [Federal] budget has to be balanced, which may mean higher taxes. For the elderly ... those are not such important issues. If they are retired, they don't have to pay much in the way of taxes. If they own their own houses, their mortgages are probably paid off. And their kids are probably already through college, so they don't have to worry about the rising costs of education.

Los Angeles Times, 5-4:(I)25.

William Schneider
Political analyst

3

Labor has far less influence on the national agenda for two reasons: One, there isn't any

money to do anything. Even if you argue for child care and help for the homeless and poor and transportation and pollution controls, you can argue until you're blue in the face—but there isn't any money. And you don't want to be caught raising taxes. So the result is that all progressive forces are on the defensive, labor among them. The second reason is the Democrat Party's inability to win Presidential elections. Labor is pretty closely tied to the Democrat Party and they've managed to hold their own on the state and local level—but haven't won a Presidential election since 1976.

Interview/
Los Angeles Times, 8-13:(IV)3.

William E. Simon
Former Secretary
of the Treasury
of the United States

4

There really is only one threat to our country and economy, and that is economic and financial excess. Most of the extremes in behavior, of course, are on the part of the government, the budget deficit in particular. Sooner or later, somebody is going to pay for the excesses, and it's always going to be you.

Time, 10-23:69.

Allen Sinai
Chief economist,
The Boston Company

5

The question is how to sustain the expansion and economic growth at near full employment without generating unwanted inflation and all of its adverse consequences. Never in the post-war period has the United States been able to finesse the full-employment zone; that is, to grow the economy and its demands at near the pace of potential supply, without igniting an unacceptably high inflation and causing punishingly high interest rates.

Nation's Business,
January:19.

Herbert Stein
Scholar, American Enterprise Institute;
Former Chairman,
Council of Economic Advisers
to the President
of the United States
(Richard M. Nixon)

1

My preference would be not to have an increase in American consumption, or not so much of an increase in American consumption. I'd rather see more investment, because I feel some obligation to my grandchildren. But it seems to me that that's about all there is to it. It's that kind of choice. It is not a matter of ruin or collapse. It's the same kind of choice that an individual makes when he decides how much to save.

The Atlantic Monthly,
February:39.

Alexander B. Trowbridge, Jr.
President, National
Association of Manufacturers;
Former Secretary of Commerce
of the United States

2

All the people [President-elect Bush has] picked for the main economic-policy areas seem to have a longstanding close relationship with George Bush. These are people he's been talking to for years, and they've been on a first-name basis with him for years. But they also know their way around Washington and the ways of government. That makes a potent combination, and we haven't had that for a while.

Los Angeles Times, 1-20:(IV)4.

Richard L. Trumka
President, United Mine Workers
of America

3

[Anti-labor-unionists] try to make us believe that each one of our disputes [strikes] is a separate little blip on the screen . . . We're here to tell them that when it affects one of us, it affects every last one of us—and we'll stand together.

At labor-union rally, Pittsburgh,
Aug. 13/
Los Angeles Times, 8-14:(I)2.

Paul A. Volcker
Former Chairman,
Federal Reserve Board

4

When I had some analyses presented to me in 1983 that showed a current account deficit rising up toward $100-billion, I said it's impossible, we can't borrow that much abroad, that's not going to happen. But things continue in government unless you feel a crisis. In fact, we didn't have a crisis, so the deficit persisted . . . I must confess what surprises me a bit about this [the deficit] is how it has persisted with less trauma than I thought was probable. Maybe it could persist another year or two years or three years. I don't think it can persist forever. Well, if you continue like this, I think we are gradually undercutting productivity and growth for the American economy, and I think we're undercutting our ability to lead the world. It now is demonstrably harder for us to propose something and expect the rest of the world to follow. I think it is hard to expect other countries to do what we would like them to do in the trade area, in the economic-policy area, as long as we stonewall them on what they think we should do about the deficit—and in fact what most of us think we should do.

Interview, New York/
Time, 1-23:50.

Paul Weiler
Professor of labor law,
Harvard University

5

[On employers' use of decertification to end unionization of their work forces]: Nothing has changed with the laws, which have been in effect for years, but in the increased readiness of employers to use permanent strike replacements in the 1980s. There is a greater respectability for union-free workplaces; it is more acceptable among employers, because of [then-President Ronald] Reagan [who eliminated the air-traffic controllers' union in 1981]. Once an employer establishes the ability to keep operating in a strike with replacement employees, the union certainly faces potential withdrawal of recognition.

Los Angeles Times,
3-12:(I)25.

William W. Winpisinger
*President, International
Association of Machinists
and Aerospace Workers*

1

With the crushing of the air controllers' organization, [then-President] Ronald Reagan sent a very vicious signal, and America went on a union-busting binge, the likes of which we haven't seen since before the Great Depression ... It's time that this nation rebuild some respect for people who exercise the right to freely form a labor organization and bargain collectively with the employer.

Interview/USA Today, 3-7:(A)7.

Jim Wright
*United States Representative,
D-Texas*

2

[On President-elect Bush's statement that he will attempt to reduce the Federal budget deficit without raising taxes]: The position [of Congressional Democrats] is give the President an opportunity to present his budget, to receive it with an open mind and to analyze it. While it may appear to many observers, including the General Accounting Office and the head of the Federal Reserve System, that it is impossible to achieve these goals without some new revenues, we shall not pre-empt him. We'll give him an opportunity to demonstrate how he feels that may be done, if he thinks it can. But it would be foolhardy for us not to think in terms of what we would do if it should develop, as most of these economics advisers indicate they feel it inevitably would develop, that we'll have to have some revenues. Now, I'm not saying we will. No. I'm not getting out front. No. But I'm trying to follow a sensible course of being prepared for any contingency.

*Interview, Washington,
Jan. 6/
The New York Times,
1-9:(A)11.*

Education

Lamar Alexander
President,
University of Tennessee

1

An eighth-grade education—in case some people haven't checked lately—is a fairly significant set of skills. If all Americans had an eighth-grade education today, we'd be leaving most of our world-wide competitors in the dust. We would still need Nobel Prize winners and our large number of higher-educated people. But our most fundamental problem is with the bottom group—those who don't have eighth-grade skills. The only way to see that everybody gets those skills is to set out goals and gradually build up. We should say no matter what else we do, every child will have third-grade skills, then fourth-grade skills, then fifth-grade skills, right on up to eighth.

Interview/
Nation's Business, April:24.

2

What business men and women can bring to the better-schools movement is a structured way of solving problems. Passion is important. Educators have the knowledge; they're the experts. But management is what is too often missing. The most critical skill that good leaders and managers have is helping people set clear goals for themselves, and developing report cards on whether they're meeting those goals. I think if business men and women all over the country would do one thing—help schools and school districts set goals for themselves and then help them measure their progress—that would be the single most important contribution business could make.

Interview/
Nation's Business, April:24.

3

There are 100,000 schools across America. Each one must develop its own goals, its own report card. Those goals will change, depending upon whether you're in Harlem or Anchorage... The most important thing the President [of the U.S.] can do is inspire Americans to set those goals... And he should set one overriding goal himself. It might be to make certain that *all* graduating students, by the beginning of the 21st century, will know and be able to do what an eighth-grade student should be able to do. That's the main difference between us and Japan. They educate the whole country. We educate one-half to two-thirds.

Interview/
USA Today, 8-14:(A)9.

Wilford S. Bailey
President, National Collegiate
Athletic Association

4

[On college sports]: The most fundamental concern is that it is necessary to achieve and maintain a true wholeness of inter-collegiate athletics and education at our institutions. We should not make conclusions that result in an undesirable imbalance of athletics and education, nor should we conclude that winning in athletics can't be a part of the educational experience. We have to maintain a balance of education and athletics.

Jan.9/
The Washington Post,
1-10:(E)4.

Robert P. Biller
Dean of admissions and
financial aid, University of
Southern California

5

[College] athletes are like musicians; they represent a certain element of the university community. We want to make sure we have an active and effective student orchestra and we want to make sure we have an active and effective basketball team.

The New York Times, 1-25:(B)7.

David Boaz
Executive vice president,
Cato Institute, Washington

1

Right now, rich parents have the clout to be customers or consumers in the education business, and if they can't get good schools in a rich neighborhood, then they can go to a private school. But poor parents don't have that clout. They're stuck with what the government offers them—lousy schools.

Interview/USA Today, 9-19:(A)13.

Ernest L. Boyer
President,
Carnegie Foundation for
the Advancement of Teaching

2

The Catholic schools' job is made simpler [than that of public schools] by self-selection [of students]. But they are also quite focused in their mission, they establish discipline and have high levels of parental involvement. Perhaps these are more difficult to achieve in public schools, but the lesson still remains.

U.S. News & World Report,
5-22:62.

3

If a health epidemic were striking one-fourth of the children in this country, if snow were piling up on the city streets, if we had heaps of garbage on the curbs—a national emergency would be declared. But when hundreds of thousands of students leave school every year shockingly unprepared, the nation remains far too lethargic. We need a larger vision [to improve education]—an urgent call to action—and the President himself must lead the way.

Before Business Roundtable,
Washington, June 5/
The New York Times, 6-6:(A)13.

David W. Breneman
President, Kalamazoo
(Mich.) College

4

The hallmark of a successful community college is trying to maximize the per-cent of the local population that crosses the door. It can be college [courses], but if that isn't selling, it will be training in the local plant, and if that isn't selling, it will be poodle grooming.

The Washington Post, 5-5:(A)16.

Barbara Bush
Wife of President of the
United States George Bush

5

In 10 years of traveling around the United States of America, visiting literary programs, libraries, kindergarten groups, day-care centers, single parent classes for high-school dropouts, public-housing projects, food banks—you name it—I've visited it. It has become very apparent to me that we must attack the problem of a more literate America through the family. We all know that adults with reading problems tend to raise children with reading problems. And when I talk about family literacy, I am talking about families of all kinds: the big and bouncing kind, the single parent, extended families, divorced, homeless and migrant.

Announcing the establishment of
the Barbara Bush Foundation for
Family Literacy, Washington,
March 6/The New York Times, 3-7:(A)8.

George Bush
Vice President, and
President-elect,
of the United States

6

[Advocating programs in which parents can choose the public school they want their children to attend]: [Choice of school is] perhaps the most single promising [new idea in U.S. education. Choice programs] give parents back their voices and their proper determining roles in the makeup of children's education, and they give schools a chance to distinguish themselves from one another . . . Almost without exception, wherever choice has been attempted—Minnesota, East Harlem, San Francisco, Los Angeles, and in a hundred other places in-between—choice has worked . . . Bad schools get better; good ones get better still . . . Any school reform that can boast

(GEORGE BUSH)

such success deserves our attention, our emphasis, our effort.

Before White House Workshop on Choice in Education, Washington, Jan. 10/Los Angeles Times, 1-11:(I)4.

1

[As President,] education will be on my desk and on my mind right from the start every day . . . Education is the key to our very competitiveness in the future as a nation, and to our very soul as a people.

To group of visiting teachers, Washington, Jan. 18/ The New York Times, 1-19:(A)13.

George Bush
President of the United States

2

Education knows no barriers, accepts no limits. Education is a ladder; it embodies self-respect, not dependency. Education can give minorities a greater voice and make sure that voice is heard.

Before United Negro College Fund, New York, March 9/ The New York Times, 3-10:(A)12.

3

Some of our states that put less money into education per capita achieve the highest scores. Which proves my thesis: that it isn't how much money you throw at a specific educational program that's going to result in the excellence we seek.

Broadcast interview/ "Learning in America," PBS-TV, 4-24.

4

[On whether parents who send their children to private schools should get a tax break]: Everybody should support the public school system. And then, if on top of that your parents think that

they want to shell out . . . tuition money [for a private school], that's their right and should be respected. But I don't think they should get a break for that.

At White House meeting with high-school students, Washington, March/ Christianity Today, 5-12:55.

5

The American people are ready for radical reforms [in education]. We must not disappoint them . . . Of course, all schools in a state will share a core curriculum and minimum standards of achievement. But the means by which that curriculum is taught, and those goals met, should be as diverse and varied as America.

At meeting of state Governors to discuss education, Charlottesville, Va., Sept. 28/ The New York Times, 9-29:(A)8.

Brad M. Butler
Former chairman, Procter & Gamble Company

6

If we continue to let children who are born in poverty fail to get the kind of education that will allow them to participate in our economy and our society productively, then some time in the 21st century this nation will cease to be a peaceful, prosperous democracy.

The New York Times, 9-25:(A)1.

Eugene C. Campbell
Superintendent of Schools of Newark, N.J.

7

I'm not saying that money is everything [in education]. Money is not everything. But [President Bush] stated that money shouldn't make a difference; and I'll tell you, for the initiatives that work, it takes money.

The New York Times, 4-26:(B)8.

103

Garrey E. Carruthers
Governor of New Mexico (R);
Chairman,
education committee,
National Governors' Association

1

[Saying the Federal government has assumed control of education from local school boards in many instances]: The decline of education—that's a fact. But the decline of education isn't the issue. I don't think education has advanced as rapidly as our needs in education. There's a difference. We're now in a world economy, competing with everybody for ideas, for products. We have not kept pace with that. If you're not in charge [of education] at the local level, how can you be blamed? If everybody else has assumed your authority, and you're on the local school board and you really have no authority, why should you be blamed?

Interview/USA Today, 9-19:(A)13.

Lauro F. Cavazos
Secretary of Education
of the United States

2

I would prefer to see all students together [regardless of their perceived abilities] and everyone taught to the highest level. One of the problems is that we don't raise enough expectations of our children. You know, "You're over here in this lower category, so we don't expect you to achieve beyond this level." Then that's exactly as far as they're going to get. But if you say to a youngster, "We expect you to achieve as well as the best," that raises expectations. Youngsters will fulfill our expectations, and if expectations are low, that's where they're going to be.

Interview/USA Today, 5-30:(A)7.

3

America's system of education was once the envy of the world. We set the standards by which many other nations compared their own systems. Our success was based on community participation in the education of our children. The school was the center of activity and a source of local pride. People recognized that the future was centered in the school house and that there was no more important job than education. More and more, through the years, we abdicated our responsibility and let the control of education slip away from us as parents, teachers and community leaders. Our place was necessarily filled by larger bureaucracies that have operated, in most instances, in the best way that circumstances would allow. But these structures cannot provide the concern and caring attention that is needed to preserve the vitality and health of educational institutions.

At Public School 117, New York,
Oct. 17/The Washington Post,
11-1:(A)24.

Colby Chandler
Chairman, Eastman Kodak
Company

4

The largest single factor holding back companies like Kodak today is education. I doubt that President Bush understands the seriousness of the problem. Five per cent of our work-force in Rochester, New York, is illiterate. There's another 10 per cent or 15 per cent, by my guess, who are far below high-school equivalency. And all of this in an atmosphere in which probably less than 2 per cent of the jobs you could call unskilled. That's replicated over and over in this country.

Interview/USA Today, 4-4:(A)7.

Joe Clark
Principal,
Eastside High School,
Paterson, New Jersey

5

I've got the most orderly high school in any city in America . . . I fight the war every day. Once I let my guard down, I see a deterioration. Teachers stop, students stop, punks and hoodlums come in. If I accomplish nothing else but to bring order here, I deserve to be crowned Lord of Lords and King of Kings . . . Reform can't be done with politicians, teachers, parents. It must come from respectful interaction between stu-

(JOE CLARK)

dents and principal. If students believe in you, no problem can't be licked. Drugs, vandalism, violence become anachronistic and an anathema. If I said a mosquito can pull a plow, students wouldn't ask me how, they'd hitch 'im up.

Interview, Paterson, N.J/
Mother Jones, January:39.

John L. Clendenin
Chairman, United States
Chamber of Commerce;
Chairman,
BellSouth Corporation

1

Each year's crop of American [high-school] dropouts costs this country an estimated $240-billion of lost earnings and taxes over their lifetimes . . . At an economic level, educational failure hurts our collective wallet. It drains money from us as individuals and as citizens of collective enterprises. And perhaps most disturbing for the long term, at a dangerously deep social level, educational failure threatens to polarize our nation and to tear apart our society's whole cloth.

Nation's Business, April:17.

2

There is an urgent crisis in education in this country. Everybody knows it. The negative statistics keep rolling out in an avalanche. As the chairman of a company which employs 100,000 people, I worry about the educational product our schools pour each year into the work pool. We see young people coming into our employment offices who lack the qualifications needed to pass tests for even the entry-level positions. We know that the highly technical jobs of the Information Age are going to make the problem even worse because the skill requirements are going up. If our young people don't have the skills necessary for the kinds of jobs existing in the year 2000, then both our domestic and foreign customers for our products and services will look elsewhere in the world, and the American economy will suffer.

Interview/
Nation's Business, June:60.

James S. Coleman
Professor of sociology and
education, University of Chicago

3

There has come to be a recognition that many of the issues in education today are not in the domain of educational psychologists, but have to do with the social structure of the school and the world outside the school. I think that now is the time for sociologists of education to shine.

The New York Times, 1-4:(B)7.

Frank DeFord
Sports commentator

4

With their cynicism and hypocrisy, as well as with their allure and flash, big-time college sports are soiling college, soiling higher education, soiling our faith in education.

USA Today, 5-19:(A)6.

Elizabeth Hanford Dole
Secretary of Labor
of the United States

5

At the same time that the jobs are going to have higher skills requirements, you have 25 per cent of young people dropping out of high school. Many who do graduate can't even read their diplomas. There are 20 million to 40 million adult Americans who have problems with literacy, and one in every 10 17-year-olds has a problem with literacy. Obviously, we are at a point where we have a very serious problem.

Interview/USA Today, 9-5:(A)11.

John Dossey
Professor of mathematics,
Illinois State University

6

American students score near the bottom in almost every important area of mathematics when compared to similar students in other nations. Our education system is producing fewer and fewer individuals who can apply mathematics in any meaningful way.

The Washington Post, 3-22:(A)4.

Denis P. Doyle
Senior research fellow,
Hudson Institute

1

[On a poll showing most Americans favor national standards for education and the ability of parents to choose which public schools their children will attend]: I think citizens really do feel we need a common glue, an intellectual cement to hold us together, and at the same time people want a choice in how to get there. There is an abiding conviction that school is important and a will to pay for it [through higher taxes].

Aug. 24/
The Washington Post,
8-25:(A)14.

Timothy J. Dyer
Superintendent, Phoenix (Ariz.)
Union High School District

2

Our schools have produced one of the greatest democracies in the world. They have accommodated the greatest melting pot the world has ever seen. It's been because people have been educated, people have been able to use skills. Without education, there can't be an orderly democratic society. Defense is important, but those people defending us have to be educated. We [in the schools] do the most important work in society. And society has to be willing to pay for those kinds of services.

Interview/
USA Today, 9-5:(D)4.

David W. Ellis
President, Lafayette College

3

We have to come to the understanding that whether you're at a major [educational] institution or [a] small one, winning [sports] teams are a big benefit in money, prestige and notoriety ... We have to understand that in our society, football and basketball are a lot more revered than Shakespeare.

The New York Times,
2-15:(B)12.

Rita Esquivel
Director of Bilingual Eucation,
Department of Education
of the United States

4

The primary purpose [of bilingual education] has always been the same, but probably my style is a little different. Our goal ... is to travel throughout the country and to tell people that the primary goal of bilingual education is to teach children English, and that there are many ways of teaching children English. Our agenda is that we want to be very open and inclusive of everyone, and our agenda is that we will use the primary language where ... possible ... keeping in mind that it's only to build a bridge to learning English.

Interview/
Los Angeles Times, 8-26:(I)20.

Joseph A. Fernandez
Superintendent of Schools of
Dade County, Fla.

5

[City school] superintendents are no longer just instructional leaders. They're also chief executives of huge business enterprises and highly visible public officials with many constituencies. But most school officials on the way up don't have any way to get a good idea of just what the job requires.

The New York Times, 6-14:(B)8.

Chester Finn
Professor of education and
public policy,
Vanderbilt University;
Director, Education
Excellence Network

6

[On charges of price-fixing among colleges]: Colleges setting their prices [tuition, student aid, etc.] to be virtually identical [from college to college] are able to cushion each of themselves against consumer resistance and allow their prices to rise faster than each could get away with [separately]. They're packaging student aid in the same amount and in the same combinations. That is equivalent to saying to me as a parent that

(CHESTER FINN)

I am not being allowed by the college to consider price, as my child and I are considering which college to choose.

The Christian Science Monitor,
9-22:7.

Barbara Foorman
Professor of educational
psychology,
University of Houston

1

[Criticizing the idea of "cooperative learning" as against individualism in students]: It goes against the American grain, the individualism that creates the entrepreneurship we as a people have historically espoused. In a utopia, [cooperative learning] would be wonderful. But education should prepare kids for life in a particular culture. In reality, the name of the game is dog eat dog. Kids have to learn that you get something through your own smarts.

The New York Times, 1-4:(B)7.

Edward B. Fort
Chancellor,
North Carolina A&T
State University

2

[On the large amount of time student-players spend on college athletics]: To me, it's nonsense. It's time to put an end to the extraordinary amount of time devoted to both football and basketball practice in Division I and perhaps even in Division II and III. Athletes, for example, who are expected to report to practice at 5 a.m . . . just simply goes too far.

USA Today, 1-10:(C)7.

William Friday
Former president,
University of North Carolina

3

[On the increasing importance of college sports]: Americans have turned sports into a religion. What we're getting pretty close to doing

is turning our universities into entertainment centers.

Interview/
The Washington Post, 8-4:(F)2.

4

A recent *USA Today* story showed yearly incomes of a million dollars in quite a few instances in professional basketball, baseball and football. That is more income in one year than most teachers could look forward to in a lifetime for 30 years of work. Whose system of values is distorted? That says loud and clear to the best and brightest of our students not to go into teaching.

Interview/USA Today, 8-23:(A)9.

Milton Friedman
Economist

5

The [Vietnam] war has had very long lasting results. Part of the deterioration in the intellectual standards and morality of American universities and colleges derives from the Vietnam war. A great many people went to colleges and universities during that period who would not ordinarily have gone there, in order to stay out of the war. And these people, who would otherwise have been businessmen or something, became, instead, academics. But they are not intellectuals fundamentally; they are really activists.

Interview/The Wall Street Journal,
1-16:(A)8.

Mary Hatwood Futrell
President, National
Education Association

6

When I came into teaching in the '60s, education was the province of women and minorities. But as these opportunities have opened up in business and private industry, many of the talented people who may have gone into teaching were directed elsewhere . . . When we ask young people why they don't want to go into teaching, they not only cite the low pay and the poor conditions, they say that teachers aren't

WHAT THEY SAID IN 1989

(MARY HATWOOD FUTRELL)

treated like professionals. Teachers are treated like very tall children and are given very little input.

Ebony, January:124,126.

1

[On President-elect Bush's proposals for giving parents choices as to which schools to send their children]: Where we begin to be leery is when people start using choice as a euphemism for vouchers and tax credits. It could be a way to open the door to use public funds to support private schools. Taking the money from private schools does not solve the issue. You are depleting the funds for schools that are already in trouble.

Los Angeles Times, 1-5:(I)22.

Keith Geiger
*Vice president, National
Education Association*

2

We need about a 25 percent pay increase [for teachers] to get us up to the average of other professions. But I don't think that's as critical an issue as the disparity of teachers' salaries. We know that probably hundreds of thousands of teachers are making less than $20,000 a year. I think we need to take a close look at those states and those communities where the salaries are so appalling that our members are eligible for food stamps.

Interview/USA Today, 7-3:(A)9.

Bernard Gifford
*Vice president for education,
Apple Computers;
Former Dean, Graduate
School of Education,
University of California,
Berkeley*

3

I would like to ask the [state] Governors and the President [Bush] to rate and rank every [educational] reform in terms of how it will

actually impact on the quality of the relationship between pupil and teacher . . . Many "reforms" haven't had one iota of impact there . . . We need to stop talking about reform from the top down and start talking about it from the bottom up.

*Interview/
The Christian Science Monitor,
9-27:15.*

George Gilder
Author, Economist

4

Our schools are pathetic, our family structure is hurting. Schools and families are critical to the new economic ideas and, unless we nurture these, we are doomed . . . [we are] teaching such things as sex education, driver's education and Indian rights instead of calculus and physics. This is frivolous stuff that you don't need to teach in high school.

*Interview/Los Angeles Times,
9-10:(IV)3.*

Paul E. Gray
*President, Massachusetts
Institute of Technology*

5

I think that the changing demographics of the nation are going to put pressure on universities with respect to enrollments, the gender and racial characteristics of their enrollments, and the composition of the whole work-force in these organizations. Something like two-thirds coming into the work-force between now and the end of the century will be either minority or women.

*Interview, Cambridge, Mass/
The New York Times, 5-17:(B)9.*

Vartan Gregorian
President, Brown University

6

[Saying many students are too preoccupied with grades and test scores]: The question is always, "What were your scores? What's your average?"—never, "What courses did you take?" Education is valued for what it will give you rather than what it can make out of you.

*Interview, Providence, R.I.,/
The Christian Science Monitor,
5-12:14.*

Gilbert M. Grosvenor
President, National
Geographic Society

1

[On the poor showing by Americans in a National Geographic Society survey of geographic knowledge]: We're going downhill and the others [around the world] are going uphill. I would like to see geography returned to the curriculum in this country . . . Geography dropped out of the school system after World War II. When it was taught, it was sometimes taught by the football coach.

Washington,
Nov. 8/
Los Angeles Times, 11-9:(A)18.

Raymond Hay
Chief executive officer,
LTV Corporation

2

I feel that education begins in the home and, until such time as we fix the social structure in this country so that kids start their education at home and have the home as the principal form of education, the population is not going to be educated. Spending more money has not done it. Hiring more teachers has not done it. I was absolutely shocked to hear that only 4.9 per cent of American high-school graduates would be accepted into many European universities.

Interview/USA Today, 6-7:(A)11.

E. D. Hirsch, Jr.
Writer on education matters

3

American traditions of educational pluralism and local autonomy will undoubtedly restrict the common core to no more than 50 per cent of the whole curriculum [in elementary schools], with the other half left to local discretion. But we still need to agree on a definite core of knowledge which each child in the nation should master in each grade. Right now our best strategy is for lots of schools and districts across the country to go ahead on their own and agree on a sensible core curriculum—any intelligent one will do—and put

it into effect while the high-echelon debate continues to go on within the establishment.

At forum on literacy in America,
sponsored by "The New York Times,"
New York, Dec. 5/
The New York Times, 12-6:(B)8.

Lou Holtz
Football coach, University
of Notre Dame

4

If you're a good coach, you'll be a good teacher. And to be good at either, you've got to have discipline. There is no way people can teach, or people can learn, if it's not in a disciplined environment. And discipline, by the way, is not what you do *to*, it is what you do *for* them . . . When it comes to discipline here, we ask three questions: Will it make him a better man? A better student? A better athlete? If the answer is yes, we make him do it. The next step is up to him. An individual has a choice when you discipline him: either to become bitter or better.

Interview, University of Notre Dame,
March 17/The Saturday Evening Post,
September:52,53.

David Hornbeck
Chairman, Carnegie
Task Force on Education of
Young Adolescents;
Former Superintendent
of Schools of Maryland

5

We suggest a heavy emphasis on science education, on the life sciences, on human biology. Anybody who's ever known a kid 10 or 15 years old knows the kind of intense interest that those kids have in themselves and their bodies, and the changes that are going on in relation to other people. One of the things that we recommend is that the curriculum [at middle schools] reflect that kind of development. One of the most important features is that we recommend high expectations for all kids. Not just for rich kids. No more dumbed-down curriculum for poor kids.

Interview/USA Today, 6-20:(A)11.

Stanley O. Ikenberry
President, University of Illinois

1

The genius of our system of higher education is its diversity, its pluralism and, frankly, the strong competition within it. [Ultimately,] it is a system designed to capture all the talent of the country.
U.S. News & World Report,
10-16:57.

Jesse L. Jackson
Civil-rights leader

2

The key to effective schools is the establishment of a foundation. Parents and teachers must constitute that foundation and form a partnership. If parents and teachers are disconnected, it's like a battery cable disconnected from the charge. You won't get any fire. You won't get any power . . . It is my position that, fundamentally, teachers don't have parent aides. Parents have teacher aides. Parents pay the taxes and hire the teachers to aid them in educating their children. Therefore, the primary responsibility for sending a child to school, for monitoring homework and for imposing discipline and ethical standards must rest with the parents. Children are not born to schools and teachers; they're born to parents.
Interview/USA Today, 8-31:(A)11.

David T. Kearns
Chairman, Xerox Corporation

3

No single feature of the education system is more shocking to business leaders than low levels of education research spending. We know more about pork bellies and soybean futures in this country than we do about our schools.
The New York Times, 8-23:(B)7.

4

We cannot compete in a world-class economy without a world-class work-force, and we cannot have a world-class work-force without world-class schools.
The New York Times, 9-25:(A)12.

James Kelly
Chairman, National Board
for Professional
Teaching Standards

5

[Calling for national board certification of teachers]: [With certification] it will be a stronger mix of professional experiences within an enriched working environment that will be more attractive to people in teaching. It will not just be 2½ million teachers who go in there at age 22 and come out at 65 and never interact. One of the ripple effects will be to encourage teachers to work with other teachers to improve their craft. That's probably one of the most powerful consequences of this. People will want to become board certified, and they will want to work in an environment where most of their colleagues become board certified if they meet the standards.
Interview/USA Today, 7-18:(A)11.

David Layzer
Professor of astrophysics,
Harvard University

6

Mathematics is taught in the way that foreign languages used to be taught. The emphasis was on memorizing grammatical rules and word lists. After two or three years of such instruction, few students could use the language.
The New York Times, 3-1:(B)7.

Sara Lawrence Lightfoot
Professor, Graduate School of
Education, Harvard University

7

[Criticizing schools for reinforcing social inequities by assuming black children are poorer students than whites]: What we demand is this: that the schools shift their focus from the supposed deficiencies of the black child, and the alleged inadequacies of black family life, to the elimination of the barriers that stand in the way of academic success among these and other children.
May 23/
The Washington Post,
5-24:(A)10.

EDUCATION

Marcia C. Linn
Professor of education,
University of California,
Berkeley

1

[On the differences between men and women
in their mathematical and special learning skills]:
The differences are now so small as to be
negligible. We should de-emphasize this issue ...
[What my research suggests] is that, in general,
there is a decline in cognitive gender differences
and, therefore, that an important part of the
variance in cognitive ability is probably a result
of experience or other influences on performance.

Before American Association for
the Advancement of Science,
San Francisco, Jan. 15/
Los Angeles Times, 1-16:(I)3.

Irving Margol
Executive vice president,
Security Pacific Corporation

2

[On the poor educational preparedness of
today's young job applicants]: We're forced to
hire the best of the worst. I'm almost taking
anyone who breathes.

The Wall Street Journal,
3-31:(R)12.

James M. McPartland
Director, Center for Research
on Elementary and
Middle Schools,
Johns Hopkins University

3

There's a real sludge of inertia in education
that is not only due to the conservativeness of
educators but also to the political and economic
forces that impact on the schools.

The New York Times, 1-4:(B)7.

Michael McPherson
Chairman, department of economics,
Williams College

4

Thinking in terms of value-added, it's very
easy for a school like Williams to take credit for

the fine quality of its graduates. But they had
almost all of those fine qualities when they came.
The real question from a social point of view is
what kind of extensions, or improvements, do we
achieve?

The Washington Post, 5-5:(A)16.

Roger Muss
Special correspondent, "The
MacNeil/Lehrer NewsHour,"
PBS-TV

5

In the Japanese system, there is a direct connection between the schools and Japanese business. There is active correlation between the
curriculum and the needs of the Japanese economy. The Japanese look at the school system not
as a social laboratory—as a place to become
popular and learn how to go out on dates. They
regard their high-school education as a contribution to the country, to the economy and to the
society ... In the United States, generally, we're
really not settled on what we think high school
ought to be. Some people want it to be used as a
place to be educated. Others want it simply to be
a place where you grow up. Others want it to be a
place to get children off the streets.

Interview/USA Today, 3-27:(A)9.

G. Dennis O'Brien
President, University of Rochester,
(N.Y.)

6

[On charges that colleges are involved in price-
fixing of tuition and student aid]: With all the
troubles of trying to run universities, upgrading
research facilities, bringing in minority students,
and deferred maintenance, and have someone
come in and say we're price-gouging and collud-
ing—it really frosts me.

The Christian Science Monitor,
9-22:7.

Leo O'Donovan
President-designate,
Georgetown University

7

[On higher education's role in the decline of
U.S. competitiveness in science and technol-

111

(LEO O'DONOVAN)

ogy]: We're certainly less competitive than we were. For President Bush to be "the education President," a great deal remains to be done in terms of funding research and student scholarships. But we shouldn't seek to be better educators in order to beat out competitors. We should seek to be better educators in responsibility to our students. And because the search for truth is, in itself, compelling. Competition may be an appropriate word for the marketplace, but it's not my favorite word to refer to educational endeavors.

Interview/USA Today, 9-21:(A)9.

Jay Oliva
Chancellor,
New York University

1

My attitude is that sports are a piece of the educational business. Coaches are teachers, and we can learn so much from sports. My job is to keep it in perspective . . . If a student wanted to come to NYU "to play basketball" I'd tell him to go somewhere else. But if they'd like to pursue athletics while they are here [primarily as students], that's fine. There are other things in life besides study.

The New York Times, 2-15:(B)12.

Robert Ornstein
Neurobiologist and
psychologist, University of
California Medical Center,
San Francisco, and
Stanford University

2

. . . our education itself is almost irrelevant to many of the changes that are taking place in the world. People are taught algebra with great precision in schools, but I've never met anyone who's used algebra after age 13. On the other hand, they're not taught probability, which is something that they need every night when they watch the news. People need to understand the nature of the world they actually live in as opposed to the world we're taught to believe in—a kind of

bucolic world that only exists now in cereal ads. And we're changing the world so fast that we believe the curriculum needs to be changed every decade. Our past is no longer a good guide to our future, and understanding what could happen in our future is what education needs to be about.

Interview/USA Today,
1-25:(A)9.

Joe Paterno
Football coach,
Pennsylvania State University

3

When a kid becomes a star athlete [in college], he automatically loses the proper perspective on academics. It's got to start back in the high schools, and high-school coaches must take the responsibility to stress academics. Kids have got to know at an early age that if they want to play college ball, they're going to have to study.

Panel discussion before Council
for Advancement and Support of
Education, Washington, July 11/
The Washington Post,
7-12:(C)5.

John Allen Paulos
Professor of mathematics,
Temple University

4

[On the term "innumeracy," which he coined]: It is the mathematical equivalent of illiteracy. Innumeracy is an inability to deal comfortably with numbers, probabilities, logic and other basic notions of math. I emphasize *basic*. You can be numerate even if you don't understand quantum mechanics . . . The term "innumeracy" covers a wide range of people, including those who are otherwise highly intelligent and knowledgeable. What's annoying to me is that, while illiterates are ashamed of their inability to read, innumerates often take a kind of pride in their mathematical ignorance. People who would never admit to not knowing anything about Shakespeare—even if that were the case—will openly boast that they can't balance their checkbooks.

Interview/People,
5-29:95.

Rudy Perpich
Governor of Minnesota (D)

1

No school district can please all students all the time. But without choice [the ability of parents to choose which school their children will go to], school districts have little incentive to change and to provide alternatives for those families that want them. We propose no rigid models. Choice needs to be debated, examined and made to fit the needs of each individual state.

At conference on choice in schooling,
Minneapolis/
The New York Times, 3-1:(B)7.

Robert S. Peterkin
Superintendent of Public Schools
of Milwaukee

2

When the military is having problems, we allocate money. When the savings-and-loans industry is having problems, we allocate money. When education is having problems, we say we could possibly allocate a few dollars.

The New York Times, 12-6:(B)8.

Donald E. Petersen
Chairman,
Ford Motor Company

3

[On the problems of education]: We need that vision that only the President can give us. That's certainly a role that the Federal government can and must play. By no means am I advocating a centrally orchestrated approach. It must really be a local initiative in the thousands of school districts. The family has to be the heart and soul.

Interview/USA Today, 8-14:(A)9.

John W. Porter
Superintendent,
Detroit Public Schools

4

You've got to have concerned parents. You've got to have motivated youngsters who are willing to come to school. You've got to have dedicated teachers who are willing to stay after school and to work with the individual youngsters. You've got to have enthusiastic support personnel, beginning with the principal. And you've got to have a supportive community that's willing to raise the money for the schools to be safe and attractive. We can talk all we want to about white folks and middle-class blacks moving to the suburbs, and about people wanting to put their kids in private schools. But it's not because they're racist necessarily—it's because they know what the desirable conditions are for effective outcomes.

Interview, Detroit/
The Christian Science Monitor,
8-11:13.

Hunter Rawlings III
President, University of Iowa

5

[Saying freshmen should be prohibited from participating in college sports]: [Freshman eligibility] sends the wrong message to these young people when they arrive on a campus, and the message they are getting is that athletics comes first. Well, academics should come first.

Interview/
The New York Times, 4-19:(B)9.

John Ray
Member, District of Columbia
Council; Candidate for
Mayor of Washington

6

[We] must require school attendance to begin at the age of five. And we must provide before- and after-school care, on the school site, for children between five and 12. We must also open up our schools in the evenings for quiet study, tutoring and family recreation. We must keep our public schools open year-round for summer enrichment programs and recreation . . . We must recognize that excellence in education is not just for the future doctors and lawyers and scientists and others bound for college. Our public education must, at a minimum, provide every child with the skills he or she needs to get a job in the basic marketplace . . .

The Washington Post, 10-27:(A)18.

Albert Shanker
President, American
Federation of Teachers

1

[On President-elect Bush's proposals for giving parents choices as to which schools to send their children]: I think choice potentially could be a very positive thing. But the idea that it can solve everything is nonsense. For years we had many manufacturers making many automobiles in this country and we had an awful lot of lemons.

Los Angeles Times, 1-5:(1)22.

2

[Saying teacher education needs to be improved]: If you ask what percentage of elementary-school teachers really understand the science they teach, the answer would be under 50 per cent. The entry standard for college in most countries requires knowing science and math and the ability to write well. It's not true for American colleges, and there's no way to catch up quickly.

The Christian Science Monitor,
8-29:7.

3

I would call for an immediate end to standardized [student] tests as they are now. What you need to do is test for things that are really important: reading, writing, computing, history. To test for depth of knowledge, you have to get away from things that are machine-gradable.

To reporters, New York, Oct. 28/
Los Angeles Times, 10-29:(A)27.

Roger Shattuck
Author; Teacher,
Boston University

4

We are absolutely hooked, in this country, on a system that assumes everyone will go to college. This is a major conflict of interest, because we're comforted into thinking that there is this other place where students will get "the rest" of their education. This downgrades and paralyzes what goes on in high school. Until the high-school

degree can be really considered a worthwhile terminal diploma that qualifies students to go to work at most jobs and to vote intelligently, we go nowhere. Everything is going to wait until it comes to college, and college is too late. Lower education will improve when we reduce, not expand, higher education.

Panel discussion/Harper's,
September:50.

Saeki Shoichi
Professor,
Chuo University (Japan)

5

I would not hesitate to tell anyone who asked that American college campuses have far more vitality than their Japanese counterparts and in general offer a more congenial environment. The lively, direct response of my American university students put to shame anything one could expect in Japan. Questions, comments, arguments and counter-arguments fly. In Japanese universities, even considerable effort on the teacher's part usually fails to elicit any response or reaction. When the teacher solicits the students' opinions, they sit in stony silence, many of them casting their eyes downward lest they be called on.

The Atlantic Monthly,
February:(A)12.

John R. Silber
President, Boston University

6

I think American primary and secondary education is at a crossroads, because Mr. and Mrs. America are not going to pay taxes for schools they are not going to use. Most members of Congress are not willing to impose that social experiment on their kids, because the schools are just not good enough.

Interview/The Washington Post,
9-5:(A)11.

7

[There should be an] abolition of all the certification rules for [public-school] teachers.

(JOHN R. SILBER)

Appointing persons competent to teach should be left to the school committees and the school superintendents. That would mean stop asking if they spent three or four years in a school of education. If they know the subject matter, and if they're willing to come under the guidance of a mentor teacher for one or two semesters, they can certainly be qualified to teach without all that delay, without all that repulsive work that has to be done at schools of education . . . It would cost nothing and it would open the doors to primary education to housewives, who have children now approaching 6 years of age and who would love to have a career they could combine with family. It would open the doors to engineers and scientists in industry who are 55 years of age or older, who could take early retirement. They know mathematics. A differential equation to one of those engineers is child's play.

Interview/USA Today, 9-25:(A)13.

1

[On President Bush's voucher plan that would allow parents to send their children to their choice of schools]: Once you start the voucher program, instead of reforming the public schools of America, you're going to destroy them. Don't believe for one moment that you're going to improve the schools when you artificially create an incentive to start new schools that are private. There'll be a lot of hucksters and sharpies out there to grab those Federal dollars. As a last-ditch effort to save the public schools, I might finally in desperation go that route, but I don't think we're at that point yet.

Interview/USA Today, 9-25:(A)13.

Lewis C. Solmon
*Dean, Graduate School
of Education,
University of California,
Los Angeles*

2

When money is committed [to education], it goes to the wrong things—to reduce class sizes by one or two kids or to raise [teacher] salaries,

which may help in the next generation but also keeps incompetents in. To me, the most crucial problem is getting better people into the profession. We can do all this fine tuning, but until we get really smart, competent, dedicated and hard-working people into the system, we're just going to be spinning our wheels.

Los Angeles Times, 10-9:(I)21.

John Thompson
*Basketball coach,
Georgetown University*

3

[Criticizing a new NCAA ruling that denies athletic scholarships to students not scoring high enough on SAT and ACT tests, saying it discriminates against minorities]: Many of the proponents of Proposal 42 [the ruling] may have laudatory academic and athletic goals in mind. However, this proposal fails to take into account the significant, detrimental effect that it will have on socio-economically deprived students. They will no longer have an opportunity to show that a poor test score in the SAT or the ACT is not a result of the lack of native intelligence, but is a result of the cultural bias of the test and the deprivation that has existed in their lives because of socio-economic and racial issues that are, unfortunately, inherent in our society today. In an effort to rekindle discussion in this proposal and to highlight the inequities inherent in it, I have decided, effective with [today's] game, that I will not be on the bench in an NCAA-sanctioned Georgetown basketball game until I am satisfied that something has been done to provide these student-athletes with appropriate opportunity and hope for access to a college education.

*News conference, Washington,
Jan. 13/
The Washington Post, 1-14:(A)7.*

P. Michael Timpane
*President, Teachers College,
Columbia University*

4

Is this nation going to find a way to put education at the top of its priorities? Will the important politicians stay involved? Will they set up a process by which they commit themselves to do whatever's necessary, whether money or leadership, or will they try to make quick improvements and divert their attention to someone else? If the answer is yes, the [recent education] summit will have been a very important event. If no, it will have been a public-relations exercise.

The New York Times, 12-6:(B)8.

Richard S. Tompson
Admissions officer,
Northwestern University

1

In every case, the high-school transcript and curriculum are the most important tools [in determining whether a student will be admitted to a college], and the SAT is just used as a way to put all that in perspective. In recent years, selective schools have de-emphasized the SAT. We have found that the three years of college preparatory work is much more useful for judging prospective students than any standardized test. There is always the hypothetical situation where you have two students who are identical except for their test scores. I have yet to see that hypothetical situation.

The New York Times,
2-4:10.

Jack Valenti
President, Motion Picture Association
of America

2

We ought to regard the English language as the singular triumph of a free people. It ought to be studied, examined, practiced and used. Sadly, it is possible to graduate from a high-quality college, having been transported from an equally lauded high school, and be functionally absent in the use of the mother tongue. How can one claim to be a civilized, educated human being and write sentences that resemble nothing so much as disordered moonshine?

At University of Texas, Austin,
Oct. 23/
Daily Variety, 11-20:10.

Arnold R. Weber
President,
Northwestern University

3

[Some argue] that a central mission of higher education should be to convey core values and concepts associated with Western civilization. These values are embedded in a certain body of literature—i.e., a "canon"—including the writings of Plato through Descartes and Nietzsche. Reforms which seek to broaden the curriculum to include exposure to non-Western, non-traditional writers and thought are viewed as evidence of indiscipline, if not moral decay. These issues are subject to earnest discussion but do not justify the quasi-hysterical conclusion that curricular innovations are instruments for the subversion of Western civilization or lead to the intellectual enfeeblement of undergraduates. Certainly the college curriculum should attempt to incorporate new ideas and changes in the external environment no matter how alien and threatening they may appear to be.

Speech, Washington/
The Washington Post, 8-8:(A)16.

Elaine P. Witty
Dean, School of Education,
Norfolk (Va.) State University

4

There often is this feeling in the black community that if a student is bright, he or she is somehow too good to be a teacher. The community will rain praise on students who say they are in engineering or pre-med programs, but the student who is in education doesn't get that kind of encouragement.

Ebony, January:124.

5

[On the need for more minority teachers]: Children look at the composition of the faculty and conclude that those people who are white are the people we can look up to for the dissemination of information, for being in charge of things, for showing authority, making decisions and exerting leadership. That's a dangerous and damaging message. [It also means that] you lose

(ELAINE P. WITTY)

the resource of minority teachers to serve as mediators of their culture for other students. For white students, we are teaching them a false view of the world. In a world that is not predominantly white, they grow up experiencing and seeing a white-controlled school system. And since we live in a global society and most of those are people of color, they need to learn there are values and intelligence in a variety of cultures and people.

Los Angeles Times, 9-27:(I)1.

Linus Wright
Former Under Secretary of
Education of the United States

1

Business people have had to get involved in education out of necessity. They are the best-qualified observers and evaluators, and they have the best-trained staffs for problem-solving. They must [help] structure a system [of education] that's built on performance results.

Nation's Business, April:17.

A. Zachary Yamba
President, Essex County
(N.J.) College

2

When we [community colleges] move students from a fifth-grade level to a different level—gainful employment—society has to recognize that as a success. Community colleges still address the concerns of those who can't go elsewhere. We were created to assuage the conscience of society . . . We say fine, we'll fight the larger societal battle.

The Washington Post,
5-5:(A)16.

Robert Zemsky
Director, Higher Education
Research Program

3

What needs to happen in American higher education is no different than what needs to happen in American industry, and is in fact happening . . . becoming meaner, a little leaner. It will be painful. It will be difficult. But it is in higher education's best interest.

The Washington Post, 9-13:(A)2.

Theodor Ziolkowski
Dean, Graduate School,
Princeton University

4

It's a high waste of national resources, not just financial but intellectual resources, to have an increasingly discouraged proletariat developing. And that's what happens when students go for too long in that terrible state of limbo of aging graduate students.

The New York Times, 5-3:(A)1.

The Environment • Energy

Wendell Berry
Agrarian poet

1

For a long time now, we have understood ourselves as traveling toward some sort of industrial paradise, some new Eden conceived and constructed entirely by human ingenuity ... Now we face overwhelming evidence that we are not smart enough to recover Eden by assault and that nature does not tolerate or excuse our abuses. If, in spite of the evidence against us, we are finding it hard to relinquish our old ambition, we are also seeing more clearly every day how that ambition has reduced and enslaved us.

At environmental symposium
at the Land Institute, Salina, Kan./
Los Angeles Times, 11-2:(E)18.

Sherwood Boehlert
United States Representative,
D-New York

2

For the first time in the history of the acid-rain battle in Congress, we have in the Oval Office a President [Bush] who acknowledges the problem exists and has made a commitment to be part of the solution rather than part of the problem. What a refreshing change.

The New York Times, 3-7:(A)14.

Wallace S. Broecker
Professor of geochemistry,
Columbia University

3

My feeling is we overestimate our ability to predict [great changes in the earth's environment]. Many of the things that are going to happen to the planet will be surprises, like the ozone hole over Antarctica. Therefore, we should be much more careful about what we are doing and much more observant of how the system works.

The New York Times,
1-17:(B)5.

George Bush
President of the United States

4

I'm determined to be an environmentalist. I *am* one, and I'm concerned that we not do irreparable damage to the environment. On the other hand, I remember some of the same arguments being made against the Alaska [oil] pipeline. And we have some radical national-security interests at stake here, and I'm one who believes we can find the balance between environmental interests and national-security interests that dictate prudent development of our domestic oil and gas resources.

Interview, Washington/
The New York Times, 1-26:(A)10.

5

[On the recent large Exxon oil spill in Alaska]: I think the Federal government moved much more quickly and more boldly than it gets credit for. I consider the United States Coast Guard a part of the United States government, and the Coast Guard moved very rapidly. What we did not want to do was to relieve the Exxon Corporation of its liability by Federalizing ... I do have a great concern about the environment. I want to do better. I want to do better and set higher standards in the environment. But I also happen to believe that the national-security needs of this country are served by having [oil] production offshore and by producing oil from [Alaska's] North Slope.

Before American Society of
Newspaper Editors,
Washington, April 12/
USA Today, 4-13:(A)13.

6

[On his clean-air plan]: Every American in every city in America will breathe clean air [by early in the next century]. Ours is a rare opportunity to reverse the errors of this generation in the service of the next. It's time to clear the

(GEORGE BUSH)

air . . . The wounded winds of north, south, east and west can be purified and cleansed, and the integrity of nature can be made whole again.

Washington, June 12/
The Washington Post, 6-13:(A)1.

1

So many of the big [environmental] problems—coastal water pollution, pesticides in ground water, urban smog and municipal garbage—aren't simply caused by large power plants and refineries. And many can't be solved by national legislation alone. Millions of small, diverse sources contribute to these problems, including the everyday behavior of people at work and at home. Such overwhelming environmental challenges can be solved by individual determination that we can do better. Local communities, businesses large and small, individual families—all can learn to generate less waste and recycle more of the waste that is generated.

At ceremony marking
Washington State's centennial,
Spokane, Wash., Sept. 19/
Los Angeles Times, 9-20:(I)23.

2

Threats to our environment have become international problems. We must develop an international approach to urgent environmental issues. One that seeks common solutions to common problems . . . And I will tell you now the United States will do its part. We have committed ourselves to the world-wide phase-out of all chlorofluorocarbons by the year 2000. We've proposed amending our own Clean Air Act to insure clean air for our citizens within a single generation. We've banned the import of ivory to protect the elephant and rhinoceros from the human predators who exterminate them for profit. And we've begun to explore ways to work with other nations, with the major industrialized democracies, and in Poland and in Hungary, to make common cause for the sake of our environment. The environment belongs to all of us. In this new world of freedom, the world citizens

must enjoy this common trust for generations to come.

At United Nations, New York,
Sept. 25/
The New York Times, 9-26:(A)8.

Remy Carle
Assistant director general,
Electricite de France

3

The nuclear [-power] issue in France was never a political one. The left side of the political scene and the right side were both, for different reasons, convinced about the necessity of nuclear energy. No politician was inclined to take this as the way of winning a battle. Certainly the fact that [the U.S. has] a Federal-state system is not good for nuclear energy because there are several levels where people can oppose energy and can try to stop it—and can succeed. In my view, the political system in [the U.S.] is really devoted to defend the individual. When somebody complains, he can stop everything. If anybody can stop anything, you go quickly to an inability to do anything.

Interview/
The New York Times, 5-8:(C)4.

John Chubb
Senior fellow,
Brookings Institution

4

[On the recent large oil spill in Alaska]: The only cry [from environmentalists] now is: "No more Alaskan oil." That's all very well, but which of the alternatives do you like? Do you like importing oil? Do you like nuclear power? Do you like coal?

The Christian Science Monitor,
4-11:7.

Harlan Cleveland
Diplomat, Futurist

5

This is the first generation in the history of the world that finds that what people do to their natural environment is maybe more important than what the natural environment does to and for them. We also have some measuring sticks for change that we never had before. And, as always happens with knowledge, as soon as you know something, you have some responsibility.

Interview/
The Christian Science Monitor,
9-1:12.

Jacques Cousteau
Naturalist

1

The survival of the human race depends on the survival of Antarctica. An oil spill in Antarctic waters can damage the food chain for decades, and this affects us even in the Northern Hemisphere. It is essential that Antarctica be declared a wilderness reserve protected by all nations. Moreover, the seas around Antarctica, which are not covered even by the old Antarctic Treaty, must be protected by a new agreement.

Interview/
The New York Times, 9-25:(A)8.

Alex Cristofaro
Director, Atmospheric and
Economic Analysis Division,
Environmental Protection Agency
of the United States

2

The environmental movement as a whole is increasingly coming to realize that we can no longer make major gains by forcing people to put widgets on smokestacks or plants. Most of the easy sources to control already have controls. To get significant reductions now means changing a number of behaviors and on such a scale that we can't do it without controlling legislation.

The New York Times, 4-3:(A)1.

Thomas J. Downey
United States Representative,
D-New York

3

[On the just-concluded first session of the 101st Congress]: Congressional sessions are like

wines. Some years are good, some years are bad. This one was terrible. The best thing you can say about it is that it came to an end early.

The Washington Post, 11-24:(A)9.

Charles Ebinger
Senior associate,
Center for Strategic and
International Studies,
Washington

4

It is instructive and sobering to recall that the 1973 oil embargo was effected by countries [in the Middle East] controlling just 6 per cent of U.S. oil supply. Today the U.S. depends on those same Middle Eastern countries for about 30 per cent of its oil supply. With over 70 per cent of free-world reserves located in the Middle East, the U.S. will become increasingly dependent on this region if an energy policy is not formulated to reduce our oil imports.

The Washington Post,
10-23:(A)12.

Donald Falk
Director, Center for
Plant Conservation,
Boston

5

I like to think that there are now two kinds of people in Washington—the ones who think it's important to conserve biological diversity for its own sake, and the ones who support biological diversity for its human benefits . . . We consider species to be like a brick in the foundation of a building. You can probably lose one or two or a dozen bricks and still have a standing house. But by the time you've lost 20 per cent of species, you're going to destabilize the entire structure. That's the way ecosystems work.

Congressional testimony, Washington/
The Christian Science Monitor, 5-26:8.

Albert Gore, Jr.
United States Senator,
D-Tennessee

6

There is an old science experiment in which a frog is put into a pan of water, and the water is

(ALBERT GORE, JR.)

slowly heated to the boiling point. The frog sits there and boils because its nervous system will not react to the gradual increase. But if you boil the water first and then put the frog in, it immediately jumps out. We are at an environmental boiling point right now. Is the destruction of one football-field's worth of forest every second enough to make the frog react and jump out of the pan? What will it take? If, as in a science-fiction movie, we had a giant invader from space clomping across the rain forests of the world with football-field-size feet—going boom, boom, boom every second—would we react? That's essentially what's going on right now.

At environmental conference
sponsored by "Time" magazine,
Boulder, Colo./
Time, 1-2:66.

1

I expect to see a dramatic change in the interaction between nations on these global environmental problems, the worst of which is the greenhouse effect, which serves as a defining metaphor to represent the impact of human civilization on the world environment with the consequent loss of species at a rate that has not occurred on Earth for the past 65 million years—the loss of forest land, the loss of the stratospheric ozone layer, the loss of topsoil, the accumulation of pollutants in the oceans and the ground water . . . There is a general tendency to dismiss problems so large and unprecedented because they are outside the scope of our historical experience, and what we call common sense. There is also a tendency to shy away from solutions that are unimaginably difficult and that require global cooperation on an unprecedented scale. But all of these obstacles mùst be overcome in the lifetimes of those now living. Or else our grandchildren will ask themselves why we didn't react. The fact is, we must.

Interview/
USA Today, 1-4:(A)11.

2

[On the giant oil spill near Valdez, Alaska]: This may be one of those defining moments that

we have heard about. A huge spill like this focuses media coverage and political attention, not only on the environment itself, but also on the larger problems for which it is a metaphor: We are spilling chemicals in massive quantities into our ground water, surface water, atmosphere and stratosphere.

The New York Times, 4-3:(A)1.

3

In the not-distant future, there will be a new "sacred agenda" in international affairs: policies that enable rescue of the global environment. This task will one day join, and even supplant, preventing the world's incineration through nuclear war as the principal test of statecraft.

At "Global Change and Our
Common Future" forum
organized by National Academy of
Sciences and Smithsonian Institution,
Washington, May 3/
The New York Times, 5-4:(A)13.

4

[On the issue of the global warming trend]: Once again, the President [Bush] has been dragged slowly and reluctantly toward the correct position when the White House should have been providing leadership. I welcome their decision finally to begin recognizing the importance of global climate change as an international issue demanding attention, but it's too early for rave reviews of a policy developed in an atmosphere of political damage control in response to Congressional pressure.

May 12/
The New York Times, 5-13:9.

John Gormley
Campaign director,
Green Party of Ireland

5

[On Dublin's air pollution]: It's disgusting. People start coughing and spluttering and people with asthma start choking. People cough up black phlegm. You can't get anything clean on the

(JOHN GORMLEY)

clothes line, the window sills are black and you have to wash your hair all the time. Even if you don't take the health risks and economic costs into account, it's just the nuisance of it all. We're meant to be the green island here, but that's a laugh.

Dublin/
The New York Times,
1-18:(A)4.

James Hansen
Director, Goddard Institute
for Space Studies,
National Aeronautics and
Space Administration
of the United States

1

[On the theory of global warming produced by a "greenhouse effect" caused by man-made changes in the environment]: Most of the scientific community would agree that the effects are going to be substantial. The National Academy of Science in the 1970s said that doubling of carbon dioxide will warm the planet someplace between one and one half and four and a half degrees Celsius. That's a huge range. But even one and a half degrees is going to make the Earth warmer than it has been in 100,000 years. Those who say the changes may be negligible are a very small segment.

Interview/
USA Today,
12-26:(A)11.

Walter Hickel
Former Secretary
of the Interior
of the United States

2

[On the massive oil spill in Alaska]: We should come down hard on the [oil] industry's laxness. But if we don't produce oil here, we'll produce it somewhere else, ship it to the U.S., and face the same risks.

USA Today,
5-10:(A)8.

Frederic D. Krupp
Executive director, Environmental
Defense Fund

3

The great failure of this [Reagan] Administration is that it blew the chance to streamline regulations and use marketplace incentives in an honest way to speed up environmental progress, lower regulatory costs and foster economic growth. Instead, the Administration abandoned any effort at progress and just accepted the weakest possible rules to protect the environment . . . We must ask the question: Is the environment better off now than it was eight years ago? The answer is clearly no.

The New York Times, 1-2:8.

William S. Lee
Chairman and president,
Duke Power Company

4

During my professional career, I have seen coal plants converted to oil for air quality, [then] oil plants converted to coal because of import concerns; nuclear plants first promoted by the Congress, then discouraged; . . . natural gas encouraged, then banned, then encouraged again as a generation fuel . . . All of which has taught our industry the virtue of being nimble.

The Christian Science Monitor,
8-8:2.

H. Jeffrey Leonard
Vice president,
Conservation Foundation

5

[On the pollution of the Great Lakes]: Millions of people in [the region] are exposed to hazardous chemicals. You drink them in contaminated water. You eat them concentrated in the flesh of the fish. You breathe them in the air. We know that these continuous exposures have a serious adverse effect on the wildlife of the region. We fear increasingly that humans, especially pregnant women, and children, may be affected as well . . . On the surface, the Great Lakes appear to be much cleaner than they were 20 years ago when Lake Erie was choking with

(H. JEFFREY LEONARD)

industrial waste and municipal sewage. The message of our report is that in subtle, and in perhaps much more dangerous ways, the Great Lakes environment is in crisis. The Great Lakes ecosystem remains a giant depository for toxic contaminants: Toxic chemicals that deform birds and fish and that are working their way up the food chain.

Chicago, Oct. 11/
Los Angeles Times, 10-12:(I)1,15.

Richard Lindzen
Professor of meteorology,
Massachusetts Institute
of Technology

1

[On an MIT study showing little or no global warming in the 20th century despite warnings by scientists about a "greenhouse effect" due to man-made changes in the environment]: As far as warming goes, we're saying we're in a situation where our models suggest there *may* be a problem. But the uncertainty in the models is very substantial—substantial enough to include the possibility that there is not a problem . . . At the moment, there's a lot of argument. Our best estimate is a half-degree rise, which almost all occurred around 1920. And nobody noticed it then. So it's hard to tell what the implications will be. It's also the case that the weather at any given position is not all that well-related to what happens over the globe. For instance, we're having a cold spell now. That's hardly a sign of global *cooling*. It's just the weather changes . . . [Atmospheric change] is potentially serious, but there is no evidence that says it's coming down our back. So we should check carefully to see what's going on, because it's a very difficult thing to do anything about.

Interview/
USA Today, 12-26:(A)11.

Manuel Lujan, Jr.
Secretary of the Interior-designate
of the United States

2

We are committed to protecting and enhancing the nation's valuable resources, as well as

proceeding with their environmentally sound development. We can do both; we do not have to choose between them.

Before Senate committee hearing
on his confirmation, Washington,
Jan. 26/
Los Angeles Times, 1-27:(I)4.

Manuel Lujan, Jr.
Secretary of the Interior
of the United States

3

[Criticizing a possible Congressional moratorium on off-shore oil drilling]: While tankers continue to spill oil into our waters, and off-shore drilling continues to provide a record of environmentally sound production, why are we attacking off-shore drilling and letting the tankers nestle into our harbors? By imposing these moratoria, the Congress is saying that we should blindly reject even the possibilities before us, burying our heads in the sands of our own ignorance.

Before Western Governors'
Association, Long Beach, Calif.,
July 18/
The Washington Post, 7-18:(A)8.

Alhaji Rilwanu Lukman
President, Organization of
Petroleum Exporting Countries

4

For many years an environment of conflict between OPEC and the West was nurtured, and it did nobody any good. Now it is time to turn the page . . . Our objective is to integrate financially and politically with the West. The West must reduce its dependence on oil. Coming from me, this seems illogical, but there is no better way to sweep suspicion . . . off the table . . . The scenario is completely changed from 10 or 15 years ago . . . The West should realize that sheiks are not as threatening to its future as they once were.

World Press Review, February:33.

Stephen McAlpine
Lieutenant Governor
of Alaska (D)

5

[On the recent Exxon oil spill in Alaska]: We're going to hold the industry's feet to the fire

(STEPHEN McALPINE)

to require them to do everything that is humanly possible to clean up . . . You're going to see the state of Alaska step in and say, "You had our trust. You had our absolute confidence. You defied that trust. And that confidence has been shattered. We are going to take over and we're not going to pay the cost. We're going to pass the cost of that on to you." There is a tremendous awareness and people are just totally repulsed by what has gone on. And they're going to demand that that anger be translated into some very strong political action.

Interview/
USA Today, 4-11:(A)11.

Edmund S. Muskie
Former Secretary of State of
the United States;
Former United States Senator,
D-Maine

1

[Public service] means protecting public health against environmental contamination. And that means strong laws on air and water pollution, toxic waste and drinking water. It means RCRA, and Superfund, the Clean Water Act, the Clean Air Act. It means raising the consciousness of the American people on the emerging challenge of global warming. It means saying no to those who seek private exceptions to pollution-control policies.

Speech in honor of just-retired
Senator Robert Stafford of Vermont,
at Environmental Law Institute/
The Washington Post, 1-6:(A)18.

Gaylord Nelson
Counselor to the Wilderness
Society; Former United States
Senator, D-Wisconsin

2

Every time some ecosystem is destroyed, it impacts people around the world. It may be indirect. What impact do all of our pollutants going into the air have on somebody in Africa, where there's no industry? Global warming is

going to affect them just as it affects everybody else. To have a magnificent ecological system destroyed by an oil spill has world-wide impact. And if you do that to every ecosystem in the world, there won't be any left. It doesn't have to be in your back yard to cause you to be dismayed about it.

Interview/
USA Today, 3-29:(A)7.

Thomas R. Pickering
United States Ambassador/
Permanent Representative
to the United Nations

3

According to current evidence, the warmest eight years of the 20th century occurred in the '80s, so obviously we are experiencing a warming trend. There is a growing consensus that pollutants, particularly gases such as carbon dioxide and methane, are increasing the degree to which the upper atmosphere absorbs heat. If this is so, and if that heat is reradiating into the lower atmosphere, we are already seeing the effects . . . We've seen maps of Florida projecting 40 years from now that show a starkly receding coastline, and some scientists think the oceans will soon become so saturated with carbon dioxide that this will have a radical effect on the warming trend. Many of the forests of the world are being mowed down as well. But the rest of the world isn't going to say, "Okay, we'll save our forests, but you Americans can keep driving all your cars!" There has to be give and take.

Interview, New York/
Cosmopolitan, September:174.

Peter Raven
Director, Missouri
Botanical Garden

4

All nations are tied together as to their common [ecological] fate. We are all facing a common problem, which is, How are we going to keep this single resource we have, namely the world, viable?

Time, 1-2:30.

William K. Reilly
Administrator, Environmental
Protection Agency
of the United States

1

People need to see the environment as a cause that is positive, hopeful and attractive. The costs that we bear to maintain the environment and improve it have to be seen as highly worthwhile investments in our future, as important as investments in education, science and defense.

Interview, Washington,
Feb. 21/
The New York Times, 2-22:(A)10.

2

One of the very disturbing realities now is that whatever we do, even if we maintain the commitments that have been made as a result of the Montreal Protocol to reduce chlorofluorocarbon manufacturing, ozone depletion will continue on for many years as a consequence of products already made that have reached the stratosphere. We're going to have to address those questions, consider the process that the protocol provides for setting higher standards perhaps over time, constantly looking at the interplay of science in public-policy responses.

Interview/
USA Today, 2-22:(A)9.

3

[Where the environment is concerned,] it's very difficult to get things done with finality. I've heard that garbage thrown into the Arctic waters takes a year to circumnavigate the pole and it's in your front yard again.

Interview/
The Washington Post, 4-28:(A)23.

4

[On President Bush's call for a move toward more clean-burning fuels for automobiles]: The President I don't think cares whether people burn ethanol or methanol, compressed natural gas or Chanel No. 5, so long as we get these pollution reductions.

Broadcast interview/
"This Week With David Brinkley,"
ABC-TV, 6-18.

Robert Repetto
Director of economic research,
World Resources Institute,
Washington

5

Just recognizing that natural resources are assets means that all of the dichotomy between environmental protection and economic growth disappears. The question of whether a country can afford to protect its resources is then seen as stupid: It cannot afford not to.

The New York Times, 6-29:(A)12.

Jeremy Rifkin
President, Foundation on
Economic Trends

6

We're finally going to get the bill for the Industrial Age. If the projections are right, it's going to be a big one: the ecological collapse of the planet.

World Press Review,
December:30.

Michel Rocard
Prime Minister of France

7

For a long time, the protection of the environment was a subject of concern to a few public figures, acting more or less in isolation, and a number of associations or movements. What we are seeing now is a more acute awareness of this requirement among political leaders.

At international conference
on Antarctica, Paris, Oct. 9/
Los Angeles Times, 10-10:(I)7.

James R. Schlesinger
Former Secretary of Energy
of the United States

8

It should be noted that, despite all our rhetoric, we Americans are doing yeoman service to restore the [OPEC] cartel's power. More than anyone else, we are adding to global demand for oil. We are allowing our domestic [oil] industry to wither and, as a consequence, rapidly raising the

(JAMES R. SCHLESINGER)

level of our oil imports. As we peer into the 1990s, we shall see a revived OPEC, one with fewer members and with power increasingly concentrated among the high-capacity producers—in brief, an inner cartel, wholly dominated by a few Persian Gulf producers. This will be brought on by the unwillingness of the consuming nations—and most notably the United States—to take the steps now that would later protect us against the worst aspects of a revival of cartel power. Regrettably, democratic societies rarely respond until a crisis has erupted. The threats of a renewed cartel upswing in oil prices lie too far in the future to spur us to action today.

Speech, London/
The New York Times, 1-4:(A)15.

Robert Stempel
President, General Motors
Corporation

1

Our [auto manufacturers'] attitude toward the environment is exactly the same as it was back in 1970. I don't know anybody in our business who is against clean water, clean air, clean earth. In our painting processes, in water runoff from our parking lots, even the water we use in building our vehicles, we return it to the river cleaner than we got it. So you get a bright, shiny car, durable finish and low emissions. But having done all of the cleanup in the car, we still get virtually no credit for it . . . Keep in mind, nobody told us how to clean up the tailpipe emissions. Nobody took the invention off the shelf. We're very proud at General Motors that our people, with a lot of blood, sweat and tears, invented the system that's used on virtually every automobile in the world.

Interview/
USA Today, 12-19:(A)11.

Margaret Thatcher
Prime Minister
of the United Kingdom

2

[On the degradation of the atmosphere by man-made chemical pollutants such as chloro-

fluorocarbons]: For centuries, mankind has worked on the assumption that we could pursue the goal of steady progress, without disturbing the fundamental equilibrium of the world's atmosphere and its living systems. In a very short space of time, that comfortable assumption has been shattered.

At international environmental
conference, London/
Los Angeles Times, 3-8:(I)6.

Crispin Tickell
British Ambassador/
Permanent Representative to
the United Nations

3

[On radioactive waste produced by nuclear power plants]: The fact that every year there is waste being produced that will take the next three ice ages, and beyond, to become harmless is something that has deeply impressed the imagination.

Time, 1-2:41.

John Wakeham
Secretary of State for Energy
of the United Kingdom

4

The developed world may well have to turn increasingly to nuclear energy to protect our environment in the years ahead and make room for more use of fossil energy in countries with less-suitable infrastructure.

At World Energy Conference
meeting, Montreal/
The New York Times, 9-25:(A)10.

Clayton K. Yeutter
Secretary of Agriculture
of the United States

5

[On the public's concern about food safety, pesticides, etc.]: We must articulate these concerns, the tradeoffs and the risk assessment that are involved in a way that the public can understand. That's the fundamental challenge. We must also be able to communicate effectively the

(CLAYTON K. YEUTTER)

degree of risk that's involved. One of the elements of the Alar apple discussion that troubled me was that so many people concluded that there might be an imminent, significant cancer risk [from Alar]. And that simply is not the case. The risk that is involved is minuscule. We have to try to avoid frightening people over these kinds of issues and try to concentrate on informing people so they can make sound judgments in an unemotional, rational environment . . . Americans should keep food-safety issues in perspective. Our food supply is safer than that of any other country in the world. Whether it is as safe as we would like it is a debatable question.

Interview/
USA Today, 4-4:(A)7.

Government

William M. Arkin
Director, national security program,
Institute for
Policy Studies
1

[On Federal secrecy and classification practices]: There is no immutable law as to what's secret. Depending on the politics of the day or how sensitive an issue is perceived at that moment or the adversarial relationship of the requester, a document may be looked at in very different ways. The idea that the bureaucracy wants to cover things up or hide certain things [to prevent embarrassment] shouldn't surprise anybody. But that shouldn't necessarily be seen as a direct political statement. I think it's a kind of philosophical lesson about secrecy, about how it can both be abused and treated in a fair manner.
The Washington Post, 3-1:(A)4.

Chester G. Atkins
United States Representative,
D-Massachusetts
2

House [ethics] rules have been set as guidelines for our behavior—standards of good conduct—but they were never meant to measure human frailty . . . If the atmosphere is poisoned—as I believe has happened in recent days [for example, the resignation of House Speaker Jim Wright because of alleged ethics violations]—excessive use of the ethics process to bring down decent but fallible officials will ensue. Unbridled negatives . . . must be checked.
Speech/
The Washington Post, 6-3:(I)23.

Donald J. Atwood
Deputy Secretary of Defense
of the United States
3

[Comparing working in government to working in private industry, where he was an executive at General Motors]: Within an industrial organiza-

tion, the supervisor has a degree of control over the activities of those that report to him without any question at all. [But in government,] when someone in DOD asks those who work for him to do something, it's the initiation of a negotiation.
Interview/
The Washington Post, 6-27:(A)21.

Les AuCoin
United States Representative,
D-Oregon
4

[On public anger over a proposed large pay increase for members of Congress]: People are ready to pick up a brick or pick up a rifle. It goes much deeper than the raise, the dollars. This has crystalized a perception that we have the rulers and the ruled. [For many people in the country, this issue has evoked] a feeling of an inability to control events.
Washington, Feb. 2/
The New York Times, 2-3:(A)8.

James A. Baker III
Secretary of State-designate
of the United States
5

[Bipartisanship] is the lubricant that enables the branches of government to overcome their natural Constitutionally designed friction, a friction that arises from our differing perspectives and our different responsibilities.
At Senate Foreign Relations
Committee hearing
on his confirmation, Washington,
Jan. 17/
The New York Times, 1-18:(A)10.

Gary Bauer
President, Family
Research Council
6

When we as a culture say that the sexual behavior and morality of our public officials is of

(GARY BAUER)

no import unless it has a direct bearing on their job performance, then we're saying to our children that matters of morality are important in some cases but not in others ... I don't think anybody sees the right to privacy as absolute. For example, any member of Congress discovered to have molested a child would quickly be turned out of office, because it's against the law and it says something about that person's moral turpitude. Almost every American has a line where the private conduct of a public official is enough to say, "I want this person out of office," even though he may be a great Congressman or Senator.

Interview/
U.S. News & World Report,
9-11:23.

Griffin Bell
Member, President
George Bush's ethics
commission;
Former Attorney General
of the United States

1

[Saying high government officials should be banned from accepting honoraria]: The evil of honoraria is so great—from the appearance of a conflict of interest. People wonder who's paying all these honoraria. It undermines confidence in government.

Washington, Feb. 22/
Los Angeles Times, 2-23:(I)20.

William J. Bennett
Director, White House Office
of Drug Abuse Policy

2

[Saying people who used drugs in their youth should not necessarily be disqualified from high Federal government office]: Do I believe it should be disqualification if someone has used drugs? No, not necessarily ... I think if somebody has used marijuana one or two or three times—back then, back then—it shouldn't necessarily be a bar ... When we look back on the

late '60s and '70s, we should think of how it was and how it was perceived. It was very easy for a lot of people just to do it, just to try it ... You have all sorts of people coming into government with youthful indiscretions. The problem is to balance that with a very clear message to young people. I think we can do that by pointing out that the '60s were one time that has long passed, not to be repeated again.

To reporters, Washington,
March 13/
The Washington Post, 3-14:(A)25.

Derek C. Bok
President, Harvard University

3

Does our present conservatism stem from a sincere conviction that we need to shift more responsibility from Washington to the grass roots and more from government hands to private hands? Or is it a lofty rationalization for selfishness, for cutting regulations and lowering taxes simply to leave us more money and freedom for our own private pleasure?

At George Mason University
commencement/
USA Today, 5-24:(A)9.

Carol Bonosaro
President, Senior
Executives Association

4

No corporation could treat its personnel like the government treats civil servants and expect to retain and attract a highly trained and qualified work-force.

USA Today, 3-30:(A)10.

William J. Brennan
Associate Justice,
Supreme Court
of the United States

5

[Referring to the late Supreme Court Chief Justice Earl Warren]: Possessed of an equal right to vote, the least of us, he thought, would be armed with an effective weapon needed to

(WILLIAM J. BRENNAN)

achieve a fair share of the benefits of our free society. In sum, he perceived that at the core of the process of government erected by the framers—unwieldy, imperfect, wearisome, sometimes maddening—lay a profound vision of justice, and that it was the duty of the Court to make that vision a reality for the least of men.

Speech, San Francisco, April 8/
The New York Times, 4-13:(A)10.

John Buckley
Director of communications,
National Republican
Congressional Committee

1

[On the current scandal about Defense Secretary-designate John Tower's drinking habits]: It's precisely the same mood of revolutionary justice that hit after [former Senator] Gary Hart was brought down [for alleged extra-marital affairs]. You don't know from day to day what the rules are. You don't know which heads will roll or when the jeep will pull up in front of your building with portable gallows. Just as in the wake of Gary Hart any politician who chased skirts had a death wish, I would venture to guess that people will give a very wide berth to the bar at the Monocle [restaurant] on the way to their dinner table.

The New York Times, 3-3:(A)12.

William Bulger
President, Massachusetts
State Senate (D)

2

Government has a tendency to push itself into all sorts of realms where it worsens situations instead of improving them. Democrats, and especially liberal Democrats who've done many, many things on a generous and good impulse, have nevertheless done things very unwisely. There's this very unfortunate sense that not to pour money into a solution is to mean that one doesn't care about the problem, one doesn't even see it as a problem. At first, I think people set forth to convince others they are sensitive and caring about various things by wanting to create a

program around them. After awhile, they've convinced themselves that they're the only ones who care. There are many ways, public and private, to show you care. All I say is, don't subsidize what you feel with someone else's money.

The Wall Street Journal,
7-12:(A)14.

George Bush
Vice President, and
President-elect,
of the United States

3

Do you think the President of the United States should have the right to go unattended to a grocery store? Would he be in better touch with what the average American faces? Would he be able to understand better the problems of the people if he could go and browse through the racks of a clothing store and look at the price tags, on sale or not on sale? . . . Would he be a better President because he can go to the house of some little kid he reads about who was hurt, without bringing a lot of cameras in there to look like he was doing it for publicity purposes? That's my question. Would the President be more in touch with the people if he can do these things from the heart in an effort to lead as normal a life as possible? Would he not be better equipped to wrestle with the problems of the American people? And I think the answer is yes.

Interview, Washington/
USA Today, 1-9:(A)11.

4

[On the staffing of his Administration]: I am particularly concerned that our search reach the men and women in America who are too often overlooked in such efforts, Americans who—let's be frank—our [Republican] Party has perhaps done too little to include in the past. I want them, too. Black-Americans, Hispanic-Americans, Asian-Americans, disabled Americans—not as tokens, but as talent.

Before Presidential Personnel
Advisory Committee,
Washington, Jan. 9/
The New York Times, 1-10:(A)11.

(GEORGE BUSH)

1

[On the members of his new Cabinet]: I'm going to tell them to think big. I'm going to tell them to challenge the system. I'm going to tell them, as each one of them has demonstrated, to adhere to the highest ethical standards. I'm going to tell them I don't like "kiss and tell" books.

Washington, Jan. 12/
Los Angeles Times, 1-13:(I)1.

George Bush
President of the United States

2

[Saying he wants to cooperate with the Democratic majority in Congress]: This is the age of the offered hand. Let us negotiate soon, and hard. But, in the end, let us produce. The American people await action. They didn't send us here to bicker.

Inaugural address,
Washington, Jan. 20/
The Washington Post, 1-21:(A)6.

3

No President, no government can teach us to remember what is best in what we are. But if the man you have chosen to lead this government can help make a difference, if he can celebrate the quieter, deeper successes that are made not of gold and silk but of better hearts and finer souls— if he can do these things, then he must.

Inaugural address,
Washington, Jan. 20/
The Washington Post, 1-21:(A)10.

4

We've been talking this week about ethics [in government]. The emphasis is not, believe me, a fad or some passing fancy; we're going to be hearing more about it, I think a lot more. In broader terms, I'm trying to set high standards for government service—duty, honor, personal sacrifice for the common good. And I want to assemble a government that the people of this nation can be proud of. That's our goal, that's our mission.

News conference,
Washington, Jan. 27/
The New York Times, 1-28:6.

5

If I say something [as Vice President] that just hurts *me,* that's one thing. [But] if I say something that might hurt the President, I would be very much concerned about that. That made me very cautious, because I didn't want to do that when I was Vice President. I think we would all agree I took a lot of shots for not speaking up in Cabinet meetings, for example [during the Reagan Administration]. Some erroneously concluded that meant I didn't have any ideas or I didn't have any opinions.

Interview,
Washington/
Time, 1-30:26.

6

I don't think about my schedule in terms of image. I think of it in terms of substance; doing things that need to be done. Today, we had a listen-and-learn session with those law-enforcement people, then a speech to re-emphasize my crime package. Then, back to the South Lawn event; then the NSC; then an RNC reception. But each one makes sense, and I do not encourage image-builders to set my schedule so that there is only one event. The proof of the pudding is in the doing, not in the *appearance.* I want to accomplish certain things, and I am less interested in image than in getting things done.

Interview,
Washington/
U.S. News & World Report,
6-26:27.

Joan Claybrook
President, Public Citizen

7

This is a democracy. The whole purpose of having the Congress subject to regular re-election is to force members to make decisions, stand behind them and accept the responsibility for them. But now the attitude is, anything to avoid the hard choices, anything to avoid accountability to the electorate, anything to avoid the possibility of ballot-box punishment.

The New York Times,
2-2:(A)13.

John Creedon
Chief executive officer,
Metropolitan Life Insurance
Company

1

I don't think ethics *per se* is going to discourage people from running for office or from aspiring to government jobs. But the climate of investigating people and putting them through the third degree in connection with possible positions [in government] may have gone too far. What could discourage people are rules on what you can do after you leave government service. Those are quite onerous. One of the reasons people go into government is to get intensive experience in a particular specialty, certainly in the law, and then use it in private practice. You can do that without doing anything wrong, without having any real conflict of interest. But to the extent that there are limitations on that, it is discouraging.

Interview/
USA Today, 6-7:(A)11.

Lloyd N. Cutler
Chairman, Federal
Pay Commission

2

While members [of Congress] have an obvious financial interest in approving salary increases [for themselves], they have a much more powerful political interest in disapproving increases.

USA Today, 2-3:(A)12.

Richard G. Darman
Director-designate,
Federal Office of
Management and Budget

3

I think it's very important for a [new] Presidency to establish a degree of the perception of its strength. If you start an Administration with a highly visible, highly advertised loss, you permanently weaken that Presidency for whatever else it might do.

At Senate Governmental Affairs
Committee hearing
on his confirmation, Washington,
Jan. 19/
The New York Times, 1-20:(A)12.

Richard G. Darman
Director,
Federal Office of
Management and Budget

4

[On recent scandals in Federal departments and programs]: There are too many people in positions of political responsibility who are infatuated by the lure of glitter and lights—and the often illusory chance to make policy . . . and too few interested in . . . the more pedestrian work of nuts-and-bolts management.

The Washington Post, 10-6:(A)22.

Thomas A. Daschle
United States Senator,
D-South Dakota

5

[On President Bush's inaugural address]: In many ways he sounded like a Democrat, talking about the homeless, poor women and children we need to reach out to . . . In contrast to [former President Ronald] Reagan, who said the government is our enemy, [Bush] knows the power of government can be used for good.

Jan. 20/
The Washington Post, 1-21:(A)11.

Edward J. Derwinski
Under Secretary for Security
Assistance, Department of State
of the United States;
Former United States Representative,
R-Illinois

6

It's one of the most curious contradictions of the Washington scene. George Shultz will go out of the Secretary of State's office on January 21 as the member of the Reagan Cabinet most influential and most respected on Capitol Hill. I believe the same will be true of [Shultz's designated successor] Jim Baker in the Bush Cabinet. It was true, too, of most of their recent predecessors. Henry Kissinger dazzled them on the Hill. Cy Vance did very well in his quieter way. Ed Muskie was regarded as one of their own. Yet their prestige never has extended to the institution that they headed. The State Department

(EDWARD J. DERWINSKI)

does not have the cozy relationships that exist between Congress and such bureaucracies as the Treasury and Agriculture Department. Among the Federal entities, the State Department ranks very low in the affections of Congress.

Interview/
The Washington Post, 1-2:(A)17.

Frank Donatelli
Political Director for
President of the United States
Ronald Reagan

1

[On why President Reagan is so popular as he nears the end of his second, and last, term]: Some people dismiss it as personality, but I would call it leadership. There's nothing a President can do to please a majority of the people all the time. He has to take too many actions, there are too many shades of gray. What makes a great President is the ability to take certain actions the public might not agree with, and still maintain their trust.

The New York Times, 1-18:(A)8.

Allen Drury
Author

2

[On recent scandals involving the private lives of government officials which have resulted in the loss of their positions or non-confirmation of their appointments to high government office]: It's not a disaster if somebody has to be reasonably sober when dealing with the public business. But the unfortunate trend now established is one must tell all and promise all and be a good, good, good boy and promise to be a good, good, good boy forever after. It's not only ridiculous, it's humiliating and sad.

The New York Times, 3-3:(A)12.

Marlin Fitzwater
Press Secretary to
President of the United States
George Bush

3

We [the Bush Administration] don't hire people that don't support our policies. That is a

hard and fast rule . . . Anybody who comes into a policy-making position is asked if they can support our policy.

Washington, Nov. 1/
Los Angeles Times, 11-2:(A)29.

Thomas S. Foley
United States Representative,
D-Washington;
Speaker of the House

4

I am Speaker of the whole House, not of one party but to each and every member of the House, undivided by the center aisle. Politics involves the clash of ideas, and we will enevitably have disagreements [between the Democratic and Republican members]. We must be careful that our desire for comity and bipartisanship does not deter us from considering contentious issues and debating them vigorously . . . Let us debate and decide with intensity, even passionate intensity, but let us debate and decide with respect, not rancor.

Before the House,
Washington, June 6/
Los Angeles Times, 6-7:(I)17.

Anthony M. Frank
Postmaster General
of the United States

5

[On whether the Postal Service will contract out some of its operations to the private sector]: Any decisions to contract out significant work elements will be difficult; they are likely to cause protest, bring political pressure, and sorely test this organization's mettle. But if some additional contracting in non-critical areas makes sense for our customers and for the long-term good of the Postal Service, then we must have the courage to make the hard decisions.

Nation's Business, March:8.

6

There's a lot of pride and a lot of love affairs between the American people and the [postal letter] carrier out there because that's the person

(ANTHONY M. FRANK)

they see, mainly. In tens of thousands of places, it is our Post Office that holds the community together and our Postmaster leads that community and represents that community. If you try to close a Post Office, then it represents the closing of a community.

Interview/
USA Today, 4-17:(A)11.

Barney Frank
United States Representative,
D-Massachusetts

1

When people are mad at the Presidency, they're mad at the President. When they're mad at Congress, they are not mad at their individual Congressman.

The Washington Post, 11-10:(A)4.

Steven Garfinkel
Director, Federal Information
Security Oversight Office

2

[On Federal secrecy and classification practices]: What remains sensitive is not a clearly objective standard. You cannot standardize what is classified and what is not classified. It is not an objective decision. From my experience, it's not unusual for two people to look at documents and come to different conclusions.

The Washington Post, 3-1:(A)4.

Leonard Garment
Lawyer; Former Adviser to the
President of the United States
(Richard Nixon)

3

[On alleged corruption among government officials and Indian tribal leaders]: Whatever corruption may exist here is what happens wherever government is given large amounts of money to dispense, great power over people's lives, and great discretion in using that power, whether it is in a poverty program or a small-business administration or the Department of

Defense. What we are seeing is not Indian corruption. It is the corruption that occurs almost universally when government has too much discretionary power and individuals too little.

Before Senate Committee on
Indian Affairs,
Washington, Jan. 30/
The Wall Street Journal, 3-9:(A)16.

Newt Gingrich
United States Representative,
R-Georgia

4

[On the ethics of members of Congress]: I've always said you have to distinguish between sin, which is private conduct, and being a scoundrel, which is public conduct. The [House] Ethics Committee's primary business is to focus on scoundrels.

The Washington Post, 10-2:(A)12.

Allan E. Gotlieb
Canadian Ambassador
to the United States

5

The most important part of diplomacy here [in Washington] is not necessarily conducted behind closed doors. I've devoted a tremendous amount of my time to [Capitol] Hill, and you work in public there. I've called on Senators on such contentious issues as hogs and cable broadcasting and corn, to find the Senators have their own cameras there. This kind of diplomacy is by nature public . . .

Interview, Washington/
The New York Times, 1-12:(A)12.

Fred I. Greenstein
Chairman, department of
political science,
Princeton University

6

[Saying that President Bush has had a low-key Administration so far]: Being unoffensive builds no credit. A sense begins to develop that there is less there than meets the eye. If Bush makes things too small, when he really wants some-

(FRED I. GREENSTEIN)

thing, people won't have any reason to pay attention. As soon as there's something to be unhappy about, they'll turn on you the way they did on Gerald Ford when he pardoned [Richard] Nixon. At some point [Bush] might start getting [Calvin] Coolidge jokes. As Dorothy Parker said when she was told Coolidge had passed away, she replied, "How did they know?"

The New York Times, 4-14:(A)9.

Lee H. Hamilton
United States Representative,
D-Indiana

1

[On the possible "peace dividend," a large saving in government expenditures for the military as a result of the current lessening of superpower tensions]: It seems clear that we will soon be faced with major choices about how to employ the peace dividend. Should it be used for deficit reduction, tax cuts, new spending programs or some combination of those purposes? Is this an appropriate occasion for a major reordering of priorities? Will the size of the budgetary savings make a difference in performance of the economy on a national or regional level, and should government policies be modified accordingly.

At Congressional Joint Economic
Committee hearing,
Washington, Dec. 19/
The New York Times, 12-20:(A)12.

Ken Hechler
Secretary of State
of West Virginia

2

[On the Electoral College]: It ought to be abolished. It's not a very good way to run a railroad. It was set up by the Founding Fathers because they didn't trust the people to make the right choice. Their initial idea was that wise men would get together and make the choice because the people, in the end, couldn't be trusted. It's time has come.

The New York Times, 1-4:(A)8.

Stephen Hess
Scholar, Brookings Institution

3

The Presidency is always a compared-to-whom position. You have the "Great Communicator" [President Reagan], and [President-elect] George Bush is never going to be able to tell the anecdote or give the set speech or wave to the crowds *a la* Ronald Reagan. But he will do better in the press conference. He's more attuned to data. Press conferences are about giving information as precisely as possible, and Ronald Reagan was basically a storyteller. He couldn't get used to that format, and he was lazy. He wasn't able to commit the time to prepare for it. The press conference is George Bush's forte.

The Washington Post, 1-14:(A)4.

Gordon J. Humphrey
United States Senator,
R-New Hampshire

4

[Criticizing a proposed salary increase for Congress, which would go into effect automatically unless voted down by Congress]: The sneaky pay raise of 1989 is more than a matter of money. A pay raise without a vote is stealing. A pay raise without a vote is more than mere greed, it is debauchery. A pay raise without a vote is more than mere cleverness, it is cowardice.

Jan. 25/
Los Angeles Times, 1-26:(I)11.

5

[Saying he will not run for a third term]: Twelve years is the right place to round it off. Eighteen years is too darn long. Serving in Congress should not be a career ... You get burned out and lose touch and less effectively serve the country.

News conference, Concord, N.H.,
March 6/
The Washington Post, 3-7:(A)14.

Jesse L. Jackson
Civil-rights leader

6

Washington [D.C.] deserves statehood status. It would end the contradiction of Congress as the occupying force over the cradle of democracy, treating it as a domestic colony. Congress, a group of people who sit above Washington, unaccountable to its people, has the power to appropriate land and to determine the form and the base for the city. It can expand or restrict the budget and can impose its will on the people . . . More people live in Washington—about 650,000 who pay billions in taxes—than live in Delaware or Vermont or North Dakota or Wyoming—and they [those states] have Senators and Congress-people who vote. So the issue of taxation without representation, as a form of tyranny, is real. While there is a tremendous focus on the Mayor's issue in Washington, the fact is that D.C. deserves two U.S. Senators, a Governor, an Attorney General, a Lieutenant Governor. Its status needs to be upgraded. It is a critical civil-rights issue.

Interview/USA Today, 7-26:(A)7.

John W. Keker
Prosecutor at trial of
Oliver North for his
involvement in the
U.S. Iran-contra scandal

1

The charges in this case . . . go to the very heart of our self-government. They involve the need for honesty in the government, especially between the branches of the government, between the Congress and the President . . . Government by deception is not a free government. Government by deception is not a democratic government. Government by deception is not a government under the rule of law. Telling the truth is an important principle in this government.

Summation at trial of Oliver North,
Washington, April 18/
The Washington Post, 4-19:(A)8.

Jack Kemp
Secretary of Housing and
Urban Development
of the United States

2

What a limited view of America to think that the Federal government is the sole repository of all answers and all resources. The great resource of this country is the people . . . the private sector of this country.

Before House Budget Committee,
Washington, March 2/
The Washington Post, 3-3:(A)5.

Robert M. Kimmitt
Under Secretary for Political
Affairs, Department of State
of the United States

3

[On those who were surprised when new Secretary of State James Baker brought in his own team of principal advisers at the State Department]: I think a big part of the problem was that this [the assumption of power by the new Bush Administration] was a "friendly takeover" from one Republican Administration to another. A lot of people assumed that they were entitled to stay and, when that didn't happen, they were disappointed. If it had been an unfriendly take-over—from Republicans to Democrats—a new team would have come in and said "throw the rascals out" and that would have been the end of it.

The New York Times, 3-27:(A)6.

Henry A. Kissinger
Former Secretary of State
of the United States

4

In government, somebody finally must say, "I've now heard all the talk, and we are going *here*." Nobody can lift that from the shoulders of the President. But he cannot avoid the curse of giving a sense of direction by hedging. That's the most important thing I learned in government. The tendency is to try to do a little of everything. Once you've decided, you pay the same price for doing the thing properly as for doing it half-heartedly.

Interview/Los Angeles Times, 4-30:(V)1.

Edward I. Koch
Mayor of New York

5

Over time, society changes. So must the government which serves it. Practices or poli-

(EDWARD I. KOCH)

cies that might have seemed unacceptable to our grandparents or unusual to our parents seem equitable, indeed necessary, to our generation. We honor the past, but we cannot be held captive to it.

New York, Aug. 7/
The Washington Post, 8-8:(A)6.

Vitaly Korotich
Editor, "Ogonyok"
(Soviet Union)

1

I was very impressed—and pleased—by how the transfer of power from [U.S. President Ronald] Reagan to [new President] George Bush was accomplished. I attended the inauguration and later, when Reagan waved farewell, two women near me began to cry. They were very upset; they wanted Reagan to stay on. I am sure that many people in the U.S. felt the same way, but he could not stay. Democracy is a strict affair . . . What I sensed most keenly in the U.S. is that people make demands on their President because they elect him by a relatively direct ballot. America has a great many shortcomings and a great many difficulties, but Americans have elected a new President and, instead of hanging up his portrait everywhere, they demand that he make America better.

Interview/
World Press Review, May:26.

Irving Kristol
Political analyst

2

[Comparing Washington with New York]: . . . Washington is a cruel town. New York is cruel in a financial way; Wall Street fires people right and left. But they can always come back and get other jobs; they haven't lost anything permanent. In New York, people pursue money, which is not a zero-sum game. No one has to lose money for you to make money. Everyone can make money. [But] the thrust in Washington is power, which is part of a zero-sum game. One accumulates power by taking it from someone else, who loses

it. That makes for viciousness. New York is ruthless but not vicious. In Washington, someone who gets cut off at the knees can never come back. If he had been the head of a Wall Street firm that went bust, he could return. This makes Washington a very cruel town for people who fall out of favor with Congress or the Executive or the media. They can't come back.

Interview/
The Wall Street Journal,
7-31:(A)12.

Jim Leach
United States Representative,
R-Iowa

3

[On the public's attitude against a pay raise for members of Congress and other Federal officials]: This was an issue that offended the sensibilities of the whole country, to an absolutely extraordinary degree. It is never easy to defy that depth of feeling. Maybe it's also true that you can afford to be a whole step ahead of the people when the national interest is unambiguously involved, but you can't afford to get even half a step ahead when it looks like self-interest.

The New York Times, 2-7:(A)10.

Carl M. Levin
United States Senator, D-Michigan

4

[On ethics legislation, which recently took effect, that puts restrictions on government employees who seek jobs in private industry]: It undermines confidence in government if people who negotiate for the government go to work on the same contract for private industry. There has to be some kind of breakwall between representing the government on day one and the contractor on day two. This law provides a two-year cooling-off period, which is reasonable.

The Washington Post, 5-23:(A)8.

Drew Lewis
Chief executive officer,
Union Pacific Corporation;
Former Secretary of Transportation
of the United States

5

. . . anybody who's really qualified for some of those jobs [in the Federal government] is fre-

(DREW LEWIS)

quently somebody with a conflict [of interest]. If you're going to hire a highway administrator, you want somebody who knows highways. And now, with all these conflict-of-interest rules, it's difficult to get qualified people to serve in the position because it turns out they have a conflict.

Interview/
USA Today, 6-7:(A)11.

1

My greatest disappointment in Washington was the caliber of the Congress. Most of the people I've seen we wouldn't hire as a warehouse manager.

Interview/
USA Today,
6-7:(A)11.

Jerry Lewis
United States Representative,
R-California

2

[On House rules in the wake of recent government ethics scandals]: Over the years, the rules have been amended to the point that they are now so complex and there are enough gray areas in them that it allows members to cross the lines without knowing it. It has created a situation where many a person finds himself charged with a violation that he never intended.

Los Angeles Times, 4-16:(I)20.

Bob Livingston
United States Representative,
R-Louisiana

3

[Saying Congressional salaries are too low]: [As a Congressman,] I live from paycheck to paycheck, like everybody else. We're surviving, but we're not saving anything. We're in greater debt today, substantially greater debt, than when we came here 12 years ago.

The New York Times, 1-5:(A)10.

Thurgood Marshall
Associate Justice,
Supreme Court
of the United States

4

The true miracle was not the birth of the Constitution, but its life—a life nurtured through two turbulent centuries of our own making, and a life embodying much good fortune that was not.

USA Today, 3-3:(A)8.

John S. McCain III
United States Senator,
R-Arizona

5

[On the Senate]: This is no longer a group of guys who get together and socialize, who go to each other's offices after a vote, sit down and have a few drinks . . . Instead, we're on planes back to our home states. Senators used to spend more time in Washington, work at a more leisurely pace. Friendships were built that crossed party lines . . . and there was a sense of protectiveness toward colleagues [that is not there any more].

The Washington Post, 3-13:(A)6.

David McCullough
Author, Historian

6

Congress, for all its faults, has not been the unbroken parade of clowns and thieves and posturing windbags so often portrayed . . . What should be spoken of more often, and more widely understood, are the great victories that have been won here, the decisions of courage and the vision achieved.

At joint session commemorating
200th anniversary of convening of
First Congress, Washington,
March 2/
The Washington Post, 3-3:(A)14.

John McDermid
Minister of Privatization
of Canada

7

[On the privatization of government-run companies and services]: If a corporation in the

(JOHN McDERMID)

possession of the government no longer serves a public-policy role and can grow in the private sector more than in the public, it is a candidate for privatization. Services have to be provided, but governments don't necessarily have to provide them.

Ottawa, Canada, July 7/
The New York Times, 7-8:27.

James McDermott
United States Representative-elect,
D-Washington;
Former Washington State Senator

1

State legislatures are the laboratories of democracy. If the states can get it rolling, they can point the way for the Federal government.

The New York Times, 1-3:(A)1.

Robert H. Michel
United States Representative,
R-Illinois

2

[On the Democratic Party's long control of the House]: Thirty-five years of uninterrupted power can act like a corrosive acid upon the restraints of civility and comity. Those who have been kings of the Hill for so long may forget that majority status is not a divine right—and minority status is not a permanent condition.

Before the House, Washington,
June 6/
Los Angeles Times, 6-7:(I)17.

George J. Mitchell
United States Senator,
D-Maine

3

It may be good government to ban honoraria. But is it good government to have a situation where only persons with very large wealth could serve in the Senate? I don't mean to minimize the problem of honoraria but, as a practical matter, it's not going to be prohibited until there's

some adjustment in compensation [government salaries].

Interview/
USA Today, 2-27:(A)9.

4

You've got a number of policy statements . . . that call for increased Federal spending in a large number of areas. And you have another one that calls for meaningful deficit reduction. We [in government] confront that all the time. Each of us determines the public interest through the prism of our private view.

The Washington Post, 3-1:(A)5.

5

[On the Senate]: The press of business, the number and complexity of the issues and the demands on time and attention are so much greater now that the image of a tightly knit social club just doesn't correspond with reality.

The Washington Post, 3-13:(A)6.

6

[President Bush] wants to be the President to go to Mars, he wants to be the education President, he wants to be the environment President, he wants to be the drug-fighting President and, of course, at the same time he wants to be the no-tax President. And all of those desires cannot be reconciled.

The Washington Post, 9-26:(A)8.

John Joseph Moakley
United States Representative,
D-Massachusetts

7

The Moakley style handling the [House] Rules Committee [which he chairs] isn't different from the Moakley style handling anybody or anything. I've learned a long time ago that the best way to get things done is not to surprise your opponents, although you don't have to give them everything they want. But just let them know what's coming out. And style, sometimes more than substance, can help you through a situa-

(JOHN JOSEPH MOAKLEY)

tion. On the big bills, we've called the Republicans, sat down with them, listened to their problems. And we gave them some of the things they wanted, rather than the old style of saying, "Hey, we've [the Democrats] got the votes. Let's vote. Screw you." I don't play that game, because we have an old Irish proverb—the people you meet on the way up the ladder are the same people you meet on the way down. I would like to be treated by some of those people the way I think I'm treating them.

Interview/
The Washington Post, 9-12:(A)19.

Edmund S. Muskie
Former Secretary of State
of the United States;
Former United States Senator,
D-Maine

1

What binds us first is a belief that there is honor, accomplishment and satisfaction in a public-service career. Politics is often reviled as a job for people who aren't qualified to do anything else. Bismarck said it ruins the character. Disraeli found no honor in it. Ben Franklin advised against going into it . . . We are also bound by a common belief in the purpose of public service. And that is the improvement of people's lives.

Speech in honor of just-retired
Senator Robert Stafford of Vermont,
at Environmental Law Institute/
The Washington Post, 1-6:(A)18.

Ralph Nader
Lawyer; Consumer advocate

2

[Criticizing Congressmen who tried to pass legislation giving themselves a large pay raise, legislation which was defeated]: I think we need a large amount of organic detergent to wash out the mouths of these pompous, arrogant members of Congress.

Washington, Feb. 7/
The New York Times, 2-8:(A)10.

3

[Arguing against a pay raise for Congress]: Members of Congress are in the public service, not in the for-profit service. If they want to make a lot of money, they can quit and go across the street to a private law firm and get more money than they deserve.

News conference, Washington,
Nov. 13/
Los Angeles Times, 11-14:(A)4.

John Palmer
Dean, Maxwell School
of Citizenship,
Syracuse (N.Y.) University

4

[On Congress' recent decision to kill a pay raise for themselves and other Federal officials]: My sense is that you have to deal with this issue in a straightforward way. There should have been plans for a straight-up vote on the raise, closely tied to a restriction on honorariums, along with a strong attempt to educate the public on the need for a raise. They never tried to make the case for why it would be a good deal [to increase salaries and stop honorariums] . . . I would have proposed a series of smaller increases phased in through the front door, instead of trying to get one lump sum through the back door.

Los Angeles Times, 2-8:(I)18.

Richard J. Phelan
Special Counsel,
House Ethics Committee

5

[Saying Congressmen should not be allowed to get away with brinksmanship in adhering to House ethics rules]: If, under any reading of these rules, this steering on the line, or near the line, or next to the line, or carefully on the line, were to be accepted and encouraged and endorsed by this Committee, not only would these rules be declared a sham, not only would they be declared a nice artifice to get around the integrity of this body and this Committee, but they would stand as precedent that when push came to shove, when interpretation came to what it ought to be, the Committee did not stand up and say,

(RICHARD J. PHELAN)

"The integrity of this House, the confidence of the American people, are here to be tested."

Before House Ethics Committee,
Washington, May 23/
The New York Times, 5-24:(A)1.

Roger B. Porter
Assistant to President
of the United States
George Bush
for Economic and
Domestic Policy

1

Most of the Presidents we eulogize are those who acted dramatically in crisis. We have tended to equate success and action. We sometimes confuse action with accomplishment. A President is instantly under enormous pressure to "do something." It is vitally important for him to have his emotions under control.

Time, 8-14:20.

Dan Quayle
Vice President
of the United States

2

[Saying the Bush Administration has been patient and prudent in setting up its policies]: We've seen over the years that even the most well-intentioned and flashy "agendas" may not be well-thought-out agendas and may have consequences that are bad for the country. Quick fixes are often bad fixes . . . Having an agenda is not inconsistent with a certain amount of patience and prudence. We do have an agenda. But it's a long-term agenda, based on planning and deliberation, looking to the long run.

Before National Press Club,
Washington, March 16/
The New York Times, 3-17:(A)14.

3

[As Vice President,] you have to watch every single word you utter. Every once in a while, you let a word or phrase out and you want to catch it and bring it back. You can't do that. It's gone, gone forever.

U.S. News & World Report,
5-29:26.

4

I think [former Vice President] Walter Mondale changed the role of the modern Vice Presidency. He was the activist, who attended all the meetings and was right on top of everything. Then [former Vice President] George Bush continued in that same vein. Presidents [Jimmy] Carter and [Ronald] Reagan both knew that was important. And now, naturally, under President Bush I have that good fortune . . . Of course, Presidents and Vice Presidents disagree. A good President wants the honest input of all the top people around him. But once a decision is made, then we all go out and support it.

Interview/
USA Today, 12-26:(D)2.

Dan Rather
Anchorman, CBS News

5

[Saying President-elect Bush may have better relations with the press than President Reagan did]: The early indications are that it's going to be better . . . that George Bush will hold more and more regular news conferences . . . The question is whether it lasts. Because, unquestionably, the new President is going to get advice from all these people who make their living being media manipulators. They're going to say to him, "All you need to do to be a success is just let me handle it. Don't do anything that I tell you not to do." They're already pounding on him about that. So we'll see if the new access [to Bush by the press] lasts. I hope it does. Because he'll be better served, and the country will be better served, if he listens to his own instincts—at least some of the time.

Los Angeles Times, 1-20:(VI)25.

Ronald Reagan
President of the United States

6

Ours was the first revolution in the history of mankind that truly reversed the course of govern-

(RONALD REAGAN)

ment, and with three little words: "We the people." "We the people" tell the government what to do; it doesn't tell us. "We the people" are the driver; the government is the car. And we decide where it should go and by what route and how fast. Almost all the world's constitutions are documents in which governments tell the people what their privileges are. Our Constitution is a document in which "We the people" tell the government what it is allowed to do . . . Man is not free unless government is limited. There's a clear cause and effect here that is as neat and predictable as a law of physics: As government expands, liberty contracts.

Broadcast address to the nation,
Washington, Jan. 11/
The Washington Post,
1-12:(A)8.

1

One of the things about the Presidency is that you're always somewhat apart. You spend a lot of time going by too fast in a car someone else is driving, and seeing the people through tinted glass—the parents holding up a child, and the wave you saw too late and couldn't return. And so many times I wanted to stop, and reach out from behind the glass, and connect.

Broadcast address to the nation,
Washington, Jan. 11/
The Washington Post, 1-12:(A)8.

2

I came here with a pretty set program in my mind of what government should be and what it was intended to be by the Founding Fathers, and where it had violated those precepts, and my determination to change it . . . [The late Democratic President] Franklin Roosevelt, when I voted for him, had a platform of reducing Federal spending by 25 per cent, returning to states and local governments and to the people the authority and autonomy that had been unjustly seized by the Federal government, and the elimination of useless boards and commissions. Well now, which [party] today is at home with that type of

program? Ours [the Republicans], not the party he was representing at that time.

Interview, Washington, Jan. 18/
The New York Times,
1-19:(A)14.

3

[Criticizing the Constitutional amendment limiting a President to two terms]: I can tell you what I feel about that amendment. Now that no one could accuse me of thinking this for myself or my own benefit [since he is about to leave office after two terms], I feel that—never mind the individual who is holding the Presidency at the time—that [amendment] is an infringement of the democratic rights of the American people. This is the only office that is chosen by all the people. And I think they have a right to vote for whoever they want to vote for and for as long. You have people 30 and 40 years sitting up in the legislature. What is so different that says to the people, "Oh, no, you can't do that for this office [the] Presidency"?

Interview, Washington, Jan. 18/
USA Today,
1-19:(A)9.

Dan Rostenkowski
United States Representative,
D-Illinois

4

[On the controversy over a proposed pay increase for members of Congress]: Each member of this House, Democrat and Republican, is worth a salary [increase to] $135,000 a year. Our decisions affect all Americans. The domestic and foreign policies of the most powerful nation in the world are shaped in the committee rooms and on the floor of this House. The responsibility we exercise is unmatched in any private-sector job. I'm not up here to sing the blues. I asked for this job and I work hard to keep it. In my home town of Chicago, they call politics a blood sport. I've been pretty successful at it. I don't apologize for getting in the arena and I'll be damned if I'll apologize for winning. Yet that is what this [salary] debate has reduced us to—apologizing for serving in the United States

(DAN ROSTENKOWKSI)

House of Representatives. That is wrong. I don't say that with any malice, just profound disappointment.

Before the House,
Washington, Feb. 7/
The Washington Post, 2-8:(A)25.

Warren Rudman
United States Senator,
R-New Hampshire

1

We are reaching a very thin line in mixing up private morality with public ethics. And when we start talking about private morality in terms of public ethics, I dare say those of us in public life had better start wearing very heavily armored vests.

Before the Senate,
Washington, March 7/
USA Today, 3-8:(A)5.

Larry J. Sabato
Professor of government,
University of Virginia

2

Democracy is messy. Democracy is never neat and never pure in a society that teems with different peoples and interests. To expect unrealistic perfection and purity is to guarantee that you will build a jerry-rig that will end up collapsing.

Interview, Charlottesville, Va./
The Christian Science Monitor,
4-27:8.

3

[On whether public officials' private lives should be public matters that affect their election chances or their continued serving in office]: If you were to eliminate everyone who exercised bad judgment, we would empty the halls of Congress. Only Mother Teresa could serve, and she's not an American citizen . . . Most people should be concerned about where candidates stand on the issues and what they really care

about. What they are like in the bedroom is purely private and is mostly on a completely separate track from their public behavior. Some people disagree very strongly with this, but many successful people operate on two tracks. [Congressman] Barney Frank [who has said publicly that he is homosexual] is an excellent example. By all accounts, here is a very able, competent, intelligent, accomplished legislator. His professional life is in order and highly successful; his private life is a mess. Well, how do you pick public officials? Do we have to insist that both their public and their private life be in perfect order? You dramatically reduce the pool of good candidates if you do that.

Interview/
U.S. News & World Report,
9-11:23.

Michael J. Sandel
Professor of government,
Harvard University

4

[George] Bush came to the Presidency with the objective of managing it responsibly, not with the objective of pursuing any overriding ideological goals. If your main objective is to manage things responsibly, your main concern is to avoid making mistakes . . . Caution has its place in the Presidency, but its place isn't everywhere. Caution cannot be a substitute for vision.

The New York Times, 8-25:(A)4.

Terry Sanford
United States Senator,
D-North Carolina

5

It is time for the Congress to end the practice of taking honoraria. No longer can we afford to have the motives and objectives of Congressmen and Senators stained by the color of money. In the last five years, members of this august body received more than $9-million worth of honoraria for their personal use. In that same period, our colleagues in the House pocketed $15.4-million in honoraria. Any taxpayer ought to be outraged at these statistics. It suggests that their representative in Washington may be indebted to moneyed interest. Surely, James Madison didn't have honoraria in mind when he wrote about competing factions in the Federalist papers. Now, of course, there may be some legitimate instances in which honoraria may be granted. But, under the present system, the potential for abuse and the appearance of abuse are just too great. Perhaps we could establish an hourly wage—maybe we could tie it to the minimum wage—so that when Senators talk before an interest group they are justly compensated for their time. But let us be sure that compensation is more than just a thinly disguised large monetary reward for little or no work.

Before the Senate,
Washington, April 13/
The Washington Post, 4-18:(A)28.

Charles E. Schumer
United States Representative,
D-New York

1

You know what I think the whole issue is for Congress when we get back [from recess]? Money. On 80 per cent of the issues to come up this fall, there will be a general consensus that we ought to do some things and no consensus on whether we spend the money. And that's frustrating.

The New York Times, 9-4:(A)1.

2

[On President Bush's relations with Congress]: There is a feeling that dealing with George Bush is a one-way street. You help him when he needs help; he doesn't help you when you need help.

Los Angeles Times, 11-9:(A)26.

Brent Scowcroft
Assistant-designate to
President-elect George Bush
for National Security Affairs

3

I don't have a quick, innovative mind. I don't automatically think of good new ideas. What I do

better is pick out good ideas from bad ideas. But I don't have an original mind. I think there is enormous satisfaction in being involved in something bigger than you are, in feeling that, however small, you're doing something that makes a difference. Maybe that's what power is all about.

Interview,
Washington/
The Washington Post, 1-3:(B)2.

George P. Shultz
Secretary of State
of the United States

4

What we have to fear today is not the imperial Congress but the chaotic Congress. Dialogue between the branches [of government] cannot yield productive results when, no matter what the apparent agreement, any fraction, any staffer, any subcommittee, any member of Congress, can delay and impede even the will of the majority ... What we have is not so much a crisis of confidence as a crisis of competence—as elements of the legislature seek to conduct the business of the Executive.

Before Citizens Network for
Foreign Affairs,
Washington, Jan. 9/
The Washington Post,
1-11:(A)19.

5

Within the Executive Branch—at a time when domestic and international issues are deeply interrelated and the perspectives of all departments are needed—we need trust that decisions arrived at through proper procedures are actually decisions and will actually be carried out ... Our decisions should be fairly made—and once they are, they should be carried out, like it or not. You live up to your oath of office not just by carrying out decisions you agree with, but by carrying out decisions you don't agree with—or else resigning.

Before Citizens Network for
Foreign Affairs,
Washington, Jan. 9/
The Washington Post,
1-11:(A)19.

Paul Simon
United States Senator,
D-Illinois

1

There has been a gradual improvement in what we demand of public officials. Daniel Webster could write to railroads and say, "If you don't pay my fee I won't introduce your bill." Today he'd be kicked out of the Senate.

The New York Times, 3-3:(A)12.

Hedrick Smith
Former Washington bureau chief,
"The New York Times"

2

[Saying White House image-builders manipulate how the President is seen by the public]: They work at it very hard . . . I think they're very harmful to the degree that they divert the public's attention away from substance to personality, and that the issues of government which are really important don't get frontally addressed.

Los Angeles Times, 1-20:(VI)25.

John H. Sununu
Chief of Staff to President
of the United States
George Bush

3

[On the new Bush Administration]: Everyone is looking for some drastic change or redirection. But there is not going to be [one] . . . This is a conservative Republican President taking over from a conservative Republican [Ronald Reagan]. You have to think of it as Republican to Republican. The important things are the style changes.

Jan. 23/
The Washington Post, 1-24:(A)4.

4

[Saying that, in the Bush Administration, ideas and proposals are argued out loud among those involved]: Because President Bush wants it that way, we have the strongest, most intense, real, focused debates they've seen around here in a long time. Maybe not too Daniel Webster-ish in eloquence, but everybody gets a chance to argue his position. The clash of ideas produces new ideas.

Interview/
The New York Times, 9-13:(A)16.

Mike Synar
United States Representative,
D-Oklahoma

5

If you don't like fighting fires, don't be a fireman. If you don't like children, don't be a teacher. If you don't like voting [on tough issues], don't run for the U.S. Congress.

USA Today,
1-9:(A)10.

Helen Thomas
Correspondent,
United Press International

6

All new Presidents promise to be more open [to the press], but eventually the door closes, and the penchant for secrecy grows.

Time, 1-30:55.

Dick Thornburgh
Attorney General
of the United States

7

[Denying that there is political bias in the Justice Department's investigations of alleged wrongdoing by government officials]: I couldn't state it more firmly. We will investigate Republicans or Democrats where there are credible allegations of wrongdoing, and we will prosecute them if the evidence indicates they are violating Federal criminal law. We have a very high stake in the integrity of this Department. During my career as a prosecutor, during the Department's history, we have never hesitated to go where the evidence leads us. If it's a Republican or a Democrat, including some of the highest offices in the land, that's our charge. It's a charge that we take seriously, and it's a charge I assure you we will be faithful to.

Broadcast interview/
"Face the Nation," CBS-TV, 6-4.

John G. Tower
Secretary of
Defense-designate
of the United States

1

[On opposition to his confirmation on grounds of alleged drinking problems and womanizing]: I suppose one thing that engenders some resentment [to the opposition] is the fact that there was no clearly defined standard against which I should be judged. The standard seemed to be developed and seemed to evolve to fit the situation ... I accept that the Secretary of Defense must adhere to a higher standard than members of the United States Senate. But my question is, how much lower an acceptable standard is there for members of the Senate? Is it an acceptable standard for Senators late in the evening who've had a few drinks in the hideaways and offices of the Capitol, a few steps away from the Senate chamber, to come on to the floor late in the evening and vote on vital issues of nuclear deterrence? Is it an acceptable standard for Senators to accept honoraria, PAC contributions, and paid vacations from special interests who have a vested interest in the legislative process? I think, in the course of formulating a standard for the Secretary of Defense or, indeed, for any other Cabinet officer, that it is time that the Congress articulated what its own standards are.

At National Press Club,
Washington,
March 1/
The New York Times,
3-2:(A)10.

Laurence H. Tribe
Professor of
constitutional law,
Harvard University

2

The future of the Constitution depends more on the hands of the people to whom we entrust its interpretation than on any sort of plastic surgery [amendments and other changes].

USA Today,
3-3:(A)8.

Paul A. Volcker
Former Chairman,
Federal Reserve Board;
Former Chairman, National
Commission on the
Public Service

3

The attitude toward Federal service has certainly changed. It's a matter of psychology and prestige. A feeling that civil servants get hammered by the political process, beginning with the last couple of Presidents. And, after a while, you have enough people swearing at you, and you don't think it's a very promising career. Salaries are of some importance, [but] when you're talking about the Federal civil service, this process of layering the career people with more and more political people has probably reached the point where it is quite important in discouraging somebody who someday wants to have a really responsible job: Why should I go into the civil service when I know I'm going to be truncated at a pretty low level?

Interview, New York/
Time, 1-23:48.

Fred Wertheimer
President, Common Cause

4

[On the controversy about whether or not Congress should increase salaries for themselves and other Federal officials]: It is quite clear that the salary issue is an impossible one for Congress to deal with. The reason is, in my view, pretty simple. Members of Congress are put in the position of having to increase their own salaries. That's inherently self-serving. It's an inherent conflict in the sense that, by definition, they are being told to feather their own nests if there are to be any increases.

Interview/
The Washington Post, 1-30:(A)6.

5

If the President [Bush] does not come forward on an honoraria ban for Congress, he's going to undermine his whole ethics package and everything he's been saying about ethics since he came

(FRED WERTHEIMER)

into office. The bottom line will be to give Congress a free ride to try to continue the corrupt honoraria system, and the Administration will be buying into the very ethics double standard in Congress that they have consistently and adamantly opposed.

April 10/
The Washington Post, 4-11:(A)6.

1

In the last six years, special interests have poured more than $400-million in PAC money, more than $35-million in honoraria fees and countless additional millions in illegal soft money and other payments into our system of government. These payments represent investments in government decision-making—investments which improperly and unfairly magnify the voices of special interests at the expense of representative government. People often ask me if I see any real difference between the ethics and corruption problems of today and the problems we have experienced at other times in our history. I believe there is a difference. We've always experienced individual cases of corruption and impropriety in government. But today we have a system of legalized, institutionalized corruption. The rules themselves allow activities to take place legally that are improper and corrupting, and almost everyone is participating in the system. It's as though the society itself were corrupt.

Washington, May 6/
The Washington Post, 5-24:(A)24.

Lawrence J. White
Former member, Federal
Home Loan Bank Board

2

I believe that you get maximum political responsibility by putting an administrative agency into the Executive Branch. You thereby have ultimately the President responsible for what happens. The risk that you run is that you get partisan politics involved. But the gain is that you get direct responsibility. If things go sour, we can all point to that Administration, that President, and say those guys are responsible.

Interview, Washington/
The New York Times, 8-17:(A)13.

Jim Wright
United States Representative,
D-Texas;
Speaker of the House

3

[On the U.S. Congress]: Contrary to certain misconceptions, this supposedly staid institution is the scene of continual change and constant turnover. A majority of the members here in the chamber today were not here at the beginning of this decade. Only about one-fifth of our membership has served for more than 15 years. In this, as in our essential character, this House reflects the nation—ever changing, ever moving and growing, struggling often uncomfortably and sometimes awkwardly to accommodate itself to the tidal onrush of events.

At opening of 101st Congress,
Washington/
The Wall Street Journal, 1-11:(A)14.

4

I don't think a person should be joining the Congress with the idea of making money. Members of Congress work harder, longer hours than members of any other profession I know. If the average one of my colleagues were to devote the same amount of time and energy into any soundly conceived business or professional enterprise, he or she would get rich. But most of the people who come to Congress just aren't motivated that way. They're highly motivated, strongly motivated, but not for money-making.

Interview/
USA Today, 2-13:(A)7.

5

[Announcing his resignation as Speaker because of allegations of ethical wrongdoing]: Let me give you back this job you gave me as a propitiation for all of this season of bad will that has grown up among us . . . I will resign as

(JIM WRIGHT)

Speaker of the House effective upon the election of my successor . . . And then I will offer to resign from the House sometime before the end of June . . . Let's not try to get even with each other. Republicans, please don't get it in your heads [that] you need to "get" somebody else because of [the Democrats' defeat of Republican John Tower's nomination for Secretary of Defense]. Democrats, please don't feel that you need to "get" somebody on the other side because of me. We ought to be more mature than that . . . The nation has important business and it can't afford these distractions, and that's why I offer to resign . . . Horace Greeley had a quote that [the late President] Harry Truman used to like: "Fame is a vapor, popularity an accident, riches take wings, those who cheer today may curse tomorrow. Only one thing endures—character."

Before the House,
Washington, May 31/
USA Today, 6-1:(A)11.

Frank E. Young
Commissioner,
Food and Drug
Administration
of the United States

1

Some of the problems that Washington produces can lead to corruption because power is very hard to hold and use correctly. But you always have to guard against corruption in any area of potentially high and unaudited power. The issues facing a pastor or university official are no different from those facing a public official: money, sex, greed and pride. The difference in government is that the opportunity for exposure is much greater than in the private sector. The political process is so intense, people have made a business of finding fault. You deal not only with the concept of wrongdoing, but also the perception of wrongdoing.

Interview/
Christianity Today,
9-8:45.

Law • The Judiciary

Leslye Arsht
Spokesman for President
of the United States
Ronald Reagan

1

[On the Quadrennial Commission's recommendation that Federal officials' salaries be increased, an idea which is supported by President Reagan]: The salary paid to Federal judges in 1969, if increased solely to match the inflation that has occurred since then, would amount to $140,340, more than the Commission recommended. Federal trial judges are currently earning less than some junior lawyers in private practice and are leaving the bench in record numbers.

Los Angeles Times, 1-6:(I)32.

F. Lee Bailey
Lawyer

2

[On the use of lie-detector results in trials]: Polygraphs are very good in bank robberies—you either were there or you weren't. But what if you were only in on the planning? Or if you were selling land in Mexico and the deal went sour? The polygraph will not be very useful in trying to determine fraudulent intent.

Interview/
Los Angeles Times, 4-26:(I)24.

Steven Brill
Publisher, "American
Lawyer" magazine

3

The day of the U.S. Attorney as superstar, by definition, is over. You can only have one superstar prosecutor every 10 or 20 or 30 years. The dynamics of that office really change when a person who is U.S. Attorney is not (a) someone who is famous, and (b) someone who wants to be famous.

The New York Times, 4-1:10.

Warren E. Burger
Former Chief Justice
of the United States

4

[Arguing against televised court proceedings]: It would be bad for the country, bad for the courts, bad for the administration of justice. We're not in show business.

USA Today, 4-27:(A)12.

Judy Clarke
Executive director,
Federal Defenders
(public-defenders organization)

5

[Criticizing the use of lie-detector results in trials]: Polygraphs are along the lines of voodoo. The machine is a detector of responses, not of lies. All it does is test one's reactions to a question. That's why people who are very good at lying like it.

Los Angeles Times, 4-26:(I)24.

Alan Dershowitz
Professor of law,
Harvard University

6

[On judges who prescribe alternative punishments other than prison for convicted criminals]: Judges are best when they apply the law and worst when they try to win Nobel Prizes for creativity.

Time, 9-11:81.

7

[On the legality of tapping and taping by law-enforcement agencies of private phone calls and other conversations]: The law is always a step behind technology but, when it catches up, it has tended to expand the rights of the government.

USA Today, 12-28:(A)8.

WHAT THEY SAID IN 1989

James F. Fitzpatrick
Partner, Arnold & Porter,
attorneys at law, Washington

1

We're entering an era where talented lawyers with large books of business will be "at play" . . . with firms bidding for their services. Star lawyers are the new "free agents" in our society, just like professional sports.

The Washington Post, 2-27:(A)1.

Orrin C. Hatch
United States Senator,
R-Utah

2

I believe it is time to pull the plug on the American Bar Association's preeminent role in judicial selection. No other private group plays so formal a role in, or exercises such power over, any other nomination.

Washington, June 2/
The Washington Post, 6-3:(A)4.

William M. Hoeveler
Judge, United States
District Court for the
Southern District of Florida

3

[Supporting an increase in pay for judges]: We can't afford to have judges on the bench who aren't as smart as the lawyers arguing before them.

USA Today, 3-30:(A)10.

Harold Levinson
Professor, Vanderbilt University
Law School

4

[On academic ethics experts who give such advice to lawyers]: If advice is given independently and in good faith, it could be an excellent measure. It becomes more delicate if the ethics advice is given by someone who appears to take an independent position and in fact is making a practice of advising law firms [for pay]. In the courtroom, the court can take care of any conflicts of interest. The classroom and law review is

where the harm may be done if people who purport to be objective actually are not.

The New York Times, 8-25:(B)8.

Arthur Liman
Lawyer

5

Most of the great trial lawyers I know are very, very scared. Fear, for an actor, stirs you to a greater performance.

Interview/Esquire, January:71.

6

I relax in the courtroom. It's a sanctuary from all the distractions of the day—the one hundred phone calls, the dozens of problems. I can remember every word that every witness says; there isn't a gesture that I miss. There's a level of concentration that you almost can't attain anywhere else.

Interview/Esquire, January:75

Stephen Markman
Assistant Attorney General
of the United States

7

In his judicial selection efforts, President Reagan has looked for judges who understand that their role is not to do justice—but to do justice under law; judges who understand that theirs is not a roving commission to impose their own personal views upon society; judges who understand that the citizenry, through their representatives, is free to make what judges might view as unsound or unwise or imprudent public policy without necessarily running afoul of the Constitution . . . We only put lawyers on the courts, not because they are more intelligent than pharmacists or physicians; not because their sense of right and wrong is more refined than shopowners or building contractors; not because they know how to organize society better than dentists or truck drivers; but because they alone are trained to read the law and that is precisely what they must restrict themselves to doing on the Federal bench.

At Eighth Circuit Court conference,
St. Louis/
The Wall Street Journal, 1-23:(A)14.

Gary McDowell
Vice president, National
Legal Center for
the Public Interest

1

[Saying U.S. Supreme Court Justice Anthony Kennedy is more conservative than Robert Bork, whom Senate liberals rejected in 1987 for the post Kennedy now occupies]: Conservatives got more of what they were looking for ideologically than they would have gotten with Bob Bork. Bork would have been a much more independent thinker, as [Justice] Antonin Scalia is. What's amazing is how the liberals thought they had won defeating Bork. What they got was really much more of what they feared was in Bork.

The Washington Post,
4-11:(A)13.

Sandra Day O'Connor
Associate Justice,
Supreme Court
of the United States

2

[On selecting her law clerks]: We have a luxury of riches when it comes to law-clerk applicants. And after I have winnowed the number down to 10 or less, I make what is the hardest decision I make every year, and that is selecting four from among the extraordinary people I have interviewed ... One thing I do look for is the person who has the ability to remain unruffled and get along. Maturity, stability and congeniality are important to me because we work long hours and every weekend and holidays, other than Christmas Day and New Year's Day ... I am the one who has to make the decisions around here, so I am not concerned or interested in the individual's particular philosophy. However, I don't want to hire someone who has a particular ax to grind in terms of legal structure. I am more interested in finding people who can be objective. So I look for the skills that any good lawyer should have—the ability to pull apart a legal problem, break it down to its logical components and analyze it.

Interview, Washington/
The New York Times,
11-3:(B)14.

Daniel J. Popeo
General counsel,
Washington Legal Foundation

3

[Saying U.S. Supreme Court Justice Anthony Kennedy is more conservative than Robert Bork, whom Senate liberals rejected in 1987 for the post Kennedy now occupies]: Anthony Kennedy's performance on the Supreme Court is what all those raving lunatics who opposed Bob Bork deserve. What's so wonderful about it is that he is so young and healthy [so he will be on the Court a long time]. Anthony Kennedy has made me very happy. The laugh is on all those people in the Senate who wanted a litmus test on Bork.

The Washington Post, 4-11:(A)13.

Stephen Presser
Professor of law,
Northwestern University

4

[On alternative sentencing, other than prison, for convicted criminals]: A lot of people think that once you depart from mathematic equations [in jail sentencing], you're violating the most profound principles of justice. But the mansion of justice has many rooms.

Time, 9-11:81.

Robert Raven
Lawyer; President,
American Bar Association

5

Our Constitution provides that Federal judges are appointed for life, recognizing that consistency and integrity in Federal law requires consistency on the bench and freedom from political pressure in decision-making. Unlike with members of the Executive and Legislative Branches, we want and need our Federal judges to stay on the bench through retirement. Failure to award reasonable salary increases to the Federal judiciary flouts the wisdom of our Constitution. Inadequate and decreasing pay forces all but independently wealthy Federal judges to forego their life tenure and market their experience and training on the bench to the more lucrative arena

(ROBERT RAVEN)

of private firms. We cannot have a quality Federal judiciary if salaries are not even remotely commensurate with the experience and abilities of those we ask to serve on the bench. The quality of our third branch of government depends on new leadership from all members of Congress to ensure adequate pay.

The Washington Post,
2-14:(A)20.

William H. Rehnquist
Chief Justice
of the United States

1

[Supporting a 30 per cent pay increase for Federal judges]: [The salary problem is] the most serious threat to the future of the judiciary . . . during my lifetime. [Without a raise,] the Federal judiciary as we know it cannot continue to meet the high standards the public has come to expect from it. Judges have suffered enormous erosion in their purchasing power as a result of their pay not having kept pace with inflation over the last 20 years. It is becoming more and more difficult [to attract qualified lawyers from the private sector and keep them as judges]. Many people feel that lawyers make too much money, [but] we're not saying offer them the same amount that they get in private practice. We're saying offer them enough so they'll be able to educate their kids.

News conference,
Washington, March 15/
The Washington Post,
3-16:(A)25.

2

[Arguing against televised Supreme Court proceedings]: I hope we don't get to the point where the members of our Court are trying to get on the 6 o'clock news every night . . . It would lessen to a certain extent some of the mystique and moral authority [of the court].

USA Today, 4-27:(A)12.

Carl B. Rubin
Chief Judge, United States
District Court for
the Southern District of Ohio

3

[Saying Federal judges' salaries should be increased]: We've been dealt with unfairly. A salary of $89,500 for a lifetime of legal experience is low pay indeed. There isn't a lawyer who appears before my court who doesn't make more than I do.

Interview/
Los Angeles Times, 2-11:(I)23.

Ellis Rubin
Lawyer

4

Law schools are teaching students that it's the job of a defense attorney to suppress the truth. That's wrong. The younger generation doesn't seem to have the same integrity and the same respect for the truth and honesty that my generation was taught. There is a cancer that has invaded the courts and that's the cancer of perjury, and it's contagious . . . Lawyers today will do anything, will say anything to win their case. To them, the end justifies the means. And the higher the fee, the more bizarre their tactics become.

Interview/
USA Today, 11-27:(A)11.

Laurence H. Tribe
Professor of constitutional law,
Harvard University

5

My thesis is that a basic understanding of the conceptual shift that has occurred in physics can help us understand and appreciate the need for a similar conceptual shift in law. An understanding of the paradigm shifts that have occurred in physics leads us to inquire into, and challenge, a conception that sees law as nothing more than a force that enters our lives on isolated instances to resolve discrete events and then moves on, leaving the rest of our social environment untouched and unaffected. It leads us to ask whether governmental actions—ranging from statutes to regulations to judicial rulings to bureaucratic programs and undertakings—oper-

(LAWRENCE H. TRIBE)

ate in a straightforward way to control some individuals and institutions, and to leave others untouched, across a social void, or whether such governmental actions, instead, exert much wider influences. We are led to ask if judicial rulings in particular, in the very act of publicly making observations about law and society, change the fabric of society itself.

Before City Bar Association, New York,
May 11/The New York Times, 5-12:(B)12.

Sol Wachtler
Chief Judge,
New York State
Court of Appeals

1

The public and politicians always talk in terms of more police and more jails. The middle part [the courts] is the invisible part. The mouth of the funnel is being made wider, but the neck is just as narrow.

Newsweek,
5-29:36.

Politics

Diane Abbott
Member of British Parliament

1

There are many differences between the British political system and the American system. In Britain, you cannot buy television ads [for political campaigns]. Each party is given so much television time according to its vote within the last election, so they might get 20 minutes each, which they can break up into little slots. And each candidate is strictly controlled on the amount of money that can be spent. In America, you need to generate huge sums. Obviously, if you've hundreds of thousands riding on a candidate, you're not going to take a risk on some black woman [candidate] with braids in her hair. In Britain, it's not like that.

Interview/USA Today, 9-12:(A)11.

Lee Atwater
Chairman, Republican
National Committee

2

[The failure of the Republican Party to attract black support indicates that] we have been fighting with one arm tied behind our back. [But] we are now presented with a very unique chance. Those very sectors which have historically given their votes to the [Democratic] Party are now beginning to realize that they have won very little in return for the allegiance . . . The other party has taken minority Americans for granted. Our Party must take them for real.

Accepting chairmanship of the Party,
Washington, Jan. 18/
The Washington Post,
1-19:(A)6.

3

Thirty years of gerrymandering by the Democrats has nearly locked in Democratic majority control, with a capital "D," of the U.S. House of Representatives. If we [Republicans] want to be the majority party in Congress, we must have a very strong Republican role in drawing new district lines after the [1990] census.

Accepting chairmanship of the Party,
Washington,
Jan. 18/
Los Angeles Times, 2-21:(I)18.

Paul Allen Beck
Political scientist,
Ohio State University

4

Young people see politics as a dirty business . . . In a democratic nation, when there is a big gulf between politics and ordinary citizens, there is real danger. It discourages talented people from going in and out of politics.

The Christian Science Monitor,
8-11:7.

Anthony C. Beilenson
United States Representative,
D-California

5

[Saying that, though he does not accept PAC money, he does not criticize colleagues in Congress who do]: In defense of my colleagues, it is easy for me to say "no," for I come from an affluent district. I can raise $100,000 each year easily from individuals. That is not true in lots of parts of the country. Many come from states with few affluent people. I don't blame them a bit for accepting PAC contributions . . . [On the other hand, and] I don't want to be unfair or judgmental, but it is just human nature to feel kindly toward people who have helped you out by making sizable contributions when you needed it. You think in terms of these people and their interests when votes come up later on. It is a decent human quality. It would be terrible if you didn't care about them.

The Christian Science Monitor,
2-22:7.

Jerry Brown
Former Governor
of California (D)

1

For most of this century there has been a steady erosion in electoral participation . . . As the political party decays as an institution to mobilize voters, more and more people decide to drop out of active political participation. Democrats have had to become more ambiguous and less partisan in order to survive [because] those who actually vote are very much more inclined to the conservative side of things. To reverse that requires not only a good candidate with a good message, but also an effective party mobilizing the vast army of non-voters.

Interview, Pacific Heights, Calif./
Newsweek, 2-27:6.

Ronald H. Brown
Chairman-elect, Democratic
National Committee

2

[On his being the first black to be chosen to head a major American political party]: We cannot ignore the history of this moment. In choosing the first American of African descent to lead one of America's political parties, you have made history . . . [But] let me speak frankly. I did not run on the basis of race, but I will not run away from it. I am proud of who I am and I am proud of this Party, for we are truly America's last best hope to bridge the divisions of race, region, religion and ethnicity. I promise you the story of my chairmanship will not be about race. It will be about the [election] races we win in the next four years.

Before Democratic National
Committee, Washington, Feb. 10/
The New York Times, 2-11:1,7.

Ronald H. Brown
Chairman,
Democratic National Committee

3

We [Democrats] have allowed our adversaries to define who we are. And in politics, as in life, when you allow your opponent to set the ground rules, it's hard to win. We've got to be willing to stand up and define ourselves as that caring party, that party of hope and opportunity. In the 1940s, '50s and '60s, if you asked someone what a Democrat was, they could tell you. Now it has become harder. Diversity is the strength of the Democratic Party. It's the strength of this country. With the right kind of message and definition and common purpose . . . we've got a real opportunity to win that White House. That's the name of the game.

Ebony, May:38.

4

I can think of no better way for this [Democratic] Party to launch a 1992 Presidential campaign than to embrace our public spirit and to become a party of community service and community action. We believe that the measure of success for America is, "Will we be better off tomorrow?" [That is unlike] the cynical, selfish question that Republicans ask: "Will I be better off tomorrow?" Not I, but we. All of our people.

Speech, Sept. 11/
The New York Times, 9-12:(A)13.

5

I think [President Bush is] a decent human being. A nice guy. Most of the polls and most of the endless analyses of polls that I've seen use phrases like "wide but not deep" in describing support. And I think that's accurate. It is support that can quickly erode and I expect that it will be eroded.

Interview/
USA Today, 12-14:(A)13.

John Buckley
Director of communications,
National Republican
Congressional Committee

6

If you ever want to know why Democrats lose the White House, it was exhibited on the floor of the House today. A quarter of the Democratic caucus told [Democratic Party Chairman] Ron Brown and [Democratic Congressman] Dick Gephardt that they are too liberal to lead their Party. It is as stunning a rebuke as there could have been.

Sept. 28/
The New York Times, 9-29:(A)10.

George Bush
President of the United States

1

... I'm determined to work with the leadership of both [the Democratic and Republican] parties, no matter who it is. That's my responsibility. I think the Republicans see it more clearly now. Some were a little bit upset that I spent maybe too much time trying to work in a bipartisan fashion, but I still feel that a President who faces a majority from the other party in both houses must try, where possible, to work together. There are some things clearly where we're not going to be able to compromise, we're not going to be able to work together . . . Do you ever remember a President who didn't get sniped for one thing or another? I can't keep everybody happy on every issue. Some [Republicans] because of my early attention to the Democrats, felt neglected, felt maybe I was spending too much time working with the Democratic leadership. I don't feel that any more at all. On big questions, we've got to have Democratic support.

Interview/
The Washington Post, 6-2:(A)20.

2

Today, special-interest political-action committees and their $160-million war chest overshadow the great parties of Thomas Jefferson and Abraham Lincoln. And as the strength of parties erodes, so does the strength of our political system. By necessity, members of Congress engage in time-consuming and often degrading appeals for money outside the party structure.

To government interns, at Library
of Congress, Washington, June 29/
Los Angeles Times, 6-30:(I)22.

3

[On whether he puts gag orders on members of his Administration to prevent them from speaking out on such issues as the recent coup attempt in Panama]: We've been blessed in this Administration by a good team who don't like the game of who's up, who's down, who's winning, who's losing, who's looking good, who's in, who's out.

And I did not have to have any gag order because all of them are singing from the same sheet of music.

News conference,
Washington, Oct. 13/
The New York Times, 10-14:8.

Carroll A. Campbell, Jr.
Governor of
South Carolina (R)

4

[On the fact that several anti-abortion Republican candidates were defeated in recent elections]: The biggest problem the Republican candidates have had is that they have allowed their Democratic opponents to define them and to state their position [on abortion] for them. The biggest mistake they made is not stating their position clearly, succinctly. The problem with Republicans is they have not gone out and said in advance what they believed in. That's one of the reasons we got into trouble and that's something we're not going to, I don't think, make a mistake on in the future.

At Republican Governors
Association conference,
Hilton Head, S.C., Nov. 13/
The New York Times, 11-14:(A)18.

Jimmy Carter
Former President
of the United States

5

I think you can equate Presidential popularity in the public-opinion polls almost exactly with press treatment [of the President]. When a President is riding high . . . he's also treated with kid gloves by the press.

At Gannett Center for Media
Studies, New York, Jan. 18/
The Washington Post, 1-19:(A)4.

Alan Cranston
United States Senator,
D-California

6

[On charges that he helps people who make large contributions to his political campaigns]: If

(ALAN CRANSTON)

we adopt the positions that you can only take money from people you don't help, then we're creating an Alice-in-Wonderland world. [But] obviously people who make huge contributions do have some advantage over those who don't. It gives them access.

Los Angeles Times, 4-20:(I)21.

Linda DiVall
Republican Party
public-opinion analyst

1

[On the Democratic Party victories in the recent national elections]: If you look at last Tuesday's results, you are hard pressed not to say . . . that the pro-choice [on abortion] coalition has indeed, definitely, become a force. If we in the Republican Party don't recognize that, we are setting ourselves up for some major defeats.

To Republican Governors, Hilton
Head Island, S.C., Nov. 13/
USA Today, 11-14:(A)20.

E. L. Doctorow
Author

2

The philosophical conservative is someone willing to pay the price of other people's suffering for his principles.

At Brandeis University
commencement, May/
The Washington Post, 9-30:(C)3.

Christopher J. Dodd
United States Senator,
D-Connecticut

3

[On President Bush's inauguration]: It did cross my mind that if we [Democrats] ever win one of these things [the Presidency] again, we're going to have to hire the Republicans to run it because there will be no Democrats alive who remember how to do an inauguration.

Jan. 20/
The Washington Post, 1-21:(A)11.

Thomas F. Eagleton
Former United States Senator,
D-Missouri

4

American politics is money and 30-second spots. The modern young candidates—the Dick Gephardts, the Al Gores—can talk in 10 seconds, 20 and 30. You can tell them what you want, and they go click, click, click, click. Old-fashioned politicians like me take three weeks to answer something.

Los Angeles Times, 1-2:(VI)14.

Don Edwards
United States Representative,
D-California

5

[On why he became a Democrat after being brought up as a Republican]: I think that, underneath, we're all creatures of family, and when you're brought up in a conservative Republican family, you're acclimated to that way of thinking. But you don't change internally if you're naturally for fair play, for the disabled. You find out on your own that Republicans don't think in those terms. And that's what made me turn into a Democrat. I just couldn't live with that elitist "trickle down" that I found a bigoted kind of view.

Interview/USA Today, 7-12:(A)9.

Susan Estrich
Former manager,
Michael Dukakis' 1988
Democratic campaign for
the Presidency

6

[On the effect of the women's vote in last fall's Presidential election, when Republican George Bush defeated Democrat Michael Dukakis]: The reality is that each year the gender gap tends to narrow as the election gets closer. It's largely a reflection of economic issues. It involves women who do not self-identify as feminists, who are not liberals or progressives and who do not necessarily belong to traditional or new women's organizations. It was not the membership of the feminist, organized women's movement that was

WHAT THEY SAID IN 1989

(SUSAN ESTRICH)

up for grabs. It was conservative women, and some went back to [Bush]. His appeal with an issue such as crime went to that constituency, not women with more liberal, progressive views.

Interview/
Los Angeles Times, 1-16:(V)2.

Martin Farrell
Chairman, department of
politics and government,
Ripon (Wis.) College

1

[The dominance of PACs] has raised the ugly head of oligarchy where it is "one dollar, one vote," instead of "one person, one vote." Those who benefit are the incumbents. They, however, are the very ones who would have to change the laws. This puts us in a Catch-22 situation which threatens democracy.

The Christian Science Monitor,
2-22:7.

Mervin Field
Public-opinion analyst

2

The historical belief was that Republicans had money and Democrats didn't. If you were doing word association, it was "Republican" equals "rich." And there are people who think that those who accumulate money do it in less than honest ways. So Democrats start out with an edge, with the public thinking they are more honest, for they are more poor.

The Christian Science Monitor,
8-4:2.

Thomas S. Foley
United States Representative,
D-Washington

3

There's a kind of split vision of Republicans. There's the good elephant that wants to wrap his trunk around you . . . But off in the distance you hear the rumble of the rogue elephant herd—the [Edward] Rollinses and the [Lee] Atwaters—

158

who want to find any Democrats they can and stomp them to death.

To reporters,
Washington, March 23/
The Washington Post, 3-24:(A)4.

Thomas S. Foley
United States Representative,
D-Washington;
Speaker of the House-designate

4

[On his being in line to be House Speaker following the resignation of Jim Wright]: . . . I am not someone who tries to undermine anyone else. I have never been driven by a desire to become Speaker. I'm not a fatalist. But I am one who thinks circumstance, happenstance, accident has a lot to do with what happens in a political career . . . I am proud to be a Democrat. But I don't particularly like to bash Republicans. I think the best partisanship is to try to persuade the unpersuaded of your point of view, to attract voters to the [Democratic] Party, to attract support to the Party and its principles and policies and not just to have a donnybrook of trashing Republicans.

Interview, Washington/
The New York Times, 6-2:(A)1.

Gerald R. Ford
Former President
of the United States

5

[On his 1974 pardon of former President Richard Nixon for his part in the Watergate scandal]: I finally decided that I should spend all my time on the problems of all Americans and not 25 per cent of my time on the problems of one man. It was an easy decision when you put it in that context.

At conference on the Ford Presidency,
Hempstead, N.Y./
Los Angeles Times, 4-8:(I)16.

Geoffrey Garin
Democratic Party consultant

6

Voters admire loyalty, but in the end you don't get much credit from the voters if you've put your

(GEOFFREY GARIN)

trust in the wrong guy. You do get rewarded for loyalty in politics and punished for being weak in your loyalties. But the truth is, what you get punished for more than anything is failure.

The New York Times, 3-10:(A)10.

Newt Gingrich
United States Representative,
R-Georgia

1

The values of the [political] left cripple human beings, weaken cities, make it difficult for us to in fact survive as a country . . . The left in America is to blame for most of the current, major diseases which have struck this society . . . You're going to see weird things coming out of [Washington] over the next few years, because you're watching the death throes of the [leftist] machine, and you're watching its power to smear and its power to intimidate.

Before Republican National
Committee, Washington,
June/
Mother Jones, October:29.

Barry M. Goldwater
Former United States Senator,
R-Arizona

2

[Criticizing Senators who are against confirmation of John Tower as Defense Secretary because of allegations about his drinking and womanizing]: People who live in glass houses should never throw rocks, and if they start investigating 100 members of that Senate as they've investigated John Tower, you people [in the press] are going to have a ball. Yes, he drank; I've had a few drinks with him . . . He chased women . . . I don't give a damn whether he did or not. If . . . everybody in this town connected with politics had to leave town because of that, and drinking, you'd have no government.

To reporters,
Washington, March 2/
The Washington Post,
3-3:(A)16.

Bob Graham
United States Senator,
D-Florida

3

[Arguing against the confirmation of John Tower to be Secretary of Defense]: It's not just [Tower's] drinking which is a problem to me. It's a pattern of bad judgment—bad judgment in the 1970s in drinking, bad judgment by placing himself in compromising positions as the U.S. arms negotiator in Geneva in the mid-80s, bad judgment in accepting large sums from the defense industry in the late 1980s.

Feb. 27/The Washington Post,
2-28:(A)11.

Fred Grandy
United States Representative,
R-Iowa

4

When I was first a staffer here on the [Capitol] Hill, there was a little [restaurant] up there that was a watering hole for members of Congress and their staffs. When [Senator] Ted Kennedy walked in, the place was all aflutter. Now, similarly, [at Hollywood restaurants such as] Ma Maison or the Bistro Garden or Spago in L.A., if Robert Redford walks in, okay, there's a passing glance perhaps—to see what he's wearing. But if Ted Kennedy walks in, or [U.S. Iran-contra figure] Ollie North, for that matter, you're talking about something truly fascinating. There is a subtle fascination with each other that is at the bottom of all this. It's almost clandestine. Politicians are fascinated by people in the arts. People in the arts, in turn, are fascinated by politicians.

Interview, Washington/
Los Angeles Times, 12-7:(Calendar)4.

William H. Gray III
United States Representative,
D-Pennsylvania

5

There is one party [the Republicans] that now wants to sell America a bill of goods that says, "There is one other political party [the Democratic] that is corrupt . . . That corruption comes from being in power too long. Therefore, they

(WILLIAM H. GRAY III)

need to be kicked out." So what do they do? They point to some people who have some problems. They are legitimate problems, I am not denying that. And therefore they say, "The whole is corrupt."

To reporters, Washington/
The Christian Science Monitor,
6-30:8.

Peter D. Hart
Democratic Party
public-opinion analyst

1

[On negative political-campaign advertising]: If the voters all said to the pollsters, "This is repulsive. I can't stand it, and I won't vote for the candidate who does it," that's the end of negative commercials. But now the candidates see that positive ads don't move the numbers, and negative ads do, so they keep on doing it.

The Washington Post,
11-6:(A)4.

Edward Heath
Former Prime Minister
of the United Kingdom

2

I think politics would be infinitely better off if politicians cared about music and the arts. If you do nothing but politics, you drive yourself into the ground, and then you're no good for the constituents you represent, because you come to wrong conclusions and support the wrong things. Balance is all-important to life.

Interview/
The Wall Street Journal,
7-3:5.

Harrison Hickman
Democratic Party consultant

3

[On recent scandals involving politicians]: First [there is] revelation, then denial, then explanation, then retrenchment—then exit.

Newsweek, 6-5:17.

Nancy Hollander
Lawyer; Vice president,
National Association
of Criminal Defense Lawyers

4

We're losing track of why we have a Fourth Amendment. The only reason the police can't come into your home whenever they want is the Fourth Amendment. Beginning in the late 1960s really, the Supreme Court began to shrink who the Fourth Amendment would protect and how it would do its protecting . . . What happens is that society's needs begin to overpower the rights of the individual. And the more discretion you give police, the closer you get to a police state.

Interview/
USA Today, 11-15:(A)13.

A. E. Dick Howard
Professor, University of Virginia
Law School

5

[Saying the issue of race is becoming less important in political campaigns in Virginia, such as the current run for Governor in which a black is the Democratic Party candidate]: This isn't the millennium, but it represents a tremendous change. There may be sputters and gasps along the road, and obviously race is still an element in politics here, but we aren't going back to the old days. Each one this time knows the first candidate to introduce race overtly into the contest will be hurt.

The New York Times, 9-25:(A)1.

Charles O. Jones
Political scientist, University
of Wisconsin, Madison

6

The Congressional Democrats have gotten used to being the opposition party to the White House Republicans. They have provided themselves with the resources aggressively to play that role. It is not at all certain that they would now work well with a Democratic President, as they did not with [Jimmy] Carter. One can make a persuasive case that the present Democratic leaders in Congress like their jobs as spokesmen

(CHARLES O. JONES)

for a legislative party whose cooperation is needed by a Republican President. Likewise, an experienced group of White House Republicans have accommodated themselves to Executive life. Despairing of ever controlling the whole Congress . . . they have become quite accomplished at managing Democratic Congresses.

Debate at American Political Science Association meeting, Atlanta/The Washington Post, 9-4:(A)5.

James R. Jones
United States Representative, D-Oklahoma

1

If we [the Democratic Party] keep sweeping under the rug that we are losing moderate votes, that we are losing adult white male voters, that we are losing white and ethnic minority voters—if we keep sweeping those statistics under the rug and failing to face up to them—we are really buying our own doom.

New conference, Washington, Jan. 30/ The Washington Post, 1-31:(A)8.

Edward M. Kennedy
United States Senator, D-Massachusetts

2

[Saying the Bush Administration has run out of ideas]: For Democrats, it represents both a danger and an opportunity—a danger because with it comes the temptation to do nothing except criticize, while waiting for the Bush Presidency to falter. In my view, that is both wrong in principle and bad politics. We dare not forget the lesson of last year: George Bush was supposed to be easy to beat . . . I hope Democrats never again fall into that trap . . . Across a range of concerns where the Administration seems frozen in the ice of its own intellectual emptiness, the creative initiative will pass over to the Democratic Party if we choose to take it. As Democrats, we have to transcend the narrow choice between bigger

deficits and lesser programs, between throwing money at problems and throwing up our hands in helpless indifference, between standing still and raising taxes . . . We have the ideas—now we have to muster the will to stand for them and run on them. If we do that—then, in 1992, we can succeed in removing a Yale President [Bush] from the White House—even if we don't succeed in replacing him with someone from Harvard.

At Yale University, March 6/ Los Angeles Times, 3-7:(I)20.

3

Whether we agreed with him or not, [former President] Ronald Reagan was a successful candidate and an effective President above all else because he stood for a set of ideas. He stated them in 1980—and it turned out that he meant them—he wrote most of them not only into public law, but into the national consciousness. It would be foolish to deny that his success was fundamentally rooted in a command of public ideas. Ronald Reagan may have forgotten names, but never his goals. He was a great communicator, not simply because of his personality or his Teleprompter, but mostly because he had something to communicate.

At Yale University, March 6/ The New York Times, 3-7:(A)16.

4

[On the Bush Administration]: This Republican President, and perhaps the Republican Party itself, have run out of ideas. The Administration has no agenda other than coping, no real budget, no major initiative and very little to say . . . [The] truth is that the Administration has more power than purpose. The Administration holds office but doesn't know what to do with it.

At Yale University, March 6/ The New York Times, 3-7:(A)5.

Celinda Lake
Democratic Party political analyst; President, Analysis Group

5

[On the effect of the women's vote in last fall's Presidential election, when Republican George

(CELINDA LAKE)

Bush defeated Democrat Michael Dukakis]: The Democrats still have an edge with women, but they don't appreciate that you can't take it for granted. They did not target women; Dukakis did not effectively target any group . . . The Republicans did not take [women] for granted. They may have responded symbolically, but they responded. The Democratic campaign did not listen and develop a strategy at the national level . . . [Bush] broke with [President] Ronald Reagan at the convention and said, "I'm not him"; he showed that he understood the modern family, and talked of day care and education, saying he was willing to use government as a tool to help; third, he said he was for change. On the eve of the election, men were for the status quo and women were for change.

Interview/Los Angeles Times, 1-16:(V)1,2.

Richard D. Lamm
Director, Center for
Public Policy and
Contemporary Issues,
University of Denver;
Former Governor of Colorado (D)

1

You've got to reform every institution that is out there. The health-care system. The education system. We've got too many farmers in America. And too many lawyers. The most dangerous animal in America is the sacred cow. It's going to kill us. I've taken on almost every constituency within the Democratic Party. I've taken on the labor unions. I've taken on the teachers. The Hispanics just go crazy because of immigration reform. The elderly are the most powerful political group in America, but they just have to be taken on; they're already getting too much, not too little. I took on death and dying. You know, everyday in hospitals across America somebody is brought back from death, and we spend a lot of taxpayers' money on them so they can die again tomorrow. There was not a Democratic constituency that was happy with me by 1982. And I won [the Governorship], by two to one.

Interview/
The Atlantic Monthly, March:50.

S. Robert Lichter
Co-director, Center for Media
and Public Affairs,
Washington

2

[President] George Bush does not want to be the Great Communicator; he wants to be the Great Administrator. He is trying to deal with the public in the same way he deals with Congress: low-key without a lot of pretense. And he has that inbred sense that it was wrong to parade himself before the public.

The New York Times, 11-22:(A)11.

Norman Mailer
Author

3

[On Republicans]: They've got to hide from the great American public the fact that they're rich guys who don't really give a damn about the country. They are not true conservatives. They are not interested in conserving anything. They're interested in ripping it all off.

Interview/
The Washington Post, 8-22:(E)4.

George S. McGovern
Former United States Senator,
D-South Dakota

4

The public gets the kind of politician it deserves. Politics is an act of faith; you have to show some confidence in the intellectual and moral capacity of the public. Sometimes that faith is rewarded, and sometimes it isn't.

USA Today, 1-25:(A)9.

George J. Mitchell
United States Senator,
D-Maine

5

[On relations between the Democratic-controlled Senate and incoming Republican President George Bush]: No one's going to suggest we sulk and pout and refuse to cooperate because of what was in many respects a dirty [Presidential election] campaign. [But there is] some sub-

(GEORGE J. MITCHELL)

stance to the idea that he doesn't enter with much of a mandate for any particular program [and there is] a determination on the part of Congress to fulfill its role as an equal partner in the operation of our government.

The Washington Post, 1-3:(A)1.

1

Where the President [Bush] acts in a manner that is right and in the national interest, he will have our [Democrats'] strong support. Where the proposals are wrong and not in the national interest, we will oppose and offer constructive alternatives. We're going to do what we think is right for the people of this country and not be consumed by the standard which, I guess you would call it, contemporary political analysis suggests be applied: that is, because the President is doing well in the public-opinion polls, we [Democrats] must be doing poorly.

The New York Times, 10-17:(A)10.

Anne Murphy
Executive director,
American Arts Alliance

2

No question about it, politicians and artists are both about the same thing. Both of them are getting the feel of society. Both are very big players in that tunnel of the present that everything needs to move through to get to the future.

Los Angeles Times,
12-17:(Calendar)4.

Ralph Nader
Lawyer; Consumer advocate

3

Reaganites say that [President] Reagan has lifted our "spirits"—correct if they mean he led the nation in a drunken world-record spending binge while leaving millions of American workers, consumers and pollution victims defenseless.

At National Press Club,
Washington, Jan. 17/
The Washington Post, 1-18:(A)21.

Sam Nunn
United States Senator,
D-Georgia

4

Democratic [Party] support is hemorrhaging in the heart of the electorate. We are losing the working and middle-class Americans who used to be the mainstay of our Party's governing coalition.

Before Democratic Leadership
Council, Philadelphia,
March 10/
Los Angeles Times,
3-12:(I)29.

Robert Ornstein
Neurobiologist and psychologist,
University of California
Medical School, San Francisco,
and Stanford University

5

The way we currently choose our leaders is a perfect example of "old-mindedness." We were designed to live in tribes of 200 or 300 people, so we're "programmed" to choose the most attractive or most commanding person. In every election except one since World War II, for instance, the taller candidate has won. It seems more and more a question of "Who do you want to watch on television over the next couple of years?" than of who has the best ideas for governing. Just think about someone trying to run for President in a wheelchair, or being bald.

Interview/
USA Today,
1-25:(A)9.

Muammar el-Qaddafi
Chief of State of Libya

6

[On new U.S. President Bush]: I know he is a man who is completely different from [his predecessor, Ronald] Reagan. He's a politician, a factual man ... Reagan used to treat the Presidency as a theatre where he performs his acts.

Broadcast interview,
Tripoli, Libya/
"Barbara Walters Interview," ABC-TV, 1-27.

163

Dan Quayle
*Vice President
of the United States*

1

After only 50 some days of the Bush Administration, we're seeing something odd: criticism [by the news media that we're] not manipulating the media, [that we're] not governing by sound bite. I'm talking about how the need to make the 7 o'clock news can lead politicians to announce initiatives that aren't well thought out, initiatives that might well make the headlines but aren't good for the health of the country. Frantic efforts to gain press attention and produce "sound bites" can distort our political process by elevating form over substance and image over reality.

*Before National Press Club,
Washington, March 16/
The New York Times, 3-17:(A)14.*

2

Any public servant, or those who aspire to public service, are well-served to have a very principled viewpoint and do not start changing it just because political winds may appear to be shifting.

*To Republican Governors,
Hilton Head Island, S.C., Nov. 13/
USA Today, 11-14:(A)3.*

Richard Rahn
*Vice president and
chief economist, United States
Chamber of Commerce*

3

[On President-elect George Bush]: He's a very open and approachable person. He sure makes a lot of phone calls. He touches base with an enormous number of people. That's always been his habit, and it was even more so in the [election] campaign. We're not going to have one of those Presidencies where the man in the White House cuts himself off. It won't be like [Lyndon] Johnson, [Richard] Nixon, [Jimmy] Carter, even [Ronald] Reagan—who all had these barriers.

*Los Angeles Times,
1-20:(IV)4.*

Ronald Reagan
President of the United States

4

Back in 1980, when I was running for President . . . some pundits said our programs would result in catastrophe. Our views on foreign affairs would cause war, our plans for the economy would cause inflation to soar and bring about economic collapse. I even remember one highly respected economist saying, back in 1982, that "the engines of economic growth have shut down here and across the globe and they are likely to stay that way for years to come . . ." Well, he and the other "opinion-makers" were wrong. The fact is, what they called "radical" was really "right"; what they called "dangerous" was just "desperately needed."

*Broadcast address to the nation,
Washington, Jan. 11/
The Washington Post, 1-12:(A)8.*

Harry M. Reid
*United States Senator,
D-Nevada*

5

It is about time that the two bodies, this body and the other body [the House], realize that we have to do something about [election-] campaign spending. Campaigns are too long; they are too costly . . . We must have some ceilings on how much money can be spent. We cannot have the Senate of the United States a body that is composed of all millionaires. We are coming to that. Why? Because it is easier for a wealthy person to run. He can spend all the money he wants. It is much more difficult for someone who is a schoolteacher or a small businessman to go out and raise the millions of dollars that it takes to be competitive.

*Before the Senate,
Washington, May 4/
The Washington Post, 5-10:(A)20.*

Charles S. Robb
*United States Senator,
D-Virginia*

6

[On the Democratic Party]: In the past 20 years, the inclusive, innovative and forward-

(CHARLES S. ROBB)

looking liberalism of the New Deal and the New Frontier have been replaced by the ideological litmus tests and programmatic rigidity of what some have called "liberal fundamentalism." Too often, this narrow outlook has become entrenched as national Party orthodoxy, enforced by activists and interest groups who exercise disproportionate influence over the Party's nominating process.

Before Democratic Leadership
Council, Washington, Nov. 13/
The New York Times, 11-14:(A)18.

1

Our [Democratic] Party has reached an impasse, because the growth of the welfare state has reached the limits of public tolerance for higher taxes and bureaucratic expansion. Either we will continue on the course of the last 20 years or we will rebuild a Presidential majority around unifying themes and principles that make sense to most Americans.

Before Democratic Leadership
Council, Washington, Nov. 13/
Los Angeles Times, 11-14:(A)26.

Edward Rollins
Co-chairman, National
Republican Congressional
Committee

2

[On the recent partisan warfare in Congress involving what some say are smear campaigns against individual members]: Our job, if we're going to be successful, is to go out and beat Democrats in the next couple of cycles. Is partisanship going to go away? I doubt it. Are the campaign tactics going to be altered? I doubt it. Is the poisonous environment that we've been dealing with in the last two months going to go away? I hope so . . . Our goal is to win Democratic seats. We're in an environment of hysteria. There's this bogeyman syndrome out there that many of the media have helped inflame. I'm not a hater, but I'm a fighter. And, obviously, I'm going to do everything that they [Democrats] do to us. But

we're just in this crazy environment, and things take on a far different role than ever before.

Interview/USA Today, 6-8:(A)11.

Shawn W. Rosenberg
Professor of political science,
University of California,
Irvine

3

The amount of attention we pay to politicians is really minimal, even during an election period, and the over-all understanding of issues is quite rudimentary. As a result, we rely on often superficial cues or pieces of information to direct our judgment of candidates and events. What people are doing is saying, "I don't really understand politics, so let me look at this person and decide if this person is trustworthy and competent." But how you look is not necessarily who you are, because that can be manipulated so readily . . . Before television, the key to election was manipulating the political-party structure. What you knew and who you knew and family connections were also important. With the advent of television politics, the content of what you have to say is much less important. The party machinery is less important. Visual impressions and image are far more important.

Interview/
Los Angeles Times, 10-29:(A)28.

Larry J. Sabato
Professor of government,
University of Virginia

4

In a democracy which places great value on personal liberty, campaign spending by interest groups and individuals is inevitable . . . When we attempt to dam the flow of political money, we simply will cause the . . . money to carve new channels around the dam . . . You cannot dam the flow of political money in a democracy.

Interview, Charlottesville, Va./
The Christian Science Monitor,
4-27:8.

5

[On the political fighting between Democrats and Republicans]: Nobody is going to turn the other cheek. That's what it takes for a truce. It is bubbling beneath the surface, and will blow again like a volcano until 1990. For Democrats, the motive is vengeance [against Republicans who drove out of office Congressmen Jim Wright and Tony Coelho on ethics charges]. For Republicans, it is the desire to become the majority. [But] I feel the Republicans will be disappointed in 1990, because there's sleaze on both sides and that will neutralize the issue. All this does is confirm to the average citizen that politics is crooked.

The Christian Science Monitor,
6-30:8.

Jose Sarney
President of Brazil

1

Politics is part reality and part fiction. I even believe that literature, by its humanistic and universal vision of the world, leads one to politics.

Interview/
World Press Review, March:35.

Arthur M. Schlesinger, Jr.
Historian

2

[On President-elect George Bush]: It has been traditional in the American sensibility that those born to wealth and privilege feel a slightly bad conscience about it and, in order to justify their circumstances, work to help others. Those who have clawed their way to the top, naturally, have thought things must be fine in a system where they could do that. I have just a slight sense that Bush may turn out to be more of a tribune of the people than he chose to suggest in the [election] campaign. We may find *noblesse oblige* replacing greed as the White House style.

The New York Times, 1-20:(A)9.

Don Sipple
Republican Party
media consultant

3

[Saying the press should pay attention to the accuracy of political advertising during election campaigns]: If reporters don't analyze the truth and falsity of the ads, it's bastardizing the role of the press, which is to inform. We [consultants] have a right to free speech, but the press has a responsibility to inform and educate voters.

The Washington Post, 1-19:(A)22.

Robert Squier
Democratic Party
media consultant

4

[Criticizing the press for not paying enough attention to the accuracy of political advertising during last year's Presidential election campaign]: The biggest failing of the press was in covering [advertising] spots and media . . . You should have been much tougher in dealing with us and the stuff we put on . . . You should treat advertising like a speech, and when a candidate says something that is untrue, say so. Don't stand on the sidelines. Be a referee.

At American Press Institute/
The Washington Post, 1-19:(A)22.

James Sundquist
Scholar emeritus,
Brookings Institution

5

[On President Reagan, who is about to leave office after serving two terms]: He was a strong President and imposed his policies on the country. He turned the whole trend of American government around. We were headed in the direction of the welfare state and all Republicans could do before was to slow the trend. Reagan halted it . . . On the domestic side, he will be judged a disaster—this horrendous deficit and the fact that we've lost our trading position in the world.

The Christian Science Monitor, 1-12:2.

Patricia Theno
President, National
Association of Business
Political Action Committees

6

[Criticizing President Bush's proposal to abolish most political-action committees]: [The

(PATRICIA THENO)

President's] recommendations on PACs are counter-productive from a public-policy standpoint and shortsighted from a partisan standpoint. They would discourage legitimate and healthy citizen participation in the political process . . . Candidates would be forced to meet ever-rising campaign costs from a dwindling supply of narrow sources . . . There would be a proliferation of . . . tactics to avoid the new restrictions. In short, what's on the table today involving many different players would go back under the table with fewer and narrower players.

The Christian Science Monitor,
7-5:7.

John G. Tower
Secretary of Defense-designate
of the United States;
Former United States Senator,
R-Texas

1

[On the controversy over his alleged drinking and womanizing problems that have cast doubt over his confirmation as Defense Secretary]: Everybody I've heard from who's been through the meat grinder in Washington says that mine is the worst meat grinder they've ever seen. I'm not even coming out coarse-ground. I'm coming out fine sausage meat.

Washington, March 4/
The New York Times, 3-6:(A)1.

John G. Tower
Former United States Senator,
R-Texas

2

[On the Senate's rejection of his nomination to be Secretary of Defense]: I will be recorded as the first Cabinet nominee in the history of the Republic to be rejected in the first 90 days of a Presidency and perhaps be harshly judged. But I depart from this place at peace with myself, knowing that I have given a full measure of devotion to my country. No public figure in my memory has been subjected to such a far-reaching and thorough investigation nor had his human

foibles bared to such intensive and demeaning scrutiny. And yet there is no finding that I have ever breached established legal and ethical standards nor been derelict in my duty.

Washington, March 9/
The New York Times, 3-10:(A)10.

Paul E. Tsongas
Former United States
Representative,
D-Massachusetts

3

My campaign theme would be, "Make America Number 1 again." Talk about America's wealth being dissipated by the [Federal budget] deficits, foreigners buying up everything. Raise those issues in a very jingoistic fashion—America's pride. Make no apologies about how you feel. Say we're going to get involved in basic education. We're going to do whatever is necessary to make the United States competitive. We're going to have capital-gains [tax] differential based on holding periods. If that's pro-business, let it be pro-business. If that means we do things Democrats have not traditionally liked, the hell with them. We're going to do it. And I think people would respond.

The Atlantic Monthly, March:58.

Guy Vander Jagt
United States Representative,
R-Michigan

4

When you're dealing with [political-] campaign reform, you're talking about one of the most precious things a Congressman deals with. You're talking about his political life or death.

Oct. 23/
The New York Times, 10-24:(A)12.

Paul A. Volcker
Former Chairman, Federal
Reserve Board

5

[On President Reagan]: You've heard this a million times from people writing memoirs: It's a little difficult to engage him in a substantive

(PAUL A. VOLCKER)

debate. He had a few relatively simple and straightforward ideas. And, in fact, I didn't see him much as the second term progressed. [White House Chief of Staff] Don Regan kept saying, "You've got to see him much more frequently. I'll arrange it." But he never did. When I saw him, it was probably as often as not at my initiative. But I didn't feel very comfortable about that.

Interview, New York/
Time, 1-12:50.

Stephen Wayne
Presidential scholar,
George Washington University

1

[On President Reagan, who is about to leave office after serving two terms]: In terms of his "presence," outlook and his ability to project a certain kind of goodness, he ranks near the top. He's made us feel good about the Presidency and the country ... [But] there may be a price we have to pay down the road for this prosperity. If historians can provide evidence that the roots of our problems were sown during the Reagan years, his evaluation will deteriorate.

The Christian Science Monitor,
1-12:2.

Paul M. Weyrich
Chairman,
Coalitions for America

2

[On the influence of conservative groups such as his on the Bush Administration]: Except in the area of public policy, we have at least as much, if not more, impact on the Bush Administration than we had on the Reagan Administration. The Bush Administration has a reputation for being more pragmatic, and, in a way, that's actually helpful. You explain an issue that would impact on them and they take it seriously and listen to you. That's unlike the Reagan Administration, which did everything they did because of the image it would project on the 6 o'clock news.

Interview/
Los Angeles Times, 10-7:(I)20.

L. Douglas Wilder
Lieutenant Governor,
and Democratic nominee for
Governor, of Virginia

3

[On running for public office]: You have to carry water. It's possible for you to jump out and say: "Guess what? I'm running!" But what have you done? Have you helped anybody? Have you helped carry someone else's water to the tub so that they can take a bath? Have you participated in building coalitions so that you can call upon them? It's important that youngsters understand that they cannot spring full-blown from the cabbage patch, like Topsy, and call themselves leaders. Leadership comes from knowing what needs to be done, then helping to do it. Rather than being concerned about whether I get a piece of the pie, I like to have my hand on the knife that cuts it. That assures that equity and justice will follow.

Ebony, November:46

L. Douglas Wilder
Lieutenant Governor, and
Governor-elect, of Virginia (D)

4

Americans everywhere want to hold the line on taxes. There was a time when Democrats were elected by campaigning against big government and high taxes. But for too long, we have let the other [Republican] party take these issues away from us—indeed, we have allowed them to hammer us with these issues.

Before Democratic Leadership
Council, Washington, Nov. 13/
Los Angeles Times, 11-14:(A)26.

Richard B. Wirthlin
Republican Party
public-opinion analyst

5

[Questioning whether the press should comment on the accuracy of political advertising during election campaigns]: The primary, if not the sole, responsibility for setting the record straight remains with the [opposition] candidate and campaign. The press should report the facts

(RICHARD B. WIRTHLIN)

as they are, but it gets on rather tenuous ground when it judges whether these are half-truths or not.

The Washington Post, 1-19:(A)22.

Jim Wright
United States Representative,
D-Texas

1

[On winning and losing elections]: Does defeat make you better, does it give you strength, does it give you a philosophical outlook, let you roll with the punches? I don't know. It depends on who you are. In order to be gracious in victory, you have to be a gentleman. In order to be gracious in defeat, you have to be a man. I think maybe that's it: "If you can meet with triumph and disaster and treat those two impostors just the same." A hard task.

Interview/USA Today, 2-13:(A)7.

2

[Saying current attacks against his ethics are politically motivated]: Because I hold passionately to certain political beliefs, I have made formidable political opponents in 40 years of active public life. But I have never sought to destroy another man's character, nor to deprive him of his dignity. In these 40 years of public life, the most unethical behavior I have witnessed is that of those who, for their own ravening ambitions, attempt to destroy the personal reputations of political opponents.

Law Day speech,
Fort Worth, Tex., May 5/
Los Angeles Times, 5-6:(I)18.

Social Welfare

Hyman Bookbinder
Former Assistant Director,
Federal Office of
Economic Opportunity

1

It is not, as some assert, that the war on poverty [in the 1960s] was not good. It was not good *enough*. It was a war we tired of too soon. It was a war we failed to adjust to new and ominous challenges: epidemic of teen-age pregnancies and broken families; drugs and crime; massive homelessness; crippling illiteracy; changing work requirements. Did *every* program of the '60s work? Of course not. Was *every* dollar used to its maximum potential use? Of course not. Should we in the '90s and the 21st century just reinstate and increase the funding of Great Society programs? Of course not . . . Has every defense contract yielded a perfect product—and at minimum cost? Has every cancer project brought us a cure? Has every space launching been successful? Why is a less-than-perfect record for social programs less tolerable to society than failed economic or military or diplomatic policies?

Before House subcommittee,
Washington, Feb. 23/
The Washington Post, 3-3:(A)18.

H. James Brown
Director, Joint Center for
Housing Studies,
Harvard University

2

We're becoming a nation of housing haves and have-nots. Increasingly, the whole issue of whether you've made it in this society seems to focus on housing. And home ownership is slipping away from thousands of people each year.

Los Angeles Times, 4-22:(I)25.

George Bush
President of the United States

3

We must protect those members of our society who are the most vulnerable—the infants, the pregnant women, children living in poverty and, yes, the elderly. We must protect the homeless. Greater support is needed for emergency food and shelter, for health service and for clinics for the mentally ill. The government . . . cannot stand on the sidelines, not in the face of the national shame of the homeless or the depressed stage of our education.

Before Business and Industry
Association of New Hampshire,
Manchester, Feb.13/
The Washington Post, 2-14:(A)6.

4

Homelessness affects a small proportion of Americans but concerns us all . . . You look out the window of the White House and see the ragged and pathetic figures huddled over the steam grates of the Ellipse. It's an affront to the American dream . . . a national shame.

At Independent Insurance Agents
of America conference,
Washington, March 14/
USA Today, 3-15:(A)4.

Mario M. Cuomo
Governor of New York (D)

5

[If Abraham Lincoln were President today,] I'd like to believe that he'd take up the challenge of narrowing the gap between the haves and have-nots in this society, of reuniting the two cities where Americans live today—one rich and glittering city on the hill, the other full of pain and despair and lost potential, the new slavery . . . Beleaguered as he was, Lincoln could never have accepted the crises we face, and their impact on the national fabric—plagues of disease and hopelessness and squalor. Surely, possessing all that we do, he would not allow this work to remain unfinished. Not Lincoln.

Speech at ceremony marking 126th anniversary
of Lincoln's Gettysburg Address,
Gettysburg, Pa., Nov. 19/
The New York Times, 11-20:(C)11.

Marian Wright Edelman
Executive director,
Children's Defense Fund

1

Preventive investment in our children and families is sound economic policy. America cannot afford to waste resources by failing to address problems that will cost billions of dollars later on. We've gotten way off balance in our investment priorities in the last decade. Billions of dollars have been cut from programs for poor children and are being invested in weapons of death. In the meantime, we've seen a growth in suffering. Now we are finally seeing a convergence between what is morally right for children and what is essential for a healthy economy.

Interview/Christianity Today,
3-17:35.

Bill Faith
Director, Ohio Coalition
for the Homeless

2

Rural homelessness is growing faster than we can keep track of it. People are living in railroad cars and tar-paper shacks. Shelters in tiny towns we've never heard of are operating at or above capacity and are turning people away.

The New York Times, 5-2:(A)1.

Barry M. Goldwater
Former United States Senator,
R-Arizona

3

People say to me, "Well, what would you do about welfare?" thinking I would stamp it out. No—but I would take a long, hard look at it. There has never been a welfare state that hasn't turned into a dictatorship. I don't see that happening, but I'm not going to live forever.

Interview, Phoenix, Ariz./
People, 2-13:72.

Raymond Hay
Chief executive officer,
LTV Corporation

4

It's hard for me to believe that entitlements have to continue going up when unemployment is going down. We're looking at 5 per cent unemployment in this country, and yet we can't do anything about entitlements.

Interview/USA Today, 6-7:(A)11.

Jesse L. Jackson
Civil-rights leader

5

We have to seize the moral initiative by dealing with the expanded base of human misery created in the last eight years. We need to attack, not react. [President] Bush proposes a savings-and-loan bailout; we should demand that he combine it with an attack on those banks' refusal to lend money in black neighborhoods. Bush says he backs a pay raise for Congress and the judges; we should tie that to a higher [national] minimum wage.

Interview/
The New York Times, 2-9:(A)12.

Sheila B. Kamerman
School of Social Work,
Columbia University

6

[On why government assistance to families with children is so generous in many countries overseas]: The concept is that people with children are making a contribution to society, in terms of producing the future labor force and the quality of that labor force, the quality of citizens—even, if you will, financing the social-security system. Children are viewed as a social resource.

Interview/
The Atlantic Monthly, August:59.

Jack Kemp
Secretary-designate of
Housing and Urban Development
of the United States

7

It is a national tragedy of appalling proportions that there are Americans without basic shelter and human services. If one person were without shelter, it would be too much, in my opinion ... I'm willing to give it the highest

(JACK KEMP)

priority at HUD . . . We've created a stunning national [economic] recovery in this nation . . . but there is a forgotten frontier in our midst—ghettos and barrios that still experience unconscionable levels of poverty, unemployment and despair.

> *At Senate Banking, Housing and*
> *Urban Development Committee*
> *hearing on his confirmation,*
> *Washington, Jan. 27/*
> *Los Angeles Times, 1-28:(I)16.*

1

[The late U.S. Attorney General] Bobby Kennedy once said, "To fight poverty without the power of free enterprise is to wage war with a single platoon, while the great armies are left to stand aside." Well, I agree with that. We need to enlist this great army of private enterprise and unleash it in our inner cities.

> *At Senate Banking, Housing and*
> *Urban Development Committee*
> *hearing on his confirmation,*
> *Washington, Jan. 27/*
> *Los Angeles Times, 1-28:(I)16.*

Jack Kemp
Secretary of Housing
and Urban Development
of the United States

2

We're going to get a terrific number of talented men and women of all ethnic and racial backgrounds coming into HUD. I want to get activists. I want to get people who will put energy and intellectual capital into this effort . . . I have to provide motivation and energy and the direction. But I am also willing to realize that . . . many people have good ideas who are out there in the field . . . I want to run it from the bottom up as much as from the top down.

> *To reporters, Washington,*
> *Feb. 16/*
> *The Washington Post, 2-17:(A)25.*

3

If a woman on welfare in the District of Columbia takes a job, she loses her welfare pay-

ment, and they tax her income to where she has to earn—this figure should be checked, but it's close—$16,000 of pre-tax income at her first entry-level job to get the equivalent of $9,000 or $10,000 of untaxed welfare payments for her and her three children. How is it possible that we could have designed a welfare system that says we want to reward you for not being able to get a job, but if you get a job you get punished? It's a terrible disincentive.

> *The Washington Post, 3-1:(A)23.*

4

You know in your life that if you work hard and you're a good citizen and you drive down the right side of the street and you stop at the signals and you study hard and you mind your mom and dad and you get good grades, stay in school and keep that first job, that you're not going to be in poverty. I mean, you just know it intuitively . . . What if this is not true for [some] people? What if there is no job at the end of the tunnel? What if education doesn't lead to anything but unemployment lines? . . . I think government has a responsibility to create [that] climate.

> *Interview/*
> *Los Angeles Times, 4-9:(I)20.*

5

[Reacting to revelations of corruption in the recent past at HUD]: I am determined that all HUD programs shall operate without favoritism and without Republican or Democratic consultants and for the fullest possible benefit of those in need and not those who are motivated by greed. We will remove the perception and the reality of influence-peddling and political favoritism in HUD programs. I want to pledge today that all decisions involving funding for our programs will be based on need and merit.

> *Before House Government Operations Subcommittee*
> *on Employment and Housing, Washington, July 11/*
> *Los Angeles Times, 7-12:(I)4.*

Joseph P. Kennedy II
United States Representative,
D-Massachusetts

6

[Saying any government rescue of the ailing savings-and-loan industry should include a pro-

(JOSEPH P. KENNEDY II)

gram for affordable housing]: The whole purpose of the savings-and-loan industry was to provide [mortgage] loans. That issue is hardly even getting mentioned. We end up providing huge amounts of government funds to an industry whose purpose has largely been forgotten.

Interview/
The Washington Post, 5-24:(A)23.

Gwendolyn S. King
Commissioner, Social Security
Administration
of the United States

1

First on my agenda is people. I want to provide that responsive and caring service that people come to us looking for. People don't come to us because they want to; they come to us for the most part because they need to. Second, of course, is protecting the trust fund. We need to continue the vigilance to ensure that dollars coming into the trust fund are protected, are not siphoned off for any reason that's unintended, and that the trust funds are there for people who retire in the future. And third, of course, a concern of mine, is keeping that very well-trained and able and committed work-force at Social Security.

Interview/USA Today, 10-9:(A)13.

Tom Lantos
United States Representative,
D-California

2

[On revelations of abuses in Federal housing programs in recent years]: There were greedy people, unethical people, sleazy people who went to HUD and found it a honey pot. Both [Secretary] Jack Kemp at HUD and we in Congress have our jobs cut out. This is gigantic . . . I don't enjoy this particular assignment [to investigate the abuses]. I would be much happier working with Jack Kemp on programs for the homeless rather than draining this swamp.

Interview/
The New York Times, 7-6:(A)15.

George Miller
United States Representative,
D-California

3

Skyrocketing reports of child abuse, new conditions resulting from crack cocaine and alcohol abuse, and homelessness among families with children are driving an increasing number of children into costly out-of-home placements with inadequate services and accountability . . . Thousands of American children have only a cell, a hospital bed or a temporary shelter to call home.

Dec. 11/
The Washington Post, 12-12:(A)1.

James Moran
Mayor of Alexandria, Va.;
Chairman,
human development policy
steering committee,
National League of Cities

4

Children growing up today are experiencing a higher level of poverty; they're experiencing a much higher [school] dropout rate. From 1979 to 1986, the rate of poverty among children went from 25.3 per cent to 29.4 per cent, from one out of four to almost one out of three. Those children desperately need more than custodial care and developmental day-care to make them competitive in our economy and certainly through our educational system.

Interview/USA Today, 8-29:(A)11.

William O'Hare
Director of policy studies,
Population Reference Bureau

5

Many of the structural changes in the family appear to be related to large-scale changes in the economy. High divorce and single parenthood rates would probably not have been possible but for the enormous economic growth of the United States after World War II, allowing the country to support a larger number of households than [is] possible in a poor economy. And increasing single-parenthood rates among both blacks and

(WILLIAM O'HARE)

whites are almost certainly explained, at least in part, by the decline over the last generation in the proportion of well-paying jobs for low-skilled men, making them less desirable marital partners.

The Washington Post, 9-5:(A)12.

Peter G. Peterson
Former Secretary of Commerce
of the United States

1

[Saying Social Security payments are too high for people who don't need them]: Let me give you an example: If things go on as they are, I'll get back from Social Security something like three or four times what I put in, *plus* my company's contributions, *plus* interest. And that's only on the retirement side. On the Medicare side, I'll get back 10 to 20 times what I put in. The average weekly-wage earner retiring today collects *all* of his Social Security and Medicare contributions, *all* of his company's contributions, *all* interest accrued, plus *all* of the Federal income taxes he paid over his entire lifetime, plus interest on those income taxes—all in the first 12 years of his retirement. In sum, the average retiree, along with his spouse, receives about 50 per cent more than he ever paid into the Federal treasury. We can't afford that . . . Let's start with the most radical proposal: that we decide on an income level for the elderly above which no one will get a subsidy from the government—i.e., no one will get more than he or she put in, plus interest. Let's assume that the American people democratically decide what that income level will be—say, between $40,000 and $100,000 a year. If a retired person earns that much, she'll receive benefits only up to the amount she's put in, plus interest. The remainder of her entitlement—her subsidy—will be taxed at 100 per cent. You and I, for example, would never get a subsidy.

Interview/Lear's, Jan.-Feb.:26.

Samuel R. Pierce, Jr.
Secretary of Housing and Urban
Development of the United States

2

We ought to get a better handle on how many of the young so-called middle-class people are

actually seeking housing. I think a lot of young middle-class people are spending more time in cities, in apartments, trying to wait before they have children. We've got to know more about their life-styles and whether they're actually looking to buy houses. What we can do, if we want to help them, is through making some changes in FHA-guaranteed mortgages [by raising the ceiling].

Interview, Washington,
Jan. 18/
The New York Times, 1-20:(A)14.

Samuel R. Pierce, Jr.
Former Secretary of Housing
and Urban Development
of the United States

3

[On allegations of improper handling of HUD monetary grants during his tenure as Secretary]: [That impression] starts because some people in Washington don't like what you're doing. And there were Congressmen that didn't like the approach I was trying to take. And there were people—not just Congress, but developers and builders and so forth—who wanted to keep programs that I wanted to get rid of because I thought they were wasteful. I think about the names I've been called in this town. I've been called Stepin Fetchit, I've been called Silent Sam, Mr. Mayor. I've been called Svengali. It shows what people will do. To be popular, you must have a lot of programs, a lot of money for everybody, including the builders and developers and consultants.

Interview/Time, 9-18:24.

Dan Quayle
Vice President-elect
of the United States

4

I want to help [President-elect] George Bush reposition the Republican Party to cast aside this stereotype image that Republicans somehow don't care about the inner city or care about the disadvantaged, that they don't care about minority opportunities or don't care about those who are less fortunate in life. I think there are a lot of things that can be done.

Interview, Washington/
The New York Times, 1-14:7.

Dan Quayle
Vice President
of the United States

1

This President [Bush] has submitted a child-care proposal. He's firmly committed to his proposal. I would say a good precedent is the minimum-wage proposal. The President said this is unacceptable as it stands. The Congress went ahead for, I believe, basically political reasons and tried to put the President in a corner. He vetoed it. As a result, we don't have a minimum-wage bill. I don't think they want to do the same thing on child care. But that will be their decision.

To reporters, Washington,
Sept. 6/
Los Angeles Times, 9-7:(I)23.

Ronald Reagan
President of the United States

2

Too many [poor people] became dependent on government payments and lost the moral strength that has always given the poor the determination to climb America's ladder of opportunity ... Twenty years ago, the government declared a war on poverty. Poverty won. Too many poor people were sucked into a system that declared that the only sin is not to have enough money.

Before Knights of Malta of America,
New York, Jan.13/
Los Angeles Times, 1-14:(I)18.

Eugene Sawyer
Mayor of Chicago;
Chairman, National Task Force
on the Next Generation

3

There's been no focus, I guess, since the late '50s on the issue of inner-city youth in general. They've done it with Social Security; they've done it with the problems of women's issues; they've done it in many categories. But it hasn't been done for young people in 30 years. It's time that we redirect our priorities, because that's our

future ... I think [drugs] is one of the problems; it's causing young people to just drift off. And the lack of hope—we've got to do something economically. Creating jobs, job-training programs, things of that nature.

Interview/
USA Today, 1-5:(A)7.

Barry Zigas
President, National
Low-Income Housing Coalition

4

[On HUD Secretary Jack Kemp's commitment to low-income housing]: I think he came wanting to bring HUD back to its original mission to give people the opportunity for decent housing. He's been weighed down by scandals [from the regime of the previous Secretary], paralyzed for months trying to cope, and I think he is being opposed within the [Bush] Administration by holdovers from [the previous] Reagan Administration who are opposed to new resources for housing assistance.

The Christian Science Monitor,
9-25:8.

Edward F. Zigler
Professor of psychology,
and Director of Bush Center
in Child Development and
Social Policy, Yale University

5

Finally, people have begun to see child care not as a welfare mothers' issue, not as a women's issue, but as a genuine national issue. A woman's productivity as a worker depends on how stable her child care is. And people with vision see that if we don't invest in good child care, workers 20 years from now will not be very productive ... Two out of three working mothers are either the sole support of their children or have a husband who makes less than $15,000 a year. Women have to work.

Interview, New Haven, Conn./
The New York Times, 6-23:(A)10.

Transportation

Glenn M. Anderson
United States Representative,
D-California

1

[On suburban traffic congestion]: Clearly, we're facing problems in the suburbs that were not envisioned years ago. As we decide the future of the highway program, we have to be aware of the need for solutions . . . The economic health of the nation depends on it.

Los Angeles Times, 1-8:(I)1.

Phil Bakes
President, Eastern Airlines

2

There is no relationship between [airline] safety and [financial] debt. Safety cannot be equated to the balance sheet, [to] debt-equity ratios or profits and losses . . . The human factor is the one area which needs improvement, and it is the one which costs the least.

The Washington Post, 10-24:(D)3.

R. Steve Bell
President, National Air Traffic
Controllers Association

3

[Saying air-traffic controllers are over-worked and the system needs reform]: I can say that the FAA has a tired and demoralized work-force that is fed up with the empty promises that have been served up in the last eight years . . . It all boils down to business as usual. And it is a very poor way of doing business.

Before House Transportation and
Public Works subcommittee, Washington,
May 25/Los Angeles Times, 5-26:(I)6.

Benjamin Cosgrove
Vice president, and
general manager of engineering,
Boeing Commercial
Airplane Company

4

[On flying safety—is it the responsibility of government, the airlines or the aircraft manufac-

turer]: There seemed to be for a while the perception that the regulatory agencies [of government] are the keeper of the keys to safety. That is not true. There is more at stake in Boeing and in the airlines in safety than any other place in the world. If the traveling public doesn't have faith in an airplane, the airplane company is not going to exist.

Interview/USA Today, 3-28:(A)11.

Robert L. Crandall
Chairman, AMR Corporation
(American Airlines)

5

[On the increase in airline traffic resulting in gridlock in the sky]: We tend to be making a conscious effort to do everything possible to restrain the transportation system that lies at the core of travel and tourism . . . Today, American [Airlines] can't compete with Eastern, Pan Am or Donald Trump between Washington and New York. We can't add flights to and from Chicago, nor can we operate the ones we already have there with the slightest assurance that they will either arrive or leave on time. Even in Nashville, our flights often sit on the ground waiting for a slot in the sky. The reality is we are making air travel harder and harder rather than making it easier and easier.

Los Angeles Times, 2-12:(I)2.

Henry A. Duffy
President, Air Line Pilots
Association

6

Let me discuss for a moment an item that we thought had been decided long ago, but is not coming around for another approach to the runway, and is again nearing a decision height. The subject is foreign [air] carriers operating in U.S. domestic markets . . . With cabotage, we wouldn't just be leaving the tent flap open to tempt the camel. We'd be inviting him in, seating him at our table, and asking him to eat our lunch . . . If your imagination fails you at this point, let me offer a

(HENRY A. DUFFY)

few examples of potential abuses: subcontracting arrangements between domestic carriers and foreign carriers, along the lines of Eastern and Orion; opening doors for anti-labor managements to move assets to foreign subsidiaries—a form of "international runaway shop" that cannot be held accountable to the Congress and to U.S. regulatory agencies. I had better stop there before I give anyone any ideas, but you get the picture. Cabotage is a declaration of war against airline labor.

Speech to aviators, New York/
The Wall Street Journal,
4-27:(A)16.

Robert Farris
Director, Federal
Highway Administration

1

[On suburban traffic congestion]: Ultimately, this local problem becomes a barrier to interstate commerce. All of these transportation issues are interrelated, and we've got to start looking at them simultaneously.

Los Angeles Times, 1-8:(I)1.

Malcolm S. Forbes
Chairman, Forbes, Inc.
("Forbes" magazine)

2

[On his love of motorcycles]: The nearest analogy to how a motorcyclist feels on his horsepower machine is the way a cowboy felt on his horse. The world is open to you . . . That feeling also frees your mind from the mundane, and your imagination is released . . . Your mind roams along with your heels. You grab the passing thoughts.

Interview/
Los Angeles Times, 7-21:(V)6.

Stephen Hayes
Vice president,
Air Transport Association

3

The idea of [FAA] independence is secondary to us. What's really important is FAA reform.

The agency should have the flexibility that private business has to procure quickly and efficiently and be able to transfer personnel more freely. At the moment, we don't see a clear way to meet those objectives without an independent FAA.

The Christian Science Monitor,
10-13:7.

Wayne E. Hedien
Chairman, Allstate Insurance

4

[On high auto insurance costs]: The big problem is automobile insurance in the cities. If you look at the Consumer Price Index and you look at auto insurance rates in urban areas, you will see that the rates have risen faster than consumer prices over-all. The factors that drive up auto insurance rates are the same factors that drive up health insurance rates—hospital room costs and doctor bills. Also, the costs of repairing cars is much greater today than in the past. The fact is, to get auto insurance rates down, we've got to get these other costs down. If we can solve the problem in the cities, we go a long way toward solving the affordability problem in insurance.

Interview/
The New York Times, 9-5:(C)2.

Soichiro Honda
Founder, Honda
Motor Company (Japan)

5

My greatest achievement was in imitating American cars . . . Japanese and American cars are like humans. Some are good in some aspects and some are bad in some aspects.

To reporters, Dearborn, Mich.,
Oct. 9/
Los Angeles Times, 10-10:(IV)9.

Robert Kiley
Chairman, Metropolitan
Transportation Authority
of New York;
Chairman, Transit 2000
Task Force

6

Automobile use is a health hazard in the U.S.A. It's not only an environmental problem

(ROBERT KILEY)

that results in medical expenses which are partly subsidized by the government, but a lot of people are killed and injured. More people have been killed by automobiles than in all the wars that we fought in this century. There's a tremendous price we pay for that, both in lost productivity and just poor health. So those are huge subsidy bucks. As consumers, we spend more on cars than we do on groceries, housing or education, and almost as much as we do on health. That's bizarre.

Interview/
USA Today, 11-30:(A)11.

Ann Klinger
Supervisor, Merced County, Calif.;
President, National
Association of Counties

1

Let's pick a topic—transportation, for example. Counties are concerned with people-movers. We're concerned with mass transit, but we're also concerned with rural America. The rural areas that have crumbling roads and bridges raise the question: "How do we get our farm produce to market?" We recognize that we have not invested and reinvested in our road system as we needed to. It becomes a very huge economic issue.

Interview/
USA Today, 9-7:(A)13.

Richard Lally
Systems vice president
of security,
Air Transport Association

2

I would say that air travel remains the safest form of travel that the world knows. It was last year. It was last weekend. It will be next week . . . It's just a fact that the American public holds air transportation to a much higher standard of conduct. Society is callous in that it will accept the 50,000 lives lost each year on the highways, but even one airline accident, or hijacking, is considered intolerable. The record speaks for itself.

Interview/USA Today, 1-3:(A)7.

Larry Pressler
United States Senator,
R-South Dakota

3

[On the eccentricities of today's air fares]: It's cheaper to fly across the nation than across South Dakota. That is bizarre.

USA Today, 6-9:(A)14.

Ian Savage
Professor of economics,
Northwestern University

4

There is a belief that financial pressure has caused some airlines to reduce expenditures on inputs to safety, such as training and maintenance. [But] people who study accidents have been unable to find any strong relationship. It is very difficult to pin down any relationship between the amount of money you spend on safety and whether or not you have accidents.

The Washington Post, 10-24:(D)3.

Samuel K. Skinner
Secretary of Transportation
of the United States

5

[On his meetings on Capitol Hill about airline deregulation]: The Hill visits have led me to the conclusion that there's great concern about the impact of deregulation on competition generally and on air fares. From all these meetings it became quite clear that we do not have a good understanding of what's going on in the airline industry as a result of deregulation. The dynamics have changed.

To reporters/
The Washington Post, 2-27:(A)7.

6

I am totally, with a big T, committed to developing a national transportation policy. We are going to have a national transportation policy in this country, or there will be a lot of dead bodies all over the [Transportation] Department. One of them will be mine.

To aviation officials, Washington/
The New York Times, 3-10:(A)12.

(SAMUEL K. SKINNER)

1

[On airport security, in the wake of last year's bombing of a Pan American Airways jet over Scotland]: I don't see how anybody in the wake of Pan Am [flight] 103 can put their head down at night and feel comfortable, unless they have done everything they can to make sure that travel on airlines in their country is safe, without regard to whose flag they carry.

To reporters, London, April 27/
Los Angeles Times, 4-28:(I)9.

2

We've got a maritime industry that has deteriorated to a very low presence in the world, yet it is very important from a national-defense posture. The U.S. Transportation Command has the responsibility of marshaling the transportation assets of this country in time of war, and using those resources to move man and materiel across the oceans. We still have enough airlift capacity to do it. Yet, we don't have the sea-lift capability that we should have. Very few ships remain U.S.-flagged. Our ship construction is at an absolute minimum.

Interview/USA Today, 7-5:(A)9.

3

So that there can be no doubt, I will not allow excessive debt in the airline industry to jeopardize the public interest—especially in the area of safety . . . [The Transportation Department wants] to be absolutely certain that any carrier is financially fit, and that safety will never be compromised. If continuing fitness is called into question, rest assured that the Department will not hesitate to make adjustments to the airline's operating certificate, or, if absolutely necessary . . . we will revoke the certificate.

Before International Aviation
Club, Washington, Sept. 19/
Los Angeles Times, 9-20:(IV)5.

4

[On the financial burdens created by airline take-overs and their effects on safety]: The pressures to pay down the principal and to meet interest payments could threaten the carrier's ability to meet its other obligations, including fleet replacement, aircraft repair and maintenance . . . Financial distress and excessive debt in a cyclical industry such as the airlines is a cause for concern.

The Washington Post, 10-24:(D)3.

Urban Affairs

Jerry Abramson
Mayor of Louisville, Ky.

1

[On the varying policies and abilities of cities to handle the homeless]: The bottom line is: without a national program, without a national response, you're just simply pitting city against city. And you're requiring those who are in those homeless ranks . . . to begin choosing the cities they can best make it in at a specific time of the year. And that's not appropriate.

At U.S. Conference of Mayors meeting,
Washington, Jan. 17/
The Washington Post, 1-18:(A)3.

George Bush
President of the United States

2

There are some who say, and you've heard it, that the state of urban America is hopeless. I say they're wrong. We've got to see past the stories on the 6 o'clock news, past the statistics. We've got to see the potential for progress. We've got to see the face of hope in our inner cities. The challenge for urban America is a challenge for all of America. It's a challenge for my Administration. Together, we must and will find a way to stop the decline in our inner cities, to restore hope and make the '90s a decade of urban renaissance.

Before National Urban League, Washington,
Aug.8/Los Angeles Times, 8-9:(I)19.

Don Fraser
Mayor of Minneapolis

3

[Praising President-elect George Bush's stated commitment to helping cities]: It's better now than we've had in the last eight years. When Bush speaks of his commitment to helping the homeless, I believe him. Ditto his pledge to work for a kinder, gentler nation. Unfortunately, resources are the key, and if I read the President-elect's lips properly, we won't be getting all the resources that we need.

Washington, Jan. 18/
The New York Times, 1-19:(A)13.

Terry Goddard
Mayor of Phoenix; President,
National League of Cities

4

We're [cities] looking forward to a new [Federal] Administration and a new leadership in Congress. We have not fared well under the prior management, and it's no secret that cities were basically devastated in terms of their relationship with the Federal government. A whole lot more went from us to the Feds than came back. And some very serious problems have emerged.

Interview/USA Today, 3-14:(A)11.

Ann Klinger
Supervisor, Merced County, Calif.;
President, National
Association of Counties

5

[Counties] have far more complexity [than cities]. When it comes to courts, corrections, welfare, hospitals and health, the heavy load is on counties. We're working with some of the most disadvantaged people in America, whether it's through job training, economic development, the welfare system, or in our jails. These are the people who need tremendous resources if they're going to become contributing members of society. The cities have a little different role.

Interview/USA Today, 9-7:(A)13.

Edward I. Koch
Mayor of New York

6

[On his losing the Democratic primary for re-election]: I believe that I've never felt better. I mean, I wanted to be the Mayor for the next four years, but I also believe that it is an enormous, wrenching job. Anyone who runs for it will only find out when they hold that job how difficult it is. So while I would have liked to be the Mayor, I'm not upset that I'm relieved of the responsibilities . . . I wanted to win [the primary]. I don't want to tell you that I did it for the game. Not at

(EDWARD I. KOCH)

all. But I'm not—I don't want to stress this too much—I'm not, as people would expect, sad or depressed. I hope I'm remembered for all the good things that I did, not just the last few days. I've been a Mayor for 12 years, in very difficult times. I hope that the span of memory covers 12 years and not just a week.

Interview, New York, Sept. 13/
The New York Times, 9-14:(A)20.

1

[On his leaving office after three terms as Mayor]: [As Mayor,] if I go out in the rain, there's somebody there with an umbrella. [But] I can hold an umbrella myself. That's not a big loss. [As Mayor,] if I go to a restaurant, there's somebody always making a reservation. [But] I know how to use a telephone; I can make a reservation. There's a chef at Gracie Mansion [the Mayor's residence]. If I didn't have that chef, I wouldn't have to lose weight. So it's pluses and minuses.

Interview, New York, Dec. 26/
The New York Times, 12-27:(A)20.

William H. Whyte
Author; Authority on
urban affairs

2

The core of the city has held. It has not gone to hell. The city remains a magnificent place to do business, and that is part of the rediscovery of the center. While we [cities] are losing a lot of functions that we used to enjoy, we are intensifying the most important function of all—a place for coming together.

Time, 8-7:9.

PART TWO

International

Foreign Affairs

Georgi A. Arbatov
Director,
Soviet Institute of U.S.A.
and Canadian Affairs

1

[On the popularity in Western Europe of Soviet leader Mikhail Gorbachev]: The "Gorbachev challenge" is a better name for it. We want to take what we call our "new political thinking" right to the people. We want them to see what we are proposing and to compare it to what has existed for so long, to what the others [in the West] are proposing . . . The man in the street is ahead of the politicians. People begin to see that we are not doomed to live under that modern sword of Damocles—the threat of nuclear war. Call it "Gorbymania" if you want, but it represents good-will toward the man and the changes that his policies have brought to our country and, in fact, to the world. This good-will, after so many years of confrontation, is itself a cause for optimism . . . We are depriving our opponents [in the West] of the "enemy image." We are leaving them without the enemy they have used to justify their policies, particularly the arms race, for so long.

Bonn, West Germany, June 13/
Los Angeles Times, 6-14:(I)6.

Moshe Arens
Foreign Minister of Israel

2

The only way to fight [international] terrorism is through the use of force, and the world will also have to learn this lesson.

To reporters/
The Christian Science Monitor,
8-2:3.

Oscar Arias
President of Costa Rica

3

We have often seen how those who led struggles against dictators themselves use the name of freedom to establish dictatorships of a different ideological hue.

At meeting of Latin American
leaders, San Jose, Costa Rica,
Oct. 27/The Washington Post,
9-28:(A)19.

James A. Baker III
Secretary of State-designate
of the United States

4

There are good reasons for both optimistic and pessimistic views of today's Soviet Union. No one can doubt that there are very real changes; many of them were unthinkable just a few short years ago. So there are reasons to be hopeful, but realism requires that we be prudent. However fascinating the twists and turns of *perestroika* [reform in the Soviet Union] may be and however riveting the details of Soviet decline as reported in Soviet newspapers, the Soviet Union remains a very heavily armed superpower. The talk is different, but the force of structure and policies that support far-reaching interests and clients have not changed commensurately. Many of those policies and those clients are hostile to American values and they threaten our interests and our allies. That is a reality. Still, I would not underestimate the impact of Moscow's domestic troubles on Soviet foreign policy.

At Senate Foreign Relations
Committee hearing on his
confirmation, Washington,
Jan. 17/
The New York Times, 1-18:(A)10.

5

There is [an] issue we must resolve . . . It concerns the relationship between the Executive and the Congress in the realm of foreign policy. Simply put, we must have bipartisanship to succeed. That is the verdict of history and that is the verdict of recent experience. On this subject let me quote [the late Secretary of State] Dean

(JAMES A. BAKER III)

Acheson. He was evidently acquainted with some of our Texas customs, because he said that there was a rule in the saloons of the old West that you never shoot the piano player. And Dean Acheson wrote that, in foreign policy, the President was the piano player.

At Senate Foreign Relations
Committee hearing on his
confirmation, Washington,
Jan. 17/
The New York Times, 1-18:(A)10.

1

[On U.S.-Soviet relations]: I am reminded of [U.S. President Reagan's] saying—"trust but verify." I don't think we ought to change that. I think "trust but verify" is a good standard. I think prudence in our approach, I think realism in our approach—all of these are good ways in which I think we could describe what should be our approach.

At Senate Foreign Relations
Committee hearing on his
confirmation, Washington,
Jan. 17/
The New York Times, 1-18:(A)11.

2

[Human rights] is one of the vary basic foundations of our foreign policy and, for that matter, our national-security policy . . . I don't think that we should distinguish in our human-rights standards in application between situations where human rights are violated on the left or situations where human rights are violated on the right. I think our standards ought to be straight and we ought to play it down the middle.

At Senate Foreign Relations
Committee hearing on his
confirmation, Washington,
Jan. 18/
The New York Times, 1-19:(A)12.

3

[On whether the U.S. has or should give financial aid to the candidate of its choice in a foreign election]: There have, I suppose, been occasions in the past where it has been in the national-security interests of the United States that parties or personalities inimical to the United States not win elections. And in duly approved covert actions, I suppose there could be instances where it would not be inappropriate. So I can't just give you a total blanket [rule].

At Senate Foreign Relations
Committee hearing on his
confirmation, Washington,
Jan. 18/
The New York Times, 1-19:(A)15.

4

I think the National Security Council's primary role is to advise the President with respect to national-security matters and to coordinate the activities of the various agencies and departments that are engaged in the national-security process . . . The Secretary of State has a statutory responsibility in the conduct of foreign policy and as the President's principal adviser with respect to foreign policy. These are statutory obligations which devolve upon the Secretary of State, and that's the way I would see my role.

At Senate Foreign Relations
Committee hearing on his
confirmation, Washington,
Jan. 18/
The New York Times, 1-19:(A)12.

James A. Baker III
Secretary of State
of the United States

5

I think if you examine American foreign policy throughout the post-war era, one truth certainly shines through. From President Truman's support for NATO to President Reagan's INF agreement, every important achievement has enjoyed sustained bipartisan support. A bipartisan foreign policy is based on honest and honorable discussion and debate. It's not based on suppressing legitimate differences. In the end, it is also, I think, based on a recognition that we are, after all, one people. We are one nation, and we must have one consistent foreign policy.

Washington, March 24/
The New York Times, 3-25:5.

(JAMES A. BAKER III)

1

[On recent changes in Soviet policies that seem to be aimed at better relations with the West]: We cannot be passive in the face of these great strategic changes, nor can we simply yield the initiative to a Soviet agenda that may not reflect the best interests of the West . . . Our policy must be to press forward with *our* agenda, to test the application of Soviet "new thinking" again and again.

Before Center for Strategic and
International Studies, Washington,
May 4/The Washington Post,
5-5:(A)21.

2

[On the current reform in the Soviet Union]: They're singing out of our hymn book . . . I mean, they are unilaterally reducing [their military forces]; we have been calling on them to do this for years. They are acknowledging the failure of their system. They are saying that their economic and political system has failed. They are having elections. They are trying to open up politically and economically. Clearly, they are coming in our direction and we ought to welcome that.

At seminar, Washington, May 15/
The New York Times, 5-16:(A)5.

3

Soviet "new thinking" in foreign and defense policy promises possibilities that would have been unthinkable a decade ago, such as deep stabilizing cuts in strategic forces and parity in reduced conventional arms in Europe. Yet *perestroika*'s [the Soviet reform program] success is far from assured. Any uncertainty about the fate of reform in the Soviet Union, however, is all the more reason, not less, for us to seize the present opportunity. For the works of our labor—a diminished Soviet threat and effectively verifiable agreements—can endure even if *perestroika* does not.

Before Commonwealth Club,
San Francisco, Oct. 23/
The New York Times,
10-24:(A)4.

Richard Barnet
Senior fellow,
Institute for Policy Studies

4

The changes in the Soviet Union and China represent a historic opportunity for a fundamental reassessment of American interests. The changes include not just those in the Communist world, but also the new global role of Japan and that of Europe becoming a unified economic superpower by 1992. Also, you have to factor in the radically changed economic position of the United States in going from the world's greatest creditor to the biggest debtor. These changes require us to rethink what we're doing . . . I am concerned that we are seeing a world in which everybody else is in motion—the Chinese and the Russians are getting together again, there's a very active diplomacy now between our allies in West Germany and the Soviet Union—and we are hanging back because we haven't figured out what the new role for the United States is. And if we wait too long, I think we're going to find the world just passes us by.

Interview/USA Today, 5-1:(A)11.

Leonid Batkin
Soviet political scientist

5

The danger of military dictatorship [in the Soviet Union] exists. But Poland has already shown—and China will, too, in a few years time—that force does not solve any problems at the end of the 20th century. It only brings closer the end of the regime that uses it.

The Washington Post,
10-21:(A)32.

Lloyd Bentsen
United States Senator,
D-Texas

6

Think how confusing it would be for a modern Rip Van Winkle—one who had fallen asleep, say, in 1969. He reads that [today] demonstrators are complaining about police brutality in the Soviet Union, and Chinese students are calling for Premier Li's resignation because he [is] going too

WHAT THEY SAID IN 1989

slowly toward democracy. It's quite a change and, from our point of view, quite a victory nevertheless.

At symposium sponsored by
National Endowment for Democracy,
Washington/
The New York Times, 5-5:(A)6.

Benazir Bhutto
Prime Minister of Pakistan

1

Everywhere the sun is setting on the day of the dictator. And for the dictators across the world, democracy is the greatest revenge.

Before U.S. Congress,
Washington, June 7/
Los Angeles Times, 6-8:(I)6.

Richard J. Bloomfield
Former United States
Ambassador to Portugal
and to Ecuador

2

A little hypocrisy is not always a bad thing in diplomacy; but a hypocrite is not a cynic. A cynic knows that what he says publicly about his motives is false; a hypocrite, in contrast, is not conscious of the discrepancy between what he says and what he wants. By and large, Americans are not cynical, so when we are hypocritical about our foreign-policy objectives, we tend to delude ourselves.

Before World Peace Foundation,
May/The Wall Street Journal,
9-22:(A)10.

David L. Boren
United States Senator,
D-Oklahoma

3

Nothing diminishes the influence of this country more than our failure to speak to the rest of the world with a single voice. Nothing is more damaging when we are dealing with sensitive international issues than to have amateur hour on the floor of the United States Senate in which each and every one of us [Senators] decide to weigh in on sensitive issues that have been delicately balanced and negotiated between our country and other nations.

Los Angeles Times, 8-5:(I)24.

Bill Bradley
United States Senator,
D-New Jersey

4

In 1985 Mikhail Gorbachev took over a country [the Soviet Union] with a rising infant and adult mortality rate; a country where 13 per cent of all deaths were due to bad water; a country that was corrupt to the core, not only in the normal sense of criminality, which was rampant, but also in the sense of people losing their faith that the system could deliver anything better for their children . . . Will *perestroika* [reform], *glasnost* [openness] and democratization [in the Soviet Union] work? It is too early to tell . . . But what if the Soviet Union really is changing? What if there's a historic transformation going on? . . . If the Soviet threat diminished, in fact, then . . . some will say [the U.S. should] find another enemy—maybe Japan, Iran, Cuba, Nicaragua. Others—and I put myself in this category—see it as an opportunity for us in a rapidly changing world to define who we are and what we believe and offer the world in a positive new vision. What should be the goal for American society? In one word, excellence.

At Rutgers University
commencement, May 25/
The Washington Post, 6-15:(A)26.

George Bush
President of the United States

5

Good-will [in foreign policy] begets good-will. Good faith can be a spiral that endlessly moves on. Great nations, like great men, must keep their word. When America says something, America means it, whether a treaty or an agreement or a vow made on marble steps.

Inaugural address,
Washington, Jan. 20/
The Washington Post, 1-21:(A)11.

(GEORGE BUSH)

1

[On Soviet leader Mikhail Gorbachev's numerous peace initiatives to the West]: I don't view it as the "Gorbachev challenge." I think if we make the mistake of assessing our relationship with the Soviet Union in terms of a personality, we'll live to regret it. You've got to make a broader assessment of Soviet intention that transcends any individual. I don't think you can shape the foreign policy of the United States based on the leader of the moment.

Interview, Washington/
Time, 1-30:26.

2

Some are saying [to me]: "You'd better hurry up. You don't want [Soviet leader Mikhail] Gorbachev to capture the high ground with his speech at the United Nations; don't want him to mold public opinion further in Europe." [But] far more important is that we do a prudent review of our foreign policy, national-security requirements, and then in concert with our allies move forward . . . I am not going to be pushed into speedy action because Mr. Gorbachev gives a compelling speech at the United Nations, and I hope the Soviets understand that.

Before Forum Club, Houston,
March 16/
Los Angeles Times, 3-17:(I)18.

3

Whenever in the world there is economic reform, the United States should be hoping that that reform succeeds. Economic reform, with its emphasis on incentive and market economics, leads to more freedom.

Before United States Chamber of
Commerce, Washington, May 1/
The Washington Post, 5-2:(A)6.

4

Wise men . . . crafted the strategy of containment. They believed that the Soviet Union, denied the easy course of expansion, would turn inward and address the contradictions of its inefficient, repressive and inhumane system. And they were right. The Soviet Union is now publicly facing this hard reality. Containment worked. Containment worked because our democratic principles and institutions and values are sound, and always have been. It worked because our alliances were and are strong, and because the superiority of free societies and free markets over stagnant socialism is undeniable . . . Our goal is bold, more ambitious than any of my predecessors could have thought possible. Our review indicates that 40 years of perseverance have brought us a precious opportunity. And now it is time to move beyond containment, to a new policy for the 1990s, one that recognizes the full scope of change taking place around the world, and in the Soviet Union itself. In sum, the United States now has as its goal much more than simply containing Soviet expansionism. We seek the integration of the Soviet Union into the community of nations. And as the Soviet Union itself moves toward greater openness and democratization, as they meet the challenge of responsible international behavior, we will match their steps with steps of our own. Ultimately, our objective is to welcome the Soviet Union back into the world order.

At Texas A&M University
commencement, May 12/
The New York Times,
5-13:4.

5

[On reform in the Soviet Union]: Make no mistake, a new breeze is blowing across the steppes and cities of the Soviet Union. Why not then let this spirit of openness grow, let more barriers come down. Open emigration, open debate, open airwaves—let openness come to mean the publication and sale of banned books and newspapers in the Soviet Union . . . Let openness come to mean nothing less than the free exchange of people, books, and ideas between East and West.

At Texas A&M University
commencement, May 12/
The Washington Post, 5-13:(A)14.

(GEORGE BUSH)

1

The Soviet Union says that it seeks to make peace with the world, and criticizes its own post-war policies. These are words that we can only applaud. But a new relationship cannot simply be declared by Moscow, or bestowed by others. It must be earned. It must be earned because promises are never enough. The Soviet Union has promised a more cooperative relationship before, only to reverse course and return to militarism. Soviet foreign policy has been almost seasonal—warmth before cold, thaw before freeze. We seek a friendship that knows no season of suspicion, no chill of distrust.

AT Texas A&M University
commencement, May 12/
The New York Times, 5-13:4.

2

I know that some are quite restless about the [slow] pace that I have set for dealing with the Soviet Union, but I think it's the proper pace. I hope I'll be forgiven for being cautious and for being prudent and for not being stampeded into something that might prove to be no good for the [NATO] alliance or no good for the United States.

At Boston University
commencement, May 21/
The Washington Post, 5-22:(A)1.

3

[Saying that, despite reforms in the Soviet Union, that country still poses a threat to the West]: I know there's almost a euphoria in some quarters [in the West] that there's no risks in the world any more. Well, I don't believe that . . . If you look at the Soviet Union modernizing its nuclear arsenal at a rather ferocious pace, I'm prudent enough to say: "Why, what's happening here? Why are they doing this? Why—if it's all euphoria and everything is rosy and nobody has anything to worry any more about—how come?" And so, let's not let down our alliance guarantees, because we are more optimistic about peace.

News conference, Washington,
Sept. 15/Los Angeles Times, 9-16:(I)1.

4

East and west, north and south, on every continent, we can see the outlines of a new world of freedom. Of course, freedom's work remains unfinished. The trend we see is not yet universal. Some regimes still stand against the tide. Some rulers still deny the right of the people to govern themselves. But now the power of prejudice and despotism is challenged. Never before have these regimes stood so isolated and alone, so out of step with the steady advance of freedom. Today we are witnessing an ideological collapse—the demise of the totalitarian idea of the omniscient, all-powerful state. There are many reasons for this collapse. But in the end, one fact alone explains what we see today. Advocates of the totalitarian idea saw its triumph written in the laws of history. They failed to see the love of freedom that was written in the human heart.

At United Nations, New York,
Sept. 25/
The New York Times, 9-26:(A)8.

5

We must join forces to combat the threat of terrorism. Every nation and the United Nations must send the outlaws of the world a clear message: Hostage-taking and the terror of random violence are methods that cannot win the world's approval. Terrorism of any kind is repugnant to all values that a civilized world holds in common. And make no mistake, terrorism is a means that no end, no matter how just that end, can sanctify.

At United Nations, New York,
Sept. 25/
The New York Times, 9-26:(A)8.

6

The United Nations was established 44 years ago upon the ashes of war and amidst great hopes. And the United Nations can do great things. No, the United Nations is not perfect. It's not a panacea for [the] world's problems. But it is a vital forum where the nations of the world seek to replace conflict with consensus, and it must remain a forum for peace.

At United Nations, New York,
Sept. 25/
The New York Times, 9-26:(A)8.

(GEORGE BUSH)

1

We have not entered into an era of perpetual peace. The threats to peace that nations face may today be changing but they've not vanished. In fact, in a number of regions around the world, a dangerous combination is now emerging: regimes armed with old and unappeasable animosities and modern weapons of mass destruction. This development will raise the stakes whenever war breaks out. Regional conflicts may well threaten world peace as never before.

At United Nations, New York,
Sept. 25/
The New York Times, 9-26:(A)8.

2

[On Soviet leader Mikhail Gorbachev's positive attitude toward pro-democracy reforms in Eastern Europe and improved East-West relations]: As I watched the way in which Mr. Gorbachev has handled the changes in Eastern Europe, it deserves new thinking. It absolutely mandates new thinking. And when I see his willingness to give support to a [conventional-forces] agreement that calls for him to disproportionately reduce his forces, and that is there on the table, I think that mandates new thinking. When I hear him talk about peaceful change and the right of countries to choose—countries in the Warsaw Pact to choose—that deserves new thinking.

News conference after meeting with
Gorbachev in Malta; Brussels,
Dec. 4/The New York Times,
12-5:(A)8.

3

[On his recent meeting with Soviet leader Mikhail Gorbachev in Malta]: Yes, I think I can trust Gorbachev. I looked him in the eye; I appraised him. He was very determined. Yet there was a twinkle. He is a guy quite sure of what he is doing. He has got a political feel. I could tell by the way he was laughing with us. A little wink now and then. He has a wonderful way of communicating with westerners. I had the feeling that I could bring up any subject at all. We had quite an animated discussion about Western values vs. democratic values. I thought they were the same thing. But he interpreted our definition of Western values to mean that we were right and he was wrong. Whereas, democratic values are what he has been working for.

Interview, Washington/
Time, 12-18:38.

Rosalynn Carter
Wife of former President
of the United States
Jimmy Carter

4

[On former President Carter's campaign for human rights abroad during his Presidency]: He believed that when the President of our country speaks out for those people around the world who are repressed, it gives them hope. And also, if countries know that to a great extent their relationship with the United States depends on how they treat their people, it makes a difference. It was a sincere effort. It was criticized a good bit, because it's very difficult to enforce human rights and demand that countries treat their citizens right. But it led the way for a human-rights movement which I think is too strong now to be stopped.

News conference, Moscow,
Jan. 16/
Los Angeles Times, 1-17:(I)8.

George Carver
Senior fellow, Center for
Strategic and International
Studies, Washington;
Former Deputy Director
of Central Intelligence
of the United States

5

[Soviet leader Mikhail] Gorbachev thinks in classical 19th-century balance-of-power terms. I think his long-range plan is to isolate us by achieving bilateral ties with all of the people we used to use as a counterweight to Soviet expansion . . . The thing that messes us up is a continuing concentration on the short term. We are sprinters competing with marathon runners in a marathon.

Los Angeles Times, 5-14:(I)20.

Fidel Castro
President of Cuba

1

Never has any [U.S.] Administration, not even [that of Ronald] Reagan, been as triumphant as this [Bush] one regarding the difficulties in the socialist camp [around the world] . . . The Bush Administration in the last few months has made statements based on the premise that the sun is setting on socialism or that socialism will end on the dust heap of history that was reserved for capitalism. [But] even if tomorrow we wake up to the news of a civil war in the U.S.S.R., even if tomorrow we wake up to the news that the U.S.S.R. has disintegrated—a thing we don't expect to happen—even under those circumstances, the Cuban people will continue fighting.

Speech at celebration of
36th anniversary of the start of the
Cuban revolution, Camaguey,
Cuba, July 26/
Los Angeles Times, 7-27:(I)8.

Dick Cheney
Secretary of Defense
of the United States

2

I don't think there is any question but what we may—and I emphasize "may"—be on the verge of a fundamental shift, or change if you will, in U.S.-Soviet relations. I would think it would be fair to say that the likelihood of war between the U.S. and the Soviet Union is probably as low as it has been in the post-World War II period—that [Soviet leader Mikhail] Gorbachev does seem to be serious about trying to change the system . . . There is clearly a lot of evidence on the table that we are dealing with a less hostile and less threatening Soviet Union.

Interview/
The Christian Science Monitor, 6-27:18.

Warren M. Christopher
Former Deputy Secretary of State
of the United States

3

[On international terrorism]: As long as the United States is powerful and has diplomats on a

world-wide basis, we'll never be finished with the hostage problem. All we can do is to deal with each case with a combination of strength and humanity.

Interview/
The New York Times, 8-9:(A)4.

Ray Cline
Former Deputy Director
of Central Intelligence
of the United States

4

[On proposed joint Soviet-U.S. efforts against international terrorism]: It is clear to me that in the back of their minds the Soviets now see terrorism is a threat to the Soviet Union, not just the United States. They would like to get on the side of the angels on this one.

The Christian Science Monitor,
10-2:8.

William J. Crowe, Jr.
Admiral, United States Navy;
Chairman,
Joint Chiefs of Staff

5

[On whether the Soviet Union is still an enemy of the U.S.]: They are a potential adversary. When you say the enemy, I don't know quite what that means. Maybe they're your enemy. They're not my enemy. I'm a military man, and we do what we have to do, but I don't particularly look at them as an enemy. Incidentally, the last major war we were in, they were our allies.

News conference, June 6/
The Washington Post, 6-7:(A)12.

Edward J. Derwinski
Under Secretary
for Security Assistance,
Department of State
of the United States;
Former United States Representative,
R-Illinois

6

In the years that I've watched it, the [State] Department has not . . . taken the trouble to

(EDWARD J. DERWINSKI)

understand each member [of Congress] as an individual—to know how the forces in his home state or district are going to affect what he can or can't vote for. A member representing an Irish-American district in the Boston area is going to have a different view of the Northern Ireland problem than State Department officials concerned about relations with the British Foreign Office. A Congressman from a Jewish district in Brooklyn will see the Mideast in very different terms from those Department officials trying to maintain good relations with the Arab world. Senators or Representatives from states with influential sugar-growing interests are not going to be sympathetic when the Department opposes domestic sugar subsidies because they hurt the economies of Third World states we are trying to influence in the Caribbean and the Far East. When State Department officials run into these attitudes, they tend to react by saying Congress is "parochial." What they fail to realize is that a member of Congress has to be parochial—that it is the essence of service to his or her district or constituency.

Interview/
The Washington Post, 1-2:(A)17.

Lawrence S. Eagleburger
Deputy Secretary of State
of the United States

1

[Soviet leader Mikhail] Gorbachev is no anti-Communist and he intends to make the Soviet Union as strong as he possibly can. Nevertheless, it is true that the changes introduced by Gorbachev offer the first realistic hope for a transformation in the nature of the Soviet system and for a qualitative improvement in East-West relations. [Already,] we are hearing it said that we need to take measures to insure the success of Gorbachev's reforms. This, however, is not the task of American foreign policy, nor should it be that of our Western partners. Our task, after all, is to devise projects which will serve our interests, whether Mr. Gorbachev succeeds or fails. And our common goal ought to be the maintenance of the security consensus which has served the West so well over the past 40 years until the process of democratic reform in the East has truly become irreversible.

At Georgetown University,
Sept. 13/
The New York Times, 9-16:5.

2

For all its risks and uncertainties, the Cold War was characterized by a remarkably stable and predictable set of relations among the great powers. A brief look at the history books will tell us that we cannot say as much about the period leading from the birth of the European nation states up through the outbreak of the Second World War.

At Georgetown University,
Sept. 13/
The New York Times, 9-16:5.

Stuart E. Eizenstat
Former Assistant to the
President of the United States
(Jimmy Carter) for
Domestic Policy

3

[On U.S. President Bush's offer of $115-million aid to Poland]: It's sad to see the head of the greatest nation on Earth go to Poland and Hungary and offer a pittance when the Japanese are putting up multi-billion-dollar Third World debt programs . . . It's a commentary less on the Administration than on the state of this country, that we are so strapped for resources, not because we don't have them, but because we refuse to pay for them. We become kibitzers, having lofty goals and let the other countries come in [and provide the money].

The Washington Post, 7-25:(A)8.

Hans Magnus Enzensberger
West German author
and journalist

4

In today's world, it is a great advantage to have more than one solution, more than one option. It's an ecological principle, really. In evolution,

(HANS MAGNUS ENZENSBERGER)

the faster the evolution occurs the more you need a whole assemblage, a whole barrage of possibilities, and not to reduce yourself to one. That partially is the problem with really big empires like the United States, even more so the Soviet Union, and even China.

Interview, Munich/
The New York Times, 9-2:11

Robert Farmer
Democratic Party treasurer

1

[Saying he supports the idea of large political-campaign donors receiving Ambassadorships]: The job of Ambassador is to serve as an American representative but, secondly, to promote business interests of America there. Generally, big contributors have had successful business backgrounds and that's why they are able to donate a lot of money. The second thing is that the host country, when they have a big problem, would probably much prefer an Ambassador who can pick up the phone and call the President of the United States. Now, no career diplomat is probably going to feel that comfortable picking up the phone . . . Somebody who is [the President's] personal friend is going to call him without a moment's notice, though.

Interview/The Wall Street Journal,
9-7:(A)16.

John R. Galvin
General, United States Army;
Supreme Allied Commander/
Europe

2

[On the Soviet Union's new willingness to negotiate arms reductions and have better relations with the West]: People look at intentions and say the intentions are changing. That may be fine for some people, but I can't look at intentions. I have to look at capability. Intentions are like moods; they can change again overnight. In the meantime, the Soviets are going through a transition which has dangers of instability, which is not really entirely predictable. I don't think the

threat as such, in terms of capabilities, is any less than it was three years ago.

To reporters, Naples, Italy,
May 23/
Los Angeles Times, 5-24:(I)13.

Hans-Dietrich Genscher
Foreign Minister
of West Germany

3

Every responsible security policy is made with the inviolable knowledge that the security of today cannot be based on the hopes and expectations of tomorrow. But it is just as correct to say that the security of tomorrow cannot be based on the assumption that everything will remain the same.

At opening of West German-American
Friendship Week,
Stuttgart, West Germany, May 7/
Los Angeles Times, 5-8:(I)13.

Gennadi I. Gerasimov
Spokesman for the Foreign Ministry
of the Soviet Union

4

We understand that the new [U.S. Bush] Administration needs time to develop policy. There are new faces there, and some of them don't know what foreign policy is about. But I think the new Administration tries to please everybody, and that's not easy. We can feel a certain influence of some of the familiar names, like [former Secretary of State Henry] Kissinger and [former National Security Affairs adviser Zbigniew] Brzezinski, who still interpret Soviet-American relations in terms of confrontation . . . The new Administration has not decided yet what position to take, what philosophical position to take.

To reporters, London, April 6/
The Washington Post, 4-7:(A)14.

Gerhard A. Gesell
Judge, United States
District Court for the
District of Columbia

5

[Sentencing Oliver North, convicted of offenses in the Iran-contra scandal, to a fine, proba-

(GERHARD A. GESELL)

tion and community service]: I believe you still lack full understanding . . . of how the public service has been tarnished. Nonetheless, what you believe is your business and jail will only harden your misconceptions. Given the many highly commendable aspects of your life, your punishment will not include jail. Instead, community service may in the end make you more conscious of certain values which at times you and your associates appear to have overlooked in the elite isolation of the White House.

Washington, July 5/
The New York Times, 7-6:(A)1.

Felipe Gonzalez
Prime Minister of Spain

1

Americans want so much to be liked [around the world]. But they also have enormous power, and that is not easily compatible with the affection of other people. This gives me a feeling of tenderness toward them.

Interview, Madrid/Time, 10-13:54.

Mikhail S. Gorbachev
General Secretary,
Communist Party of the
Soviet Union; President of
the Soviet Union

2

New forms of cooperation in the world process [are needed] . . . Internationalization of problems is needed. This is why we attach such an importance to the United Nations organization, which has long been unable to bring into play its possibilities. But it has been waiting for its hour, and it has come.

Before Trilateral Commission,
Moscow, Jan. 18/
Los Angeles Times, 1-19:(I)9.

3

Recently, many things have changed in East-West relations: There is less suspicion and fear, and more trust. Political and cultural iron curtains are now falling apart. But economic as well as scientific and technological ties can also be a litmus test, showing whether one's policy is sincere and whether one's deeds match one's words.

To West German businessmen,
Cologne, June 13/
The New York Times, 6-14:(A)6.

4

Everywhere, people want changes for the better. Everywhere, people are tired of war. Everywhere in the world, people want our global problems resolved. We [Soviets] are trying to do that and that is why people receive us so warmly.

News conference,
Bonn, West Germany, June 15/
Los Angeles Times, 6-16:(I)6.

5

The Cold War has ended, or is ending, not because there are victors and vanquished but because there is neither one nor the other. Therefore, it is perfectly possible to avoid a period of "cold peace" and to proceed with greater courage toward a period of peace for human history.

At banquet, Rome, Nov. 29/
The New York Times, 11-30:(A)13.

6

We [Communists] have abandoned the claim to have a monopoly on the truth. We no longer think that we are the best and that we are always right, that those who disagree with us are our enemies.

Speech, Rome, Nov. 30/
The New York Times, 12-1:(A)10.

Alexander M. Haig, Jr.
Former Secretary of State
of the United States

7

We have to view [international] terrorism in a new way: that this is an on-going war between law-abiding nations and terrorist nations . . . We

(ALEXANDER M. HAIG, JR.)

have to negotiate, but we can't get too hung up on the moralist issue . . . We can't make too many compromises.

Interview, Washington/
Los Angeles Times, 9-6:(VI)7.

Lee H. Hamilton
United States Representative,
D-Indiana

1

[On the Bush Administration's slow responses to recent Soviet peace initiatives]: This is a very, very cautious Administration, despite Bush's and [National Security Adviser Brent] Scowcroft's long experience in foreign relations. But my sense is that we've reached the point where we need to stop reflecting and start acting. We have to get at it—respond to [the Soviet's] proposals, test their intentions, advance our own proposals, keep the guard up, be wary but make a start.

The New York Times, 4-7:(A)4.

2

I think Oliver North [who was recently convicted for his involvement in the Iran-contra scandal] is a scapegoat. That does not excuse him . . . But I don't have any doubt at all that Ollie North was used by his superiors [in the Executive Branch] to carry out a lot of activities that they knew or had a very strong suspicion that he was carrying out.

Broadcast interview/
"Meet the Press," NBC-TV, 5-7.

John Lawrence Hargrove
Executive vice president,
American Society of
International Law

3

[On the new U.S. decision allowing the FBI to capture U.S.-wanted fugitives in foreign countries without those countries' consent]: In general, one country doesn't go into another country and exercise its law-enforcement functions in

any way without consent. You can envision a variety of legal and political consequences, including the United States [placing] itself in the position of being an international law-breaker, even though in a just cause.

Interview, Oct. 13/
The New York Times, 10-14:5.

Francois Heisbourg
Director, International
Institute for
Strategic Studies, London

4

[Saying U.S. efforts to oust Panamanian strongman Manuel Noriega have diminished U.S. attention to more strategic areas, such as Europe]: I think Europeans understand the importance of America's backyard to Americans, but that the trivia in Panama can take up so much of the Administration's time and energy raises questions about the way political institutions [in Washington] operate.

Los Angels Times, 10-28:(A)1.

Jesse Helms
United States Senator,
R-North Carolina

5

You cannot deal with rattlesnakes, and you cannot deal with Communist governments. There is no such thing as a moderate Communist government. They are all still rattlesnakes and they will turn around and bite you when the occasion arises.

Los Angeles Times, 6-6:(I)9.

Richard Helms
Former Director of Central
Intelligence of the United States

6

[On the long-standing ban on CIA involvement in the assassination of foreign leaders]: It was a bad policy for the U.S. to go around assassinating foreign leaders. Not only for moral reasons but also because in the U.S. nothing can be kept secret for very long.

Time, 10-30:54.

(RICHARD HELMS)

1

A coup d'etat seems to be confused by some people with an immaculate conception. Coups involve violence, blood and killing, and they often go in unpredictable directions.

Time, 10-30:54.

Henry J. Hyde
United States Representative,
R-Illinois

2

[On former Assistant Secretary of State Elliott Abrams]: I'm a charter member of the Elliott Abrams fan club. It is an elevating experience to find someone who believes in something and is willing to fight for it . . . Diplomacy is the art of the compromise, the art of the possible. His virtues to us are vices to others. He wasn't temperamentally able to back and fill and grovel. To succeed in diplomacy, one's grovel quotient has to be fairly high—and his wasn't.

Los Angeles Times, 1-23:(I)6.

Bobby Ray Inman
Former Deputy Director
of Central Intelligence
of the United States

3

[On proposals that the intelligence budget be separated from the defense budget so that Congress could vote on a publicly announced figure for intelligence spending]: My worry is that as we start a new cycle of draw-down in the Pentagon, we will once again incrementally take a slice off intelligence [by not having the two budgets separated]. There is much less hazard in letting people know how much money we spend on intelligence than in letting the cuts get made almost accidentally.

The New York Times, 11-28:(A)12.

Toshiki Kaifu
Prime Minister of Japan

4

No country can replace the United States in its position and role as leader of the Free World. We expect that the United States can respond to various problems with confidence, and at the same time Japan will do its utmost to continue cooperating with and supporting American leadership.

Before Japan Society of Northern
California, San Francisco,
Aug. 30/
Los Angeles Times, 8-31:(I)8.

Phillip A. Karber
Vice president,
B.D.M. Corporation
(U.S. Defense Department
consultants)

5

Two years from now, if [Soviet leader Mikhail] Gorbachev succeeds [with his reform program in the Soviet Union], we are going to look like a bunch of pikers for not forecasting how radical his changes turned out to be. If he fails, all of our hopes are going to look terribly naive. No matter what we say now, it's probably going to be wrong, so the ambiguous position is probably the most realistic.

Sept. 27/
The New York Times, 9-28:(A)6.

Igor V. Kasatonov
Vice Admiral and First
Deputy Commander-in-Chief
of the Northern Fleet,
Soviet Navy

6

Seas and oceans do not only separate continents, they also unite peoples living on these continents. We stand for converting the seas and oceans of the earth into the zone of cooperation, of mutual assistance and friendly contacts.

Norfolk, Va., July 21/
Los Angeles Times, 7-22:(I)15.

John W. Keker
Prosecutor at trial of
Oliver North for his
involvement in the U.S.
Iran-contra scandal

7

When time came for Oliver North to tell the truth, he lied. When time came for him to come

(JOHN W. KEKER)

clean, he shredded [documents]; he erased; he altered. There is a difference between keeping [government] secrets and telling lies. And you don't have to tell lies to keep secrets.

Opening argument at trial,
Washington, Feb. 21/
USA Today, 2-22:(A)1.

George F. Kennan
Former United States
Ambassador to the Soviet Union

1

[On Soviet leader Mikhail Gorbachev's reform program in the Soviet Union]: What we are witnessing today in Russia is the breakup of much, if not all, of the system of power by which that country has been held together and governed since 1917 . . . A new Russia is going to emerge from all this confusion which will not much resemble one we have known for the past seven decades . . . Whatever reasons there may once have been for regarding the Soviet Union primarily as a possible, if not probable, military opponent, the time for that sort of thing has clearly passed. That country should now be regarded essentially as another great power like other great powers, [and differences with the U.S. should be settled] by the normal means of compromise and accommodation.

Before Senate Foreign Relations
Committee, Washington, April 4/
The Washington Post, 4-5:(A)22.

Hiroshi Kimura
Director, Slavic Research Center,
Hokkaido University
(Japan)

2

Now that he has been facing difficulties domestically and internationally, my personal view is that the West should take a slightly more positive attitude toward [Soviet leader Mikhail] Gorbachev and *perestroika* [reform in the Soviet Union] than it has been. We should not squeeze him, nor should we help him unconditionally. But "wait and see" is now too passive a position . . .

Nobody knows whether Gorbachev will survive—and any country would want to deal with a more stable power. It's in the United States' and Japan's interest to see him survive.

At symposium/Newsweek, 5-15:29.

Henry A. Kissinger
Former Secretary of State
of the United States

3

I believe that the '90s, whatever we do, will be a period of tremendous structural change in international relations . . . I think that the dominance of the two superpowers will erode in the '90s. You will have various powers. You will have the U.S., Soviet Union, China, India, Europe. All of which will be simultaneously economic, political and military powers; and a little later I wouldn't exclude that Brazil and Mexico could be at least at the second rank of such a world. This requires that we look at the world in a different way than we did in the post-war period.

Interview/
The Christian Science Monitor,
1-6:19.

4

It's interesting, for example, that in George Kennan's containment policy [toward the Soviet Union] there is no statement of what we should do on the magic day that the Russians appeared and said that the United States now has a position of strength and they were ready to negotiate. Nor do you find it in the writings of Dean Acheson or John Foster Dulles. Now, by God, here they [the Russians] are saying we *have* such a situation of strength and they *do* want to negotiate. And the West does not know exactly what it wants. But because we are at about the point that everybody wanted in 1948, I'm fundamentally more optimistic. It is a more normal world. There will be other centers of power, meaning other centers of responsibility. We don't have to make all the decisions, which is another way of saying we should make only those decisions of greatest importance to us. We don't have to mix into every pettifogging problem around the world.

Interview/Los Angeles Times, 4-30:(V)6.

Robert H. Kupperman
Senior adviser, Center for
Strategic and International
Studies, Georgetown University

1

[The Soviet Union's] problems [with international terrorism] are in some ways even greater than the United States'; especially their emerging problems with Islamic fundamentalism. Some of their client states are also going to get weapons of mass destruction, and the Soviets are going to have trouble controlling them. Libya's [alleged] chemical-weapons plant is just the beginning.

At U.S.-Soviet conference on terrorism,
Moscow/Los Angeles Times, 1-27:(I)10.

2

[On the recent arrests and convictions of international terrorists]: We are looking at minor victories in the criminal arena to substitute or to solve major national-security problems. We may convict all the terrorists we can get our hands on, but it's not going to make the foggiest bit of difference to terrorists or the pattern of terrorism. The reality is that we will have done nothing to thwart the actions of large countries that support terrorism.

Los Angeles Times,
5-19:(I)10.

John J. LaFalce
United States Representative,
D-New York

3

The time has arrived for us to reconsider the sensitive issue of MFN [most-favored-nation status], and the Jackson-Vanik amendment. Among the advanced industrial nations, the United States stands alone in its dogged adherence to the notion that the politics of economic denial, from high import tariffs to export controls, somehow advances Western security and foreign-policy interests.

At National Issues Forum on East-
West Relations, sponsored by
Brookings Institution/
The Washington Post,
11-29:(A)26.

Richard Lally
Systems vice president
of security,
Air Transport Association

4

[On terrorist attacks against civilian airliners]: Maybe it is time for the government to engage in a more active, hands-on kind of role to defend against international terrorism, based upon the fact that acts of international terrorism are, in reality, acts intended to achieve political goals or to make a political statement. Those political goals are intended to influence the actions of government, the policies of government. Governments are the objectives, the airlines convenient and vulnerable surrogate targets.

Interview/
USA Today, 1-3:(A)7.

Frank R. Lautenberg
United States Senator,
D-New Jersey

5

[Criticizing those in the U.S. who are calling for cuts in the number of Soviet Jewish emigrees allowed to enter the U.S. after the Soviet government began granting more exit permits]: I think it would be misguided in the extreme to have encouraged people to take a step toward freedom and then close the door on what they believed was a safe haven in this country. What we started with our campaign to free Soviet Jewry is something that we ought to finish.

Sept. 6/
The Washington Post, 9-7:(A)19.

Christopher Layne
Lawyer;
Authority on
international relations

6

The trick of statesmanship is to turn the inevitable to one's own advantage.

Interview/
The Atlantic Monthly,
June:51.

Robert Legvold
Director, Harriman Institute
for Advanced Study
of the Soviet Union,
Columbia University

1

[On criticism that the U.S. Bush Administration has not responded fast enough or positively enough to favorable changes in the Soviet Union under Mikhail Gorbachev]: I think what we have in Washington today is a highly competent leadership with no vision, but it is a highly competent leadership with no vision in historic times. Therefore, it is going to be pushed along by these times. I would have hoped that we would have led these times. But we are not going to resist them— that is the critical point. You watch—when [U.S. Secretary of State James] Baker begins his meetings with [Soviet Foreign Minister Eduard] Shevardnadze, the times will push him. Only a comatose Administration would fail to respond to this moment.

The New York Times, 5-8:(A)4.

Nguyen Van Linh
General Secretary,
Communist Party of Vietnam

2

The fact that the imperialists—especially the U.S. imperialists—are leaving no stone unturned in an attempt to affect the situation of a number of socialist countries with the aim of driving them into the free world of capitalism is a sufficient proof of their wolfish nature.

Before Vietnamese Communist
Party Central Committee, August/
The Washington Post, 9-15:(A)24.

Roderick MacFarquhar
Professor of government, and
director, Fairbank Center,
Harvard University

3

It is very difficult for a government to interfere in the internal affairs of another country, even when it's a country you don't like, as [U.S.] President Bush is finding in Panama and Nicaragua. When it's a friendly country, whether South Korea, China or whatever, you find it much more difficult and, indeed, your whole relationship is on the line.

U.S. News & World Report, 6-5:27.

Malcolm Mackintosh
British authority
on the Soviet Union

4

I'm totally against those who say, "Let's make it more difficult for the Soviet Union by not helping them out, because they'll eventually come around on their knees." The West should be ready to make maximum use of all the new spirit that's coming out of [Soviet leader Mikhail] Gorbachev's administration. There's a lot to be said for bringing them into areas where we can work together. In principle, there's even something to be said for the idea of a Marshall Plan [for the Soviet Union], but in practice it's somewhat different. Because of the nature of the system, it will take so long to carry out Gorbachev's economic reforms that however much money we shovel into the Soviet Union coffers, it would go down some endless well that might produce something in another 30-40 years.

Interview/
Los Angeles Times, 6-10:(I)18.

Herbert Meyer
Former Vice Chairman,
National Intelligence Council,
Central Intelligence Agency
of the United States

5

There is no question that in the past the Soviet Union has been a key player in state-sponsored terrorism. They have provided support through training facilities and other means. If the Soviet Union still supports those states which engage in terrorism—Iran, Libya, Syria, Yemen, North Korea—then the idea of cooperation [between the U.S. and the Soviet Union] is insane. On the other hand, if the Soviet Union has withdrawn all support to state-sponsored terrorism, including the shutting down of all training camps in Eastern Europe and elsewhere, that is an enormously important news story that I have not yet read.

The New York Times, 4-7:(A)5.

George J. Mitchell
United States Senator,
D-Maine

1

[On U.S.-Soviet relations]: What has concerned me is the emergence in recent weeks of a negative tone within the [U.S. Bush] Administration . . . a [tendency] to respond to [Soviet leader Mikhail] Gorbachev's initiatives by engaging in name-calling. [It is] particularly non-productive [to] say what he [Gorbachev] is doing is intended to influence public opinion. Of course it is. So are actions that we take every day . . . There is a spectacular irony in the fact that here in the closing years of the 20th century we are experiencing the triumph of democratic capitalism and the failure of Communism. Gorbachev has been dealt a losing hand, and President Bush comes to office having been dealt a winning hand. And yet Gorbachev is playing as though he has the winning hand—Bush's hand; and Bush is playing as though he has Gorbachev's hand—the losing hand.

Interview/
The Washington Post, 5-20:(A)4.

2

[We have] concern about the capacity of our society to absorb all of those who wish to come here from other countries. It seems to me very clear that the answer is that we cannot simply accept everyone who wants to come. We have always, in our society, distinguished between those seeking refugee status . . . and those who are immigrants solely for economic reasons. Increasingly, the lines are converging, and it's not as easy now to distinguish.

To reporters, Washington/
The Christian Science Monitor,
8-7:7.

3

There appears to be a basic ambivalence within the [U.S.] Bush Administration about the dramatic transformation now under way in the Eastern Bloc. This ambivalence is difficult to understand. For over 40 years, the United States has demanded that the Soviet Union change its political system and loosen its stranglehold over the countries of Eastern Europe. The Western alliance, formed to confront the threat of Soviet totalitarianism, has consistently urged the Soviet Union to decentralize its political and economic system and grant every citizen the right to speak, to worship, to emigrate freely. What we have demanded for over four decades is beginning to occur. This is unquestionably a triumph for the United States. Now is the time for the United States to encourage and capitalize upon the changes we have sought for so long. [But] instead of encouragement and engagement, the [Bush] Administration has adopted an almost passive stance. "Show me," the President says. His officials warn of the unpredictability of change. The Bush Administration seems almost nostalgic about the Cold War and the rigid superpower relationship that divided the world into two hostile and isolated camps.

Before the Senate, Washington,
Sept. 18/
The New York Times, 9-19:(A)4.

Oliver L. North
Lieutenant Colonel,
United States Marine Corps

4

[On his being convicted of three of 12 counts for his involvement in the Iran-contra scandal]: After more than 2½ years and over 40 million of our taxpayers' dollars spent on investigations, Congressional inquisitions, and a special prosecutor who has likened me to Adolf Hitler—we now face many months, perhaps years, fighting these remaining charges . . . We will continue this battle—and with the support and prayers of the American people, I will be fully vindicated.

News conference, Washington,
May 4/
The Washington Post, 5-5:(A)10.

5

[Addressing the judge at his sentencing for his role in the Iran-contra scandal]: Your Honor, I have devoted nearly two decades to the service of our country and I would never knowingly do anything to hurt it or any of its institutions. Over

(OLIVER L. NORTH)

these years, there have been some success[es]. But I have always believed that those accomplishments were more the result of the efforts of the good people I was privileged to work with rather than myself. I also recognize that I have made mistakes and as a result of those mistakes I have been convicted of serious crimes. I have also lost a chance to ever again serve as a Marine. In his paperwork, the prosecutor said that I feel no remorse. In that he is wrong. For I grieve over what happened. And I truly do pray about it every day. One should not confuse a smile or a wave toward the ever-present press cameras that seem to follow me around for a lack of sensitivity over what has happened or lack of care for the consequences.

Washington, July 5/
The New York Times, 7-6:(A)14.

Sam Nunn
United States Senator,
D-Georgia

1

We cannot prevail as a great power if either our enemies or our allies look to Washington and see division. Our nation cannot afford a separate Democratic and Republican foreign policy.

Los Angeles Times, 3-11:(I)18.

2

We have, no doubt, the best intelligence capability in the world in terms of technical intelligence. But I have a haunting fear that the more we improve our technical intelligence, our human intelligence has begun to slide.

Aug. 2/
Los Angeles Times, 8-3:(I)11.

Javier Perez de Cuellar
Secretary General
of the United Nations

3

World opinion is enraptured by the two big powers [the U.S. and Soviet Union]—it has an inferiority complex. We do not need the two great powers to settle all problems. Sometimes I get the impression that some people would like to go back to a kind of directorate of the superpowers, that they are willing to hand over to them the management of world affairs. The superpowers carry a great deal of military weight, of course. But one cannot say that the Soviet Union is swimming in prosperity. And the U.S. is the most deeply indebted country in the world. As for the Europeans, they are a bit lazy. They should constitute a true third force, to broaden the picture a bit.

Interview/
World Press Review, May:50.

Thomas R. Pickering
United States Ambassador/
Permanent Representative
to the United Nations

4

[On international terrorism]: The world community is reacting much too slowly. Uniquely targeted against innocent people, terrorism is simply an effort to create horrible problems to get the world's attention for a particular issue ... Over the long term, regional peace settlements have an effect on terrorism. After all, a lot of the terrorists are activated because they feel they're wronged victims in their own countries. You have to deal with those sources as well.

Interview, New York/
Cosmopolitan, September:174.

Richard Pipes
Russian-history scholar,
Harvard University;
Former Director, Soviet and
East European Affairs,
National Security Council
of the United States

5

[On the current pro-democracy reforms in Eastern Europe and the Soviet Union]: For years [American liberals] told us that the Communists were stable, that we had to placate them or face the prospect of nuclear war. We conservatives have been saying the Soviet Union is a giant on clay feet. You [now] see our ideals triumphing.

Newsweek, 12-18:25.

Muammer el-Qaddafi
Chief of State of Libya

1

[On the new U.S. Bush Administration]: I think the new American Administration is going to be very sane, very wise. I don't think that this President or any other President would like to walk out of the White House on the bodies of dead Americans. I think that [current President] Reagan is walking out on the dead bodies of more than a thousand Americans that have been killed all over the world, walking out on the destroyed reputation of the United States, and I think that he's left America hated by everyone.

Interview/USA Today, 1-10:(A)9.

2

[On his vision of world revolution]: Governments and classes, parliaments and parties will disappear. Armies and the police, all the instruments of official repression, will disappear. The masses alone will take their place. Libya with full self-confidence is capable of supporting its international revolutionary program.

*Before Libyan General People's
Congress, Tripoli, Sept. 1/
The New York Times, 9-2:3.*

Dan Quayle
*Vice President
of the United States*

3

[On Soviet leader Mikhail Gorbachev]: A "drugstore cowboy" in a sense connotes a bit of phoniness. And there is a bit of phoniness about the [Gorbachev arms-reduction] proposals. He is perceived as making radical proposals out there when they are really marginal . . . [Having a Soviet leader who is] very pleasing to the West, has an easy mannerism to him, who is very good from a public-relations, press, p.r. point of view, makes it harder for the U.S. to gain public approval that is needed to maintain some of its defense postures. [Gorbachev] has a tremendous advantage [in the competition for shaping the world opinion]. He can just throw a proposal out one day, take it back the next day. He can make a proposal without consulting anybody. He

doesn't have to worry about public opinion [at home] or about his allies . . . [Because of his country's over-all military superiority,] he is able to play those cards quite well. And all of a sudden people say, "Oh, he wants to reduce [arms]."

*To reporters, Washington, May 19/
The Washington Post, 5-20:(A)4.*

Ronald Reagan
President of the United States

4

. . . we have, the past few years, forged a satisfying new closeness with the Soviet Union. I've been asked if this isn't a gamble, and my answer is no, because we're basing our actions not on words but deeds. The detente of the 1970s was based not on actions, but promises. They'd promise to treat their own people and the people of the world better, but the gulag was still the gulag, and the state was still expansionist, and they still waged proxy wars in Africa, Asia and Latin America. This time, so far, it's different: [Soviet] President [Mikhail] Gorbachev has brought about some internal democratic reforms and begun the withdrawal from Afghanistan. He has also freed prisoners whose names I've given him every time we've met . . . What it all boils down to is this: I want the new closeness to continue. And it will as long as we make it clear that we will continue to act in a certain way as long as they continue to act in a helpful manner. If and when they don't, at first pull your punches. If they persist, pull the plug. It's still trust, but verify. It's still play, but cut the cards. It's still watch closely and don't be afraid to see what you see.

*Broadcast address to the nation,
Washington, Jan. 11/
The Washington Post, 1-12:(A)8.*

5

. . . I've always believed that the Lord put this great continent here for those people, wherever they may be in the world, who had a special love for freedom and courage to uproot themselves, leave family and friends and come to this country to start a new life. And I still believe that this country should offer that . . . We've always offered a refuge, we've always had and set quotas

(RONALD REAGAN)

of refugees that we were willing to take, but do we come to a point in which we just plain can't handle them? Doesn't that then say that what we should be doing is even more in trying to replace totalitarianism and persecution with democracy in these other countries to where they won't have to be refugees? . . . [And] I think there is an area where we should also collaborate with our allies and other democracies to make sure that everybody is doing their bit in this—that maybe we're going to have to redirect refugees to other countries that are also willing to take them.

Interview, Washington,
Jan. 18/
The New York Times, 1-19:(A)14;
USA Today, 1-19:(A)9.

Max Robinson
Consul General of the
United States in Moscow

1

[On the increasing number of Soviets wanting to leave that country and emigrate to the United States]: We cannot be the sole destination for those who want to leave. If someone feels they must move soon, but they do not have a close relative in the United States, they should consider another country. It's a matter of priority. I do not see any contradiction between our principled stand on the basic right of people to be allowed to emigrate and the fact that there simply is only a certain number of people we can accept and humanely process in a given period of time.

Moscow/
Los Angeles Times, 10-4:(I)14.

Dennis Ross
Director of Policy Planning,
Department of State
of the United States

2

The United States emerged from World War II with unparalleled power—politically, economically and militarily. Today, we do not have unparalleled power. [Foreign-] policy planning is more complicated now. As we shape our re-

sponses, we have to recognize our real assets and our real strengths. That doesn't mean that we don't have a potential to lead, but that we have to lead in partnership.

Interview, Washington/
The New York Times, 11-17:(A)12.

Michael J. Sandel
Professor of government,
Harvard University

3

[President] Bush ran for election offering experience and competence, not any distinctive conception of America's role in the world. [Ronald] Reagan and [Jimmy] Carter, [Richard] Nixon and [former Secretary of State Henry] Kissinger, all came in with visions of the world. Call them naive, simple-minded or overly ambitious, but they were visions nevertheless . . . Reagan's rhetoric obscured the fact that the world had changed. America no longer stands astride the world as an unrivaled power. We are now one important power among several. [Secretary of State James] Baker's foreign policy will have to come to terms with this. Jim Baker is Secretary of State of a debtor nation, and debtor nations sooner or later have to confront their limits.

The New York Times, 2-9:(A)12.

4

[Saying Soviet leader Mikhail Gorbachev is besting the U.S. Bush Administration around the world in public relations]: They [the Administration] are criticizing Gorbachev for conducting foreign policy in precisely the same way the Bush people conducted their election campaign, which was to manipulate the media with public-relations gimmicks and subordinate the substantive policy debate. Now they are suddenly the wounded ones. No wonder they are angry. They are being beaten at their own game. What the Bush people are missing is the unavoidable connection between electoral politics and governance. They thought they could win the Presidency by manipulating the media, but that governing and conducting foreign policy would be another matter, where they could just ignore symbols and

(MICHAEL J. SANDEL)

rhetoric and public relations. That is now coming home to roost.

The New York Times, 5-18:(A)6.

James R. Schlesinger
Former Director of
Central Intelligence
of the United States

1

[On Soviet leader Mikhail Gorbachev's program of reform in the Soviet Union and his popularity in Western Europe]: . . . one of the realities is that the Soviets have generated a certain responsiveness in Western Europe and elsewhere. For us [in the U.S.] to appear both passive and impassive to Gorbachev is a problem. One needs to strike a balance between caution before making fundamental changes in policy and a visible degree of understanding and responsiveness to the changes going on in the Soviet Union. The [U.S.] Bush Administration may have erred too much toward the first.

The New York Times,
5-8:(A)4.

Brent Scowcroft
Assistant to President of the
United States George Bush
for National Security Affairs

2

[On Soviet leader Mikhail Gorbachev's recent peace initiatives]: I think the cold war is not over. There may be, in the saying, light at the end of the tunnel. But I think it depends partly on how we behave, whether the light is the sun or an incoming locomotive. [Gorbachev] badly needs a period of stability, if not definite improvement in the relationship so he can face the awesome [economic] problem he has at home . . . I also think he's interested in making trouble within the Western alliance and I think he believes the best way to do it is a peace offensive, rather than to bluster the way some of his predecessors have.

Broadcast interview/
"This Week With David Brinkley,"
ABC-TV, 1-22.

3

The President runs the government. He has expert advice from [the] State and Defense [Departments], and it is my job to ensure the integration of that advice, to fill in where there are holes and, hopefully, to help provide a strategic concept which covers the whole field of national security.

Interview, Washington/
The New York Times, 11-3:(A)12.

Georgy Shakhnazarov
Senior Advisor on Eastern
Europe to Soviet leader
Mikhail Gorbachev

4

During the 1960s and '70s, we had a period of East-West detente. But this was only a temporary warming of the international climate which was followed by even worse relations than before. What's happening now [with Soviet and East European reforms] is not simply a temporary thaw. It's the end of one era and the beginning of another. Ever since the first states emerged 3,000 years ago, relations on the world arena have been determined by confrontation between countries. Now a new era is beginning when the essence of international relations is not confrontation, but cooperation. We are entering a transitional period in which the interests of the two superpowers [the U.S. and Soviet Union] are becoming closer. Of course this won't happen all at once. But over the next 10, 15, 20 years, we can expect common problems to come to the fore. We will think less of our egoistic interests and more about common global problems: terrorism, the fight against AIDS, ecology, the search for new energy resources.

Interview/The Washington Post,
11-10:(A)40.

Eduard A. Shevardnadze
Foreign Minister
of the Soviet Union

5

Perestroika [reform in the Soviet Union] has been becoming a fashionable conversation piece in the West. Now and again some incorrect com-

(EDUARD A. SHEVARDNADZE)

parisons of one socialist country against another can be heard. We stick to the principle whereby every fraternal country can arrange socialism in its own national colors.

East Berlin, June 9/
Los Angeles Times, 6-10:(I)4.

1

If it is obligatory for us [in the Communist world to be tolerant] in our attitude toward the [new non-Communist] government of Poland, why are others [in the West] so intolerant toward, for example, Cuba? And if a non-Communist Prime Minister is possible in a socialist country [such as Poland], why should the appearance of a Communist as head of a Western government be perceived as heresy? That's something we shouldn't exclude.

At United Nations, New York,
Sept. 26/
The New York Times, 9-27:(A)6.

2

[On *perestroika*, the Soviet reform program]: The peoples of the world associate with our *perestroika* their hopes for peace, for the settlement of global problems and for the improvement of their general well-being. This may flatter our national ambitions or irritate others, but it is a fact . . . The world interprets *perestroika* as a living symbol of faith. It has long ceased to be our internal affair, and it is now seen as a truly universal cause. People are not indifferent to the way the process of renewal struggles ahead, for they associate our internal stability with global stability . . . There is no exaggeration here—it is really that way.

Before Supreme Soviet, Moscow/
Los Angeles Times, 10-29:(A)10.

George P. Shultz
Secretary of State
of the United States

3

There is an idea afoot that America is in decline and we're in decline because we are engaged abroad. "Over-extended," the prophets of decline call it . . . They touch the old American inclination to withdraw from the world in order to regain economic or moral security. They play to the darker side, to the idea that America no longer has anything to give the world. They are wrong. We have something to give the world. Moreover, it's not simply a choice of deciding to be engaged and taking risks or disengaging and not taking risks. We are either going to be a source of progress, stability and harmony, or stand aside to watch conflict, instability and the decline of international order. That's the real stake overlooked by the prophets of decline. In our world, we shall not find our souls or the solution to our economic problems in retreat; we may very well find chaos instead. So let's reject the school of decline, which, if believed, cuts off the very rationale for public service.

Before Citizens Network for
Foreign Affairs, Washington,
Jan. 9/The Washington Post,
1-11:(A)19.

Dmitri K. Simes
Senior associate,
Carnegie Endowment
for International Peace

4

[On Soviet leader Mikhail Gorbachev's program of reform in the Soviet Union]: There [used to be] a very powerful feeling [in the U.S.] that Gorbachev was more style than substance. Now everyone agrees: Gorbachev is for real . . . At this point I am still not ready to be critical of their [the U.S. Bush Administration's] pace [which some have criticized as being too slow to accept change in the Soviet Union]. But if nothing has changed [in the Bush Administrations's attitude] a year from now, I would begin to worry. What is missing now is music—a sense that we may once again be present at the creation.

The New York Times, 5-8:(A)4.

5

[On President Bush's foreign-policy technique]: If you are satisfied with an Administration avoiding mistakes, they have done it very

(DMITRI K. SIMES)

well . . . This Administration is at its best when it has to react, rather than act. I think, however, we're moving into a new stage, where the Administration may have to display new skills— skills like daring, like creativity, imagination, a sense of direction.

USA Today, 12-4:(A)8.

Helmut Sonnenfeldt
Former senior member,
National Security Council
of the United States

1

The U.S. will remain a political leader [in the world] because, in most respects, we'll remain a leading economic power. It depends on how you define leadership, of course. We can't crack the whip and make people fall into line any more. But . . . everyone still looks to us to do something, and that's a good definition of leadership.

At symposium/Newsweek, 5-15:29.

Ronald I. Spiers
Under Secretary General of
the United Nations;
Former American diplomat

2

If you listen to the debate in the [UN General] Assembly, you realize that it is really a global village town meeting. At a town meeting in Vermont, what people worry about are things like crime, clean neighborhoods and how to help the poor. When you translate that into the UN's global agenda, the main concerns are drugs, environment, terrorism. These are problems that can't be solved by single countries acting in isolation. They require a collective effort . . .

The Washington Post, 10-24:(A)10.

Joyce Starr
Co-chairman, United States
Global Strategy Council;
Senior associate, Center for
Strategic and International
Studies, Georgetown University

3

I think you need to see [international] terrorism the way you see the Mafia. It's industry.

They make money. It's also ideological. But, believe me, there are many fewer ideologues involved in terrorism than there are money-hungry people who couldn't make it for one reason or another in the real world . . . I think most terrorism, somewhere behind the scenes, is a desire for profit. Most of the people who perpetuate terrorist acts—it is a profession for them. It is what they know. Yes, at the front ranks, there might be ideologues; but after a while, I think, it stops being ideological and for most of them it becomes a life-style, a way to earn money, a way to maintain their self-esteem, and I think the ideology is lost.

Interview/
USA Today, 3-15:(A)9.

Dick Thornburgh
Attorney General
of the United States

4

[On whether there is as much espionage activity against the U.S. today, during an era of reform in the Soviet Union, as there was in the past]: There is a level of relations between countries—friend or foe—that tends to find areas of common agreement which can be fashioned into a more peaceable and safe world community, but every nation maintains its own intelligence-gathering apparatus. Whether that activity is any greater or less is difficult to assess because it is by nature clandestine. There are a lot more Soviet nationals in this country today than there were before this era began to unfold.

Interview/
USA Today, 7-25:(A)9.

Sosuke Uno
Foreign Minister, and
Prime Minister-designate,
of Japan

5

Allies trust each other in all matters. That is what an alliance is . . . Raising a club to conduct negotiations is simply not permissible.

News conference,
Tokyo, June 2/
Los Angeles Times, 6-2:(I)12.

Brian Urquardt
Former Under Secretary
General of the United Nations
for Special Political Affairs

1

In terms of what the UN has done over the past year, the verdict has to be "So far, so good." But the UN and its associated agencies have to go beyond that if they are to prove their relevance to the global agenda of the 1990s. In the years just ahead, something like 85 per cent of UN activities will involve not the peace-keeping and mediation associated with armed conflicts but activities of a social and economic nature in areas such as the environment, narcotics trafficking and helping the have-not nations achieve a greater ability to compete with the haves. If the UN is to have relevancy, it must undergo a transition that will test whether it can work effectively on these problems or whether something else is needed.

The Washington Post, 10-24:(A)10.

Richard Viguerie
Chairman,
United Conservatives

2

Communism would have been dead 50 years ago if the Western establishment had let it die. The multinational companies, David Rockefeller, the International Monetary Fund and foreign aid continue to prop Communists up. Without this group, Communism would have died a natural death. East minus West equals zero.

Interview/USA Today, 3-8:(A)11.

William H. Webster
Director of Central Intelligence
of the United States

3

[On Soviet leader Mikhail Gorbachev's programs of reform and openness]: There's been an awful lot of predicting whether it's going to fail or not. It's easy to say it's going to fail, because there are so many obstacles that he has to overcome. But it would be a great mistake if we just declared him lost. He's an extraordinary leader.

He's demonstrated cleverness and boldness, and he has moved aggressively to obtain the sinews of power, to reorganize the Soviet government so that he will not be blocked by bureaucracy. He has opened up with *glasnost* [openness]. He has kept us at times off balance by his surprise foreign-policy initiatives. We're always reacting to him, and that all works in his favor.

Interview/
USA Today, 1-12:(A)7.

4

[Saying the CIA should be given greater latitude to operate in situations abroad that may result in the death of foreign leaders, such as supporting coups to overthrow dictators]: The United States does not engage in selective, individual assassination. But the United States has other important overriding concerns about security and protecting democracy in areas of the world where it has a legitimate claim of interest. And when despots take over, there has to be a means to deal with that, short of making us to be hired killers.

Interview, Washington,
Oct. 16/
The New York Times, 10-17:(A)1.

5

It is clear that those assumptions under which we have operated—the existence of a bipolar world divided into East-West alliances, the economic supremacy and dominance of the West and the competition for global strength through ideology and military power—are no longer unquestioned. As the hard edges of the world recede, the threats we face have become more numerous, more diffuse and more difficult to define. Intelligence is critical, as policy-makers determine what course to follow in a world which may become more dangerous because it has become less predictable.

At National Press Club,
Washington, Nov. 29/
Los Angeles Times, 11-30:(A)6;
The New York Times, 11-30:(A)18.

Paul Wolfowitz
*Under Secretary
for Policy,
Department of Defense
of the United States*

1

Amidst all the "new thinking" in the Soviet Union, there's a lot of "old policy" on regional conflicts. The Soviet Union and its allies continue to supply large amounts of sophisticated military equipment to countries like North Korea, Nicaragua and Libya, which threaten their neighbors and support international terrorism . . . Does the [Soviet] withdrawal of troops from Afghanistan and other countries reflect a recognition that the peoples of these countries are entitled to governments of their own choosing? Or does it simply reflect a decision to pursue the same ends by different, less costly, and less controversial means? Unfor-

tunately, today the weight of evidence still appears to support the latter conclusion.

*At conference sponsored by University of
Pittsburgh and the Chautauqua Institution,
Pittsburgh, Nov. 2/
The New York Times, 11-3:(A)4.*

Alexander N. Yakovlev
*Member, Politburo, Communist Party
of the Soviet Union*

2

Official political thinking in the West continues to make use of the concepts of hostility and confrontation [toward the East]. Movement in Western thinking is only just beginning. It is a long way from full understanding that the policy of military strength has no future, and even more from rejecting it.

*Tblisi, Soviet Union, Feb. 27/
Los Angeles Times, 3-1:(I)5.*

Africa

Adebayo Adedeji
Executive Secretary,
United Nations Economic Commission
for Africa

1

Education and health have at best stagnated on a continent [Africa] where the population is growing at more than 3 per cent a year. Just think of what Africa will be like in 20 or 30 years. We will have fewer people educated . . . than we do now.

At meeting of United Nations
Economic Commission for Africa,
Addis Ababa, Ethiopia/
The Washington Post, 4-15:(A)15.

Martti Ahtisaari
United Nations Special
Representative to Namibia

2

[On the current transition period of Namibia from South African colony to independence]: The people of Namibia have waited long years for this day, and it is the eve of an era: an era of all of the people of Namibia. Namibia has truly been a wound in the side of Africa. But it also has a special place in the hearts and minds of the whole world.

News conference, Windhoek, Namibia,
March 31/Los Angeles Times, 4-1:(I)14.

Boris A. Asoyan
Deputy Chief, Department of
African Countries,
Foreign Ministry of the
Soviet Union

3

In our opinion, we doubt that [anti-apartheid] revolution in South Africa is possible, if you're talking of revolutionaries storming Pretoria. We support the ANC and we regard it as the main force in contemporary political life in South Africa. But we also believe that there is really no alternative to a peaceful solution.

The New York Times, 3-16:(A)1.

Les Aspin
United States Representative,
D-Wisconsin

4

[Saying the recent U.S. shooting down of two Libyan fighter planes over the Mediterranean may have been deliberately precipitated by Libyan leader Muammar Qaddafi to gain sympathy in the world for his claims that the U.S. is planning to destroy a Libyan plant the Americans say will be used to produce chemical weapons]: He has been milking the alleged threat to his chemical plant for all it is worth to garner Arab support. The fact that the clash takes place far from Rabta [site of the plant] minimizes the chances that Rabta would be a focus of retaliation. Two planes is a cheap price to pay so that Colonel Qaddafi can tune in his television to hear outpourings of fervent backing from all over the Arab world.

Washington, Jan. 4/
Los Angeles Times, 1-5:(I)8.

James A. Baker III
Secretary of State-designate
of the United States

5

I really don't see the possibility . . . for the United States normalizing relations with South Africa without there being real progress toward dismantling [South Africa's apartheid] system. I think our [economic] sanctions have amplified that message, but I think we ought to all be candid enough to recognize that the sanctions we've imposed haven't produced the desired result; and, by themselves, they probably cannot produce the desired result. It seems to me, based on the studying I've done since I was nominated for this post, that those sanctions haven't weakened the resolve of the Afrikaners; they haven't increased black bargaining power. And white voters have shifted to the right, if you believe the polls down there, and repression has intensified. So we do need to review the situation in South

(JAMES A. BAKER III)

Africa; we need to review our policy in South Africa.

> *At Senate Foreign Relations*
> *Committee hearing on his*
> *confirmation, Washington,*
> *Jan. 17/*
> *The New York Times,*
> *1-18:(A)10.*

1

In my view, national reconciliation [in Angola] means the emergence of a government that reconciles the competing views of the present government and the movement that Dr. [Jonas] Savimbi represents [the UNITA rebels that have been fighting the government], in a manner that is satisfactory to both . . . I don't think we can step in and put an objective standard there. I think national reconciliation means that the two forces there, that are not reconciled now, reconcile on a basis that's mutually satisfactory.

> *At Senate Foreign Relations*
> *Committee hearing on his*
> *confirmation, Washington,*
> *Jan. 18/*
> *The New York Times,*
> *1-19:(A)12.*

Pauline Baker
Authority on Africa,
Carnegie Endowment
for International Peace,
Washington

2

[On new South African President Frederik de Klerk]: The world seems to think of de Klerk as the [Soviet leader Mikhail] Gorbachev of South Africa, a man committed to reform the [apartheid] system. But we don't want reform of apartheid—we want it to be abolished. De Klerk is certainly a much more nimble politician than his predecessor [Pieter Botha]. He may take some halfway measures which the United States will applaud, and get caught in the middle.

> *Los Angeles Times,*
> *9-23:(I)14.*

Allan Boesak
President, World Alliance of
Reformed Churches
(South Africa)

3

All the evidence points to the fact that the South African government will only move [to change its policy of apartheid] if it has no other option, only if the pressures are such that it has to do what is right in that particular case. Right now, the South African government is around the table negotiating about the future of Namibia. And that happened because of the pressures put on it—diplomatically, politically—by the U.S.S.R., the United States and the United Nations. Because of even the limited [economic] sanctions imposed on South Africa, they put such a strain on the South African economy that it simply can no longer afford the war—either in Angola or in Namibia.

> *Interview/*
> *USA Today, 5-18:(A)11.*

4

I am convinced that the South African government [and its apartheid system] in its present form will not last long . . . We are going into a down curve. You are watching the death throes of the beast . . . The end will come quicker upon [the country's white leaders] than they think or they can understand. There has never been anything in our history like now.

> *Interview, Cape Town/*
> *USA Today, 9-13:(A)11.*

Pieter W. Botha
President of South Africa

5

My entire life bears testimony to the reform [of the apartheid system] that I have initiated, and I still believe that it should be pursued with two conditions . . . I am for reform, but not for handing over [power to the black majority]. I am for reform, but against the undermining of stability and order.

> *Broadcast address to the nation,*
> *March 12/*
> *The Washington Post, 3-13:(A)1.*

WHAT THEY SAID IN 1989

(PIETER W. BOTHA)

1

[On the Cabinet's overruling his wanting F. W. de Klerk, his successor as head of the National Party, to obtain his permission before meeting Zambia's leader Kenneth Kaunda]: It is evident to me that after all these years of my best efforts for the National Party and for the government of this country as well as the security of this country, I am being ignored by ministers in my Cabinet. I consequently have no choice other than to announce my resignation.

Broadcast address to the nation,
Aug. 14/
The New York Times, 8-15:(A)5.

Roelof F. Botha
Foreign Minister
of South Africa

2

[On the current transition period of Namibia from South African colony to independence]: We are leaving Namibia with a feeling that we have fulfilled our commitments here with dignity ... I cannot imagine a country that has a better hope of making a success of independence than this one.

News conference,
Windhoek, Namibia,
March 31/Los Angeles Times,
4-1:(I)14.

J. Emmanuel Bowier
Minister of Information
of Liberia

3

[On U.S. insistence that his country pay off the debts it owes the U.S.]: We are saying our relationship goes beyond money. But if, after 130 or 140 years, the U.S. will look at us and say, if you don't pay down to the last brass copper we will pull out and close down everything, then we know now that for them a relationship, a friendship, has a monetary value, has a dollar sign.

Interview/
The New York Times, 4-28:(A)4.

Frank Chikane
General secretary,
South African Council of Churches

4

[On anti-apartheid activism against the current South African elections in which blacks cannot participate]: The first lie about these elections is that they are general elections. They are exclusive and racist ... The impression that those who want to register their protest are disrupting the democratic process is a disgraceful lie. Apartheid elections are a sinful ritual which will always leave this country divided, bitter and nearer the brink of disaster.

The Washington Post, 9-5:(A)14.

Herman J. Cohen
Assistant Secretary-designate
for African Affairs,
Department of State
of the United States

5

If we do nothing else in Africa during the next four years, we must work every day to promote a negotiated, non-violent transition to a new constitutional system which will guarantee equal political rights and equal economic and social opportunity for all South Africans regardless of race or ethnic affiliation ... We have a major role to play by pushing all parties in South Africa toward the imperatives of dialogue, negotiation and compromise.

At Senate confirmation hearing on
his nomination,
Washington, May 3/
The Washington Post, 5-4:(A)21.

William S. Cohen
United States Senator,
R-Maine

6

[On U.S. charges that Western countries are helping Libya build an alleged chemical-weapons plant]: This willingness to wear moral blinders, whether it be on the part of the companies which provide this expertise or the nations which condone it, is simply unacceptable. By citing the West Germans, I do not mean to suggest that

(WILLIAM S. COHEN)

they are alone or that they are displaying a greater willingness than any other nation to look the other way in the face of what is clear evidence of what the Libyans are doing. Japan has shown a similar lack of resolve, and so have the other nations whose firms have provided this assistance. What, then, can and should the United States do? Idle threats are not the answer. We should not come to be regarded as a nation which speaks loudly but carries a small stick. At the same time, we should not act rashly or without full regard for potential consequences of whatever action we might take.

Los Angeles Times, 1-4:(I)14.

Chester A. Crocker
Former Assistant Secretary
for African Affairs,
Department of State
of the United States

1

[On the ruling National Party of South Africa]: The National Party has been in power without any serious challenge for the past 41 years. The Party has used its 1948 victory to assure the permanent empowerment of the Afrikaner mainstream. They brought into being an Afrikaner nationalist revolution, and they have been magnificently successful at empowering their own people economically. If the Afrikaners stay together as a tribe, they can dominate politics and the whole country. If the Party is not doing well, that's because they are not united any more.

Interview, Washington, Sept.6/
The New York Times, 9-7:(A)10.

Frederik W. de Klerk
Leader, National Party
of South Africa

2

[Criticizing the two other major political parties in South Africa]: The contrast is clear. The Conservative Party stands for a minority [white] government in a South Africa that will, by their own admission, in perpetuity be populated by a majority of people of color. It is unfair and does

not pass the test of justice. The Democratic Party stands for a majority [black] government. In a country with such a massive and wide diversity as ours, this is unfair toward the smaller peoples and population groups. Their policy, too, fails the test of justice.

Before South African Parliament,
Cape Town/
The Washington Post, 5-13:(A)12.

Frederik W. de Klerk
President of South Africa

3

[On his efforts to open up more public areas to blacks]: The government is not playing games. There is no alternative for South Africa but the road of reconciliation and of creating opportunities for all people of this country in a way which is just, fair and equitable.

To Presidential advisory group,
Cape Town, Nov. 16/
Los Angeles Times, 11-17:(A)1.

4

The past 10 years was a crucial period during which it was realized by many that apartheid cannot succeed. The National Party has now accepted that all South Africans—black, white, Colored and Indian—will permanently share power . . . All South Africans must have a vote. We must get away from white domination, inasmuch as it exists. But to exchange that for a situation where the white minority or some other minority suddenly becomes dominated would also not be a solution. There must be a balance . . . [But] we are not, as in the past, ideologically bound to a rigid definition of "group" along racial or ethnic lines.

Interview/
Newsweek, 12-4:70.

Samuel K. Doe
President of Liberia

5

[On U.S. insistence that his country pay off the debts it owes the U.S.]: In my mind, I think it is America that owes us; we don't owe them. I think

(SAMUEL K. DOE)

the only thing America has not done to me is to shoot my plane down.

Speech, April/
The New York Times, 4-28:(A)4.

Jose Eduardo dos Santos
President of Angola

1

[Addressing Cuban troops who are starting to withdraw from Angola]: You have fulfilled your mission with honor and glory, and your contribution to our country is unforgettable and indestructible. Those of your colleagues who have died [fighting anti-government rebels in Angola], we have engraved their names on this soil. For the rest, your names are engraved in the memories of the Angolan people.

Luanda, Angola, Jan. 10/
The Washington Post, 1-11:(A)15.

2

We have just cooperated with the United States in a complex process for the pacification of southwestern Africa. We have done a number of things that the United States requested us to do in order to normalize our relations. The government of the United States used to tell us that the withdrawal of the Cuban troops [from Angola] was what was required to normalize relations ... The Cubans are now leaving. But still there is no normalization, and still there is no cessation of the [U.S.] assistance to [Jonas] Savimbi and [his] UNITA [rebels fighting the Angolan government]. It is an attitude [by the U.S.] that we consider to be unfriendly, and which goes against the whole spirit of those agreements.

News conference, Luanda, Angola,
Sept. 29/
The Washington Post, 9-29:(A)48.

Jadalla Azouz Ettalhi
Foreign Minister of Libya

3

[On U.S. charges that Libya is building a chemical-weapons plant]: I don't think our know-

how will enable us, even if we decided to do [it], to produce chemical weapons in the very near future. We have never had a plan to produce chemical weapons ... We have not the intention. We have no plan for the time being.

Broadcast interview/
"Face the Nation,"
CBS-TV, 1-8.

Laurent Gbagbo
Ivory Coast historian
and dissident

4

Ivory Coast needs democracy the way a human body needs oxygen ... We are also the country with the highest per capita debt in Africa. We are also the country with the most millionaires. That means we have the most thieves. The more [President Felix] Houphouet ages, the more his collaborators sense an end of the regime, and the more they steal. In all countries there is corruption. The difference is that in a liberal democracy, the press can denounce and the prosecutors can indict. Here there are no counterweights.

The New York Times, 2-27:(A)4.

Gennadi I. Gerasimov
Spokesman for the Foreign Ministry
of the Soviet Union

5

[Criticizing the U.S. for shooting down two Libyan fighter planes in a dogfight over the Mediterranean]: Such actions, which are a show of political adventurism and state terrorism, can produce very serious consequences. We cannot agree that the United States, which is a permanent member of the UN Security Council, usurps the right to pass sentence on this or that sovereign state, in this case, Libya. Irrespective of pretexts, the use of force contradicts international law and runs counter to the efforts of the world community to find political solutions to existing conflicts.

To reporters,
Jan. 5/
Los Angeles Times, 1-6:(I)14.

Gerald Kaufman
Member of British Parliament

1

[On the U.S. downing of two Libyan fighter planes in a dogfight over the Mediterranean]: The Americans ought to show the utmost caution, and they really will need to justify this activity if they're going to get any support or even understanding from our country.

BBC-TV interview,
London, Jan. 4/
Los Angeles Times, 1-5:(I)5.

Gene R. La Rocque
Rear Admiral, United States
Navy (ret.);
Director, Center for
Defense Information

2

[Criticizing the U.S. downing of two Libyan fighter planes in a dogfight over the Mediterranean]: It seems again that we want to pick a fight with the Libyans and that [U.S. President] Reagan will go out fighting. We're setting it all up. We've been trying to create the environment that will justify our taking out the chemical plant [in Libya that the U.S. says will be used to make chemical weapons]. The Libyans were out there trying to defend their country, which is their right. It would even be prudent for them to be flying out there.

Jan. 4/
Los Angeles Times, 1-5:(I)5.

Ernest Lefever
President, Ethics and Public
Policy Center, Washington

3

[Saying tougher U.S. economic sanctions against South Africa to protest its apartheid system will hurt, not help]: We should have a little humble patience [because] usually when things happen too fast in history, they tend to reverse themselves. If you go too fast and in the wrong way, the forces we oppose may react and reverse the good that has been achieved.

USA Today, 9-13:(A)11.

Yoweri Museveni
President of Uganda

4

I've got a mission—to transform Uganda from a backward country to an advanced country. The economy is the base of stability. It affects your social programs, your political stability, everything . . . The biggest problem is the vicious circle. We have a population without skills. While we retrain, we must import skills from the advanced countries. For that you need dollars. But to have dollars you have to produce exports. To produce exports you need people with skills.

Interview,
Entebbe, Uganda/
Time, 11-6:54.

Sam Nujoma
Leader, South-West Africa
People's Organization
(Namibia)

5

[On his return to Namibia from exile now that the country is becoming independent from South Africa]: No words may express my happiness at joining my family, friends and comrades. The years spent abroad have at times been . . . lonely. [But] we never lost sight of our principal objective—freedom and independence for Namibia.

News conference,
Windhoek, Namibia,
Sept. 14/
Los Angeles Times, 9-15:(I)15.

6

[On his organization's winning Namibia's recent election]: We stand ready to be guided by the democratic principle of open discussion and decision by majority . . . Certainly SWAPO will not impose its will on others, nor a one-party state against the wishes of the people. [But] if the Namibian people choose a one-party state and it is done democratically at the polls, it should be so because of the will of the people.

News conference,
Windhoek, Namibia,
Nov. 15/
The New York Times, 11-16:(A)3.

Muammar el-Qaddafi
Chief of State of Libya

1

[On the shooting down of two Libyan fighter planes by the U.S. over the Mediterranean]: If America has prevailed because it is a superpower in the air and the sea, it will inevitably be defeated on land. We, as well as the fish, are awaiting them ... The revolutionaries of great Libya will not bow their heads and will not abandon their principles and the objectives of their eternal motherland of unity, liberation and the building of progress. They will meet challenge with challenge.

Jan. 4/
The New York Times, 1-5:(A)5.

2

[On the U.S. Reagan Administration's hostile attitude toward Libya]: I think during the days of the [forthcoming Bush Administration in the U.S.], relations will improve. We should bury this silly and stupid policy with the previous Administration ... They should erase the policies based on power and force ... I believe that America has learned enough lessons to abandon such policies, to adopt new policies. When the new Administration takes over, I think it is possible to have a dialogue and to understand each other, because none of us is going to change the other's views by force.

Interview/USA Today, 1-10:(A)9.

Randall Robinson
Executive director,
Trans-Africa (U.S.A.);
Member, Council on
Foreign Relations

3

[On acting South African President Frederik de Klerk, who took over for ailing Pieter Botha]: F. W. de Klerk is not a liberal, not even by South African standards. Compared to P. W. Botha, he is not fundamentally, politically different at all. He's simply polished, well-educated, very bright, smooth. Botha is a beer-hall pol who, with a high-school education, bullied his way to power. He has been ousted by a man who gives South Africa

a different kind of image, but not a different kind of policy [toward apartheid].

Interview/USA Today, 9-6:(A)9.

Ivan Van Sertima
Professor of African studies,
Rutgers University

4

Africa's a shattered world. It's a shattered diamond. It's an exploded star. You have to go back to what was essentially Africa before it was devastated by European colonization and slavery ... [The devastation] started in the 15th century and it spread over 200 to 300 years. It's still going on in parts of Africa, like southern Africa ... Invasion, colonization, fragmentation of people, repartitioning, control of its resources. Millions of young people were torn out of the belly of Africa and transported. All of us knew what effect this had on the transplanted blacks, but few of us are aware of what it did to Africa. Empires disintegrated, family life was tremendously affected. Tribes were torn asunder and the borders were reset, causing tremendous friction later on.

Interview/USA Today, 2-23:(A)9.

George P. Shultz
Secretary of State
of the United States

5

[On U.S. charges that Libya is building a plant to produce chemical weapons]: ... they do have a plant and it's designed to produce chemical weapons. We have found out about it and made that known, so that's made them antsy, and they should be antsy. That's one of our objects, to make them feel uncomfortable about the fact that they have this hot potato on their hands. Also, to do everything we can to prevent its getting itself into the shape where they can really start production. They haven't been able to do that yet, and if we can make it hard for them to get the additional expertise to make it go, that's what we want to do ... It's not illegal to build a chemical-warfare plant ... But it is very undesirable, and [Libyan leader Muammar] Qaddafi's known connections to terrorist groups and the potential

(GEORGE P. SHULTZ)

for the use in that connection is ominous.
Interview, Washington,
Jan. 4/
The Washington Post, 1-5:(A)31.

Walter Sisulu
Former general secretary,
African National Congress
(South Africa)
1

The apartheid regime [in South Africa] faces a deep and irreversible crisis today. All its strategies for reforming apartheid have failed dismally. The ANC has captured the center stage of political life in South Africa. More and more people, black and white, are being inspired by the ideals of the ANC.
At anti-apartheid rally,
Soweto, South Africa, Oct. 29/
Los Angeles Times, 10-30:(A)1.

Desmond M. Tutu
Anglican Archbishop of
Cape Town (South Africa)
2

The [anti-apartheid] struggle [in South Africa] from the beginning has been non-violent and peaceful. The African National Congress for the first 50 years of its existence was non-violent. It was only after it was banned that it resorted to armed struggle. In instance after instance, we have come into tense situations, and we have helped to defuse these.
Interview, Cape Town/
USA Today, 9-13:(A)11.

Stoffel van der Merwe
Minister of Information
of South Africa
3

We [in South Africa] have to go through a very fundamental process of considering how the government of this country should be structured. But the power distribution should be such that it will not matter what the color or origin of a particular incumbent is, especially when one comes to the more symbolic positions.
To reporters/
The Washington Post, 3-23:(A)34.

Desmond Watkins
Director, Shell Petroleum
4

[On apartheid in South Africa]: I believe that most genuinely international businesses, certainly Shell, share most of the objectives of the anti-apartheid campaign. Apartheid is incongruous with the aims and practices of business; capital is colorblind and the search for profit and economic growth is a rationalizing force. We have hopes that market forces will bring about fundamental changes in the U.S.S.R. So with South Africa. The present South African state system is protectionist, bureaucratic, inefficient and wasteful. In this it is anti-business. Left to itself, the market system will seek to develop the black community and market, train black businessmen, develop black entrepreneurs, sweep away the artificial prejudices and distinctions which inhibit economic success.
At International Business Conference,
London/
The Wall Street Journal,
9-19:(A)28.

The Americas

Elliott Abrams
*Assistant Secretary for
Inter-American Affairs,
Department of State
of the United States*

1

I don't think we [the U.S.] need a new policy [toward Cuba]. I think the policy's working. It's a policy of putting pressure on [Cuban President Fidel] Castro to isolate him, to make his economic situation difficult, to try to force him out of Angola, to try to force him to make human-rights concessions. That's what's working . . . [Castro is] a first-generation Communist leader . . . who is unable to countenance a reduction in his personal power, real democracy, real change. It will take the next generation coming, I think, for there to be real change in Cuba.

*Broadcast interview/
"Good Morning America,"
ABC-TV, 1-2.*

2

You can argue that a [public-relations] mistake was made in going for [U.S.] *covert* aid for the contras [rebels fighting the Sandinista government of Nicaragua]. Most Americans have the wrong idea about covert activity. They think that if we weren't ashamed of what we were doing, we'd do it publicly, when in fact our reason for secrecy is to protect third parties. As a result of this misunderstanding, when our covert aid to the contras was publicized, the effect was somewhat tainted. [From the beginning, U.S. President Reagan should have said,] "We cannot have a Communist government in Nicaragua," and done whatever was needed to get rid of it, including a naval blockade or possibly even an invasion. We shouldn't have started out saying that our main purpose was to interdict supplies for the Communist guerrillas in El Salvador. Instead, we should have said it was to get rid of a Communist government and to permit democratic institutions to grow in Nicaragua.

*Interview/
Los Angeles Times, 1-4:(I)10.*

Elliott Abrams
*Former Assistant Secretary for
Inter-American Affairs,
Department of State
of the United States*

3

[Criticizing Panamanian strongman Manuel Noriega for annulling recent elections in which Panamanians voted against his rule]: We have just seen free elections in the last few months in Chile, Paraguay and Bolivia. The Panamanian election fraud is a rarity in Latin America these days. It would seem to me to be useful to take this to the OAS to isolate Noriega more within Latin America.

Los Angeles Times, 5-9:(I)14.

4

[On the current U.S. invasion of Panama aimed at ousting Panamanian dictator Manuel Noriega]: The [U.S. Bush] Administration was out of options. It was either military intervention or do nothing. And doing nothing was becoming less possible after Americans [in Panama] started getting killed. This could have a very positive effect beyond Panama. It sends a message around the world, to [Soviet leader Mikhail] Gorbachev, and everyone else, that this President [Bush] will defend American interests. In that sense, it may be Bush's Grenada, or Bush's Tripoli [referring to former President Reagan's military attacks on Grenada and Libya during his Administration].

Los Angeles Times, 12-21:(A)5.

Adolfo Aguilar Zinser
Mexican political analyst

5

There is a clear gap between the institution of the [Mexican] Presidency and the prestige of the party. Elections have never been a key element in our culture for determining the credibility of our President. This is a *caudillo* culture in which you believe in the *caudillo*, the strongman who exer-

(ADOLFO AGUILAR ZINSER)

cises power, even though you don't believe he came to power through a legal process . . . I think people feel confident with a President who exercises power, but they don't feel confident with the system in which all this operates.

Los Angeles Times, 8-20:(I)1.

Raul Alfonsin
President of Argentina

1

Latin America is the only part of the developing world in which democracy is growing. We cannot risk going back to our old ways [of dictatorship].

The Washington Post, 3-13:(A)23.

Oscar Arias
President of Costa Rica

2

[Soviet leader Mikhail Gorbachev should] be consistent with what he wrote in his book, *Perestroika.* If he supports sincerely the Central American peace plan, he has to persuade Fidel Castro not to keep on supporting the guerrillas in El Salvador. War has taught us in Central America that violence is not the solution. I think we have learned that we must change bullets for ballots, and we can only do this with the support of the Cubans and the Soviet Union.

To reporters,
Washington, April 4/
The Washington Post, 4-5:(A)24.

3

. . . we cannot expect [Cuban President] Fidel Castro to change in a few months after 30 years of dogmatism . . . But he has to find out that sooner or later he has to step down from the mountains . . . I think he's beginning to understand this. I think that he knows that he's more isolated today than ever before. He knows that he's no longer the revolutionary romantic of the '60s . . . admired by youth all over the world. That is not the case any more.

Interview/
The Christian Science Monitor, 4-18:2.

Ricardo Arias Calderon
Leader of opposition to
Panamanian strongman
Manuel Noriega

4

[On efforts to remove Noriega from office]: At no point would the representatives of the regime consider any formula under which General Noriega would retire from his position as Commander-in-Chief [of the armed forces and de facto head of government]. He has been, he is and he will remain the key unresolved issue, the great obstacle to solving the Panamanian crisis and the great obstacle to Panama's being able to democratize its political life.

News conference, Washington,
Aug. 23/
The New York Times, 8-24:(A)3.

5

[On Francisco Rodriguez, the new President of Panama]: He is a functionary of the regime, personally related in friendship and service to General Noriega. The appointment is equivalent to a *coup d'etat,* leaving the country completely without constitutional government. This becomes the seventh front-man for General Noriega in seven years. It will only increase the crisis. They will gain nothing politically. There will be no sector of Panamanian society that will diminish its opposition.

The Washington Post, 9-2:(A)22.

Bernard W. Aronson
Assistant Secretary for
Inter-American Affairs,
Department of State
of the United States

6

[On the current large-scale rebel offensive in El Salvador]: This was a typical FMLN operation. It was bold and reckless. They were willing to risk their lives. But it also shows how isolated they are from the population. They talked themselves into the delusion that they have a mass popular base in the country, when they've never been so isolated.

Nov.14/
The New York Times, 11-15:(A)6.

WHAT THEY SAID IN 1989

(BERNARD W. ARONSON)

1

[On the recent killing of six Jesuit priests in El Salvador, which he attributes to right-wing death squads]: The FMLN [left-wing rebels fighting the U.S.-backed Salvadoran government] systematically tried to get the death squads to come out of the closet in 1989 and start killing again. [The rebels] got what they wanted. The right-wing death squads probably did come out of the closet . . . The people responsible for this crime are murderers and barbarians. They must be brought to justice and punished for their crimes. The terror of the FMLN is no excuse for the terror of the violent right.

Before Senate Foreign Relations
Committee, Washington, Nov. 17/
The New York Times, 11-18:1,6.

James A. Baker III
Secretary of State-designate
of the United States

2

The overwhelming blemish [in Central America] remains—the terrible draining conflict between Nicaragua and her neighbors and between the Nicaraguan Marxists [the ruling Sandinista government] and their own people, some of whom have taken up arms and merited American support. Starting in 1987, all of the governments of the area stepped back from the brink long enough to agree on a set of principles for peace. The Esquipulas Agreement, known as Esquipulas II and authored by President Arias of Costa Rica, expresses well everyone's objectives. It is a good platform for peace, but what it lacks, in my view at least, is a mechanism for enforcement. Clearly, we need a different approach. We need an approach that must be bipartisan here in Washington if it is to succeed there in the region. Events have shown that only such bipartisan action influences the Sandinistas.

At Senate Foreign Relations
Committee hearing on his
confirmation, Washington, Jan. 17/
The New York Times, 1-18:(A)10.

3

Our neighbor, Mexico, is deeply in debt and faces some serious challenges to its social fabric.

But Mexico also has many assets—the capabilities of its people and its significant natural resources. The Mexican government, led by President Salinas, is taking the road of economic and political reform. It's a difficult road, and we are determined to help. It is in our interest to do so. It is time that we regarded Mexico with the respect and the seriousness it warrants. Whatever the past, we must all be aware that America's relationship with Mexico means a very great deal. I happen to believe that it is as important as our relationship with any other country in the world.

At Senate Foreign Relations
Committee hearing on his
confirmation, Washington, Jan. 17/
The New York Times, 1-18:(A)10.

4

Recently, working with Canada, we were able to achieve a free-trade agreement, something both nations had sought for 100 years without success. In my view, the free-trade agreement is in our mutual interest, and there are geopolitical implications that go far beyond the economic significance of this agreement. The United States-Canada agreement represents a signal success in a strategy designed to move all nations toward a more [free] trading system.

At Senate Foreign Relations
Committee hearing on his
confirmation, Washington, Jan. 17/
The New York Times, 1-18:(A)10.

5

Despite guerrilla efforts, the democratic political process has been established in El Salvador. There have been five free and honest elections since 1982. And we have another election scheduled for March of 1989. There's a free press; there's open access to the media; and there's freedom for parties to organize and campaign. Over the long term, I think the trend has been indisputably downward in terms of politically motivated violence—even though it seems to be rising a bit now, which is disturbing just as we're moving into an election cycle. [But] you should not worry about the new [U.S. Bush]

(JAMES A. BAKER III)

Administration going soft on human rights in El Salvador, because that is simply not going to happen.

> *At Senate Foreign Relations*
> *Committee hearing on his*
> *confirmation, Washington, Jan. 17/*
> *The New York Times, 1-18:(A)11.*

James A. Baker III
Secretary of State
of the United States

1

If you ask the United States to forgo unilateral initiatives and work instead in good faith with the democratic nations of Latin America in a new cooperative diplomacy to support democracy, then we ask you [Latin American democracies] to join with us in good faith to turn the promise of that democracy into reality throughout this hemisphere. All those who advocate diplomacy and political solutions to the region's conflicts have a responsibility to prove that this is the best and surest route to achieve our common goals. We invite Latin America's democratic leaders to join us in this challenge.

> *At seminar on Western Hemisphere*
> *affairs, Jimmy Carter's Presidential*
> *Center, Atlanta, March 30/*
> *Los Angeles Times, 3-31:(I)17.*

2

The Soviet Union bears a special responsibility [for insurrections in Central America] because its arms and money, moving through Cuba and Nicaragua, continue to support violence, destruction and war. Shipments of Soviet rocket-propelled grenades to the [guerrillas in El Salvador] are incompatible with the new thinking [in the Soviet Union]. Soviet behavior toward Cuba and Central America remains the biggest obstacle to a full across-the-board improvement in relations between the United States and the Soviet Union.

> *Before Organization of American*
> *States foreign ministers,*
> *Washington, Nov. 13/*
> *The Washington Post, 11-14:(A)32.*

Enrique Bermudez
Military commander of the
contras, rebels fighting the
Sandinista government
of Nicaragua

3

[On the precarious position the contras find themselves in]: I do not know if it is because of arrogance or incapacity, but the United States [the contras' chief backer] does not know how to negotiate [with the Sandinistas]. To negotiate, the United States pressures its allies and not its enemies. They cut out aid, but allow the Sandinistas to continue to receive more than $500-million a year in Soviet and Cuban aid. I think we in the military fulfilled our obligations, but we lost on the political front, where we did not have great capacity. We were defeated in Washington, not on the field of battle.

> *Interview/*
> *The Washington Post, 4-12:(A)8.*

Larry Birns
Director, Council on
Hemispheric Affairs

4

[Saying the U.S. was correct not to intervene in favor of the rebels during the recent failed coup attempt against Panamanian strongman Manuel Noriega]: The U.S. happens to be in Panama, but it has no special privileges, no "right" to a military option. The U.S. should get out of the business of installing and taking other governments out ... [As for Noriega,] history shows that against unspeakable odds, a population, if it has sufficient resolve, will get rid of its oppressor.

> *The Christian Science Monitor,*
> *10-10:7.*

David L. Boren
United States Senator,
D-Oklahoma

5

[Saying the U.S. should have helped dissident Panamanian soldiers in their failed coup against strongman Manuel Noriega, who is wanted by the U.S. for drug trafficking]: Here you have brave people in Panama trying to rid themselves

(DAVID L. BOREN)

of a drug dealer and thug who's taken over their country; and for the United States, with all of our strength and force and all of our belief in democracy, to stand by just two miles away, as the crow flies, and do nothing and allow these people to fail, personally I think is wrong. Today we had an insurrection of some very courageous people . . . and the United States did nothing.

To reporters, Washington,
Oct. 3/
Los Angeles Times, 10-4:(I)12.

Bill Bradley
United States Senator,
D-New Jersey

1

[On Mexico's debt]: I hope we'll get [a debt-reduction] agreement that will give Mexico the room to grow because that growth is critical to the United States as well as to Mexico. Mexico is a country where half the population is under the age of 15, and where, if they don't invest domestically, they don't create the jobs. And if they don't create the jobs, you end up with a lot of illegal immigration [to the U.S.]. It's important because if they are not growing, they are not buying our exports. If they are sending money into banks for principal and interest payments, they don't have the money to buy our exports. Frankly, the more difficult their economic circumstances are—not only in Mexico but all over—the less democracy is strengthened.

Interview, New York/
The Christian Science Monitor,
7-19:8.

Philip Brenner
Professor of international
relations, American University,
Washington

2

[Saying the current U.S. invasion of Panama aimed at ousting Panamanian dictator Manuel Noriega will have adverse effects on U.S. foreign policy]: What this means is that every Latin American leader will now feel compelled to take an anti-American stance. And all the countries in which we have bases now are going to think about how we are going to use the troops on those bases.

Los Angeles Times, 12-22:(A)9.

George Bush
Vice President, and
President-elect,
of the United States

3

[The flow of Central American refugees into Texas and Florida] is causing an over-burdening of facilities like schools and hospitals. This is a sorry commentary on what's happening in Central America and Nicaragua, and we've been seeing this for a long, long time. When I become President, we're going to take a hard new look at the immigration policies, but there is no easy answer to it. The final answer is democracy and freedom in Nicaragua. When people are fleeing tyranny, the United States has to be generous. But no one community can suffer an overload without some support.

News conference,
Islamorada, Fla., Jan. 13/
Los Angeles Times, 1-14:(I)16.

George Bush
President of the United States

4

The Soviet Union . . . has an obligation and an opportunity to demonstrate its new thinking. In other regional conflicts, it's adopted a welcome new approach. But in Central America what we've seen . . . is only old thinking. The Soviet Union has no legitimate security interests in Central America. The United States has many. We reject any doctrine of equivalence in the region.

Washington, March 24/
The New York Times, 3-25:5.

5

[On the recent elections in Panama which went against Panamanian leader Manuel Noriega, who nevertheless remains in power]:

(GEORGE BUSH)

There has been a massive voice of the people heard. There has been a statement for democracy so loud and so clear that perhaps even General Noriega will listen to it. And I would like to think that he will heed the call of the people and that he would listen to the international outcry that is building and that he would step down from office, in which case the relations with the United States would improve dramatically and instantly.

News conference, Washington,
May 9/
The New York Times, 5-10:(A)6.

1

This past week the people of Panama, in record numbers, voted to elect a new democratic leadership of their country. And they voted to replace the dictatorship of General Manuel Noriega. The whole world was watching. Every credible observer—the Catholic Church, Latin and European observers, leaders of our Congress, and two former presidents of the United States—tell us the same story: The opposition won. It was not even a close election. The opposition won by a margin of nearly 3 to 1. The Noriega regime first tried to steal this election through massive fraud and intimidation, and now has nullified the election and resorted to violence and bloodshed. In recent days, a host of Latin American leaders have condemned this election fraud. They've called on General Noriega to heed the will of the people of Panama. We support and second those demands. The United States will not recognize nor accommodate with a regime that holds power through force and violence at the expense of the Panamanian people's right to be free.

Washington, May 11/
The New York Times, 5-12:(A)4.

2

[The U.S. will not normalize relations with Cuba] as long as [Cuban President Fidel] Castro violates the human rights of his own people, as long as he, almost alone in the entire world now, swims against the tide that is bringing sweeping change, democracy and freedom to closed societies around the world. As President, I will look for signs that Castro wants to move away from subverting his neighbors, move toward more openness, more freedom for his own people. But until I see such demonstrable change, there will be no improvement in relations with Cuba. It simply cannot be.

Republican fund-raising address,
Miami, Aug. 16/
The Washington Post, 8-17:(A)5.

3

[On criticism that the U.S. did not aid the recent failed coup attempt against Panamanian leader Manuel Noriega, whom the U.S. wants out of office]: I have not seen any fact, in all the reports that have come out, that would make me have done something different in terms of use of force. And I reiterate that. Now, in terms of procedures, I'll simply say, any time we can make improvements, so much the better. But there has not been an intelligence gap that would have made me act in a different way. And I repeat that. And there's been endless interviews and discussions and stories, many of which are false, that come out as to what we were asked to do or not to do. But I've seen no fact that would make me change my view. And I've seen allegations that when I said I wanted Noriega to get out [of] there, that implied use of force [by the U.S.]. I hope I would never be reckless enough as a Commander-in-Chief to make a blanket commitment to use of force without knowing the facts regarding some coup attempt . . . I wouldn't mind using force, and if it could be done in a prudent manner. So, in other words, I am not ruling out the use of force for all time. I'm reiterating the fact that it was not proper to use force under the existing circumstances.

News conference,
Washington, Oct. 13/
The New York Times, 10-14:8.

4

[On the current large-scale rebel offensive in El Salvador]: I want to tell you how upset I am that in a time when we are all trying to build peace

(GEORGE BUSH)

in Central America through diplomatic means, the FMLN in El Salvador, aided and abetted by Nicaragua and the Cuban government, has reverted to senseless bloodshed in gross violation of all the agreements reached to promote peace in Central America.

At Organization of American States,
Washington, Nov. 14/
The New York Times, 11-15:(A)6.

1

[On the current U.S. invasion of Panama aimed at ousting Panamanian dictator Manuel Noriega]: Fellow citizens, last night I ordered U.S. military forces to Panama. No President takes such action lightly. This morning, I want to tell you what I did and why I did it. For nearly two years, the United States, nations of Latin America and the Caribbean have worked together to resolve the crisis in Panama. The goals of the United States have been to safeguard the lives of Americans, to defend democracy in Panama, to combat drug trafficking and to protect the integrity of the Panama Canal Treaty. Many attempts have been made to resolve this crisis through diplomacy and negotiations. All were rejected by the dictator of Panama, General Manuel Noriega, an indicted drug trafficker. Last Friday, Noriega declared his military dictatorship to be in a state of war with the United States and threatened the lives of Americans in Panama. The very next day, forces under his command shot and killed an unarmed American serviceman, wounded another, arrested and brutally beat a third American serviceman and then brutally interrogated his wife, threatening her with sexual abuse. That was enough. General Noriega's reckless threats and attacks upon Americans in Panama created an eminent danger to the 35,000 American citizens in Panama. As President, I have no higher obligation than to safeguard the lives of American citizens. And that is why I directed our armed force to protect the lives of American citizens in Panama, and to bring General Noriega to justice in the United States . . . I took this action only after reaching the conclusion that every other avenue was

closed and the lives of American citizens were in grave danger. I hope that the people of Panama will put this dark chapter of dictatorship behind them and move forward together as citizens of a democratic Panama with this government that they themselves have elected [the new government of Guillermo Endara whose election earlier this year was voided by Noriega]. The United States is eager to work with the Panamanian people in partnership and friendship to rebuild their economy. The Panamanian people want democracy, peace and the chance for a better life in dignity and freedom. The people of the United States seek only to support them in pursuit of these noble goals.

Broadcast address to the nation,
Washington, Dec. 20/
The New York Times, 12-21:(A)9.

Adolfo Calero
President, national directorate,
Nicaraguan Democratic Force

2

[On his being a leader of the contras, rebels fighting the Sandinista government of Nicaragua]: At age 50, I looked forward to an easy life, to retirement and looking after my investments. Seven years later, I'm even less eager for war. I would be very happy to end it. But we have to be very careful how we deal with the lives of thousands of [contra] fighters. We must remain a viable force up to the last minute.

Interview, Feb. 15/
Los Angeles Times, 2-16:(I)6.

Dante Caputo
Foreign Minister of Argentina

3

[In the 1970s,] social conditions, domestic politics and international relations [allowed] terrorism to find support in our [Latin American] countries. Today, terrorism in Argentina is isolated. There is not a single political party which has an ambiguous or ambivalent position on it. They have all condemned it, as have the trade unions, and this was not at all the case earlier . . . Since the beginning of the '80s, there has been democracy as never before in Latin Amer-

(DANTE CAPUTO)

ica. This is the new phenomenon at the end of the 20th century, the phenomenon of the impoverished democracy.

Interview/
The New York Times, 2-20:(A)6.

Jorge G. Castaneda
Mexican author and educator

1

Mexico can never afford to forget that the U.S. exists. It can never stop thinking for a single moment that the U.S. is there, on the border, next door. This is an inevitable consequence of the tremendous asymmetry that exists between Mexico and the U.S. We have to think obsessively, constantly, recurrently about the U.S. The U.S. only thinks about us every now and then, and most of the time for the wrong reasons.

Interview/
Time, 8-7:56.

Fidel Castro
President of Cuba

2

Today, we say with more force than ever: socialism or death, Marxism-Leninism or death!

Jan. 1/
USA Today, 4-5:(A)12.

3

There are two kinds of survival and two kinds of peace. The survival of the rich and the survival of the poor; the peace of the rich and the peace of the poor. That is why the news that there may be peace, that there may be detente between the United States and the Soviet Union, ·does not necessarily mean that there is going to be peace for us.

At armed-forces celebration/
The New York Times, 1-11:(A)4.

4

[Criticizing the changes in the Soviet Union resulting from that country's reform program]: In

their press and media, there is not a single word about internationalism and anti-imperialism. You do not see these two notions at all in the Soviet media today. Instead, they are trying to participate together with capitalist countries, in splitting the profits made at the expense of the Third World. If we [Cuba] are destined to remain the only socialist country in the world, so be it. We will fight to the very end to protect the gains of socialism.

At rally honoring Cuban soldiers
who died in Africa/
Los Angeles Times, 12-9:(A)14.

Alfredo Cesar
Member of campaign committee,
National Democratic Union
(political opposition to
Sandinista government
of Nicaragua)

5

[On next year's scheduled Nicaraguan elections]: Whatever results we have in the February 25 election—if they are held, if they are not postponed and if they are fair—the game is over in Nicaragua for one player [the Sandinistas]. From then on, you're going to need two to tango. And so the basic point is: Is the government ready? [Is it] ready to confront such a challenge, risking power in the election or winning by a small margin?

At forum, Carter Center,
Emory University,
Atlanta, Nov. 14/
The New York Times, 11-15:(A)6.

Dick Cheney
Secretary of Defense-designate
of the United States

6

[On the Sandinista government in Nicaragua]: Those familiar with history will be aware that tactics similar to those of the Sandinistas were used by the Nazis during Hitler's rise to power in Germany. I find it almost too ironic for words that a government whose political tactics are beneath contempt can be considered credible when it promises to democratize or that it can be

(DICK CHENEY)

considered deserving of support by those in the United States who claim they are friends of political and economic freedom and justice.

The Washington Post, 3-14:(A)4.

Dick Cheney
Secretary of Defense
of the United States

1

[On critics in the U.S. who say the U.S. should have militarily helped those in Panama who recently staged a failed coup attempt against strongman Manuel Noriega]: I have never seen so many bloodthirsty people as I've experienced over the last week . . . who say we should have used force. I think there's a lot of Monday-morning quarterbacking going on. There are more Monday-morning quarterbacks per square mile in Washington than any other city in the nation. The fact of the matter is, given what we knew then, and what we know now, I still think we made the right decision [not to intervene] . . . [Using U.S. military force] would have involved going in against the rebels and taking Noriega from them. I never thought that was a very good idea, but we told [the American military commander in Panama] to be prepared in case he got the order to do so. And then, shortly after that, the coup fell apart.

Broadcast interview/
"Face the Nation," CBS-TV, 10-8.

2

[On the current U.S. invasion of Panama aimed at ousting Panamanian dictator Manuel Noriega]: I think we as a government bent over backward to avoid having to take military action. I think the record is replete with the patience and forbearance of the United States government in this instance. When we reached the point, however, when it was clear that American lives were at risk, when it reached the point where it was clear that General Noriega had created an environment in which his troops felt free to terrorize and brutalize Americans who had every legitimate and lawful right to be in Panama, that was a

fundamentally different set of circumstances.

Press briefing,
Washington, Dec. 20/
The New York Times, 12-21:(A)10.

Violeta Barrios de Chamorro
Candidate for President
of Nicaragua in the 1990 election

3

We Nicaraguans defeated a cruel dictatorship [by overthrowing Anastasio Somoza in 1979], but the [now-governing] Sandinistas betrayed us by imposing Marxist-Leninist tyranny. We're fighting for democracy, just like people in Poland and all over the world. Forget about the Sandinistas. They're obsolete.

Interview, Sept. 3/
The New York Times, 9-4:(A)1,4.

Alan Cranston
United States Senator,
D-California

4

[On the recent killing of six Jesuit priests in El Salvador, which some people attribute to right-wing death squads]: The war in El Salvador [between left-wing rebels and the U.S.-backed government] has been reduced to the level of street thugs butchering each other. There is no U.S. national-security interest in using our tax-payer dollars to bankroll such a conflict. Military forces are involved in acts of murder. Salvadoran President [Alfredo] Cristiani is unable to control this indiscriminate violence. He is unable to control right-wing death squads operating under the protection of U.S.-armed military forces.

Nov. 17/
The New York Times, 11-18:6.

Alfredo Cristiani
President of El Salvador

5

The only privileged people in our society will be the very poor.

Inaugural address, San Salvador,
June 1/
The New York Times, 6-2:(A)3.

Christopher J. Dodd
United States Senator,
D-Connecticut

1

[Saying the U.S. should not abrogate the treaty that calls for turning over control of the Panama Canal to Panama in 1999, despite the current rule of Panamanian dictator and drug-trafficker Manuel Noriega]: They hate Noriega in Panama, but abrogate the treaty and they'd build monuments to him in every village.

The New York Times, 5-11:(A)6.

2

[On the recent killings of six Jesuit priests in El Salvador, which some observers have attributed to the army or right-wing death squads]: The time has come for [Salvadoran] President [Alfredo] Cristiani to evidence his commitment to controlling those officials within his own party who are in very large part responsible for the civil conflict in El Salvador. President Cristiani is either in control of his government or he is not... President Cristiani either deserves our support, or he does not.

Nov. 17/
Los Angeles Times, 11-18:(A)19.

Enrique Dreyfus
Nicaraguan businessman

3

[Nicaragua's] economy is the biggest problem we have, but politics is priority Number 1. For [the economy] to recover to a level anywhere near what should be normal for us, will take a giant national effort. It will need all Nicaraguans—not just those in opposition or government but truly all of us—or it simply will not work. The government cannot will an economy to work.

The Christian Science Monitor,
1-3:3.

Lawrence S. Eagleburger
Deputy Secretary of State
of the United States

4

[On Panamanian leader Manuel Noriega's throwing out the results of an election in which

the people of Panama voted against him]: The Latins are always going to be edgy about [the U.S.] response in the sense that they are always worried about intervention in the internal affairs of states in Latin America. In this particular case, however, I think it's fairly clear that there is going to be almost universal condemnation of Noriega's [election fraud], and I think we will find very substantial Latin American support for our [limited] response.

Broadcast interview/
Los Angeles Times, 5-12:(I)14.

5

Countries that provide safe haven or support for the international drug-trafficking cartels menace the peace and security of this hemisphere, just as surely as if they were using their own military forces to attack our societies. [Panamanian leader Manuel] Noriega has turned Panama into a haven for drug traffickers and a center for money laundering and the transshipment of cocaine. Will General Noriega be permitted falsely to wrap himself in the flag of Panamanian sovereignty while the drug cartels with which he is allied intervene throughout this hemisphere? That is aggression as surely as Adolf Hitler's invasion of Poland 50 years ago.

Before foreign ministers of
Organization of American States
members, Washington, Aug. 24/
Los Angeles Times, 8-25:(I)10.

Mickey Edwards
United States Representative,
D-Oklahoma

6

[Criticizing a Central American agreement that would disband the contras, rebels fighting the Sandinista government of Nicaragua, before elections are held in that country]: This agreement is a complete violation of our understanding up to this point that demobilization of the contras and democratization in Nicaragua were going to be simultaneous. It strikes me as a sellout of the contras by the Presidents of the Central American countries, who decided to cut their losses, knowing that the contras would not be get-

WHAT THEY SAID IN 1989

ting a lot more assistance from the United States . . . If we just back off and say to the contras, "Nice try but it's over now," then an awful lot of young men down there died for nothing.

Aug. 8/
The New York Times, 8-9:(A)8.

Guido Fernandez
Minister of Information
of Costa Rica

1

It is our belief that now that the United States has assumed a policy toward Central America that will give a real chance for peace, it is time for the Soviets to adopt the same attitude. It is time for the Soviets to suspend any military aid to Nicaragua in order to contribute to the creation of an environment propitious to a peace settlement in Central America. If the Soviets now keep supplying arms to Central America to be used in Nicaragua, or through Cuba, to guerrilla movements in El Salvador and Guatemala, it is going to be very difficult for Central Americans to promote a real peace.

Interview, San Jose, Costa Rica/
The New York Times, 3-30:(A)6.

Mikhail S. Gorbachev
General Secretary,
Communist Party of the
Soviet Union;
President of the Soviet Union

2

We want a Latin American solution to the conflict [in Nicaragua] without any interference from any outside party. We are against doctrines which justify the export of revolution and counter-revolution or any kind of foreign interference in the internal affairs of sovereign states.

Before Cuban National Assembly,
Havana, April 4/
USA Today, 4-5:(A)1.

3

The Soviet Union does not seek for itself political, strategic or military advantage in the Western Hemisphere . . . The Soviet Union has not and does not intend to have naval, air force or missile bases in Latin America, or deploy nuclear or other weapons of mass destruction there.

Before Cuban National Assembly,
Havana, April 4/
Los Angeles Times, 4-5:(I)9.

Peter Hakim
Staff director,
Inter-American Dialogue

4

[U.S.] sanctions were initially applied [in Panama] under the mistaken assumption that they would create an intolerable level of pressure on the [regime of Panamanian leader Manuel Noriega] and dislodge him quickly from office. They have not worked that way. Instead, they have devastated the Panamanian economy, which has contracted by more than 25 per cent in the past year; imposed severe hardship on the people of Panama, who have suffered widespread job losses, reduced income and drastic declines in their standard of living; and pushed many U.S. businesses in Panama to the edge of bankruptcy . . . It may now be useful to consider distinguishing among different kinds of sanctions. For example, we could decide to lift punitive measures—such as the freeze on Panamanian government assets in the United States, the withholding of payments to the Canal Commission, and the prohibition of U.S. companies paying taxes in Panama—but, at the same time, continue to deny Panama the benefits of fully normal commercial and economic relations, such as trade preferences, foreign assistance and sugar quotas. We could, in short, significantly reduce the suffering of the Panamanian people and avoid further damage to U.S. business, while continuing to make clear our distaste for the Noriega regime.

Before two House Foreign Affairs
Subcommittees, Washington,
July 26/
The Washington Post,
8-1:(A)20.

Rafael Hernandez Colon
Governor of Puerto Rico

1

[U.S.] statehood [for Puerto Rico] . . . is unworkable because it . . . does not take into account . . . that Puerto Ricans form a people, a distinct society, with its own culture, ethos and language . . . This most unequal of states would resist to meld or blend. It would be a state with a different primary language, marching under its own flag.

The Christian Science Monitor,
7-18:8.

Robert E. Hunter
Senior fellow,
Center for Strategic and
International Studies,
Washington

2

I don't see a future for the contras [rebels fighting the Sandinista government of Nicaragua]. Everything [U.S. President] Bush has done so far indicates a desire to try to place Nicaragua in some broader context which will help him avoid an early political dispute and possible failure. He is concerned about Nicaragua, but to use an old Lyndon Johnson expression, "This dog won't hunt."

Los Angeles Times, 2-16:(I)7.

3

[On how to deal with the problem of Panama's strongman Manuel Noriega, a dictator allegedly involved in drug trafficking]: The best solution is for the Latin Americans to do it. The next best is for us to do it with them. Absolutely the worst is for us to do it by ourselves . . . Last time, we got into this backward. [Former U.S. President Ronald] Reagan didn't have an answer to the drug issue—who does?—so he found it useful to point a finger at Noriega, a drug kingpin who always lives up to his evil reputation. Trouble is, no one figured out what we would do if Noriega refused to go. So [current U.S. President] Bush inherited this problem, and I salute him for his calm approach this far. He's smart to try not to get himself stuck to this tar baby.

The New York Times, 5-11:(A)6.

Fred C. Ikle
Former Under Secretary for
Policy, Department of Defense
of the United States

4

The war in Nicaragua was lost by the [U.S.] Congress, not by the contras [U.S.-backed rebels fighting the Sandinista government]. The last major installment of [U.S. aid for the contras] approved by Congress was extremely effective: The Sandinista regime was in deep, deep difficulty, and it probably would have been toppled had Congress approved another $200-million or so of aid. Continued support would have made the contras more effective, and, even more important, it would have convinced the people of Nicaragua that the United States was on the contras' side. Expectations matter a great deal in such a conflict; people want to be on the winning side.

Interview/
The Washington Post, 7-12:(A)22.

Patrick J. Leahy
United States Senator,
D-Vermont

5

[On the guerrilla war in El Salvador]: There is brutality and murder on both sides. The right justifies it in the name of the Lord, the left justifies it in the name of liberation, and the people die in the middle.

Washington, Nov. 17/
The Washington Post, 11-18:(A)18.

Rensselaer Lee
President,
Global Advisory Services

6

[On the U.S. fight against illegal drugs from South America]: We [in the U.S.] are asking these countries to stop producing coca and cocaine, yet people are making their living that way [by growing it], especially in Bolivia, Peru and parts of Colombia . . . You cannot have a drug strategy and ignore the economic fallout. We are taking a military and law-enforcement approach to a problem that is economic and

WHAT THEY SAID IN 1989

(RENSSELAER LEE)

social . . . I would like to see us tone down this drug "war" . . . build up their legal economies and strengthen their criminal-justice institutions.

The Christian Science Monitor,
9-8:2.

Francisco Lopez
Director, National Institute
for Social and Economic Investigations,
(Nicaragua)

1

The [Sandinista] revolution [in Nicaragua] now finds itself at a crossroads. The government has thrown so many bones to the producers and the professionals that they've become elites . . . It's a total contradiction of our revolutionary ideals.

The Christian Science Monitor,
1-25:1.

Abraham Lowenthal
Executive director,
Inter-American Dialogue

2

If radical, nationalist anti-Americans took over in Mexico—even if they weren't Communists—it would be awful for the United States. What could cause this? A prolonged, profound economic crisis in which the U.S. is seen as indifferent.

The Christian Science Monitor,
1-18:7.

Connie Mack
United States Senator,
R-Florida

3

[Criticizing the treaty by which the U.S. will relinquish control of the Panama Canal to Panama]: We made a mistake in 1977. We have given up our interests in the Canal based on the idea that our show of friendship would bring about peace and tranquility in Central America. The opposite has occurred. The message was one of weakness—that the United States no longer

considered Panama to be a vital interest to the United States. That's why we have gotten into the difficulties that we have . . . I am one individual who has called for the abrogation of the treaty. I think it was wrong. I believe the treaty is being violated on a day-to-day basis, and I think we ought to abrogate it . . . We entered into this agreement wrongly, but we entered into it with the understanding that there would be a free, fair, open government, a democracy in place in Panama. And that simply has not occurred. It's been 12 years now and, if anything, the situation has gotten worse [such as the emergence of Panamanian dictator Manuel Noriega].

Interview/
USA Today, 5-10:(A)9.

Alfredo Maduro
President, Chamber of Commerce
of Panama

4

[On U.S. economic sanctions against Panama as a protest against that country's leader, Manuel Noriega]: Economic sanctions are not going to kill this government. They haven't killed Nicaragua or Cuba. They only hurt the people they are trying to help.

The Christian Science Monitor, 5-3:2.

Michael Manley
Prime Minister-elect
of Jamaica

5

Our position is that Cuba is part of the hemisphere, but that our fundamental relationships are with our big trading partners—the United States, Canada, Central America and countries in Latin America. Cuba should be recognized by all countries . . . and we would do that . . . What we would never do again is allow the level of the relationship to become a source of either internal tension or tension with Washington.

Interview/Newsweek, 2-20:29.

Hugo Margain
Former Minister of Finance
of Mexico

6

[Mexico's] domestic debt is less conflictive than the foreign debt because it is ours, it's in the

(HUGO MARGAIN)

family, and we can do whatever we have to do, with fellow Mexicans. It shouldn't exceed certain limits, but it does not rob me of my sleep the way the foreign debt does.

The New York Times, 6-5:(C)16.

Lorenzo Meyer
Political scientist,
Colegio de Mexico

1

[Local] elections [in Mexico] serve as barometers to measure how far [President Carlos] Salinas is committed to democracy. The problem [for Salinas] is that, for many Mexicans, the only way he can prove his democratic credentials is by losing. The system has lost so much credibility that any PRI [Salinas' party] victory would be considered a fraud.

The Christian Science Monitor,
6-29:1.

Herbert Muller
President, Central Bank
of Bolivia

2

[On Bolivia's role in drug trafficking]: Even if Bolivia were to eradicate all its coca, be sure that tomorrow there will be coca grown in another country. And Bolivia will be left without the social cushion of the 250,000 jobs the coca and cocaine economy provides.

The Christian Science Monitor,
9-6:6.

Aryeh Neier
Vice chairman,
Americas Watch

3

[On Cuba's crackdown on human-rights workers]: Cuba seems determined to crush this movement. It seems apparent that the Cubans no longer feel under any international pressure on human rights . . . This is another indication that Cuba is intent on suppressing any independent

activities and [is] simply interested in operating as a completely totalitarian state.

The New York Times, 8-10:(A)9.

Manuel Antonio Noriega
Commander of the armed forces
of Panama

4

Refusing U.S. demands that he resign in the wake of his recent election loss and charges that he is involved in drug trafficking]: We have made it a point of our doctrine that this is not one man's struggle, but the struggle of many men and many people here at the shore of the [Panama] Canal. It's Panama's fight against an empire [the U.S.] that has to leave . . . Today it's Panama, tomorrow it will be the other countries [of Latin America], because this is a United States mechanism for aggression.

Broadcast interview, May 17/
The New York Times, 5-18:(A)4.

5

[On the recent failed coup attempt against him by some members of the Panamanian armed forces]: The United States was involved before, during and after the coup. They [U.S. officials] had to make the contacts, woo them, convince them. It's a lot of work before you've hooked the fish. But they were the hook and the useful fools were the fish.

Interview, Panama City,
Oct. 11/
Los Angeles Times, 10-12:(I)1.

6

[Saying that before 1968, the U.S. controlled many aspects of Panamanian life]: They put in and took out Presidents, monitored the electoral process, and sent troops when the members of the wealthy oligarchy asked for them. Before [Panama took charge of its own affairs], no ordinary citizen had access to public office, university education, or health care. These were monopolies of the oligarchy, and this was and still is the basis of colonialism . . . Those were the times when the Presidents, named by the oligarchy,

231

were supported by the commanders of the National Guard. Well, all of this and much more has changed now. Neither I nor any of my men . . . will ever take orders from a President who oppresses the people or who takes orders from the White House [in Washington]. [The U.S.] will never give up this paradise, from which it can destabilize Latin America, destroy any government that does not obey it absolutely. [The U.S.] realizes that the era of decolonization has begun and is trying to find out if it can control this decolonization, which for us is an irreversible process.

Interview/
World Press Review, December:52.

Richard Nuccio
Senior associate,
Inter-American Dialogue,
Washington

1

[On Latin American reaction to the current U.S. invasion of Panama aimed at ousting Panamanian dictator Manuel Noriega]: The Latin Americans are going to make political judgments based on how neat and clean or messy the situation in Panama is over the next few days. They must [outwardly] express outrage at a violation of Panama's sovereignty, but in private they are saying, "Thank goodness Noriega is gone." But if [U.S.] troops have to stay in Panama a long time, fighting a guerrilla war against Noriega's men or creating a new Panamanian army, then the [Latins'] adherence to principles will be stronger and many of them will not recognize [Guillermo] Endara [who won this year's Panamanian Presidential election that was voided by Noriega and who is now, after Noriega's ouster, assuming the Presidency]. That will put them on a collision course with the United States.

Los Angeles Times, 12-21:(A)12.

Daniel Ortega
President of Nicaragua

2

Now is not the time to establish socialism [in Nicaragua]. We're convinced that our model should not be the countries of Eastern Europe or Cuba. [It should be the Scandinavian countries.] They're small; they have a heavy emphasis on social programs; the state has a role in the economy, but so does the private sector.

Interview/Time, 2-6:46.

3

We have a crisis provoked by the United States in Nicaragua, in El Salvador, in Panama. Where is this going to stop? We are ready to work with the United States on negotiated solutions to all these problems, but first we have to sit down and talk . . . The United States is not going to be hurt by talking to us. It would be exhalted by such a gesture.

At ceremony marking 10th
anniversary of Sandinista rule in
Nicaragua, Managua, July 19/
Los Angeles Times, 7-20:(I)12.

4

[On the contras, U.S.-backed rebels fighting his Sandinista government]: We aren't interested in taking revenge against them [if they put down their arms]. The majority of them have also been victims of the yankees . . . The contras are Nicaraguans defending a position that isn't Nicaraguan. They are doing the work of the yankees.

Speech, Pantasma, Nicaragua,
Aug. 15/
The New York Times, 8-16:(A)6.

5

[Saying he will allow official U.S. observers at next year's Nicaraguan elections only if the U.S. agrees to help finance the elections and disband the contra rebels]: I told them they could send delegations of the North American government, but they have to comply with these two requirements. It's absurd that we should accept observers of a government that carries out an ambiguous policy—that on one hand says it favors the electoral process and on the other hand is financing mercenaries to murder the Nicaraguan people . . . They have to take away the

(DANIEL ORTEGA)

financing they are now giving the contras to attack the Nicaraguan people and . . . use these funds to demobilize the contras. When they send food, clothing and boots to the contras, they are giving support to continue their attacks.

Speech, San Jacinto, Nicaragua,
Sept. 13/
Los Angeles Times, 9-14:(I)9.

1

[On his opposition in the forthcoming 1990 elections]: We are not going to worry about those who are willing to serve as political mercenaries of the United States, because we are going to beat them anyway. In the same way we defeated the armed mercenaries, we will defeat the political mercenaries . . . They are nothing but instruments. My real opposition is the North American government [the U.S.]. My latest adversary is named [U.S. President] George Bush. He is the other candidate in Nicaragua . . . I am ready to debate him in Washington or Managua, or we can debate by satellite . . . He knows what he wants, so we can talk. With the others [running in the 1990 election] there is nothing to discuss.

News conference, Managua,
Sept. 26/
Los Angeles Times, 9-27:(I)8.

2

[Saying his government is considering resuming its war against the contra rebels after a 19-month cease-fire]: The United States government wants to keep the contras around indefinitely to exert pressure against Nicaragua. This is a source not only of continuing criminal attacks against the Nicaraguan people [but], in the face of inevitable Sandinista [government] victory in the coming elections, the contras are trying to torpedo the voting process.

News conference,
San Jose, Costa Rica, Oct. 28/
Los Angeles Times, 10-29:(A)12.

3

[On U.S. President Bush's opposition to Nicaragua's Sandinista government]: It's true that President Bush is tall, something like six feet-four inches. He has a Gulliver complex, and President Bush shouldn't forget that the dwarf tied up Gulliver. It's possible that President Bush, with his Gulliver complex, looks upon Latin Americans as dwarfs, [but] he shouldn't forget that we are proud and dignified people. I feel proud to be a tiny little man of the great [Nicaraguan] people. I'd be ashamed to be a Gulliver Bush, bullying and doing damage to little countries.

Speech, Rivas, Nicaragua,
Oct. 29/
The Washington Post, 10-30:(A)19.

4

[On U.S. criticism of his government's decision to end its cease-fire with the contra rebels]: [U.S.] President Bush, we are not going to prolong the cease-fire. We are not a state of the United States . . . The United States has no reason to dictate to the Nicaraguan people what they should do in the face of criminal attacks [by the contras] that it promotes. Even Christ lost patience and felt the right to take the whip to run the money-changers from the temple.

News conference,
Managua, Nov. 1/
Los Angeles Times,
11-2:(A)13.

5

[On his government's decision to end the 19-month-old cease-fire with the contra rebels]: To suggest that this is a scheme to cancel the [1990] elections is absurd. To the contrary, it would be a greater threat to the elections if we stood with our arms folded and allowed the contras to continue committing crimes. No country would countenance this type of terrorist activity [by the contras] . . . We had to take action, even with the risks and costs to Nicaragua's image. We knew we would have to pay a price, but the lives of Nicaraguans are worth much more.

Speech and interview,
Managua, Nov. 1/
The Washington Post,
11-2:(A)50.

Luiz Pazos
Professor of economic theory,
National Autonomous University
of Mexico

1

The main problem facing the Mexican government is not the interest due on the foreign debt, but payment of the interest due on the internal debt. If something is not done about this quickly, we are going to see the economy turn into Argentina or Brazil. Fresh money from abroad can only postpone the day of reckoning, not solve the problem . . . You can declare a moratorium on payment of the foreign debt, or you can renegotiate it. For the internal debt, you can do neither of those things. The only options are to print more money or let the debt grow, and that is a promise of inflation.

The New York Times, 6-5:(C)16.

Carlos Andres Perez
President of Venezuela

2

The new government of the United States has the immense and challenging possibility of recognizing our continent as an open zone of fertile dialogue, even on those issues that in the recent past have been fiery points of conflict . . . The possibility of a profound encounter between the United States and Latin America will be strengthened to the extent that we recognize each other as firm friends and not in anti-historic relations of subordination.

Inaugural address,
Caracas, Feb. 2/
Los Angeles Times, 2-3:(I)1.

3

The ghost of Communism has done much damage to relations between the U.S. and Latin America. Under the pretext of defending the region from Communism, the U.S. supported military dictatorships. This was a terrible error. Now we don't need to look for ghosts. We have realities. If the problems that our countries face are not resolved, the social explosions would be of a magnitude previously unimagined. I'm not just imagining this. The world today is much more complex. Before the days of mass media, radio and television, the poor were more resigned to their fate. Without television, they didn't have any possibility for comparison. That's why today's poverty is more dangerous and could provoke terrible social upheavals—a Latin America in effervescent rebellion. We are facing certain danger. If we don't deal with this catastrophe, military dictatorships could come back.

Interview/Time, 11-27:14.

Dan Quayle
Vice President
of the United States

4

The Sandinista dictatorship [in Nicaragua] will make all sorts of attractive promises about pluralism and democracy—promises they have made time and again, and have betrayed time and again. Unfortunately, the Sandinistas have friends in this country [the U.S.] who always seem to be willing to give them the benefit of the doubt. The moment the Sandinistas fail one test, these friends always come up with another test, and another and another.

At Conservative Political Action
Conference, Washington, Feb. 24/
The Washington Post, 2-25:(A)17.

Sergio Ramirez
Vice President of Nicaragua

5

The international interest in Nicaragua and our revolution is sociological as well as political. The [ruling] Sandinistas are a phenomenon of the changing Third World, as well as victims of U.S. arrogance. This will not change, even if the U.S. attitude toward us does.

Interview/
The Christian Science Monitor,
1-3:3.

Charles B. Rangel
United States Representative,
D-New York

6

[Criticizing the current U.S. invasion of Panama aimed at ousting Panamanian dictator

(CHARLES B. RANGEL)

Manuel Noriega]: As much as I would like to get rid of the bum in Panama, I don't see the legal authority of the use of the military. I am of course distressed that prior to our action, an American was killed [in Panama], an American arrested, an American brutally beaten, and an American military wife was threatened with rape. [U.S.] President Bush said, "That was enough." If that is so, far more than that happens on the streets of New York every day and night; and I say, that, too, is enough. Why are we not providing massive assistance to our state and local police, in our cities and towns, where the real war on drugs is being waged?

Dec. 20/
The New York Times, 12-21:(A)11.

Ronald Reagan
President of the United States
1

[Criticizing the U.S. Congress for not providing strong support for the contras, rebels fighting the Sandinista government of Nicaragua]: We haven't changed our mind about the need to help those people . . . But again, we come down to the problem of the division here in our own government of a Congress that refuses to acknowledge that need for those freedom fighters [the contras] and thus, in a way, is on the side of the Sandinistas in Central America . . . who . . . have a totalitarian state. And I've never been able to understand it.

Interview, Washington,
Jan. 18/
USA Today 1-19:(A)9.

Otto J. Reich
Former United States Ambassador
to Venezuela
2

[Cuban President Fidel] Castro is trying to ruin the superpower relationship emerging from the last two [U.S.-Soviet] summit meetings. He's a convinced ideologue, and the demise of Marxist-Leninist ideology is not in his interest. He is doing what he can, from his small island in

the Caribbean, to stop the rapprochement between the superpowers.

Dec. 4/
The New York Times, 12-5:(A)9.

Raul Roa
Deputy Foreign Minister
of Cuba
3

A [U.S.] policy to isolate Cuba is a non-policy. There can be no coherent U.S. policy toward Latin America without a new policy toward Cuba.

The Washington Post, 4-3:(A)30.

Riordon Roett
Professor of Latin American
studies, School of Advanced
International Studies
4

[On the recent failed coup attempt against strongman Manuel Noriega by army dissidents in Panama, in which the U.S. did not participate]: If this is really a national-security question, and the President [of the U.S.] is concerned about the [Panama] Canal and about drug-money laundering [by Noriega], then it seems to me [the U.S. should] take whatever national-security measures are required. You plan, you do it correctly, and you use the appropriate levels of force in a coordinated kind of way . . . If the U.S. has finally decided to do something, then it should do it right, and win.

The Christian Science Monitor,
10-10:7.

Ileana Ros-Lehtinen
United States Representative,
R-Florida
5

[On whether the U.S. should open diplomatic relations with Cuba]: I'm totally against it because the only winner in that proposition would be [Cuban President] Fidel Castro. He has shown time and time again that he does not honor any commitment unless it's to his advantage. So I see that the United States would have little to

235

(ILEANA ROS-LEHTINEN)

gain and just about everything to lose if we were to open up diplomatic relations with Castro . . . He goes his own way. He has not complied with any previous agreements and there's really no reason for us to be entering into any kind of diplomatic situation with someone who has such a total lack of concern about human rights or any other concerns.

Interview/
USA Today, 9-11:(A)13.

Jeffrey Sachs
Economist,
Harvard University

1

[Saying general U.S. economic aid to such countries as Bolivia and Peru would accomplish more to eradicate drug trafficking there than pouring money in direct drug-fighting programs]: Our government was negligent not to have studied the economic aspect. A sensible economic strategy looks more realistic than all the nonsense that has happened so far. For all the posturing, all the brave talk, there has been no serious attempt to come to grips with the coca economy and the human realities it creates . . . It is a tragedy that what appears to be the most promising alternative hasn't been explored. If there were a U.S. commitment of a couple of billion dollars, over three or four years, and if it were shown to lead to a significant cut in the supply of cocaine, it would not be much money. Two billion dollars for what Americans regard as their most important problem is a small amount of money.

Interview/
The Atlantic Monthly, July:76.

Elizardo Sanchez
Chairman, Cuban
Commission on Human Rights
and National Reconciliation

2

[On the forthcoming meeting between Cuban President Fidel Castro and Soviet leader Mikhail Gorbachev in Cuba]: There will be many public smiles. Gorbachev will say that Castro is a great leader of Cuba, Latin America and the Third World, and did many good things for Cuba. But behind closed doors, there will be a very serious discussion. The Soviets will ask what the Cuban government has managed to accomplish after 30 years with the unprecedented economic support of Moscow. Castro will have to explain his rejection of Gorbachev's reforms [of the Soviet system].

To reporters, Havana, March 31/
The Washington Post, 4-1:(A)20.

Jose Sarney
President of Brazil

3

[On the day I was born,] God said, "Jose, go and accomplish what is before you. Write books, love, experience days made up of the purest joy . . . Have friends, have a love of the earth, plants and animals. And then become President of the Republic."

Interview/
World Press Review, March:35.

Patricia Schroeder
United States Representative,
D-Colorado

4

[On the current U.S. invasion of Panama aimed at ousting Panamanian dictator Manuel Noriega]: We should remember, first, that the [U.S.] Bush Administration fumbled a clear opportunity to assist the attempted Panamanian coup [that might have ousted Noriega] last October, and second, that Noriega himself is the toxic waste of a polluted [former U.S. President Ronald] Reagan-Bush foreign policy. Noriega was A-O.K. as long as he did our bidding. As the present example has shown, you reap what you sow.

Dec. 21/
The New York Times, 12-22:(A)14.

George P. Shultz
Secretary of State
of the United States

5

I think the most frustrating area for us has been Central America and Panama. There has been

(GEORGE P. SHULTZ)

the emergence of a bipartisan consensus on many aspects of what should be done, but not on Nicaragua. And we've paid a considerable penalty because we haven't been able to get that. On [Panamanian leader Manuel] Noriega, of course, there isn't any disagreement about what ought to happen [getting him out of office] . . . but it is not so easy to get it to happen.

To reporters enroute to Vienna,
Jan. 16/
Los Angeles Times, 1-17:(I)6.

Carl Tham
Director, Swedish
International Development
Authority

1

[Criticizing U.S. policy against the Sandinista government of Nicaragua]: Small countries should be protected against intervention, aggression and phony wars sponsored by big powers. The Sandinistas have made so many political and diplomatic mistakes. But it's easy for outsiders to tell them what to do. Small countries have a right to find their own way without having to face the destabilizing forces that are at work here.

Managua, Nicaragua/
The New York Times, 1-17:(A)6.

Dick Thornburgh
Attorney General
of the United States

2

[On the possibility of the U.S. sending military aid to Colombia to help that country in its fight against Colombia-based international drug-traffickers]: I think we have to look at any request that we get for either law-enforcement or military assistance seriously. If in Colombia they feel, hypothetically, that they may have reached the point where they can no longer operate under the rule of law and have to use the rule of force, then they're going to require all the help they need against internal threats from drug traffickers . . . I don't think we ought to respond, as some

suggest, willy-nilly with a military response. But I do think that's an option that we have to keep open.

Broadcast interview/
"Meet the Press," NBC-TV, 8-20.

Jacqueline Tillman
Director, Washington office,
Cuban-American Foundation

3

[On the probability that Cuba will be invited to rejoin the OAS, from which it was barred in 1962]: I am dismayed. I don't know why one of the world's last remaining Stalinists [Cuban President Fidel Castro] belongs in the OAS. The OAS is supposed to stand for democratic principles, and the human-rights record in Cuba is so bad that it should be of concern to all the members.

Interview/
Los Angeles Times, 10-29:(A)13.

Margaret D. Tutwiler
Spokesperson for the
Department of State
of the United States

4

[On Francisco Rodriquez, the new President of Panama]: [Panamanian leader Manuel] Noriega's latest puppet President is an unknown within Panama with no political following and whose chief qualification for the position seems to have been his long-time friendship with Noriega, and his slavish loyalty to the dictator. Noriega's naming of a so-called "provisional government" is completely outside Panama's Constitution and is, in effect, a thinly disguised *coup d'etat.* Noriega's is an outlaw regime.

Sept. 1/
The Washington Post, 9-2:(A)1.

Joaquin Villalobos
Commander, Farabundo
Marti National Liberation
Front (rebels fighting the
government of El Salvador)

5

[Asking for political reforms in the Salvadoran government in exchange for a cease-fire]: We are

(JOAQUIN VILLALOBOS)

not asking the government of the republic to step down [or that President Alfredo] Cristiani give up the legitimacy he says he obtained through elections. What we are asking is that, for the sake of peace, it be put to a test . . . We have said we are willing to integrate ourselves into the political life of the nation, understanding that if the causes for the war cease to exist, then there is no sense to remaining armed.

News conference,
Mexico City, Sept. 13/
Los Angeles Times, 9-14:(I)1.

William J. Walker
United States Ambassador
to El Salvador

1

[On the recent killings of six Jesuit priests in El Salvador, in which the Salvadoran Army has initially been implicated]: This is a crime of such repugnance that to say that I condemn or deplore seems inadequate. It is a barbaric act that has brought shame to El Salvador. I have difficulty in imagining what sort of animals would, in cold blood, execute priests and other innocents.

Press briefing,
San Salvador, Nov. 16/
The New York Times,
11-17:(A)9.

Richard Allan White
Research fellow,
Council on Hemispheric Affairs,
Washington

2

[On the recent coup in Paraguay overthrowing strongman Alfredo Stroessner]: If you think of Paraguay as run by a Mafia, then you'll understand it better. This is like one family in a Mafia organization fighting against another . . . This coup may prevent a real democratic change, which people hoped would happen once Stroessner died or left power. Now it looks like things have changed to remain the same.

The Washington Post,
2-4:(A)19.

John Hoyt Williams
Professor of
Latin American history,
Indiana State University

3

[On Paraguay's new leader, Andres Rodriguez, who took power in a military coup]: General Rodriguez has an exceedingly unsavory reputation. I mean really bad, and that's an understatement. He has been implicated time and time again by U.S. and international drug organizations as a kingpin of the drug trade. Rodriguez has reportedly provided protection, airfields and an air-taxi service to people smuggling drugs northward. That's an allegation, but it's common knowledge on the streets of Paraguay, and I have read about it many times in reports published by authoritative research organizations.

Feb. 3/
The New York Times, 2-4:5.

Jim Wright
United States Representative,
D-Texas

4

From a purely economic standpoint, the stark poverty that stalks the southern tilt of our hemisphere is the biggest single impediment to developing markets for goods made in [the U.S.] . . . The most challenging opportunity we have is to provide true debt relief. In Mexico and Brazil, as well as in a score of smaller countries, the level of external debt is so high that the interest charges alone consume the nations' total export earnings. Such a condition would be intolerable to any nation. Debts of this magnitude tend to be self-perpetuating and self-defeating. It is difficult, almost impossible, in fact, for a country to dig itself out. It is economic quicksand. The new investments that ultimately could pay off the debts are blocked, while the money that could launch them is siphoned away by the need simply to meet interest payments. It is a form of indentured servitude.

Before Center for National Policy,
April 7/
The Washington Post,
4-12:(A)22.

Enrique Zileri
Editor, "Caretas" magazine
(Peru)

1

Peru embodies many of the most acute problems of the Third World. We have suffered eight years of terrorism from the Shining Path guerrilla group and others. We are faced with a huge foreign debt and all of the accompanying complications, including a decline of new investment. Inflation has accelerated. Population growth continues. Our long tradition of military intervention adds a further worry . . . [But] we have fabulous economic frontiers. We know the location of immense mineral treasures but don't exploit them. We have potential riches in fishing, where state-owned operations now work at half-capacity. We have a huge state-owned dry region awaiting irrigation. As Chile and New Zealand discovered, Southern Hemisphere countries have natural advantages as winter produce exporters . . . If we all worked together, we could make a lot of investors, and ourselves, rich.

Interview/
World Press Review,
January:33,35.

Asia and the Pacific

Lal Kishanchand Advani
President, Bharatiya Janata Party
of India

1

[Advocating Indian production of nuclear weapons]: Ever since the Chinese invasion of 1962, and since China and Pakistan went nuclear, we feel that *realpolitik* demands that we also become nuclear . . . I would be happy if the whole world becomes non-nuclear. But the situation being what it is, even though nuclear weapons may not be used, they do give political leverage to a country, particularly in the limited relationships and communications we have with Pakistan and China.

Interview/The New York Times, 11-28:(A)5.

Sergei F. Akhromeyev
Chief, Soviet Armed Forces
General Staff

2

The Soviet Union was never planning to solve the Afghanistan problem with the help of its armed forces. It was fantasy to think that a military solution could be achieved by deploying a contingent of 100,000 in a mountainous country with a territory of 652,200 square kilometres [251,800 square miles]. It was obvious at first glance to military and political leaders that the task was to support the Afghanistan regime. But every action follows its own rules. It is easy to deploy forces, but objective realities then compel you to take other decisions. From this point of view, the armed forces were pushed into participating in long-term military activities, and, of course, we could see that there was no prospect of a military solution. There were political reasons, too, but that was a major reason that our troops were withdrawn.

Interview/Time, 11-13:59.

Corazon C. Aquino
President of the Philippines

3

[On the death of former Philippine President Ferdinand Marcos]: Speaking for the nation, I

can say that he touched the life of every Filipino who was his contemporary as no other Filipino leader did before him. His rule changed our country. In what ways he changed it, I leave for now to others and ultimately to history to describe.

Manila, Sept. 28/
Los Angeles Times, 9-29:(I)1.

4

What is happening now [in the Philippines] is people would like to have the benefits of a dictatorship at the same time living under a democracy. When they refer to me as being weak and ineffective, they would like to see the forcefulness of a dictator. But they are not willing to give up their freedoms either, in exchange for the rapid decisions of the dictator.

Interview, Manila/
The Washington Post,
10-27:(A)24.

Georgi A. Arbatov
Director, Soviet Institute
of U.S.A. and Canadian Affairs

5

[On Soviet reaction to the recent crackdown by the Chinese government on pro-democracy demonstrators in Beijing, including the use of military force]: Our relations with China have a difficult and controversial history. They are of tremendous importance to us in the world, and therefore we have to be very cautious and reasoned in our approach. We must abstain from any interference in their affairs. In the past, we tried to tell them what to do . . . In this complex situation, we do not want to make easy judgments without all the facts.

Los Angeles Times, 6-19:(I)10.

6

[On the Soviet troop pullout from Afghanistan]: Afghanistan is at our borders. I have a feeling that Americans cannot forgive us that we

(GEORGI A. ARBATOV)

got out of Afghanistan without losing face, and they wanted us to repeat the [U.S.] Vietnam experience. And they go on arming groups which have actually no support in Afghanistan itself. Instead of seeking for an end, there's hostilities. We have committed a mistake. We should tell it to the people often, and draw lessons from it.

Interview/
USA Today, 11-16:(A)7.

Michael H. Armacost
United States Ambassador
to Japan

1

All we seek is similar opportunities for our companies to sell in Japan's market, and to compete openly to provide goods and services for the benefit of the Japanese consumer . . . Though living standards have improved dramatically, there have been limits on the extent to which Japanese consumers have benefited from this "economic miracle." Perhaps we could say that America needs to give its producers a prod, while Japan needs to give its consumers a break.

At symposium sponsored by
Chicago Mercantile Exchange,
Tokyo, May 30/
The Washington Post,
5-31:(F)1,4.

Chester G. Atkins
United States Representative,
D-Massachusetts

2

[Criticizing U.S. support for the Khmer Rouge taking part in a transitional government in Cambodia, despite the Khmer Rouge's reputation for barbarism]: It would seem to me that there is no reason we would want to insist that the Khmer Rouge be part of a settlement other than the fact that [Cambodian Prince Norodom] Sihanouk wants it. It would seem that in light of the outcome in Paris [at the recent Cambodian peace talks] that Sihanouk is increasingly playing a personal agenda which relates to his own

political aggrandizement and less of a nationalist Cambodian agenda.

At House Asian and Pacific Affairs
Subcommittee hearing,
Washington, Sept. 14/
The New York Times, 9-15:(C)20.

James A. Baker III
Secretary of State-designate
of the United States

3

. . . there is progress toward a Vietnamese withdrawal from Cambodia, perhaps not as rapid progress as we might have liked, and maybe they didn't quite get to the 50,000 troop withdrawal that they had estimated they would achieve by the end of 1988; but they are, nevertheless, leaving. The objectives, of course, of the United States in that area are to see a Vietnamese withdrawal without seeing a return to power of the Khmer Rouge, and we will be working to achieve that.

At Senate Foreign Relations
Committee hearing on his
confirmation, Washington,
Jan. 18/
The New York Times,
1-19:(A)12.

James A. Baker III
Secretary of State
of the United States

4

[Defending the U.S. Bush Administration against charges that it has not spoken out more forcefully on the recent violent crackdown on pro-democracy demonstrators in China]: Human rights has got to be a fundamental keystone and basis for American foreign policy, but there are also other considerations in the formation and implementation of American foreign policy that must be taken into account. And the geopolitical [and] economic relationship between the People's Republic of China and the United States is important. Many people, both in the People's Republic of China and the United States, have worked for many years, 10 to 12, 15 years, to improve what had been a very poor relationship

241

(JAMES A. BAKER III)

between these two countries, and significant progress had been made.

Before House Foreign Affairs
Committee, Washington,
June 22/
Los Angeles Times, 6-23:(I)12.

1

The time has arrived for Japan to translate its domestic and regional successes more fully into a broader international role with increased responsibility. Japan has become a world power. We applaud this achievement, which holds so much promise for the future. But to make the most of that promise, the United States and Japan must build a new and truly global partnership.

Before Asia Society,
New York, June 26/
The New York Times,
6-27:(C)1.

2

[On the recent violent crackdown on pro-democracy demonstrators in China]: China has suffered a tragic setback, but the story is not over . . . China's rendezvous with freedom, like its rendezvous with the advancing nations of the Pacific, cannot be long delayed. We will be there to help when the day follows the night.

Before Asia Society, New York,
June 26/
Los Angeles Times, 6-27:(I)8.

3

The strength of our [U.S.] support for any Cambodian government will directly and inversely depend on the extent of Khmer Rouge participation, if any, in that government . . . The United States strongly believes that the Khmer Rouge should play no role in Cambodia's future.

At international conference on
Cambodia, Paris,
July 30/
The New York Times,
7-31:(A)1,4.

A. Doak Barnett
Political scientist, Paul Nitze
School of Advanced
International Studies

4

[On the U.S. suspension of military sales to China to protest that country's recent violent crackdown on pro-democracy demonstrators]: The resolution of the present conflict within the Chinese leadership will ultimately be determined by forces within China, not by what any outside power does. Nevertheless, the signal that this action [suspension of military sales] represents is worth sending, to both hardliners and moderates in China. I believe, however, that it would be a severe mistake to impose economic sanctions on China or to cut our economic ties—which will be damaged enough without any U.S. government action—because the effects of this would, in my judgment, weaken rather than strengthen the moderates in China—that is, the professionals, liberals and technocrats who are committed to reform and liberalization—and, to the extent that such action would exacerbate China's already immense economic problems, they would damage the interests of ordinary Chinese more than the position of China's present hardline leaders.

June/The Washington Post,
7-5:(A)16.

Benazir Bhutto
Prime Minister of Pakistan

5

As a representative of the young, let me be viewed as one of a new generation of leaders unshackled by the artificial constraints and irrational hatreds of the past. As a representative of women, let my message be to them, from the villages of Baluchistan to the universities of Lahore, Paris and Boston: "Yes, you can." As an adherent to Islam . . . let my message be about a compassionate and tolerant religion, teaching hard work and family values under a benevolent God, for that is the true Islam which we cherish.

Before U.S. Congress,
Washington, June 7/
Los Angeles Times, 6-8:(I)6.

Alexander I. Bovin
Soviet political commentator

1

[On the improved relations between the Soviet Union and China]: We don't need anything concrete, no agreements, no pieces of paper. We have to learn how to talk, how to talk with each other as comrades, how to come and go without a big deal, how to live as good neighbors, helping each other. We need to develop a feel for one another as neighbors, as socialist countries, as great powers. But we have to do all this in a way that we do not frighten others, particularly in the United States, Japan or Europe, and make them think we are plotting a campaign to spread world revolution . . . That we no longer are treating each other as enemies does not make us allies like we were in the 1950s.

Interview, Moscow/
Los Angeles Times, 5-14:(I)18.

Roger A. Brooks
Director of Asian studies,
Heritage Foundation

2

Washington should welcome the thaw between Moscow and Beijing. The web of relations among the three countries is no longer a zero-sum game. The United States does not necessarily gain if Chinese-Soviet relations are cool, nor does the U.S. necessarily lose if those relations improve. American relations with Moscow have been rapidly improving, so we can hardly look askance at the Chinese for following the U.S. lead.

The New York Times, 5-15:(A)4.

Dale Bumpers
United States Senator,
D-Arkansas

3

[On the U.S. military presence in South Korea]: Where do you get the most applause, Republicans and Democrats alike, when you go home and speak to the Rotary Club? When do they applaud the loudest? When you talk about burden sharing. Why do our allies not help themselves? Why is the United States, with a $160-billion to $170-billion deficit this year, spending

$2.6-billion for that kind of presence in Korea, when South Korea has twice as many people as North Korea?

Before the Senate, Washington,
September/
Los Angeles Times, 10-19:(A)18.

Barbara Bush
Wife of President
of the United States
George Bush

4

Just seven days ago we returned from a long, exciting trip to Asia and we saw there two countries, Japan and [South] Korea, whose economies are soaring. In 40 years or less they have gone from war-torn rubble to become great economic powers, and we know that one very important aspect of that rise is directly related to an educated, literate work-force.

Announcing the establishment of
the Barbara Bush Foundation for
Family Literacy, Washington,
March 6/
The New York Times, 3-7:(A)8.

George Bush
President of the United States

5

Both democracy and economic liberty work [in South Korea]. Thirty years ago, such progress was unimaginable. It stands as a testament to the Korean people and our commitment to them. Those ideas, once thought to be strictly American, have now become the goal of mankind all over Asia.

Speech after returning from Asia,
Andrews Air Force Base, Feb. 27/
The New York Times, 2-28:(A)6.

6

[On the massacre of pro-democracy demonstrators in Beijing by the Chinese military]: I'm convinced that the forces of democracy are going to overcome these unfortunate events in Tiananmen Square. On the commercial side, I don't want to hurt the Chinese people [by cutting com-

(GEORGE BUSH)

mercial contacts to show our disapproval of the massacre]. I happen to believe that commercial contacts have led, in essence, to this quest for more freedom. I think as people have commercial incentive, whether it's in China or in other totalitarian systems, the move to democracy becomes more inexorable. So what we have done is suspend certain things on the military [-aid] side . . . I don't want to see a total break in this [U.S.-Chinese] relationship, and I will not encourage a total break in the relationship. This relationship is, when you see these kids struggling for democracy and freedom, this would be a bad time for the United States to withdraw and pull back and leave them to the devices of a leadership that might decide to crack down further. Some have suggested I take the [U.S.] Ambassador out. In my view, that would be 180 degrees wrong. Our Ambassador provides one of the best listening posts we have in China. He is thoroughly experienced. And so let others make proposals that in my view don't make much sense. I want to see us stay involved and continue to work for restraint and for human rights and for democracy [in China].

News conference,
Washington, June 5/
The New York Times, 6-6:(A)7.

1

From Main Street to Wall Street, America loves the Philippines, and America loves [Philippine President] Cory Aquino. You deserve our help, and you will get it.

To visiting President Aquino,
Washington Nov. 9/
The Washington Post, 11-10:(A)24.

Robert C. Byrd
United States Senator,
D-West Virginia

2

If the United States is to play a new role in Southeast Asia, that role must be based on a solid, bipartisan, fully debated and understood consensus. Surely we have learned from our experience in Vietnam, if nothing else, that if we are to succeed in a new policy toward that region, it cannot be achieved through secret policymaking, secret military programs, secret arms transfers, or secret deals.

Before the Senate,
Washington, June 2/
The Washington Post, 6-3:(A)12.

Tran Ngoc Chau
Executive editor, "Tuoi Tre"
(Communist Party youth
newspaper of Vietnam)

3

[Saying Vietnam's troop withdrawal from Cambodia has not led to an end to the U.S. economic boycott of his country]: Many Vietnamese had high expectations after the troop withdrawal for international aid to help alleviate all the difficulties in the economy. [Now] we are frustrated with the American government. We take it as a fact that the American government still considers Vietnam an enemy [from the days of the Vietnam war]. America has to share the responsibility that Vietnam is such a poor country now.

The Washington Post, 10-5:(A)64.

William J. Crowe, Jr.
Admiral, United States Navy;
Chairman, Joint Chiefs of Staff

4

There's both a military and a political content to our [U.S.] presence in [South] Korea, one that has served us very well now for many years. It has kept, at least contributed to, the stability of that region. On the other hand, I must tell you, as a military man, that with the kind of fiscal constraints that we are having put on us, then everything in our inventory is open to looking at and certainly being re-examined every year.

At National Press Club,
Washington, July 7/
The New York Times, 7-13:(A)12.

Dalai Lama
Exiled former ruler of Tibet

5

[On Tibet]: The world community has a responsibility to preserve one of its ancient cul-

(DALAI LAMA)

tures ... You look at our Tibetan refugees, as well as people inside Tibet, and despite their hardships, on their face there is peace, there is joy. That is something quite precious. This culture is worth saving.

Interview,
New Delhi, India, March 21/
The New York Times, 3-22:(A)3.

1

If Tibet took arms [against Chinese control], followed the violent course, that's almost like suicide. I understand that there are desperate feelings, [but] I always believe that non-violence is something important. The best way to solve human conflict is through understanding, not fighting. Patience.

News conference, Newport Beach, Calif.,
Oct. 5/
Los Angeles Times, 10-6:(I)18.

Derek Davies
Editor, "Far Eastern
Economic Review"

2

Very few people in the non-Asian world understand much about Asia. They tend to view it through Westernized eyes, with a propensity for irrelevant labels for countries that never really fit into American/European political pigeonholes of left, right and so on. That was especially true during the Cold War. We are still getting things wrong, applying the touchstone of how pro-West, or how anti-Moscow or pro-Chinese, states are. This has led to ghastly miscalculations. What has occurred is the rise of a vast middle class with a desire not to be told what to do and think. We have labeled it "democracy," but whether in East Asia it ends up in systems recognizable in terms of the U.S. Constitution, or the Westminster model, seems questionable. The systems that Asians throw up will be different but not less democratic.

Interview/
World Press Review,
September:34.

Deng Xiaoping
Senior leader of China

3

[On the government's recent use of the Chinese military to crack down on pro-democracy demonstrators in Beijing]: This disturbance [by the demonstrators] was something beyond anyone's control. A very small number of people created turmoil, and this eventually developed into a counter-revolutionary rebellion. They are trying to overthrow the Communist Party, topple the socialist system and subvert the People's Republic of China so as to establish a capitalist republic. In putting down the counter-revolutionary rebellion, the People's Revolutionary Army, the armed police and the public-security officers have been conscious of their duties and have overcome the challenge.

To military commanders,
Beijing, June 9/
The New York Times, 6-10:(A)1.

4

I once told foreigners that our worst omission of the past 10 years was in education. What I meant was political education, and this doesn't apply to schools and students alone, but to the masses as a whole. And we have not said much about plain living and the enterprising spirit, about what kind of a country China is and how it is going to turn out. This is our biggest omission. Is there anything wrong to the basic concept of reforms and openness? No. Without reforms and openness how could we have what we have today? There has been a fairly satisfactory rise in the standard of living, and it may be said that we have moved one stage further. The positive results of 10 years of reforms must be properly assessed even though there have emerged such problems as inflation. Naturally, in reform and adopting the open policy, we run the risk of importing evil influences from the West, and we have never underestimated such influences.

To military commanders,
Beijing, June 9/
The New York Times, 6-30:(A)4.

5

[On the recent pro-democracy demonstrations in Beijing and the government's harsh

(DENG XIAOPING)

crackdown on those involved]: The nature of the matter became clear soon after it erupted. [The demonstrators] had two main slogans: to overthrow the Communist Party and topple the socialist system. Their goal was to establish a bourgeois republic entirely dependent on the West. Of course we accept people's demands for combatting corruption. We are even ready to listen to some persons with ulterior motives when they raise the slogan about fighting corruption. However, such slogans were just a front. Their real aim was to overthrow the Communist Party and topple the socialist system.

To military commanders,
Beijing, June 9/
The New York Times, 6-30:(A)4.

1

[On last June's pro-democracy demonstrations in Beijing which were violently put down by the government]: Frankly speaking, the United States was involved too deeply in the turmoil and counter-revolutionary rebellion that occurred in Beijing not long ago. We hope that China and the United States will solve as soon as possible the problems in their relations, [but] it is up to the U.S. to take the initiative. The U.S. is capable of making some initiatory moves . . . In the past decade and more, China has not done one single thing harmful to the United States.

At meeting with visiting former
U.S. President Richard Nixon,
Beijing, Oct. 31/
The Washington Post,
11-1:(A)40.

2

[On his decision to retire]: I want to take this opportunity to formally say goodbye to my political career . . . It may be impolite if I refrain from meeting some old friends when they visit China in the future. In that case, I can visit them at the place where they stay. We will chat about friendship and non-political affairs . . . The Party, government and army leaders should be given a free hand in their work, and I will not meddle in

their affairs. This is essential for their growth and work.

To visiting Japanese businessmen,
Beijing, Nov. 13/
Los Angeles Times, 11-14:(A)8.

Joseph Estrada
Philippine Senator

3

It is the only way [in the Philippines]: the iron hand. Martial law could have been the best thing for this country if [deposed President Ferdinand] Marcos had only followed through and if he could have been a benevolent leader. Democracy is not perfect, and it is not applicable to our country now.

Interview/
The New York Times, 2-25:4.

Fang Lizhi
Chinese dissident

4

[On the current pro-democracy demonstrations in China]: These events are very important. This is the first time students, intellectuals and ordinary people know they have the right to criticize the government. That has never happened before . . . I only expected students and intellectuals and a few workers, but I was very surprised there were so many ordinary people [who] joined. That means they've already approached that stage where the people demand political reforms . . . In the short term, I don't think we can easily change a lot. Maybe to change a small step is possible. For instance, this time we can get a little bit of freedom of the press . . . In the long term, we need the older generation of the [Chinese government] leadership to go, like [senior leader] Deng Xiaoping. If they leave, the situation will be better. More democracy.

Interview, Beijing, June 2/
The Wall Street Journal,
6-13:(A)18.

5

[On the Chinese government's violent crackdown on pro-democracy demonstrators in Beijing

(FANG LIZHI)

last June]: Some people say that the terror that has filled Beijing since June can't help but make one feel pessimistic. And I must admit to such feelings of pessimism myself. But I would also like to offer a small bit of encouragement. Remember that . . . it may well be that those who are most terrified are those who have just finished killing their fellow human beings. We may be forced to live under a terror today, but we have no fear of tomorrow. The murderers, on the other hand, are not only fearful today; they are even more terrified of tomorrow. Thus, we have no reason to lose faith. Ignorance may dominate in the short term through the use of violence, but it will eventually be unable to resist the advance of universal laws. And this will come to pass just as surely as the Earth turns.

The Washington Post, 11-21:(A)24.

Marlin Fitzwater
Press Secretary to
President of the United States
George Bush

1

[On the relatively mild protests by the U.S. of the recent violent crackdown on pro-democracy demonstrators in China]: [China] is a country of a billion people and is a sizable portion of the world's population and cannot be closeted off and ignored . . . It has an important role in regional conflicts . . . They are a superpower. They are a force that the United States cannot ignore.

June 21/
The Washington Post, 6-22:(A)32.

Edward Friedman
Professor of political science,
University of Wisconsin;
Authority on China

2

[On the recent massacre of pro-democracy demonstrators in Beijing by the Chinese military]: [The Chinese leaders who ordered the massacre] have made their choice, and they had to know what the consequences would be in

terms of shutting off new [foreign] investment and technology flows. There may well be people in the leadership who may want to use this crisis to orient China's economy away from the West . . . The leaders in Beijing know they will get Hong Kong, that the British have no options but to go ahead with the deal [which provides for China's takeover of Hong Kong in 1997]. But who will want to invest there with the uncertainty hanging over China? They may be in the process of killing the goose that lays the golden eggs before they ever get their hands on it.

Interview/
The Washington Post, 6-5:(A)21.

Sam Gejdenson
United States Representative,
D-Connecticut

3

[Criticizing U.S. President Bush for sending a top delegation to visit the Chinese leadership even though last June the Chinese government violently cracked down on pro-democracy demonstrators in Beijing]: The butchers of Beijing have been consolidating their power, increasing tyranny in China, and the [Bush] Administration sends two of its top people to China. What kind of message is this to those in the East Bloc who want to use military force to crush the democratic movements [in Eastern Europe]? Is this a statement by the Administration that it has one standard for human rights in Eastern Europe [where the U.S. has praised democratic reforms], and another standard for human rights in Asia?

Los Angeles Times, 12-13:(A)12.

Mikhail S. Gorbachev
General Secretary,
Communist Party of
the Soviet Union;
President of the Soviet Union

4

[On his current visit to China, designed to improve Soviet-Chinese relations]: Over these few days, an event is taking place in the Chinese capital that is extraordinary by any standards. What is happening is a shift in relations between two of the world's major countries, which share a

(MIKHAIL S. GORBACHEV)

common border 4,660 miles long, into a stable and healthy period. We are here at the first meeting of leaders of our two socialist countries in three decades. The road that led us to it was not easy and demanded of both sides wisdom and responsibility, as well as persistence in over-coming negative ideas and prejudices that bur-dened our relations for so many years. Today we have every right to say that these relations are entering a qualitatively new stage, both because our two countries have changed and because the world around us is different.

At banquet in his honor,
Beijing, May 15/
The New York Times, 5-16:(A)4.

1

[On pro-democracy demonstrators in China]: We are struggling with similar phenomena. We [Soviets] also have hotheads who, in most cases, favor the renewal of socialism, but who are more intent on that renewal than on the leadership of the Party which began the policy. They want it all done in one night. This is not the way it happens in life. This happens only in fairy tales.

At meeting with Chinese
Communist Party leader
Zhao Ziyang, Beijing, May 16/
The New York Times, 5-17:(A)4.

2

[On the apparent reconciliation between the Soviet Union and China]: A few erroneous deci-sions taken in disregard of a partner's interests, attempts to impose on him one's own views and an escalation of mutual grievances to the political level as well as elevating ideological disputes and disagreements to the point of confrontation be-tween states may result in dividing one-time friends by a wall of suspicion and animosity . . . Let me express in confidence that the leaders and peoples of our two countries will make sure that such errors, so difficult to correct, are not repeated.

Before Chinese intellectuals,
Beijing, May 17/
Los Angeles Times, 5-17:(I)15.

3

The Cambodian settlement is gradually taking on a realistic shape. The main principle on which it can and must be based is the principle of self-determination, which is the only correct one. Only the Cambodians—and no one else—can find the formula of agreement and of the future political structure of their country. The Soviet Union is ready to take part in the appropriate international guarantees and to respect any choice of the people of Cambodia and their coun-try's course of independence, neutrality and non-alignment.

Speech, Beijing, May 17/
Los Angeles Times, 5-17:(I)15.

Mohammed Hakim
Mayor of Kabul, Afghanistan

4

[On the war between Afghan rebels and the Soviet-backed Afghan government]: We only hope that [U.S. President] Bush and the people of the United States [which backs the rebels] take a good look at us. They think we are very fanatic Communists, that we are not human beings. We are not fanatics. We are not even Commu-nists . . . I look forward to when the war is over, when everyone, tourists from all over the world, can come to Kabul and see it as a beautiful place. I hope for the day when the world will help us develop this poor city and our backward coun-try. But unless both the big powers . . . help us in a political way instead of sending more war, this war, I'm afraid, will go on a long time.

Interview, Kabul, April 21/
Los Angeles Times, 4-22:(I)13.

Han Xu
Chinese Ambassador
to the United States

5

[On the recent massacre of pro-democracy demonstrators in Beijing by the Chinese mili-tary]: My government believes that it confronted a serious insurrection in Beijing. My govern-ment has stated that a mob led by a small number of people prevented the normal conduct of the affairs of state. For example, demonstrators

(HAN XU)

marred the important visit of the Soviet President, Mikhail Gorbachev. And after a protracted period of patience, with considerable advance warning, military forces dispersed the mob. There was, I regret to say, loss of life on both sides. I wonder whether any other government confronting such an unprecedented challenge would have handled the situation any better than mine did. I know that most of you would describe the events differently than my government does. This is understandable. I am afraid the media have not been able to present the complete picture—namely, the very important historical context . . . The causes [of the unrest in China] are complex and many. The transition from the old economic structure to the new gives rise to a degree of market chaos. Some corrupt officials and speculators have taken advantage of the situation. The resulting income disparity has caused much complaint. An overheated economy plagued by ever greater demand eventually touched off runaway inflation. And the rapid spread of television has created rising expectations that cannot be met. The ensuing frustration has proved incendiary. There are also people who wish to copy alien political institutions and introduce them to China overnight. In short, China now manifests all the social tensions that are generated by rapid economic development.

Before Forum Club of the Palm
Beaches, West Palm Beach, Fla.,
July 24/
The New York Times, 8-21:(A)15.

Harry Harding
Specialist on China,
Brookings Institution,
Washington

1

China is already close to the point where it's arguing that China must be included in international discussions affecting matters in the region. Through arms sales, it's also extending its sphere of diplomatic involvement to include the Middle East. It wants to be a major power that is involved in global issues.

The Christian Science Monitor,
1-18:2.

2

The Chinese find themselves more and more isolated [as a result of the violent crackdown on pro-democracy demonstrators in Beijing last June]. They're left with Romania, North Korea and Cuba, which is an alignment that only illustrates China's isolation. For any thinking Chinese, it's an embarrassment. This is what China's reduced to, welcoming [Cuban leader] Fidel Castro.

Los Angeles Times,
12-11:(A)1.

Bob Hawke
Prime Minister of Australia

3

[On the killing of pro-democracy demonstrators in China by the Chinese military]: I call on the Chinese government to withdraw its troops from deployment against unarmed civilians and to respect the will of its people. To crush the spirit and body of youth is to crush the very future of China itself . . . We watched in horror the unyielding forces of repression brutally killing the vision of youth.

At memorial service for those killed,
Canberra, Australia, June 9/
Los Angeles Times, 6-10:(I)13.

Shintaro Ishihara
Japanese politician

4

I think Japan will be one of the major players that will build a new world history. It can't be done by Japan alone. Active interaction with other countries will enhance technological developments. In this respect, the U.S. will remain Japan's most important partner. There's no doubt the U.S.'s position as a global leader will continue. But from the Japanese viewpoint, the U.S.'s desire to keep Japan or other countries in the palm of its hand is annoying. The Americans should dispassionately put the present world in historical perspective. Their failure to do so will jeopardize not only their future but also that of the rest of the world.

Interview/Time, 11-20:82.

249

Jiang Zemin
General Secretary,
Communist Party of China

1

Failure to stick to the socialist road, while using the blood and sweat of laborers to fatten the capitalist class, will plunge most of the Chinese people into extreme poverty once again.

Speech at National Day celebration,
Beijing, Sept. 29/Time, 10-9:44.

Henry A. Kissinger
Former Secretary of State
of the United States

2

In Asia we are coming up against something that can best be compared to the British role vis-a-vis Europe in the 19th century. In Northeast Asia, we have the Soviet Union, Japan and China, in a rough sort of equilibrium. In Southeast Asia, the same applies to India, China and Japan, with the United States and the Soviet Union in the second line. And what all of this requires is something that American intellectuals have rejected and our policy-making apparatus isn't well suited to: a definition of the national interest that is permanent. We need to think and talk, not about a final condition called peace, but about a process in which we ameliorate situations, move them to more stable conditions, but never pretend to ourselves that the process at any one point is finished.

Interview/
Los Angeles Times, 4-30:(V)1.

Tommy T. B. Koh
Singaporean Ambassador
to the United States

3

[There is a] deteriorating relationship between the United States and Japan. A recent public-opinion poll showed that more Americans regard Japan as a threat than the Soviet Union . . . For many of us who have a stake in the continuation of good relations between Washington and Tokyo, we are worried whether the leaders in these two countries will be able to manage the evolution of this relationship in a way that

prevents it from breaking down. The bottom line is, there has to be a new high-level concord between Washington and Tokyo on both burden-sharing and power-sharing. American leaders have been addressing burden-sharing without simultaneously being willing to talk about power-sharing. The Japanese leaders must be more sensitive than they have been to the need to internationalize the Japanese economy.

Symposium/Newsweek, 5-15:30.

Rajni Kothari
Indian social scientist

4

[On Indian Prime Minister Rajiv Gandhi's just-announced resignation]: His vision of society was an extremely alien model. It was not politically thought through. I used to say that if, when [former Prime Minister Indira] Gandhi was assassinated, we had asked the United Nations to send a body to run India, it wouldn't have been very different from Rajiv Gandhi's government. It has no roots in this society.

Nov. 29/
The New York Times, 11-30:(A)4.

Laurence W. Lane
Publisher, "Sunset" magazine;
Former United States Ambassador
to Australia

5

Australia today is not unlike what this country [the U.S.] was 100 or 150 years ago as settlers streamed across the prairie and the Rocky Mountains. The cowboys and settlers were lured by a promise, the same kind of promise that's alive in Australia today . . . It's important for the U.S. to recognize that Australians resent and will strike back at being treated as the little brother to the U.S. Australians resent being perceived as backward and in the shadow of the U.S.

Interview/Los Angeles Times, 6-19:(IV)3.

David Lange
Prime Minister
of New Zealand

6

[On the strained U.S.-New Zealand relations as a result of New Zealand's refusal to allow U.S.

(DAVID LANGE)

warships that might be carrying nuclear weapons into its ports]: There has been some concern from the United States that New Zealand might try and pretend that we have edged back to what is referred to as "business as usual." To ensure that there is no misunderstanding, I think it best to say clearly that as between the United States and New Zealand, the security alliance is a dead letter.

At Yale University/
Los Angeles Times, 7-29:(I)5.

Simon Leys
Professor of Chinese studies,
Sydney University (Australia)

1

[On the current pro-democracy demonstrations in China]: The main result of the uprising— a result that is of momentous significance—is not that it "changed the nature of politics in Communist China," but that it exposed the true nature of Chinese Communist politics, in its naked reality. The regime has become a complete anachronism; it has lost its grip upon reality; it is corrupt and inefficient; it has run out of ideas and policies. It is not even able to renew its language. The most dusty and antiquated accusations are being recycled to denounce the dissenters: "counter-revolutionaries," "anti-Party conspiracy," etc. Who knows? Good old "agents of U.S. imperialism" might even be resurrected soon! Unfortunately, there is still one field in which Chinese Communism has real competence, expertise and efficiency—and that is repression. For this reason, the immediate aftermath of the uprising will be very grim indeed. The confrontation between the people and the government will benefit only the army and, more specifically, the security organs. Such a development, needless to say, is ominous. In the long term, however, it will prove utterly ineffectual and irrelevant. A police state cannot any more hope to tackle the real issue of China; it will more ensure that the next— and unavoidable—explosion of political discontent be violent.

Interview/
The Wall Street Journal,
6-6:(A)22.

Li Peng
Prime Minister of China

2

Democracy is a good thing, but it must arise from the conditions within a country. As far as China is concerned, we want to build a democracy, and we think that if we do this work well, it will contribute to economic development and social stability. On the other hand, if the democratic process is carried out in haste, or excessively, then it will certainly affect our stability and unity. If stability is undermined, that will impair our work of reform and national construction.

News conference,
Beijing, April 3/
The New York Times, 4-4:(A)4.

3

We don't think that capitalist countries have a monopoly on freedom, democracy and human rights. People in socialist countries should also enjoy freedom, democracy and human rights. China is prepared to improve these aspects of its political reform.

To visiting Soviet leader Mikhail
Gorbachev, Beijing, May 16/
The New York Times, 5-17:(A)1.

4

[On pro-democracy demonstrations now taking place in China]: Questions and suggestions raised by the [demonstrating] students have exerted positive influence on improving the work of the [Communist] Party and government. But demonstrations, protests, boycott of classes, hunger strikes and other forms of petition have upset social stability, and will not be beneficial to solving the problems. Moreover, the situation now is not developing in line with the subjective wishes of the students and is going in a direction that runs counter to their intentions. It has become more and more clear that the very few people who attempt to create turmoil want to reach their political goals—negating the leadership of the Communist Party of China and the socialist system and violating the Constitution— goals that they could not reach through demo-

251

(LI PENG)

cratic and legal channels ... Comrades, our Party is a party in power and our government a people's government. To be responsible to our sacred motherland and to the entire Chinese people, we must adopt firm and resolute measures to end the turmoil swiftly, maintain the leadership of the Party as well as the socialist system.

To Chinese Communist Party
officials, Beijing, May 20/
The New York Times, 5-20:4.

1

[On the recent pro-democracy demonstrations in Beijing, which were put down by the military]: Quite a lot of rioters are yet to be apprehended, and we can in no way leave them unpunished and let them stage a comeback. Anyone who had conducted beating, looting and robbery, or took part in murdering soldiers and police, no matter if he is a student or not, will be dealt with without mercy.

At meeting with families of soldiers
killed during the crackdown,
Beijing, June 19/
The New York Times, 6-20:(A)6.

2

[On the West's criticism and sanctions against China as a result of the crackdown on the recent pro-democracy movement there]: We have made a proper analysis of the anti-China tide and will withstand the pressure. So long as we persist in the independent foreign policy of peace and reform ... in a situation of political stability and steady economic development, we will certainly tide over temporary difficulties.

At Cabinet meeting, Beijing/
The Washington Post, 8-17:(A)35.

3

[On the recent pro-democracy demonstrations in China which were crushed by the government]: These two aspects, dissatisfaction and rebellion, must be separated. I think that the

danger of action to overthrow the government has not been totally eliminated, neither overseas nor in China itself. I fear that we must still continue the struggle against subversion and infiltration ... Our primary task is to allow this population to feed and clothe itself. This is much more important than empty words about human rights.

Interview/
The New York Times, 9-7:(A)4.

4

[On whether there will be changes in China resembling those taking place in Eastern Europe, such as a more pro-democracy and less-Communist outlook]: We opted for socialism because socialism can provide the Chinese people with better living standards and economic prosperity. Therefore, China will continue to adhere to the socialist system, and there will be no change in China's system and policies because of the developments in Eastern Europe.

News conference,
Rawalpindi, Pakistan, Nov. 16/
The New York Times, 11-17:(A)9.

Kenneth G. Lieberthal
Director, Center for
Chinese Studies,
University of Michigan

5

[On the current anti-government unrest in China and the use of the military to try to quell it]: While Westerners have tended to think of China as under firm rule, [Chinese leader] Deng [Xiaoping] tends to see the potential for chaos, and may often feel the central government is hanging on by its fingernails. He wants reform, but not at the price of chaos.

The New York Times, 6-1:(A)9.

James R. Lilley
United States Ambassador
to China

6

[On the U.S. response to the recent massacre by the Chinese military of pro-democracy demonstrators in China]: We've gone through many

(JAMES R. LILLEY)

ups and downs with China, and I think right now we're going through a down. But I don't think we should sort of give up on it; I think that would be a terrible mistake . . . At the moment, you have an overwhelming desire [by Chinese leaders] for survival, and that takes precedence over anything. What we do is we play for the long term, and we don't look for a quick fix—a "feelie-goodie" about this thing. We look for a long-term solution . . . I don't think we want irritants in the Chinese-American relationship. But we Ameicans stand for certain things, and I don't think we're going to change. And I think the Chinese stand for certain things, and they're not going to change.

Broadcast interview, Beijing/
"Face the Nation,"
CBS-TV, 6-11.

1

Especially troubling have been [China's] attempts to shift blame for domestic, social and economic problems onto Western nations. How can we square Chinese insistence that the policies of reform and opening up will not change, at the same time they accuse the West of trying to undermine China through "peaceful evolution"— or using our technology and investment as a Trojan horse to infect China with such corrosive influences as respect for human rights? I say to my Chinese friends: You can't have it both ways. You can't instantly emote anti-foreign rhetoric and then hope to lure tourists to view your precious relics. And since [last June's violent crackdown on pro-democracy demonstrators in Beijing's] Tiananmen [Square], Beijing has tried to hang responsibility for its domestic economic woes on Western nations' limited economic sanctions. We are not responsible for the fall of tourism. Perceptions of Tiananmen, armed guards, martial law in Beijing are the causes and are within Beijing's power to change. This shifting of blame just won't wash. The domestic problems China faces are of its own making.

Hong Kong, November/
The Wall Street Journal,
12-6:(A)14.

Nguyen Van Linh
General Secretary,
Communist Party of Vietnam

2

Democratization [in Vietnam] is now essentially directed at the economic domain. It is not our policy to hasten renovation of the political system while preparations are still inadequate. Neither is it our intention to effect limitless democratization. That would mean political liberalization.

Speech, Sept. 2/
The Washington Post, 9-19:(A)22.

Roderick MacFarquhar
Professor of government,
and director of the Fairbank
Center, Harvard University

3

[On the current use of the military to attack pro-democracy demonstrators in China]: The way the Chinese leadership has put down the student movement is an absolute disaster. The students will become martyrs. The Communist Party will never live this down. And the People's Liberation Army will come to be regarded as the Army of the People's Oppression . . . The [Chinese] regime is held together by Scotch tape, and the name of that Scotch tape is [Chinese leader] Deng Xiaoping. Deng may still have enough stature to hold everything together for a while and impose his will, but he's an old, sick man. And once he's gone, all kinds of scenarios are possible—and most of them spell trouble.

Los Angeles Times, 6-5:(I)15.

Mike Mansfield
United States Ambassador
to Japan

4

Japan has achieved maturity and majority. Japan is one among equals, one of the two superpowers of the world economically, one of the great powers of the world, generally speaking. And with more of the burden which we want them to assume, more of the responsibility which they must and are able and willing to undertake, must go also I think a greater share in the decision-

253

(MIKE MANSFIELD)

making [with the U.S.]. So that matters can be worked out on a cooperative basis and not brought up all of a sudden and through a statement laid down as established fact and/or policy.

Interview, Washington/
The Washington Post,
1-16:(A)19.

William Maynes
Editor, "Foreign Policy"
magazine

1

[On continuing U.S. support for the rebels fighting the Soviet-backed government in Afghanistan, even after the Soviets have pulled out their troops]: The policy has become an embarrassment [for the U.S.]. The [Bush] Administration is riding a dead horse that has fallen to the ground, and it's still beating it and can't figure out why it won't get up.

The New York Times, 11-29:(A)19.

George J. Mitchell
United States Senator,
D-Maine

2

[Saying President Bush has not reacted strongly enough to the crackdown on pro-democracy demonstrators in China, including the executions of many of the demonstrators' leaders]: I am saddened by the President's refusal to give outlet to the feelings of the American people about these executions which have now reached the point which can only be described as organized murder—terror by the government against its own people, seeking to intimidate them, to permit that government to remain in power. I understand and appreciate the delicate situation in which the President finds himself, and I support his stated desire to maintain, if possible, some relationship with the Chinese government. But I ask—I urge—the President to condemn these actions personally and in the strongest possible terms.

The New York Times,
6-23:(A)6.

Akio Morita
Chairman, Sony Corporation
(Japan)

3

All Japanese know that we don't have any natural resources, we don't have enough oil and we don't have enough food. Unless we acquire foreign currency [through export], we cannot survive. That is a simple thing, which everybody knows and everyone can see.

The Washington Post, 2-22:(A)24.

Keith Morrison
Correspondent, NBC News

4

[On the pro-democracy demonstrations and violence taking place in China]: This is such an amazing story, like nothing we've run across in years and years. And there's something new every hour. In between the bursts of gunfire that you hear out the window, the story changes. It's gone from a peaceful movement for democracy, to a crackdown on student dissidents, to military units fighting each other, to rumors of military coups, to fears of actual civil war. The country is literally descending into chaos.

Interview, Beijing, June 6/
Los Angeles Times, 6-7:(VI)1.

Ryohei Murata
Japanese Ambassador-designate
to the United States

5

Japan will never be the nation which leads the world, but will be a nation which can play a very useful role—perhaps as best second fiddle, if we have a good concertmaster [the U.S.].

Interview, Tokyo/
The Washington Post, 11-29:(A)29.

Vladimir S. Myasnikov
Deputy director,
Soviet Institute of
Far Eastern Studies

6

The poor relations that the Soviet Union and China had for so many years undeniably con-

(VLADIMIR S. MYASNIKOV)

tributed to world tensions, and the evidence of this is quite abundant. We hope that the improvement of our bilateral relations will now help reduce international tensions. That is certainly one of our goals and, I believe, one of China's, too . . . We can already see a new situation emerging in Asia in better relations between China and India, between India and Pakistan, in the withdrawal of Soviet forces from Afghanistan, in the search for a solution in Kampuchea [Cambodia], even to some extent in relations between China and Vietnam.

Interview, Moscow/
Los Angeles Times, 5-16:(I)11.

Najibullah
President of Afghanistan

1

[Afghanistan] is a multi-nationality country. We always proceed from the principle that there should be equal rights for all nationalities in the political, cultural, economic and social spheres. It is on the basis of this rational policy that there have been positive moves on the part of some nationalities to support our political policy.

The Christian Science Monitor,
6-26:3.

Andrew J. Nathan
Professor of political science,
Columbia University

2

[On the Chinese government's recent crackdown on pro-democracy demonstrators, including the use of military force]: I don't know how long this situation will last, but I have a feeling now that the transition from dictatorship to some Chinese form of democracy is going to be very, very protracted and very, very painful and violent. And yet I cannot envision how the trend in that direction can be totally stemmed. This is an indication that this is going to be a very bloody and long struggle. It's a serious setback, but not permanent. It's not the end of the story.

The New York Times,
6-19:(A)4.

Richard M. Nixon
Former President
of the United States

3

Shall China turn away from greatness and consign itself to the backwater of oppression and stagnation? Or does it continue to venture forth on the open seas on a journey which may at times be rough but which leads to progress and peace and justice for its people? The United States must decide whether it wishes to persist in the arduous journey begun 17 years ago. Does it wish to be involved in the development of a nation whose values and traditions differ from ours? Or does it wish to disengage itself from a quarter of mankind who are destined to be one of the superpowers of the 21st century.

At banquet in his honor, Beijing,
Oct. 30/
Los Angeles Times, 10-31:(A)5.

4

[Addressing Chinese Prime Minister Li Peng on his government's violent crackdown on pro-democracy demonstrators in Beijing last June]: The cultural, political and ideological differences beween us, Mr. Premier—you a Chinese Communist who believes in Leninist rule, I an American conservative who believes in capitalism and democracy—are too great to permit a common understanding of this tragedy. But let us not become mired in endless and fruitless recriminations over the seeming impasse that has now developed between our two countries.

At banquet in his honor, Beijing,
Oct. 30/
The New York Times, 10-31:(A)3.

5

[On the Chinese government's violent crackdown on pro-democracy demonstrators in Beijing last June]: The fact is that many in the United States, including many friends of China, believe the crackdown was excessive and unjustified. The events . . . damaged the respect and confidence which most Americans previously had for the leaders of China . . . As a result [of the subsequent U.S. sanctions and criticism of China],

255

(RICHARD M. NIXON)

some Chinese now exhibit a distrust of the United States that is reminiscent of the period before 1972. The death of innocent people [in June's crackdown] was a great tragedy, but another tragedy would be the death of a relationship and of policies that have served [the U.S. and China] so well. We must not permit our real enemies—misunderstanding, fruitless resentment, endless recrimination—to close the door we opened with such high hopes 17 years ago.

At banquet in his honor, Beijing,
Nov. 1/
Los Angeles Times, 11-2:(A)7.

Michael Oksenberg
Professor of China politics,
University of Michigan

1

[On the recent massacre of pro-democracy demonstrators in Beijing by the Chinese military]: Let the reason for this global retreat or withdrawal from China be clearly understood. It is not the product of a conspiracy led by the United States [to force other countries to back off from their support of China because of the massacre]. It is not due to a coordinated policy of Western governments. It is not the result of the improvement of Sino-Soviet relations. It is not attributable to hostile Western journalists filing distorted dispatches from China. It is not the consequence of a plot by a small number of Chinese intellectuals. It does not stem from students failing to leave the [Tiananmen] Square [sight of the massacre] at the right time. Nor is it the outcome of a struggle for power, in which one defiant leader—Zhao Ziyang—stimulated a mass movement that otherwise would have been handled deftly. These are the reasons that the leaders of China offer for their debacle. And I suspect that the leaders believe their own explanation. They are unprepared to accept the real reasons for their domestic and foreign plight: their own lapse of judgment; their isolation; their tragic failure to understand and respond to the profound changes caused by their own economic reforms and openness to the outside world; and

their lack of concern for the world-wide reaction to the violent suppression of the demonstrations.

Before House Foreign Affairs
subcommittee, Washington, July 19/
The Wall Street Journal, 8-24:(A)10.

William H. Overholt
Director of research,
brokerage division,
Bankers Trust Company,
Hong Kong

2

[On China's recent forceful crackdown on pro-democracy demonstrators]: People [in the West] had convinced themselves that China was heading for capitalism. There's been a great disillusionment. If they had listened to what the leaders were saying, they would have understood that there was a very important market-oriented reform, but a very limited one, and democracy is not what they had in mind.

The New York Times, 6-14:(A)8.

Suvinai Pornavalai
Professor,
Thammasat University
(Thailand)

3

[On the increasing economic influence of Japan]: When I was a child, I knew only [U.S. and European companies such as] Singer, Philips and GE. I knew only Oldsmobile and Cadillac. I didn't know about Toyota, Honda and Sony. But what has happened now? Japan has replaced the position that the Americans occupied in the post-war periods—rich and helpful.

Interview, Bangkok, Thailand/
The Christian Science Monitor,
11-15:3.

Dan Quayle
Vice President
of the United States

4

One of the things that's very interesting to the people I've talked to thus far is what is [Japan's] role going to be in national security. They [Asian

(DAN QUAYLE)

3

leaders] are not asking, nor do I think it would be prudent, for a re-emergence of an offensive capability for Japan from a military point of view. But there are a lot of things that [Japan] can do from a defensive point of view: thousand-mile communications from the shore [of Japan]; ASW; radar, surveillance and things of this sort would be very helpful. Japan is a vital link to stability in the Pacific . . . With its emergence as a world economic power—and it's going to stay there—there are certain responsibilities.

Interview, Singapore, May 2/
Los Angeles Times, 5-3:(I)8.

I've come to Japan as a friend, as someone who wants to see us get through the friction of our relationship so that it does not rub the relationship raw . . . The fact of the matter is that until Japan's trade barriers—whether they're regulatory, cultural, structural, whatever—until they're lowered, the focus in the U.S., is not going to be on whether American companies have the quality products Japanese consumers want to buy, but that the Japanese system won't let Japanese consumers buy them.

To business leaders, Osaka, Japan,
Oct. 28/
Los Angeles Times, 10-28:(A)4.

Leticia Ramos-Shahani
Philippine Senator

1

[Addressing and criticizing the U.S. on its treatment of the Philippines]: America's only colony is the weakest economic performer in Asia. The economic foundation you helped to establish in Taiwan, South Korea and other places was not done here. It's an indictment, and the United States has to deal with that.

The New York Times, 10-20:(A)4.

Ronald Reagan
Former President
of the United States

2

[On the democracy movement in a number of Communist countries, including China, where pro-democracy demonstrators were massacred recently by the Chinese military]: You can't massacre an idea. You cannot run tanks over hope. You cannot riddle a people's yearning with bullets. Those heroic Chinese students who gave their lives have released the spirit of democracy, and it cannot be called back. That spirit is loose upon the world this spring. This spring, the seeds of democracy have been planted. It may take years or even decades before the people of these countries can sit in the shade of democracy, but sit in the shade of democracy they some day will.

Before English-Speaking Union,
London, June 13/
Los Angeles Times, 6-14:(I)10.

Charles S. Robb
United States Senator,
D-Virginia

4

[Supporting U.S. military aid to non-Communist factions in Cambodia in wake of the scheduled pull-out of Vietnamese forces from that country]: No one can contend that the cause of a negotiated settlement will be advanced by leaving the non-Communist resistance weak and vulnerable in the face of two ruthless and heavily armed Communist adversaries. By adding the non-Communist resistance, we advance the prospects for a successful outcome. But if we do nothing, we only increase the likelihood of further civil war and heighten the possibility of the return of the murderous Khmer Rouge regime.

Before the Senate, Washington/
The Christian Science Monitor,
7-24:1.

Roh Tae Woo
President of South Korea

5

[On recent anti-government violence in South Korea]: It has become evident that lurking behind the flames that kill young people are violent revolutionaries who indulge in murder, arson, kidnaping and destruction with the goal of overthrowing our democratic society. If violence and lawlessness imperil democracy and the future of the nation in spite of the best efforts of

(ROH TAE WOO)

the government and the general public, I will have to consider invoking the emergency powers vested in the President by the Constitution.

Broadcast address to the nation,
Seoul, May 3/
Los Angeles Times, 5-4:(I)20.

1

If present economic difficulties [in South Korea] persist, grave problems will appear next year . . . and our economic achievements of the past 30 years will burst like a bubble . . . Production setbacks caused by labor disputes may be directly to blame for the difficult economic situation. But the never-ending demands of even doctors, teachers, bankers, clergymen and journalists—not to mention farmers and laborers—have become a key element aggravating the economy.

To party and government leaders,
Seoul, June 19/
Los Angeles Times, 6-20:(I)6.

2

There is still some unrest in [South Korea]. Our society has many issues to resolve as it moves from authoritarianism to democracy . . . However, I am not pessimistic about the situation because it represents the pain of creating a new democratic order.

To reporters, Seoul, June 28/
The Christian Science Monitor,
6-29:4.

3

[Arguing against a cutback in U.S. forces in South Korea]: It is the most economic investment strategically for America to maintain this forward deployment of its military forces. There is a saying in America: "If it ain't broke, don't fix it." I think it neatly applies to this situation.

News conference, Seoul, June 28/
The New York Times, 6-29:(A)7.

4

The United States troops in [South] Korea not only defend South Korea against a possible

attack from North Korea. But they are an important factor in the over-all military balance of power in Northeast Asia. There can be a slight modification as time goes by, but the general level of the American presence is not a subject for any possible change.

Interview, Seoul, Oct. 12/
The New York Times, 10-14:3.

5

I will say firmly that there is at present nobody who can be defined as a political prisoner [in South Korea] or a prisoner of conscience. Only those who committed specific acts have been arrested. I don't think that even in the United States they would be called political prisoners.

Interview, Seoul, Oct. 12/
The New York Times, 10-14:3.

Alan D. Romberg
Authority on Japan,
Council on Foreign Relations

6

If we [the U.S.] want Japan to bear more of the burden [in world affairs], we are going to have to let them take on more of the responsibility. It's unrealistic to think we're going to be able to call the tune all the time. For years, we have been urging the Japanese to speak up more, and getting very chagrined when they don't. Now the Japanese are beginning to play a serious role, and, all of a sudden, people [in the U.S.] view it as a threat.

Los Angeles Times, 2-26:(I)16.

Andrei D. Sakharov
Dissident Soviet physicist

7

[Criticizing the Soviet Union's recent 10-year military intervention in Afghanistan]: I deeply respect the Soviet Army and Soviet soldiers. I never insulted the heroic Soviet soldiers who served there. But the war itself was a criminal adventure and a huge crime by our country that cost the lives of almost 1 million Afghans. It was a war of annihilation, a terrible sin.

Before Congress of People's Deputies,
Moscow, June 2/
Los Angeles Times, 6-3:(I)8.

Saw Maung
Chief of State of Burma;
General, Burmese armed forces

1

[On his seizing power last year]: Do you think that I'm assuming power today because I hunger for power? The job that I want most is commander of the armed forces. These [governmental] responsibilities are burdens that I had to take on because of historical need . . . In the next general election, none of us [in the armed forces] is going to stand for election.

Interview/
World Press Review, April:44.

Robert Scalapino
Authority on Asia,
University of California,
Berkeley

2

There is no single area of the world that is more critical to the U.S. than Northeast Asia. It's the one area where all the major powers come into close touch, except for the European Community.

The Christian Science Monitor,
2-22:1.

Eduard A. Shevardnadze
Foreign Minister
of the Soviet Union

3

Today there are no Soviet troops in 26 of the 32 provinces of Afghanistan, but the [Soviet-supported] regime in Kabul continues to exist, despite all the malevolent predictions [that the regime would fall to anti-government rebels after the Soviets leave]. Beyond that, its contacts and cooperation with the opposition are broadening, and coalition organs of government are being formed in place. I again solemnly declare that both we and [Afghan] President Najibullah do not want Soviet troops to remain, and we firmly intend that their withdrawal should make possible the restoration of peace, not lead to new skirmishes, new victims.

Kabul, Afghanistan,
Jan. 15/
The New York Times, 1-16:(A)3.

4

[Saying that, despite the Soviets' withdrawal of troops from Afghanistan, his country will continue to support the Afghan government against attacks by anti-government rebels]: If a war is imposed on the Afghan government despite the common sense and logic of national interests, [the Soviet Union] will be forced to counter this with a force of arms, and it has this force. The present regime has every opportunity to withstand, and, in case the war goes on, the Soviet arms supplies will also be continued.

Interview/
Los Angeles Times, 1-16:(I)1.

5

[Saying the recently ended Soviet military intervention in Afghanistan was wrong]: We violated the norms of proper behavior. We went against general human values. I am talking, of course, about the dispatch of troops to Afghanistan. We committed the most serious violations of our own legislation, our Party and civilian norms . . . The decision, with such serious consequences for our country, was taken behind the backs of the Party and the people. The Soviet people were presented with a *fait accompli.*

Before Supreme Soviet, Moscow,
Oct. 23/
The New York Times,
10-24:(A)4.

6

[On the long-time Soviet military involvement in Afghanistan, from which it recently withdrew]: When more than 100 UN members for a number of years were condemning our action, what other evidence did we need to realize that we had set ourselves against all of humanity, violated norms of behavior, ignored universal human rights? I am referring, of course, to our military engagement in Afghanistan. It should teach us a lesson that, in this case, gross violations of our own laws, intra-party and civil norms and ethics were allowed.

Before Supreme Soviet, Moscow,
Oct. 23/
The New York Times, 10-25:(A)6.

WHAT THEY SAID IN 1989

Norodom Sihanouk
Exiled former Chief of State
of Cambodia

1

The Romans had their Janus god, with two faces, for peace and war. But there are two or three or four Sihanouks. [Still,] I am not "the changeling prince," as the Western press calls me. I have to use my imagination and my intelligence to find any reasonable solution possible for Cambodia—but one based on fact and the realities on the ground.

Interview, Beijing/
The New York Times, 12-19:(A)3.

Jaime Sin
Roman Catholic Archbishop
of Manila

2

The old politics has come back [to the Philippines], to the dismay of us all—the positioning for power, the corruption, the grandstanding, the jet-setting, the influence-peddling, the petty bickering. It seems we have gone back to life as usual, to what we really are: a nation of easygoing people, rascals, braggarts, thieves. It is we who are the problem.

Sermon/
Los Angeles Times, 6-12:(IV)4.

Stephen J. Solarz
United States Representative,
D-New York

3

[On the apparent reconciliation between China and the Soviet Union]: I think one reason for the absence of a reaction in Washington is due to the fact that Moscow was prepared to meet the Chinese conditions for a summit, and those conditions very much suited important American objectives. Those were a withdrawal of Soviet troops from Afghanistan and a withdrawal of Soviet-backed Vietnamese troops from Cambodia. When you add to that the fact that both countries are going through a process of democratic reforms, with more benign foreign policies, their rapprochement is seen as being

far less threatening than it would have several years ago.

The New York Times, 5-17:(A)4.

4

[Criticizing the Chinese government's use of military force against pro-democracy demonstrators in Beijing]: Our ability to influence the course of events in China is very limited, but there is much more at stake. If we appear to be indifferent or insensitive to the human rights of one-fifth of the human race, then I think it'll be very difficult for us to plausibly contend that we are in favor of democracy and human rights all over the world.

Broadcast interview/
"Face the Nation," CBS-TV, 6-4.

5

[On the recent massacre by the Chinese government of pro-democracy demonstrators in Beijing]: It is not unknown in history for tyrants to do their killing in the silence of the night, but this is the first time I recall them publicly boasting about the massacre of innocent civilians. [Chinese leader] Deng Xiaoping, who might have gone down in history as a modernizer, will now be remembered as the Butcher of Beijing.

The New York Times, 6-10:(A)5.

6

[Calling for U.S. military aid to the non-Communist resistance in Cambodia]: History will not forgive us if we stand idly by as Pol Pot once again turns Cambodia into an Asian Auschwitz. So long as there are Cambodians willing to fight, who are determined to prevent the Khmer Rouge from returning to power, don't we have a moral obligation to help them out?

The Washington Post, 6-13:(A)23.

7

[On just-held elections in Taiwan]: The entire world can see the contrast between Taiwan and the P.R.C. [Communist China]. In the P.R.C., when the people ask for democracy, they are

(STEPHEN J. SOLARZ)

greeted with a hail of bullets, and Beijing is drowned in a river of blood. In Taiwan, when people demand democracy, they are given an opportunity to participate in an electoral process and can vote for the candidates of their choice.

Taipei, Taiwan, Dec. 3/
The New York Times, 12-4:(A)3.

Richard H. Solomon
Assistant Secretary for
East Asian and Pacific Affairs,
Department of State
of the United States

1

[Defending the U.S. support for the Khmer Rouge taking part in a transitional government in Cambodia, support which has drawn criticism in the U.S. Congress because of the Khmer Rouge's reputation for barbarism]: We are not school-children in this business. The chances of avoiding continuing conflict are not very good. But we firmly believe that the chances are much better to get this problem under control if you have a struc-tured political settlement than if you just leave a situation that is totally unstructured or uncon-strained, where civil conflict is almost a certainty.

Before House Asian and Pacific
Affairs Subcommittee,
Washington, Sept. 14/
The New York Times,
9-15:(C)20.

Tam Yiu-chung
Member, City Legislative
Council of Hong Kong

2

[On the coming 1997 reunification of Hong Kong under Chinese control in light of current anti-government, pro-democracy protests in China]: The latest events in China have made Hong Kong people realize that Hong Kong is closely connected with China, and only when there is democracy in China will Hong Kong have a future.

The Washington Post,
5-23:(A)19.

Robert G. Toricelli
United States Representative,
D-New Jersey

3

[Saying the U.S. is too silent on the pro-democracy demonstrations in China, because it doesn't want to offend the Chinese leadership]: [U.S.] President Bush is balancing the chances of offending an 84-year-old Communist leader [Deng Xiaoping] during his last days in power with speaking to the aspiration of one billion Chinese people. I don't think the two should be weighed on the same scale ... A democratic revolution is taking place [in China], and the world's leading democracy will be remembered as being silent and the Soviet Union will be remembered as the source of change.

Los Angeles Times, 5-23:(I)15.

Margaret D. Tutwiler
Spokesperson for the
Department of State
of the United States

4

[On the recent massacre of pro-democracy demonstrators by the Chinese military in Beijing]: The whole world has seen what happened in Tiananmen Square. Large numbers of peaceful protesters were killed by army units. We con-demn the use of live fire against unarmed civilians, which is what happened in Tiananmen Square. The demonstrators were seeking basic human rights, such as freedom of association, of the press and of expression. Labeling such people "counter-revolutionaries" and "hooli-gans" will do nothing to alter the reality of what happened in Tiananmen Square on June 3.

Washington, June 12/
The Washington Post,
6-13:(A)20.

Bharat Waliawalla
Member, Indian Institute for
Defense Studies and Analysis

5

[There was a] decay of institutions and the rise of cult of personality under [the late Indian Prime Minister] Indira Gandhi. [Her predecessors]

WHAT THEY SAID IN 1989

(BHARAT WALIAWALLA)

Mahatma Gandhi and Jawaharlal Nehru were builders of institutions. Indira Gandhi, through the years, destroyed those institutions and made personality all important. So now you have these palace intrigues dominating political life [under current Prime Minister Rajiv Gandhi], rather than real issues. A more fundamental problem, though, is the secrecy of government . . . Where you have secrecy, you have intrigues, and although India is the largest democracy in the world, it is also the world's most secretive democracy.

Los Angeles Times, 3-31:(I)16.

Wang Yizhou
*Associate professor, Institute
of Marxism, Leninism and
Mao Tse-tung Thought
(China)*

1

The level of freedom of speech, freedom of action, freedom of criticism that is now officially permitted in the Soviet Union is higher than in China. There is a kind of pressure now from below, from intellectuals, from citizens, demanding that China must have reform, must have change, especially change like that in the Soviet Union, including the discussion of historical questions, the replacement of old cadres with younger people and crackdowns on corrupt officials . . . Many leading Chinese intellectuals evaluate the Soviet elections very highly and

have spoken of them at rallies . . . This is one of the important reasons why the demand to push forward with political reform in China is getting stronger and stronger.

*Interview, Beijing/
Los Angeles Times, 5-15:(I)13.*

Yang Shangkun
President of China

2

[On Soviet leader Mikhail Gorbachev's visit to China aimed at improving Soviet-Chinese relations]: Chinese-Soviet relations traversed a tortuous course in the past. Today, we have come to a new starting point. It has not been easy for leaders of our two countries to come to this historic meeting. We on both sides must value and safeguard what has already been achieved and continue to address the remaining problems . . . Ten years ago, we [in China] embarked on the road to reform and opening up, and since then China has undergone great changes. Despite various difficulties, twists and turns we may still encounter on our road of advance, we are confident that we will overcome all difficulties, free ourselves from poverty and backwardness and attain our anticipated goals, so long as we adhere to leadership by the Communist Party and to the socialist road, persist in reform and the open policy and continue to blaze new trails by relying on the united struggle of the Chinese people.

*At banquet in Gorbachev's honor,
Beijing, May 15/
The New York Times, 5-16:(A)4.*

Europe

Leonid I. Abalkin
*Vice Prime Minister of the
Soviet Union; Chief economic
advisor to Soviet President
Mikhail Gorbachev*

1

[On the Soviet economic reform program]:
The important thing to know is when will people
[in the Soviet Union], sitting around their kitchen
tables, finally be able to say, "Oh, life is much
better now than it was." I think this will happen
only by 1995, and we will be reaping the first
palpable changes by then.

*News conference,
Moscow, Jan. 25/
The Washington Post, 1-26:(A)1.*

2

Our studies show clearly that if the [Soviet]
economy is not stabilized over the next year or
two and at least the start of an improvement is not
achieved, a rightward swing by society is inevitable. Society will be destabilized. The estimate,
again, is one to two years at a maximum, and then
something unpredictable will be begun. The form
[of the upheaval] is unpredictable, but it will be
inevitable.

*News conference,
Moscow, June 16/
Los Angeles Times, 6-17:(I)4.*

3

[On economic reforms in the Soviet Union]:
Everyone is waiting for everything to turn for the
better immediately, and it may be the residue of
fairy tales. Each time we [Soviets] face difficulties, however, flying saucers become the topic of
the day and faith healers appear. People really
seem to think some guy is going to climb out of a
UFO and explain the best way to develop
socialism.

*At economic conference, Moscow,
Nov. 15/
Los Angeles Times, 11-16:(A)13.*

Yuri Afanasyev
*Soviet legislator; Rector,
Historical Archives Institute*

4

[On Soviet leader Mikhail Gorbachev's reform program]: Things are not working out the
way he thought they would. Nothing has gotten
better. The economy, inter-ethnic conflicts, the
psychological mood of the people—all of it has
deteriorated. I think Gorbachev feels a sense of
his own powerlessness to change things sometimes, and that is an unpleasant feeling for any
head of state. I think that is what is causing the
inconsistency in his behavior and causing him to
ignore, and even shut off, the constructive voices
around him.

*Speech at Historical Archives
Institute, Moscow, Oct. 31/
The Washington Post, 11-1:(A)36.*

5

[On the Communist system in the Soviet
Union]: Teachers and utopian thinkers used to
believe that a society of universal justice and
prosperity could be built simply by thinking it
out. But the epic of conscious construction of
ideal societies died in Western Europe a long
time ago. Even with the French Revolution there
was an attempt to take deliberate action, but it
failed disastrously. And they went back to their
normal course of development. But *we* have been
in this state of deliberate, conscious construction for 70 years. It has to be given up.

The New York Times, 12-6:(A)23.

Abel Aganbegyan
*Director, Institute of Economics,
Soviet Academy of Sciences*

6

The picture in different spheres of *perestroika*
[reform in the Soviet Union] differs very widely
. . . In the areas of foreign policy and disarmament, there has been a great breakthrough.
Hardly anyone would have expected that by

(ABEL AGANBEGYAN)

1989 the Soviet Union would have reduced military production by 19.5 per cent. But together with the pleasant surprises, life has handed us some bad ones. The country's financial situation has worsened. The budget deficit has increased. The gap between available money to the population and availability of goods has grown, and shortages in the consumer market have also increased. Then, of course, we were hit by very sad events: the earthquake in Armenia and, after, in Tadzhikistan. Life to us is very contradictory. It's a mosaic and certainly not to be viewed in a rosy light.

Interview, Boston/
The Christian Science Monitor,
3-21:4.

Sergei F. Akhromeyev
Chief, Soviet Armed Forces
General Staff

1

The U.S. should thank God for its geographical position. Such threatening neighbors it has— Canada and Mexico! . . . Americans are living in safety. Except for nuclear weapons, an enemy cannot reach the U.S. Our [Soviet] political and geographical situation is completely different. We are located between Europe and Asia and are encircled by American bases. No matter what conflict might arise in the world, the U.S. can quite easily deploy its armed forces without rushing. No such thing for us. If the situation became serious, we would be forced to change to wartime organization quickly. That is why we need to have very well-trained reserves and armed forces organized on the basis of the draft.

Interview/Time, 11-13:60.

Georgi A. Arbatov
Director, Soviet Institute of
U.S.A. and Canadian Affairs

2

Our problems [in Eastern Europe] are more than 50 per cent economic. Why are the [Soviet Baltic] republics speaking so much about independence, for example? Because things are not good in the economy. We were successful with politics before we were successful with a lot of things. [Soviet leader Mikhail] Gorbachev is a democrat, but we have not yet found the answers to some of the economic problems. But maybe it is necessary to hit the bottom and then you can do it. And we almost have hit the bottom.

Interview/USA Today, 11-16:(A)7.

William T. Archey
International vice president,
United States Chamber
of Commerce

3

[On the coming 1992 economic unification of Europe]: The motivating factor behind 1992 is a fear on the part of the Europeans that they were falling further behind the U.S. and Japan in the ability to compete in a global economy. They concluded that only through uniting the European market will they be able to develop the economic vitality necessary to make them a world-class competitor . . . European companies are going to become world-class. U.S. companies in those markets ought to start planning for a tremendous increase in competition from Europe.

Interview/
Nation's Business, June:24.

4

Until now we have not supported projects in Eastern Europe because of the lack of viable private-sector business organizations that could carry them out. But the changing economic climate in the Communist world has allowed us to take another look at the situation. The collapse of Marxism as an ideology and the bankruptcy of Soviet-style economies have opened the way for a flowering of organizations devoted to building free-enterprise systems in their nations, with Poland and Hungary leading the way.

The Washington Post, 9-19:(C)1.

Egon Bahr
Official, Social Democratic
Party of West Germany

5

All this talk about reunification [of East and West Germany] is crazy nonsense. Both sides

(EGON BAHR)

know it's not in the cards. The United States is the only country that could live with a united Germany because [the U.S. is] big and powerful enough to handle it. None of our neighbors want it. It is absolutely impossible for [Soviet leader Mikhail] Gorbachev to give up [East Germany] . . . If you speak of European unity and West European economic union, you do not speak of German unification . . . The Americans in West Germany are the very best guarantee the Russians have that these crazy Germans will not do anything wild.

The Washington Post, 7-27:(A)26.

Wladyslaw Baka
President, Bank of Poland

1

We [in Poland] have several problems which need foreign assistance. The first is stabilization and having a convertible currency, which needs foreign-exchange support. The second is structural changes in the economy, including new investment and replacement of used equipment. The third is money to change ownership of our economy and to support the private sector. And the fourth is to assist the introduction of market forces.

Interview, Washington/
The Christian Science Monitor,
10-5:9.

James A. Baker III
Secretary of State-designate
of the United States

2

This year marks the 40th anniversary of the founding of NATO, the most successful alliance in history. But today's Western Europe is not the exhausted Europe recovering from its own devastation, nor is it yet the single Europe of the political visionaries. A new appreciation is needed on our side and theirs of how we can adapt to changing circumstances as a force for peace. Certainly in the first instance, it requires, as [U.S.] President-elect Bush has suggested, a meeting of our minds on how we proceed with a

changing Soviet Union. The stakes haven't changed. Our commitment to NATO is stronger, because we as nations are stronger. As long as Europe remains the most heavily armed continent, where American and Soviet troops face each other on the front lines, the Atlantic Alliance will be our first line of defense.

At Senate Foreign Relations
Committee hearing on his
confirmation, Washington, Jan. 17/
The New York Times, 1-18:(A)10.

James A. Baker III
Secretary of State
of the United States

3

We hope that whatever happens with respect to the desire on the part of the people in the [Soviet] Baltic states for more autonomy and more self-determination and more freedom happens peacefully. Should there be self-determination? Should there be freedom? Should there be more autonomy? Yes—but it should not take place in the context of major instability, bloodshed and that sort of thing. That's our policy.

The New York Times, 9-28:(A)6.

4

[On Soviet leader Mikhail Gorbachev's reform program in the Soviet Union]: Gorbachev has not been deterred by the failure to produce economic results. To the contrary, at least so far, his recourse when facing obstacles, as we saw once again this summer, is to use problems to further consolidate his authority. Then he takes [new] steps to press political and economic reforms further. He doesn't fold, he doesn't call, he simply raises the stakes.

At Senate hearing, Washington/
Los Angeles Times, 10-9:(I)6.

5

We want *perestroika* [Soviet reform] to succeed at home and abroad because we believe it will bring about a less aggressive Soviet Union, restrained in the use of force and less hostile to democracy. A *perestroika* that resulted simply in

(JAMES A. BAKER III)

a more efficient and more capable Soviet state would indeed be a more formidable and dangerous competitor. But I do not believe that *perestroika* can succeed without increasing measures of free markets, free speech and institutions more accountable to the people . . . That means a more democratic society, more respectful of human rights and legal norms which could provide a lasting foundation for more constructive, less dangerous Soviet behavior abroad; a society that produces not subjects who are to be acted upon but citizens who participate in policy; and a society where citizens have a say in what their government does at home and abroad.

Before Foreign Policy Association,
New York, Oct. 16/
The New York Times, 10-17:(A)8.

1

As Europe changes, the instruments for Western cooperation must adapt. Working together, we must design and gradually put into place a new architecture for a new era. This new architecture must have a place for old foundations and structures that remain valuable—like NATO—while recognizing that they can also serve new collective purposes. The new architecture must continue the construction of institutions—like the EC—that can help draw together the West while also serving as an open door to the East. And the new architecture must build up frameworks . . . that can overcome the division of Europe and bridge the Atlantic Ocean. This new structure must also accomplish two special purposes. First, as a part of overcoming the division of Europe, there must be an opportunity to overcome through peace and freedom the division of Berlin and of Germany. The United States and NATO have stood for [German] unification for 40 years, and we will not waver from that goal. Secondly, the architecture should reflect that America's security—politically, militarily and economically—remains linked to Europe's security. The United States and Canada share Europe's neighborhood.

At Berlin Press Club, Dec. 12/
The New York Times, 12-13:(A)10.

2

Americans will profit from access to a single European market [after the 1992 European economic integration is completed], just as Europeans have long profited from their access to a single American market. As Europe moves toward its goal of a common international market . . . the link between the United States and the European Community will become even more important.

At Berlin Press Club,
Dec. 12/
Los Angeles Times, 12-13:(A)16.

3

[On current pro-democracy reforms in Eastern Europe]: After the streets empty of demonstrators, after the people select new leaders, after governments become the servants of the people, after all this—the economies must put food on the table and goods on the shelves of stores. New economic reform plans must break with 40 years of stagnation to unleash private market forces. Here is where we [in the West] can help, indeed must help, if we are to meet the call of history.

At meeting of foreign ministers,
Brussels, Dec. 13/
Los Angeles Times, 12-14:(I)1.

Gerald L. Baliles
Governor of Virginia (D)

4

[On the forthcoming 1992 economic unification of the European Community]: Increasingly, 1992 is receiving the coverage it merits in the American press. It has taken a while, but this is natural in a country that not so long ago traded with itself more than it traded with others. Now it's a new ball game. The rules have been changed. The dimensions of the economic playing field have increased dramatically. The effort by the 12 nations of the European Community—which has quickly progressed during the past two years—to remove internal economic barriers and to proceed toward the status of a unified superpower, is historic and full of implications for the U.S. Some view these developments with concerned apprehension; others happy anticipa-

(GERALD L. BALILES)

tion. But regardless of how one looks at it, the stakes for America are immense.

July 3/The Washington Post,
7-11:(A)24.

John Barnes
Lecturer in government,
London School of Economics
(Britain)

1

[On British Prime Minister Margaret Thatcher]: As we move toward the mid-1990s we will see the whole European issue putting a strain on British politics. Thatcher is not the one to handle that issue. She's managed to ride both horses very well until now, but she will have trouble riding one horse as Britain is drawn into Europe.

The Christian Science Monitor,
1-3:6.

Janos Berecz
Former chief ideologist,
Communist Party of Hungary

2

[On political reform in Hungary]: We [the Communist Party] have to become a real political party. In the past, our basic role was to control economic production. The problem was how best to influence the bureaucracy. Now we have to aim at the citizens, because they are the voters. We have to enter into disputes and discussions at the grass roots and have tolerance for people who shout back.

The Washington Post, 4-17:(A)24.

Algirdas Brazauskas
First Secretary, Communist
Party of Lithuania

3

[On calls for economic independence for the Soviet Baltic republics of Lithuania, Estonia and Latvia]: Everyone wants great haste. Everyone wants decisive breakthroughs. Everyone thinks that in making these changes we can move as fast as a person might around his own house, that we

are rearranging the furniture, so to speak, in working out quite fundamental changes. But the balance in the Baltics, and in the Soviet Union as a whole, is rather delicate at this moment, and we must take care that we make real progress and do not sacrifice real gains for speed.

Interview/
Los Angeles Times, 5-14:(IV)7.

Visvaldis Brinkmanis
Leader, Latvian
independence movement

4

[Advocating independence for the Soviet Baltic states of Latvia, Estonia and Lithuania]: We do not demand more freedom and more democracy. We demand complete freedom and complete democracy as the Western world enjoys it. There can be no greater disaster for a nation than being incorporated into the Soviet empire.

At conference on Baltic states'
independence, Riga, Latvia,
U.S.S.R., Aug. 21/
The Washington Post, 8-22:(A)1.

Harold Brown
Former Secretary of Defense
of the United States

5

I think we have to recognize that [Soviet leader Mikhail] Gorbachev, however sincere he may be [in his program of Soviet reform], is a shrewd enough political animal to want to gain whatever he can in the way of the weakening of [NATO] alliance ties, of separating Western Europe from the United States. We need to be cautious about that. Well, what does that mean we should do? It doesn't mean that we should stick to the present form of the alliance indefinitely. It does mean that we should make changes cautiously; that the Europeans, as they form a more independent pillar, actually do what they need to do to maintain their military capability and to maintain political cohesion; that the United States, if, in the long run—as I think most of us think—it is going to have less of a presence in Europe at some point, should do so as part of arms reductions and as part of political change in the relationships between East and West, and should not do so precipitately.

Symposium/Newsweek, 5-15:29.

Zbigniew Brzezinski
Former Assistant to the
President of the United States
(Jimmy Carter) for
National Security Affairs

1

[On Soviet leader Mikhail Gorbachev's reform program in the Soviet Union]: There's no doubt that the impulse for greatness, for a great many Russians, was enhanced by the alleged universality of the Communist ideology. That, I think, has been stripped away. The question then remains, will their nationalism suffice? The Russians are a great nation. So I think the desire to be Number 1 will probably motivate quite a few great Russians. But I also suspect that, right now, very many of them would be also very conscious of the fact that they have a . . . long way to go—much longer than they thought. A few years ago, they thought they were riding the crest of history. I think now they know that they are risking sliding into the dustbin of history. That is an egregiously serious preoccupation. This is why Gorbachev can now say with unabashed apocalyptic pessimism: "*Perestroika* [reform] is our last chance." If it doesn't work, it is the death of socialism.

Interview, Washington/
The Christian Science Monitor,
3-20:8.

2

[On recent pro-democracy reforms in Eastern Europe]: No successful precedent exists of transition from a Communist, dictatorial system to a pluralistic, democratic system. Some countries have moved in that direction, particularly Poland and Hungary, but their success is far from certain. It is especially difficult to restructure a statist centralized economy into a functioning market system. The latter involves not only an intricate set of economic relationships but also

the emergence of an entrepreneurial culture. If these transitions succeed, a major step will have been taken in building a common European home.

Before Soviet Foreign Ministry's
Diplomatic Academy, Oct. 27/
The New York Times, 11-15:(A)25.

3

You cannot end the division of Europe without ending the division of Germany. If you want to end the division of Germany, you need to end the fears that it generates.

The New York Times, 11-16:(A)9.

4

[On the pro-democracy reforms in Eastern Europe]: I can imagine a Soviet intervention in East Germany, where the Soviets have a lot of troops on the ground and therefore on the spot. If the East German Communist regime were to collapse through violence and if the Soviets were to remain passive, then the whole thing would collapse—in Poland, Hungary and Czechoslovakia. The Soviets know that if they let go of East Germany, Poland is lost. That's why it is so urgent for us, the West, collectively, to give this turbulence a chance to work itself out constructively in the direction of some form of pluralist democracy. So far, we have not responded in a manner that does justice to the magnitude of the opportunity, or, alas, to the magnitude of the threat inherent in these truly earthquake-like political phenomena.

Interview/Time, 12-18:10.

Fyodor Burlatsky
Soviet political scientist;
Candidate for the Congress
of People's Deputies
of the Soviet Union

5

[On the new multi-candidate elections in the Soviet Union]: When you consider how we used to justify those old, one-candidate elections as expressions of the "people's approval" for [Communist] Party policy, then you will realize

(FYODOR BURLATSKY)

how fundamental a change multi-candidate elections are for us. The new structure, though still a one-party system, is based on pluralism, not the political monotheism of the past. Now candidates must put forward their own programs, Party policies will be judged on their merits against other alternatives and Party members must compete with everyone else. That is the starting point, and it can make the Supreme Soviet our central political institution where all trends, all opinions and alternative programs converge.

Los Angeles Times, 3-6:(I)12.

George Bush
President of the United States

1

[Saying the U.S. plans to offer economic aid to Poland]: We're not going to offer unsound credits. We're not going to offer aid without requiring sound economic practices in return. And we must remember that Poland still is a member of the Warsaw Pact. I will take no steps that compromise the security of the West. While we want [U.S.-Polish] relations to improve, there are certain acts we will not condone or accept—behavior that can shift relations in the wrong direction: human-rights abuses, technology theft and hostile intelligence or foreign-policy actions against us.

Speech, Hamtramck, Mich.,
April 17/
Los Angeles Times, 4-18:(I)12.

2

Nowhere will the ultimate consequences of change have more significance for world security than within the Soviet Union itself. What we're seeing now in the Soviet Union [reform and openness] is indeed dramatic. The process is still ongoing, unfinished. But make no mistake, our policy is to seize every—and I mean every—opportunity to build a better, more stable relationship with the Soviet Union, just as it is our policy to defend American interests in light of the enduring reality of Soviet military power. We

want to see *perestroika* [change in the Soviet Union] succeed, and we want to see the policies of *glasnost* [openness] and *perestroika*—so far a revolution imposed from top down—institutionalized within the Soviet Union.

At U.S. Coast Guard Academy
commencement, May 24/
The New York Times,
5-25:(A)4.

3

Conventional forces alone have not guaranteed peace in Europe, and nuclear weapons continue to play a key role in demonstrating to any aggressor that war in Europe is unthinkable.

Before North Atlantic Council,
Brussels, May 29/
Los Angeles Times, 5-30:(I)10.

4

For 40 years, the seeds of democracy in Eastern Europe lay dormant, buried under the frozen tundra of the Cold War. And for 40 years the world has waited for the Cold War to end. And decade after decade, time after time, the flowering human spirit withered from the chill of conflict and oppression. And again, the world waited. But the passion for freedom cannot be denied forever. The world has waited long enough. The time is right. Let Europe be whole and free . . . so when I visit Poland and Hungary this summer, I will deliver this message: There cannot be a common European home until all within it are free to move from room to room. And I'll take another message: The path of freedom leads to a larger home, a home where West meets East, a democratic home, the commonwealth of free nations.

Speech, Mainz, West Germany,
May 31/
The New York Times, 6-1:(A)7.

5

We have a great and historic opportunity to shape the changes that are transforming Europe. Working with our allies in Europe, we set a course for the future. And we must move to ful-

(GEORGE BUSH)

fill that promise, moving beyond containment, moving beyond the era of conflict and Cold War that the world has known for more than 40 years, because keeping the peace in Europe means keeping the peace for America.

At Pease Air Force Base,
Portsmouth, N.H., June 2/
Los Angeles Times, 6-3:(I)3.

1

[Supporting greater economic and political reforms in Poland]: Poland has a special place in the American heart and in my heart, and when you hurt, we feel pain; and when you dream, we feel hope; and when you succeed, we feel joy. It goes far beyond diplomatic relations; it's more like family relations. And coming to Poland is like coming home. This special kinship is the kinship of an ancient dream, a recurring dream, the dream of freedom . . . So I say follow your dream of a better life for you and your children. You can see a new and prosperous Poland—not overnight, not in a year, but yes, a new and prosperous Poland in your lifetime. It's been done by Polish people before. Hopeful immigrants came to that magical place called America and built a new life for themselves in a single generation, and it can be done by Polish people again; but this time it will be done in Poland.

Speech, Gdansk, Poland, July 11/
The New York Times, 7-12:(A)5.

2

[On the current mass exodus of East Germans to the West]: We are riveted, and I am moved, by the tens of thousands of East Germans sacrificing all that they own, leaving everything behind, to find their way to a West that offers the promise of freedom and opportunity. I also look forward to the day that Germans will not have to climb fences, freeze in Embassy courtyards or dodge bullets in order to enjoy the fruits of a free society.

At White House gathering,
Washington, Oct. 5/
Los Angeles Times, 10-6:(I)10.

3

These [pro-democracy] changes we're seeing in Eastern Europe are absolutely extraordinary, but I'm not going to be stampeded into overreacting to any of this. Democrats on Capitol Hill have been calling me "timid." I have other, better words, like "cautious," "diplomatic," "prudent."

Interview, Washington,
Oct. 24/
The New York Times, 10-25:(A)1.

4

[On criticism by some in the U.S. that he is not responding with sufficient decisiveness or aid to the democracy movement in Eastern European governments]: The fact that some critics are out there equating progress with spending more money doesn't bother me in the least. Look at the dynamic changes that are taking place around the world. And well, I'd like to hear some specific suggestions other than triple the spending on every initiative. We are working closely with our allies. We are trying to facilitate the change. I don't hear complaints coming out of our allies or indeed out of Hungary or Poland or Eastern Europe.

News conference,
Washington, Nov. 7/
The New York Times, 11-8:(A)6.

5

[On East Germany's decision to allow freedom of travel for its citizens, who may now visit the West and cross the Berlin Wall]: Of course I welcome the decision by the East German leadership to open the borders to those wishing to emigrate or travel. If it's implemented fully, it certainly conforms with the Helsinki Accords, which the G.D.R. signed. And if the G.D.R. goes forward now, this wall, built in '61, will have very little relevance. It clearly is a good development in terms of human rights.

News conference,
Washington, Nov. 9/
The New York Times, 11-10:(A)10.

6

[Addressing Lech Walesa, whose Solidarity trade union has formed a non-Communist gov-

(GEORGE BUSH)

ernment in Poland]: You were called a "no-body". But Lenin and Stalin have been disproved, not by presidents or princes but by the likes of an electrician from Gdansk and his fellow workers in a brave union called Solidarity. The Iron Curtain is fast becoming a rusted, abandoned relic, symbolizing a lost era, a failed ideology.

Presenting Walesa with the Medal
of Freedom, Washington, Nov. 13/
The New York Times, 11-14:(A)9.

1

[On recent pro-democracy reforms in Eastern Europe and the Soviet Union]: Immediately after my [coming] visit with [Soviet] President [Mikhail] Gorbachev, I will go to Brussels to consult with our partners in NATO, the very alliance that has kept the West free for 40 years. I will assure them that no matter how dramatic the change in Eastern Europe, or in the Soviet Union itself, the United States will continue to stand with our allies and our friends. For, in a new Europe, the American role may change in form but not in fundamentals. After all, the Soviet Union maintains hundreds of thousands of troops throughout Eastern Europe. Study the map, review history and you'll see that this presence, with the Soviet Union's natural advantage of geography, cannot be ignored. So even if forces are significantly reduced on both sides—a noble goal indeed—we will remain in Europe as long as our friends want and need us.

Broadcast address to the nation,
Washington, Nov. 22/
The New York Times, 11-23:(A)8.

2

[On recent pro-democracy reforms in Eastern Europe, including the opening up of the Berlin Wall]: [In the past,] the world was haunted by the images of watchtowers, guard dogs and machine guns. In fact, many of you had not even been born when the Berlin Wall was erected in 1961. But now the world has a new image, reflecting a new reality, that of Germans, East and West, pulling

each other to the top of the wall, a human bridge between nations. Entire peoples all across Eastern Europe, bravely taking to the streets demanding liberty, talking democracy. This is not the end of the book of history, but is a joyful end to one of history's saddest chapters.

Broadcast address to the nation,
Washington, Nov. 22/
The New York Times, 11-23:(A)8.

3

[On the pro-democracy reforms in Eastern Europe]: I think if there's a worry, the worry is: Can it be managed properly? [I am] trying not to listen to those that are out there encouraging flamboyant action, but rather to respond prudently, as a great power must, to change. And you know and I know that I've been criticized for timidity. Some have wanted me to go jump up on top of the Berlin Wall [which was recently opened allowing East Berliners into West Berlin]. Well, I never heard of such a stupid idea.

To European reporters/
The Washington Post,
12-1:(A)38.

4

[On the popular uprising in Romania that has resulted in the ousting, capture and execution of dictator Nicolae Ceausescu]: Well, I'm just amazed and respectful of the change that has taken place. We did say that we were concerned that the trial of Ceausescu should have been more open, but that's their matter. They went forward, and I think now it could bring the remaining holdouts, security forces, to bay. The army seems to be doing that, and my concern is for tranquility and freedom in Romania. And you know what touched me, was hearing this guy singing a Christmas carol. It was reported that it was the first time . . . in some 40 years that a Christmas carol was allowed to be heard on Romanian TV. It made a dramatic statement to me.

To reporters,
Corpus Christi, Texas,
Dec. 27/
USA Today, 12-28:(A)9.

Oleg Bykov
Deputy director, Soviet
Institute for World Economy
and International Relations

1

Perestroika [Soviet reform] is doomed neither to failure nor to success. The process depends on people and the decisions they take. If *perestroika* fails, it won't simply be a matter of going back to stagnation. It will be catastrophe. Some countries are smug where they are, but we are not. We have eaten up whatever we had and also eaten up much of our future.

The Washington Post, 12-1:(A)38.

Marian Calfa
Prime Minister
of Czechoslovakia

2

[The long-term goal in Czechoslovakia] is to prepare a transition to a market economy, to insure economic stability, and increase the living standard of the population and the rational use of natural resources. We cannot afford to experiment with some kind of as-yet-untried economic system based on a combination of principles whose compatibility has never been proven. We have to accept the market economy with all its advantages, but also its disadvantages. The market is based on the freedom of people within the framework of valid laws, assuring equal rights for all. It gives every individual the opportunity to follow his own interests and at the same time to benefit all others.

Before Czechoslovak Parliament,
Prague, Dec. 19/
The New York Times, 12-20:(A)9.

George Carver
Senior fellow, Center for
Strategic and International
Studies, Washington;
Former Deputy Director of
Central Intelligence
of the United States

3

[Saying the Soviet Union will ultimately crack down on Hungary, which is allowing East Ger-

mans to pass through its territory on their way to West Germany]: I would love to see the Soviet empire break up. But empires seldom break up without a lot of tension and bloodshed . . . Things may be different than [when the Soviets cracked down on Hungary in] 1956, but I don't think we should count on it. We are always hoping that world opinion will force these guys to behave— baloney.

Los Angeles Times, 9-12:(I)12.

Nicolae Ceausescu
President of Romania

4

[Rejecting pro-democracy reforms for Romania, such as are occurring in other Eastern European countries]: The [Communist] Party cannot give up its revolutionary responsibility; it cannot surrender its historical mission to another political force. The Party is the vital center of our nation, the patriotic revolutionary consciousness of the entire people.

At Romanian Communist Party
Congress, Bucharest, Nov. 20/
The Washington Post, 11-21:(A)21.

Dick Cheney
Secretary of Defense
of the United States

5

[On Soviet leader Mikhail Gorbachev's reform policy in the Soviet Union]: I started out as a real skeptic, frankly, about Mr. Gorbachev. Having watched over the last few years, having visited the Soviet Union and [having] visited with him on a couple of occasions and watched this process unfold—sitting in my office last week with the Soviet Ambassador discussing the election returns in the Soviet Union, something I never really anticipated having the opportunity to do—I've become a believer in the notion that Gorbachev wants fundamentally to reform Soviet society economically. In order to achieve economic change, he's also going to have to push certain political reforms, i.e. elections. How all that translates into an altered military posture is still an open question.

Interview, Washington, April 4/
The Washington Post, 4-5:(A)12.

(DICK CHENEY)

1

[On Soviet leader Mikhail Gorbachev]: My personal view is that the task he set for himself of trying to fundamentally reform the Soviet system is incapable of occurring. If I had to guess today, I would guess that he would ultimately fail. That is to say that he will not be able to reform the Soviet economy to turn it into an efficient, modern society. And that, when that happens, he's likely to be replaced by somebody who will be far more hostile than he's been in terms of his attitude toward the West.

Broadcast interview/
"Evans & Novak," CNN-TV, 4-29.

2

Once you start negotiations [with the Soviets] on short-range nuclear forces [in Europe], if you can't resist the political pressure to get into the negotiations, how do you resist the political pressure that is clearly going to be there to accept the first Soviet offer, which is going to be not 50 [short-range nuclear missiles for each side], but probably zero? The proposition we're faced with now is a single track: "Don't deploy; negotiate." That's what the Germans have, in effect, presented to us. We've made it clear we find that unacceptable. The British obviously find it unacceptable as well.

Before Senate Armed Services
Committee, Washington, May 3/
The Washington Post, 5-4:(A)30.

Vladimir N. Chernega
Vice rector, Diplomatic
Academy, Foreign Ministry
of the Soviet Union

3

If the governments of Eastern Europe want it, we [Soviets] must withdraw our troops from their territory. We can do this even unilaterally. As for American troops—I would leave that up to the Western European governments. I know that some circles in Western Europe feel their security is greater with American troops. It's an understandable position. Let them have it. We have a historical chance now and we have to make the most of it. In this context, a certain presence of American troops—a limited presence—poses no danger. For us, this is not just reducing military spending and reallocating resources to civilian purposes. It is a matter of structural reorganization of our whole economy. Forty per cent of our machine-tool industry and 75 per cent of our spending on science go to the military. This is no basis for a normal economy.

The New York Times, 11-30:(A)12.

John L. Clendenin
Chairman, United States
Chamber of Commerce;
Chairman, BellSouth Corporation

4

[On the coming 1992 economic unification of Europe]: I think that 1992 may indeed compound some of the problems that exist in that area [fair international trading]. We can't afford to let EC92 evolve into the "Fortress Europe" that many people are concerned about—the closed market that favors its own products to the exclusion of others. That concern is real. A Fortress Europe would be very damaging to the economic health of our country. We have to speak forthrightly and early to make sure that doesn't happen.

Interview/
Nation's Business, June:62.

William S. Cohen
United States Senator,
R-Maine

5

[U.S.] President Bush went to West Germany two weeks ago. He said the Berlin Wall must come down. He was clear; he was unambiguous. He said that wall stands as a scar against the conscience of humanity. Take it down. [Soviet leader Mikhail] Gorbachev was reported, in today's paper, saying that nothing is eternal in this world; the [Berlin] Wall can disappear once the conditions that created the need for it disappear. What is he saying? What is Mr. Gorbachev saying? Did he mean that once the people of the Eastern bloc stopped yearning for freedom, they would no longer have to stay in

(WILLIAM S. COHEN)

jail? Is that what he means by "once the conditions disappear, the Wall will disappear"?

Before the Senate,
Washington, June 16/
The Washington Post, 6-22:(A)26.

Francesco Cossiga
President of Italy

1

[On Italy's frequent changes of Prime Ministers and Cabinets]: In Italy, a leader has to conquer respect and authority day by day, every day. Italians do not look at authority and power with sacred respect, as do countries that have strong traditions of government, like England, or countries that are the product of great revolutions, like the United States.

Interview, Rome/
The Washington Post, 10-10:(A)21.

William J. Crowe, Jr.
Admiral, United States Navy;
Chairman, Joint Chiefs of Staff

2

I returned from my trip [to the Soviet Union] with basically the same view that I have had before I went, and that is I think that there's change afoot in the Soviet Union, but that we should move warily and carefully, exploiting opportunities as they present themselves, [and] that we should be very deliberate in our actions and take steps as the horizon clears . . . I do not question the genuineness or the sincerity of what they're about. Change is everywhere. You can hear it, you can smell it, you can see it. But the task they've taken on is immense, it's ambitious, it's risky. I think they have underestimated the task.

Broadcast interview/
"Meet the Press," NBC-TV, 7-2.

3

[On his recent visit to the Soviet Union and the reforms taking place there]: I grew up watching the Soviet Navy grow into a global role. I never,

in my wildest imagination, thought I would be aboard Soviet ships at sea [as he was during the visit] and have an opportunity to look at their exercises. When I went aboard the Soviet cruiser and they played *The Star-Spangled Banner,* I found that quite an amazing event. In my mind, it's very symbolic. Everywhere you go in the Soviet Union, you can smell change. You can feel it. You can hear it.

Interview/USA Today, 7-17:(A)9.

Jacques Delors
President,
European Commission

4

The European countries will insure their material prosperity and defend their identity and independence only if they someday have a common defense policy. But achieving that means waiting for the right time. For the moment, it is more a matter of convincing Europeans to adopt a common attitude, a shared analysis of things, made up of openness and vigilance regarding the East and [Soviet leader] Mikhail Gorbachev's initiatives. I see the future construction of Europe in a broader sense, as a dialectic between strengthened political-economic integration on the one hand and an opening up to other European countries on the other. We should open up not only our expanded market but also new forms of economic, scientific and cultural cooperation. We don't want to give up our plan of a European union, but we cannot forget that Europeans around us want to make it clear politically that they belong to the same historical vein that we do.

Interview/World Press Review,
September:28.

5

[On pro-democratic reforms taking place in Eastern Europe]: We're just coming out of the Cold War. The Cold War was intellectually convenient. It was easier to manage than the present period. There was a balance of terror. You could evaluate the relative strength of each side, you could take your precautions, and two precautions were better than one. Now we are in a diffi-

(JACQUES DELORS)

cult situation. We ask ourselves: Where will [Soviet leader Mikhail] Gorbachev go [with his reform program]? Will the Poles be able to improve their economy? Will the Hungarians destroy everything by a too rapid political evolution? And so on. In this context, the existence of a peaceful, prosperous [Western] European community will be an element of stability . . . The events of the East should force us to accelerate our social, political and economic integration. Europeans must become responsible for the other Europeans. It's not just for the Americans and Russians to decide, *ex cathedra*, what we're going to do in Europe. That's over.

Interview, Cambridge, Mass./
The Christian Science Monitor,
10-2:4.

Hans Magnus Enzensberger
West German author
and journalist

1

There is a sea change between Europe and America. It's something almost geological. It's not something you could stop by any measure. It's not a wish on the part of Europeans to get away from the alliance; I don't believe that at all. It's just a more normal relationship. This is a polycentric world. That's one of the facts of life you have to deal with and not hang onto a solution which was found, after all, in 1945.

Interview, Munich/
The New York Times, 9-2:11.

Marlin Fitzwater
Press Secretary to President
of the United States
George Bush

2

[On the forthcoming Solidarity-led non-Communist government in Poland]: We do encourage and support the process of pluralism, and it appears that that is the general direction that they are aimed. Certainly a non-Communist government would be a remarkable and history-making occurrence and, while we are generally suppor-

tive of the process, we're very reluctant to involve ourselves in a more direct fashion.

Kennebunkport, Maine, Aug. 17/
The Washington Post, 8-18:(A)28.

Joseph Fromm
United States chairman,
International Institute
for Strategic Studies

3

[British Prime Minister] Margaret Thatcher, an implacable foe of European integration and passionate English nationalist, is the least promising candidate for "president of Europe" [following 1992's European economic unification]. The best bet: not [current West German Chancellor] Helmut Kohl but a future Chancellor of West Germany, which will rank as the dominant power in a united Western Europe politically, economically and militarily.

USA Today,
7-14:(A)13.

John R. Galvin
General, United States Army;
Supreme Allied Commander/
Europe

4

I don't want to see us ever do away with our nuclear capability in Europe. My Number 1 mission is to deter war, not simply win one. For 500 years, every European generation had had to learn anew about war. Now, for four decades, we haven't had one here. I don't think it's a coincidence that this period has coincided with the nuclear age. The logic for nuclear weapons in Europe has always been two-fold. First, they have compensated for the conventional-force imbalance between the [NATO] alliance and the Soviet bloc. Second, and more important, they are a deterrent. They raise the level of uncertainty in the mind of a potential aggressor. He has to consider that the cost of war may be too high. It's the element of unpredictability of what might happen in a nuclear exchange that keeps war from happening. So, regardless of whether we can ever get conventional-force parity, I believe nuclear weapons have an indispensable peace-

(JOHN R. GALVIN)

keeping value irrespective of the conventional balance.

Interview/Time, 5-29:78.

1

If we look at the difference between the danger that we [NATO] faced as an alliance a few years ago, and the situation now, the military situation is roughly the same. The Soviets seem to have started some reductions, but they've given themselves two years to do it. But that would only be a 10 per cent reduction, leaving a Soviet and Warsaw Pact force that is still much larger than NATO. At the same time, there has grown into this equation an element of unpredictability, of potential instability. Definitely, if we were to have a loss of the current leadership in the Soviet Union, that would be a potentially very dangerous situation for the world.

Interview/USA Today, 10-2:(A)13.

Bronislaw Gemerek
Chief policy-maker of Solidarity
(independent Polish trade union)

2

[On Solidarity's sweeping success in just-held Polish national elections]: Solidarity has many times emphasized that it is a part of the opposition, and shall remain so. It is an opposition against the system of rule as it has existed to now. I would like to say that when the system of rule changes, when the heritage of the Stalinist system and the Communists' right to appoint leaders falls, room will be created for new political solutions. But this is not a matter for today or tomorrow ... In my personal view, I do not see the conditions existing for Solidarity and its citizens' committee to serve as a basis for forming a coalition government, a government with participation of Solidarity representatives. At the same time, Solidarity bears full responsibility for the fate and future of the country, and stands ready to support reform-oriented policies and the change of the system.

June 5/The New York Times,
6-6:(A)4.

Hans-Dietrich Genscher
Foreign Minister
of West Germany

3

An undivided Europe without the Iron Curtain, without the [Berlin] Wall and barbed wire, again appears attainable, and it will come ... Freedom, tolerance, dialogue, human rights and democracy must form the foundation of the common European home. It must be a home with open doors and windows in which everyone can arrange his apartment as he pleases, in which everybody can freely visit the others.

At Conference on the Human
Dimension of the Conference
on Security and Cooperation in
Europe, Paris, June 2/
Los Angeles Times, 6-3:(I)5.

4

[On the tide of East Germans fleeing their country for the West]: What has happened shows that we are in a historical period of change which cannot be reversed and will continue. I hope that the East German leadership realizes this and will not isolate itself by refusing to change. [Soviet leader Mikhail] Gorbachev is coming [to East Germany] and I hope he will convince East Germany that reform lies in its best interests, that reform means more, not less, stability.

Oct. 1/The New York Times,
10-2:(A)4.

5

[On calls by East German citizens for reunification of the two Germanys]: The word unity has been mentioned for the first time aloud yesterday [during pro-democracy demonstrations in Leipzig]. They didn't only say, "We are the people." They said, "We are one people," and that means we are one people together with the Germans in the Federal Republic of [West] Germany—and this is, after all, a reality. We are one nation, in spite of the fact that we have been separated from each other for decades.

Broadcast interview, Washington/
"Good Morning America,"
ABC-TV, 11-21.

Gennadi I. Gerasimov
Spokesman for
the Foreign Ministry
of the Soviet Union

1

[Some in the West] ask whether our policies will change overnight, as they might have sometime in the past. In the past, policies ran counter to the principles declared by the Soviet state, and so there was skepticism. In the future, all major foreign-policy decisions will be taken only after thorough discussion in the Supreme Soviet and, for the most important decisions, in the Congress of People's Deputies. That is the guarantee that our policies will not change overnight.

Moscow, May 30/
Los Angeles Times, 5-31:(I)10.

2

[On the Soviet approval of the pro-democracy reforms and increased independence of Poland and Hungary]: The Brezhnev doctrine is dead . . . You know the Frank Sinatra song, *My Way?* Hungary and Poland are doing it *their* way. We now have the Sinatra doctrine.

Time, 11-6:42.

3

[Criticizing talk in West Germany about German reunification in light of East Germany's recent pro-democracy reforms]: Bonn should take into account that any policies considering changes in borders would not be suitable to any government in Europe and would cause deep mistrust. A new regime has started on the East German side of the border, but the border does remain . . . [Likewise,] to convert East Germany into a neutral Austria is just hypothetical. Why should East Germany be considered an Austria when this is our firm ally? The NATO forces are dangerous, and to compensate we should count on the Warsaw Pact. The G.D.R. is our strategic ally.

Moscow, Nov. 10/
The Washington Post,
11-11:(A)23,25.

Manfred Gerlach
Leader, Liberal Democratic Party
of East Germany

4

Despite the problems, socialism has also brought many achievements to this country. We have social security, no unemployment, low inflation—this is the result of socialist development. In the entire world, there are no better-fed refugees [than the large number of East Germans who have recently fled to the West]. They arrive [in the West] in their own cars. And once the stagnation and encrustation [of the East German government and economy] have been dealt with, I don't know why people would reject socialism here.

Newsweek, 11-20:32.

Felipe Gonzalez
Prime Minister of Spain

5

We [in Spain] made the economic crisis one of our priorities. False ideological debates between progressive and conservative attitudes have slowed down many governments. Demagogic attitudes have proved incapable of improving the economic situation. They were not a part of this Administration. As early as the campaign of 1982, I had the courage to announce that before the International Monetary Fund dictated what to do with Spain's economy, we would do it ourselves. That is what we did, and the effort was worth it because the indicators began to change in 1985. It is true that the international economic climate has improved, but if this had not coincided with an improvement at home, it would not have helped us. In fact, since the middle of 1985, jobs have been created at a rate of 1,000 a day, the same rate at which we were once losing them.

Interview/World Press Review,
March:25.

6

Social democracy will continue to gain ground. It is on the move now in Germany and in Sweden. In France, the socialists have returned to their winning ways. In Greece, Prime Minister Andreas Papandreou has ruled through two par-

(FELIPE GONZALEZ)

liaments. In Italy, the Socialist Party is drawing even with the Communists for the first time. But I do not believe that when a socialist party wins an election this is a groundswell for socialism—or that when a conservative party wins [it is one for conservatism], either.

Interview/World Press Review,
March:25.

1

[On Spanish-U.S. relations]: They are much better today than they have been for a long time. When we had a dictatorship, our relations with the U.S. were, shall we say, "special." It could not have been particularly agreeable for the U.S. to deal with an authoritarian regime, but they considered it necessary from a geostrategic viewpoint. We have gone through a difficult period when we had to negotiate a new agreement [with the U.S.] on a different footing. The former regime [of dictator Francisco Franco] posed no problem for the U.S., but that comfortable relationship was lost. Now we have one of mutual acceptance and respect . . . I used to have little faith in the U.S., and this was still true when I came into office. I held the Americans responsible for the duration of the Franco dictatorship. But I changed as I came to know the U.S. a little more.

Interview, Madrid/Time, 10-23:54.

Mikhail S. Gorbachev
General Secretary,
Communist Party
of the Soviet Union;
President of the Soviet Union

2

If you listen to Western radio talk—and they are not jammed now—they say that the longest we can give Gorbachev [to remain in office] is a year, as if that were the issue. They have been trying to pin everything on one personality. Of course, personnel is important. We need personnel, but that is not the issue. The issue is, the entire country has adopted the policy of reforms [which Gorbachev launched], and the people will

not allow it all to be thrown to the wind. We have this singular chance, and it will not be missed.

To industrial workers, Feb. 14/
The Washington Post, 2-17:(A)30.

3

We [Soviets] still lag behind the developed countries, both large and small, in the productivity of labor in agriculture, in the yield of our harvests, in livestock productivity and in the diversity and quality of food products. The gap, rather than narrowing, is growing wider. The food shortages create social tension, and they are generating not just criticism but actual discontent. [The] food problem [is now] our society's biggest wound.

Before Soviet Communist Party
Central Committee, Moscow,
March 15/
Los Angeles Times, 3-16:(I)14.

4

[Saying some in the Communist Party are finding his reform programs difficult to handle and wish for a return to hard-line, more dictatorial rule]: Some of our Party committees have found themselves in the position of a military commander whose regiment or division has launched an offensive while he himself is still stuck in his trench, sliding back into it and unable to find any bit of support to get out. And so he sits in the trench while it is time to catch up with the offensive.

Before Soviet Communist Party
Central Committee, Moscow,
April 25/
Los Angeles Times, 4-27:(I)1.

5

[On criticism from within the Soviet Communist Party of his *perestroika* (reform) and *glasnost* (openness) programs]: Some have already gone so far as to say that, in a manner of speaking, both democracy and *glasnost* are very nearly a disaster. And the fact that [the public has] begun to act, that they no longer wish to remain silent and insists on their demands, is per-

(MIKHAIL S. GORBACHEV)

ceived as a defect of *perestroika*. I for one, comrades, see this as a success of *perestroika*.

Before Soviet Communist Party
Central Committee, Moscow,
April 25/
The New York Times, 4-27:(A)1.

1

As a Communist, I categorically reject hints that I am trying to concentrate power in my own hands. This is alien to me, to my views, to my outlook and my character. I, as General Secretary [of the Party] and President [of the nation], have no other policy than the restructuring of society, and promoting democratization and openness. In this I see the point of my life and my work.

Before Congress of People's
Deputies, Moscow, June 9/
Los Angeles Times, 6-10:(I)4.

2

There is an understanding both in the East and the West of the role of the United States in Europe. I can't imagine a realistic policy of the Soviet leadership that would have the objective of pushing the United States out of Europe, of hampering the interests of the United States in Europe.

News conference,
Bonn, West Germany, June 15/
Los Angeles Times, 6-16:(I)6.

3

[On the Berlin Wall]: The wall was raised in a concrete situation and was not dictated only by evil intentions. [East Germany] decided this as its sovereign right, and the wall can disappear when those conditions that created it fall away. I don't see a major problem here.

News conference,
Bonn, West Germany, June 15/
The New York Times, 6-16:(A)1.

4

Europeans can meet the challenge of the coming century only by pooling their efforts. We are convinced that what they need is one Europe, peaceful and democratic—a Europe that maintains all its diversity and common humanistic ideas, a prosperous Europe that extends its hand to the rest of the world, a Europe that confidently advances into the future. It is in such a Europe that we visualize our own future . . . I strongly believe that it is high time that Europeans brought their policies and their conduct in line with a new rationality—not to prepare for war, not to intimidate one another, not to compete in improving weapons . . . but rather to learn to make peace together, and together to lay a solid basis for it.

Before Council of Europe,
Strasbourg, France,
July 6/
Los Angeles Times,
7-8:(I)14.

5

Perestroika [reform in the Soviet Union] is changing our country, advancing it to new horizons. That process will continue, extend and transform Soviet society in all dimensions—economic, social, political and spiritual, in all domestic affairs and human relations . . . As a result, you and your governments [in the West], your parliaments and your peoples will soon be dealing with a totally different socialist nation than has been the case before. And this will have, and cannot but have, a favorable impact on developments through the entire world.

Before Council of Europe,
Strasbourg, France,
July 6/
Los Angeles Times,
7-8:(I)14.

6

It is important that our society understands that intolerance and force are not methods for solving problems. One can, on the contrary, only move away from the solution of a problem and complicate it. In the conditions of a democratic state under the rule of law that we are striving for, there cannot and must not be any method of political action except reliance on law and the

WHAT THEY SAID IN 1989

(MIKHAIL S. GORBACHEV)

desire to resolve any problems first of all through consensus.

Before Supreme Soviet, Moscow,
Sept. 25/
Los Angeles Times, 9-26:(I)4.

1

[Saying the West should not gloat over democratic reforms now taking place in Eastern Europe]: It is useless to shout about victory in the Cold War, about the collapse of this or that social system. Everything should be analyzed realistically and interests should be balanced. When accusations [by the West about the Soviets] "exporting revolution" are replaced by calls [by the West] for "exporting capitalism," this is a dangerous product of the old thinking.

At meeting with French Foreign
Minister, Moscow, Nov. 14/
The New York Times, 11-15:(A)1.

2

[Saying the Soviet Union is not ready for private property]: I do not think the working class will support those authors who want to start making our society capitalist. I know the opinions and moods of the workers; I myself am from that environment. And I cannot help myself; no matter what you do with me, I am not going to forsake this position. Perhaps later, as our society develops a little bit further and our economy is reformed, we will develop a new type of economy, perhaps there will appear forms that will in some way resemble small-scale private property. I don't exclude this possibility. But to make it a program—I would not do this. I've said it before and I'm telling you now.

At conference with Soviet students,
Nov. 15/
The New York Times, 11-17:(A)9.

3

[On the current pro-democracy reforms in Eastern Europe, including a lessening of influence of the various Communist Parties]: In

some socialist countries the situation has been unconventional. Fraternal parties are no longer ruling in Poland and Hungary. Our friends in the [East] German Democratic Republic and Czechoslovakia have largely lost their positions. New political forces have emerged on the arena. They include both those who support the socialist idea and those who seek other ways of social development . . . The Soviet Union is building its relations with East European countries—whether they have been carrying out transformations for quite some time, or have only embarked on the road, or are yet to do it—on a single position of respect for sovereignty, noninterference and recognition of freedom of choice. We proceed from the fact that any nation has the right to decide its fate itself, including the choice of a system, ways, the pace and methods of its development.

Before Soviet Communist Party
Central Committee, Moscow,
Dec. 9/
The New York Times, 12-12:(A)10.

4

In the final analysis, we envision Europe as a commonwealth of sovereign democratic states with a high level of equitable interdependence and easily accessible borders open to the exchange of products, technologies and ideas and wide-ranging contacts among people . . . Respect for the people's national, state, spiritual and cultural identity is an indispensable condition for a steady international environment that Europe and the world now need to cross the historic watershed and attain a new period of peace.

Speech, Rome/Time, 12-11:37.

5

[Criticizing the Lithuanian Communist Party's decision to break away from the national Party]: The decisions of the Lithuanian 20th congress with its organizational and charter positions are illegal . . . The delegates to this congress were given a mandate for *perestroika* [reform in the Soviet Union], not a split of the Party . . . Therefore, they are illegitimate . . . A number of comrades believe the decisions of this congress

(MIKHAIL S. GORBACHEV)

should be recognized as a *fait accompli* by allowing the events in the republic to take their own course, by limiting our reaction to political assessment. More than that, they do not even see anything dramatic in these developments, thinking that the logic of democratization of the Soviet federation sooner or later will bring us similar steps in other republics as well . . . [But] we have to clearly draw up limits beyond which one cannot go because going beyond them means, in advance, the planned breakup of efforts to build a federation, and the destruction of *perestroika* in its entirety. One such limitation is the impossibility of rejecting the single structure of the Communist Party. Otherwise, our Party would turn into an amorphous federalist club consisting of separate independent party groups. Isn't it clear that if we cross this line we will deliberately be heading toward the disintegration of the Soviet Union and that this would be a historic blind alley for all the peoples of the Soviet Union?

Before Soviet Communist Party
Central Committee, Moscow,
Dec. 25/
The New York Times, 12-27:(A)10.

Alexander S. Grossman
Member, editorial board,
"Issues of History" magazine
(Soviet Union)

1

[For the Soviet people,] perhaps the most serious consequence of [World War II] was disillusionment over unrealized expectations after it was over. We are talking about a Soviet people who expected that after destroying fascism—triumph—a better life would be instituted inside the country, and we would maintain good relations with the great powers who were our allies during the war. But life proved to be just as demanding and difficult as the Cold War settled in. And owing to this Cold War, a difficult life inside the country was justified by citing the need to maintain our defenses. So the hopes which people nourished in the post-war period failed to materialize.

Los Angeles Times, 8-29:(I)8.

Gregor Gysi
First Secretary, Communist Party
of East Germany

2

[Saying that, in view of the pro-democracy reforms currently under way in his country, the U.S. should help to keep East Germany from being reunited with West Germany]: I have never been in America in my life, but I think it is a country that should not give up its responsibility for Europe. If the continued independence of the German Democratic Republic [East Germany] is in the interests of stability in Europe, then you should think about whether you want to leave help for the G.D.R. up to a single neighbor country [West Germany], and thereby create dependency, or whether it wouldn't be better to share the responsibility, to prevent the re-emergence of Greater Germany.

Interview, East Berlin, Dec. 14/
The New York Times, 12-15:(A)1.

Arthur A. Hartman
Former United States Ambassador
to the Soviet Union

3

My greatest worry is about Eastern Europe. If there is going to be a durable peace in the world, the Soviet Union has got to clearly change its attitude and let these countries choose their own system of government.

The Christian Science Monitor,
1-10:3.

Pierre Hasnner
Scholar, French Institute of
Political Science

4

[French President Francois] Mitterrand so far has seemed more interested in not being outdistanced by the Germans than in formulating a clear policy toward the East. His cardinal sin is having a rhetoric which celebrates human rights and a diplomacy which, because it is inspired by *Realpolitik*, remains timid toward tyrannical regimes.

The Christian Science Monitor,
1-18:4.

Vaclav Havel
Czechoslovak dissident leader

1

[On the pro-democracy movement in his coun-try]: One week ago, a people's movement began in Prague. For seven days, Prague and the entire republic have been living through great drama. After 40 years of totalitarian rule that manipu-lated them, citizens have started to think and act freely. On behalf of [his organization] the Civic Forum, I can announce that what we have been calling for has happened: Dialogue has begun between the power [the state] and the people . . . We know what we want—truth, humanity and freedom. From now on, we are all participating in the management of this country and we are responsible for its fate.

Speech at rally, Prague, Nov. 26/
The New York Times, 11-27:(A)6.

Francois Heisbourg
Director, International
Institute for Strategic Studies,
London

2

There's no question about it. If NATO does not sketch out a strategy for the future, it will be-come an increasingly irrelevant body—withering at best and, at worst, a deadening encumbrance.

Los Angeles Times, 4-3:(I)7.

3

If Germany moves toward unity in a self-centered, neo-nationalist sense, that would be disastrous. Conversely, it's quite different if it's Germany acting as part of the EC, acting in consultation with the other 11 members. The change can be managed in a peaceful and benign fashion if the rapprochement is handled as a collective European issue.

Newsweek, 10-26:52.

Ed A. Hewitt
Editor, "Soviet Economy"
(U.S.-based journal)

4

[On recent Soviet reforms]: It's possible that the biggest advance the Soviets have made so far

in the economic field has been their ability to set aside ideology. Some of them still can't use words like "private property" without stuttering, but the progression is amazing.

The Washington Post, 10-5:(A)50.

Erich Honecker
First Secretary, Communist Party
of East Germany

5

We are committed to a lesson of history: No more war will emanate from German soil. We seek good neighborly relations between the Ger-manys [East and West]. But to pursue other goals would be fireside dreams. The reality is the exis-tence of two independent, different German states, with two different orders of society, be-longing to different alliances.

Interview/Newsweek, 6-19:45.

Zdenek Horeni
Editor, "Rude Pravo"
(Czechoslovakia)

6

We are in a period in which more important roles are being taken by small and medium-sized nations. You see the special role of France and West Germany, and countries in our part of Europe. Europe in this sense is truly new, and it is demonstrating that it can be new without being influenced by the different political systems. Recently, we had a meeting in Prague of seven ministers from seven neighboring states. That is something unique. The issue was the environ-ment. It will not mean anything to citizens of Los Angeles, but to people in this region, it sounds like music of the future.

Interview, Prague/
Los Angeles Times, 6-10:(I)18.

Milos Jakes
First Secretary, Communist Party
of Czechoslovakia

7

[On the reform movements in several Eastern European countries]: [Restructuring] certainly does not mean edging away from the ideals of

(MILOS JAKES)

socialism ... We keep a close eye on those developments [in Hungary and Poland], which in many respects give us concern, and draw the necessary lessons—for example, that the [Communist] Party as the leading force in society must not lose control over the situation.

Interview/Newsweek, 10-16:46.

1

[On the pro-democracy demonstrations in his country, following pro-democracy reforms elsewhere in Eastern Europe]: For a week, our capital [Prague] lives in a feverish atmosphere accompanied by large demonstrations. The tension is gradually spreading to other places in the republic. We must openly say that our country is at a fateful crossroads. We have underestimated completely the processes taking place in Poland, Hungary and especially recently in East Germany, and their effect and influence on our society.

Speech, Prague, Nov. 24/
The New York Times, 11-25:6.

Wojciech Jaruzelski
First Secretary, Communist Party
of Poland

2

Today we will draw directions of democracy which will include some pluralistic solutions ... The priority goal is radical and irrevocable reconstruction of social life so that ... there is a place in it for all citizens who recognize the supreme interests of our country and the unchangeable shape of its essential framework.

Before Polish Communist Party
Central Committee, Warsaw,
Jan. 16/
Los Angeles Times, 1-17:(I)9.

3

The [Polish] economic situation should not for a moment escape our attention and concern. An atmosphere of militant disputes and unrestrained claims must give way to attitudes of

co-government, co-management and co-responsibility for the destiny and development of Poland's prospects.

Before Polish Communist Party
Central Committee, Warsaw,
Jan. 16/
The New York Times, 1-19:(A)4.

Wojciech Jaruzelski
Prime Minister of Poland

4

[Saying he will not run for the newly created office of Polish President]: I know well that public opinion associates me more often with martial law and less often with the line of reforms ... I must take into consideration social reality ... When there is an obstacle to reconciliation, to uniting social forces, there is only one possible solution—even if that obstacle is Wojciech Jaruzelski.

To Polish Communist Party
leaders, Warsaw, June 30/
Los Angeles Times, 7-1:(I)1.

Karl Kaiser
Director, (West) German
Council on Foreign Relations

5

[On the possibility of reunification of East and West Germany]: You [in the U.S.] have taken our reunification debate far more seriously than we have. Inevitably, Germany is shifted into a new position with reform in East Europe and the end of the Cold War. But the thought that the future of Germany's economy lies in the East makes the German businessman smile. Germany's choice between East and West was made 40 years ago.

The Washington Post, 7-27:(A)26.

David Kemme
Chief economist, Institute for
East-West Studies, New York

6

[On economic reform in Eastern Europe]: The biggest issue is egalitarian income distribution. Only Poland and Hungary have had experience

(DAVID KEMME)

with haves and have-nots . . . A basic issue in the whole reform process in Eastern Europe is giving up the notion of equity for all. The Poles and the Hungarians have gone further in this than the others. They are trying to convince themselves that there is some merit—some benefit to society—in the notion of unequal distribution of income, or just inequality.

The New York Times, 12-11:(C)1,6.

George F. Kennan
Former United States Ambassador
to the Soviet Union

1

[On the possibility of German reunification in light of current pro-democracy reforms in East Germany]: Russia would never assent to a united Germany with forces such as those now existing, which would make Germany the strongest military power on the continent. People would ask, "What did we fight the [Second World] war for?" I doubt whether even the other Western European powers would accept it.

The Washington Post, 11-30:(A)56.

Jeane J. Kirkpatrick
Former United States
Ambassador/Permanent
Representative to the
United Nations

2

[On the effect of pro-democracy reforms in Eastern Europe on NATO and the Warsaw Pact]: NATO and the Warsaw Pact are the military expression of the division of Europe. NATO reflects a concern on the part of Western European nations and the United States about a possible Soviet expansion into Western Europe. If the Soviet Union is non-expansive, then there is no need for NATO or for the Warsaw Pact forces. However, the opening of the German border doesn't really deal with the question of the necessity of NATO and a Warsaw Pact because the question is bigger than that. There were open borders when Adolf Hitler was governing Germany. And it would have been nice to have some

forces that might have contained him . . . Our NATO allies are going to be concerned about the possibility of any negotiation that leads to a withdrawal, not only of foreign troops from the soil of Germany, but also from the withdrawal of the United States from Europe. Let's be clear that the Soviet Union is not going to withdraw from Europe. And our allies are not going to want to be left with the Soviet Union the only strong power in the area.

Interview/USA Today, 11-13:(A)11.

Henry A. Kissinger
Former Secretary of State
of the United States

3

In [Soviet leader Mikhail] Gorbachev's *perestroika* [reform program] and in all the Soviet public statements—nobody pays much attention to this in [the U.S.]—they keep talking about the European "house" that goes from the Urals to the Atlantic . . . Now, a Europe from Moscow to the Atlantic will lead to one of two things: either the Soviet Union will be the permanent drain on its resources if its economy doesn't improve, or the Soviet Union will become so strong that all of Europe will become Finlandized, and America will be gradually separated from Europe . . . And once this gets established in people's minds that Moscow is part of Europe but Washington is not, the '90s could get very uncomfortable.

Interview/
The Christian Science Monitor,
1-6:19.

4

It must be in the Soviet interest not to be the permanent policeman of Eastern Europe, thereby jeopardizing a relaxation with the West. We have to find a way to give the Soviets assurances of security within their 1941 borders, and convince them that it is in their interest to get out of physical control of Eastern Europe—which, however, can be turned into a zone to make military attack against them impossible. We need a concept for Germany, for the evolution of Eastern Europe and for defense in a new political

(HENRY A. KISSINGER)

environment. We've gotten ourselves obsessed in the West. We were so militarized in our thinking that we're now militarized in our diplomacy—on both sides. And we have to get away from that.

Interview/Newsweek, 10-16:45.

1

[On the East German government's recent granting of permission for its citizens to travel and emigrate to the West]: If the border [between East and West Germany] is open, there are only two possibilities. Either economic conditions will be equalized on both sides of the border, or most of the East German population will move to West Germany. Why should they stay in East Germany at a standard of living less than half of the Federal Republic [West Germany]? And why should the Federal Republic subsidize a state [East Germany] that the vast majority of the German people do not want?

*Before Philadelphia World Affairs
Council, Nov. 14/
The New York Times, 11-16:(A)9.*

Tommy T. B. Koh
*Singaporean Ambassador
to the United States*

2

It's clear that the reduction of the Soviet threat to Western Europe is beginning to pose challenges to the cohesiveness of the Atlantic Alliance. The glue that has cemented NATO for 40 years is the collective perception of the Soviet threat and, as that diminishes, some of the inherent differences between member states of NATO are coming to the fore.

Symposium/Newsweek, 5-15:29.

Helmut Kohl
Chancellor of West Germany

3

[On bringing down barriers between East and West Germany]: Time is working for us. [East German leader Erich] Honecker can dig himself in; he can refuse to allow in magazines from the

West, and now magazines from Moscow, but time will march on over his head. The Germans are entirely normal people . . . What do they want? They want to live in peace. They want to live in freedom. They want social justice. They want a good livelihood. They want happiness in life. They want to be glad; they don't want to walk around stressed, confronted from morning to evening with the burden of history. There are, however, people who want to persuade us that we should not be allowed to do this.

*Interview, Bonn, West Germany/
World Press Review, May:31.*

4

In recent weeks much has been said and written about German-American relations. It has been suggested that the post-war era has finally come to an end and that the German-American, indeed the European-American relationship, is undergoing a fundamental change. Changes do, of course, take place in relations between nations, [and] the present generation did not experience the post-war era [and] take much of what has been achieved for granted. [But firm bonds cement relations] even if we disagree on this or that political issue, whether now or in the future.

*At dinner for visiting
U.S. President Bush,
Bonn-Bad Godesberg, West Germany,
May 30/
The New York Times, 5-31:(A)6.*

5

[On the differences voiced between Britain and West Germany during the recent NATO summit conference]: [British Prime Minister] Margaret Thatcher stood up for her interests, in her temperamental way. We have different temperaments. She is a woman and I'm not.

U.S. News & World Report, 6-12:15.

6

[On German guilt about World War II]: Hitler had wanted, planned and unleashed the war. There was not and cannot be any doubt about

WHAT THEY SAID IN 1989

(HELMUT KOHL)

that. [But] we should beware of making hasty judgments from today's vantage point. Who among us can say with a good conscience that, confronted with such evil, he would have summoned the strength to be a martyr?

Before West German Parliament,
Bonn, Sept. 1/
The New York Times, 9-2:1.

1

It is clear for us [Germans] that developments in Germany, and in the other part of Germany [East Germany], make it urgently necessary that we push the process of European unity further forward. German problems can only be solved under a European roof. We are not wanderers between the worlds. Our place is in the Western community of values.

News conference, Bonn, Nov. 3/
Los Angeles Times, 11-4:(A)9.

2

[On the possibility of the reunification of Germany in the wake of the current mass exodus of East Germans to the West]: Let us avoid the temptation to assume that a solution to the German question can be arranged in advance with a script and a calendar. History doesn't follow a schedule. The precondition for reunification in freedom is the free exercise of the right of self-determination by all Germans. I am certain that if they get the chance, they will choose freedom and unity . . . We have less reason than ever to be resigned to the long-term division of Germany into two states. [But] the Federal Republic of [West] Germany will remain irrevocably anchored in a strong and lasting relationship with the Atlantic Alliance and in the community of values of the free peoples of the West.

Before West German Parliament,
Bonn, Nov. 8/
The New York Times, 11-9:(A)1.

3

[On the possibility of German reunification in light of pro-democracy reforms taking place in

East Germany]: A policy based on the division of nations is anti-historical and hence, implausible and unjust. But it would also be anti-historical and implausible to assert that it is a matter for the Germans alone whether and how they freely determine their fate. The truth is that we Germans, as a people living in the heart of Europe, know today that this question, and our answer to it, is not something toward which our neighbors in East and West are indifferent.

At Catholic University,
Lublin, Poland, Nov. 13/
The Washington Post, 11-14:(A)35.

4

[Saying his country would give economic aid to East Germany if that country continues its pro-democratic reforms and changes its economy]: We don't want to force our opinions on anyone, but nobody can deny that socialism has shown itself to be a failure. I say again—economic aid will be in vain unless there is an irreversible reform of the [East German] economic system, an end to a bureaucratically planned economy, and the introduction of a market economy.

Before West German Parliament,
Bonn, Nov. 16/
Los Angeles Times, 11-17:(A)15.

5

[On relations between East and West Germany in light of recent pro-democracy reforms in the East]: The nearness and the special character of the relations between both German states require an increasingly tighter network of agreements in all sectors and at all levels. This cooperation will also increasingly require common institutions. Existing common commissions can assume new tasks; further commissions can be created. I am thinking especially of the economy, transport, environmental protection, science and technology, health and culture. It is self-evident that Berlin will be fully included in this cooperation. I urge all social groups and institutions to participate in the formation of such a community. We are also prepared to take a further decisive step, namely, to develop con-

(HELMUT KOHL)

federative structures between the two states in Germany in order to create a federation. A legitimate democratic government in East Germany is a prerequisite.

Speech, Bonn, Nov. 28/
The New York Times, 11-29:(A)11.

Vitaly Korotich
Editor, "Ogonyok"
(Soviet Union)

1

[On Soviet leader Mikhail Gorbachev's program of *perestroika,* reform in the Soviet Union]: If *perestroika* fails, it will be a catastrophe. My prediction is only positive. I do not think there is any alternative, and we have to do everything for it to win. The entire history of the Soviet Union and of mankind proves that there is no alternative to democracy. We have to live in a democracy; that is the only decent life . . . [Gorbachev's political fate] depends mostly on the economic results of reform. But the movement that he has launched will prevail in any case. The democratic process can be stopped only temporarily, not forever. I think the history of the 20th century proves that.

Interview/World Press Review,
May:24.

Egon Krenz
First Secretary, Communist Party
of East Germany

2

[On opposition movements in East Germany]: Let's get rid of this idea of opposition. Let's say that there are citizens in the German Democratic Republic who have ideas about how we can go forward in this country. Every idea is needed and no one is excluded from an exchange of ideas, if they stand by the East German Constitution.

To reporters/
The Christian Science Monitor,
10-27:3.

3

Our society already has enough democratic forums in which different interests from various parts of the population can express themselves . . . Socialism is not negotiable.

Broadcast address to the nation,
East Berlin/Time, 10-30:61.

4

[On pro-democracy demonstrations in East Germany]: Many people are out on the streets to show that they want a better socialism and the renovation of society. I consider this to be a very good sign, an indication that we are at a turning point in the life of the German Democratic Republic . . . We will take up every idea that is expressed. I cannot, of course, promise that we will solve all the problems, but we should not just be making promises, but getting down to work.

News conference, Moscow,
Nov. 1/
Los Angeles Times, 11-2:(A)18.

5

[The Berlin Wall is a historically necessary] border between two social systems, a border between two military blocs . . . a kind of protective shield. [As far as any idea of tearing down the wall is concerned,] we should not live in a world of dreams.

News conference, Moscow, Nov. 1/
The Washington Post, 11-2:(A)44.

6

[Saying there will be reforms in his country, in the wake of mass demonstrations and the exodus of great numbers of East Germans to the West]: That there is some impatience in the country is understandable and can even serve the cause. But there is also a danger: It is not possible to correct in a few days or even a few weeks developments that have piled up over the years to a cluster of serious contradictions and symptoms of crisis . . . We want full sovereignty for the people of the German Democratic Republic. Our aim is to reform the political system. At its center is the mature citizen, his democratic participation and his free self-expression.

Broadcast address to the nation,
East Berlin, Nov. 3/
The New York Times, 11-4:(A)5.

(EGON KRENZ)

1

[On the possibility of German reunification in light of pro-democracy reforms taking place in East Germany and elsewhere in Eastern Europe]: Today we have a unique opportunity to contribute to the construction of the "European home." This seems to me a more constructive approach than to give priority to the unity of Germany. It is obvious that the citizens of the Federal Republic [West Germany] have no interest in joining a socialist society, while people in this country do not want to change their socialist society into a capitalist one. Besides, the existence of two German states is a stabilizing factor for European security. To be perfectly frank, despite differences in views, I know of no serious politician, either in the East or the West, who is interested in the unification of the two states.

Interview, East Berlin/
Time, 12-11:47.

Alman Kulcsar
Minister of Justice of Hungary

2

[On the Soviet Union's attitude toward possible democratic changes in Hungary]: The Soviet Union is not in a position to cause too many problems here. In September, I was invited to speak to the Soviet Justice Minister and made it clear to him what type of legislation we were preparing. He was interested in our ideas. It's not the same situation as some years ago, when they gave orders. Put yourself in their position. They want to see how political reform works in a small country, what problems we face.

Interview, Budapest/
The Christian Science Monitor,
6-30:4.

Jacek Kuron
Polish opposition activist;
Candidate for the Polish Senate

3

[On whether the opposition should be mounting a more aggressive campaign against the ruling Communist Party in Poland]: I don't think that is

a good idea. I have studied revolutions, and I don't think that is what we need here. Right now we have people standing in line for meat; but if we have a revolution, there will be no meat at all. What we want is an evolutionary rebuilding of the system with the cooperation of the Communists, because only the Communists can guarantee peaceful change. Perhaps we will be proved wrong, but there is no other way but to try.

Campaigning for the Senate, Warsaw/
Los Angeles Times, 5-29:(I)12.

Marju Lauristen
Member, Congress of People's
Deputies of the Soviet
Union; Leader, Estonian
independence movement

4

[On Estonia's quest for independence from the Soviet Union]: During this past year we have come even closer to the ideals that our people have carried in their hearts for 50 years. Why this shift? Why are we talking more openly about these things? Because all of us want to have freedom, and freedom without independence is impossible.

The New York Times, 8-24:(A)10.

Nigel Lawson
Former Chancellor of the Exchequer
of the United Kingdom

5

[Saying Britain should join the European Monetary System's exchange-rate mechanism]: Britain's destiny lies in Europe . . . I have little doubt that we will not be able to exert [maximum British] influence [in the European Community] as long as we remain largely outside the EMS . . . For economic and political reasons alike, it's important that we seek the earliest practical time to join, rather than the latest for which a tolerable case can be made.

Before House of Commons,
London, Oct. 31/
The New York Times, 11-1:(C)7.

6

[Criticizing British Prime Minister Margaret Thatcher for assuming too much power over her

(NIGEL LAWSON)

Cabinet ministers]: For our system of Cabinet government to work effectively, the Prime Minister of the day must appoint ministers that he or she trusts, and then leave them to carry out policy. When differences of view emerge, as they are bound to do from time to time, they should be resolved privately and, wherever appropriate, collectively.

Before House of Commons,
London, Oct. 31/
The Christian Science Monitor,
11-6:3.

Christopher Layne
Lawyer; Authority on
international relations

1

Wars are not caused by nations having armies. Wars are caused by political conflicts that create crises that spin out of control. Now, the Soviets are not going to wake up one morning and say, "Let's invade Europe today." That's just not going to happen. But their being in Eastern Europe prevents the natural political evolution of the Eastern European countries. Thus political tensions within those countries fester—they have no safety valve. Sooner or later, under these conditions, an explosion will happen; popular unrest will break out. What will the Soviets do then? Will they sit back and watch their empire disintegrate, or will they be tempted to launch a war against the West to save the empire?

Interview/
The Atlantic Monthly, June:51.

Sol M. Linowitz
Lawyer; Former
American diplomat

2

[Saying the U.S. should do more in support of Eastern European countries that are reforming in favor of democracy]: We need to applaud early, clearly and emphatically every sign of movement toward democracy. Countries that choose to follow our path have the right to expect something more than words, and they aren't getting it.

Even if we step up aid to Poland now, the world sees us as giving in, kicking and screaming, and we lose all credit for aligning ourselves with the forces of freedom.

The New York Times, 10-2:(A)14.

Gerald Livingston
Director, American Institute for
Contemporary German Studies,
Johns Hopkins University

3

[On the mass exodus of citizens from East Germany to the West]: Those of us who claim to be experts have to 'fess up in this case because all of us were surprised. East Germany has been, until a few months ago, the most stable Communist country in Eastern Europe. All of us so-called experts deduced all sorts of reasons why that was so: the deep roots of Communism in pre-war Germany, which were centered in what is today the German Democratic Republic [East Germany]; the high standard of living; the fact that East Germans have not really known any democracy since 1933—they passed from Hitler's dictatorship right into the Communist dictatorship. So there were all kinds of reasons that looked, on the surface, to give Communism a firmer base in East Germany than elsewhere. But we really have learned how wrong we were . . . We did, of course, recognize there was this, what you might call, "existential threat." That was the fact that right next door to East Germany was this rich, free and successful capitalist West Germany. I guess we underestimated the drawing power that West Germany had for East Germans.

Interview/
USA Today, 11-7:(A)11.

Simon Lunn
Analyst; North Atlantic
Treaty Organization

4

Politically, there is a consensus that for deterrence to work, there must be some option below strategic weapons and there must be some European sharing of risks. We Europeans must ask ourselves what we want for reassurance in the era of [Soviet leader Mikhail] Gorbachev.

WHAT THEY SAID IN 1989

(SIMON LUNN)

And the Americans must ask what they require from the Europeans in terms of risk-sharing.

The New York Times,
5-24:(A)4.

Michael Mandelbaum
Authority on Eastern Europe,
Council on Foreign Relations

1

[On new Polish Prime Minister Tadeusz Mazowiecki, Poland's first non-Communist leader in over 40 years]: As Prime Minister, Tadeusz Mazowiecki is going to have two problems: First, he is going to have to stab his adversaries and then he is going to have to stab his supporters. To rationalize the Polish economy, he is going to have to abolish the parasitic class of Communist officials who sop up so many resources and man key economic positions for which they are not qualified. These people are not going to go quietly. At the same time, he is going to have to shut down inefficient, overmanned state enterprises, such as the Gdansk shipyards, where Solidarity [the trade union backing Mazowiecki] was born, or some mines and steel mills, and that is going to hurt his core constituency.

The New York Times,
8-25:(A)4.

2

[On recent changes in Eastern Europe away from Communism, such as the new non-Communist government in Poland]: The real test is Germany. If you have a Polandization of East Germany, you are not only talking about a change of regimes, you are talking about the very existence of the state. The end of Communism in East Germany immediately raises the prospect of German reunification. And since East Germany is both at the center of Europe and the strategic anchor of the Warsaw Pact, these changes would be extremely difficult, perhaps impossible, for Moscow to accept.

The New York Times,
9-28:(A)6.

Ante Markovic
Prime Minister of Yugoslavia

3

Our reality [in Yugoslavia] is very complex. We are one country with two alphabets, three religions, four languages, five nationalities, six republics and 23 million incorrigible individualists.

Interview, Belgrade/
The New York Times, 10-9:(A)5.

Tadeusz Mazowiecki
Prime Minister-designate
of Poland

4

[On the forthcoming government he will most likely lead, the first non-Communist government in Poland in more than 40 years]: It won't be easy. I think the most difficult task will be to make people think that it [life in Poland] can be better—even though it cannot be better immediately—and make them believe that their work is not wasted . . . I am afraid of many things. But if I were only afraid, I would be a total pessimist. Somebody has to try it. I am a believer and I believe providence cares for us.

Warsaw, Aug. 18/
Los Angeles Times, 8-20:(I)8.

5

[On the forthcoming government he will most likely lead, the first non-Communist government in Poland in more than 40 years]: We must believe that this nation, a wonderful nation, can reach the stage where life will be better in Poland, so that no one lacks anything in Poland, that no one leaves it. Today, when we open this historic chapter, we must reject a feeling of hopelessness and helplessness. It must be rejected because no one can do anything without believing that it can be done.

Speech, Gdansk, Poland, Aug. 20/
The New York Times, 8-21:(A)1.

Tadeusz Mazowiecki
Prime Minister of Poland

6

[On his new non-Communist government]: The transformation now taking place would not

(TADEUSZ MAZOWIECKI)

have been possible if it were not for the support of Communist Party members. They deserve credit for initiating the roundtable talks last year. These reform-minded Party members paid a high price for this in last June's Parliamentary elections. It so happens that sometimes in politics and history, the ones who pay are not the ones who are at fault. I told President Wojciech Jaruzelski last week that the success of my government will depend on his help. I don't think Communism will disappear, but I believe it will undergo a transformation.

Interview, Warsaw/Time, 9-11:35.

1

The average standard of living [in Poland] is lower today than it was 10 years ago. And the fear of poverty has expanded in the countryside as well as the cities. The economy is in the noose of foreign debt. Industrial capacity is quickly being worn out. The breakdown in the housing industry is deepening, which particularly affects young people. The ecological crisis in some parts of the country has taken on catastrophic dimensions. For the first time since 1982, a rapid drop in production has begun . . . The spiral of wages and prices, which is infecting the whole economic organism, has joined these phenomena in recent months. We are threatened by an enormous inflation that could lead to complete economic chaos. We are determined, as soon as possible, to halt this process and to make a turn in the economic situation of the country.

Before Sejm (Parliament),
Warsaw, Sept. 12/
Los Angeles Times, 9-13:(I)5.

2

Yesterday I talked with a leading Western European politician, and he said that he perceived grateful reactions in Poland to the West's offers of assistance, even though he thought these offers were too low. The point is that to master inflation and reform our economy, we must have several factors acting simultaneously—both the element of releasing social and economic energy

inside the country and the element of economic cooperation with other countries. Obviously, if one of these factors is missing, there is the threat that this process will collapse.

Interview,
Warsaw/
Newsweek, 10-9:46.

3

[On his new non-Communist government]: We do not want a free ride. But I hope, above all, that friends of Poland will understand that they shouldn't wait until we are drowning. We must initiate cooperation that will enable our economy to emerge from the quagmire, to help us overcome our tragic environmental situation, and to assist this nation in getting on the road to modernity in culture and science. Fairly quickly, our experts will have to spell out our expectations. They must meet with experts from Western countries and from the International Monetary Fund to discuss our problems. In science, for instance, we are far behind. Our cultural institutions are falling apart. My government will not be able to finance all of that right away.

Interview/
World Press Review,
October:17.

Roy A. Medvedev
Member, Congress of People's Deputies
of the Soviet Union

4

[On Soviet leader Mikhail Gorbachev's announcement of the "real" Soviet military budget]: The real reason the figure was secret [in the past] was that government was secret. Everything the government, not just the military, did was secret. Budgets were secret, military spending was secret, the size of the armed forces was secret . . . Everything was secret because that is the way we were governed—through secrecy. That is why saying now what is what, how much is spent and so forth, is important. No longer will we be governed by secrecy.

Moscow, May 30/
Los Angeles Times,
5-31:(I)10.

291

Vadim A. Medvedev
Member, Central Committee,
Communist Party
of the Soviet Union

1

[On the reform program in the Soviet Union]: The people demand that the [Communist] Party should be guiding them more boldly, more decisively and more successfully. Great expectations have been aroused, but the situation, due to a combination of a number of unfavorable factors, has become more difficult . . . The speed and scope of reform is clearly lagging behind the demands of [economic and social] development. Many enterprises, ministries and organizations continue to work in the old style . . . It is clear that we cannot go on without further efforts to dismantle this "braking mechanism."

April 21/
Los Angeles Times, 4-22:(I)15.

2

[On whether reform in the Soviet Union will lead to a multi-party system]: There is no contradiction, as experience shows, between multi-party politics and socialist society. But the single-party system does not stand in contradiction to democracy, either. There is nothing to prevent the [Communist] Party from acting democratically, subject to the rule of law and the scrutiny of the people. What matters is the means available for expressing the interests of individuals and groups, and for responding to them. At our country's present stage of development, we feel a need for a single unifying force, which the Party provides. Attempts to upset or weaken it are nothing but attempts to hamper *perestroika* [reform].

Interview/World Press Review,
September:23.

Vladimir I. Melnikov
First Secretary, Komi Oblast
Committee, Communist Party
of the Soviet Union

3

[On Soviet leader Mikhail Gorbachev's program of *perestroika,* reform in the Soviet Union]:

On the whole, we don't have the grounds today to appraise with total optimism the course of *perestroika.* Mass refusals to work, hunger strikes, unsanctioned meetings and demonstrations, and even strikes, have become realities of our life. At times, they arise at the urging of extremist-minded elements and representatives of various organizations who come to us from the center and other regions. Their appeals find fertile soil among the population only because the people today do not have confidence in tomorrow . . . Comrades, look at our movies and our journals. Where's the patriotism, the civic attitude? Where's the labor discipline? How are we going to educate our young? We are educating them in an entirely different mien. Can this really not worry the ideological staff of the Central Committee and Politburo?

At meeting of Soviet Communist
Party Central Committee,
Moscow, April 25/
The New York Times, 4-28:(A)6.

Gianni De Michelis
Deputy Prime Minister
of Italy

4

There is a new and troubling imbalance in Europe today. The U.S.S.R. is active, resourceful and peacefully aggressive. The [U.S.] Bush Administration is passive, reactive, unimaginative. It's incredible, but [former U.S. President] Ronald Reagan seemed to understand what's going on better than Bush does.

Interview, May 26/
The New York Times, 5-29:4.

Gianni De Michelis
Foreign Minister of Italy

5

[On the changes taking place in Europe, including the coming 1992 economic unification of the West and the current pro-democracy reforms in the East]: We have to build mechanisms to integrate this new Europe. The new realities are social, political, economic, artistic. For 1,000 years, European equilibrium was built in Central Europe, starting with Charlemagne.

(GIANNI DE MICHELIS)

For the last 80 years we have lacked a workable system, with obvious results; but now we have a chance once again to build it.

The New York Times, 11-23:(A)9.

Leszek Miller
Secretary, Central Committee,
Communist Party of Poland

1

If the economic situation [in Poland] does not get better, and if there is growing tension in society as a result, it is easy to imagine a wave of anarchy and chaos and the eventual predominance of demagogues ... You're in a country where everything is possible.

To reporters, Warsaw,
Feb. 3/
The Washington Post, 2-6:(A)15.

Francois Mitterrand
President of France

2

I am not afraid of reunification [of East and West Germany]. If the Germans want to be a single nation in a single state, this must be founded on the will of the German nation, and nobody can oppose it. What counts is what the Germans want.

News conference,
Bonn, West Germany,
Nov. 3/
The New York Times, 11-20:(A)19.

Hans Modrow
Prime Minister-designate
of East Germany

3

[Saying the East German government has been too slow in implementing democratic reforms]: What is at stake at this time is the existence of the [Communist] Party and the existence of socialism in our country. Instead of showing consequent action and responsibility as the governing party, we further speeded the loss of confidence in us by waiting and hesitating. The

turnabout originated in the street, and we must not forget the Leninist principle that a party that does not recognize and admit its errors loses the power to lead.

Before East German Communist
Party Central Committee,
East Berlin, Nov. 9/
The New York Times, 11-13:(A)8.

Hans Modrow
Prime Minister
of East Germany

4

[On his government's reformist philosophy]: In its understanding of Constitutionality, the government assumes that, for citizens, everything that is not expressly forbidden should be allowed and, for the state, only what is expressly permitted should be allowed.

Broadcast address to the nation,
East Berlin, Nov. 17/
The New York Times, 11-18:4.

Dominique Moisi
Co-founder, French Institute
for Foreign Relations

5

[On France's attitude against a total denuclearization of Europe]: The long-term prospect of a denuclearized world cannot be seen in the same light in Paris and Bonn. [West] Germany's hope remains France's fear.

The Christian Science Monitor,
5-26:6.

6

[On international worries about the possible reunification of Germany in light of pro-democracy reforms in East Germany]: Nothing is more dangerous than to say to Germans today, "We fear you." If we do that, we will create a Germany according to that image, the kind of Germany we would deserve.

Panel discussion sponsored by
"Time" magazine,
Brussels/
Time, 12-18:26.

Walter F. Mondale
Former Vice President
of the United States

1

[Saying the U.S. should respond more decisively to the reforms being undertaken in Eastern Europe and the Soviet Union]: Now is the time to strike. I think the circumstances are such that we need a much more rapid U.S. policy response. The people of Poland speak to us of the joy of democracy and freedom. We come back with the language of bookkeepers and bureaucrats.

At reunion of officials from the
Jimmy Carter Administration,
Washington, Nov. 6/
The New York Times, 11-7:(A)8.

Danny Morrison
Spokesman for Sinn Fein,
political arm of
Irish Republican Army
(Northern Ireland)

2

We agree with the efficacy of armed struggle [against the British in Northern Ireland], that it can bring about political benefits, and that ultimately it will be the armed struggle that saps the will and ends the British occupation of Northern Ireland.

Los Angeles Times,
3-13:(I)9.

Robert A. Mosbacher
Secretary of Commerce
of the United States

3

[On the reform programs in Eastern Europe and the Soviet Union]: Unless an economy can satisfy the most basic needs and desires of a people . . . there can be no stability. We want the bold programs . . . in Hungary and in Poland to succeed. And we want *perestroika* [reform] to succeed in the Soviet Union.

At Institute for East-West Security
Studies conference,
Frankfurt/
The Christian Science Monitor,
10-23:3.

Giorgio Napolitano
Foreign-policy chief,
Communist Party of Italy

4

[On the Italian Communist Party]: We are not something half East and half West. We are a fully-fledged Western European party of the left, and we want to contribute to the policies of the European Community and NATO as a party which believes in the importance of Western European integration, and believes in a European pillar within the Western alliance.

The Christian Science Monitor,
5-16:4.

Aleksandr M. Obolensky
Member, Congress of People's
Deputies of the Soviet Union

5

For the next few years the main task for all of us is to build the law-governed state [in the Soviet Union] . . . Just the way the question is put is terrifying—I mean that we have to build it yet, and in the kind of state we are now living in. Here's what I consider the priorities: First, prohibit from now on all departmental law-making practices. The only basis for the life of the country should be the laws passed by us, the legislative power. All norms and regulations adopted up till now by ministries should be null and void. I mean their legal validity, but they can be used as recommendation. If we do not do this, our *perestroika* [reform program] will continue idling as before. Next is the establishment of a constitutional court . . . So far, I haven't heard of anything better than the jury system for independence of the Court of Justice . . . For the Constitution to be really the basic law, I think everybody will agree that it should be revised and abridged. Over 150 articles is too much. Only those that are the basis of our life should remain. It should be adopted in the course of a series of public referendums. It should be free from the control of any representative bodies.

Before Congress of People's Deputies,
Moscow, May 25/
The New York Times,
5-26:(A)7.

Achille Occhetto
Leader, Communist Party
of Italy

1

Our Party isn't a member of a particular political-ideological camp. It's not part of the so-called Communist camp. On the contrary, I maintain that there is no longer a real Communist movement, and the traditions we represent in Italy are our own . . . We want democracy, no longer as a means to achieve socialism, but to achieve democracy as a universal end in itself. If our Party were in America, we might call ourselves the Liberal Party.

Interview/The Washington Post,
5-16:(A)12.

Lionel H. Olmer
Former Under Secretary for
International Trade,
Department of Commerce
of the United States

2

[On the coming 1992 economic integration of the European Community]: My fear is that, as European governments seek to balance political interests among the 12 member states, the legitimate interests of outsiders will be the first to be traded off. Fortress Europe may not be a realistic outcome, but selected protectionism will be defended as necessary . . .

Nation's Business, June:20.

Robert O'Neill
Former director,
International Institute for
Strategic Studies, London

3

This is a major opportunity for Britain and Western Europe to build a positive relationship with Eastern Europe that can solve the long-term security problem that has confronted Western Europe throughout this century, and even during the 19th century. Eastern Europe has been the cradle of the major wars of Europe in the 20th century, and now Europe has got to face the challenge of solving the old Eastern question without the Soviets guaranteeing everything, as they have in the past.

Symposium/Newsweek, 5-15:29.

Mark Palmer
United States Ambassador
to Hungary

4

While we want ultimately to see changes in structural systems [in Eastern Europe]—the legalization of Solidarity [trade union] in Poland, for instance—and should work away at that, we should also do concrete things. We should be working away at what makes the tenor of the societies more livable and normal . . . We should get off our black-and-white attitude and get our private sector thoroughly involved in Eastern Europe. We're doing things in terms of increasing travel and American business involvement, but we're doing that very half-heartedly.

The Christian Science Monitor,
1-10:7.

5

[Encouraging private U.S. contacts with Eastern Europe to encourage democratic reforms there]: Our policy should be to throw so many bridges over the East-West divide that the Iron Curtain becomes irrelevant.

Newsweek, 7-17:33.

Burton Yale Pines
Authority on Europe,
Heritage Foundation, Washington

6

[On the possibility of German reunification in light of East Germany's pro-democracy reforms]: We would be nuts to try to oppose German reunification—there is nothing to be gained by antagonizing Germany—but we would be equally nuts to keep our hands off and say that German reunification is only a question for the German people. Because of the instabilities a united Germany has created in this past century, it is absolutely appropriate for Moscow and Washington to begin talking now, along with Britain and France, about how Germany should be reunified—what sorts of weapons it should be allowed to have, what limitations on its troops should be imposed and how it would relate to its neighbors.

The New York Times, 12-7:(A)14.

Gavriil K. Popov
*Member, Congress of People's
Deputies of the Soviet Union;
Economist*

1

[Criticizing new government proposals for planning the Soviet economy]: This planning system reminds me of egg production: This hen will produce 180 eggs this year, 183 eggs the next, then 185. Why don't we finally leave this hen alone and let her live with her rooster? Thanking us for her independence, this hen will provide us with enough eggs.

*Before Congress of People's Deputies,
Moscow, Dec. 13/
Los Angeles Times, 12-14:(A)1.*

Imre Pozsgay
*Member, Politburo,
Communist Party of Hungary*

2

[On the reforms now going on in Eastern Europe]: A crisis prevails in Eastern Europe. There is no political or even geographical unity. What you call the East bloc is an artificial linkage, a hybrid imposed after Yalta. The crisis of Europe lies in its division. Protracted problems here will lead to protracted problems in Western Europe as well ... We have seen no sign that Moscow wants to pull us back [from the reforms now taking place]. To the contrary, [Soviet leader Mikhail] Gorbachev's *perestroika* [Soviet reform program] is a wind at our back. Hungary has reached a point where there is no going back.

Interview/Newsweek, 10-16:46.

Charles Price II
*United States Ambassador
to the United Kingdom*

3

Although the Anglo-American relationship rests on the sturdy pillars of common purpose and common principle, we should not assume that these alone will perpetuate it. Our partnership requires vigilance and care. It needs constant attention.

The Christian Science Monitor, 1-20:6.

Dan Quayle
*Vice President
of the United States*

4

[On how the West should react toward the current reform in the Soviet Union and Eastern Europe]: I think we have to get away from the wild euphoria that somehow this transition and change is going to come in the real near term. We are very heartened by what's happened in Poland. Poland has made tremendous progress. We're heartened by what is beginning to happen in Hungary. But we're also realists and look at statements that are coming out toward the Baltic states [which are demanding independence from Moscow] ... Let us remind ourselves that we're still dealing with a totalitarian government [in the Soviet Union] and there are going to be bumps along the transition.

*To reporters, Washington,
Sept. 6/
Los Angeles Times, 9-7:(I)23.*

5

[On the possibility of German reunification in light of the recent pro-democracy reforms in East Germany]: Once the East German Communist system goes by the wayside, then there becomes a less convincing reason why it should be a separate country. That's what keeps it separate ... East Germany is East Germany because of the Communist system. Do away with the Communist system, and it's "German."

*To Republican Governors,
Hilton Head Island, S.C.,
Nov. 13/
Los Angeles Times, 11-14:(A)13.*

Mieczyslaw Rakowski
Prime Minister of Poland

6

[On current changes in the Polish economic system]: It depends what you mean by the system. What led to the past political structures, a certain method of running the economy, yes, this is past. But I warn against burying the Communist formulation. There's no simple road to development.

The New York Times, 4-26:(A)19.

Mieczyslaw Rakowski
First Secretary, Communist
Party of Poland

1

[On current reforms in Communist-ruled Eastern Europe]: Lenin and Marx could not foresee everything. We should not kneel before Lenin and his teachings. We have different problems, different times and different values. At the time Lenin lived, we didn't have atomic bombs and guided-missile cruisers . . . The main priority [now] is putting the interest of the people first . . . The fact is that today's transformations mean a moving away from the concept of Communist parties that grew up in the 1930s, away from the Third International. But the question is still open what will be the end result of the transformation.

Moscow, Oct. 11/
Los Angeles Times, 10-12:(A)13.

2

[On the new non-Communist Polish government led by Solidarity]: Poles would like to work in socialism but live in capitalism. We like the demands on us to be low. Most Poles are attached to the peaceful life. The greatest barrier to reform lies in people's psychology, what I call the "awareness barrier." Changing this is not a matter of a year or five years; it will take a generation. As it is, the system has demoralized people. I may be wrong, but after the first radical steps [by the Solidarity government], and the subsequent social reaction, the new government will retreat.

Interview/Newsweek, 10-16:46.

Rozanne L. Ridgway
President, Atlantic Council;
Former Assistant Secretary
for European and Canadian
Affairs, Department of State
of the United States

3

[On the pro-democracy reforms currently taking place in Eastern Europe]: What is happening is a people's revolution—in Poland it was the leadership of Solidarity [trade union] and Soli-

darity members who pushed for nine years; in Hungary it was the reformers in the [Communist] Party; and in East Germany it is the people, half a million people in Alexanderplatz. You can call all the meetings you want to talk about change, but the people in the streets apparently have their own agenda . . . Some people say that it is frightening and you have to get control of it but, in truth, how do you get control of it? I don't think you do.

The Washington Post, 11-30:(A)56.

Nikolai I. Ryzhkov
Prime Minister
of the Soviet Union

4

[On the Soviet economy]: Our high import needs and our limited abilities to pay for them have already led to a foreign debt exceeding by two times the revenues we have from exporting goods and services. Due to that, we have to negotiate short-term credits in increasing amounts. All our revenues from oil are not enough to pay the interest. The government considers that an inflated foreign debt could bring dangerous economic and political consequences.

Before Congress of People's
Deputies, Moscow, June 7/
Los Angeles Times, 6-8:(I)8.

5

People so far do not see the results of *perestroika* [reform in the Soviet Union] in their standard of living, and some even feel that it would be better to return to the old order-giving method of managing the economy. But there is no turning back. Those methods will lead only to an impasse and will not get society out of the difficult situation we are now in.

Before Supreme Soviet, Moscow,
Oct. 2/
Los Angeles Times, 10-3:(I)14.

Andrei D. Sakharov
Dissident Soviet physicist

6

[On Soviet leader Mikhail Gorbachev's program of *perestroika*, reform in the Soviet Union]:

WHAT THEY SAID IN 1989

(ANDREI D. SAKHAROV)

[*Perestroika* is] absolutely necessary. There is no other solution. This doesn't mean that you have to support Gorbachev without reservation. To associate *perestroika* 100 per cent with his name would not be fair. Gorbachev could come under pressure. He could have other ideas. The restructuring has to be supported in general without worrying whether some people are going to be upset. For the Soviet individual today, the question of collective rights is more immediate than individual rights.

Interview, Moscow/
Los Angeles Times,
1-27:(I)8.

1

I am afraid that something like what is happening in China [the Chinese government's crackdown on pro-democracy demonstrators, including the use of military force] could happen in the Soviet Union. The political activity of the masses has increased greatly in the Soviet Union, and the political leadership is getting scared. [Soviet leader] Mikhail Gorbachev must gather enough common sense and realism—not to create new causes for conflict, but to solve the outstanding problems instead. That is the only way to avoid disaster. Our country, too, is on the brink of catastrophe.

During visit to the Netherlands/
Los Angeles Times, 6-19:(I)1.

2

The Soviet Union is the last colonial empire in the world. It rests on national contradictions that have always existed but have not been apparent because they were suppressed for so long. There was the oppression of [internal Soviet] republics by the Soviet Union as a whole. Then within the republics there was the suppression of small nationalities. The roots of national contradictions lie very deep indeed, and the problem is that whichever way one goes, there are terrible dangers. To maintain this structure will lead to

terrible dangers, but so will loosening it. Great upheavals are more or less inevitable.

Before Royal Institute of
International Affairs, London,
June 20/
World Press Review,
August:32.

Valery T. Salkin
Mayor of Moscow; Member,
Central Committee,
Communist Party
of the Soviet Union

3

[On Soviet leader Mikhail Gorbachev's program of reform in the Soviet Union]: It is strange, but many have accepted democratization as all-permissiveness, as a delegated right to ignore our legal and moral norms. Strange, but pluralism of opinion has been taken by many as a legal and open opportunity for wholesale disparaging of all socialist values, all achievements of socialism, of everything associated with the Communist Party. It should be said that a massive attack at the hearts and souls of people has been launched in this direction.

At meeting of Soviet Communist
Party Central Committee,
Moscow, April 25/
The New York Times,
4-28:(A)6.

Max Schmidt
Director, Institute for
International Politics and
Economics (East Germany)

4

[Saying Germany is one entity despite its split into East and West]: I am a German Communist. I live in a state that is German, and I am of German nationality. To say that the G.D.R. [East Germany] is a nation was a theoretical mistake. We are not two states like any other two states. There is an ethnic component, and that is a perspective we must respect.

Time, 11-27:40.

Franz Schoenhuber
Leader, Republican Party
of West Germany

1

During the war [World War II], I was not an enemy of Hitler. No matter what they said later, 80 per cent of the Germans went along with Hitler—even though he brought us to the greatest catastrophe for our country and the whole world . . . I still have the soul of a soldier. We were great soldiers because the Germans are born warriors. But we are born losers. However, we cannot shorten our history only to those 12 years of Hitler. Germany is greater than that.

Los Angeles Times, 8-28:(I)12.

Raymond G. H. Seitz
Assistant Secretary for
European Affairs,
Department of State
of the United States

2

[On the current pro-democracy reforms in Eastern Europe]: I guess history comes in waves, and this is one that is clearly cresting. It is not coups we are talking about. It is mass movements, people in the streets. What it has lacked up to now, thank goodness, is a feature that always gives history its real pungency, though. That is violence and barricades—*Les Miserables.* So we may not get on-Broadway plays out of this moment, but we'll definitely get off-Broadway.

The New York Times, 12-7:(A)14.

Simon Serfaty
Executive director,
Johns Hopkins Foreign
Policy Institute

3

The evolution of the [NATO] alliance doesn't reflect the decline of American power. To the contrary, it indicates that American power was well used. It helped bring about the evolution we wanted—a stronger, more independent united Europe, the reform of the Soviet system, the breakup of the Soviet empire in Eastern Europe. This is exactly what is happening, and what do we do? We panic. Bizarre.

Symposium/Newsweek, 5-15:30.

Eduard A. Shevardnadze
Foreign Minister
of the Soviet Union

4

[On the human-rights accord that emerged from the Conference on Security and Cooperation in Europe]: The Vienna accord is a landmark on the way to a fundamentally new Europe. [The meeting] shook the "Iron Curtain," loosening its rusted joints, piercing still more holes in it, and enhancing its corrosion. It warmed the cold-war channel with the swell of new currents. Europe may only welcome this.

Vienna, Jan. 19/
Los Angeles Times, 1-20:(I)16.

5

Pursuing its declared fundamental objective of removing any foreign military presence and bases from the territory of other countries, the Soviet Union will withdraw from Central Europe military formations and units with all their organic armaments, including tactical nuclear weapons.

At Conference on Security and
Cooperation in Europe, Vienna,
Jan. 19/
The New York Times, 1-20:(A)4.

6

[Criticizing calls for the autonomy of the Georgian Republic and other Soviet republics]: Every river, even the broadest, has its banks. Every popular movement, even the broadest, has, or should have, its inner and outer limits.

Before Georgian Communist Party,
April 14/
The New York Times, 4-17:(A)4.

7

[On the reform program in the Soviet Union]: We in our country are not just repainting the facade, but rebuilding the entire structure in which the rules of living together must and will be based on the supremacy of law, people's power, openness to the outside world, inter-ethnic harmony. In every sphere of the common life of our

299

(EDUARD A. SHEVARDNADZE)

state and our people, the national economy, the political system, the intellectual endeavor of our people, rejection of the ossified relics of the past goes hand in hand with the enthusiasm of new construction. And even though, in the words of a poet, there may be a gloomy day or two, we are confident that *perestroika* [reform], which began as a revolution of hopes, will keep these hopes alive. Our people, our nation will keep *perestroika* going, for it embodies the aspirations that they cherish.

At United Nations, New York,
Sept. 26/
The New York Times, 9-27:(A)6.

1

It is no secret that we were not enthusiastic about the election setback of the Polish Communists. Nor should it be a secret that we hope that they can overcome the crisis. Nevertheless, we see nothing threatening in the fact that, in accordance with the will of the Polish people, a coalition government has been formed. We are in no way prejudiced against that government. We wish it every success and are ready to cooperate with it most actively. Tolerance is the norm of civilized behavior.

At United Nations, New York,
Sept. 26/
The New York Times, 9-27:(A)6.

2

[On the pro-democracy reforms taking place in East Germany and other Warsaw Pact countries]: We have to hail the bold, innovative steps of the German Democratic Republic [East Germany]. They meet the interests of socialism, of Europe as a whole, of the East German people and of the Warsaw Pact . . . We support the course of the renewal of democracy in the German Democratic Republic and wish our friends and allies success.

Before foreign-policy committees of
Supreme Soviet, Moscow,
Nov. 17/
Los Angeles Times, 11-18:(A)3.

Yuri F. Solovyev
First Secretary of the
Leningrad region, Communist
Party of the Soviet Union

3

[Criticizing Soviet leader Mikhail Gorbachev's reform program in the Soviet Union]: It's no secret that it has gone so far that people carrying Party membership cards openly speak against the CPSU, against its vanguard role in the society, and stand for turning the Party of action into a party of discussion clubs.

At meeting of Soviet Communist
Party Central Committee, Moscow,
April 25/
The New York Times, 4-28:(A)6.

Ferenc Somogyi
Deputy Foreign Minister
of Hungary

4

[Saying his country's allowing East Germans to flee from Hungary to West Germany will be good for Hungarian relations with the West]: We want to open up and diversify relations with Western Europe and the West in general. We are fully aware that in some cases the conditions are not yet ripe for us to be a full-fledged member of that community. Our economy is not yet at that level. But in humanitarian concerns we are closer to the West than in the economy . . . We think in the long run we have to be persistent to keep what little we have, that is, our prestige and respect in the international community. We can solve our internal problems only if we are integrated in a wide set of international relations.

Interview, Budapest, Sept. 14/
The New York Times, 9-15:(A)4.

Helmut Sonnenfeldt
Former Member, National
Security Council
of the United States

5

[On Hungary's allowing East Germans to pass through its territory on their way to West Germany]: Obviously, this is a major complication in Hungary's relations with the GDR, and it

(HELMUT SONNENFELDT)

obviously complicates empire management for the Soviet Union ... Partly they [Hungarians] are being good guys. You can't really open up the system and gradually remove repression, as the Hungarians hope to do, and then play the game with the East Germans of sending these people back. I assume they also have it in mind that the West Germans will repay them in some form. It is part of the Hungarian effort to convince the outside world ... that they are a different breed of cat from the rest of Eastern Europe. From the Hungarian standpoint, it is probably a worthwhile exchange.

Los Angeles Times, 9-12:(I)11.

Romuald Spasowski
Exiled former Polish Ambassador
to the United States

1

[On the moves toward democracy in Poland]: I am full of cautious optimism. If nothing is changed in a year, there will be a violent explosion. Not only in Poland, but all through East Europe. The Iron Curtain is rusting, the system cannot be repaired. The times are like the mid-1800s in the strong movement of people to free themselves of their tyrants.

Interview/
The Washington Post, 9-8:(B)1.

Michael Sturmer
Director, Ebenhausen Foundation
(West Germany)

2

[On the increase in East Germans seeking asylum in West Germany since some border-crossing barricades and fences were removed in parts of Eastern Europe earlier in the year]: It is the greatest embarrassment possible. The East German government has pretended for years that capitalism is a decaying system and that East Germany is building on the moral high ground. Now the people are voting with their feet, as they have done before. Nothing can persuade them otherwise ... The people who are leaving are the folks the GDR needs to have any hope of

working. They are the young, the active and the technically skilled people. East Germany cannot afford to lose them. They are the kind of people who went to America in another time.

Interview/
The New York Times, 8-22:(A)1,3.

Stephen S. Szabo
Professor of European affairs,
National War College,
Washington

3

Let's be frank. We and the British and French like the status quo in Europe. It has kept the peace for 40 years, it has managed the German problem, and produced a great deal of prosperity for us. We have not exactly suffered from the division of Europe. The Soviets got East Europe. We got West Europe. The Soviets got Poland. We got Germany. If the bipolar world fragments, some argue, so does our [the U.S.'] dominant position in Europe. If we diminish our military and political role in Europe, it means we will have less leverage on the European Community—right at a time when it is moving toward economic integration in 1992 and we are going to need all the leverage we can muster.

The New York Times, 4-28:(A)4.

Matyas Szuros
Acting President of Hungary

4

[On his country's declaring itself an independent republic]: This is a prelude to a new historical age. The Hungarian republic is going to be an independent, democratic and legal state in which the values of bourgeois democracy and democratic socialism are expressed equally.

Speech, Budapest, Oct. 23/
Los Angeles Times, 10-24:(A)8.

Margaret Thatcher
Prime Minister
of the United Kingdom

5

[Addressing Soviet leader Mikhail Gorbachev]: Both our countries know from bitter experience that conventional weapons do not deter war in Europe, whereas nuclear weapons have done so for over 40 years.

April/
The New York Times, 4-27:(A)6.

1

[Defending her government's hard-line policies against terrorism in Northern Ireland, which some have criticized as eroding civil rights]: To beat off your enemy in a war, you have to suspend some of your civil liberties for a time. Yes, some of those measures do restrict freedom. But those who choose to live by the bomb and the gun, and those who support them, can't in all circumstances be accorded exactly the same rights as everyone else. We do sometimes have to sacrifice a little of the freedom we cherish in order to defend ourselves from those whose aim is to destroy that freedom altogether.

Los Angeles Times, 4-6:(I)7.

2

[Addressing Soviet leader Mikhail Gorbachev on his reform program in the Soviet Union]: We are pleased when families are reunited and those who want to emigrate can do so, but we also look forward with keen anticipation to the changes in the law of which you spoke in your New York speech, which make these the rights of every person so that they can be claimed and enforced and not given as privileges which one day can be taken away. I think that is one of the most exciting prospects of the things which you have enunciated in your new thinking. We embrace the principle of freedom of choice. It is fundamental to our own society. We want to see it fully applied in all aspects of national and international life.

April 6/The Wall Street Journal,
4-17:(A)10.

3

[Addressing Soviet leader Mikhail Gorbachev]: In barely more than four years since your first visit, we have seen changes in the Soviet Union which could only be described as a "peaceful revolution." We very much admire the vision and the boldness which have inspired those changes. We do not for a moment underestimate the scale of the problems which remain to be overcome. There will be setbacks; there always are. People like to believe that the future is a Promised Land which will arrive if you just sit and wait for it; but it is not like that at all. It has to be earned by effort—not someone else's effort, but the effort of each and every person . . . Your recent elections, sir, were followed almost as closely in this country as in the Soviet Union. Public opinion was given the chance to express itself through Constitutional means, and the results were exciting. Above all, they were a firm endorsement of your new thinking. To us, it seems that they brought out hitherto untapped qualities in the Soviet people. It is only through the exercise of democracy that *perestroika* [reform in the Soviet Union] will be made irreversible. That is what you are trying to do, Mr. President, and with all our mind and strength, we want you to succeed.

At dinner for Gorbachev, London/
The Washington Post, 4-19:(A)18.

4

America has allies throughout Europe and throughout the free world. I would like to think that we [in Britain] pride ourselves on being among the foremost of United States' friends, and we will always be . . . In time of great crisis or danger, you [the U.S.] have always been able to count on [Britain]. And I can say to you rather solemnly tonight, you will always be able to count on Britain—when there is danger, when you need us. That is why the relationship is special.

To reporters at dinner for visiting
U.S. President Bush, London,
June 1/
The New York Times, 6-2:(A)6.

5

They [liberals] talk of a "social" Europe—they mean and want a socialist Europe. We Conservatives want a Europe of enterprise,

(MARGARET THATCHER)

applying in the European Community those policies which have made Britain prosperous and brought down unemployment.

The Christian Science Monitor,
6-14:4.

1

In 1979, we [the Conservative Party] knew that we were starting a British revolution. In fact, we were the pioneers of a world revolution. We did not know it at the time, but the torch we lit in Britain which transformed our country—the torch of freedom that is now the symbol of our Party—became the beacon that has shed its light across the Iron Curtain into the East [of Europe]. The messages on our banners in 1979—freedom, opportunity, family, enterprise, ownership—are now inscribed on the banners in Leipzig [East Germany], Warsaw, Budapest and even Moscow.

At British Conservative Party
conference, Blackpool, England,
Oct. 13/
Los Angeles Times, 10-14:(A)4.

2

[Saying Britain should not join the European exchange-rate mechanism until reforms take place in certain European countries]: We shall join the exchange-rate system when there are no foreign-exchange controls, when there's freedom of movement of capital, when their insurance and pension funds are run as openly and freely as ours are, and when the subsidies are gone. You can't have a currency like sterling playing under that higgledy-piggledy set of rules . . . We believe in an open economy, but [some European countries] have artificial and cultural barriers which are going to be very difficult to get down. I really can't have Britain worsted by other people having a different set of rules from us. Of course, I fight for Britain and, of course, I'm combative; I shall go on doing it. But they simply must be fair.

Broadcast interview,
London, Oct. 29/
The New York Times, 10-30:(C)6.

3

[On the current pro-democracy reforms in Eastern Europe]: These developments put a special responsibility on those of us who are members of the European Community. While continuing to build up cooperation among the 12 [members], we must not allow ourselves to become obsessed with the details of the Community's internal business as though nothing were happening elsewhere. We must not take a narrow, blinkered approach. We have to remain open and outward-looking, ready to help, looking at these changes in Eastern Europe as part of the eternal battle between freedom and central control. We must stretch out the hand of cooperation, and develop new forms of association with the emerging democracies of Eastern Europe— Poland, Hungary, East Germany—and we hope others will follow. After all, the European Community is a powerful example of how European states can work together in freedom, and it would be natural for the Eastern European countries to believe they will benefit from closer contact with it.

At Lord Mayor's banquet, London/
The Washington Post, 11-15:(A)20.

4

[On her reluctance to have Britain join the European Monetary System's exchange-rate mechanism]: We believe in Europe, a Europe based on a free economy, a deregulated Europe under the rule of law—not a regulated bureaucracy dictating to [the British House of Commons] from Brussels.

Before House of Commons,
London, Oct. 31/
The New York Times, 11-1:(C)7.

Kurt Tiedke
Member, Central Committee,
Communist Party of East Germany

5

[Arguing against economic or political reforms in East Germany that might stem the flow of refugees to the West]: Why should we be in favor of a "socialism" that adopts the basic evils of capitalism? Surely, "new thinking" cannot mean

303

(KURT TIEDKE)

copying bourgeois policies or cribbing from Social Democratic programs which nowhere lead to socialism. There will never be a return to the capitalist society of unjustice. There is nothing—repeat, nothing—that persuades us to correct our course.

Los Angeles Times,
8-31:(I)16.

Jerzy Urban
Spokesman for the
government of Poland

1

It is only the Soviet Union that guarantees our [Polish] frontiers. And it is only the Soviet Union that secures us with all raw materials that we need. Also, the experiences of the past indicate that the only foundation of the stability in the region is the Polish orientation toward the Soviet Union. Over the past 300 years, Poland existed with a different orientation for 20 years only. So both we and the opposition, people who do not love the Soviet Union, believe that this alliance with the Soviet Union is inviolable, untouchable.

Interview/
USA Today, 4-6:(A)9.

Miklos Vasarhelyi
Hungarian writer
and dissident

2

[On the pro-democracy reforms in Eastern Europe during the past several months]: What was most surprising was the speed with which it happened. Since last May, we thought and hoped there would be changes. But what's happening now, and especially in Berlin, is a major surprise. Nobody dared to think about such big changes. Even to have mentioned such things three months ago would have seemed crazy. What is so unusual is that it was all the will of the people. It was not figured out by intellectuals or politicians or diplomats.

Interview,
Washington/
The New York Times, 11-18:4.

Trivimi Velliste
Director, Estonian
Heritage Society

3

The Soviet government now accepts that the Nazi-Soviet pact [in World War II] was a crime, but refuses to liquidate the consequences of that crime [by freeing the Baltic states]. So the citizens of Latvia, Lithuania and Estonia will do it for them. We will not stop until we are free again.

At rally, Tallinn, Estonia, U.S.S.R./
Newsweek, 9-4:30.

Sergei Vikulov
Editor-in-chief, "Nash Sovremenik"
(Soviet Union)

4

In 1917, following the October Revolution, the Russian people sacrificed everything—their well-being, their standard of living, even their culture—to help every one else [in the Soviet Union]. We poured our sweat and blood and our money into Central Asia, into the Baltics, to raise them up, to give them an economy, to provide literacy and, later, to beat back the Germans. Russians did that. And now what has happened? The Russian Republic is the least developed part of the whole country. And we are called "occupiers," "lazy people," "the ruin of the country."

Moscow,/
The Washington Post, 7-31:(A)1.

Yuri P. Vlasov
Member, Congress of People's
Deputies of the Soviet Union

5

We're already four years away from the beginnings of *perestroika* [reform in the Soviet Union], and everything happening in the country now is to a significant extent the responsibility of the direct activities of our current leadership. One of the richest countries in the world is making ends meet in times of peace with food coupons—which is to say, ration cards. We lack the most elementary provisions. Our ruble is pitiful in the face of any other currency. There is a lot of corruption, lawlessness, arbitrariness in the

(YURI P. VLASOV)

country. The country is drowning in irresponsible decisions. A great country is abased. It's impossible to fall to lower depths. Anything further will be breakdown. The guilty in such cases usually resign—and not just one of them, but all, as the people who have made a mess of things.

Before Congress of People's
Deputies, Moscow, May 31/
The New York Times, 6-1:(A)8.

Heinrich Vogel
Director, Federal Institute for
East European and
International Studies
(West Germany)

1

[On international worries about the possible reunification of Germany in light of pro-democracy reforms in East Germany]: If reunification should happen, where is the threat to the rest of Europe? Please, let us stop thinking of reunification producing a Fourth Reich built on the ashes of NATO.

Panel discussion sponsored by
"Time" magazine, Brussels/
Time, 12-18:27.

Vladimir Voinovich
Exiled Soviet author

2

I miss Russia, not the country I left, but the country I have now come back to [visit]. But I also cannot forget that they took everything from me in 1980: my apartment, my citizenship, my life. They talk about restoring the citizenship of exiles as a gesture of magnanimity. I need justice. Some people seem to think that anyone born in Russia should want to be buried beneath our birch tree. Birch trees are of course important, but they are not as important as freedom. If I have to choose between freedom and my homeland, I will always choose freedom.

Interview, Moscow/
The Washington Post,
5-2:(D)4.

Richard von Weizsacker
President of West Germany

3

We in the Federal Republic of Germany are irrevocably imbedded in the European Community and the Atlantic Alliance. We are not a great power. But we are also not a playing-ball for others. It is to our great benefit to have found friends and partners. But for their part, the Alliance, Western Europe and the whole continent are decisively dependent on our contribution. Our political weight derives from our central location, the special situation of Berlin, the size of our population, our productivity and our stability.

At ceremony marking the 40th
anniversary of the West German
Constitution, Bonn, May 24/
The New York Times, 5-25:(A)10.

Lech Walesa
Chairman, Solidarity
(independent Polish
trade union)

4

[Saying the Polish government should reinstate the Solidarity union]: The authorities will grant the union, whether they want to or not. Only will it be by force or without, and what will be the costs? Legalization of Solidarity is the key issue. I repeat: We do not want to overthrow the authorities. A compromise is in our common interest. The interest of Poland is the order of the day. This is the supreme cause. That's why we must come to agreement with each other. We agree there cannot be constant strikes, struggle, any attempts at [the union] taking over power [from the government]. We can guard against this. However, we shall not allow ourselves to be divided, to be left without guarantees that we can maintain our independence.

Interview/
The New York Times, 1-5:(A)5.

5

[Asking for political and economic reform in Poland]: We know that the country is ruined. But it wasn't a goblin that ruined it, but the political

(LECH WALESA)

system, which stripped people of their rights and wasted the fruits of their work . . . After running around to the shops and standing in long lines and then coming home to count how much money they have left until the end of the month, people are in no mood to listen to long speeches [because they want positive steps taken].

At meeting between Solidarity and the government, Warsaw, Feb. 6/ Los Angeles Times, 2-7:(I)8.

1

I didn't come to Rome with hat in hand or to ask for charity, but to explain the process of democratization that's beginning in Poland. It's a new road in which we ask you [Italians] to invest . . . It's you, the great democracies of the West, who must understand that a historic chance, possibly unrepeatable, has been created in Poland. We need help to construct a Poland that is freer, more just and closer to Europe.

Rome, April 20/ The Washington Post, 4-21:(A)23.

2

[Disagreeing with U.S. President Bush's more cautious attitude in dealing with Soviet leader Mikhail Gorbachev's reforms in the Soviet Union and Eastern Europe]: The Iron Curtain is coming down and some people are looking in like a young man looking at a pretty girl, saying "Should I or should I not [pursue her]?" I tell you to come and see.

Interview, Strasbourg, France/ The Christian Science Monitor, 5-15:4.

3

We [in Poland] have found ourselves today in a situation in which political reform was necessary because a slave worker never makes a good worker. And also for another reason: because today's progress of civilization cannot develop in an atmosphere of restraining monopoly [by the Polish government]. So, we're shaking off that

ugly hump of totalitarian Stalinism, and we're trying to catch up with the rest of Europe and the whole developed world, which is getting farther and farther away from us. We are heading toward democracy and pluralism. But all this makes it necessary for us to keep in mind the proportions that must exist between the reforms in the economic sphere and those in the political sphere. Changes must occur at the same time in both of these fields, at the same time and equally . . . If the proportions are not respected, we will not be able to succeed.

Speech, Gdansk, Poland, July 11/ The New York Times, 7-12:(A)5.

4

[On Poland's new non-Communist government and its plans for the economy]: Nobody has previously taken the road that leads from socialism to capitalism. And we are setting out to do just that, to return to the pre-war situation when Poland was a capitalist country, after having gone through a long period of socialism. But it is an uncharted road. We have Western nations as an economic and political model. But we do not know how to transpose your [the West's] experiences to our reality.

Interview/World Press Review, October:15.

5

[Calling for U.S. loans and investment in Poland, which has recently instituted pro-democracy reforms]: Sometimes I feel we are swimming chained hand and foot, trying to summon all our energy just to make it safely to shore; and on the shore there is a cheering crowd of people who offer us their admiration instead of simply throwing a lifebelt. I know that investing money in Poland requires a bit of courageous thinking or maybe even a bit of imagination . . . Investing money in dictatorships always turns out to be short-term business. Investing money in a democratic country is always profitable, even if it does not bring immediate results.

At AFL-CIO convention, Washington, Nov. 14/ The New York Times, 11-15:(A)10.

Manfred Woerner
Secretary General, North Atlantic
Treaty Organization

1

It is a measure of our success that the East today looks to us [in the West] for inspiration and support in their struggle to inject new vigor into their own societies. NATO has been a great success, and *glasnost* [Soviet openness] is a measure of it. But we must look ahead. In carrying out new policies toward the East, we must have informed, supportive publics in our countries. I fear that [Soviet leader Mikhail] Gorbachev has somehow been able to take credit for initiatives actually begun by the West. We have to devote more effort to winning battles for the minds of our European voters.

Interview,
Brussels/
Los Angeles Times, 6-10:(I)19.

Boris N. Yeltsin
Candidate for
the Congress of
People's Deputies
of the Soviet Union

2

The official view is that *perestroika* [reform in the Soviet Union] must be pushed forward in every direction, that it must enhance everything. But I believe we don't have enough options and resources for this. We are not mature enough. We have not yet gone through psychological restructuring in regard to the democratization of society. So we have to move forward by stages. I favor this approach. One stage yields one result, then the next stage yields another, thus forming a chain of restructuring. Of course, one of the first links in the whole chain is that of the political system. Starting here, we must then improve living standards and concentrate our resources on this, even if it means reducing investments, financial allocations or expenditures in other areas, so that people can come to believe in the process. Psychologically, we have certainly started to live slightly better, and that's *perestroika*. But by heading off in every direction at once, as we have been doing for 3½ years, we

have hardly made any progress at all as far as the standard of living is concerned.

Interview/
Time, 3-20:45.

Boris N. Yeltsin
Member, Congress of
People's Deputies
of the Soviet Union

3

[Criticizing Soviet leader Mikhail Gorbachev's being both Soviet President and Communist Party chief]: Against the background of a deteriorating economy and the sharpening of social issues, we see an increase in the personal influence and the personal power in the hands of the head of state. This can lead to the temptation to solve our complex problems with force, and we can again find ourselves in the sway of a new authoritarian regime, a new dictatorship, without noticing it.

Before Congress of People's
Deputies, Moscow,
May 31/
Los Angeles Times, 6-1:(I)1.

4

The situation in the [Soviet Union] is extremely alarming. Anti-*perestroika* [anti-reform] forces have become active and are consolidating, the shadow economy is growing, corruption and crime are on the rise, the moral standards of society are becoming diluted, the problems of youth are becoming more acute ... The principles of social justice and social equality are not being realized, the number of poor people is growing, the Soviet people's belief in the real results of *perestroika* is falling, the contradictions in ethnic problems are becoming sharper ... With chaos in our consumer sector, inflation, queues and ration coupons, the threat of a financial collapse has become real. The system of economic administration by command has not been broken. Power still belongs to the [Communist] Party apparatus and the bureaucracy.

Before Congress of People's
Deputies, Moscow,
May 31/
Los Angeles Times, 6-1:(I)28.

WHAT THEY SAID IN 1989

(BORIS N. YELTSIN)

1

[On Soviet leader Mikhail Gorbachev's reform program in the Soviet Union]: If we speak in sports terminology, Gorbachev has dropped in the standings among the people. It's clear that our reforms have been delayed. The economy is in crisis; our finances are in crisis; the Communist Party is in crisis; the nationalities are in crisis. The standard of living has not gone up a bit after four years of *perestroika* reforms. An American President's term is four years; more than four years have passed [of Gorbachev's time in office], and after such a time a person should account for his work—what has been done and what has not. And why not, too? It's high time that Gorbachev did that and told us why the situation has not improved.

Interview, Moscow,
Sept. 6/
The Washington Post,
9-9:(A)1.

The Middle East

Bassam abu Sharif
Senior adviser to
Palestine Liberation
Organization chairman
Yasir Arafat

1

[On Israel and the PLO]: The issue is not the PLO's flexibility. We have shown our commitment to a peace settlement by renouncing terrorism, accepting Israel's right to exist behind safe and secure borders and by accepting [UN] Resolutions 242 and 338. What we now want to know is whether [Israeli Prime Minister Yitzhak] Shamir will accept 242 and 338. If the Israelis will accept 242 and 338 and the right of the Palestinians to live in their own independent state, then everything, I repeat, everything else would be negotiable, including the modalities of elections and timetables.

Interview, Cairo/
Los Angeles Times, 4-15:(I)4.

Mustafa Amin
Egyptian political
commentator

2

[On Libyan leader Muammar Qaddafi's new overtures of friendship toward Egypt after years of enmity]: If he is really changing, we should welcome it, but the change is too sudden to trust. What can you say about a man who wants to shoot you in the morning and then hug you in the afternoon, except . . . that he is crazy?

Los Angeles Times, 6-30:(I)9.

Michel Aoun
Christian Army Commander
of Lebanon

3

[Criticizing Syria's involvement in the civil war in Lebanon]: I am not the Christian leader who is going against the Syrians. I am the Lebanese [leader], who is defending his rights on his own territory. The Syrians have no rights in Lebanon. They are an occupying army, and the world has to support us.

Interview, Beirut/
The Christian Science Monitor,
4-6:3.

4

[On Syria's involvement in Lebanon's civil war]: That is what Syria is doing—to keep the country under fire and to make mutual understanding among the Lebanese impossible. In keeping the tension high, no one can think of reforms. The Lebanese can't compromise, they will get killed . . . We cannot stop fighting until liberating the country. I know it is very tough, very tough. There is a disequilibrium of forces in favor of Syria, but it will not be the first time that the weaker one wins. We are very motivated. The Syrians are not.

Interview, Beirut, Aug. 31/
The Washington Post, 9-2:(A)14.

5

[Criticizing the U.S. for closing its Embassy in Beirut and withdrawing diplomatic personnel]: By leaving Beirut, these Americans have left the doorway to all of the Middle East, and they may never find a window from which they could re-enter.

Interview, Beirut, Sept. 7/
The Washington Post, 9-8:(A)26.

Yasir Arafat
Chairman, Palestine
Liberation Organization

6

We make a very clear distinction between terrorism and national struggle, armed struggle. In fact, we [Palestinians] are victims of terrorism—the terrorism of the Israeli state, organized against our children, women and old people. More than 600 Palestinians have been killed in the uprising [against Israeli occupation of the

309

(YASIR ARAFAT)

West Bank and Gaza]. We have 29,000 wounded. Almost 30,000 people are being detained. Homes have been destroyed or sealed up . . . Recently, the Jewish state passed a law to step up the iron fist in the occupied territories, and they have given orders to the armed forces to use firearms without restriction or prior command. Israel has also authorized Jewish settlers to use their weapons against our people. It has prohibited medical treatment by hospitals in Palestine or children wounded in the *intifada* [anti-Israel uprising]. This is pure racism. Under the Geneva Conventions, even enemy soldiers are entitled to treatment. How can you deny wounded children medical attention?

Interview/World Press Review,
April:29.

1

I dream of [a Palestinian homeland] as a free land for one of the world's free peoples, a democratic state where the rule of law prevails, a country that will be an oasis of democracy and freedom, a state in a peaceful land, the land of Palestine—the land of messages, messengers and prophets; the land of history.

Interview/World Press Review,
April:29.

2

As for the Covenant [in the Palestinian National Charter which called the State of Israel illegal], I believe there is an expression in French, "C'est caduque [null and void]."

Paris, May 2/Time, 8-7:31.

3

Nothing and nobody can deter the PLO from attacking its main enemy, Israel.

June 8/Time, 8-7:31.

4

[Criticizing increased Japanese trade with Israel]: Recently, trade relations between Japan and Israel have expanded. Have you [Japan] forgotten the 200 million Arabs and the friends of the 200 million Arabs in the world? Do you know how much of the oil you import comes from the Arab world? It is not necessary for you to think of our interests. Think of your own interests.

At Japanese Foreign Ministry,
Tokyo, Oct. 2/
Los Angeles Times, 10-3:(I)7.

Moshe Arens
Foreign Minister of Israel

5

We are convinced that establishing contacts or, worse yet, extending recognition to the PLO cannot possibly promote peace in the Middle East. It is bound to encourage extremism and further acts of violence.

News conference,
Jerusalem, Jan. 3/
The Washington Post, 1-4:(A)1.

6

The peace process in the Middle East is one which moves at a glacial rate. It took Egypt 30 years and five wars to come and negotiate with Israel. Ten years have gone by and no other Arab country has come forward . . . I think the conclusion that was reached by [then Israel Prime Minister Menachem] Begin and [then Egyptian President Anwar] Sadat 10 years ago at Camp David was that the gap in perceptions, aspirations and fears was too wide to be bridged immediately and a permanent settlement reached. But rather, you had to go toward an intermediate settlement which would create a better atmosphere and bring about a narrowing of gaps—and only then go on to negotiations on a final settlement. I think it is right at the present time, if anything even more correct than it was then.

Interview/
The Washington Post, 2-24:(A)18.

Mubarak Awad
American Palestinian activist

7

Many people believe a Palestinian is born a terrorist because he is a Palestinian. I go around

(MUBARAK AWAD)

the country [the U.S.] and I say if I were fighting Communists we would be called "freedom fighters." But since we are fighting Israelis and the U.S. is allied with Israel, we are "terrorists."

At "Voices of the Intifada"
conference, Crystal City, Virginia,
April 14/
The Washington Post, 4-17:(B)4.

Tarik Aziz
Foreign Minister of Iraq

1

There is no doubt whatsoever now that nuclear weapons have been introduced into this region by Israel's possession of nuclear weapons, as well as of chemical weapons and missiles that can reach many Arab cities, including cities in Iraq. In this respect, Israel constitutes a serious threat to Arab national security, to the safety of the countries of the region and to the nuclear non-proliferation [treaty]. A situation such as this calls for effective international measures to be rapidly taken in order to remove nuclear weapons from this region. Iraq believes that any call for a comprehensive ban on chemical weapons must be coupled with a parallel and similar call for a comprehensive ban on nuclear weapons.

At conference on chemical weapons,
Paris, Jan. 8/
Los Angeles Times, 1-9:(I)10.

James A. Baker III
Secretary of State-designate
of the United States

2

The Arab-Israeli conflict has long engaged America's attention, its resources and good-will. Now [U.S.] President Reagan has authorized a dialogue with the PLO. Dialogues bring messages. And we are bringing a message to the PLO about terrorism and about the need for even more realism, realism that makes practical progress on the ground possible. But the existence of the dialogue should not lead anyone to misunderstand our over-all policy or to question our enduring support for the State of Israel. Nor have

we altered our belief that an independent Palestinian state will not be a source of stability or contribute to a just and enduring peace.

At Senate Foreign Relations Committee
hearing on his confirmation,
Washington, Jan. 17/
The New York Times,
1-18:(A)10.

James A. Baker III
Secretary of State
of the United States

3

We [the U.S.] have not made a policy decision that we are going to take a stand that [Israel] must [negotiate with the PLO]. At the same time, I think it would be a major mistake . . . for us to categorically, absolutely, totally and completely rule out, under any and all circumstances, any dialogue that might lead us toward peace. That happens to be my view. It was my view last week; it is my view this week. I think it is a very reasonable view, particularly in light of what happened since our [the U.S.'] own dialogue [with the PLO] began.

Before House Foreign Affairs
Subcommittee on International
Operations, Washington,
March 21/
The Washington Post,
3-22:(A)22.

4

The United States vigorously opposes the admission of the PLO to membership in the World Health Organization or any other UN agencies. We have worked, and will continue to work, to convince others of the harm that the PLO's admission would cause to the Middle East peace process and to the UN system. To emphasize the depth of our concern, I will recommend to the President that the United States make no further contributions, voluntary or assessed, to any international organization which makes any change in the PLO's status as an observer organization.

May 1/The New York Times,
5-2:(A)6.

WHAT THEY SAID IN 1989

1

First, the United States believes that the object of the peace process [between Israel and the Arabs] is a comprehensive settlement achieved through negotiations based on United Nations Security Council Resolutions 242 and 338. In our view, these negotiations must involve territory for peace, security and recognition for Israel and all of the states of the region, and Palestinian political rights. Second, for negotiations to succeed, they must allow the parties to deal directly with each other face to face. Third, the issues involved in the negotiations are far too complex and the emotions are far too deep to move directly to a final settlement. Accordingly, some transitional period is needed, associated in time and sequence with negotiations on final status. Fourth, in advance of direct negotiations, the United States and no other party inside or outside can or will dictate an outcome. That is why the United States does not support annexation or permanent Israeli control of the West Bank and Gaza, nor do we support the creation of an independent Palestinian state. I would add here that we do have an idea about the reasonable middle ground to which a settlement should be directed. That is, self-government for Palestinians in the West Bank and Gaza in a manner acceptable to Palestinians, Israel and Jordan. Such a formula provides ample scope for Palestinians to achieve their full political rights. It also provides ample protection for Israel's security as well.

Before American Israel Public
Affairs Committee, Washington,
May 22/
The New York Times, 5-23:(A)7.

2

[Addressing Israel]: Now is the time to lay aside, once and for all, the unrealistic vision of a "greater Israel" . . . Forswear annexation [of the West Bank and Gaza]. Stop settlement activity [by Israelis in those areas]. Allow [Palestinian] schools to reopen. Reach out to the Palestinians as neighbors who deserve political rights.

Before American Israel Public
Affairs Committee, Washington,
May 22/Time, 6-5:32.

3

[On U.S. plans to sell tanks to Saudi Arabia]: Let me simply say that we have a long-standing security relationship [with] Saudi Arabia. It is in our interest and in the interest, we think, of peace, that moderately oriented Arab governments feel secure and capable of dealing with threats from radicals. We don't contemplate sales like this to any Arab government without first taking into account the question of Israel's security. We are committed to maintaining a qualitative edge for Israel and that commitment simply is not going to change.

News conference,
New York, Sept. 29/
The New York Times, 9-30:2.

Hanan Bar-On
Israeli scholar and
former Israeli Foreign Ministry
official

4

Persistence in the political and military status quo not only has consequences in the military and political field but tends to make any society, ours first and foremost, irrelevant to a world which is today entering a new environment. The Middle East status quo could make this part of the world into a backwater with very little relevance to the world at large or even the Jewish people.

Los Angeles Times, 12-22:(A)15.

Yossi Beilin
Deputy Minister of Finance
of Israel

5

For the last two, 2½ months there have been clear and official negotiations between the Israeli government led by [Prime Minister] Yitzhak Shamir and the PLO, by way of the Americans . . . Whoever doesn't know [about the contacts], whoever doesn't recognize this, whoever hides from this, is like a child who closes his eyes and thinks the world doesn't see him.

Broadcast interview,
Israeli Army Radio, July 13/
Los Angeles Times, 7-14:(I)8.

Yosef Ben-Aharon
Cabinet Secretary for
Israeli Prime Minister
Yitzhak Shamir
1

[Criticizing the continuing contacts between the U.S. and the PLO]: The United States is weaving iron chains around us. This is not good. If we say that Israel cannot talk to the PLO, and the United States keeps talking to them, this applies pressure on us. If this is the course that is going to be followed, we are headed for a full-dress, head-on collision with the United States. It was a big blunder to open talks with the PLO.
Los Angeles Times, 3-31:(I)18.

2

We do have a very real argument with the United States . . . because they insist on working in such a way that will involve the PLO [in Israeli-Palestinian peace initiatives] . . . We have people telling us that we are closing our eyes to reality, that the PLO is there and must be taken into account. This is the pragmatic American way of looking at things. But we say we are very realistic; there is no way we are capable of coming to grips with what the PLO is saying and what they represent.
Interview, Jerusalem/
The Washington Post, 10-30:(A)1,21.

Benazir Bhutto
Prime Minister of Pakistan
3

[On the death of Iranian spiritual leader Ayatollah Ruhollah Khomeini]: Leaders like Imam Khomeini are born but once in centuries. The people of Iran have lost a divine guide and the world of Islam a spiritual leader of unique qualities and strength.
June 4/Los Angeles Times, 6-5:(I)13.

George Bush
President of the United States
4

Egypt and the United States share the goals of security for Israel, the end of the occupation [of

Arab land by Israel], and the achievement of Palestinian political rights. These are the promises held out by a sustained commitment to a negotiated settlement, toward which a properly structured international conference could play a useful role at an appropriate time . . . There is a need now for creativity, demonstrable commitment and the application of sound principles; creativity in order to look again at old problems and then devise imaginative ways of solving them; commitment to face the challenges and risks of making peace, rather than throwing up our hands and giving up. A new atmosphere must be created, where Israelis and Arabs feel each other's willingness to compromise so that both sides can win.
To reporters, Washington,
April 3/
The New York Times, 4-4:(A)1.

5

[On U.S. relations with Iran]: They keep calling us the Great Satan. That doesn't bother us. Sticks and stones, you remember the old adage, will hurt your bones; the names don't hurt you. But performance is what we're looking for. And I don't see, so far, any sign of change . . . We want better relations with Iran. I remember when we had good relations. We like the Iranian people. We have a lot of Iranians living in this country. [In my inauguration address] I said to Iran, Look, you want better relations? Do what's right. Do what's right by people that are held against their will [as hostages in the Middle East]. And we've seen no movement. I would repeat that offer tonight.
News conference,
Washington, June 8/
The New York Times, 6-10:(A)12.

6

[On whether he is willing to negotiate in his efforts to free American hostages held in Lebanon]: I'm not talking about terms, I'm talking about talking to get people out that are held against their will. And I think I covered that pretty well in my inaugural address when I said "good-will begets good-will." And if ever there

(GEORGE BUSH)

was a clearer signal, in my view that's it. So I repeat it. And if there are changes taking place, and signals that are shifting, I don't want to miss a signal. The life of every single one of these people is too precious for me to be sticking my head in the sand and miss some subtlety in this highly complicated corner of the world. So we are in touch with as many people as possible, anyone that I think can help either me or the Secretary of State or others who are in contact with them. We're going to keep on doing that.

To reporters, Washington,
Aug. 9/
The New York Times, 8-10:(A)6.

1

[On U. S. hostages being held in Lebanon]: If I could find some action—diplomatic, military, private-sector, public-sector—that I thought would help get the hostages out, or guard against future hostage-taking, I would take such action. Military action—I'd like to know that what action we took was not going to victimize a lot of innocent people . . . So when you look at the action that the United States can take, I don't want to be responsible for the loss of innocent life. I also must weigh, if we considered military action, the lives of the Americans that were being asked to carry out that action. So it's just not clear yet, but if I could find a way to take those hostages, get them and bring them out, and that required using the military force of the United States, make no mistake about it, I would do it in an instant.

News conference,
Washington, Aug. 15/
The New York Times, 8-16:(A)8.

2

I'll tell you [something] that really kills me. It's the agony I feel in my heart about Lebanon. Having been there in the early '60s on business and seeing this mecca, this oasis, and then to see what's happened there now [as a result of the civil warfare there]. It just [hurts]. I don't know why I take it almost so personally. Some of it, I think, is

the fact that Americans are still held there against their will [as hostages], and it's Christmastime.

Interview, Washington/
U.S. News & World Report,
12-25:34.

Farouk Charaa
Foreign Minister of Syria

3

[Saying his government could not be expected to renounce the use of chemical weapons unless Israel renounces nuclear weapons]: It is unacceptable, given continued Israeli occupation and the disequilibrium existing in our region, to adopt selective concepts and methods aimed at disarmament concerning only one kind of mass-destruction weapon without taking into account the need of disarmament concerning other forms.

At conference on chemical weapons,
Paris/The Washington Post,
1-13:(A)24.

Dick Cheney
Secretary of Defense
of the United States

4

The United States cannot permit Iran to control [Persian] Gulf sea lanes or to engage in oil blackmail directed against United States allies. Nor can the United States sit idly by while the Soviet fleet sails into the Persian Gulf to give the Soviet Union the power to bring pressure to bear on countries in the region which have previously shown a willingness to cooperate with the United States.

The Washington Post, 3-14:(A)4.

William L. Dickinson
United States Representative,
R-Alabama

5

[On the killing of an American hostage by his Muslim kidnappers in Lebanon]: [U.S. President Bush] made it very clear that until the facts are known—at least more facts than we have now—there's no way you can make a definitive decision. It's an exercise in frustration. If you do

(WILLIAM L. DICKINSON)

nothing, it's the wrong thing to do. If you go to military action, it's the wrong thing to do. And if you negotiate, it's the wrong thing to do. What can you do in a situation like this?

Washington, July 31/
Los Angeles Times, 8-1:(I)8.

Robert J. Dole
United States Senator,
R-Kansas

1

[Criticizing Israel for abducting a Lebanese Shiite Muslim leader alleged to be involved in Middle East terrorism, which led to the announced killing of an American hostage in Beirut]: Perhaps a little more responsibility on the part of the Israelis one of these days would be refreshing. [U.S. President Bush should try to arrive at] some understanding with the Israelis about future conduct that would endanger the lives of Americans. I know the Israelis had good motives but certainly they know where the leverage is. The leverage is with the United States. When these [Muslim] fanatics want a response, they're going to attack an American or kill an American.

Before the Senate,
Washington, July 31/
The New York Times, 8-1:(A)6.

Abba Eban
Former Foreign Minister
of Israel

2

I do not advocate [a Palestinian state], but I am not afraid of such an outcome. We must not allow fear to become the central theme of our lives. I'm concerned when people like the Prime Minister speak with such pessimism. Whoever claims that we can expect destruction at the hands of the Palestinians is guilty of a historical insult to Zionism. From a pragmatic point of view as well, such pessimistic talk acts to destroy our deterrent power.

Interview/
The Washington Post, 5-30:(A)18.

Daniel Elazar
President, Jerusalem Center
for Public Affairs (Israel)

3

This [Israeli] government, like every government in the world, has discovered that it can't provide a complete and comprehensive welfare state and still maintain economic growth.

The Christian Science Monitor,
1-5:1.

Mohammed Hussein Fadlallah
Leader of Hezbollah,
pro-Iranian Lebanese faction

4

The conditions put forward by [Iranian President Hashemi] Rafsanjani for restoring relations with the U.S. are the same ones he put forward during the life of [the late Iranian spiritual leader, Ruhollah Khomeini]. They are that America should stop its aggressive policy against Iran and that America can express that by releasing the frozen Iranian assets . . . I see the problem of the frozen assets as an indication of whether there is a change from a hostile policy. Naturally, this may have an effect on building Iran, but I believe that Iran, which is already rich with its own natural resources, will not relinquish its freedom in exchange for any amount of money.

Interview/
Time, 10-9:58.

Charles E. Grassley
United States Senator,
R-Iowa

5

[Arguing against U.S. talks with PLO members who have been involved in terrorism against Americans in the past]: Do we expect the American people to have collective amnesia on all these unjustified acts of murder by terrorists against American citizens? Are we running an amnesty program for terrorists? We simply cannot elevate terrorists to diplomats. That is the message to the PLO: We will not talk to those who have blood on their hands.

The New York Times,
7-19:(A)4.

David Hartman
Director, Shalom Hartman Institute
for Jewish Study
(Israel)

1

[On the current *intifada,* anti-Israeli violence by Palestinians in the West Bank and Gaza]: In the Six-Day War [of 1967] and even in the war in Lebanon, people told stories of heroism about our [Israeli] soldiers. With the *intifada,* we have not one story of [Israeli] heroism. There's no sense of triumphalism or victory or power. Just the opposite. There's a horrible, helpless feeling.

The Washington Post, 1-30:(A)14.

Hussein I
King of Jordan

2

[Criticizing the Israeli government for refusing to negotiate with the PLO]: It is tragic that Israeli public opinion supports a dialogue with the PLO, yet the leadership in Israel is unable to move with enough vision and enough courage to seize this opportunity for making progress toward the establishment of a just peace.

Interview, Amman/Time, 1-23:32.

3

The forum for a negotiated comprehensive [Israel-Palestinian] settlement is a peace conference under the auspices of the United Nations. Any steps taken should lead to such a conference if our efforts to arrive at a comprehensive settlement are not to be diverted.

Washington, April 19/
Los Angeles Times, 4-20:(I)13.

Martin Indyk
Director,
Near East Policy Institute,
Washington

4

[Tthe U.S. Bush] Administration has learned from experience that if you begin your Middle East diplomacy by putting forward some high-blown peace plan, all the parties to the conflict just sit back and take potshots at it. Instead of the

parties moving themselves, they wait for the United States to move and then criticize it for not moving. So we get all the blame and no action. [U.S. Secretary of State James] Baker seems to be saying to the Israelis and Palestinians: "You are the guys who are going to have to move. We understand that it is going to be difficult, so we are going to begin with some small, concrete steps so you get used to the idea and in that way build some momentum toward negotiations."

The New York Times, 3-16:(A)7.

Paul Jabber
Former director of the
Middle East program,
Council on Foreign Relations

5

[On Israel's refusal to negotiate with the PLO or its chosen representatives]: Who are you going to negotiate with if not your opponent? No one is asking Israel to sit down with [PLO leader] Yasir Arafat . . . [U.S. Secretary of State James] Baker, the Egyptians, the PLO, and everybody else, have been bending over backwards to try to find some formula that would enable the Israelis to say "yes" . . . I don't think we're going to make any significant progress unless the Israelis bite some very hard bullets—just as the PLO and others have who have undergone some agonizing reappraisals.

The Christian Science Monitor,
11-15:2.

Brian Jenkins
Director, research program on
subnational conflict
and political violence,
Rand Corporation

6

[On Americans being held hostage by terrorists in the Middle East]: The [American] public has, to a certain extent, become immune to terrorism. In the last 13 years, there have been only 258 days on which American citizens were not being held hostage by terrorists somewhere in the world. In the last five years, there have been only 22 days when Americans were not being held hostage by terrorists somewhere. In that

(BRIAN JENKINS)

sense, while everyone sympathizes on the humanitarian level, the plight of the hostages simply does not have the pull on the American public. We cannot allow the Iranians and the captors in Lebanon to overrate the pull of the hostage issue on the American public. To put it in words that no U.S. official can afford to say, to put it bluntly, "Washington can wait."

Interview/USA Today, 8-1:(A)9.

Ahmed Jibril
Secretary general,
Popular Front for the
Liberation of Palestine—
General Command

1

Israel is America's Mideast aircraft carrier. You [Americans] keep the Jews on our [Palestinians'] lands to protect your oil interests, and at $3-billion a year in American aid, your ship on land is a bargain . . . In time, it will sink like the Crusader kingdom did.

Interview, Damascus, Syria/
U.S. News & World Report,
7-10:40.

John Paul II
Pope

2

In the name of God, I address Syria and appeal to its authorities to stop the bombardment aimed at destroying the capital of Lebanon [Beirut] and the entire country . . . In reality, we are faced with a threat to the entire order of international life. It is a threat of a moral nature, so much more so because it is a weaker state that is feeling the violence and indifference of the stronger.

Rome, Aug. 15/
The Washington Post, 8-16:(A)1.

Jean-Paul Kauffmann
French journalist;
Former hostage of terrorists
in Lebanon

3

[On his having been a hostage in Lebanon]: One thing is certain, all this you hear in the

press—that he's in the Iranian Embassy in Beirut, for instance—is rubbish. Our abductors have a sense of clandestinity that even the Syrians can't penetrate. It was impossible for the American, French or even the Israeli intelligence services to know where we were. I was moved 18 times. They must laugh, these Lebanese, when they read this stuff.

Interview/Newsweek, 6-5:42.

Salah Khalaf
Deputy chief,
Fatah faction of Palestine
Liberation Organization

4

We believe in direct meetings [with Israel]; we are ready for such meetings, and we say it publicly, on any level. Let the Israelis come and meet us secretly, openly or any other way. We are anxious for such meetings, not because we are in despair. Quite the contrary, it is because we are strong, because we have confidence in ourselves and in the need for peace, because we seek this peace with every faith in it, that we have arrived at a truth that we hope the Israeli leaders will also arrive at before it is too late. This is the truth which says that two peoples and two states must coexist on this land.

Taped address at symposium
sponsored by International Center
for Peace in the Middle East,
Jerusalem, Feb. 22/
The Washington Post, 3-7:(A)24.

Ali Khamenei
President of Iran

5

In setting the conditions for the resumption of [U.S.] ties [with Iran], the American President [Bush] should know that we, not they, have conditions to set. These are our conditions: Stop being aggressive, stop your arrogant actions, discontinue the transgressions against the rights of the Iranian people and return what you owe us.

Prayer service at
Teheran University,
Jan. 27/
The Washington Post, 1-28:(A)15.

WHAT THEY SAID IN 1989

(ALI KHAMENEI)

1

Next to the usurper regime [Israel] ruling over occupied Palestine, you [the U.S.] are the most cursed government in the eyes of the Iranian people. No one in the Islamic Republic will hold talks with you . . . Our nation is alert, alive and strong. We do not need the American government in order to rebuild our country. If some people in the world think that our country's officials would beg the United States for help, they are absolutely mistaken.

To families of Iranian prisoners of
war held in Iraq, Aug. 14/
The Washington Post, 8-15:(A)12.

Ruhollah Khomeini
Spiritual leader of Iran

2

[On Salman Rushdie, author of *The Satanic Verses,* a book which allegedly is blasphemous to Islam]: Even if Salman Rushdie repents and becomes the most pious man of all time, it is incumbent upon every Muslim to employ everything he has, his life and wealth, to send him to hell . . . If a non-Muslim becomes aware of his whereabouts and has the ability to execute him faster than a Muslim, it is incumbent upon Muslims to pay a reward or a fee for this action.

Feb. 19/Los Angeles Times,
2-20:(I)1.

3

I will never let this country fall into the hands of the liberals. I reject those ignorant clerics who believe we should change our slogans under the pretext that they isolated us from the rest of the world. The Western world hates Islam. I will never accept that we compromise on our revolutionary principles in order to re-establish relations with Western or Eastern countries.

The Christian Science Monitor,
3-28:3.

Teddy Kollek
Mayor of Jerusalem

4

We [Jews] for 3,000 years have believed that [Jerusalem] is our capital, and we have acted accordingly. We prayed for it three times a day, and we have never given up the idea. Jerusalem was never the capital of any Arab state. Not everything [the Palestinians] want can they get.

Los Angeles Times, 2-27:(I)13.

Bernard-Henri Levy
French philosopher

5

[On the visit of PLO leader Yasir Arafat to France to meet with French President Francois Mitterrand]: Yasir Arafat is my enemy. He is the enemy of all the Jews. I understand totally those who are revolted by the visit. That said, let's get serious. It is with one's enemies, not one's friends, that one negotiates.

Paris, May 1/
Los Angeles Times, 5-2:(I)13.

Clovis Maksoud
Chief Arab League
representative to the
United Nations

6

[Saying the PLO's status as a non-state observer at the UN should be upgraded]: More than 90 countries recognize the PLO state . . . The PLO is a full member of the Arab League, the Non-Aligned Movement and the Islamic Conference. We think this should be reflected in the UN General Assembly. It is a logical step reflecting a new reality.

The Washington Post, 11-28:(A)9.

Hosni Mubarak
President of Egypt

7

[Criticizing Israel's proposal to have peace talks only with Palestinians in the occupied territories, not with those from outside those areas]: I do not know what is so complicated about this delegation [which would include externally based Palestinians]. Can you hold a dialogue with residents of the occupied territories without Palestinians from outside? I'm presenting you [Israelis] with a challenge. You Israelis are like people banging their heads against a wall.

(HOSNI MUBARAK)

Don't you understand that residents of the territories can do nothing without the go-ahead from Palestinians living outside the territories?

To Israeli journalists,
Cairo, Sept. 20/
The New York Times, 9-21:(A)10.

1

[Saying Israel should be willing to give up occupied Arab land in exchange for peace]: Only you Israelis are complicating the issue, and I emphasize this. I call on Israel to tell its government to agree with the principle of territories for peace. Don't you have to give me something for peace?

Interview/
The Washington Post, 9-21:(A)39.

Hisham M. Nazer
Minister of Planning
of Saudi Arabia

2

In charting the development of Saudi Arabia, we were very much aware that ours is and will remain a conservative religious Islamic society. That was the consensus from the King on down. We always had reservations about mixing things like modernization and Westernization, a mistake that in my opinion many Westerners make out of an ethnocentric view of the world.

Interview, Riyadh, Saudi Arabia/
The New York Times, 4-17:(A)7.

Benjamin Netanyahu
Deputy Foreign Minister
of Israel

3

We [Israelis] have two problems. The first is the [occupied] territories and the Arabs. And the second is the survival of the country. We shouldn't try to solve the first problem at the expense of the second.

Interview, Feb. 8/
The New York Times,
2-9:(A)7.

Mohsen Nourbakhsh
Minister of Finance and
National Economy of Iran

4

We [Iran] don't have any diplomatic relations with the United States. We are not counting on any kind of economic relationship with the United States. Political issues take precedence over economic issues.

Interview, Washington, September/
The Christian Science Monitor,
10-11:9.

Sari Nusseibeh
Professor of philosophy,
Bir Zeit University,
Israeli-occupied West Bank

5

[On the *intifada,* the current anti-Israeli violence in the West Bank and Gaza]: In previous uprisings, we were reacting to something Israel did or was trying to do. Now they [those involved in the current uprisings] sense themselves to be in control of events and shaping them. They sense that they hold genuine power and desire to wield it until they get what they're after. They have their own strategy, their own plan; they carefully calculate the reactions of the outside world to their moves. There's never been anything like this.

The Christian Science Monitor,
1-20:2.

Ehud Olmert
Minister Without Portfolio
of Israel

6

[Criticizing his government's forceful reaction to anti-Israeli violence by Palestinians in the West Bank and Gaza]: The [Palestinian] casualties must weigh on us from the moral point of view and also because it creates difficulties for Israel to cope in the political arena [abroad]. When I get up in the morning and hear an Arab boy has been killed [by Israeli soldiers], I don't get up with it well. I don't sleep with it well. I certainly support the use of force, but there must be some kind of general policy that will reinstate

319

(EHUD OLMERT)

order and lower the number of casualties.

Israeli broadcast interview, Jan. 16/
Los Angeles Times, 1-17:(I)1.

Mohammed Oteibi
Professor of sociology,
King Saud University
(Saudi Arabia)

1

[On the wealth brought to his country by oil sales]: There is very rapid change; and for me, it's scaring me, to tell the truth. We used to have values, we used to have a lot of things, and we are missing it. The sky rained a lot of money on this area, but the social fabric is fading away.

Interview/
Los Angeles Times,
11-14:(A)18.

Reza Pahlavi
Exiled son of the late
Shah of Iran

2

[On charges of brutality by the Iranian secret police during his late father's reign as Shah]: All I have to say is that there was brutality. There was torture and there were unjustified actions by some people. But that doesn't mean that it was a state policy in Iran to have torture or violence. You have police brutality in New York City, too, but that doesn't mean that [U.S.] President Bush should be held responsible for it.

Interview/People, 4-3:50.

Avi Pazner
Spokesman for Israeli Prime Minister
Yitzhak Shamir

3

We believe that [Israel's] most important problem is not the problem that we face inside our country with the Palestinian *intifada,* or uprising ... The most serious problem that Israel faces is the problem of our relationship with the Arab world which, apart from one country, Egypt, does not recognize us and still finds itself,

41 years after our creation, in a state of war against us.

Washington, April 5/
Los Angeles Times, 4-6:(I)13.

Shimon Peres
Vice Prime Minister of Israel

4

I know deep in my heart that we shall not be able to achieve peace [with the Palestinians] without a historic compromise involving a rearrangement of territories and boundaries, of governance and security. We have to negotiate with Palestinians as they are. They should select their representatives; we shall reject their guns ... They shall govern themselves, as we shall govern ourselves.

News conference,
Jerusalem, March 21/
The Washington Post, 3-22:(A)23.

Muammar el-Qaddafi
Chief of State of Libya

5

We [Arabs], for our part, cannot accept responsibility for the atrocities of Hitler. We cannot accept Jews on our land ... Let them go to Alsace-Lorraine. Let them go to Alaska. Let them go to the Baltic states. Let them go to any of these places. The United States is encouraging Jewish emigration from Russia to Palestine. If you accept a Jewish state in Palestine, let us change the map of the whole world. We, the Muslim people, wish to live in New York because we like to live in New York. Why not? The Jews like Palestine, so we like New York as a place to live.

At meeting of non-aligned nations,
Belgrade, Yugoslavia, Sept. 5/
Los Angeles Times, 9-6:(I)8.

Dan Quayle
Vice President
of the United States

6

[On the U.S. attitude toward the PLO and its leader, Yasir Arafat]: Let me tell you, my friends,

(DAN QUAYLE)

we need more than press-conference statements and semantics. We need to see real evidence of concrete actions by the PLO—actions for peace and against terrorism—before changing our fundamental [negative] attitude toward the PLO . . . Once again, simple prudence obliges us to monitor Mr. Arafat and his organization very carefully and to probe his words very closely before arriving at a final determination.

Before National Executive Committee
of Anti-Defamation League of B'nai B'rith,
Palm Beach, Fla., Feb. 10/
Los Angeles Times, 2-11:(I)14.

1

We believe that the Arab-Israeli conflict is not intractable, and that compromises on all outstanding issues can be found. But the responsibility for making the compromises, for finding the solutions, rests with the parties themselves. Anyone who tries to shift the primary peacekeeping responsibility to the United States, who thinks that we can somehow be persuaded into pressuring Israel to accept a pre-cooked solution is only kidding himself. Israel knows what is in its national-security interests and we will support Israel.

Before National Executive Committee
of Anti-Defamation League of B'nai B'rith,
Palm Beach, Fla., Feb. 10/
The New York Times, 2-11:3.

Yitzhak Rabin
Minister of Defense of Israel

2

[On the anti-Israeli violence by Palestinians in the West Bank and Gaza]: As long as the residents of the [occupied] territories aren't ready to sit down at the negotiating table, as long as they respond with violence, rocks and bottles, they will not make us run away, they will not make us surrender. They will suffer. As long as they say, "We will continue with violence." their violence will be met with force. What is Israel to do?

Before the Knesset (Parliament),
Jerusalem, Jan. 18/
Los Angeles Times, 1-19:(I)6.

Hashemi Rafsanjani
Speaker of the
Iranian Parliament

3

The people of Palestine . . . must avenge the blood [of the estimated 461 Palestinian deaths in the Israeli-occupied West Bank and Gaza]. If in retaliation for every Palestinian martyred in Palestine they will kill and execute, not inside Palestine, five Americans or Britons or Frenchmen, [the Israelis] would not continue these wrongs . . . Those who give $10-billion a year to preserve Israel and know what they are doing—is their blood worth anything? It is not hard to kill Americans and Frenchmen. It is a bit difficult [to kill] Israelis, but there are so many [Americans and Frenchmen] everywhere in the world.

At prayers, Teheran, May 5/
Los Angeles Times, 5-6:(I)1,15.

Hashemi Rafsanjani
President of Iran

4

[On the U.S. hostages held by terrorists in Lebanon]: I wish to say—I address the White House—that Lebanon has a solution; the freedom of the hostages is solvable. They have intelligent and manageable solutions. One cannot solve the issue with such bullying ways [by the U.S.], with arrogant confrontations and tyranny. Come along wisely; we then will help you to solve the problems there so that the people of the region may live in peace and tranquillity.

Prayer sermon, Teheran, Aug. 4/
The New York Times, 8-5:1.

Abdul Ahmed Rahman
Chief spokesman,
Palestine Liberation
Organization

5

[Criticizing Iranian Parliamentary Speaker Hashemi Rafsanjani for advising Palestinians to hijack Western airliners and take Western hostages to combat alleged Israeli repression in the West Bank and Gaza]: We are against this poisoned advice to the Palestinian people to commit international terrorism against innocent

(ABDUL AHMED RAHMAN)

people. We are against terrorism. We are against the advice from Rafsanjani to take hostages and hijack airplanes. These are uncivilized methods.

Tunis, Tunisia, May 7/
The Washington Post,
5-8:(A)28.

Ronald Reagan
President of the United States

1

[On the Americans who have been held hostage by Middle Eastern terrorists]: It preys very heavily on me, and has from the time they were taken hostage. I think it's one of the cruelest, most cowardly, barbaric things that any group of people can do. And to those who have taken them I feel that way. I hope and pray that if it can't be us, that it can soon be the next [U.S.] Administration that will see them come home.

Interview,
Washington, Jan. 18/
The New York Times,
1-19:(A)14.

Charles E. Redman
Spokesman for the
Department of State
of the United States

2

[Criticizing Israel's expulsion of Palestinians involved in anti-Israeli violence in the West Bank and Gaza]: As a strong friend of Israel, we are gravely concerned about these most recent expulsions. Deportations are an unacceptable practice under the Geneva Conventions. Moreover, they are counter-productive, and we do not believe they are an appropriate form of punishment. Instead of enhancing Israel's security, deportations increase Palestinian resentment and add to tensions. If individuals are accused of having committed criminal acts, they should be afforded full and public judicial process to defend themselves. If found guilty, they should be punished properly.

Jan. 3/
The Washington Post,
1-4:(A)12.

Yitzhak Shamir
Prime Minister of Israel

3

[On the anti-Israeli violence by Palestinians in the West Bank and Gaza]: Neither murders nor stones nor Molotov cocktails will destroy the will of the nation of Israel to redeem the Land of Israel and settle it with many Jews.

Brakh, Israeli-occupied West Bank,
Jan. 12/
Los Angeles Times, 1-13:(I)12.

4

[On possible Arab-Israeli peace talks]: I don't believe in conferences and things like that. But if it can help someone that these negotiations be held under some formal auspices of the superpowers or the UN, I don't mind—as long as the negotiations themselves are direct and on condition that the external bodies do not intervene in the content of the negotiations. Maybe it can help . . . The main thing is to get to negotiations. I know very well that the road from negotiations to a settlement is a long one, but if we don't start down this road, we will never reach an agreement.

Interview/
The Washington Post, 1-14:(A)14.

5

[On anti-Israeli violence by Palestinians in the West Bank and Gaza]: Those who throw stones and gasoline bombs at us do that not because we are sitting in Nablus. They do that because we are in the Land of Israel and we want to be an independent people and live in peace . . . One of the angers I have against these people of the *intifada* [the uprising] is that they make us sometimes kill people we don't want to kill.

To Israeli reservists,
Nablus, Israeli-occupied West Bank,
Jan. 17/
Los Angeles Times, 1-18:(I)12.

6

Our government is united in its opposition to the creation of a Palestinian Arab state west of the River Jordan. We are opposed to negotia-

(YITZHAK SHAMIR)

tions with the PLO because it will inevitably lead to a demand for a state.

At conference of World Jewish leaders,
Jerusalem, March 20/
The Washington Post,3-21:(A)15.

1

[On the *intifada,* anti-Israeli violence by Palestinians in the West Bank and Gaza]: The *intifada* is, above all, a new means of Arab struggle against Israel. After having tried every other method of war—conventional war, terrorism, economic boycott—the Arabs realized that they were getting nowhere. The *intifada* is an expression of that disappointment. I am not saying that it was conceived outside the country, but the Arabs quickly encouraged it and discovered Israel's weakness: its inability to break this movement by indiscriminate means. We cannot, for example, open fire on crowds of hundreds or thousands of people. We think that this *intifada* does not serve the interests of the Palestinians. If they want to improve their lot, even politically, that can be achieved through negotiation. But if they want a Palestinian state immediately, they will not get one. They will not get one by negotiations or by force.

Interview/
World Press Review, April:27.

2

[On why his government refuses to negotiate with the PLO even in light of that organization's statement of recognition of Israel]: A government—a state—can change its policy. But a political or ideological movement whose whole reason for being is the disappearance of Israel is not going to change from one day to the next. Change its whole philosophy, its ideology? That is impossible! We know that the PLO's shifts are merely tactical. The organization remains faithful to its ideology. Its leaders say so, for that matter. The PLO is not trying to convince Israel that it must make concessions. The PLO thinks it must convince the U.S., because it thinks Israel is an American puppet. To convince the U.S., the

Palestinians have to go through certain motions. [PLO leader Yasir] Arafat has to say that he recognizes the existence of Israel, that certain terrorist acts are held in abeyance for a time. But not for good. They have said so.

Interview/
World Press Review, April:28.

3

First, we propose an effort to make the existing peace between Israel and Egypt, based on the Camp David accords, a cornerstone for expanding peace in the region. Second, we call upon the United States and Egypt to make it clear to the Arab governments that they must abandon their hostility and belligerency toward Israel. Third, we call for a multinational effort under the leadership of the United States, and with substantial Israeli participation, to finally solve the Arab refugee problem. Fourth, in order to launch a political negotiating process, we propose free and democratic elections, free from the atmosphere of PLO violence, terror and intimidation, among the Palestinian Arabs of Judea, Samaria [The West Bank] and Gaza.

To reporters, Washington, April 6/
The New York Times, 4-7:(A)5.

4

For us [Israelis], the carnage in Beirut, the use of poison gas against civilians and acts of terrorism and fanaticism are not news from afar. They are events happening around the corner. If there is one mistake Israel cannot afford to make, it is the mistake of forgetting where we live.

USA Today, 4-10:(A)10.

5

[Criticizing calls for Israel to give up the Palestinian territory it occupies in the West Bank and Gaza]: The slogan "territories for peace" implies that if we give up these areas, we shall have peace. But the truth is that if we withdraw, there will be a PLO state on the outskirts of Tel Aviv and Jerusalem, and war. We cannot relinquish control over these areas and survive.

Before American Society of
Newspaper Editors, Washington,
April 13/
The Washington Post, 4-14:(A)22.

WHAT THEY SAID IN 1989

1

Israel is under many pressures and threats, especially related to her security. I would say to ourselves: "Let's keep things in proportion." The truth which we have to see and come to terms with is that the Arabs have not yet reconciled themselves to our existence and our independence. The expression of this is the violence and the insane hatred we have to stand up against [such as the current anti-Israeli violence by Palestinians in the West Bank and Gaza].

Broadcast interview/
Los Angeles Times, 5-11:(I)14.

2

[On U.S.-Israeli relations]: Loyal and firm allies are important to every country and under all circumstances. This applies especially to a superpower, and especially because of the constantly changing circumstances. Israel is such an ally of the United States, and our alliance is as steadfast as ever.

Before Los Angeles World Affairs
Council, November/
Los Angeles Times, 12-22:(A)14.

3

Among our [Arab] neighbors, democracy is still unknown. Totalitarianism, religious fanaticism, violence and terror still prevail . . . And immense energies are wasted on attempts to isolate and delegitimize our state and mobilize an international coalition against us.

Speech/
Los Angeles Times, 12-22:(A)15.

Ariel Sharon
Minister of Trade and Industry
and former Minister of Defense
of Israel

4

From my childhood, I have believed Jews and Arabs can live together, and I believe now they should live together. I was taught by my parents from a very early age one very important thing. If that would be understood, all of us could live in

peace. It is that all the rights to this country, to the land of Israel—especially Judea and Samaria—are Jewish. I am talking about rights over the land. But everyone who lives in the country should have all the rights of the country.

Interview/Time, 4-17:40.

5

Jordan is Palestine. The capital of Palestine is Amman. If Palestinian Arabs want to find their political expression, they will have to do it in Amman. The land west of the Jordan River, between the Jordan River and the Mediterranean, is Israel. Judea, Samaria—the so-called West Bank—and Gaza are Israeli. We will never give them up. There will be no second Palestinian state west of the Jordan River.

Interview/Time, 4-17:41.

6

[On the intifada, anti-Israeli violence by Palestinians in the West Bank and Gaza]: We have to stop using slogans, dishing out promises and handing out tranquilizers. The time has come to deal with terror and violence. I think we are in a war—a different kind of war, but a war. The most important thing is to restore law and order, to bring an end to terror and violence, to what is called here the intifada, and to eliminate the heads of the terrorist organizations, and first of all [PLO leader Yasir] Arafat. As long as that will not be done, I don't see any real possibility to arrive at peace or even to start a peace process.

To reporters,
Golan Heights, July 17/
Los Angeles Times, 7-18:(I)13.

Eduard A. Shevardnadze
Foreign Minister
of the Soviet Union

7

Israel no longer has even a semblance of a pretext for refusing to start a dialogue with [the PLO], which is recognized by the international community as the sole legitimate representative of the Palestinian people . . . It is precisely because the Middle East is becoming a major

(EDUARD A. SHEVARDNADZE)

obstacle to the further development of the process of disarmament, on which most of the world's nations place their hopes for a better future, that it is necessary to internationalize the search for a settlement in the Middle East.

Speech, Cairo, Feb. 23/
The Washington Post,
2-24:(A)12.

1

There was a time when the world community helped the Jewish people to exercise their free choice—to establish the state of Israel. Today, Israel has no right to deny freedom of choice to the Palestinian people [who wish to establish a Palestinian homeland].

Speech, Cairo, Feb. 23/
The Washington Post,
2-24:(A)14.

2

Unless a peaceful, comprehensive political settlement is found to the Arab-Israeli conflict, developments in the region will follow a spiral wound by the logic of military confrontation.

Speech, Cairo, Feb. 23/
Los Angeles Times, 2-24:(I)16.

Dan Shomron
Lieutenant General
and Chief of Staff,
Israeli Armed Forces

3

[Saying the *intifada*—anti-Israeli violence by Palestinians in the West Bank and Gaza— cannot be put down militarily in an acceptable way]: People ask why we don't end the *intifada*. Anyone who wants to end the *intifada* must remember that there are only three ways to achieve· this: transfer, starvation or physical elimination—that is, genocide.

Speech to business people,
Jerusalem, June 15/
Los Angeles Times,
6-17:(I)18.

Zehdi Labib al-Terzi
Palestine Liberation
Organization representative
to the United Nations

4

A Palestinian state cannot be established as long as there is an [Israeli] army of occupation [in the West Bank and Gaza] whose presence de- prives the population of freedom. This military occupation will be liquidated. It need not happen overnight or in one stroke of the hand. This may sound like self-destruction to some Israelis, but what I am saying is that, after 40 years, they should know better: Israel has nothing to fear from the military point of view. It defeated all the Arab armies together but failed to realize one thing: It is impossible to defeat the Palestinians. I view the partition [of Palestine] as a punishment that will result in the birth of inseparable Siamese twins joined by a common economic spine. I do not see any grave economic problems. After all, the 120,000 people crossing [into Israel proper] every day will continue to do so—but without any reservations. They may even rent flats close to their jobs instead of traveling home every night. I see nothing wrong with trying everything where economic cooperation is concerned.

Interview/
World Press Review, February:17.

Margaret D. Tutwiler
Spokesperson for the
Department of State
of the United States

5

Any improvement in relations between [the U.S. and Iran] will be contingent on Iranian willingness to act responsibly in the world arena, to include efforts to resolve the hostage issue [U.S. hostages held in Lebanon] once and for all, by producing the release of our hostages, and by also making it clear that they have turned away from support of terrorism.

Aug. 4/
The New York Times, 8-5:5.

6

[Saying the U.S. opposes upgrading the status of the PLO from non-state observer at the UN]:

WHAT THEY SAID IN 1989

(MARGARET D. TUTWILER)

We feel so strongly about this that we will cut off funding [for the UN if the upgrading is approved]. The United States opposes any enhancement in the UN of the status of the self-proclaimed state of Palestine [as the PLO would be known if upgraded]. [The U.S. does not recognize a Palestinian state because] it does not satisfy the generally accepted criteria under international law for statehood.

Nov. 27/
The Washington Post,
11-28:(A)9.

Ali Akbar Velayati
Foreign Minister of Iran

1

In the last few years, we [Iran] have done a lot to help countries which have had hostages in Lebanon. Sometimes we could do something, but sometimes we failed. So when we consider the past history of the hostage crisis in Lebanon, we find that there are some events that are out of the reach of Iran and many other countries. If the U.S. releases our frozen assets we will do our best; we will try to help as much as we can. But it doesn't mean we can guarantee 100 per cent the releasing of hostages, because the hostages are not in our hands.

Interview,
New York/
U.S. News & World Report,
10-9:30.

Ezer Weizman
Minister of Science,
and former Minister of Defense,
of Israel

2

[On Israel's relations with the Palestinians]: The most important thing is who is the authority on the other [Palestinian] side—who can sign on the dotted line and deliver the way [the late Egyptian President Anwar] Sadat delivered [in his peace pact with Israel]. And the PLO are the ones, whether we like it or not . . . If we want to achieve peace, we'll have to sit down, and I think we will sit down with the PLO and [its leader Yasir] Arafat.

Interview/
The Washington Post, 3-25:(A)10.

James Zogby
Executive director,
Arab-American Institute,
Washington

3

[On anti-Israeli violence by Palestinians in the West Bank and Gaza]: The uprising is the expression of the national will of the Palestinian people, that they will be free and that they, and only they, will determine their destiny as a people. It is their call for identity, for national self-determination, for respect. It has created an irreversible tide in the relationship between Palestinian and Israeli people. Israelis have clearly gotten the message, whether they . . . will admit it or not.

Interview/USA Today, 9-18:(A)13.

PART THREE

General

The Arts

Berenice Abbott
Photographer

1

Photography is the least mechanical of arts. There's no other art in which you can shoot your guts out so much. It is learning to see the way the lens sees, which is altogether different: how high, how far, how low, where to put the camera, to know that this background is better, that that foreground is worse. The camera is a lousy instrument designed to protect your silver salts, on which the picture is made, from too much light. The paintbrush is a better instrument for an artist.

Interview,
Monson, Maine/
The New York Times,
10-4:(B)5.

Les AuCoin
United States
Representative,
D-Oregon

2

[On the controversy over the NEA's funding of obscene or politically oriented art]: When it comes to art, I think the fact that public funds are involved should not mean that the freedom of the artist is somehow diminished. I think we should fund artistic expression to allow more artists to stretch further to give us more art—art which challenges, art which inspires and, yes, at times and occasionally, art that shocks. But you are ultimately operating in a political sphere and some judgment and restraint is required so you don't jeopardize the best mechanism we have for promoting and extending the arts. My interest has been in trying to keep [these] blips in the NEA's history from being turned into swords that will be plunged into the gut of the NEA so as to kill it.

Interview/
Los Angeles Times,
11-16:(F)13.

Livingston Biddle
Former Chairman, National
Endowment for the Arts
of the United States

3

The Chairman [of the National Endowment for the Arts] expresses the commitment of our nation to the arts. The person who holds the job is at once regarded as Santa Claus by the whole arts community, whatever the season, or Scrooge, hoarding his resources. He is also regarded as the Oracle of Delphi when it comes to the arts.

The New York Times, 3-20:(A)1.

Theodore Bikel
Actor; Former member,
National Council on the Arts

4

[Criticizing Congressional efforts to stop NEA funding of "objectionable art"]: We managed what I consider some very sane decisions regarding the arts. We gave support to people with some kind of track record, but we wanted to branch out into new and uncharted waters. Everybody is going to go the safe way now, even if Congress backs off from this horrendous notion of prior restraint. We assume a 90 per cent failure rate in the sciences. But in the arts, as a society, we want only success.

Los Angeles Times, 9-9:(I)17.

Fernando Botero
Colombian painter

5

Every artist has an obsession, and the greater, the better. If you think of Titian or Matisse, it is color; of Giotto, form. One does not repeat oneself; one gets even deeper into the problem. Of course, after Picasso, everyone thinks he has to change his style every week. But painting is always obsession and evolution because an artist is always working on the skin of the canvas. A painter's maturity consists of his radicalism. The more sectarian a painter's beliefs, the better,

WHAT THEY SAID IN 1989

because sectarianism involves renunciation, and renunciation is maturity. Obviously, this radicalism brings a lot of enemies. Thus it is impossible for painters to be friends. Each has his own obsessions. Friendship between artists is the enemy of enthusiasm. I avoid them like lepers.

Interview/
World Press Review,
August:61.

J. Carter Brown
Director,
National Gallery of Art,
Washington

1

If an artist is great enough, each period sees in him or her where they're coming from. So Rembrandt has never been out [of style]; each generation has found something else to admire in Rembrandt. And this is what happens with someone of the stature of Cezanne. Someone with less stature may be the darling of one age and then can't make it into the next . . . as Cezanne seems able to do.

The Christian Science Monitor,
2-1:10.

2

In 1984, the total of contemporary art sales in New York was $12-million. Last year, it was $104-million. So we do have a boom psychology here. Many people ask why. Basically, I suppose it's easy to say it's supply and demand. The supply, except for the contemporary field, where artists are producing more, is limited by finite groups of objects, and more and more of them are ending up in permanent collections in museums, or being restricted by export restrictions. And therefore, it isn't easy, even if you're as rich as the Getty Trust, to find them to spend your $50-million a year pocket money on.

Interview,
Washington/
The Christian Science Monitor,
7-26:10.

3

A great art collection is like a garden. A bit of judicious pruning is necessary—though some blossoms fall.

Aug. 8/
The Washington Post, 8-9:(C)10.

George Bush
President of the United States

4

Art defines our civilization and opens new worlds for us, as many worlds as there are writers, dancers, musicians. The arts are the product of the diversity of our democracy; a colorful reflection, like the multi-colored mirror of our history.

At National Medal of Arts awards
ceremony, Washington, Nov. 17/
The New York Times, 11-18:12.

Chuck Close
Painter

5

Being an artist today is a lot harder than it was in the past. There is a sense of raised expectations today, due to art schools and other institutions [with] which artists are associated. You see Frank Stella have a one-man show when he's 21, or Julian Schnabel have a retrospective when he's 30. If you've been hanging in there and haven't achieved any measurable success, you begin to ask yourself, "What do I have to point to that shows I'm a professional, too?"

The Christian Science Monitor,
10-10:16.

Milton Cummings
Professor of political science,
Johns Hopkins University

6

[On the National Endowment for the Arts]: I think that, overall, the record is good. It was really a novel thing for the Federal government to take on when they created the Endowment . . . I think that you would have had the incredible flowering with the arts that has occurred in the last 25 years if you had not had the NEA, but I do

(MILTON CUMMINGS)

think they made a difference that justifies the expenditures. I think the symbolism of our country caring enough about the arts to spend modest amounts of money [on them] is good.

Los Angeles Times, 9-9:(I)17.

John C. Danforth
United States Senator,
R-Missouri

1

[On proposals that the NEA not fund obscene or controversial art]: Maybe there shouldn't be any National Endowment for the Arts. Maybe the government should never be in the business of making judgments of taste, because that's what the NEA does. I think that it's an arguable position. But the question isn't whether the NEA should do it or shouldn't do that. We've already decided that. The NEA is in that business. The question is whether we in the Congress of the U.S. should try to establish some criteria by which we define what is or is not suitable art . . . and how do we draw those definitions, and should we really write definitions on the floor of the Senate which cover *Godspell* and *Tom Sawyer* and *The Merchant of Venice* and *The Color Purple* and *The Godfather* . . . I think that the answer is no.

Before the Senate, Washington,
Sept. 28/
The New York Times, 9-30:12.

Philippe de Montebello
Director, Metropolitan
Museum of Art, New York

2

Art, especially great art, is difficult to access. It is so easy in the visual arts to take in an image in a split second and move on. We have to fight this. If I spend a certain amount of time in front of a work, it reveals all sorts of secrets to me. So people should come and look at just a few things well. Otherwise, they're sort of doing an inventory and getting a quick thrill—the punch line rather than the unfolding story.

Interview, New York/
Cosmopolitan, March:147.

John Dixon
Chairman, Corcoran School
of Art, Washington

3

Politicians have not looked at artists as messengers. Artists are generally perceived as being disconnected—some extremity out there that's interesting. Artists are sensitive to the environment they are in. They are signaling things in the society that are either right or wrong.

Los Angeles Times, 9-29:(VI)19.

Elliot W. Eisner
Professor of education and art,
Stanford University

4

Artists speak to us in a language that carries meaning that cannot be conveyed through words. Will our children be able to understand what they have to say? Even more, will they know their messages exist?

The Christian Science Monitor,
3-13:12.

Joseph Esherick
Architect

5

Comic ideas have an analogy to architecture. You set someone up *here,* and then the punch-line is over *there.* That sudden abrupt flip can be a revelation, or a Joycean epiphany—which is close to what architecture is.

Interview/
Connoisseur, August:74.

Martin Freedman
Director, Walker Art Center,
Minneapolis

6

Periodically, the issue is bound to arise concerning works of art, artists and programs sponsored by the NEA. Things have come out that have been disturbing, but the function of artists is not to sedate. When you have openness and freedom, there will be incidents, but the real issue is artistic freedom.

Los Angeles Times, 6-23:(VI)9.

331

John E. Frohnmayer
Chairman-designate,
National Endowment
for the Arts
of the United States

1

Very often the art that is deemed historically to be the most significant is not necessarily popular when first introduced. In my definition, entertainment is accessible to everybody, and I don't think art is accessible without some degree of education. That is why I think arts education is so important, because unless we are literate to color and composition and form and content and sound, then the tools for appreciating much of art are not there.

Interview,
Washington, Sept. 11/
The New York Times,
9-12:(B)3.

2

My response to people who argue that the Federal government has no legitimate role in supporting the arts is that we're not here just to be protected. The government doesn't exist just to put an impregnable ring of missiles around the United States, because there has to be something in the middle there—something we're protecting. And that is the ability of Americans to exercise artistic freedom. To learn through the arts that there are a number of different ways to look at things, which is the fundamental basis of cooperative society . . . One dream scenario would be that, in every community in the country, there are imagination celebrations and art teachers in the schools who really turn kids on to creativity, and music teachers who can work with the kids as alternatives to gang life. The objective is to see the U.S. as a nation where people are really practicing the arts. It's not corny to sing. It's not wimpy to paint. You shouldn't get derision if you do ballet. There needs to be a sense that creativity and the arts are normal things to do. That's the ultimate of a creative society.

Interview,
Portland, Ore./
Los Angeles Times, 9-22:(I)10,11.

John E. Frohnmayer
Chairman, National
Endowment for the Arts
of the United States

3

[On the controversy surrounding the NEA's withdrawal of a grant for an exhibition about AIDS because of what it says is the political nature of the exhibit]: I'm doing my best to make my position clear. I hope it's coming through that it's because I care so passionately about the Endowment that I think it's essential that we remove politics from grants and must do so if the Endowment is to remain credible to the American people and to the Congress. Obviously, there are lots of great works of art that are political. Picasso's *Guernica* and the plays of Bertolt Brecht are strongly political. But the question is, should the Endowment be funding art whose primary intent is political? The NEA has always steered clear of that.

Interview, Nov. 9/
The New York Times, 11-10:(B)13.

4

[On the recently enacted law barring NEA funding of obscene or controversial art]: We are feeling our way along in a situation which none of us really wanted, under a law which none of us think is necessary. The law is unnecessary and we will certainly work for its removal.

News conference,
New York, Nov. 15/
The New York Times, 11-16:(B)4.

Leonard Garment
Lawyer; Former Adviser to the
President of the United States
(Richard Nixon)

5

[On the National Endowment for the Arts]: When the Endowment's budget was increased quite dramatically under President Nixon, with Nancy Hanks as Chairman of the Endowment, that was a certain time and place. She was right just then, and President Nixon was interested for reasons that were again peculiar to that time and place. Now, nearly a quarter of a century later,

(LEONARD GARMENT)

times have changed, and one has to find out what is right for this time and place. Are there comparable opportunities today? I think the education of children is central to the solution to problems of health, crime, delinquency and general social pathology, and if arts organizations get involved in education they can become part of a broad new coalition. I don't mean the Endowments should give up everything else they're doing, but I think education offers a possibility for an announced, focused moving into areas that everybody is concerned about, not just people who have a very strong feeling for chamber music. For most children, producing art is their introduction to work. They discover what powerful satisfaction work can give. These are the impulses people need if they are to be productive members of society. Furthermore, if children are to become innovative, they must be at home in the world, and nothing better suits them for that than a broad education which includes the arts ... What I'm saying is that to justify the expenditure of government funds for art, you have to show what it can do. The new flag for the National Endowment for the Arts should say on it what Lincoln said in his second inaugural: "Think anew; act anew." Those are timeless words.

Interview,
Washington/
The New York Times, 4-11:(B)3.

Dana Gioia
Poet

1

It's true: In some ways bad art responds much better to analysis than good art, because in good art there is almost always a mystery which remains beyond explanation ... [Critics] have reduced the literary experience to an analytical, intellectual experience. I've always felt that part of being a true critic is responding to a work of art with the fullness of your humanity, of which your intellect is only part.

Interview,
White Plains, N.Y./
Connoisseur, March:110.

Ernst Gombrich
Art historian; Former director,
Warburg Institute, London

2

We search for one common denominator, which says, for example, that Cubism relates to relativity, or that Mannerism was the result of the deep spiritual crisis of the age. But I don't like those intellectual shortcuts. Culture has no such monolithic character. Art is the product of individual artists, and sometimes it's even they who influence history.

Interview/
The New York Times,
2-23:(B)2.

Fred Grandy
United States Representative,
R-Iowa

3

[On the controversy over NEA's funding of obscene or politically oriented art]: To me, the [recent] decision to yank the grant [for a controversial art exhibit about AIDS] ... is directly related to the debate that we had on the potential of NEA funding and whether or not taxpayer dollars should go to fund works that may be extensively political in nature, homoerotic or distasteful. What this is going to require ultimately is the Federal government is going to have to give a little bit more on the imagination side and the artistic community is going to have to get a little more politically hip.

Los Angeles Times,
11-16:(F)13.

Oswaldo Guayasamin
Ecuadoran painter

4

All the painting I do is born 8,000 years ago. I don't believe myself the author of these works. I am the most surprised of anyone when I finish painting something. From where do so many things come? When I am painting, I am completely outside myself; things are surging from inside me that I don't even know myself.

Interview/
Los Angeles Times, 11-29:(F)8.

333

Jesse Helms
United States Senator,
R-North Carolina

1

[On those who criticize his efforts to prevent the National Endowment for the Arts from funding certain "objectionable" material]: What they [arts advocates and news media] seem to be saying is that we in Congress must choose between absolutely no Federal presence in the arts or granting artists the absolute freedom to use tax dollars as they wish, regardless of how vulgar, blasphemous or despicable their works may be. If we indeed must make this choice, then the Federal government should get out of the arts.

Before the Senate, Washington/
Los Angeles Times, 9-9:(I)16.

2

[On his proposal to keep the NEA from funding obscene or controversial art]: Censorship is not involved. I've said over and over again, the issue is solely this: Any artist can produce anything he wants to, but nobody has a pre-emptive right to raid the pocketbooks of the American taxpayers . . . Just remember that we become a part of what we condone. We have condoned too much. And so much has been said about who's going to decide. We've had an organization that we've been funding for a long time called the National Endowment for the Arts. Sure, I want to put the blocks to them; I want them to exercise their responsibility instead of exercising irresponsibility. I'm not prepared to condone forcing the taxpayers to support this kind of thing . . . A vote against this amendment [to limit the NEA's funding discretion] is a vote for pornography.

Before the Senate,
Washington, Sept. 28/
The New York Times, 9-30:12.

Josef Herman
British painter

3

. . . there is a certain misunderstanding about "monumentality" [in painting]—that one always associates it with physical scale. But true monumentality has, rather, a spiritual ingredient independent of physical size. So a drawing of four inches can be big, while a painting of three yards can be very small.

Interview,
London/
The Christian Science Monitor,
1-12:10.

Charlton Heston
Actor;
Former member,
National Council on the Arts

4

I think a National Endowment [for the Arts] funded by taxpayers' money has two responsibilities. First, it has to preserve and expand the appreciation of the great works of the past, which obviously are more extensive than the great works of the present. You're pretty safe with Michelangelo, Mozart and Shakespeare. But you must also encourage new work. It's very hard to do, especially given the political considerations that you have to split [the money] up according to states. And that inevitably is a political consideration—along with ethnic background and religious background.

Los Angeles Times,
9-9:(I)16.

Howard Hodgkin
Painter

5

I've talked ad infinitum about how I want my pictures to be totally self-contained physical objects. Sometimes the subject is so ineffable— almost uncatchable—you need to make sure that, for the viewer and for itself, it is contained in something inviolable. I'm trying to think of a parallel. I can think of a really stupid one! Like the little urns in ancient Greece that were made to contain tears. If you think of the life of a picture in the world and what people will do to it, and where it'll be hung, and so on, it needs to be like a sort of clenched fist, like a safe jewel case.

Interview,
London/
The Christian Science Monitor,
4-13:10.

Frank Hodsoll
Chairman, National
Endowment for the Arts
of the United States

1

... the big downside to me is that the arts that we support, all the cultural heritage and most of the contemporary expression, aren't really part of the lives of most Americans. In part, it's a question of [lack of] education and understanding and comfort level going out of the schools and, in part, due to the extraordinary power of the entertainment industry in capturing our leisure time.

Los Angeles, Feb. 16/
Los Angeles Times, 2-18:(V)10.

Farouk Hosni
Minister of Culture of Egypt

2

Being an artist doesn't just mean that you create things but that you are a person of vision and imagination ... The problem is not the artist's visionary point of view but the means—the material tools—to carry out his dreams.

Interview, Marina del Rey, Calif./
Los Angeles Times, 7-26:(VI)3.

Keith Jarrett
Jazz musician

3

I think most artists have a greater responsibility than most artists would like to know. And it goes far beyond the art they are involved in. It has something to do with perceiving more than they thought. When an artist is on the brink or could ever get close to showing that, what else is more important to a creative person than perceiving deeper or more of what they thought was everything? In an age when there's no real father figure—there's no church saying this is right and this is wrong, and if they did, no one would believe it anyway—and when there's no faith in teachers or a path that everyone would agree, "Here's a wise man ... ," all that's left is the arts. There's nothing else.

Interview/
Down Beat, February:19.

Garth Jowett
Professor of radio and television,
University of Houston

4

There is a mystique about American popular culture that has been dominant this century and particularly since the end of World War II. One only has to look at the impact of American movies. More than 60 per cent of screen time throughout the world is still devoted to the showing of Hollywood product. People may resent the United States militarily, and throw eggs at our soldiers, but they love its popular forms.

The Christian Science Monitor,
2-16:10.

Jonathan Katz
Executive director, National
Assembly of State Arts Agencies

5

[On a proposed Congressional bill that would prohibit the National Endowment for the Arts from funding controversial and obscene arts projects]: One of the reasons it's such a difficult issue is that ideas and issues will always be controversial to some citizens and some legislators, and that's one reason that free access to the broad range is practical. Otherwise, you have to identify some mechanism that is going to limit the range, and the American public from the time that the Constitution was formed through the present has always acted against the limiting of its access to ideas and images. Who would want to be the person to say, "This image is to be denied public access," or "This idea is too controversial for the American people." I wouldn't want to do it, and I wouldn't want to be the Representative or Senator responsible.

The Washington Post, 7-29:(C)5.

Jeff Koons
Artist

6

It used to be that if you weren't good enough to make it in the art world, you'd go into advertising; but now it's the other way around. Advertising is much more politically effective than art at this point. As to why I haven't gone into adver-

(JEFF KOONS)

tising, I try to incorporate the tools used in advertising and the entertainment industry in my work. Artists must incorporate these things, otherwise we'll become a completely impotent profession. And right now, art is impotent and totally non-threatening, and that's why it's commanding the [high] prices we've been seeing lately. Its political statement is almost blank, so corporations can buy it without worrying that it will alter anything at all. Artists used to be the ones who knew how to manipulate, control and meet the needs of the masses, but we've lost our power. And I want to bring the power back.

Interview, Beverly Hills, Calif./
Los Angeles Times, 1-22:(Calendar)5.

Bella Lewitzky
Choreographer

1

[On the growing influence of the Pacific area in the arts]: I happen to believe that the arts must help people lose their egocentricity and recognize that we of Anglo-European backgrounds are not the dominant culture in the world. We have been wonderfully influential, but it's time we discovered that the world is more than just round—it's round with a lot of facets.

Los Angeles Times,
3-19:(Calendar)66.

Alan Lomax
Music historian

2

Man's biggest contribution on the planet is the invention of a multitude of cultures, each suited to a certain environment and time. Each culture's complex of artistic patterns sums up the healthy modes of survival. We have to think into the future how to maintain all the potential that the human spirit has spun out in the last 90,000 years. To have only one culture would be like facing the Atlantic with a storm on the way—and with just one lifeboat.

Interview,
New York/
The New York Times, 3-7:(B)3.

William H. Luers
President, Metropolitan
Museum of Art, New York

3

[Criticizing the Senate decision to cut off National Endowment for the Arts support for art works considered too controversial or obscene]: I lived for years in the Soviet Union, and I watched how the government tried to establish itself as arbiter for what is and what isn't art. It's frightening that at a time when the rest of the world seems to be discovering freedom and liberty for all people to express their ideas, we seem to be giving it up. Somehow, culture is seeming anti-American.

July 27/
The New York Times, 7-28:(B)1.

Witold Lutoslawski
Composer

4

A piece of music is true when it reflects a personal, original artistic conviction without regard for the consequences. You may wonder whether this position is not utterly egocentric and whether society needs art created on the basis of such principles. It is my deep conviction that society needs only such art. A work based on lies, on the abandonment of principles for the sake of transitory, capricious aims like pleasing the tastes of critics or the public, just to get applause or fame or money—those are the works that are not the products of purely artistic motivation.

Interview/Los Angeles Times,
8-6:(Calendar)55.

Naguib Mahfouz
Egyptian author; Winner,
1988 Nobel Prize in Literature

5

Art is for people. If art is not assimilated, it remains truncated and nebulous. That is why [James] Joyce's departure from the novel was dangerous. He is still not considered a writer with a large audience. Art must be pleasure, diversion and escape.

Interview/World Press Review,
January:61.

Wynton Marsalis
Jazz musician

1

. . . music is a medium for expression. It has a history and tradition. Music—and culture, in general—allows us to see ourselves through the eyes of our most enlightened people, the artists of each generation.

Interview, New York/
The Christian Science Monitor,
2-22:11.

Gian Carlo Menotti
Artistic director,
Spoleto Festival U.S.A.

2

[On why the Spoleto Festival takes place in Charleston, S.C., rather than a large city such as New York]: Years ago, [New York's] Mayor Koch asked me to bring the Spoleto Festival to New York, and I told him, "Sure, why not?" because I knew he wasn't serious. But if he had been serious, I wouldn't have done it. It's impossible, in a city as big and culturally rich as New York. In an arts festival, you should be meeting the same people again and again as you do at the great festivals like Salzburg and Bayreuth. The atmosphere of an arts festival should be like that of a very beautiful mansion which you and other guests have been invited to enter. You must have one person who is at the head of the mansion, a *padrone di casa*. That's the atmosphere of the Spoleto Festival U.S.A., and that's why I gave up the Spoleto Festival in Melbourne, Australia, after three years. The city was too big. It was not a place where I could get people to mix.

Interview, New York/
The New York Times, 5-23:(B)1.

Arthur Miller
Playwright

3

What worries me is that at home [in the U.S.] as well as here [in Britain], we're turning to popular culture not just for entertainment but for education. Superficial stereotypes dominate so many people's thinking, and they lead to serious misunderstandings.

Interview, Norwich, England/
The Washington Post, 5-15:(C)8.

Kevin Mulcahy
Professor of political science,
Louisiana State University

4

[On the National Endowment for the Arts]: I don't think the NEA has ever had much of a vision of what the American cultural condition should look like and what its role should be. Budget is not the issue necessarily. The Endowment has pretty much accepted, on a leadership level, that the goals of cultural institutions should be the goals of public culture. It serves the purposes of institutional survival; that isn't necessarily the public's interest. And the future is still a problem. We are becoming a multi-cultural society, and that has tremendous consequences for public culture and tremendous opportunities. I don't think the Endowment has been very much in the forefront of providing leadership in some of these issues.

Los Angeles Times, 9-9:(I)17.

Anne Murphy
Executive director,
American Arts Alliance

5

The value of art is never determined by the generation that creates it. The permanent value of art is determined by succeeding generations, who vote to keep it in the human repertoire, who say, "This is worth passing on to the next generation."

The Christian Science Monitor,
7-17:11.

6

The [National] Endowment [for the Arts] was not created to create great art. That's not its job. Its job was to find the best and put it in front of the American people so they would have exposure to it and be part of the judgement about whether it should go on to the next generation.

Los Angeles Times, 9-9:(I)17.

Joyce Carol Oates
Author

7

[On Senator Jesse Helms' bill that would prohibit the National Endowment for the Arts

(JOYCE CAROL OATES)

from funding controversial and obscene arts projects]: It's a very subtle issue. I know that some of my work would be violently disliked by Mr. Helms and some of his friends, and I'm not sure I would want them to like it. Serious art often concerns itself with the exploration of what we call taboo. It's an anthropological term, and what Freud meant by taboo is that which is in violation of the conscious. Naturally, this upsets people. I think the related issue is, should the constituency of a nation support this effort. That's the most subtle issue. In a democracy, the constituency has its own ideas, of course, about what it wants to support.

The Washington Post, 7-29:(C)1.

Peter Palumbo
Chairman, Arts Council
of Britain

1

A great number of people in [Britain[have made a great deal of money. And they should be encouraged to give back something of what they've gained [by contributing money to the arts]. We shall try to persuade government to provide as much as it can, but we shall have to look increasingly to the private sector to help us . . . If you want to furnish a great capital with a great symphony, a great theatre, a great opera house, they are costly things. But they are flagships—they are what we are judged by in the eyes of the world. I believe passionately that it is in the interest of the country to continue their support.

Interview, London/
The New York Times, 5-6:12.

Joseph Papp
Stage producer

2

[Criticizing moves that would restrict National Endowment for the Arts funding of obscene or controversial art]: To keep art alive it needs people taking extreme positions. There is no question that the artist should be allowed to do what he will, and the government's respon-

sibility is to support the extremes that come about, which make the center possible. The fact is that the government of the United States has taken it on itself to support the arts, as an act compatible with any country that believes in its past, present and future as expressed by art. It's generally accepted that art plays a fundamental role in our lives. The nature of extreme expression is essential.

Panel discussion,
New York, Sept. 14/
The New York Times, 9-16:12.

Jon Pareles
Popular-music critic,
"The New York Times"

3

Why separate culture from the rest of what the school is teaching—math, science, history? Our problem with trying to give people culture is that they get the idea that it is separate from daily life—that music is something in a concert hall listened to in silence, or that art is something you see in a museum.

Panel discussion/
Harper's, September:44.

Alain Robbe-Grillet
French author;
Motion-picture writer
and director

4

Not only is a work of art different for all people, but it is different at different moments for the same person. I think it was Roland Barthes who said, "The great work is not one that imposes the same meaning on numerous observers, but rather one that develops numerous meanings in one observer."

Interview, New York/
The New York Times, 4-17:(B)3.

Dana T. Rohrabacher
United States Representative,
R-California

5

[Supporting restrictions on National Endowment for the Arts funding of obscene or contro-

(DANA T. ROHRABACHER)

versial art]: When you get in bed with the government, you can't expect to have a good night's sleep. Those people who believe that art can be Federally funded without Federal control are living in a dream world. It is not proper for the government to spend the taxpayers' money on art that is morally repulsive to them ... When as a Congressman I'm having trouble coming up with money for pre-natal care and so forth, to be spending money on art is questionable, but to be spending it on indecent and obscene art is outrageous ... If you want funds for the arts, take it out of the hands of the Federal government. I believe in keeping tax breaks, so people can give money as they choose rather than centralizing it in the Federal government. Let the taxpayers make their own decisions.

Panel discussion,
New York, Sept. 14/
The New York Times, 9-16:12.

1

[On the controversy over NEA funding of allegedly obscene or controversial works]: The NEA people should have their own standards for what is decent and what is indecent. If they are so far off the wall that they end up endorsing things that are no better than what you find at a porno bookstore, then you have to say their values on this are out of touch and they shouldn't be the ones making the decisions.

Interview, Los Angeles/
Los Angeles Times, 9-27:(VI)8.

William Rubin
Director emeritus of painting
and sculpture,
Museum of Modern Art,
New York

2

Cubism is without question the most important but also the most difficult and demanding art movement of the last two centuries. The great cubist pictures of the period 1911-12 are the nearest thing to a Rembrandt, in their quality and metaphorical use of shadow and light, that the 20th century has produced. Like a Rembrandt, they require prolonged participation. So you look and you look and you look, and eventually you find in these paintings illumination about human nature and psychology, about how we grasp the world, about what mind means.

Interview/
U.S. News & World Report,
10-23:68.

Witold Rybczynski
Architect

3

Architecture is not a particularly well-paying profession, yet there is an enormous interest among young people in the field, in large part because the work is a lot of fun. There is a very lighthearted atmosphere in most architectural offices. A good part of what architects do is thinking in miniature, and working with architectural models is a kind of play. People are always fascinated with these models because they are like toys. The tiny buildings peopled with pocket-size figures recall the dolls' houses and lead soldiers of our childhood. We have all spent hours sprawled on the floor playing with toy blocks, and built little houses with construction toys. We have all been little architects.

Interview/
U.S. News & World Report,
7-3:55.

Arturo Schwarz
Curator, Palazzo Reale,
Milan, Italy

4

Surrealism is a state of mind that rejects the cliches of life everywhere it manifests itself. And every Surrealist painter is completely different from another. The only thing that unites them is a common involvement with the unconscious to shed more light on man's personality, to express his dreams and desires.

Interview,
Rapallo, Italy/
The New York Times,
8-30:(B)3.

339

Peter Sellars
Stage director

1

I think the Pacific will emerge as a major force in the arts over the next 200 years in the way European arts have had a tremendous period of hegemony that is just finishing. The world is shifting and the culture reflects that. Dante and Shakespeare are fine. But if you want to call them up to work on new projects, they're not available.

Los Angeles Times,
3-19:(Calendar)66.

Giuseppe Sinopoli
Orchestra conductor

2

The ambition of the artist is to *try,* not to achieve. An artist is not a taxi driver, whom you can tell to go to 46th Street and, when he arrives, he has "achieved." Artists never achieve. The religion of an artist is to doubt what he does.

Interview, New York/
Ovation, March:28.

Stephen Sondheim
Composer, Lyricist

3

The fact is, popular art dates. It grows quaint. If it has a certain something, like Gilbert and Sullivan, there will always be people who feel strongly about it. But how many people feel strongly about Gilbert and Sullivan today compared to those who felt strongly in 1890? Today we tend to have Gilbert and Sullivan societies. To stay popular is a real trick, because you have to move away from what you're about; you move away from your roots.

Interview, New York/
The Washington Post, 6-19:(B)1.

Hugh Southern
Acting Director, National
Endowment for the Arts
of the United States

4

[Criticizing a Senate Appropriations Committee vote to ban for five years National Endowment grants to two arts organizations that helped support exhibitions of controversial material]: [Banning grants to specific arts organizations is] a dangerous precedent which goes against the long and widely respected system of Federal support for the arts through a competitive peer-review process. Both of these organizations have made important contributions for many years to the arts in their states and regions. Enactment of this provision would be the first instance since the Endowment's founding nearly 25 years ago of direct congressional involvement in awarding or prohibiting specific grants.

July 25/
The New York Times, 7-26:(B)1.

Ted Stevens
United States Senator,
R-Alaska

5

[Supporting a cutoff of National Endowment for the Arts funding of art works considered controversial or obscene]: The art community is the judge of what is good art. But they are not the judge of what art we should spend Federal money to disseminate around the country. They cannot accept the line that they cannot cross using taxpayers' money. I do not see any reason to disseminate the work of weird, crude minds.

The New York Times, 7-28:(B)9.

Paul Taylor
Choreographer

6

The artist is unfettered by precedents. He doesn't know what's been done. He starts from scratch and comes up with things that a person would never think of.

Interview/
Dance Magazine, April:37.

Maurice Tuchman
Senior curator of modern and
contemporary art,
Los Angeles County
Museum of Art

7

Being a curator is a long-haul job. You help collectors for years in the hope they'll finally

(MAURICE TUCHMAN)

leave their works to the museum. You don't know the outcome of your efforts for decades. You just keep at it every day, like brushing your teeth. We've never had an endowment for acquiring art for the collection. I've had to raise every penny and solicit every donation . . . I am by nature a matchmaker. I've always seen it as part of my function to introduce artists to dealers and dealers to collectors and museum people. I like to put people together.

Interview/
Los Angeles Times,
10-22:(Calendar)4.

John Updike
Author

1

[On the controversy over National Endowment for the Arts funding of "objectionable" works]: Whenever the American government starts to directly subsidize the arts, I think you're in trouble. I'm not sure the entire disappearance of the NEA would be a terrible loss. I don't think ours is a bad government, but I think with this one and this democracy, there are going to be repercussions often. I'd rather not feel the government looking over my shoulder.

Nov. 15/
The Washington Post,
11-16:(A)23.

Esther Wachtel
President, Los Angeles
Music Center

2

An arts organization is a very special thing, and creative people need a great deal of individual freedom. No matter how much money we raise, no matter what our government relations are, we [administrators] cannot do what our artists do. They are supreme here and have to be given tremendous freedom in order to create.

The Christian Science Monitor,
9-11:11.

Stephen E. Weil
Deputy director, Hirshhorn
Museum and Sculpture
Garden, Washington

3

Art does not set out to be acceptable. It often deals with the extremes of the human condition. It is not to be expected that, when it does that, everyone is going to be pleased or happy with it—particularly museum art which people are free to come to see, or not see. Many museums show things that are not palatable to everybody. It is really important to understand that art often bites, it can really touch raw nerves. *Crime and Punishment* and *Hamlet* are not about pretty things.

The New York Times, 6-15:(B)3.

Pat Williams
United States Representative,
D-Montana

4

[On proposals to stop NEA funding of obscene or controversial art]: We ought to examine as a Congress and a public the two potentially irreconcilable forces that are coming at each other. First is the absolute necessity to protect the freedom of artistic expression in America. The other force . . . is the right of taxpayers to decide through their elective representatives how their money shall be spent. I have no preconceived notion that the NEA should survive. I like what it has done, I believe that it has the potential to be of great assistance to art in America for decades to come, but in fact it may be so flawed and ripe for use by Congressional censors that it should not survive. That's kind of a bizarre twist that drives my art friends crazy.

The Washington Post, 9-26:(A)16.

Journalism

Roone Arledge
President, ABC News

1

[On the high salaries paid to TV network news anchors]: The objective of ABC News is to be financially healthy. You do that by having programs that people want to watch. People with track records are clearly successful at doing that. On the level of a network star journalist, who is desired by other networks, the amount of money [salary] doesn't really matter. Numbers don't always tell the story.

The New York Times, 2-20:(C)7.

David Conant Bartlett
President, Radio-Television
News Directors Association

2

[Saying journalists should not cooperate with the government in its investigation of information leaks to the press]: Any journalist who hasn't just dropped in from Mars knows that he should in no way help a leak investigation. That's what we do for a living, the last time I checked.

The Washington Post, 9-13:(A)23.

James Batten
President,
Knight Ridder newspapers

3

[On the problem of attracting young readers to newspapers]: We're still just at the top of the first inning in even thinking about how to attack it. Cosmetic touches, which a lot of papers—including some of ours—have done don't really go at the heart of this question. This is a demographic group that's different in all kinds of ways from those that went before, and I think that we have to understand them better than we do and really be wide open to approaches that may be radically different from what we've done before. Anybody who is not actively concerned about [young readers] . . . is living in a dream world.

Los Angeles Times, 3-16:(I)29.

Martin Bell
Chief Washington correspondent,
BBC-TV

4

I've been here [in Washington] 11½ years and there has not been a time until now when we didn't have the feeling that Washington was the world's predominant news center. Now it's only one of several news centers. This is a wonderful country, but it's not undergoing a process of dynamic change.

The Washington Post, 6-8:(A)21.

Saul Bellow
Author

5

A good many writers are having trouble placing longer fiction in the magazines. I think the magazines have failed the public badly in this respect. They've gone political; they've gone social; they've dealt with health and with sex and with sports, and really they have no patience for fiction. They ration it now; even the very best magazine will have one small story in every issue. They run a token poem or story—if it's minimalist it's even better, because it takes up less space. If I had written a journalistic piece of the same length I would have had no trouble placing it.

Interview, Chicago/
Publishers Weekly, 3-3:59.

Berke Breathed
Newspaper cartoonist

6

[On why he stopped doing the *Bloom County* comic strip]: I'm 32. That's too young to coast. I could draw *Bloom County* with my nose and pay my cleaning lady to write it, and I'd bet I wouldn't lose 10 per cent of my papers over the next 20 years. Such is the nature of comic strips. Once established, their half-life is usually more than nuclear waste. Typically, the end result is lazy, rich cartoonists . . . [Cartoonist] Charles Schulz

(BERKE BREATHED)

said it once: You only have to be a halfway good artist and a halfway good writer to be a cartoonist. I know my limitations. I could never make it as a writer, and I could never make it as a fine artist. Thus, the world of cartooning was waiting for me to come along. I have plenty of partial ability.

Interview/Time, 12-25:10.

Otis Chandler
Chairman, executive committee of the board of directors, Times Mirror Company

1

You might be surprised to know that the newspaper business is the largest employer of any industry in the United States. This year the *Los Angeles Times* will turn the corner and become a billion-dollar-a-year business, with over 10,000 employees.

*Interview/
Los Angeles Times, 8-13:(IV)5.*

Shelby Coffey
Editor, "Los Angeles Times"

2

[On newspaper writing]: Clarity is first. Accuracy is a must. Elegance is wonderful when it's the kind of story that calls for it. But pace . . . A 60-inch or 90-inch story that leaves you wanting 20 more inches—that's good pacing.

*Interview, New York/
USA Today, 1-9:(B)8.*

William H. Cowles III
President, American Newspaper Publishers Association

3

Sunday newspaper circulation and readership have kept pace with the growth in the adult population and the growth in households in the 1980s. Daily circulation has not quite kept pace with the growth in households. The net result is that newspaper circulation is the same now,

basically, as it's been for three or four years; that is, 63 million copies every day. Now, that's not losing; that's maintaining a steady number in terms of circulation . . . What our industry worries about is some of the same things that others in communications worry about, and that is being relevant, being essential, by providing news, entertainment, opinion.

Interview/USA Today, 4-25:(A)11.

John E. Cox, Jr.
President, Foundation for American Communications

4

Let's face it, the free press is the one institution that's going to keep our nation free. It is the institution which is trying to police the private and public institutions. If it hasn't got credibility—if people stop believing the press because they think journalists are just a bunch of sensation-oriented people who want to make the biggest buck for the biggest headline or the most impressive story on the air—the public will end up shooting the messenger.

Interview/USA Today, 5-15:(A)9.

Michael J. Davies
Publisher, "The Hartford Courant"

5

[Calling for changes in newspapers to be more in line with today's readership requirements]: I don't mean to be an alarmist, but it seems to me we should periodically remind ourselves that we have no Constitutional right to stay in business. Because we are strong today doesn't mean we will be strong tomorrow.

*At American Newspaper Publishers
Association convention, Chicago,
April 26/
The New York Times, 4-27:(C)14.*

Linda Ellerbee
Broadcast journalist

6

There are fewer women [newscasters] on air at the networks now than there were in 1975 when I went to work at the networks. All the attention that's being paid to Connie Chung, Mary Alice Williams and Diane Sawyer is giving the wrong message. The message it seems to be giving is, "Boy, women have come a long way. Look at these big salaries and big jobs" . . . The fact is that those of us who were there are still there. So when the networks decide they need a woman for this or that, they're not saying they need more women—they're trying to fill a quota, and the list is short these days.

Interview/
USA Today, 4-10:(A)11.

Max Frankel
Executive editor,
"The New York Times"

1

We've [newspapers] got to be important in people's lives. They've got to need us, and once we get them hooked—and preferably if we get them hooked early enough—then it will be a lifelong habit that they have to at least look at us every day.

Los Angeles Times,
3-16:(I)28.

Marion Goldin
Broadcast journalist;
Former producer,
"60 Minutes," CBS-TV

2

Maybe I'm romanticizing, but I seem to remember a day when [working in TV news] was more collegial. When people did help and did compliment you, and didn't look at you as a worse competitor than somebody from another network. And now that doesn't exist. Now there is that sense, sometimes overt, certainly covert, of that old Hollywood phrase: Better my colleague here should fail than my worst enemy . . . It was as soon as news became part of big business, as soon as news was made into ratings, as soon as you could never come in the next day or the next week and have what you did honestly critiqued, because if it got super ratings, then it

was good, and if it got dumpster ratings, well, then it couldn't be very good.

Panel discussion/
Mother Jones, June:46.

Robert Gottlieb
Editor, "The New Yorker"
magazine

3

The editor of *The New Yorker* sets the tone, the course, the way. And he's treated as a living god.

Newsweek, 10-23:23.

Barbara A. Henry
Editor, "Rochester (N.Y.)
Times-Union" and
"Democrat and Chronicle"

4

The quality and credibility of our newspapers depend on a diverse work-force, and we don't have one. I'm concerned, and other editors should be, that a majority of minorities [say] race is a major obstacle to promotion. Blacks, especially, said this. Editors need to address that concern openly and honestly. There's a fear in newsrooms of talking about race and gender, and talking about promoting minorities. But it's good for our newspapers, and it's good for our readers.

Interview/USA Today, 6-6:(A)11.

Paul Johnson
Author, Historian

5

Most journalists are scoundrels. They can't tell the difference between hard news and scandal, except that they like scandal because it makes money. They should all be locked up.

Interview, London/
Connoisseur, February:78.

Marvin Kalb
Director, Barone Center on
the Press, Politics and
Public Policy,
Harvard University.

6

[On the practice of TV networks luring broadcast journalists away from other networks and

(MARVIN KALB)

paying them high salaries]: We are watching a profound shift in the way networks function. It is similar to what is happening in professional baseball or basketball. Journalists are exchangeable commodities; the highest bidder wins.

Time, 4-3:70.

Garrison Keillor
Author

1

People who talk about the fear on the streets and the drug problem and so on are talking about things that undoubtedly are true, but most of them are talking about things that are not their own experience. They're talking about stories that they've read in the paper. Part of the purpose of the press in all of its history has been to scare us, to our delight.

Interview, New York/
Los Angeles Times, 9-7:(V)12.

Edward M. Kennedy
United States Senator,
D-Massachusetts

2

[Saying journalists should reveal the honoraria they receive for speaking before private groups, just as members of Congress must reveal *their* honoraria]: As Justice [Louis] Brandeis said years ago, sunlight is the best disinfectant . . . It *is* an invasion of privacy for reporters, just as it is for members of Congress. But it goes with the territory in this day and age.

Radio broadcast/
The Washington Post, 4-14:(A)1.

James J. Kilpatrick
Political columnist

3

[Saying one can't compare honoraria received by journalists for speaking to private groups with honoraria received by members of Congress for the same thing; that he approves for the former but not the latter]: [There is a] tremendous difference between a Congressman on the Banking

Committee who goes out and speaks to the bankers association . . . He's doing more than expressing opinion, which is all the rest of us can do. Those guys on the [Capitol] Hill can vote on the interest of that trade association.

The Washington Post, 4-14:(A)8.

Andrew Kohut
Former president,
Gallup Organization

4

[On surveys that show public confidence in the fairness and accuracy of the press dropping sharply but also show the public still views the press favorably]: Why, in the face of declining believability, do people still like the press? Because people like the watchdog role of the press, and they like the product.

Los Angeles Times, 11-16:(A)18.

Vitaly Korotich
Editor, "Ogonyok"
(Soviet Union)

5

To a large extent, Soviet journalism does not favor facts as much as interpretations of facts. Whereas in the West a newspaper includes a large number of facts, we usually have hardly any. In the past, people in the Soviet Union could not read a speech by [U.S. President] Ronald Reagan or other prominent Americans; they read only commentaries on the speeches. Now *Ogonyok* has begun to print people verbatim . . . [U.S. newsman] Dan Rather, the scientist and author Carl Sagan, and Reagan himself—without commentary. We choose people who are interesting to Americans. The Soviet press is becoming more interesting, but commentaries, rather than facts, still predominate. That is probably the main difference [between Soviet and Western journalism]. Second, we have no press law. The rights of editors and writers are poorly defined. I think that when we get a press law, journalists will be able to do a lot more, both in their relations with the censor and in their relations with the leadership. For now, too much depends on the personality of the editor and on the personality of the person who approves the issue for publica-

(VITALY KOROTICH)

tion. But I am very pleased that so many people today are trying to create a new Soviet press. I am one of those people.

Interview/
World Press Review, May:25.

Jim Lehrer
Co-host, "MacNeil/Lehrer
NewsHour," PBS-TV

1

I am concerned when we of the press beat the brains in of any political figure who really does tell the truth. Defense Secretary Richard Cheney was the latest victim, saying he believed [Soviet leader Mikhail] Gorbachev would fail in his reforms. Chastised by everyone, [Cheney] later admitted he was guilty of too much candor. Guilty of too much candor: Think about that, please.

At Southern Methodist University
commencement/
The Christian Science Monitor,
6-12:13.

Bill Moyers
Broadcast journalist

2

I think I am looked to by viewers as a sojourner, a reporter who takes them with me on assignment . . . It's all connected: journalist, journal, journey.

Interview, Huntsville, Texas/
Esquire, October:139.

3

[Lamenting the "entertainment" factor that has become part of TV news]: Network journalism has been destroyed from within, by producers and journalists who had no principle more important than satisfying their own ambition. They've created shows that succeed neither as entertainment nor journalism, and they've been willing to subvert journalism in the mistaken notion that nobody would notice. But the American people are more discriminating than that. It's

precisely that significant portion of Americans who've opted out of voting, who've opted out of watching commercial TV, who feel betrayed.

Interview, New York/
Los Angeles Times,
11-12:(Calendar)84.

Henry Muller
Managing editor,
"Time" magazine

4

Any reporter who is reporting a story substantially differently from his colleagues is sure to get a lot of calls from the home office asking why. He's sure likely to get a lot of skepticism from his home office and maybe even some guidance to file stories that come closer to the mainstream view.

Los Angeles Times, 8-25:(I)33.

Jack Nelson
Washington bureau chief,
"Los Angeles Times"

5

Suppose I wrote that the [U.S. President] Bush NATO summit trip was a failure. The editor would say, "Hey, wait a minute . . . AP says it's boffo. UPI says the same thing. The network anchors seem to all agree that it was a success." Suppose I wanted to go against the grain . . . I didn't happen to go against the grain on that, but I would imagine that I would meet with some resistance.

Los Angeles Times, 8-25:(I)33.

Robert Novak
Political columnist

6

There seems to be . . . less individuality [in news reporting] today than there was 25, 30 years ago. [Newspeople] tend to create a more conventional reportage because they're much less characters than they used to be . . . much less apt to go off the deep end on an interesting or an outrageous position . . . You can go on [a Presidential] . . . trip without ever having a conversation with anybody other than another journalist.

Los Angeles Times, 8-25:(I)33.

Norman J. Ornstein
Resident scholar,
American Enterprise Institute

1

The public likes the idea that the press is there, that it is playing the role of watchdog of society. But the confidence that the press is an objective reporter of the news is declining. Let's face it, the basic currency of the institution has to be its credibility. If that continues to decline, it's going to require some very serious soul-searching on the part of the journalists and others associated with the profession.

Interview/USA Today, 11-22:(A)13.

Dan Rather
Anchorman, CBS News

2

Public criticism [of TV anchormen] can be a brutal process. This is already a lonely business. You spend a lot of time on the road. A lot of time at work. And not only do we live in a glass house, but also, because of the vast audience for TV news, all the glass is magnifying glass. That can make life stressful . . . You have to have a good support system on the job and at home, and a hide like a rhinoceros. If you don't develop one, you'll bleed to death.

Interview/Ladies' Home Journal,
January:82.

3

Bold, aggressive reporting has gone a tad out of fashion, and that makes it easier for conventional wisdom. It's hard to get in trouble if you ride along with conventional wisdom . . . Even if you're wrong, your editor will probably shrug his shoulders and say, "Well, you know, what the hell, everybody else was wrong on that story."

Los Angeles Times, 8-25:(I)33.

George E. Reedy
Professor of journalism,
Marquette University;
Former Press Secretary to the
President of the United States
(Lyndon B. Johnson)

4

[The late President Lyndon] Johnson held press conferences a couple of times a week; he

met reporters in the Oval Office; he had them over on Saturday mornings; he took them for walks on the South Lawn. It drove everybody crazy . . . I finally asked Johnson to stop. He loved those Saturday morning sessions because I think he just became lonely and wanted to talk. But a lot of papers didn't publish on Sundays. It was too late for the news magazines. There was no chance of really hitting television. They went on and on. They really were horrible from every standpoint. Bureau chiefs were pleading with me to get him to stop. He finally stopped.

Interview/
The New York Times, 1-26:(A)12.

John Rohrbeck
General manager,
KNBC-TV, Los Angeles

5

[On TV news]: Should you try to make something dull in order to become journalistically responsible? I don't think showing an elephant for 20 seconds at the end of the sportscast trivializes the news portion. There are nights when I want to put my head under the pillow because the news is so dreadful: a plane crash, a murder, another gang shooting. To come in with something that is fun and at least lets you go to sleep with a smile rather than the feeling that it would be better if the world ended tonight, I don't think there is any conflict at all.

Interview/Los Angeles Times,
1-22:(Calendar)3.

Ann Rubenstein
Correspondent, NBC News

6

[On her advice to a young woman just entering a career in TV journalism]: Hang onto her own code of ethics. Do not depend upon those of her employers. They'll ask her to do things that you shouldn't do. You must really decide for yourself what you're going to do and not do. And what price you are willing to pay for whatever they're offering. Otherwise, you're going to find yourself one day standing out in the snow with a microphone and sticking it in the face of a woman who's just had her son killed and asking her how

(ANN RUBENSTEIN)

she feels about it, because somebody told you that's the way to get to the top.

Panel discussion/
Mother Jones, June:29.

Timothy J. Russert
Executive vice president,
National Broadcasting Company

1

[On leaks to the press of confidential information]: Every reporter, every investigative reporter, is by definition of that role very conscious of the agenda of the leaker. That's what it is to be a journalist, to understand that and to factor it in when coming to a legitimate conclusion about whether you have a story.

The Washington Post, 8-12:(A)4.

William Safire
Political columnist

2

[Saying he approves of journalists receiving honoraria for speaking to private groups]: I think it's a wonderful thing, free speech in action. It gets you out of town. You get to meet some real people. They get to ask questions; you get to ask them questions. It gets you out of the ivory tower.

The Washington Post, 4-14:(A)8.

Bernard Shaw
Anchorman,
Cable News Network

3

[To be a journalist,] you've got to have an almost religious respect for the printed word. If you don't have that going in, it's doubtful that you're going to have it in broadcasting—where some people do not spell words correctly, where they spell them phonetically in scripts. If you're a stickler for correct spelling, presumably you're going to be a stickler for facts. Which is basic to journalism. I see a lot of it [misspelling]. A lot of it. And whoever has that weakness is a threat to journalism.

Interview/Los Angeles Times,
4-30:(Calendar)8.

Alan K. Simpson
United States Senator,
R-Wyoming

4

[Saying that, as there has been much criticism in the press of members of Congress receiving honoraria, journalists who receive payments for speaking before private groups should reveal *their* honoraria]: Their [readers and viewers deserve] to know if they pick up a fat check from a group they report on. It's basic fairness. It applies to Congress, and it sure as hell ought to apply to this elite press corps in Washington.

Radio broadcast/
The Washington Post, 4-14:(A)1.

James D. Squires
Editor, "The Chicago Tribune"

5

The pressure of the marketing challenge forced [newspaper] editors to decide they'd better tear down the barriers [between the business side of the newspaper company and the news department] and learn to master the whole paper or be totally at the mercy of the business side. It is in no way a compromise of editorial integrity. It is, in fact, the assurance of it ... The great threat is that all decisions that impact content, staff—everything—tend to be made from the marketing point of view. The threat is of the business strategy dominating the paper.

Interview, April 11/
The New York Times, 4-12:(B)2.

William Sullivan
Professor of philosophy,
La Salle University

6

If we are to have a society that, in any sense, is to be understood and directed by its citizens, collectively . . . citizens have to get crucial information and be able to make some sense of that information. The print press clearly represents the best source of not just news, in the simple sense, but of commentary and understanding that we have. What newspapers are about, in their best sense, is the formation of public debate and public opinion. It seems fairly

(WILLIAM SULLIVAN)

clear that electronic media are far less effective as sources of coherence or intelligibility.

Los Angeles Times, 3-15:(I)14.

Bill Thomas
Former editor,
"Los Angeles Times"

1

If you want the skimming of the news, you can watch television; so my theory is that in every area, we've [newspapers] got to be accurate and [as] complete as possible, never dreaming for a minute that all of our readers are interested in everything we are offering them, which was the old-style newspaper. If you're interested in a science story, [if] you're a doctor or engineer, you may not be interested in a third, at least, of what else is in the paper in depth. But the few stories in your area that you want to read, you want them to be accurate and complete, or what the hell good are we to you?

Interview/
Los Angeles Times, 1-1:(I)18.

Dick Thornburgh
Attorney General
of the United States

2

[Saying journalists should cooperate with the government in its fight to crack down on information leaks to the press]: Our effort to uncover leaks would be immeasurably aided if the media would cooperate in the investigations of the type that we're carrying out. We'd have every leaker out of town before sundown. If we had that kind of cooperation, I think we'd all be the better for it.

Aug. 2/
The Washington Post, 9-13:(A)23.

George Watson
Washington bureau chief,
ABC News

3

Quite simply, next to the anchorperson, the White House correspondent is the most visible and productive and consequential part of a national-affairs broadcast. It is really the summit of national journalism.

USA Today, 1-18:(D)1.

Literature

Jeffrey Archer
Author

1

I am a storyteller, someone who has the ability to tell a yarn. It's an ability versus a gift. When I tell you I'm a storyteller versus someone who writes literature, it's not a put-down. It's just that I know I'm incapable of winning the Nobel Prize.

Interview/
The Writer, June:5.

Margaret Atwood
Canadian author

2

[On being a writer in Canada]: It's different here from the way it is in the [United] States. There writers have the luxury of saying, "My art, it's the expression of my individual soul. I'm not interested in politics." I think that would be wonderful; I *long* for that. But here, being a small country, we are, perforce, community-minded.

Interview, Toronto/
Mother Jones, April:30.

Paul Auster
Author

3

I seem to be afflicted with this disease, which is that words come very slowly to me. I don't have ready access to language. There's always a gap. I feel as though I'm falling into a void every time I try to fish up the next sentence. I *know* there are other writers who can sit down and just blast it out. I've never been able to do that. I prefer to inch along. I have a much better grip on what I'm doing. I feel satisfied if I can get one page out of the day. It's a page that is pretty good but that will need a real careful going over later.

Interview, New York/
Publishers Weekly, 3-3:81.

Julian Barnes
British author

4

I don't take too much notice of the "but-does-he-write-proper-novels?" school of criticism, which I get a bit, especially in England. I feel closer to the continental idea—which used to be the English idea as well—that the novel is a very broad and generous enclosing form. I would argue for greater inclusivity rather than any exclusivity. The novel always starts with life, always has to start with life rather than an intellectual grid which you then impose on things. But at the same time, formally and structurally, I don't see why it shouldn't be inventive and playful and break what supposed rules there are.

Interview, London/
Publishers Weekly, 11-3:73.

John Barth
Author

5

I see the feast of literature as truly a smorgasbord. I wouldn't want a world in which there were only Balzac and Zola and not Lewis Carroll and Franz Kafka. The idea that because we [in the U.S.] live in a large and varied country we therefore ought to write the sweeping, panoramic novels is like arguing that our poets all ought to be like Walt Whitman rather than Emily Dickinson.

Time, 11-27:78.

Saul Bellow
Author

6

I don't think writers are very close to each other in this country any more. They used to be more so in my younger days. Nowadays, they live solitary lives in various corners of the country. When I was in my 30s and 40s, a publishing house like Viking used to be a meeting place for all kinds of writers. You'd run into people like Gene Fowler or John Steinbeck and you'd sit down and have a chat. Now publishing houses belong to conglomerates and there are none of these colorful old editors to attract the writers to the publishing house itself. Editors are just middle-level executives in a big corporation.

Interview, Chicago/
Publishers Weekly, 3-3:60.

(SAUL BELLOW)

1

There is no intention on my part to be formidable. I write about who we are and why we are here and what this life is about—the psychic unity that embraces us all . . . You pick up the paper and it carries your mind in 50 directions— toward terrorism, toward the budget, toward a notorious trial or to the cooking pages or the sports pages.

Interview, Chicago/
People, 3-27:66.

James H. Billington
Librarian of Congress
of the United States

2

I think the qualitative development of books first of all depends on people reading a great deal more than they write. People aren't reading as much as they used to. That's where we and other great libraries come in. Books transmit knowledge, but they generate wisdom, and the best books are produced by wise people who are not merely knowledgeable, but have the common right of quality.

Interview/
Publishers Weekly, 1-13:26.

Roy Blount, Jr.
Author

3

A word is like a person, and to herd them all into solemn little groups is to oppress them. It seems to me that words should be allowed to frolic around a little bit.

The Writer, October:4.

Kate Braverman
Author, Poet

4

I write. I rewrite. I lecture. I teach. I review. I edit. I perform. I don't watch television. I don't read a newspaper. I don't read magazines. I have few conventional pastimes. I have to protect myself from the toxicity of this culture. I read

poetry out loud every day. I read my work out loud. I meditate. It appears that writing is a sedentary form, but in fact it requries incredible physical, emotional and spiritual stamina. When I finish writing at the end of a serious day of work, I feel like I've been mountain climbing. I remember A. Alvarez said about Sylvia Plath, "Poetry of this order is a murderous art."

Interview/Time, 11-20:19.

Joyce Brothers
Author, Psychologist

5

[On book-promotion tours by authors]: The book tour cures you from wanting to write a book for a long time. I believe if Shakespeare had to go on tour to plug *Romeo and Juliet, Macbeth* never would have been written.

USA Today, 6-2:(A)11.

Camilo Jose Cela
Spanish author; Winner,
1989 Nobel Prize in Literature

6

A young man once said to Flaubert, "Give me an argument and I'll write a novel." Flaubert agreed and said, "Write this down: A man and a woman love each other. That's the story. Now you have to provide the talent." That's what I think. You need patience and minimal talent.

Interview,
Guadalajara, Spain/
The New York Times, 11-7:(B)2.

Tom Clancy
Author

7

To pick out one or even 10 would not even begin to enumerate those from whom I have learned [about writing] and to whose standards I have aspired. Writing isn't like science, where one man makes a single great discovery upon which others build. The body of literature is built by many, much as medieval cathedrals were built over generations by countless masters, each of whom contributed a mark for posterity.

Esquire, July:87.

Mary Higgins Clark
Author

1

[On writing her suspense novels]: I get the main character first, of course. My protagonist is always a woman, and there's always an important, strong man. And I always know what happened and why it happened. I don't understand how some writers can not know who did it, who killed a person, when they start. If someone dies, you have to have a motive. Why does someone love/hate, hate/love someone so much that they're driven to the ultimate act?

Interview, New York/
Publishers Weekly, 5-19:64.

Jackie Collins
Author

2

I am a storyteller. After 20 years and 12 books, all of them still in print, I really don't have to write any more. I do it because I genuinely love it. And *that's* the secret of success!

Esquire, July:83.

E. L. Doctorow
Author

3

Writers are supposed to write only what they know about, and that's usually interpreted to mean you can only write about your own experience. But there are various ways you know things, and one of them is intuition. Speculation. You know things by means of imagination. Imagination is a form of knowledge.

Interview, New York/
The Washington Post, 2-28:(B)2.

4

Books, even in this country [the U.S.], are censored all the time by local school boards and parents worried the children will read four-letter words in some teen-age novella in the high-school library. My own feeling is that children have a lot more to worry about from the parents who raised them than from the books they read.

Interview, New York/
Los Angeles Times, 4-5:(V)5.

5

You have to surrender to the act of writing. Give up to it, and trust that if you have anything, *it* will discover it for you. Whatever is your ordinary self is just shucked, and then you're not only *in* the lines you're writing, you *are* the lines.

The Writer, June:5.

6

I learned a very valuable thing as a writer: to maintain my anxieties in the face of all good fortune.

The Writer, November:5.

Umberto Eco
Italian author and philosopher

7

I have always thought that the policy of the high advance [paid by a publisher to an author] is negative for the author. Okay, you get the advance, but if by chance your next book doesn't go so well, the publisher is discouraged. Next time, you shift to another publisher, then to another publisher . . . I think that when you stay with the same publisher, they know you and are interested in supporting you. The policy of the high advance is too much adventurous!

Interview, New York/
Publishers Weekly, 10-27:51.

8

The [book-buying] public [in the U.S.] has changed enormously in the last two decades. You see boys going into the bookstore and buying Proust. They want a difficult experience. They have had enough of Yogi Bear or *Dallas* or Harold Robbins—there is plenty of easy, precooked experience available. The most interesting reactions I get from readers in the United States don't come from New York or San Francisco but from the Midwest or from the mountains. They were happy to be involved in a complex reading experience that demanded a certain effort and that gives, it seems, a certain reward.

Interview/
U.S. News & World Report,
11-20:79.

Joni Evans
Publisher, adult-trade division,
Random House, publishers

1

Quality fiction and non-fiction [are hot right now]. A literary novel by Anne Tyler or Gabriel Garcia Marquez can be a Number 1 best-seller. That's a very big difference from what sold two years ago and certainly five years ago. It started with *The Closing of the American Mind,* by Allan Bloom. That trend probably explains not the demise of but the cloud over commercial television. People want quality—and not just what's fed to them. You need a balance, and more people are coming to books for that balance.
Interview,
New York/
Cosmopolitan, April:130.

2

I always understand the bottom-line responsibility of a book, because I knew how much it cost to run a publishing house and how much it cost to pay for a lunch at the Four Seasons. Very early on, I saw profit-and-loss statements on every book, and I was fascinated to see that some books, perceived as successful, didn't even pay for the light bulbs. That hit my stomach on some level. I've always viewed publishing as a business as much as a creative form. I think authors feel the same way. They want to make money.
Interview, New York/
Cosmopolitan, April:135.

Athol Fugard
South African playwright

3

The written word, and the spoken word, is infinitely more powerful and effective a means of affecting change than any of the forms of violence that are so appallingly alive at this moment—bombs, and stones, and assassinations, and God only knows what.
Interview,
Washington/
The Christian Science Monitor,
12-7:11.

Dana Gioia
Poet

4

[On his switching away from comparative literature courses in college]: I felt that my teachers had developed powerful methodologies to analyze literature, but their abilities to judge the quality of literature had atrophied. This is not such a problem if you're a classicist, but if you're interested in modern and contemporary literature it leads you into dismissing works of excellence which don't fit into your methodology as well as elevating works of mediocrity, because they respond to your methodology. So the more deeply I got into comp. lit., the more uncomfortable I felt.
Interview, White Plains, N.Y./
Connoisseur, March:110.

Nikki Giovanni
Poet

5

I'm very conscious of the rhythm in my poems, which is why I consider myself a lyricist—I write lyrical poetry. You should be able to tap your foot when you read most of my work. James Joyce teaches us that you must write on the human breath. This is the reason people get confused when they read *Ulysses* or *Finnegans Wake.* There are no breaks, so people don't understand how to read them. But Joyce wrote as he breathed. And you should write the way you breathe.
Interview/
Writer's Digest, February:32.

Linda Grey
President, Bantam Books,
publishers

6

The overly big guarantee [being demanded from publishers by authors through their agents] might put a lot of money in an author's and agent's pockets on a short-term basis. But the publishers cannot consistently lose money and stay in business. Remember the fable about killing the goose that lays the golden egg?
The New York Times, 1-19:(B)2.

353

WHAT THEY SAID IN 1989

Donald Hall
Poet

1

Reviewing is in terrible shape. There's more poetry than ever—more readings, more books, more *sales* of books—and less reviewing. And worse reviewing. Literary journalists like Malcolm Cowley, Louise Bogan and Edmund Wilson made their livings, in large part, by writing book reviews. Their descendants have tenure, instead, and teach Linebreaks 101. *The New Yorker,* by appointing Helen Vendler, resigned from reviewing poetry. *Atlantic* and *Harper's* and the old *Saturday Review* reviewed poetry regularly; no more. *The New York Review of Books* isn't interested in poetry and it is stupid when it pretends to. *The New York Times* is at its worst on poetry, especially under the current editor. What's left? *The New Republic* and *The Nation* are honorable; there are the quarterlies, each of them read by few people. *APR* reviews little. We suffer from a lack of intelligent *talk* about poetry. I don't know why. Maybe it's the same cultural separation that splits creative writing and literature in the university, an epidemic of ignorance, willful know-nothingism.

Interview/
The American Poetry Review,
Jan.-Feb.:45.

Donald Harington
Author

2

. . . I don't feel that creative writing can be taught. All of these graduate schools turning out MFAs by the thousands—that's not the way to become a writer . . . [I would say to students,] "If you want to write, get yourselves a dictionary and a thesaurus and go out and write!"

Interview/
Publishers Weekly, 3-31:39.

Seamus Heaney
Poet; Professor of rhetoric
and oratory,
Harvard University

3

I believe it is an abuse of poetry to think that you can live [financially] unaided as a poet. I

myself was four years as a free-lance writer. At that time I was depending to some extent on poetry readings as a means of earning my daily bread. [However,] I think to be reading your poetry as a breadwinning activity . . . it commits some sin against the freedom of poetry. I do believe that poetry is in the realm of the gift and in the realm of the sacred. Poetry is earned spiritually. It's earned with silences. It's earned, it isn't arrogated.

Interview/
The Christian Science Monitor,
1-9:16.

Lawrence Hughes
Chairman,
Hearst Trade Book Group

4

The [book-publishing] industry always seems to go through cycles, where prices [of authors' contracts] go crazy, and we're in one of those cycles right now where the economics are out of line for big books. One reason is the shortage of big-name authors, and the competition for them among the publishing conglomerates.

The New York Times, 4-17:(C)8.

John Irving
Author

5

I've read about myself that I am not to be taken seriously because I am a shameless entertainer, a crowd pleaser. You bet. I am. My feeling is I'm not going to get you to believe anything if I can't get you to finish the book . . . I have a very simple formula, which is that you've got to be more interested on page 320 than on page 32 . . . Let no one forget that when I say I'm only a storyteller, I'm not being humble.

Interview/
The New York Times, 4-25:(B)1,3.

P. D. James
Author

6

I don't think any writer can ever explain how we invent characters. It's impossible really to

(P. D. JAMES)

describe. But it often seems to me that the people and the plot, everything about them, exists in some limbo of my imagination. And what I'm doing is quietly and with humility waiting for them to get in touch with me so that I can get their story down in black and white on paper. It seems to me often that it's far more a process of revelation, rather than creation.

At American Booksellers
Convention, June/
The Christian Science Monitor,
8-4:12.

Paul Johnson
Author, Historian

1

[In writing,] structure is everything. When authors come to me complaining of writer's block, it means they are too lazy to work out a structure either in their lives or in their work. Which is not to say that every writer doesn't have his own, idiosyncratic procedures. Mine begins with three basic stages: research, structure and writing. The writing part often takes the least time. I do all the reading and note-taking for some months, or years if it's a long-term project with other books in-between. Then I work on the structure for a long time. By the end, it becomes a visual process, which I often do on the floor.

Interview, London/
Connoisseur, February:78.

Erica Jong
Author

2

Most first novels use the materials of the author's life. Sometimes they're disguised. Perhaps the author went to Barnard, and says Vassar in the book. Nearly every first novel is autobiographical, and years later you cannot remember any more the things you change.

The Writer, October:4.

Ward Just
Author; Former journalist

3

Nowadays, few journalists leave Washington for something as obscure as writing novels, a leap

I took in the early '70s. When I started out in journalism, everyone worth his salt had a novel in his desk drawer, and publishing it was what reporters aspired to do. Each one wanted to be another Ernest Hemingway or Stephen Crane. Today, a journalist might have a thriller in his drawer, but more often the manuscript is a screenplay, a screen treatment or some elaborate book of non-fiction that will fetch $500,000 or more. The novel is no longer enough.

Interview/
U.S. News & World Report,
2-20:60.

Galway Kinnell
Poet

4

[On poetry]: It's the only art in which one person says directly—without intermediaries and other characters—in words what is going on inside.

TV broadcast/
"Moyers: The Power of the Word,"
PBS-TV, 9-15.

Julia Knickerbocker
Publicity director,
Simon & Schuster, publishers

5

The average [book] reviewer is deluged with books daily, some junk, some worthy, and all the press releases look pretty much the same. Anything that makes them blink, that makes them take a second look—oh, please let them take a second look—anything that makes them maybe read the letter that goes with the book, maybe even read the book, is worth it.

The Wall Street Journal, 1-19:(A)8.

Dean R. Koontz
Author

6

[As a writer,] never, never try to "scope" the market. If you say, "They want science fiction so I'll write science fiction, or they want mysteries so I'll write mysteries," you're doomed. You've got to write what you're passionate about. Other-

355

WHAT THEY SAID IN 1989

(DEAN R. KOONTZ)

wise you'll produce juiceless, flavorless fiction. I sold my first short story when I was a senior in college, and to some extent I regret that I started selling so young. Because "young" and "naive" are two words that often go together, as are "young" and "stupid"—at least in my case. A lot of that early work is poorly formed because I was inexperienced and floundering, but I *was* passionate, all right, and never scoped the market.

Interview/
Writer's Digest, November:36.

Judith Krantz
Author

1

Sometimes my characters are bitchy, unfaithful, cruel, ruthless. I've met these people in ordinary life. I love villains. Villains provide the plot points in a novel. When good people interact, it's boring. Put a villain or villainess in and things happen.

Interview/
The Writer, January:5.

John le Carre
Author

2

[On how he keeps up with the world of secret intelligence, which he has written about in his novels]: I just imagine it. If it were otherwise, I wouldn't lie to you. I have no sources; I know nothing. But it's like this: If a veteran journalist gave up his work tomorrow, even 20 years from now he could pick up a magazine or newspaper and sense instantly the way that paper is structured and why stories are handled in a certain way. So, when I see something occur in the world of intelligence, I get a kind of imaginative readout of what probably happened—and, quite likely, it's right. It has always been my concern not to be authentic but to be credible, to use the deep background I have from the years I spent in intelligence work to present premises that were useful to my stories and that I knew were rooted in experience. It's terribly easy to imagine an operational context when you've done a few

operations; it's as if you were asking a sailor how he kept up with the sea. Of course, what I didn't know I just made up.

Interview/
U.S. News & World Report,
6-19:59.

3

There is an enormous difference between the respect that is accorded writers in the Soviet Union and the way our brothers are seen in the West. By and large, we [in the West] have a rather indifferent attitude toward writers. In the U.S.S.R., as well as in Russian history before it, the intelligentsia, writers, artists and thinkers have held a special place in the life of society. They have a sense of high social responsibility, a need to speak for the people and to address the people. In the West, because we have a social history of expressing ourselves more openly and vociferously, writers have not performed such a public function.

Interview/
World Press Review, October:28.

Gordon Lish
Editor, "The Quarterly"
magazine

4

That's why so many writers drink or take drugs: It's fear, it's fear, it's fear, it's fear, it's embarrassment, it's anxiety, it's fear, it's fear.

Interview/Esquire,
March:162.

Naguib Mahfouz
Author; Winner, 1988 Nobel Prize
in Literature

5

[On whether he writes from inspiration]: Yes. That is why writers write. They get excited and start writing. Novelists who study contemporary society to see what they can use for their novels will fail in artistic expression. They will not be producing artistic portrayals of that society.

Interview/
World Press Review, January:61.

Norman Mailer
Author

1

[Criticizing Iranian leader Ayatollah Ruhollah Khomeini's call for the assassination of author Salman Rushdie because of what Rushdie's book, *The Satanic Verses,* implies about Islam]: The Ayatollah Khomeini has offered us [writers] an opportunity to regain our frail religion, which happens to be faith in the power of words and our willingness to suffer for them. He awakens us to the great rage we feel when our liberty to say what we wish, wise or foolish, kind or cruel, well-advised or ill-advised, is endangered. We discover that, yes, maybe we are willing to suffer for our idea. Maybe we are even willing, ultimately, to die for the idea that serious literature, in a world of dwindling certainties and choked-up ecologies, is the absolute we must defend.

At meeting of authors,
New York, Feb. 22/
USA Today, 2-23:(A)9.

2

Novelists have to combine opposites in themselves that most people can't tolerate: extraordinary interest in people and a great need for isolation. You have to have a huge interest in power as something to write about, together with the ability to step away from power completely. If one has no interest in power, one tends to write anemic little novels.

Interview/
The Washington Post, 8-22:(E)4.

Tom McGuane
Author

3

[As a writer,] it's nice to decoy oneself by making outlines and planning, but all the writing you're able to keep comes up just the way phrases come up for musicians. But for some reason, you have to pretend that it's plannable and go through a certain number of mnemonic devices just to get started.

Interview,
New York/
Publishers Weekly, 9-29:52.

4

There are readers who abandoned me over the feeling that my writing has become relatively lusterless. But your literary style is kind of like your face—you can't do much to change it. I just hope that you can look at a shelf of my books and say, "This is a 40-year struggle to understand the human race."

Interview, Montana/
Time, 12-25:70.

James A. Michener
Author

5

I think the top category in literature is the sort of work like *Madame Bovary,* where you sit alone in a room and brood about this woman. I don't think the Bronte sisters ever consulted a library once.

Interview, Coral Gables, Fla./
The New York Times, 11-14:(B)2.

Arthur Miller
Playwright

6

I cannot accept that each man is an island and that literature, theatre, is something done altogether for the pleasure of the artist and altogether to divert people from real life. I think there is a mission. It may be terribly subtle, it may be buried deep, but literature has a job that has to do with the way we live, the way we organize ourselves.

Interview/
The Writer, November:5.

Czeslaw Milosz
Author

7

Wild escapades of 20th-century literature into cruelty and ugliness, under the guise of so-called complete freedom of art, probably will be assessed by the future as simple lapses of taste.

At University of
California-Berkeley commencement/
The Christian Science Monitor,
6-12:13.

357

WHAT THEY SAID IN 1989

Susanna Moore
Author

1

I don't believe the notion that out of suffering comes a story, and I find it an offensive idea. The suffering isn't worth the book—life is more important than art.

The Writer, August:5.

Bill Moyers
Broadcast journalist

2

Poets in their solitary pursuit are the most ardent champions of the social contract, because what they remind us of are things we have in common which usually are the ordinary and mundane things, whether a flower, parents, a passage, a transcendence, a pain or a trip.

Interview/
The New York Times,
9-13:(B)4.

3

... poets live the lives all of us live, with one big difference: They have the power—the power of the word—to create a world of thought and emotion others can share. We have only to learn to listen. Listening's the thing ... When we hear it, we say: "I know that, and didn't even know I knew it."

TV broadcast/
"Moyers: The Power of the Word,"
PBS-TV, 9-15.

V. S. Naipaul
Author

4

My work has been a search for myself, yes, but also for the world itself. Every book is a discovery. All books are. Without an element of surprise and discovery, there is no writing. I don't analyze myself, because my work is a matter of accident, intuition and instinct. That is my stock in trade.

Interview,
New York/
Los Angeles Times, 3-15:(V)1.

Lynn Nesbit
Literary agent

5

The [literary] agent has become increasingly central in a writer's life. The publishing world is in such flux. How many editors can you name who have been at the same company for 10 years? Publishing houses merge, are bought and sold. The agent is the constant in a writer's life.

Interview, New York/
Cosmopolitan, October:154.

S. I. Newhouse
Owner, Random House,
publishers

6

From the beginning, I felt that Random House was a special place where good writing and new ideas, particularly those fighting their way into existence from dark corners of the world, would always be published just for themselves. In these days of hype and commercialism, I believe this is more important than ever.

Newsweek, 11-13:74.

Cynthia Ozick
Author

7

One must avoid ambition in order to write. Otherwise, something else is the goal: some kind of power beyond the power of language. And the power of language, it seems to me, is the only kind of power a writer is entitled to.

Interview/
The Writer,
March:3.

Frederik Pohl
Author

8

If you read enough science fiction, nothing will ever take you by surprise; it's the best prophylactic against future shock.

At discussion sponsored by
"The New York Post,"
New York, Sept. 17/
The New York Times, 9-18:(B)2.

358

Martha Ramsey
Poet

1

Poets and storytellers were the first human beings to interpret the world, and they still have that power. There's a magic to the sharing that goes on when people read poetry. It fulfills a spiritual need that can't be met in any other way.
The Writer,
August:5.

Bernard Rath
Executive director,
American Booksellers
Association

2

A lot of bookstores are still family-run. But instead of being run by Mom and Pop, they're run by Dick and June, who may be former professors, trial lawyers, investment bankers or librarians doing it as a second career. And they're applying knowledge from their careers to the business of selling books.
The New York Times,
6-12:(C)8.

Richard Rhodes
Author

3

Too much writing today lacks passion for the subject. Without passion, the writing can't come alive. So find the story, and then find a way to afford to write it, and do it. Writing gives such joy. It's where everything happens. It's where, if you're split as a human being—and most of us are—you become one again. If you love words, love to read, and have read all your life, you've already had a full-time course in writing. I think the main thing holding people back is not technique, but fear. It's not a question of training; it's whether you dare. Most people don't dare. Some never find the courage. They think, "who am I to speak?" Well, goddamn it, you're a human being. Of course you have a right to speak. Get started. Do it. Fools rush in.
Interview/
Writer's Digest,
July:29.

Anne Rice
Author

4

Literary reputation is everything. I want to be read. I want to be valued. That is perhaps the only shot at immortality a human being can have.
Esquire, July:84.

5

What do I hope to achieve [as a writer]? Well, I remember the second time I read Mary Renault's *The Last of the Wine* I didn't want it to end. I walked for hours in the rain carrying that book because I couldn't bear to read the last chapter. If I could make someone feel what Mary Renault made me feel that day—I believe that's what writing is about. I want people to carry dog-eared copies of *Interview with the Vampire* [Rice's book] in their backpacks. I want my books to live, to be read after I'm dead. That will be justification enough for all the pain and work and struggling and doubt.
Interview, New Orleans/
Lear's, October:155.

Adrienne Rich
Poet

6

Some of the worst political poetry I know is written by white poets who go to places like the Caribbean on a two-week vacation and write poems about the beautiful bougainvillea and the palm trees and the beautiful women and choose not to see, choose not to write about or even consider the poverty and misery of those countries . . . It should pass for being non-political but I say it's political because that kind of poem not only excludes but distorts reality so frighteningly.
Interview, Santa Cruz, Calif./
Los Angeles Times, 5-21:(V)3.

May Sarton
Author

7

In America, I think I'm pushed aside as that awful thing called a sensitive feminine writer. The very ingredient that makes me universal has

(MAY SARTON)

kept me from being interesting to the critics. You can't say that I'm a Maine writer, or a New England writer. I'm not regional. I can't be labeled as a lesbian writer because only one of my books deals with that subject. Poets consider me a novelist. Novelists consider me a poet. It sounds so dull, but I feel that what I write about is the human condition. I hope I'm a good writer, but the critics have no handle on what I am because not many distinguished writers work in as many forms as I do. That's why I feel I'm brushed aside by the most important reviewers, not taken as seriously as I'd like. I never went to college. Anne Sexton and Sylvia Plath did. Both of these women were enormously talented, so I'm not saying the people who get the prizes don't deserve them. I'm just saying that sometimes people who do deserve them don't get them, which is my case, I think.

Interview, York, Maine/
Writer's Digest, March:48.

Robert Sayre
Professor of English,
University of Iowa

1

Autobiography is both history and fiction. It is not just a mirror; it is a painting.

U.S. News & World Report,
10-23:64.

Sidney Sheldon
Author

2

To me, the act of creating is the most exciting thing in the world. In a sense, every writer is God. What else could be more exciting than that?

Esquire, July:85.

Susan Sontag
Author

3

[Saying she does not seek to be a "public figure"]: Think of the things that I don't do. I don't appear on television. I don't write for any newspaper or magazine regularly. I'm not a journalist. I'm not a critic. I'm not a university teacher. I don't speak out on most public issues. If I wanted to play a pundit role, I would be doing all of these things. Still, the legend goes on. My life is entirely private. My interests are not those of a pop celebrity. My only interest is in literature and doing work that, if I have the talent and the energy and the devotion to accomplish it, will be a permanent part of literature.

Interview, New York/
The New York Times, 1-26:(B)1.

4

I think that the glory of being a writer is that everything is relevant. I don't do "research"; I'm just *being* all the time, and paying attention. That's what a writer does, on the whole: pay attention to the world. I *am* sort of all over the place. But what I want for essays is for them to be very condensed and very lively at the same time. Sometimes I think that what I'm doing is turning soup into bouillon cubes.

Interview/
The Writer, May:3.

Danielle Steel
Author

5

It's an odd life, this solitary life as a writer. A life of intense involvement and caring, of endless hours clacking along in the silence of the night on my 1948 manual typewriter. But there are moments when it all goes well, as if you are doing an elegant slalom down a grand mountain . . . and then that final moment, that incredible, wonderful pinpoint of light and time when everything is perfect, you've done it, and it's over.

Esquire, July:86.

Gay Talese
Author

6

[Criticizing the appointment of Timothy Healy, a priest, to the presidency of the New

(GAY TALESE)

York Public Library]: A priest should offer moral guidance. But I don't want moral guidance from a librarian . . . It's the biggest library in the most secular city in the world, and we want to keep the fingerprints of the church—any church—off its shelves.

The Washington Post,
4-21:(C)1.

Mary Wesley
Author

1

[Writing] is like having a dual life. Once at Mass I was praying very hard for someone, and then I laughed. The person I was praying for was a character in my book.

The Writer,
November:5.

Lanford Wilson
Playwright

2

[On his early days writing poems]: I was wrassling with poems. I'd see them as if it was war, and I was a general. You only get the initial moment of creation once. I would have the initial impulse but I didn't know how to craft it. Once you achieve surety, you don't worry about crafting because you know that later on you will have the chance.

Interview/Esquire, April:123.

Tom Wolfe
Author, Journalist

3

I'm a journalist at heart; even as a novelist, I'm first of all a journalist. I think all novels should be journalism to start, and if you can ascend from that plateau to some marvelous altitude, terrific. I really don't think it's possible to understand the individual without understanding the society.

Interview/Time, 2-13:92.

Medicine and Health

Gerald L. Baliles
Governor of Virginia (D)

1

[On illegal-drug use]: When drugs become as pervasive as they've become in recent years in every state of the union, it has an impact on the ability to produce a work-force that is reliable, upon students who are alert, upon recruits into the [military] services. It has a pervading effect on all levels of society. That has the ultimate effect of weakening our nation at many different levels and in many different ways . . . A nation that is economically strong, a nation that is physically strong, a nation that is intellectually strong can be a world leader. Weaken any of these links in our chain of strength, and you will find some very enormous problems for our future. So while others may characterize it in different ways . . . it is certainly a threat to our future.

Interview/
The Christian Science Monitor,
10-16:7.

Lloyd Bentsen
United States Senator,
D-Texas

2

[On those who criticize Medicare's catastrophic-coverage plan]: Some folks say the odds are they're not going to need this coverage. There's only a half-percent chance your home is going to burn, but most of us buy fire insurance.
USA Today, 4-26:(A)10.

Erwin P. Bettinghaus
Member, National
Cancer Advisory Board

3

[The decrease in smoking in the U.S. is] the most dramatic social change that has occurred in America in the last 40 years. What we're down to is heavy smoking amongst the poorly educated, the poorly employed, the individuals in the lowest socioeconomic class, the minority groups within our society, and, unfortunately, young adolescent women.

Feb. 8/
Los Angeles Times, 2-9:(I)22.

Joseph R. Biden, Jr.
United States Senator,
D-Delaware

4

Right now, the drug-education message is reaching only 50 per cent of the kids in the country . . . Drug education is the only vaccine we have against drug abuse among the young. Can you imagine vaccinating only 50 per cent of America's children against polio or smallpox?
Broadcast address to the nation,
Washington, Sept. 5/
USA Today, 9-6:(A)5.

Steven Blair
Director of epidemiology,
Institute for Aerobics Research,
Dallas

5

I don't think exercise by adults is a fad. It's gone on too long with too many people having adopted it. I don't think we're going back where we were 20 to 30 years ago . . . My guess is we're going to continue to see more people adopting exercise habits as a way not only to improve their health but also as a way of maintaining a higher level of function throughout life, so as you get into the older years, you can lead a more active lifestyle.

Interview/
USA Today, 1-10:(D)4.

Brendan Brady
Deputy chief executive,
Tobacco Institute of Australia

6

[On anti-tobacco sentiment in Australia]: If they want to ban the various marketing outlets

(BRENDAN BRADY)

[tobacco] companies use for tobacco, which is a legal product, then where does it end? The next step is to move on to alcoholic products, pharmaceutical products, or products with high levels of cholesterol. Consumers must be given more credit for making their own choices.

The Christian Science Monitor,
10-25:6.

James S. Brady
Vice chairman,
National Organization on
Disability;
Former Press Secretary to the
President of the United States
(Ronald Reagan)

1

Disabled people are the nation's largest minority and a great untapped resource. We don't want sympathy; we do want opportunity. We do not want acceptance. We want to participate and be included . . . I will be calling on the President, members of Congress and other national leaders to ensure disability remains high on the national agenda . . . I will call on our Governors and state legislators to bring their disability statutes up to date, to remove discrimination and to open opportunity. I will call on Mayors and community leaders across America to break down attitudinal and physical barriers in their localities, to provide jobs and include disabled people in worship, education, voting and other activities . . . I'll be calling on educators to expand educational opportunities and make our schools and colleges more accessible to disabled students. I'll call on business leaders, in companies large and small, to hire qualified disabled people and to make work-places accessible . . . And tonight, my friends, I call on you [the press]—who are the gatekeepers and opinion-makers in our country—to help our minority make up for lost time by telling our story and telling it often. We need your help to help improve attitudes.

Before American Society
of Newspaper Editors, April 14/
The Washington Post, 4-28:(A)24.

Samuel Broder
Director,
National Cancer Institute
of the United States

2

You can't say that because you can't cure a disease with a drug that it doesn't work. Such a drug might be controlled to prolong life or lessen symptoms, and the fact that you can't cure a patient doesn't nullify what you've done. You've got to keep people alive with the tools you have.

Interview, Bethesda, Md./
The New York Times, 2-7:(B)7.

3

In a certain context, prevention is the most important priority of the Cancer Institute. There are a number of things that we will try. One of them relates to smoking prevention. I think not many people in this country know that lung cancer, which is one of the many diseases caused by smoking, was an exceptionally rare disease at the turn of the century. For example, as a vignette that I might share with you, in 1919 an entire class of medical students at Barnes Hospital [in St. Louis] was summoned to the autopsy room to see a postmortem on a man who had died of lung cancer. They were summoned because their professors felt they would not see another case in their lifetime. So lung cancer was a rather rare disease in this country at one time, and I think it's possible for it to become a rare disease again.

Interview/
The Saturday Evening Post,
May-June:50.

4

I think that in both basic [cancer] research and prevention, in early diagnosis and treatment, in all of those areas there's been a lot of progress. But there's also bad news, and I think that that's something people have come to terms with. The bad news is that we do not have a unifying molecular explanation for cancer. We do not have a cure for all cancers in an advanced state. And, in fact, for some cancers we really do not have effective treatment of any kind . . . Even when we have certain knowledge about some

363

(SAMUEL BRODER)

things, we sometimes still don't have the ability to take it to heart. Smoking is the best example of that.

Interview/
The Saturday Evening Post,
July-August:42.

Michael D. Bromberg
Executive director,
Federation of American
Health Systems

1

[Criticizing a White House Budget Office proposal to cut Medicare spending by $8-billion]: Congress is going to fight this budget. If you keep drying up money for health care, services will have to be reduced. Either you close emergency rooms and trauma centers, or you fire nurses and technicians.

The New York Times, 12-1:(A)1.

Alan Brownstein
Executive director,
National Hemophilia
Foundation

2

[Saying many hemophiliacs are afraid to be tested for AIDS]: We have people who feel healthy and don't want to face the potential of knowing they've been exposed to a deadly virus. We also have other people—a large percent-age—who are concerned about potential dis-crimination. People have told me they are more fearful of social isolation than they are of death from AIDS. It's quite staggering when you hear that.

Los Angeles Times, 1-2:(I)18.

George Bush
President of the United States

3

[Addressing school children on drug abuse]: Every day, with a thousand small decisions, you're shaping your future. It's a future that ought to be bright with potential, and most of you

are doing the right thing. But for those who let drugs make their decisions for them, you can almost hear the doors slamming shut.

Broadcast address,
Washington,
Sept. 12/
USA Today, 9-13:(A)6.

Arthur L. Caplan
Director,
Center for Biomedical Ethics,
University of Minnesota

4

We have built gigantic castles of intensive-care technology. And we have trained hordes of people to go into those technical utopias and use their skills as aggressively as possible [to keep people alive, even if only in a technical sense]. The ethic of medicine has become: If you *can* do something, you *must* do something.

The Washington Post,
8-8:(A)8.

John H. Chafee
United States Senator,
R-Rhode Island

5

We [in the U.S.] face extraordinary problems in our health-care systems today. The number of Americans, especially children, without insur-ance coverage and, therefore, without access to services, has been growing in the past few years. Something is desperately wrong in a country where we spend more than $500-billion per year on a health-care system that does not even come close to being comprehensive and fails to reach too many. The focus of our system is on high-technology care, mostly for people who are already sick. There is a decided lack of emphasis on preventive and primary-care services. This results from the mistaken notion that people can afford prevention and primary care, but not acute care. This is not true—not for the working poor, not for the unemployed and not for low-income families.

Before the Senate,
Washington, June 16/
The Washington Post, 6-20:(A)22.

Horace B. Deets
Executive director,
American Association of
Retired Persons

1

What we need is universal access for all Americans to affordable, quality [medical] care. You've got to see it as a continuum, going from pre-natal care right up through hospice care for chronic and acute patients. This is not something that can be put in place overnight with one piece of legislation. But if we don't get the plan and begin constructing such a system, we're going to continue to have problems like this, where you have disagreement about how it should be paid for. Health care is basic human need, and we think that just like we've addressed certain other common needs in this country— police protection, education, fire protection, national defense—there should be a national plan for health care which covers everyone and which has its cost spread over the entire population.

Interview/
USA Today, 10-25:(A)11.

Barbara Drinkwater
President, American College
of Sports Medicine

2

One area that is very hot is fitness for the older adult. We are looking into the role that physical activity plays in maintaining the independence of older adults—balance, flexibility. You can't turn back the chronological clock but you can do a lot to slow down the biological and physiological changes that appear to occur with aging. A good bit of those changes are due to being sedentary.

Interview/
USA Today, 1-10:(D)4.

David Durenberger
United States Senator,
R-Minnesota

3

[On a proposed change in Medicare payment procedures by which some medical providers will be paid more and some less, with more emphasis on primary care rather than surgical and specialist care]: This will very quickly be adopted across the board by the private sector. It's a rationalization of the system. It says that this country has let specialization and technology get out of hand, and there's no longer a reasonable relationship between the dollars we pay and what we're getting.

The New York Times, 10-13:(A)10.

David Eddy
Professor of health policy and
management, Duke University

4

Current medical logic tells doctors, "When in doubt [about performing surgery], do it."

Time, 6-26:71.

Jeff Goldsmith
National health-care adviser,
Ernst & Young, accountants

5

There is a staggering amount of waste in our health-care system, not in the sense of fraud so much as in the failure to apply technology to a stage of illness where it does the patient the most good. There are huge amounts of acute care that are unnecessary, not because patients don't need it, but because there was no one to help them early in the disease process, before they became acutely ill. I think that is the most serious problem that we face as a society.

Interview/
The Wall Street Journal,
11-13:(R)31.

Ward O. Griffen, Jr.
Executive director,
American Board of Surgery

6

[On the possibility that a glut of surgeons may be resulting in too few operations per surgeon to maintain competency]: I subscribe to the bicycle theory of surgery: I think if you learn an operation correctly, especially when you're younger, you'll do it okay forever. [But] I agree that there's a certain amount needed to keep up skills, and

(WARD O. GRIFFEN, JR.)

some urban surgeons may be getting near the danger point.

The New York Times, 11-7:(B)5.

Tom Harkin
United States Senator,
D-Iowa

1

[Saying the states have not used the more than $700-million in Federal funds available for fighting drug abuse]: We have three-quarters of a billion dollars just sitting there, not being used for education, treatment and rehabilitation. When you look at the size of some of these states that have not used this money—California, New Jersey, Ohio, Maryland—it's inexplicable . . . The entire anti-drug effort has focused on interdiction. Education, treatment and rehabilitation have been left on the back burner.

Interview/
The New York Times, 4-17:(A)8.

James Hawdon
Sociologist,
University of Virginia

2

As a nation, we [the U.S.] glorify certain drugs. [Advertising tells us that] "weekends are made for Michelob" [beer]. In fact, "nights are made for Michelob"; you don't even have to wait for the weekend any more. "Be a coffee achiever." All these marketing campaigns glorify drugs. [People have come to expect that] if you are sick, we can cure you. If you have a headache, we have a pill. If you are too fat, we have a pill. If you are too skinny, we have a pill. No matter what your mood is, we are taught that some substance can cure this, whether a physical or a mental ailment.

The Christian Science Monitor,
4-26:7.

Malcolm Hodkinson
Professor of geriatric medicine,
University College, London

3

Society is slowly coming to realize that the general increase in life span will bring huge

problems as well as great benefits. The health of the elderly has been, for too long, a fourth-division field. It must now be elevated to the top of our priorities.

World Press Review, February:32.

Daniel Hoth
Director,
AIDS program,
National Institute of Allergy
and Infectious Diseases

4

[Saying hemophiliacs are reluctant to take part in a testing program for a new anti-AIDS drug]: I think the hemophiliac population is having a difficult time coping with the reality of what is going on here. A very large fraction of the hemophiliac community is infected, and this trial offers them the best possible hope of avoiding the consequences of [AIDS] infection. But most patients are saying: "Being in a clinical trial will remind me that I'm infected—so if I'm not involved, I don't have to think about it."

Los Angeles Times, 1-2:(I)1.

Stephen C. Joseph
Health Commissioner
of New York City

5

Nobody expects in his professional life to live in the center of a millennial event. AIDS is a millennial event. I am living in the center of it. It's hard to describe that . . . Do I really comprehend the magnitude of what's going on around us in this? No. Maybe better than most people. But you do the best you can and try to understand where you are in this. I don't think any of us really understands the total picture of this.

Los Angeles Times, 2-16:(I)29.

6

[On the drug-abuse problem]: It is nothing short of a Molotov cocktail. This problem doesn't stand in isolation from anything; it is the central knot in the seamless web of our problems . . . For the first time, in the first quarter of '88 we had more new cases of AIDS among intravenous

(STEPHEN C. JOSEPH)

drug abusers than from gay men. There is no doubt, and the data shows it graphically, that the driving engine for the future of the epidemic is drug abuse.

The New York Times, 5-10:(A)17.

Lewis Judd
Director,
National Institute of Mental
Health of the United States

1

[On the biggest problem facing people with mental illness]: The stigma. The intense misunderstanding about the true nature of mental illness. Myth often substitutes for information. The result is that mental disorders are not given the same kind of attention and priority that other disorders might be given . . . Not long ago, the National Alliance for the Mentally Ill, one of the major advocacy organizations for mental illness, did a survey in one of the states. Seventy-one per cent of the respondents felt that mental illnesses were due to emotional weakness. Approximately one-third felt they might be due to sinful behavior. About 40 per cent felt that they were brought on by the patients themselves and that patients could wish it away if they wished.

Interview/USA Today, 10-5:(A)9.

Ann Klinger
Supervisor,
Merced County, Calif.;
President, National
Association of Counties

2

I'm a big booster of county hospitals. In my county, we've been in the hospital business for 115 years continuously. We run 167 beds routinely. We see this as a real responsibility of county government. Many of them did close several years ago, and some of the smaller hospitals now are at risk because of the way Medicare payments are being implemented. But, overall, the county hospitals will be here because they're very needed institutions.

Interview/USA Today, 9-7:(A)13.

C. Everett Koop
Surgeon General
of the United States

3

With about two-thirds of Americans calling themselves drinkers, the U.S. is unlikely to ever again ban alcohol, and it shouldn't. But most Americans are like me and drink relatively little, yet we all pay for alcohol-related [car] crashes.

News conference, Washington,
May 31/
The Washington Post, 6-1:(A)4.

David F. Musto
Professor in the Child Care
Center, psychiatry and the
history of medicine,
School of Medicine,
Yale University

4

[Drug abuse today is] a two-tier system. You have a fundamental change of attitudes among the middle class and a growing bewilderment that anybody still uses drugs . . . But then you have the world of the inner city where there isn't the education, the jobs or the other kinds of things that give people a reason to stop using drugs.

The Washington Post, 1-3:(A)3.

Hiroshi Nakajima
Director General,
World Health Organization

5

If steps are not taken to check the transmission of the AIDS virus, then we are going to have much to fear. In 1987 the estimated number of those who tested positive for the AIDS virus [including those not exhibiting symptoms] was about 5 million. So we can predict that the total number of AIDS-afflicted persons will be more than 1 million at the end of 1991. These figures are independent of the number of new infections that will have surfaced in 1988 or later . . . It is particularly important [at this time] to check heterosexual transmission through education and public information. If necessary, systematic screening of target populations can be added—but carried out in a spirit of good-will without

(HIROSHI NAKAJIMA)

using force. In the developing countries, these measures should be integrated into the delivery of primary health care ... I am absolutely convinced that a humanist approach is entirely compatible with the pragmatic objectives of public health, and we do have proof of this. Discrimination against people affected or thought to be so is dangerous, because it slows the effectiveness of measures intended to prevent the spread of the virus.

Interview/
World Press Review, March:52.

1

The developed world has the resources and technology to end common diseases world-wide. By just increasing the health spending in the developing countries, which is about $5 per capita, by only $2 per head, we could immunize all their children, eradicate polio and provide the drugs to cure many of all their diseases. Not making these tools available is like turning your head while people are dying.

Interview/USA Today, 9-26:(A)13.

John J. O'Connor
Roman Catholic Archbishop
of New York

2

[Criticizing the medical profession, and others, for the way they approach AIDS prevention]: The truth is not in condoms or clean needles. These are lies; lies perpetrated often for political reasons on the part of public officials ... by some health-care professionals who believe they have nothing else to offer persons with AIDS or [who are] at risk. Sometimes I believe that the greatest damage done to persons with AIDS is done by the dishonesty of those health-care professionals who refuse to confront the moral dimensions of sexual aberrations or drug abuse. Good morality is good medicine.

At AIDS conference,
Vatican City/
Los Angeles Times,
11-16:(A)7.

David Owen
Leader, Social
Democratic Party of Britain

3

[Criticizing what some say is British Prime Minister Margaret Thatcher's plan to "privatize" Britain's National Health Service]: The commercialization of health care is the primrose path down which inexorably lies American medicine: first-rate treatment for the wealthy and 10th-rate treatment for the poor.

The New York Times, 2-1:(A)1.

Judy Park
Director of legislation,
National Association of
Retired Federal Employees;
Co-chair,
Coalition for Afforable Health

4

We must set some priorities for long-term [health] care, the Number 1 issue among the senior community. We must decide who is to be covered. What is to be covered? How will it be paid for? And how much are seniors willing to pay? This is not just a senior issue. It can wipe out any family—young or old—when someone in the family needs long-term care.

Interview/
USA Today, 10-25:(A)11.

Charles B. Rangel
United States Representative,
D-New York

5

[Criticizing HUD Secretary Louis Sullivan for supporting programs that would distribute clean needles to illegal-drug users to help stop the spread of AIDS]: It is a tragic indictment of our national policy that the nation's top health official is advocating free needles to addicts as his first anti-drug proposal before even developing a policy for how to treat addicts. [Needle programs] would keep addicts out of sight, out of mind, and even sweep them under the rug instead of restoring their dignity and giving them drug-free lives.

March 9/The New York Times,
3-10:(A)8.

Arnold S. Relman
Editor, "The New England
Journal of Medicine"
1

[On referrals by doctors to medical facilities in which they have a financial interest]: I am concerned about the increasing prevalence of this. The crucial point is not whether it involves 40,000, 50,000 or 100,000 doctors, but that it's unethical and it's wrong and it's not in the public interest.

Los Angeles Times, 4-29:(I)22.

Elliot L. Richardson
Former Secretary of
Health, Education and Welfare
of the United States
2

It is characteristic of us that if a new and better [medical] treatment is available, we want it as soon as we can get it and we really don't care what it costs.

USA Today,
8-10:(A)12.

David Rothman
Professor of social medicine,
Columbia College of
Physicians and Surgeons
3

[On whether certain patients should be permitted to use new drugs that have not been sufficiently tested for effectiveness and safety]: Many drugs will be released with less knowledge [under these circumstances]. But if you were a patient facing a terminal illness, wouldn't you want the ultimate right to make choices of risk and benefits? My answer would be: absolutely . . . In all human experimentation, there is always conflict between the interests of the particular patients and the research community and outside society. Delays [in drug approval] may ultimately benefit all future patients—but not this particular patient at this particular moment. But should this particular patient be required to sacrifice his interest for the larger social good?

Los Angeles Times,
9-7:(I)20.

David Roy
Director, Center for Bioethics,
Montreal
4

The whole death-dying dilemma and euthanasia will become controversial in the next 10 years. And there are conflicts ahead with fetal surgery and the rights of the woman, fetal-tissue transplants, and how the tissue is obtained. With organ transplants in general, there may well be a change in attitude about burying healthy organs. And there is pre-symptomatic genetic testing. It's an area that will explode in the 1990s. If we can determine that you have a genetic predisposition to a disease, who should have access to the information? Family, employer, insurer?

World Press Review, December:32.

James H. Sammons
Executive vice president,
American Medical Association
5

I believe it is a critical comment on the state of our legal system that even one patient would not receive care because physicians fear being sued [for malpractice].

USA Today, 10-18:(A)8.

Pat Schoeni
Director of public affairs,
Health Insurance Association
of America
6

We do not believe the American public wants a monolithic [national] health-care system. I think there's certainly problems with the [current health-care] system . . . Certainly, [there are] people [who] are not covered. But the vast majority of people have health care, and everybody has access to emergency care. You may be able to fix the pieces that are wrong without having to redo the whole system.

Los Angeles Times, 1-12:(I)26.

Patricia Schroeder
United States Representative,
D-Colorado
7

When you look at the Federal dollar and how it's spent on medical care, a very high per-

(PATRICIA SCHROEDER)

centage of it is spent on the last few days of a person's life. It should not be either/or, and you should not pit one age group against another. But we've totally ignored one age group: children.

March 1/
The New York Times, 3-2:(A)14.

Alan K. Simpson
United States Senator,
R-Wyoming

1

[Criticizing those senior citizens who have called for repeal of the catastrophic-illness law which involves a surtax to help pay its costs]: The whole U.S. has been swung around on their tails by the 5.6 per cent who don't want to pay for these benefits. We're not confused; we're terrorized ... Yes, it's a social experiment; it's called pay for what you get.

Washington, Oct. 6/
The Washington Post, 10-7:(A)10.

David Sobel
Director of preventive medicine,
Kaiser Permanente
Medical Care Program
in Northern California

2

Pleasure is a vital nutrient, and many people today are not getting their minimum daily requirement. Improving your health doesn't necessarily mean giving up things you love, doing arduous exercises or constantly worrying about everything you do. It's often just a question of following the things that give you pleasure. Things like listening to music, smelling sweet scents, even going shopping may have unrecognized health benefits.

USA Today, 6-8:(A)2.

William M. Stahl
Chief of surgery,
Lincoln Hospital, New York

3

... drug [-abuse] related violence is becoming a more prominent feature of life here [at the

hospital] ... When we take a slug out of somebody here, chances are a month or two later they'll be back again with something else, maybe worse. All of the expensive things in the health-care system are being expended on people whose cause of illness is not natural—drugs. We are pouring blood, medicines, antibiotics into a large drug-patient population that requires intensive care.

The New York Times, 5-10:(A)17.

Fortney H. (Pete) Stark
United States Representative,
D-California

4

Medicare, patients and the taxpayer are paying tens of millions of dollars for needless tests, caused by doctors referring patients to centers from which the doctor makes a profit because of his referral. It's a blatant and gross avoidance of present law that must be stopped.

The New York Times, 4-29:7.

Martin A. Strosberg
Professor of health-care
management, Union College,
Schenectady, N.Y.

5

[Saying intensive-care units at hospitals are overflowing, in part because new technologies allow more elderly and otherwise terminal patients to cling to life indefinitely]: Most ICUs are filled to the brim, much more pressed than they were five years ago ... That means that other patients may be denied intensive care. The unseen victims are the people who are dying outside the unit on the hospital floor.

The New York Times, 8-22:(B)5.

Louis W. Sullivan
Secretary of Health and
Human Services
of the United States

6

Although the general decline in [illegal] drug use indicates that our national media campaigns, school- and community-based prevention pro-

(LOUIS W. SULLIVAN)

grams and intervention efforts in the work-place are having an impact, the most difficult and challenging part of the drug-abuse problem is now apparent. We need to strengthen our efforts to reach those who require more intensive prevention efforts and those who need treatment. For instance, we need to help those young people who are the most vulnerable to drug abuse because of drug abuse in their families, limited opportunities to succeed in school and the attraction of a drug underworld whose immediate promise of material benefits appears deceptively to outweigh the long-term advantages of education and employment.

July 31/
The Washington Post, 8-4:(A)22.

Robert W. Sweet
Judge,
United States District Court
for the Southern District
of New York

1

[Calling for legalization of now illegal drugs]: . . . mind-altering by alcohol has been part of Western culture. Not so marijuana, cocaine, heroin and crack. However, these substances, to a greater or lesser extent, and in varying degrees, do alter one's consciousness, one's view of the world. Even as alcohol dulls the suppressor and enhances one's view of oneself, cocaine gives a sense of exhileration, heroin a glow, a warmth, and marijuana a sense of relaxation and ease. What then is wrong? . . . The gamble would have to be that addressing the underlying causes, providing safe narcotics and treating the users, would ultimately result in a healthier America. If it is otherwise, it will be because our citizens have lost the capacity to act affirmatively and to control their individual addictions. The present climate seems to me to be optimistic: There is an emphasis on health, diet and what one ingests. If our society can learn to stop using butter, it should be able to cut down on cocaine. If it cannot, no prohibition can be effective.

At Cosmopolitan Club, New York,
Dec. 12/
The New York Times, 12-13:(A)16.

Margaret Thatcher
Prime Minister
of the United Kingdom

2

[On criticism that she plans to "privatize" Britain's National Health Service]: The National Health Service will continue to be available to all, regardless of income, and to be financed mainly out of general taxation. We aim to extend patient choice, to delegate responsibility to where the services are provided and to secure the best value for money.

Jan. 31/
The New York Times,
2-1:(A)1.

Stanley Weiss
Member, department of
preventive medicine,
University of
Medicine and Dentistry
of New Jersey

3

If you talk to people in middle-class America, AIDS seems a significant threat because a lot of their other problems are under control. But if you approach the poor in the inner cities, they don't see the disease as such a threat. They have so many problems besides AIDS that it is hard to focus on this one issue.

Time, 1-30:61.

John E. Wennberg
Professor of community and
family medicine,
Dartmouth College
Medical School

4

There's a double standard of truth in medicine today. We have this big apparatus to screen the medicines we allow on the market but no comparable system to evaluate almost everything else doctors do. As a result, we don't know what works and what doesn't.

U.S. News & World Report,
1-30:70.

Michael E. Whitcomb
Dean,
University of Washington
Medical School

1

We should make it clearer to first-year medical students what our expectations are in terms of the ethical and moral behavior of physicians. If you come to this school and you refuse to care for an AIDS patient, or some similar problem, that is grounds for dismissal, just as you say if you cheat, you are out.

The New York Times,
10-3:(B)7.

Nadine Winter
District of Columbia
Councilwoman

2

In the 1960s and 1970s many educators and their respective schools of thought impressed on many of us that substances heretofore considered "recreational" were not particularly dangerous. Marijuana and cocaine were "fun" drugs of the beat generation, the new generation, the now generation and the me generation. So here we are today with the dead generation. I was never impressed with the liberalization and public toleration of chemical self-destruction then, and I am certainly not pleased with having to pick up the pieces today. I look at my 12-year-old grandson and pray that he will be spared active exposure to and the consequences of such "fun."

Before Senate Appropriations
Subcommittee on
the District of Columbia,
Washington, April 4/
The Washington Post,
4-20:(A)18.

Sidney Wolfe
Director, Public Citizen
Health Research Group,
Washington

3

[Criticizing the current U.S. health-care system]: Those who say, "It ain't broke; don't fix it," are wrong. Our country is in a world-wide scandal with its failure to act. It's the only industrialized country outside South Africa that does not have national health insurance ... Anyone who says we don't need national health insurance is just off the wall.

Los Angeles Times,
1-12:(I)27.

James Wyngaarden
Director,
National Institutes of Health
of the United States

4

Virtually every major achievement in medical research in the past century has depended, in one way or another, upon the use of animals. I cannot envision how progress in our successful research efforts to improve human health could be maintained without continued reliance upon experimental animals. This is why I feel a sense of deep outrage that the biomedical research community is being harassed and threatened by a small segment of society that is opposed to the use of laboratory animals ... As costly as acts of vigilante vandalism already have been, their effects will be increased many fold if we as members of the biomedical research community permit ourselves to be intimidated and fail to carry out urgent research because animals are required. For the true victims of the illegal acts of terrorism [against animal research] are not only research institutions and staff, but all members of society. The ultimate cost is levied against those who wait for better treatments or preventive measures for disease and disability—whose very lives may be at stake.

News conference,
New York, April 21/
The Washington Post,
4-24:(A)14.

Irvin D. Yalom
Psychiatrist,
Stanford University

5

I see psychotherapy as a truth-seeking venture, and in therapy we are all the time trying to force patients to look at their own responsibility

(IRVIN D. YALOM)

for what happens to them... Basically, for myself and for my patients, my rosary is the Socratic epigram, "The unexamined life is not worth living." More than anything else, I want the patient to examine his or her life with as much honesty as possible, and I think that, ultimately, illusion about significant portions of life ends up weakening the human spirit rather than enriching it.

Interview/
U.S. News & World Report,
10-30:67.

Frank E. Young
Commissioner,
Food and Drug Administration
of the United States

1

[On quick FDA approval of new drugs for patients with life-threatening diseases]: My highest priority since I came to the [FDA] is to get drugs to the desperately ill and people that need them as quickly as possible. For those people, it is clear they are prepared to take a different set of risks when a disease threatens their lives.

The Washington Post, 2-2:(A)4.

The Performing Arts

BROADCASTING

Tom Brokaw
Anchorman, NBC News

1

[On technical problems, such as occurred during the recent San Francisco earthquake, that blacks out TV coverage]: The new satellite technology is wonderful, but it's made us hostage to our expectations that information can be instantaneous.

Time, 10-30:47.

Allan Burns
Producer

2

With few exceptions, *The Cosby Show* for one, almost all [TV] series that have had any longevity have not started out very quickly or promisingly [in the ratings] ... *MASH, Lou Grant, Mary Tyler Moore.* The network executives have got to be willing to stick with the talent and shows they believe in. Short-term six-episode commitments are going to be the death of us all, or certainly the death of television.

At TV forum,
University of California,
Los Angeles/Daily Variety, 3-20:6.

Johnny Carson
TV talk-show host

3

There's a big difference between being a movie personality like Paul Newman and being a television personality like me. Fans, seeing Paul Newman in a public place, might whisper or even point, but they don't approach him, because Paul Newman is a movie star, bigger than life—eight feet by ten. Me, I'm 21 inches [the size of a TV screen]. People don't hesitate to come up to me and say, "Hi, Johnny, nice to see you."

Interview/
Cosmopolitan, March:186.

Barbara Corday
Executive vice president,
CBS Entertainment

4

[On what she looks for in TV programming]: Intelligent, thoughtful shows that are about something. I don't mean soapbox programs, but I think every show, even if it's a silly half-hour comedy, can have value. I'm just beginning to develop shows for next fall. We'll have 130 scripts by February. Twenty-five or so will be made into pilots by the end of April. A handful— maybe seven—will get into the schedule ... Look, I would love to make quality shows. But they'd better be entertaining.

Interview, New York/
Cosmopolitan, January:110.

William H. Cowles III
President,
American Newspaper
Publishers Association

5

Television is becoming vastly fragmented. The audiences for television are becoming more segmented, more specialized as time goes by. Just look at the 35-channel or 108-channel cable systems that are in most cities in the country. Television is becoming segmented, as magazines and as perhaps newspapers will have to be.

Interview/
USA Today, 4-25:(A)11.

Phil Donahue
TV talk-show host

6

[On criticism by newspaper journalists of shows like his which they say frequently verge on "trash"]: I do not apologize for wanting to draw a crowd. I am as interested in ratings as the people

(PHIL DONAHUE)

in this room are interested in circulation. I also believe that there is an unbecoming elitism here within our own journalistic community.

*At seminar at American Society of
Newspaper Editors convention,
Washington, April 12/
The New York Times, 4-13:(B)4.*

John P. Foley
*Roman Catholic Archbishop
of Philadelphia*

1

[Saying consumer boycotts of advertisers and networks is appropriate as a method of protesting alleged pornography in TV programming]: If freedom of speech exists, then the individuals who receive the pictures or words in their homes also have freedom of speech in which they can make their attitudes known to those who produce or make possible the production of such programs. It's their right to do so, and if they feel that certain things are damaging to their children, then perhaps it is even their duty to do so.

*To reporters, Rome, May 16/
The New York Times, 5-17:(A)3.*

Edward O. Fritts
*President,
National Association
of Broadcasters*

2

In 1984, when Congress passed the Cable Act, cable [TV] characterized itself as a struggling, infant industry. That Act, which in essence removed all regulatory oversight, has become the communications equivalent of anabolic steroids. Today, cable-television operators enjoy an unregulated monopoly. Amazingly, only 32 of more than 8,000 cable systems have any direct competition.

*Before Senate Judiciary
Subcommittee on Antitrust,
Monopolies and Business Rights,
Washington,
April 12/
Los Angeles Times, 4-13:(IV)2.*

Janice Gretemeyer
*Director of press relations,
American Broadcasting
Companies*

3

The viewer expectancy has been modified by all the TV choices they have. That doesn't mean that we'll ever see the networks pandering to the same tastes as cable, but we do have to recognize that people just expect to see more on TV nowadays.

Christianity Today, 3-3:45.

Lawrence Grossman
*Former president,
Public Broadcasting Service*

4

[On financing of public-TV programs]: It's brutal. In public broadcasting the money lies under different rocks all over the place—the private sector, corporate underwriters, non-profit foundations and government agencies. But no one is ever in a position to fund the whole thing, so the fanatic who wants to put together a public-television series that involves major amounts of dough has to become a wandering beggar trying to put these things together.

The New York Times, 5-8:(B)2.

Sherman Hemsley
Actor

5

You don't realize how many years you've been doing [a TV series] until you look back. To me, a character is a job, whether it lasts 10 years or two days ... In TV, you never get a chance to do the same show twice; you don't have that flow. It's always changing from week to week, so you never feel comfortable. *I* never do. Sometimes I just barely make it through.

*Interview/Emmy Magazine,
March-April:21.*

Jim Henson
Puppeteer

6

At least with us, we tend to work a little bit more spontaneously in television [than in

(JIM HENSON)

movies]. Things will happen [in TV] because you're working very fast and because it's easier. Tape is rolling, and you try a couple of different kinds of things. With film, particularly if you do a big, expensive movie, by the time you're shooting it, you've been working on the script for a year, and it's gone through x number of revisions. You've examined every little line, and you've talked about it, and you've heard it read. You don't even know if it's funny any more because you've forgotten when you're supposed to laugh. I think comedy through this whole process is very difficult because everything is zeroed down and you know exactly what you're going to shoot, and you have to break from that. You have to consciously try not to get yourself locked into that way of thinking. But the system tends to do that to you. On the other hand, I think that film in a theatre is a whole different experience from watching something on television. I would think that experience is the major difference. There's no way you can get that in terms of television.

Interview/
American Film, November:21.

Aletha C. Huston
Professor, University of Kansas;
Co-director, Center for
Research on the Influence of
Television on Children

1

[On how TV violence affects young viewers]: There is more research on this topic than on almost any other social issue of our time. Virtually all independent scholars . . . agree. We keep pumping children with the messages that violence is the way to solve their problems—and some of it takes hold.

The Washington Post, 9-19:(D)5.

Jesse L. Jackson
Civil-rights leader

2

[Saying his planned new TV talk show will not be like tabloid-TV programs which tend to choose odd or sensational topics]: [With the

other shows] you got your goat with the eye in the middle and two-headed puppies and all kind of personal sexual habits and private fantasies and all kind of perversions and eroticism . . . There are a number of shows that appeal to people whose interest is in these kind of subject matters, which I, you know, find important because people are expressing their feelings about marriage and double-dating and divorce. Good. There's obviously room for that. [But] there's another market over here, too. There's some magazines in the racks with naked ladies and sexual whatever, and there's a market for that. There's also a market for *Time* and *Newsweek* and *Ebony* and *Jet,* too. There's a market for tabloids and there's a market for the *Los Angeles Times* and *New York Times*-type papers, too. This [new talk show] is about expanding the market. We're not really competing with people who do [tabloid-TV].

Los Angeles/
Los Angeles Times, 12-5:(F)2.

Hal Kanter
Television writer

3

It's getting harder and harder to turn out a show on a weekly basis. It seems to me that the networks have greater input today than ever before. [This input] leads to rewrites and changes that are unnecessary. I don't know why it is. When I began working in TV, a half-hour show could be turned out every week by one producer, a director, and, at the most, four writers. Today, look at the credits on a TV show, and you'll find four to six producers. I have no idea what these people do.

Interview/
Emmy Magazine, Sept.-Oct.:49.

Larry King
TV and radio talk-show host

4

I think radio is a constant because of the automobile. Radio goes with you. Radio is personal. It's like that couch you like and that favorite pair of shoes. It's kind of like always going home.

The New York Times, 6-27:(B)2.

David Letterman
TV talk-show host

1

All I ever wanted to do is to have a television show. And I've got one. So from that standpoint I feel like I've succeeded . . . I think once this show is canceled or once I get fired, you'll never see me again in another TV show of my own. It's just too much work, too heartbreaking, and if you've done it once, congratulations.

Interview, New York/
Time, 2-6:68.

Joseph L. Mankiewicz
Director, Screenwriter

2

[Criticizing today's TV writing]: Today, the WGA has 10,000 members. There haven't been 10,000 writers since Homer. [Today's dialog is] all cartoonists' balloons. Everybody has a joke; nobody is a straight-man. The question is how much you are going to stand for. You are the ones who sit at home and watch this drivel.

Upon receiving Akira Kurosawa
Award at San Francisco Film Festival/
Daily Variety, 3-20:8.

Robert Mulholland
Director, broadcast division,
Medill School of Journalism,
Northwestern University;
Former president,
National Broadcasting Company

3

The competitive situation [for broadcasting] has dramatically changed in the United States, while the regulatory environment has not. [The] underlying issue is not money but access. Over half of all Americans now receive their television broadcasting through a wire [cable]. A vertically integrated company controlling production, cable and syndication has an enormous advantage over broadcast operations that essentially are restricted, such as the networks.

The Christian Science Monitor,
6-9:6.

Preston Padden
President, Association of
Independent Television Stations

4

Cable [TV] program services are available only to those with the financial ability to pay. By contrast, broadcast stations are the quintessential democratic medium, available equally to the rich and the poor . . . The pay medium that lives off the free medium should not be permitted to simultaneously undermine that free medium . . . Like a 20th-century Trojan horse, cable rode into the American living-room on the promise of enhanced reception of free over-the-air programming. Now that cable is safely entrenched in more than half of all American homes, it has set about to remove popular events from free over-the-air broadcasting and place those, instead, on pay cable services.

Congressional testimony/
The Washington Post, 7-14:(B)2.

Dennis Patrick
Chairman, Federal
Communications Commission

5

We would all like to see the finest quality in children's [TV] programming. The question is: How do you define what that is? It's easy to be a demagogue, but it's an extraordinarily subjective question as to what constitutes good children's programming.

Interview/
Los Angeles Times,
1-20:(VI)27.

David Puttnam
Producer; Former chairman,
Columbia Pictures

6

Those who sincerely believe—as I do—that television's true role is [the] fundamental part it plays in our nation's social life, find themselves, all too frequently, having to remind themselves of the obvious—that the marketplace exists to serve the needs of society, not the other way 'round . . . We all know in our heart of hearts that society must not be manipulated into serving the needs of

(DAVID PUTTNAM)

the marketplace. If necessary, society even needs protection . . .

*At "Television 1989—Will More
Mean Less" debate,
England, February/
Daily Variety, 3-30:10.*

Linda Ronstadt
Singer

1

Radio's been taken over by a corporate mentality, and the personality jocks who spring from the community have been systematically eliminated because they're harder to control. Radio is completely formatted now, and this change has had a profound impact on music. Radio used to be a democratic process where you put the music out there and the people judged it. No matter how much payola, coke or hookers were delivered, you still couldn't get a hit if the people didn't like your music. Now, with formatting, what the people do or don't like doesn't come into play because they don't even get to hear anything that isn't already an approved part of the format. It's really destroyed radio, and it's now left to things like festivals to preserve any kind of democracy in music. They're the keepers of the flame now.

*Interview, Los Angeles/
Los Angeles Times,
10-29:(Calendar)48.*

Quentin Schultze
*Professor of
communication arts and sciences,
Calvin College*

2

The [TV] networks are increasingly competitive, given their dwindling audience in the face of cable and VCR markets. Their goal is to maximize ratings, period. We can be optimistic, but if they wanted to do something [about limiting violence in programming], they would do it on their own and not need to get together [to make sure all three networks would do something and thus not be at a competitive disadvantage with each other].

Christianity Today, 2-17:48.

Jane Seymour
Actress

3

[On TV miniseries]: I believe they are the artform of our time. They offer the chance to present to the vast public book adaptations that they would never otherwise know. I also think they encourage people to read and re-read the classics . . . Most feature films today are for 17-year-olds, prizefighters and vigilantes. The best roles are in television.

*Interview, Santa Barbara, Calif./
The Saturday Evening Post,
May-June:42.*

Tom Shales
*Television critic,
"The Washington Post"*

4

[On TV talk shows that critics say frequently verge on "trash"]: It's not a question of what's journalism and what's not journalism as what's good taste and what's bad taste, what's good manners and what's bad manners. And television now is overrun with bad taste and bad manners.

*At seminar at American Society of
Newspaper Editors convention,
Washington, April 12/
The New York Times, 4-13:(B)4.*

Alfred C. Sikes
*Chairman, Federal
Communications Commission*

5

If Congress decides to reinstate [the broadcast Fairness Doctrine], we would enforce it because Congress makes the law. I do not favor the Fairness Doctrine. I was a broadcaster and I have seen the practical effects of the Doctrine. Broadcasters were so afraid that they would be cited if they carried more news on one subject, or editorialized, and that they would have to hire a slew of Washington lawyers to defend them. As a consequence, many broadcasters stayed out of the editorial business. Fundamentally, I think that broadcasting should be shielded by the First Amendment.

*Interview/
The New York Times, 10-3:(C)2.*

Fred Silverman
Producer;
Former TV network executive

1

In network television, if you snap your fingers, 200 people do it for you, but here [as an independent producer] you do it yourself. Being on the selling side is completely different. The hardest thing is that you have something in your head [an idea for a TV program], and you try to move it into the buyer's head. They just look at you and say no. And that's it.

Interview, Los Angeles/
The New York Times, 6-5:(C)1.

Howard Stringer
President, CBS Broadcast Group

2

We [TV networks] must rethink our relationship with cable. They have an endless cash flow . . . They take our programming—for which the three networks spend $4-billion in Hollywood—and get it for no cost whatsoever, and then charge viewers for it. Then they take that money and go after our best programming. This is nuts, not just for us but for the American people, who now seriously run the risk of seeing our most cherished national events and programs that have always been available on universal free television become restricted to a pay-TV service for our most affluent population.

Before CBS affiliates/
The Washington Post, 7-14:(B)2.

Ted Turner
Chairman, Turner Broadcasting System

3

I'd rather do something that appeals to adults, that has a little meat on the bones, and you couldn't do that with theatricals [motion pictures]. You usually lose your shirt if you try to do something of social or historical significance. There's so much of that sort of thing on TV, why should people go to theatres to see it? Particularly if kids aren't as interested. But the television audience is mainly adults, so I'm making the stuff I want to make, which is appealing to adults. I don't have to do these bloody murder things that theatrical people have to do.

Interview/Daily Variety, 3-1:(F)16.

Jack Valenti
President,
Motion Picture Association
of America

4

There can be no question that cable-TV lacks effective competition in the U.S. . . . The motion-picture studios that comprise the MPAA are among the biggest producers and distributors of motion pictures in the world. But they compete with one another . . . in a rough and tumble marketplace in which the consumer is sovereign. [But with cable-TV companies,] each has its aggregation of franchised fiefdoms, impermeable to competitive threats.

Before Senate Antitrust
Subcommittee, Washington/
Daily Variety,
5-9:19.

5

[Criticizing Europe's plans for quotas on U.S. TV programming]: When restrictions go on, they never come off, and they are usually a floor, not a ceiling. Quotas are like a fungus. They never go away. They grow, they slowly get worse, and some day they are going to hurt.

Brussels, Oct. 31/
Los Angeles Times,
11-1:(F)6.

Donald E. Wildmon
Media critic

6

[On gratuitous sex and violence on TV]: The networks are in a game of exploitation. And when you exploit, you always have to go one degree further and one degree further. The people who are responsible call themselves the "creative community." From time to time they do have something that's creative. But it's less work and a lot easier to exploit than to create . . . In our minds, television has the potential to be the most constructive medium man has ever devised. The goal we would like to see is that television reach the potential instead of being used in a destructive manner as it currently is.

Interview/Time, 6-19:54.

379

MOTION PICTURES

Don Ameche
Actor

1

Performers are the worst judges of their own material. If we had the studio system now, no telling how much better the business might be today. Of course, we might not have the [Irving] Thalbergs, the [Darryl] Zanucks and the Sam Goldwyns . . . I went to [Zanuck] once about *Alexander's Ragtime Band* with suggestions about my part. I went to him again about another picture. In both cases he said, "I think you're wrong and I'm going to ask you to do it my way." In both cases he was right. I went to him the third time and he said, "I think you are right but I'm going to Europe. I wish you'd do it my way again. If I'm wrong, I'll make it up to you" . . . The film stank and Zanuck did make it up to me.

Interview/Films in Review, January:31.

Roseanne Barr
Actress

2

These people in Hollywood, these are chinless folk with car phones. And they just don't *like* women. They want us to be drag queens. Hollywood is comfortable to show women raped and beaten, but they don't want to show the power of a woman in a family, to show real women's problems. Or to show real women.

*Interview, New York/
The New York Times, 12-4:(B)4.*

George Bush
President of the United States

3

I can always say, to understand the heart of America just look at the American film.

*At 25th anniversary celebration of
American Film Institute,
Washington, Sept. 27/
The Washington Post, 9-28:(D)8.*

Glenn Close
Actress

4

My characters are people you just meet, like anybody else. It takes time to get to know them. I sometimes feel so shy in front of them that I have to force myself to speak their words. When I walk into the first rehearsal I sometimes feel I have no personality at all—it's like a prevision of insanity. It's because I don't yet know who the character *is*. You have to look at the world through the character's eyes—not yours.

*Interview/
Esquire, November:140.*

Rob Cohen
Producer

5

We [in films] work in an industry where everyone has the same profile, the same judgments and the same interests. In tone, Hollywood is a white, male, college-educated, Jewish milieu full of ambitious guys who want to play out their fantasies in the largest possible forum. You rarely see people come out of screenings debating the film itself. Everyone debates whether the film will do $20 [-million] to $30-million—or $40 [-million] to $50-million. When that's the largest you're aiming for, films about minorities or venturesome topics only get made out on the fringe, after long, bloody battles—or they don't get made at all.

*Los Angeles Times,
4-16:(Calendar)24.*

Francis Ford Coppola
Director

6

The trouble with American film-making is that producers don't allow the risk of failure. If a good

(FRANCIS FORD COPPOLA)

film can't risk being a failure, it won't be really good.

Interview, Cannes, France/
Films in Review, March:155.

Brian De Palma
Director

1

[Violence is] an aesthetic tool, part of the palette . . . Many movies are exciting and exhilarating because of their use of violence: Chase movies. Boxing movies. Stalk-somebody-and-kill-them movies. That's why it exists.

Interview, New York/
The Washington Post, 8-18:(D)6.

Clint Eastwood
Actor, Director

2

Movie-making to me is something that happens in the present tense. I find with a lot of films, if they're overly set up, or if the director insists on a lot of takes, or if things just move along real slow, the lack of energy shows. They become vacant films. They're technically nice, but their soul is gone. I just like to keep everything moving, keep everything alive, so that you make decisions on reflex, without over-thinking it. The more time you have to think things through, the more you have time to screw it up.

Interview/Los Angeles Times
5-21:(Calendar)26.

Willis Edwards
President, Beverly Hills/
Hollywood (Calif.) branch,
National Association for the
Advancement of Colored People

3

[On how blacks are portrayed in films]: There has been no balance. We are looked upon as comedians, not as people who have families and intimacy. We have love affairs as well as whites do. In the movies, we don't see blacks going to bed. It's like we don't go to bed. Hollywood has

never wanted us to have love interests. They feel it won't sell in Peoria or in Mississippi.

Ebony, April:42.

Michael D. Eisner
Chairman, Walt Disney
Company

4

U.S. films capture 87 per cent of the box-office in Australia, 70 per cent in Greece, 80 per cent in the Netherlands and 92 per cent in Britain. Why? My contention is audiences world-wide want to see the American way of life. For viewers outside our boundaries, the United States is the place where the individual has a chance to choose. That is a very powerful message for people in other countries.

At Denison University commencement/
The Christian Science Monitor,
6-12:12.

Douglas Fairbanks, Jr.
Actor

5

[On today's movies]: If they are losing their sense of good taste, if they're excessively violent, I blame the public. The motion-picture business is an industry which, like Detroit making cars, supplies the public with what they want and what they think they want, and what they'll buy. And if they won't buy more decent and conventionally romantic films, but insist on more violent and/or more tasteless scenes of sex, or whatever, I have no answer except to blame the public. 'Cause that's the only thing they'll buy.

Interview, Washington/
The Christian Science Monitor,
11-17:10.

Harrison Ford
Actor

6

I'm a technical actor. For me, acting is part intellectual, part mechanical. It's being in control of your mind and body at the same time. The emotions you show may be spontaneous, but the bricks have to be carefully laid to fit with the other pieces. You don't fool around with the work.

Interview/Time, 5-29:84.

Penny Fuller
Actress

1

Like everything else you do, you bring a compilation of life [to acting]. I think actors are sponges. You see something and say, "Oh, I'm going to use that some time." Often it's not even conscious. Unlike the painter, whose colors are on a palette, *you're* the palette. You're the sculptor and the clay. And everything you bring to it is your own.

Interview, Los Angeles/
Los Angeles Times, 1-19:(VI)5.

David Geffen
Producer

2

[On concerns about Japanese influence on U.S. motion pictures resulting from such buyouts as Sony Corporation's announced purchase of Columbia Pictures]: It's not bad for the movie business and it's not bad for Columbia, but I wonder if it's bad for America . . . The question is, where does it all stop? If the Japanese came in and bought all the textbook manufacturers in this country, you can be sure someone in Congress would complain about the potential for abuse. Well, a giant part of the education of young people in this country comes from film and TV, and someone should be paying attention to what's going on.

The Washington Post, 9-27:(B)1,5.

Larry Gelbart
Playwright, Screenwriter

3

In motion pictures, unless you're willing or able to also direct and/or produce your film, once you [the screenwriter] hand in the pages, other people are going to make the key decisions, including whether or not it is your work that will finally be on the screen. And as often as not, you find yourself sharing screen credit with anyone, from a friend—and your friendship might be strained as a result—to a total stranger.

Interview, New York/
Los Angeles Times, 12-3:(Calendar)6.

Frank Gilroy
Screenwriter, Director

4

The right to make your own mistakes—it's all an independent film-maker does have, certainly very little money. It's getting harder and harder to make independent pictures, but I only have to listen to the lamentations of my fellow writers with major studios to know that I've made the right decision. I get too involved with the money side, but I console myself with what [the late director] John Huston said: "Never mind, kid. We made the picture." I can't tell you how much better and cheaper films could be if they incorporated the writer into the production process.

Interview/
Films in Review, May:298.

Jean-Luc Godard
French director

5

[On the French New Wave directors of 30 years ago]: We were the first for whom cinema had a past. For a director at Paramount 50 years ago, the cinema had no history. But we knew that it had a past; we were children who realized we had parents. We never thought we could do better than our parents. We thought we could do better than the bad films, but not better than the good. Myself, I never thought I would do better than John Ford or Orson Welles, but I thought I could perhaps do what Godard was meant to do on earth.

The New York Times, 8-11:(B)7.

Dave Grusin
Composer, Arranger

6

[On his music scores for motion pictures]: A lot of what I do has to do with being the audience

(DAVE GRUSIN)

for a film. The structured steps are fairly straight-forward. After looking at the film, I gain an idea as to the style of music I should write. I study the movie to determine what we are supposed to get people to feel at certain parts of the story, and determine which areas of the film would benefit by music. From then on, its mathematical, fitting in a certain amount of music to fit the scenes. Getting the script ahead of time is useful to determine whether it's a project I can contribute to; but my real inspiration comes from actually viewing the film, not what the director tells me about it.

Interview/Down Beat, July:25.

Taylor Hackford
Director

1

Hollywood's biggest problem today is that it's so blockbuster oriented. They focus so much attention on the big movies that I'm not sure they know how to market more unique pictures. The studio executive is a very timid breed—and maybe rightfully so. Ultimately, Hollywood becomes an arithmetical business.

Los Angeles Times,
4-16:(Calendar)4.

Gene Hackman
Actor

2

All of us, from ditch-diggers to bus drivers to shoe salesmen, have a need to create something. I'm blessed that I found a profession that lets me do so. Once in a while, a piece of artistry flows by me or through me, but it's a mistake to think of myself as "artistic." It looks relaxed, easy, but I work very hard . . . Acting is a selfish profession. You have to be selfish with your time, your thoughts, and hope the people around you won't suffer too much.

Interview/Time, 1-9:62.

Tom Hanks
Actor

3

When I say comedy takes care of itself, I mean it's an assumption the actor has to make—and

then pay no attention to. You have to go on to the more specific tasks of actors: to actually walk in this world, to reflect what's going on in society, to be a breathing character others can recognize. I consider myself an actor before I consider myself a comedian, but I'm certainly aware that I'm funny and that my movies are comedies. I disagree with the guy who said comedy is an intellectual process. People who intellectualize about it aren't funny. That's true about acting in general. But comedy's more instinctual. I don't know if it's possible to have a specific "approach." I don't have a system or even think about it very much. Something happens, but it's always different. A lot of it's just common sense.

Interview, Burbank, Calif./
Film Comment, March-April:18.

Mollie Haskell
Film critic

4

In recent years, the French cinema has lost its pre-eminent place in American film culture. It hasn't been replaced by any other national cinema. But everything is so English-oriented now and audiences are lazy and parochial; nobody wants to read subtitles, not even students. And what we're getting is not authentic French cinema but French films recycled for American audiences—English-language remakes of French hits, which usually don't work, because the idiom can't be translated from one culture to another.

Interview/
The New York Times, 8-4:(B)5.

John Hurt
Actor

5

I often say with interviews there are only about six questions and all of them are "How do you act?" Dame Edith Evans gave the best answer, really, when being interviewed by a young man from TV. He said, "Dame Edith, how do you approach your parts? How do you go about researching? How do you fill . . ." She just stopped him and said, "I pretend, dear boy." And in a sense, she's absolutely right. A lot of it's

(JOHN HURT)

waffle, don't forget. I once said in front of [director] Lindsay Anderson, "Well, come on, Lindsay, let's face it. Acting's just a more sophisticated way of playing cowboys and Indians." And he went bananas: "How *could* you say that? How *could* you say that?" I knew that would rile old Lindsay something rotten. That's why the Method School, I think, is barking up the wrong tree. Everybody has their own method of getting to the truth. But I don't think you can put too much store in research, in observation. All of those things you have to do, of course you do; but the essential thing that takes the audience on the journey that you want them to go on is imaginative. That's what flies. Or something changes because of whoever you're working with.

Interview/
Film Comment, March-April:67.

William Hurt
Actor

1

Acting is about actions. It's not pretending. Acting is not *looking* like you're doing, it's *doing*. The problem begins when you get into adjectives in acting. Acting is not about adjectives. It's about verbs and adverbs.

Interview, New York/
The Washington Post, 1-25:(C)10.

Lawrence Kasdan
Director

2

If you can actually get a job directing, it's not that hard to finish the job. You may not do it well, but essentially it runs itself because everybody is there to get it over with. You can be amazingly competent. The hardest part is getting the job, and that takes ambition and politics, which have nothing to do with telling an actor how to play a scene.

At "The Director in Action" seminar,
sponsored by Directors Guild of America
and Independent Feature Project/
Film Comment, Jan.-Feb.:30.

Stanley Kramer
Producer, Director

3

[All my films] had something to do with a human sense of values . . . I never learned differently than to follow my own tastes and desires and dreams. Sometimes it works and sometimes it doesn't. I think of a film as a failure if it fails to reach an audience . . . I don't think a film can change someone's mind. You can provoke people to talk about [an issue]. You can plant a seed. In [today's] tumultuous times, you look for your own truth and what you usually find is a part of the truth.

Daily Variety, 4-28:12.

Andrew Laszlo
Cinematographer

4

How do you translate words into images? Sometimes you have to experiment, with no guarantees of success. You ignore what your light meter says, and expose the film in a way that doesn't seem to make a lot of sense. But you know instinctively it's the right thing to do. That's when the genie comes out of the bottle and the magic happens . . . It's only when I see the assembled cuts that my doubts melt away and I know my instincts were right. Why do I take chances? Because I care. If you don't care, you should be in another line of work.

Daily Variety, 3-20:5.

David Lean
Director

5

I think the cinema is mainly good for telling a story in pictures. I have the impression that nowadays, for economic reasons, television tells the stories through dialogue. But I think the great films tell their stories with pictures. I love the flow of images. Of course, good dialogue is vitally important. But as far as I am concerned, it is secondary. I take the greatest care with it, but that is not what I enjoy the most.

Interview/
World Press Review,
August:59.

(DAVID LEAN)

1

I suppose round about *Lawrence of Arabia* I got quite good notices [from film critics]. Then, as I went on, *Doctor Zhivago* got *the* worst notices you could ever see. *Ryan's Daughter* was absolutely torn to shreds by the critics and I thought, "What the hell am I doing?" When you're the movie director, the only people that you really believe are the critics. You mistrust your friends because you think they're being nice, but there in black and white with the power of the printed word it says you stink and you have no idea of what you're doing.

Interview, London/
The New York Times, 10-17:(B)1.

Spike Lee
Director

2

I'm a film-maker. I feel that's what I was put on earth to do. But there are certain issues I have opinions about. Film's the most powerful medium in the world. I think I should have been shot if I didn't use this advantage to talk about things that affect us [blacks], being a black American today.

Newsweek, 10-2:37.

Jack Lemmon
Actor

3

In my opinion, acting is basically a mental process of uncovering why a character says or does something. Once you know what motivates him, the next step is showing the audience something you've already found out. And the greatest thing for any actor is to reach the point where you're not afraid to expose yourself, no matter how risky it seems.

Interview, Los Angeles/
Los Angeles Times, 4-25:(VI)1.

Shirley MacLaine
Actress

4

Film is analogous to life. To study film and character and camera and cutting and choices,

emotional range and the canvas of being human [represents] exactly the same problems we all have when we study how to be better humans. To make a really good film is analogous to making a really good life.

On receiving career achievement award of
Los Angeles Film Teachers Association,
Universal City, Calif., Jan. 10/
Daily Variety, 1-12:3.

5

In general, I don't see much movement in Hollywood toward movies about women. The leading-lady parts tend to be vacuous; they're still defined in terms of the men they play opposite. In many cases, stories don't even need an end, *per se*. In real life people don't know how things are going to turn out. I'd like to see more slice-of-life stories where boy meets girl, boy and girl fall in love, but boy and girl don't necessarily get married.

Interview, New York/
Ladies' Home Journal, April:86.

Louis Malle
Director

6

One of my obsessions when I'm making a film is that the camera shouldn't show; it shouldn't be one of the characters. I like the spectators [audience], in a matter of a minute if possible, to forget that there is a camera. And by doing so, it seems to me, it brings them infinitely closer to the characters and the emotions of the story.

Interview/American Film, April:24.

7

Actors are the ones who are important. I keep telling my crew, "These people are on the screen." When I'm going to say "action," there will be these people, usually terrified, alone in front of the glass eye. And frankly, I wouldn't like to be in their place. It's very hard to be a film actor. They need to be loved and protected and helped in any way possible, and they make the difference.

Interview/American Film, April:28.

WHAT THEY SAID IN 1989

Frank Mancuso
Chairman,
Paramount Pictures Corporation

1

I believe in getting the audience's responses early. The audience will make the final decision anyway; you'd better listen to them early on, while you can still shape the film in the cutting process. Some film-makers are wary of it. It can be extraordinarily painful to make changes. But most of them come to rely on it. They admit it gets better as you go along.

Interview, Los Angeles/
Los Angeles Times,
9-10:(Calendar)23.

Joseph L. Mankiewicz
Director, Screenwriter

2

[The old studio moguls were] Medicis compared to today. [Louis B. Mayer would say,] "That picture made a little money. Let's let Mankiewicz make a couple more." Today, someone like [actor Sylvester] Stallone gets $12-million just to sign a contract because they think he's sure to get $250-million at the box-office.

Upon receiving Akira Kurosawa Award
at San Francisco Film Festival/
Daily Variety, 3-20:8.

Robert McKee
Teacher of screenwriting

3

[On his screenwriting course]: On the first day of class, they look like stunned mullets. I mean, they don't know what hit them. On the second day, depression sets in—when they realize how hard it is. And then on the third day, I give them a shot in the arm, inspire them, because screenwriting is the most difficult writing form of all—because there is no place to hide.

Interview, Los Angeles/
Los Angeles Times, 2-26:(Calendar)24.

Jonas Mekas
Director, Anthology Film Archives,
New York

4

[On the mission of his organization, which is dedicated to supporting and preserving non-commercial independent films]: The world is so practical these days, and so full of this craving for "entertainment," that seriousness is not very popular. Taking a stand for the poetic principal in life, for poetry in life, is not very popular. You hide; you practically blush. To deal with the essence of life—with what life is really all about in the end—is avoided. Here we will be stressing the need of art to uphold the principle of poetry in life—which has to do with *inner* experience, *inner* life. It has to do with the one word that people are perhaps more afraid to say than anything else today: the *soul* of man. In the end, serious art has to do with the development of human beings. We stand for that.

Interview, New York/
The Christian Science Monitor,
6-20:10.

Bette Midler
Actress

5

I intended to be a movie star because I thought it was the high end. I thought it was where the work would survive, that if you had something beautiful and good to offer, it was worth the effort. I still feel that way, but not as strongly. Because I know how hard it is to make something good and beautiful. With your own personal vision. You almost have to be a giant of some sort.

Interview/Los Angeles Times,
2-12:(Calendar)27.

Jonathan Miller
Artistic director,
Old Vic, London

6

[On making films adapted from literary works]: The question is why, in fact, have we attempted to translate literature into visual images, for literature, in fact, conjures mental images. The images we have as a result of reading, recalling or imagining are of a different logical order than the kind of impressions we have when confronted by images on the screen . . . In text, we can refer to the past in a quick and effortless change of tense, without having to revert to a flashback. Proust

(JONATHAN MILLER)

can extend, for 58 pages, long arcades of habitual tense—"On Saturday, Swann and Odette would visit the Luxembourg Gardens"—which sets up an atmosphere of how things were in general. Then he can say, "On the Friday when Odette introduced Swann to the Verdurins, the following occurred." This is a wonderful punctuality for which there is no equivalent in film.

Before Folio Society, London,
Feb. 9/
The New York Times, 2-11:12.

Thom Mount
Producer

1

If you want to see what signals cultural trends, you look to cartoon strips, followed by pop music and, lastly, film, simply because it takes so incredibly long to respond to something and get a film made . . . The cultural winds are changing—and studios do respond to those changes. The only problem is sometimes they forget to stick their fingers in the air to see which way the wind is blowing.

Los Angeles Times,
4-16:(Calendar)26.

Bill Murray
Actor

2

[On his currently directing a film]: Directing is where the action is. It's like being the catcher in baseball. I was the catcher when I played, and you were in on every play. You called every play. Actually, making movies is a group effort. Any one person can mess up at any moment. Any one person can mess it up for everyone else.

Interview, New York/
The New York Times, 8-24:(B)1.

Paul Newman
Actor

3

[On his being a celebrated actor]: If people tell you you have power but don't feel powerful, then what good is the power? If everybody tells you that you are accomplished but you don't feel accomplished, then what the fuck good is that? If people tell you that you are a great lover but you don't feel like a great lover, then what is that? They make that up about you, but it has nothing to *do* with you, and so it strengthens the opinion that you have of yourself—that you are simply nothing but an accumulation of characteristics that you've picked up from playing other people. And you really have to go off in a corner and sit down for about 15 or 20 minutes and say, "I'm not Earl Long or General Groves" [characters that, as an actor, he may currently be playing] and I don't have to embrace their ideas." I simply behave like them for a little period out of every day and then I can go back and I can be whatever this other thing is . . . a kid from Shaker Heights who benefited from the luck of the draw.

Interview, Winnfield, La./
Esquire, October:166.

Sven Nykvist
Cinematographer

4

Light [in a film] can be gentle, dreamlike, bare, living, dead, clear, misty, hot, dark, violent, springlike, falling, straight, slanting, sensual, subdued, limited, poisonous, calming and pale. I discovered the many qualities of light while making some 20 movies with Ingmar Bergman. How do you choose the right light? The answer isn't easy to put into words. The decision is personal. It comes from inside . . . I always tell the cast what I am doing and why. I tell them the truth is in their eyes. If you show their eyes, you can bare their souls. If the chemistry is right, you can capture an inner beauty on film. And that's pure magic.

Interview/Daily Variety, 6-9:7.

5

[On cinematography]: The most important thing is to change the style for each picture. I ask myself how can I help the audience to look at the right thing: is it the actors, or the dialogue, or the mood, or so on. I am not a good technician, although that's my background . . . If I have a

(SVEN NYKVIST)

good lens and a camera that is steady, that's enough. I'm not crazy about the new toys that come up each year. I like simplicity. It's taken me 30 years to come up with simplicity.

Interview/
Film Comment, Sept.-Oct.:53.

Joyce Carol Oates
Author

1

[On her writing a screenplay of one of her novels]: It's an enormous challenge, because one has to transcribe virtually from one dimension to another. In prose fiction, the writer is really writing about language. In a screenplay, there is no language. Just dialogue. Everything is visual. I don't think I found it as difficult as I do prose fiction. It's not that it's easier. I don't find writing easy at all. It's always challenge, an uphill struggle. But writing novels is very lacerating to the soul, and I'm really very exhausted. When I do a screenplay, I'm taking something I already have written. I know the characters like members of my own family. I know the ending. I don't have the anxiety of the original writing. So the screenwriting is a delightful excursion into another dimension.

The New York Times, 1-13:(B)2.

Laurence Olivier
Actor

2

[To become a great actor,] you need talent, luck, stamina and sex. By sex, I don't mean the person has to be wildly attractive—only that he or she have a certain amount of sex appeal. Of all these, the most important is luck. By far.

Interview, London/
Ladies' Home Journal,
December:126.

Alan Pakula
Director

3

The best of this [film] business is the collaboration and the worst of this business is the col-

laboration. The collaborative effort is so much a part of it that you have to keep reminding yourself who *you* are.

Interview, New York/
Los Angeles Times,
3-5:(Calendar)4.

4

As a director, you can orchestrate performances but you can't give them. You can make a good actor look bad, but you can't make a bad actor look good. The trick is knowing when to say something, and when not to.

Interview, New York/
Los Angeles Times, 10-12:(F)7.

Alan Parker
Director

5

I've never understood the philosophy that a director should make 20 versions of the same film throughout his career. Every time I go into a new area, I learn more. It doesn't seem very interesting to me to always plow the same furrow . . . Most of my decisions about what [films] to do are instinctive and intuitive, rather than trying to force things into an intellectual pattern. There are certain things in a project that I require to fire me up and excite me to justify making the film at all. It's far too hard doing what we do to have it left behind like an empty tub of popcorn. It's great to think you can reach a large audience, but it's also nice to think that you can affect people's lives in some way. So when they write the three-line biography of me in *The London Times* when I'm 83, they can say I tried, even if sometimes I didn't succeed. I'd be happy with that.

Interview/
American Film, Jan.-Feb.:12,15.

Gregory Peck
Actor

6

There's been a lot of glamorous financial news in the papers lately [involving entertainment companies]. Multimedia conglomerates . . . It may be that, in a few years, all pictures and all

(GREGORY PECK)

television will be made by two or three of these behemoths who happen also to own magazines, newspapers and cable stations, and [who] manufacture and distribute videocassettes. If these Mount Everests of the financial world are going to labor and bring forth still more pictures with people being blown to bits with bazookas and automatic assault rifles, with no gory detail left unexploited, if they are going to encourage anxious, ambitious actors, directors, writers and producers to continue their assault on the English language by reducing the vocabularies of their characters to half a dozen words, with one colorful but overused Anglo-Saxon verb and one un-beautiful Anglo-Saxon noun covering just about every situation, then I would like to suggest that they stop and think about this: Making millions is not the whole ballgame, fellows. Pride of workmanship is worth more. Artistry is worth more.

Upon accepting Life Achievement Award
of American Film Institute,
Beverly Hills, Calif., March 9/
The New York Times, 3-11:12.

Harold Pinter
Playwright, Screenwriter

1

The excitement for me in transposing a novel into a film has always been . . . to go from one medium to another. You are not simply recording a novel. The big question is and remains: how to keep faithful to the book while creating a new form for the ideas . . . The responsibility of the screenwriter in adapting a book is to find the visual focus and condensation. The one thing a book does not have is the eye. You are reading words but you are seeing *what*? Surely when you look at a film, the hand of an actor falling away over the arm of a chair can tell us as much as five pages in a book. Of course, these five pages may be brilliant and evoke the life of a man whose business is collapsing, whose wife has left him, whose children are drug addicts . . . But in classic terms—and Griffith, Eisenstein, Pudovkin knew this—the hand falling over a chair says it all.

Interview, London/
Film Comment, May-June:20,21.

Sydney Pollack
Director

2

For a long time, directors have been confused about whether they belong to management or labor. It has been quite a dance, but I've concluded the director is part of management. If you're going to control the project, you've got to [be a producer].

At "The Director in Action" seminar,
sponsored by Directors Guild of America
and Independent Feature Project/
Film Comment, Jan.-Feb.:30.

Tom Pollock
Chairman,
MCA Motion Picture Group

3

It's almost impossible to get a film made about a serious subject when the average picture costs $15-million to $17-million. If films cost $1-million to make, you'd see a lot more adventuresome stories being told. But the system is rigged against doing serious films simply because of the costs.

Los Angeles Times,
4-16:(Calendar)5.

David Puttnam
Producer; Former chairman,
Columbia Pictures

4

Good or bad, [movies] tinker around inside your brain, they steal up on you in the darkness of the cinema to form or confirm social attitudes. They can either help to create a healthy, informed, concerned and inquisitive society, or, in the alternative, a negative, apathetic, passive, ignorant one.

At "Television 1989—
Will More Mean Less" debate,
England, February/
Daily Variety, 3-30:39.

5

Today there is the whole notion of the home-run movie—the one movie where you [the producer] never have to work again. The home-run movie completely alters the nature of risk. The old moguls could take a roll on a picture and know that if it didn't work, it wasn't going to bring the studio down. There was a regular cinema audience. Today, as I learned to my cost at Columbia, almost every time you come to bat, you're making a $20-million, $30-million or $50-million bet. That's not an environment that encourages risk or adventurous, creative decisions.

Interview/Time, 5-1:62.

1

Cinema is insidious in a way. You're on your own in the theatre, seeing images that are bigger than life. It almost steals into your subconscious. Like a great teacher, cinema can provide something you refer back to year after year.

Interview/Time, 5-1:62.

Ronald Reagan
Former President
of the United States

2

[Saying he favors Sony Corporation of Japan's purchase of the U.S. film company Columbia Pictures]: I'm not too proud of Hollywood these days with the immorality that is shown in pictures, and the vulgarity. I just have a feeling that maybe Hollywood needs some outsiders to bring back decency and good taste to some of the pictures that are being made.

Japanese broadcast interview,
Oct. 25/
The Washington Post, 10-26:(A)1.

Isabella Rossellini
Actress

3

[On her films]: The films are not a portrait of my life. They are not an autobiography whatsoever. I believe it's true for any actor. The fun of being an actress is to be in a situation that isn't your own and portray a person that isn't you and to make that person real . . . [In analyzing a

character,] my mind starts trying to find ways to make this person richer. I even analyze the words, you know, because the words this person uses is also [a] key. It's a key to that personality. In a good script, each person has a different vocabulary. Everything is a key to understand a character.

Interview, New York/
The Washington Post, 2-20:(D)13.

Claude Sautet
French director

4

In making a movie, I think it's the first 20 beats that set the tone. You cannot change the tone after that. The thing is to keep a sense of unity in your work—it's what I look for in other peoples' movies. This requires a *huge* discipline! But then, as Tristan Bernard [the 18th-century writer] said, "Art is when you surprise people with what they already accept."

Interview, Los Angeles/
Los Angeles Times,
6-25:(Calendar)23.

Paul Schrader
Director, Screenwriter

5

[Comparing film criticism with film-making]: They are very different disciplines. Criticism is essentially cadaverous. Like a coroner, you examine the cadaver to see how or why it lived. And film-making or film writing is embryonic: Something is being born, something whose shape you do not know, something you have to nourish so that it will come out a full-blooded creation. You cannot afford the judgmental prerogatives of a critic. You just can't. You have to take the critic, put him in the other room and lock the door. So I've never been bothered by the fact that I've been involved in films that I would not have approved of as a critic, because I just felt it was an entirely different state of creation. And not that one is easier or better than the other. I mean, good criticism is certainly as difficult and as rare as good film-making.

At American Film Institute seminar/
American Film, July-Aug.:16.

Neil Simon
Playwright, Screenwriter

1

[Saying he prefers writing for the theatre to writing for films]: Many [film] actors today will say, "I like this [script]; let me see the next draft." I'm constantly being auditioned for films now by actors. It drives me crazy. I'll rewrite for directors. I'll rewrite for producers. I'll rewrite for the studio. But I can't rewrite for actors because I don't always trust the actors' instincts. I don't mean to say that they're selfish. But I don't think they have the overview of the whole piece. They're saying, "Well, my character isn't right." I want the *piece* to be right. So I have more trouble and less desire to do film today.

At "An Evening With Neil Simon,"
sponsored by West Coast Friends
of Brandeis University,
Beverly Hills, Calif.,
Nov. 27/
Daily Variety, 11-30:8.

Steven Spielberg
Director

2

I've done 14 films, and none of them haven't had major stars. And I've never not had control ... In most cases, movie stars hire themselves out because they trust and are seduced by the character they want to play. The idea of real luxury to intelligent movie stars—and most of them are intelligent—is to find a director they can trust, so they can bury themselves in the part they are playing ... I don't mean you don't clash. But I've worked with people who are supposed to be the toughest, going all the way back to Burt Lancaster, who had a fiendish reputation, and that was when I was a kid. Barbra [Streisand], [Al] Pacino, [Robert] Redford, [Paul] Newman, Faye [Dunaway], Meryl [Streep] ... I've worked with people who have reputations. You think, "Boy, oh boy, you are gonna get into a big pissing contest." It's just not true. Or it's not true unless something is wrong.

Interview,
Universal City, Calif./
Los Angeles Times,
12-3:(Calendar)8.

James Stewart
Actor

3

[On the old studio system, when actors were under contract to the major studios]: I've always felt that was the real way to make movies. [Today's] idea of being independent and waiting around for someone to send you a script... [Under the studio system,] you went to work every day, got home at 6. If you weren't in a picture, you exercised in the gym, or you were doing a [screen] test with someone they wanted to take a look at, or you were out on the road publicizing a movie you might not even have been in. The heads of the studios—they called them moguls, which is embarrassing—they loved the movies and they insisted on variety. You had The Three Stooges on one lot and *Romeo and Juliet* on another. It'll never come back. Now they're owned by all sorts of people, like Coca-Cola.

Interview, Washington/
The Washington Post, 9-20:(D)15.

4

[On people recognizing him on the street]: I consider it part of my job. I look on the people who recognize me as the audience. And I've always had a feeling that the audience is much more than customers. They're partners. Because if they don't come and see you, you ain't got no job.

Interview, Washington/
The New York Times, 9-21:(B)2.

Meryl Streep
Actress

5

I really have a great respect for, and an understanding of, the craft of acting. So many people who write about the movies don't understand either the process or the creation of the actor. They don't know what it is. I've been thinking about this for a long time. I always wanted to get together a group of actors and talk about the process and then write it all down and send it to all the major critics so they'd know what actors do. I don't think they do know. They judge it, yet they don't know what it is that they are looking at.

WHAT THEY SAID IN 1989

(MERYL STREEP)

Most of them—even the most sophisticated—are swept away by whether it's a character they like or dislike. They confuse the dancer with the dance.

Interview/
The Saturday Evening Post,
July-Aug.:53.

Lucian K. Truscott
Author

1

Writing a novel I've always thought of as writing a letter to somebody. Movies are like sending a postcard.

At program sponsored by
Folio Society, London/
The Writer, June:5.

Ted Turner
Chairman, Turner
Broadcasting System

2

I'm almost relieved that I don't have to do theatricals [motion pictures] because the movie-going audience is mainly kids. Everybody knows that, so most of the movies have got to appeal to kids. Over half of them. And in order to get the kids into theatres, you got to do these ghoulies and ghost-buster type things.

Interview/Daily Variety, 3-1:(F)14.

Jack Valenti
President, Motion Picture Association
of America

3

One of the strange anomalies of the movie business is the public indifference to screenwriting. Directors occupy their own nirvana. Actors are world famous. The producer's name sometimes inhabits an "above-the-title" stature. But names of the writers blur before the viewer's eye . . . The fact is that nothing in the movie world begins without a script. "In the beginning was the word" is not only a biblical injunction, it is a mandate of daily life in Hollywood. Words are the threads which weave the movie tapestry. Without a latticework of words finely caught, braced and knit with dramatic narrative, nothing happens. Nothing. I am not aware of any great film that was constructed from a bad script. I know of no superior director who was able to conceive a splendid movie from an awkward, loose-fibered screenplay. It doesn't happen.

At University of Texas, Austin,
Oct. 23/Daily Variety, 11-20:10.

MUSIC

Julie Andrews
Actress, Singer

1

[On why she wants to do concert tours]: I need to sing. I don't mean necessarily the emotional desire, which is always there, but the actual physical need to keep my vocal cords really working. If I don't air my voice enough, I'm quite frightened that I will lose it. It's one thing to practice around the house, where dogs disappear and cats scream and children close their doors, but that's never the amount you need to keep in good shape.

Interview, Los Angeles/
Los Angeles Times, 7-20:(VI)1.

Daniel Barenboim
Music director-designate,
Chicago Symphony Orchestra

2

I have a number of ideas about the role of the musicians, and the orchestra in general. It is time now to look back and see how the symphony orchestra has developed. We have made really tremendous progress in the last 50 years in improving the social position of musicians. However, because of the need for more concerts—and more audiences—the life has become a little too much based on routine.

Interview, Paris/
Los Angeles Times,
2-5:(Calendar)64.

Herbert Blomstedt
Music director,
San Francisco Symphony
Orchestra

3

I never read reviews. They are dangerous. If they are good, you might start to think they are true—and think you are somebody and stop working. If they are bad, it gets you upset and you think you are nobody, you have no talent; that also puts the brake on your ability to make progress.

Interview/
Christianity Today, 3-3:62.

Rose Brampton
Opera singer

4

The greatest quality required [of an aspiring opera singer] is stick-to-it-iveness. Have courage, take disappointments in stride, be patient. Anything that's meaningful costs you something, and working in music has to be a kind of obsession. As a teacher, you hope some of your enthusiasm will get across. Self-confidence comes through experience and having people enjoy what you do, so singers have to forget themselves to a degree and really be involved in what they're doing. From that, your sense of personality and charisma will grow.

Interview, New York/
Opera News, 3-18:13.

John Browning
Pianist

5

. . . what we [pianists] do is exhibit publicly what we work on in private. And it's the private work which, I think, makes or breaks you. So many people, particularly students, are in love with what they think is the glamour. They want to be on the stage, or they want to be applauded, but those things aren't really very important. It's your relationship to the art which you do alone. So it's really a very lonely job.

Interview, Washington/
The Christian Science Monitor, 8-23:10.

WHAT THEY SAID IN 1989

Gary Burton
Jazz musician; Staff member,
Berklee College

1

Trends keep changing over the years. When I first started playing jazz in the early '60s, the concept of what audiences were used to hearing was the more traditional jazz ensemble sound, which was a single comping instrument, a single melody instrument, and just basically swingtime jazz structures. Over the years, audiences have gotten used to—because of records and changing trends—the sound of a larger rhythm section. They no longer hear a piano trio as being a big sound any more. That would strike them as something very light and perhaps even kind of dated. People are now used to larger rhythm sections with guitar and piano or two guitars with overdubs and extra percussion and everything else. So, to some extent I try to imagine what the average listener out there—who after all is my target—will feel most comfortable relating to.

Interview/Down Beat, April:21.

Jheryl Busby
President, Motown Records

2

We're [record companies] in the image business. Being able to sing well is not necessarily a criterion for signing artists. We are not just in the music and record business, we're in the entertainment business. Image is so important. Being a good singer isn't necessarily part of having the right image or being a good entertainer. Look at rappers. They can't sing. Yet we sign rappers. Singing is just one thing you look for.

Interview/Los Angeles Times,
7-2:(Calendar)4.

Bob Buziak
President, RCA Records

3

Three years ago, no one thought about [large record companies] distributing independent labels. Now I think it's going to be the future. The more viewpoints you can have attached to a large business, the more opportunities for success and for creativity you're going to have.

Los Angeles Times, 9-11:(VI)6.

John Cage
Composer

4

My favorite music is the music I haven't heard yet . . . I don't write music that I hear; I write music to hear what it sounds like.

At Cage-Fest retrospective,
Rockville, Md., May 6/
The Washington Post, 5-8:(B)7.

Jose Carreras
Opera singer

5

[On his choosing a recital rather than an opera as a return vehicle after fighting leukemia for the past year]: One needs to be fit physically for opera. The acting, the costumes, the pacing, the *tessitura* all can be very strenuous. That is why I decided instead to give concerts at first. But which really is more difficult? To sing *Tosca*, where the tenor has 25 minutes of music, or a full recital that has 25 songs—25 little dramas, each with its own atmosphere, its own problems and its own poetry? In a way, the recital is more difficult. It exposes one more. It requires more concentration.

Interview, Seattle/
Los Angeles Times, 5-9:(VI)7.

Sergiu Celibidache
Conductor, Munich
(West Germany)
Philharmonic Orchestra

6

Music has nothing to do with sound. Sound is the vessel, the glass, the vehicle. So is rhythm, so is harmony, so is everything. The purpose of music is not to be beautiful. Music is not beautiful. Music is truth. Music is reality.

Interview, New York/
The New York Times, 4-20:(B)3.

Ray Charles
Jazz musician

7

You've got to give them credit, these singers who came up in the early years—who were so

394

(RAY CHARLES)

unique they could say one word and you knew who they were. One word! You never had to ask who was singing when Ella Fitzgerald opened her mouth. You didn't have to ask anybody. And that's the thing I miss today in our modern society, because I have trouble knowing who I'm listening to. The record companies want [youngsters] to sound like whoever had the last hit. I'm not knocking it, my friend, I just wish we could go back to a time when an artist or a band could play two chords and you knew who it was. We're in a kind of lull, right now. I don't think it's the end of the line, but I think there comes a time in life when there's a pause to see which direction we are going to go—maybe that's what we're into right now. I'm very saddened because I don't see a lot of youngsters coming up where you can say, "Hey man, give this guy another three or four years and he's going to be a bitch." I'm talking about originality. I'm talking about somebody who has a sound of his or her own—they've got it, it belongs to them. That's what I'm looking for and that's what I'm not seeing.

Interview/Down Beat, January:19.

1

A lot of people are into music just because it's something to do, and they say, "Well, I'm gonna get out of it next year. I done made enough money." My thing is not that way. See, music to me is my *blood*, it's my breathing, it's my *everything*. I don't wanna ever in life do nothing else but what I do. *Per-i-od.*

Interview, New York/
The Wall Street Journal,
8-22:(A)13.

Judith Christin
Opera singer

2

[In opera,] sometimes you go over too far. Sometimes you go under too far. Comedy is especially difficult to play. There are nights when the audience doesn't get it—either they miss it, or you're overdoing it, and so all night you're adjusting. That's when you become self-con-

scious and you start watching your performance, and that's bad. The good times are when you stop watching yourself and you just go into it. Once you set up a certain mood, if it's right from the very beginning, the audience is listening every time you speak. They're ready to laugh, and you can just ride that wave.

Interview/Connoisseur, April:78.

Van Cliburn
Pianist

3

When [the late pianist Artur] Rubinstein gave a concert, no one went because of what he was playing. You were happy to take what he had on his platter that evening . . . The composer is at the top in the scheme of things, but it is a *person* who brings the music to life.

Interview, Fort Worth, Texas/
The New York Times, 3-27:(B)4.

J. C. Combs
Professor of percussion,
Wichita (Kansas)
State University;
Jazz musician

4

Music video is a wonderful tool if used properly—like Michael Jackson does. There a video and an artist seem to meet, with video and music going hand in hand. But often it's as if a poem you were proud of was set to music that overpowered it to the point no one even cared about the words. The visual part runs in its own direction to hype the product as much as possible. It's two different idioms.

The Christian Science Monitor,
2-16:11.

Lella Cuberli
Opera singer

5

[Metropolitan Opera conductor James Levine] is most supportive—not in terms of vocal suggestions, but in terms of what he hears. That's vitally important, because singers don't hear the sound the audience hears. In the final analysis, our performances are molded by conductors and directors. I work well with them. This is no accident. One has to be musically and mentally grounded, to be open to suggestion, be willing to try and try again. Then one can begin to be an artist.

Interview/Opera News, 1-21:18.

Suzanne Danco
Opera teacher; Former singer

1

I must say, some of my pupils really depress me. They don't even seem to know how to sing a scale properly—and these are students with diplomas! I suppose it's not their fault. The world is running on so fast. They just don't have time to master the rudiments thoroughly. These days I have students from everywhere, even Japan. But no matter how diligent and hardworking they are, they are alien to our culture, and they all seem stamped from the same mold. They're too careful to dot every "i" and cross every "t," and in the process the music eludes them. Undoubtedly today, many of the best opera singers come from America and Britain. But surely Italian opera ought best to be sung by Italians? It is a curious thing that Italy, now such a prosperous country, has hardly any singers any more. Of course there's Pavarotti and Ricciarelli, but in my day there was not only Di Stefano, there was also Del Monaco, and not only Tebaldi but also Carosio, Favero and Albanese. Where have they all gone? Perhaps I'm being unduly pessimistic.

Interview/Opera News, 4-15:32.

Neil Diamond
Singer, Songwriter

2

I know it's not just me that they [his fans] come to see. I know it is the songs, which is why I have to cut back this time on the [talk and effects] to do more songs. My original heroes weren't rock singers or any kind of singers. They were songwriters . . . The truth is I've been kind of like a racehorse with blinders on ever since the beginning . . . There is a crowd on the sideline and I hear them—but I'm looking to that finish line,

that goal of writing the best songs I can.

Interview, Cincinnati/
Los Angeles Times,
6-25:(Calendar)84.

Charles Dutoit
Conductor

3

[As a conductor,] you don't talk too much to an orchestra. What I use the most is conducting technique itself. If you want the most floating, transparent sound, and you beat time like a schoolmaster, you will not get it.

Interview/The Wall Street Journal,
8-15:(A)13.

Harry "Sweets" Edison
Jazz musician

4

When I recorded with [Count] Basie in the '30s, we had only one microphone, but the sound came through. If you made a mistake, you had to make the whole thing over again. The microphone was hanging over the middle of the band, so the soloist would have to stand up. Nowadays it's so technical. They have the producers, the electrician, the men on the board—they can make you sound bad or sound good. In [the old] days, everybody that recorded could play any way, so the control man didn't have any control over you at all. Either you played a good solo or you didn't.

Interview/Down Beat,
March:45.

Maria Ewing
Opera singer

5

It is very rare for everything to work in an opera production, of course, but when a conductor or a director appreciates you [the singer], as you appreciate *his* way of expressing himself, then anything is possible; and even if you think slightly differently, it's bound to be an interesting conversation—and perhaps by the end of it, you will have learned more, and expanded upon what *you* think, by virtue of what that person has had to

(MARIA EWING)

say. There's an equality, and you ultimately see eye-to-eye.

Interview, East Sussex, England/
Ovation, May:27.

Tom Freston
President, MTV (music video
cable TV channel)

1

There's a world music today, a world pop culture and sensibility among 12- to 34-year-olds. If you take 23-year-olds in Australia, Austria and the United States, they have more in common with each other than they do with their parents. They have a viewpoint, attitude, consumer habits that have been shaped by the last 25 years of advances in technology, communications and transportation. They wear the same clothes, drink Coca-Cola, watch movies made in France, the U.S. and U.K. And as for music, there's no entertainment form that crosses boundaries more readily and successfully than popular rock and roll.

The Christian Science Monitor,
2-16:10.

Marthalie Furber
Education director,
Opera America

2

Story-sharing and story-telling are important ways we learn to cope. They teach us the lessons of life, and that is one of the essentials of opera . . . The "glory" of opera is what it communicates to people. Opera deals with basic human conflicts. This is the reason opera appears in some form in almost every culture.

Opera News, November:36.

Hakan Hagegard
Opera singer

3

Musicians spend so much time in airports, and in transit, that we have very little time to slow down and learn new things. Ours is not an effi-cient profession. Most of us spend 85 percent of our time reproducing what we have done in the past, and very little time investing in the future. No other business could survive with that kind of policy. And artistically, it's not healthy.

Interview, New York/
The New York Times, 1-9:(B)3.

Thomas Hampson
Opera singer

4

I learned there's something terribly subjective and intangible about singing. The scientific study of the voice, in my opinion, is slowly but surely its inevitable downfall . . . I believe the voice functions best by control of its resonance and its sound board. If you start worrying about what's actually happening in the throat—well, a pianist isn't going to be a better pianist by knowing exactly how the hammer hits the strings. That's all well and good, but it should still be about playing music. They trained the voice differently even 15 or 20 years ago—and more correctly, I believe. The sound was higher-placed, more resonant, more open to the unique sounds of the singer. If you listen to the old recordings, every person sounds different. Today, in general, you have the "sound of a baritone."

Interview,
New York/
Opera News, 2-4:10.

Keith Jarrett
Jazz musician

5

One of the greatest fallacies in the laymen's concept of [jazz] improvising is that it's something that takes you over: You're talented and you just go, man, you just play; it's a gift. That's maybe true on the beginning level. But nobody is really an improvisor unless they throw away all their position papers, all their theses that they might have come up with—all the things they use to justify their work and consciously make the music do something. Some of them aren't even musical in the traditional sense.

Interview/
Down Beat, February:17.

Quincy Jones
Composer, Musician

1

Once you taste the blood of Number 1 records, it takes a lot of guts to change. But when you surrender your instinct and start guessing what someone *else* will love, you're in a lot of trouble. I can't anticipate someone else's goose bumps. I have to feel mine first.

Interview, Los Angeles/
USA Today, 12-7:(D)2.

Ardis Krainik
General director,
Lyric Opera of Chicago

2

I'm not a prophet, but I know that good things don't die, and I can't imagine that opera is going to die . . . I think it's going to flourish. How, depends upon the individuality of the people who are writing the music and who are producing it and who are running the opera companies. That individuality is always going to have an opportunity to be expressed. So I'm very confident about the future. What it will be, I have no idea, and I don't think it matters. I just know it's going to be good. And if that sounds like Pollyanna, okay! Just call me Pollyanna Krainik!

Interview, Chicago/
The Christian Science Monitor,
1-11:11.

Nikolaus Lehnhoff
Opera director

3

I always think and dream of an audience that is intelligent, unaffected and ready to explore new waters. Opera buffs who get carried away by high Cs are as unbearable as audiences who are happy when they see what they already know. One should not go into an opera house to forget about the tensions and problems of life. Opera is about human communication. Opera gives answers—it fills in a lot of the gaps in our society. It should tell us and make us think about fundamental aspects of our lives.

Interview, New York/
Opera News, 3-4:45.

Witold Lutoslawski
Composer

4

What I understand by truth in a piece of music is a genuine, honest expression of what you have to convey to others. Loyalty to yourself, to your own aesthetics, to your own aims . . . A piece of music is true when it reflects a personal, original artistic conviction without regard for the consequences.

Interview/Los Angeles Times,
8-6:(Calendar)55.

Zdenek Macal
Conductor, Milwaukee
Symphony Orchestra

5

[When picking up the baton, I'm] not just handling a well-balanced piece of silky-finished wood. I'm really handling a piece of history. It's a conduit to another place, another time, another person. When I conduct, I feel a close presence of the composer. I instinctively *feel* the type of person he was. Every individual sends out waves. Some people are able to receive them; some are not, although they could learn to . . . by developing the consciousness. It's a very delicate thing. Many don't know about it. If people would only listen more to their emotions.

Interview/Horizon, March-April:18.

Joseph L. Mankiewicz
Screenwriter

6

The old studio moguls were Medicis compared to today. [Louis B. Mayer would say,] "That picture made a little money. Let's let Mankiewicz make a couple more." Today, someone like [actor Sylvester] Stallone gets $12-million just to sign a contract because they think he's sure to get $250-million at the box-office.

Upon receiving Akira Kurosawa
Award at San Francisco Film Festival/
Daily Variety, 3-20:8.

7

Something's got to give [in what U.S. films show about America]. Somebody has got to do

(JOSEPH L. MANKIEWICZ)

something about the source of the way the rest of the world sees America. What they are seeing of this country is singularly silly.

Upon receiving Akira Kurosawa
Award at San Francisco Film Festival/
Daily Variety, 3-20:8.

Wynton Marsalis
Jazz musician

1

[On his taking time to lecture on music at high schools and colleges]: I'm just trying to give [youngsters] criteria to be more objective in their understanding of American musical culture, because a lot of propaganda is involved. You know, $5-billion is made every year off the sale of records, and at least $1-billion is put into publicity, I'm sure. Those who are trying to make more billions are not concerned with any kind of cultural education; they never have been.

Interview, New York/
The Christian Science Monitor,
2-22:10.

Paul McCartney
Musician; Former member of
the Beatles

2

It's strange to think what life would have been like without the Beatles years. Those were great years ... People never understand [that] the thrill wasn't just being in the Beatles, but helping create what *made* the Beatles ... the magic of creating something, making a rabbit come out of a hat ... It was also the excitement of the times ... the way all the bands excited each other. The [Rolling] Stones came out with *Satisfaction*, and that made a lot of people go, "Wow, fuzz guitars." When [Bob] Dylan came out, that tumbled it all into poetry. [Jimi] Hendrix, the Who. There was always something going on to inspire you.

Interview, London/
Los Angeles Times,
6-17:(V)8.

Gerry Mulligan
Jazz musician

3

[One] thing I try to get across to young musicians is: Don't disregard your history. One of the things I liked about jazz, and this was 40-50 years ago, was that there was a tradition going on, and I liked the tradition. I admired very much the musicians who went before: Louis Armstrong, Jack Teagarden, the bandleaders, the writers, Sy Oliver—wonderful people like that. Everybody was putting in their best efforts. Everybody was trying to make his own mark, but there was a feeling of a concerted effort for an over-all excellence. People were trying their best, and I think they did it. There is a mainstream, and each succeeding generation becomes part of the mainstream. But don't lose sight that the mainstream goes a long way back. I think it's a good idea to explore it and be able to understand why the music had the attraction it did. What is the magnetism that made the music what it is?

Interview/Down Beat, January:25.

Riccardo Muti
Conductor,
Philadelphia Orchestra

4

When I started here [in the U.S.], I was not familiar with American music and now I know much more about it. But there is a lot to do in this country. Many composers work in universities and they are fine musicians, but they seem to have a life that is separate from the real world of performing. It's difficult for them to be performed. And television doesn't help here. There is a distance, a wall, between the public and the composers ... If the government would decide to help this situation, it would be a very great help to the culture.

Interview, New York/
Los Angeles Times,
5-14:(Calendar)97.

Jarmila Novotna
Opera singer

5

Of course there are many important things in life besides music, but that doesn't make music

WHAT THEY SAID IN 1989

(JARMILA NOVOTNA)

unimportant. If you love music, what would life be without it—can you imagine? Art is what brings beauty into life. Look at the young people, always listening to music—different from ours, but it's music. Even if you just hear a little bit of a bird's singing, it's something lovely.

Interview/Opera News, 12-23:12.

Mel Powell
Composer, Pianist

1

Jazz is a pure performer's art. Serious music, if I can use that term without offense, is a composer's art. When I hear a [serious-music] composition, I honestly don't care who plays it. I assume he'll play the notes indicated on the score. It's the composer to whom I listen. When I hear jazz, I don't care what the tune is. It's the musician to whom I listen. The avenues of jazz and serious music are absolutely exclusive of one another, and I try to be comprehensively schizoid about that.

Interview/The Wall Street Journal,
11-7:(A)26.

Richard Rodzinski
Executive director,
Van Cliburn International
Piano Competition

2

[On piano competitions]: Name me the important pianists of this generation whose careers have not evolved out of the competitive process, and I'll show you a very short list.

The New York Times, 3-6:(B)1.

Linda Ronstadt
Singer

3

[On music and politics]: I consider myself an informed person, but artists aren't obliged to be informed. It's the artist's responsibility to deliver a good show, and musicians don't have to address social issues in their work—not that it's bad to do that, but I don't think it's required. The music I do

is a reaction to my own life. It's a comment or compensation, and an attempt to put it in some kind of logical order. That's what I concern myself with in my work—and believe me, that's really quite enough.

Interview, Los Angeles/
Los Angeles Times,
10-29:(Calendar)47.

Mstislav Rostropovich
Music director,
National Symphony Orchestra,
Washington

4

In the United States, orchestras depend on the kindness of generous strangers. The advantage is that the system keeps the government from having power over the orchestra. The disadvantage is that the system does not always work.

Interview, Washington/
The New York Times, 10-13:(B)2.

John Rutter
Conductor, Cambridge Singers
(Britain)

5

[On the increasing popularity of choral singing]: People are beginning to realize that the voice is the only instrument that you don't have to pay for; nor do you have to plug it in; nor do you necessarily even have to have lessons before you can use it.

Interview/
The Christian Science Monitor,
5-26:11.

Essa-Pekka Salonen
Music director-designate,
Los Angeles Philharmonic
Orchestra

6

My experience is that you have to combine things in a way that shows contemporary music is a result of certain historical and stylistic developments in traditional or older music. If you manage to create combinations that are interesting enough, then it works in terms of attracting audiences.

The Christian Science Monitor,
8-24:10.

Doc Severinson
Jazz musician

1

It bothers me to hear some musicians saying, "Only this is pure," and, "This is not jazz." If it's good, it's good whether it's plugged in or acoustic. Why squelch creativity by saying, "I don't understand it so it's not any good?" I'd guarantee that if Duke Ellington were a kid growing up today, he'd be fooling around with electronic machines and making marvelous new music.

Interview/Down Beat, February:28.

Hugh Southern
General manager-designate,
Metropolitan Opera,
New York

2

Opera is going through a period of enormous change. For one thing, recent history has seen a great enlarging of the public for opera in the U.S., viewed over, let's say, a 20-year span—increases in the number of companies and the performances they put on, in the nature of the repertory, which I think has become more adventurous, more performances of American opera in recent years, and more premieres across the country of contemporary American and world-wide works as well. It's a lively time in the opera firmament in the U.S.

Interview/Opera News,
November:16.

Ringo Starr
Rock musician;
Former member of
the Beatles

3

I'm not the greatest singer. People know that.

What people get from me when I sing is a feeling of fun and good spirits. It's not great singing but people can connect with it. What I do best is connect with the audience. If I can convey this good feeling when I sing, and touch people with it, then I've done what I've set out to do.

Interview, Beverly Hills, Calif./
Los Angeles Times, 8-31:(VI)4.

Dean K. Stein
Executive director,
Chamber Music America

4

What is the state of the chamber-music world? It's not exploding in the way it was a decade ago. But it is still seeing significant growth. One reason is that it's more economically feasible to present a chamber group than an orchestra. And I think people are looking for more intimate concert experiences today.

The New York Times, 1-26:(B)3.

Seymour Stein
President, Sire Records

5

[On the mergers of independent record companies with larger ones]: When I started in the business, there were record companies of importance in every major city. Small record companies, independents, are the lifeblood of the business. It's where the new artists and trends tend to come from . . . I think [the mergers] are going to stifle creativity. I'm very frightened.

Interview, London/
Los Angeles Times, 9-11:(VI)1.

David Stivender
Chorus master,
Metropolitan Opera,
New York

6

To me the greatest conductors have always come out of the theatre. In the old days, they *all* came first out of the theatre. Technically, after all, opera's the hardest medium. So many things can go wrong. The pit's 20 miles from the stage, the orchestra's spread out all over, the singers are

(DAVID STIVENDER)

on another wavelength and working from memory, always a tricky matter. Anything can happen. But if you've had your training in the theatre, your antennae stay atingle every minute.

Interview/
Opera News, 2-18:17.

Yoav Talmi
Music director-designate,
San Diego Symphony
Orchestra

1

We don't know exactly why, but Americans have been going to concerts less in the past three-four years. We have to find a *modus vivendi* to convince people to go to one or two concerts a month. It's a necessity, not a luxury. Some people think that all they need is the television, [but] you need concerts for your soul and your well-being.

Interview,
Tel Aviv, Israel/
Los Angeles Times, 9-15:(VI)25.

Al Teller
MCA Music Entertainment
Group

2

My guess is there will be fewer true [music] superstars to emerge from the '80s. One reason is video. I don't want to denigrate music video. I'm still a fan of them, if they are used properly. But there is no free lunch with any of this, and perhaps one of the handicaps of music videos is they have lessened the [motivation for young bands to be great live acts]. If you go back to the covered-wagon days of the '60s and '70s, part of breaking-in an artist was touring that artist, club to club, city to city, so people could see the artist and spread the word. Now that [exposure] is done primarily through videos and that is a highly controlled environment. With videos, you can redo the song and edit it, etc. That's why artists have been able to come from being unknown to selling 2, 3 million copies without having to go through

the important step of playing and winning fans live.

Interview/Los Angeles Times,
9-10:(Calendar)60.

Yuri Temirkanov
Chief conductor,
Leningrad Philharmonic
Orchestra

3

I think a baton is something artificial. The great conductors conduct wonderfully using batons—von Karajan, for example—but I feel musical phrasing more intensely using my fingers and wrist . . . When I conduct, I dance and move my body. English critics think this is not necessary. They think I do it to entertain the public, to make the public like me. Of course, any artist wants the public to love him, because we work for the public, not critics—critics are more pious Catholics than the Pope.

Interview/Airport, April:30.

James VanDemark
Bassist

4

One of the problems a bassist faces is that touring with this instrument is like traveling with a three-hundred-pound egg. It's really quite fragile, and it's in constant need of repairs, major or minor.

Interview/
Connoisseur, March:92.

Jerry Wexler
Record producer

5

All those great R & B singers [of the past] learned to sing in church. Singing gospel was an incredible training ground for singers. Kids don't go to church and sing in church like they used to in the old days. They're too busy rapping on the street corners. So R & B [today] goes in that direction.

Interview/
Los Angeles Times,
7-2:(Calendar)4.

Bob Wilbur
Jazz musician

1

I think there is a new division of jazz. The old categories—the revivalists vs. the moderns—if they applied at all, are definitely outmoded now. Now we have a new breed of jazz where swing is not one of the objectives ... Jazz has gotten away from the dance and has become a concert music, which I kind of lament. I like the idea of the "joint is jumpin'," of a communal art where everybody is taking part.

Interview/
Down Beat,
July:51.

Dolora Zajick
Opera singer

2

For me, interpretation doesn't mean adding a lot of stuff. I make my voice as big and beautiful as possible to follow the score as accurately as I can. With great composers, especially Verdi, the drama is in the notes. Even the acting is in the scene, though often hidden. You have to look for clues. Sometimes, if there's an accent or some other marking in an odd place, I'll discover that a gesture of some sort works well there. Figuring out an interpretation from the score is like putting together a puzzle.

Interview/Connoisseur, September:108.

THE STAGE

Edward Albee
Playwright

1

The theatre is in serious trouble, especially for any extended run. It gets harder and harder to find actors of a certain age willing to commit for any length of time on stage. They've been bought away by movies and television. Even if they're willing to work, they'll say, "I'll give you four months, sandwiched in between my film titles."

Interview, San Diego/
Los Angeles Times,
3-26:(Calendar)4.

Mikhail Baryshnikov
Ballet dancer

2

Dance rewards me in terms of my experience with modern choreography. Being a dancer doesn't mean you have to walk around in white tights all the time. I think I can dance barefoot, in heels, maybe even in high heels . . . You never know; the night is young.

Interview/Connoisseur,
January:73.

Pina Bausch
West German choreographer

3

I think that for many years now, all of the members of [her dance] company have understood that their role in a performance depends on what is being expressed. Everybody, including myself, must submit to the imperatives of expression. To understand what I am saying, you have to believe that dance is something other than technique. We forget where the movements come from. They are born from life. When you create a new work, the point of departure must be contemporary life—not existing forms of dance.

Interview/World Press Review,
October:91.

Victor Borge
Musician, Humorist

4

I have always worked for two audiences at the same time. One is sophisticated, the other not musically oriented. I notice that the ones who laugh most are composed of professionals, as when I do my act with orchestras. But my jokes must be understood by everybody. Nobody must be bored. It is a fine line that I walk.

Interview, Greenwich, Conn./
The New York Times, 12-5:(B)3.

Robert Brustein
Artistic director,
American Repertory Theatre,
Cambridge, Mass.

5

[On the cut in government financial aid to small theatre companies]: Without as much funding, the box office has become more important. As a result, a lot of adventurous theatres turned to safe and conventional material. So, along with the financial deficit, you have what people are calling an "artistic deficit." There's not much daring any more. Many theatres look for "products" they can create and send to more lucrative venues.

Interview, Cambridge, Mass./
The Christian Science Monitor,
1-31:10.

Therese Capucilli
Principal dancer,
Martha Graham
Dance Company

6

Some people fail or succeed in their careers because of some great opposition—whether it's your parents or a teacher or even life itself. For

(THERESE CAPUCILLI)

me, this was never true. I've always been sur-rounded by people who believed in me, and lots of doors were opened for me. And yet self-doubt has always stalked me. Doubt is harbored in me—and it won't go away. *That's* my opposi-tion . . . But once on stage, I'm transformed. I can experience every emotion. I can hurl myself into these larger-than-life roles with total abandon and become the person that I could never in a million years be in real life. It's because, to me, movement means self-expression. Movement is my tool. In real life, I don't have that tool.

Interview/Dance Magazine,
March:54.

Richard Eyre
Artistic director,
Royal National Theatre,
London

1

[On staging the classics today]: We're united in the feeling that you can't impose a conceit that belongs to 1989 on a piece that was written cen-turies ago. You have to go back to the original, and through a process of conversion and transla-tion come up with something that speaks to today's audience. People try to force a superfi-cial relevance on a play. My taste precludes a kind of theatre that is reductionist, that diminishes a play in order to corral it within a concept.

Interview, London/
The New York Times, 9-18:(B)3.

Martin Feinstein
General director,
Washington (D.C.) Opera;
Former executive director of
performing arts,
Kennedy Center for the
Performing Arts, Washington

2

The Congressional mandate [for the Kennedy Center] calls for the best in ballet, the best in music and the best of all the things that are going on around the country. But you have to go for the commercial ventures in order to make a profit to present the things you should be presenting. In Ottawa [Canada], the national cultural center gets very strong support from the Canadian government. In New York, Lincoln Center gets a good sum of money from the New York State Arts Council, as well as from the city. Here [in Washington], nothing is subsidized.

The New York Times, 11-30:(B)3.

William Forsythe
Artistic director,
Frankfurt Ballet
(West Germany)

3

Ballet . . . has always been about one person's ability to imagine an organizational body. Basically, what we're doing here is showing how a ballet organization can transcend its origins to be what the dancers imagine it to be. Not what I imagine it to be. Because what we produce comes out of the dancers.

Interview/Los Angeles Times,
6-4:(Calendar)54.

Athol Fugard
South African playwright

4

All serious plays are political. Chekhov's plays are as profound a political analysis of the disintegration of a feudal society, a society that was going to be shattered by the revolution, as any political tracts written in that time. You read Chekhov, and you read politics. All serious writing, all good writing, inevitably involves something of a diagnosis, a dissection of the society that creates it. I believe that very strongly. That's why I think it's such a misnomer, really, to single out a particular playwright for being political . . .

Interview, Washington/
The Christian Science Monitor,
12-7:10.

Penny Fuller
Actress

5

For me, the continual attraction of theatre is that it's really about your participation as an

WHAT THEY SAID IN 1989

audience . . . We tend to be a very visual society today—we watch things, rather than participate in them. Theatre makes you participate . . . Somewhere between the stage and the audience, in that ether between the two—*that's* where the play really takes place.

Interview, Los Angeles/
Los Angeles Times, 1-19:(VI)5.

Frank Gilroy
Playwright

1

Size has become a synonym for quality. Once, you could produce wonderful little comedies on Broadway. Now, to draw the crowd, start by gutting the theatre or putting the whole cast on skates.

Interview/
Films in Review, May:299.

Martha Graham
Modern-dance choreographer

2

When I cast a role, I look for avidity, an eagerness for life, a blood memory in the sense that the dancer remembers and can call upon more of his or her life than has yet been lived. There has to be a hunger and a need in the dancer. Of course, the formal training must be there, but there also has to be courage, a willingness to explore unknown feelings and daring to feel them and let them become part of your being. It's scary. Terrifying. But you do it because you have no choice. The composer Varese once told me that he believed that everyone had genius. But some people have it only for a few minutes. I don't use the word genius, but I think what he meant was that we all have the capacity to live up to our ultimate selves, but most of us don't, or won't. I look for the dancer who will.

Interview, New York/
Dance Magazine, May:52.

3

[On whether Soviet audiences will understand her company's kind of dance when they visit the Soviet Union later this year]: I'm not interested in understanding. I'm interested in feeling. I think everyone is capable of being understood if they have an "anxiety" for the energy that sustains work and that we call the universe. You can call it Santa Claus. You can call it God. But the energy is a physical thing that creates its own shape and puts it into motion.

Interview, New York/
The New York Times, 5-11:(B)3.

Stewart Granger
Actor

4

[On his forthcoming debut on the Broadway stage, after being retired from film acting]: I don't worry that I can't act. I don't worry that I've lost the technique of timing and projecting. It's the lines. Can I remember the lines? And I fear the discipline. Have I got the discipline to go out every night, and twice on Wednesdays and Saturdays, and get my brain working so it says, "Hey, you've got to go to the theatre now"? You must never retire, my boy. You must never retire. You should improve as you mellow.

Interview, New York/
The New York Times, 8-31:(B)3.

A. R. Gurney
Playwright

5

If you're going to write for the theatre, you might as well embrace the medium. I don't think you should write, saying, "Oh, this is going to make a great *movie*." I think you should write, saying, "I'm going to make this as good a *play* as I can." And to capitalize on the immediacy of the form. I think what's happening in the theatre today is that playwrights are becoming slightly tribal. They're speaking to particular ethnic groups. They're speaking to particular constituencies. That's a good thing and a bad thing. You have . . . a really strong sense of audience as that group responds to its signals. What you lose is that wonderful groping for generalization that you get in Arthur Miller or [Eugene] O'Neill or in some of Tennessee Williams.

Interview, New York/
The Christian Science Monitor, 1-23:17.

Marie Hale
Artistic director,
Ballet Florida

1

One of the things that's important to us is that we want dancers in our company who are not only a joy to watch, but a pleasure to know. There aren't any prima donnas—morale is fantastic, and I believe we have 15 "stars." Another thing is that when we choose choreography, it must be meaningful for the audience, and equally good for the dancers' technical and artistic growth. Some companies don't work to strike this balance, but we believe it is vital.

Interview/Horizon, Jan.-Feb.:21.

Julie Harris
Actress

2

I think of working on a new play as being the most intensely exciting kind of work that you can do. There are some moments in the play when you think, "I don't really know how to do this," but you keep plodding along, like a painter keeps making strokes. And you know it's not right, but you keep making them because you've got to do something. Then, one day it sort of comes together, but you don't know it's going to come together; you just have to keep going.

Interview,
San Francisco/
The Christian Science Monitor,
3-21:11.

Mary Beth Hurt
Actress

3

You can't make a living [acting in theatre in New York]. I am happy with my career, but it's very hard to maintain. I don't sing. I can't do musicals. The only way I can make a living doing theatre is on Broadway. And it's a terrible situation. There aren't many straight plays on Broadway. And Broadway needs straight plays. They provide a special voice that shouldn't be stilled.

Interview,
New York/
The New York Times, 11-2:(B)3.

Glenda Jackson
British actress

4

It's always exciting for me to work with Americans. They're so direct. American audiences are immediate in their responses. In England [they] tend to wait until the curtain comes down to express an opinion, which is too late for me. I like to know what's happening while it's happening.

Interview, Los Angeles/
Los Angeles Times,
10-1:(Calendar)4.

Bernard Jacobs
President,
Shubert Organization

5

[Criticizing calls for the Tony Awards to encompass Off-Broadway productions and not be limited, as they are now, only to Broadway shows]: If they're the best plays and they're done Off-Broadway, they go to Broadway. If they're not good enough to go to Broadway, they're not the best play. My opinion is that Off-Broadway does not belong in the Tonys. The Tony is Broadway's award. The Tonys are all about Broadway's desire to promote Broadway. Off-Broadway has the Obie. Two different awards for two different jurisdictions.

The New York Times, 3-1:(B)3.

6

This [Broadway] has always been a cyclical business. If you think you can explain the cycle, you're much smarter than I am ... When it's bad, it doesn't mean anything, and when it's good, it doesn't mean anything. When it's bad, people always say the theatre's dying. When it's good, they say the theatre's prosperous. And the truth is, the theatre stumbles its way through, whether it's a better season or a poorer season. And thus it will always be.

The New York Times, 9-5:(B)1.

Glynis Johns
Actress

7

New York, London, Toronto—a theatre is a theatre to me. Any good theatre is a good theatre

(GLYNIS JOHNS)

to me. An audience is an audience. My happiness has more to do with the play and the characters than the theatre. Theatre is just as good away from London and away from Broadway, and everybody's idea of Mecca shouldn't be, "Oh, I must get to Broadway." You can do good stuff in other places.

Interview, New York/
The New York Times, 8-31:(B)3.

Darci Kistler
Ballerina,
New York City Ballet

1

You were asking why I like to dance . . . I hate to be confronted with *me*. And in dance you aren't. You're always aiming *at* something. What I love is dance where it can become so simple that it's just the music. [The ballets of George Balanchine] are so musical that they do everything for you. The music tells you when to move, where to look. It tells you everything.

Interview/Connoisseur, June:108.

Rocco Landesman
Producer;
President, Jujamcyn Theatres

2

We [in the Broadway theatre business] need a top-to-bottom reorganization. We are in the ridiculous position of ticket prices being actually too low. If they reflected our costs and the rate at which we should pay back investors, a musical would cost $100 a ticket, but of course, that's out of the question . . . If a baseball team needs a new stadium, the city will throw in millions of dollars, but nothing for the theatre. Out-of-town tourists come to New York to see Broadway theatre, not [baseball's] *Yankees*. Besides, more people go to the theatre every year than to sporting events . . . I think the only way we'll bring costs down is to be willing to take a strike. The stagehands' union has a lot of leverage—their members can get other jobs in films and television—but I don't think they will go to the point of destroying the theatre. Everyone has to be willing to take cuts:

owners and producers as well as the unions. I think it's great to have musicals like *The Phantom of the Opera* and *Jerome Robbins' Broadway*, but they've raised the stakes and set a dangerous precedent. An $8-million musical is fine if you're selling out, but what about those that come along later and only do 80 percent of capacity? They used to be hits, but now they would never pay back their investors.

Interview, New York/
The Wall Street Journal,
5-4:(A)16.

3

[On a proposal to cut production costs and ticket prices on Broadway so that smaller, serious plays could be staged there]: This plan is in a general way an attempt to make serious drama on Broadway competitive with Off-Broadway. The whole thrust is for us to be able to compete with what is going on at the [smaller, serious venues such as the] Promenade Theatre, the De Lys, the Houseman. All of us—the unions, the guilds, the producers, the theatre owners—are looking at empty Broadway houses and saying that something is wrong here, that we should be utilizing all our resources. We have wonderful spaces in which to do work, and we should do work in them.

The New York Times, 12-1:(B)6.

Archibald Leyasmeyer
Associate professor of English,
University of Minnesota;
Former member, executive board,
Guthrie Theatre, Minneapolis

4

[Supporting the Guthrie Theatre's plan to attract actors to its company by, among other things, raising salaries]: I see a circling back to the original assumption that theatre is an actor's medium. [In the absence of good salaries,] the two great support systems for actors are unemployment [checks] and [acting in] commercials . . . The actor becomes a gypsy traveling from place to place.

The Christian Science Monitor,
9-13:11.

Lar Lubovitch
Choreographer

1

Dance is an obsession. Everything I do in life has to do with dancing. My dances are dictated by a very strong passion. It is a passion for existence, for improving existence, for pointing out the highest manifestation of humanity. I want to provoke something positive.

Interview, Berkeley, Calif./
The Christian Science Monitor,
3-20:11.

Kelly McGillis
Actress

2

. . . regional theatre in America is the place where you as an artist can take the biggest chances. I can take a chance on doing comedy, which is not something that people readily identify me with. And if I'm not funny, it's not going to be the end of the world. It's okay for me to fail. I feel it's not okay for me to fail in New York. If I failed in New York, I would fear that I'd never work again—even though that probably isn't true.

Interview, Washington/
The New York Times, 10-12:(B)3.

Amanda McKerrow
Principal dancer,
American Ballet Theatre

3

I think that some perfectionist quality drove me to dancing in the first place, but you can try so hard to be right that you don't do anything at all. Technique isn't the only thing now. I'm after—well, "abandon" is probably the word. I come away so much more fulfilled, even if a balance doesn't go just so, because I feel more emotionally committed in my performances. There are ballets where technique is paramount because they're about technique. But now the idea is to feel like it's really happening, like there's a web of involvement with the music and the steps and the audience.

Interview/
Dance Magazine, April:43.

Terrence McNally
Playwright

4

After *The Ritz*, everybody expected me to write farce. After *It's Only a Play*, they expected me to write drawing-room comedies. Now with *Frankie and Johnny*, everybody expects me to write blue-collar romance. You could argue that any writer's just trying to write the same play over and over. First as a comedy; then as a musical; then as a tragedy. I don't know. I just think it's fun to work in all these forms. When I see a bare stage, I want to write for *that*.

Interview, New York/
Los Angeles Times,
3-5:(Calendar)49.

Arthur Miller
Playwright

5

Broadway is not a theatre any more. It is just a lot of shows . . . Nothing originates in New York any more. No sane producer will open a play on Broadway for the first time . . . It may be that theatre is being thrust back to where it belongs [small regional companies], with actors playing to 200 people at a time. Maybe we got too big for our own good.

Interview, Norwich, England/
The Washington Post, 5-15:(C)8.

6

Because my plays in general have reference to contemporary society as a society, not simply as individuals, the assumption is that I'm always writing about social problems in a way that Ibsen was . . . There are critics who have decided that that's what they're about. There's never a problem with the audience—they don't respond that way, because they're not interested in putting tags on stuff.

The Writer, June:5.

Rudolf Nureyev
Ballet dancer

7

I am here to perform, not read reviews. If you read reviews, they will influence your perfor-

(RUDOLF NUREYEV)

mance. Reviews are not written for me. They are written for the public. All I demand is that they are written in good English.

Interview, Hartford, Conn./
Los Angeles Times,
11-26:(Calendar)7.

Jerome Robbins
Choreographer; Co-director,
New York City Ballet

1

[On his decision to resign as co-director of the New York City Ballet, saying he does not wish to be an administrator]: I have no great ambitions to babysit a board, temperamental dancers, feisty unions and economic pressures. I've seen many creative people sink under these burdens. I'm essentially a choreographer. That's my talent, and I'd like to save my juices for that.

Interview, New York, Nov. 5/
The New York Times, 11-6:(B)2.

Stephen Sondheim
Composer, Lyricist

2

Musicals get quaint. They are very much a product of their time. Very much the only decent musical theatre that's going to be interesting in 50 years, if the world lasts another 50 years, will be *Porgy and Bess*. I think everything else will seem quaint, at best. Operas last longer because from generation to generation they're a chance for singers to show off. So they're a performer's medium. And that's why perfectly dreadful operas are done over and over and over again, in major opera houses all over the world, because each generation of singers comes along and uses them. Musicals don't lend themselves to that. They become old-fashioned very quickly because popular musical tastes change quickly. So, you look at a Victor Herbert show today and it's quaint. Rodgers and Hammerstein have become quaint already, and it's only a generation later.

Interview, New York/
Los Angeles Times,
1-8:(Calendar)5.

3

I don't despair about the development of talent [for the theatre], only the lack of outlets. I mean, open the newspaper and look at the wide choice of movies—everything from *Chocolat* to Arnold Schwarzenegger. Would that it were true of the theatre! The theatre should be like a supermarket—where you can see a silly sex farce, right next to Shakespeare, next to an Arthur Miller, right next to a British musical, an American musical, a lighthearted musical, a serious musical and an experimental musical. But it's not working out that way.

Interview,
New York/
The Washington Post,
6-19:(B)4.

4

The problem with theatre is that once a show is closed, it's closed. And though it still may exist on tape, it's not like a movie. You can't go back and revisit it until somebody puts it on. And putting on a musical is very, very expensive, so you can't just revive them whenever you would like to.

Interview,
New York/
The New York Times,
11-27:(B)1.

Peter Stone
President, Dramatists Guild

5

[Saying the Tony Awards, until now confined to Broadway shows, should be expanded so that Off-Broadway productions are eligible]: There's no getting away from the fact that the Tonys mean a great deal. It's a glamorous thing. There's no question playwrights do covet it, because it sits in the national myth . . . They are the absolute parallel of the Oscars and the Emmys and the Grammys. And many of America's leading dramatic voices are not eligible because of a parochial system that has got to stop, that has got to bend. The hypocrisy of geography controls the Tony Awards. It's as if Hollywood were to say that the only pictures that are eligible for the

(PETER STONE)

Oscars are the ones that are made in the West Coast studios, and films made in New York or Europe or Minnesota, or small-budget films, are not eligible.

The New York Times,
3-1:(B)3.

Twyla Tharp
Choreographer,
American Ballet Theatre

1

[On the ABT's connection with the Paris Opera]: The challenge comes from pushing the bounds of technique. To do that, the school has to have a close connection with the company. When my company was in existence, I could never raise enough money to create a school in which to develop the right kind of dance talent. Small companies have become economically unworkable. Joining ABT is an attempt to find a solution to the problem. At the Paris Opera, the problem doesn't exist. The resources are astounding. They give five classes in the morning. There are people who are committed to watching the dancers every day and helping them develop . . . to seeing that the dancers achieve more than they even know they can. The excitement of dance for me comes from the here and now, from taking risks. With wonderful dancers, that's possible.

Interview,
Paris/
The Wall Street Journal,
1-31:(A)13.

2

The thing about a rehearsal is you can only expect people to work as well as you do. So if you're focused, you're concentrated, you mean business, they should, too. If you're slow with your notes, you're not focused, you're having to go back and forth, humma, humma, humma, they are, too. Regard for one's craft and for the people that you work with is the point of the whole business. If there isn't that, then, really, there's no point in working. Because the point is to make

progress, and the only way you can do that is by having great regard for what you do.

Interview, New York/
Los Angeles Times, 3-5:(Calendar)62.

Vladimir Vasiliev
Ballet dancer,
Bolshoi Ballet (Soviet Union)

3

What I find strange is that I'm finding much more emotion in modern dance than I'm finding in classical dancing. Maybe it's not so strange, though. First of all, I find we are moving away from folklore and character or national dancing, which was formerly an important part of classical dance. And now we have a sort of leveling, where everyone becomes sort of equal in the ballet. I don't want to say anything bad about [the late American choreographer, George] Balanchine, but there is a sort of leveling in his ballets, a certain mechanization. Maybe I haven't seen that much ballet, but there has been a leveling of styles.

Interview,
New York/
The New York Times,
11-9:(B)3.

Oleg Vinogradov
Artistic director,
Kirov Ballet (Soviet Union)

4

[On the exodus of well-known Soviet dancers to Western countries]: Obviously, I cannot speak for the dancers and for their reasons for leaving, but I can understand people possess unique abilities—truly unique, and this they have proved to the world—but [have a] repertoire so limited that they had nothing to dance. No more than 10 or 15 percent of their creative abilities were utilized by the [Soviet] theatre—and they wanted to work. This you cannot reproach them for. They have proved this in the West, dancing every possible repertoire. But why weren't these ballets available to them in the Kirov? [Mikhail] Baryshnikov, for example, chose Bournonville's *Sylphide* as one of the first ballets he danced in the West. But why couldn't he dance it [at the

WHAT THEY SAID IN 1989

(OLEG VINOGRADOV)

Kirov] in Leningrad? The directors of the theatre didn't want such changes. It took such extraordinary circumstances, as the loss of the best dancers, to make the situation clear to them.

Interview/Dance Magazine,
July:42.

Lanford Wilson
Playwright

1

I haven't read Shakespeare, I haven't read Ibsen, Williams, O'Neill—none of those guys.

But I feel confident enough, now, in terms of my voice to read those guys without being influenced. Writing is a process of self-discovery. You make discoveries about yourself and your relation to the world. You get to the point where your demons, which are terrifying, get smaller and smaller and you get bigger and bigger. They're mere pests. *Psst!* Get away from me! As your spirit gets larger, you say to your demons, "I used to be terrified of you—now get out of my way." It's a great feeling. Then you turn around and there is a whole new set, twice as big.

Interview/Esquire,
April:126.

Philosophy

Daniel Bell
Sociologist,
Harvard University

1

How do you have order in any society? It goes back to Rousseau and the Social Contract in which he says man can never rule by might and might alone. You have to turn might into duty and right into obligation. In effect, societies are ruled either by coercion or manipulation, by deceit, cheating, ideology, or by power. How do you get to normative order that avoids the excesses of these things? That is the basic problem.

Interview, Cambridge, Mass./
The New York Times, 2-7:(B)2.

Robert Bellah
Sociologist,
University of California,
Berkeley

2

We Americans find ourselves in a poignant double-bind. When sociologists ask, "Would you like to spend your life married to one other person?" we find absolutely, consistently in surveys conducted over the last 30 years that something like 90 per cent of the respondents say yes. But then we ask, "Do you expect to spend your life with one other person?" and the affirmative answer drops to about half. This is painful. People want what they think they can't have. This suggests that, though they might not put it into words, they have a problem with individualism. Individualism emphasizes "what's in it for me" and "you don't meet my needs; so, baby I'm splitting"—attitudes that make it very hard to sustain a lifetime relationship with another person.

Interview/
Christianity Today, 2-3:24.

3

It's important to recover a way of speaking that doesn't just immediately, any time any value question is raised, say, "That's just up to individuals and whatever they feel." Of course, many Americans talk that way because they possess the virtue of tolerance. They don't want to reject everybody who isn't exactly like them. But the ability to have a broad, sympathetic understanding of diversity does not require us to give up all objective moral judgment. And we tend, in America, to make that equation: If you accept other people, then you can't come to any conclusions at all about how they're behaving. Our moral practices are being stunted by a constricted moral language.

Interview/
Christianity Today, 2-3:24.

Saul Bellow
Author

4

People have a feeling of "Give it to me quick." The contemporary mind feels a kind of relief when it sees things rapidly consummated.

Interview, Chicago/
People, 3-27:69.

Douglas Besharov
Resident scholar,
American Enterprise Institute

5

I think what we are seeing is what you might call trickle-down morality. The elites of the country changed their behavior, at least outward manifestations, in the 1950s. Everyone else is following. Across the board there has been a total loosening of the old Puritan standards by which we grew up. Changes in our social structure are more complex than just the fact of people not being able to find jobs. People today value early marriage less, value having children less and value having a career of their own—and some fun before settling down—more highly. The explanation has as much to do with the social atmosphere as economics. Scholars simply don't understand the reasons very well.

The Washington Post, 9-5:(A)12.

Samuel Broder
Director,
National Cancer Institute

1

I do fear there are so many times we make "the perfect the enemy of the good," and we end up with discussions about whether something is absolutely perfect or absolutely certain when we're way off the mark. Even in areas where there's a lot of consensus, we want to do the right thing; we want to be good but still shooting for perfection. I think that perfection can be a source of paralysis for all of us. I'm paraphrasing Winston Churchill, of course, but I think that those are realistic goals.

Interview/
The Saturday Evening Post,
May-June:51.

Joseph Brodsky
Poet

2

[Addressing students]: A substantial part of what lies ahead of you [in life] is going to be boredom. When hit by boredom, go for it. Let yourself be crushed by it. For boredom speaks the language of time, and it is to teach you the most valuable lesson of your life—the lesson of your utter insignificance.

At Dartmouth College
commencement, June 11/
The New York Times, 6-12:(A)11.

Zbigniew Brzezinski
Former Assistant to
the President of the United States
(Jimmy Carter)
for National Security Affairs

3

[Karl] Marx made a good point—he wasn't always wrong—that consciousness lags behind reality. Communism as an ideology doesn't die as a human being dies. An ideology dies progressively—it loses its vitality, its appeal. It's fragmented, it disintegrates, it gets discredited, it fades away. That's what we're saying. That's the death of Communism. You're going to have fringe groups calling themselves Communists for

a long time. Into the next century, you're going to have Communist Parties calling themselves Communists, except they will not be practicing Communism. A lot of that is already happening in Hungary and Poland. Where do you think children of Polish [Communist Party] Central Committee members go when they're about three weeks old? To the church to be baptized.

Interview/
USA Today, 3-8:(A)11.

George Bush
President of the United States

4

We are not the sum of our possessions. They are not the measure of our lives. In our hearts, we know what matters. We cannot hope only to leave our children a bigger car, a bigger bank account. We must hope to give them a sense of what it means to be a loyal friend, a loving parent, a citizen who leaves his home, his neighborhood and town better than he found it. And what do we want the men and women who work with us to say when we're no longer there? That we were more driven to succeed than anyone around us? Or that we stopped to ask if a sick child had gotten better—and stayed a moment there to trade a word of friendship.

Inaugural address,
Washington, Jan. 20/
The Washington Post, 1-21:(A)6.

5

We know what works: Freedom works. We know what's right: Freedom is right. We know how to secure a more just and prosperous life for man on earth—through free markets, free speech, free elections and the exercise of free will unhampered by the state.

Inaugural address,
Washington, Jan. 20/
The Washington Post, 1-21:(A)6.

6

We live in a time when we are witnessing the end of an era: the final chapter of the Communist experiment. Communism is now recognized,

(GEORGE BUSH)

even by many within the Communist world itself, as a failed system, one that promised economic prosperity but failed to deliver the goods; a system that built a wall between the people and their political aspirations. But the eclipse of Communism is only half of the story of our time. The other is the ascendancy of the democratic idea. Never before has the idea of freedom so captured the imaginations of men and women the world over. And never before has the hope of freedom beckoned so many: trade unionists in Warsaw, the people of Panama, rulers consulting the ruled in the Soviet Union. And even as we speak today, the world is transfixed by the dramatic events in [Beijing's] Tiananmen Square [mass pro-democracy demonstrations]. Everywhere those voices are speaking the language of democracy and freedom, and we hear them, and the world hears them. And America will do all it can to encourage them.

At U.S. Coast Guard Academy
commencement, May 24/
The New York Times, 5-25:(A)4.

1

Some historians argue that Marxism arose out of a humane impulse. But Karl Marx traced only one thread of human existence and missed the rest of the tapestry—the colorful and varied tapestry of humanity. He regarded man as helpless—unable to shape his environment or destiny. [But] man is not driven by impersonal economic forces. He is not simply an object acted upon by mechanical laws of history. Rather, man is imaginative and inventive . . . Man is dynamic, determined to shape his own future.

At Karl Marx University of Economics,
Budapest, Hungary, July 12/
Los Angeles Times 7-13:(I)1.

Steve Carlton
Former baseball pitcher,
Philadelphia "Phillies"

2

I don't have a trophy room and I don't pay much attention to that kind of thing. Peoples'

lives—when they start to reflect, they stop. I never want to look back, because the good ol' days are for people who are dead. It means you're not living now; these are the good ol' days. It's a trap. If you're going to live a long life, you better be creative. If you start reflecting, you start to die.

Interview,
Clearwater, Fla./
USA Today, 7-28:(C)2.

Nicolae Ceausescu
President of Romania

3

We can and we must assess most strongly the fact that socialism has proved its might and creative capability. Socialism is the future of the whole of mankind, and we must do our utmost to build a world free of exploiters, of oppressors, in which the people should live in full liberty and independence and secure their welfare and happiness.

At Romanian Communist Party
conference, Bucharest,
Nov. 20/
Los Angeles Times, 11-21:(A)7.

Harlan Cleveland
Diplomat, Futurist

4

The option is always temptingly there for each of us to drift along—watching the initiatives of others, not taking the lead, not reaching for, or even accepting, broader responsibilities as our lives and careers move on. The choice is always there—to modify a John Gardner metaphor—to sit on the telephone wire until it's quite clear where the rest of the birds are going. But each of us who does think that he or she has the quality of leadership will be more than fully employed. World-wide, the need for people who can bring other people together to make something different happen is growing much faster than the supply.

Before World Future Society,
Washington, July 16/
The Christian Science Monitor,
9-1:12.

415

Glenn Close
Actress

1

Our daughter is one year old. She is a brilliant actor because she lives absolutely and truthfully moment to moment. She's not interested in the movie that may or may not be made. She could care less about the deal that may or may not fall through or the part that may or may not be offered. She is interested in lunch, a beautiful flower, a tiny speck on the rug, the wind in high branches, a bird flying across the setting sun. She has taught me that after all the compulsion and ambition and anxiety, the little moments are the sum of our lives, not the huge klieg-light, earth-shattering events. Life is now.

At College of William and Mary
commencement/
The Christian Science Monitor,
6-12:13.

John J. Curley
Chairman and president,
Gannett Company

2

Success is feeling good about yourself. If you're low on self-esteem, no job or amount of money in the world is going to make you feel good.

At Simpson College commencement/
USA Today, 5-24:(A)9.

Dalai Lama
Exiled former ruler of Tibet

3

The source of peace is within us; so also the source of war. And the real enemy is within us, and not outside. The source of war is not the existence of nuclear weapons or other arms. It is the minds of human beings who decide to push the button and to use those arms out of hatred, anger or greed.

Speech, Costa Rica, June/
The Wall Street Journal,
7-17:(A)10.

4

[On his being awarded the 1989 Nobel Peace Prize]: I very much appreciate that kind of recog-nition about my beliefs. In fact, I always believed in love, compassion and a sense of universal respect. Every human being has that potential. My case is nothing special. I am a simple Budd-hist monk—no more, no less.

Newport Beach, Calif., Oct. 5/
The New York Times, 10-6:(A)6.

Robertson Davies
Canadian author

5

Today, there is a lot of interest in myths, and I think that is related to the breakdown of conven-tional religion. Mythology and psychology have rushed in to fill up the hole among many quite sophisticated people. I'm told that in New York, near Wall Street, there is an area full of palmists, astrologers, tarot-card readers and the like, where you can go and have a reading that takes 15 minutes. At lunchtime, apparently, it is full of young people from the financial world, not the top brass, getting their reassurance. Now, that is very much how things were in the 200 years or so before the birth of Christ, when the Roman world was absolutely gnawed down to the core by all sorts of superstition. We tend to think of Romans as noble, incorruptible characters, but they were the greatest bunch of omen-seekers, card-readers and lucky-day choosers who ever lived on earth—and we're getting to be just like them.

Interview/
U.S. News & World Report,
1-16:61.

Milovan Djilas
Author; Former Vice President
of Yugoslavia

6

Communism is contrary to human nature. The Communist party is monopolistic and totalitarian in its structure. Human nature is pluralistic in its being. Human nature is sinful. If human nature were perfect, Communism might be possible; but that would be a "dead" society . . . Capitalism functions better because it is closer to human nature. It permits the human being to express more freedom. Communism has failed and will fail because human nature cannot live without

(MILOVAN DJILAS)

freedom, without choices, without facing alternatives. If man is not creative, if he does not change, does not have ideas, he cannot exist, he cannot be truly alive. This is the difference between human beings and animals.

Interview/
The Washington Post, 5-31:(A)22.

E. L. Doctorow
Author

1

We're always attracted to the edges of what we are, out by the edges where it's a little raw and nervy. And gangsters bring that quality right into the heart of the society, and we who are law-abiding have this mythic attachment to the irreverent law-breakers and the audacious dissenters, asocial, non-social, anti-social. It reflects that atavism we all still have in us for the idea of transgression, breaking the rules.

Interview, New York/
Los Angeles Times, 4-5:(V)5.

Malcolm S. Forbes
Chairman, Forbes, Inc.
("Forbes" magazine)

2

I don't waste too much time philosophizing about wealth. I just recommend it to everyone.

Interview/Los Angeles Times, 7-21:(V)6.

Milton Friedman
Economist

3

Everybody looks at the world through his own glasses, and those glasses mean more than the facts you are looking at.

Time, 1-30:47.

John W. Gardner
Professor-designate of public
service, Stanford University;
Former Secretary of Health,
Education and Welfare
of the United States

4

I think that all human systems require continuous renewal. They rigidify. They get stiff in the joints. They forget what they cared about. The forces against it are nostalgia and the enormous appeal of having things the way they have always been, appeals to a supposedly happy past. But we've got to move on.

Interview/
The New York Times, 7-21:(A)6.

Mikhail S. Gorbachev
General Secretary,
Communist Party of the Soviet Union;
President of the
Soviet Union

5

[On reforms being carried out in various Communist countries, and public demonstrations for democracy taking place now in China]: Renewal is a painful process, but this reaffirms that it is a profound change, not cosmetic repairs. Some people regard this as "the crisis of socialism." I believe actually that it reflects a very serious turnaround in world socialism. This process is under way in varying degrees in the Soviet Union, China, and other socialist countries, and its main thrust is revealing the potential of socialism through democratization.

Beijing, May 17/
Los Angeles Times, 5-18:(I)1.

6

[On the reforms taking place in his country and in Eastern Europe]: Having embarked upon the road of radical reform, the socialist countries are crossing the line beyond which there is no return to the past. Nevertheless, it is wrong to insist, as many in the West do, that this is the collapse of socialism. On the contrary, it means that the socialist process in the world will pursue its further development in a multiplicity of forms. Let us leave it to experts in anti-Communist propaganda to rejoice in the "triumph of capitalism" in the Cold War.

Speech, Rome/Time, 12-11:37.

Martha Graham
Modern-dance choreographer

7

The past is not dead; it is not even past. People live on inner time; the moment in which a deci-

(MARTHA GRAHAM)

sive thought or feeling takes place can be at any time. Timeless feelings are common to all of us. A work is dated if it doesn't speak to us about those timeless feelings. It doesn't matter when the work was done, or when those feelings are experienced. The past can be as fresh as now.

Interview, New York/
Dance Magazine, May:55.

Gus Hall
Chairman, Communist Party
U.S.A.

1

Not only is Communism not dead, it is the way of the future for all human societies. If you look at the United Nations, there are no new capitalist countries. All new societies are socialist or countries moving in the direction of national liberation and socialism.

Interview/
USA Today, 3-8:(A)11.

T. George Harris
Editor-in-chief,
"American Health" and
"Psychology Today" magazines

2

We've spent too much of our serious research looking for agony, when Mother Nature has been teaching us the exact opposite. It's very clear that Mother Nature is a very gentle lady, and she coaxes us along with the extreme pleasure of sexuality and good food and playful behavior. If we don't learn the lesson of pleasure, the species dies. What nature's teaching us all the time is that what feels good is generally good for you, unless civilization has screwed it up.

USA Today, 6-8:(A)2.

Roger Heyns
President, William and Flora Hewlett
Foundation

3

The safest thing you can say about the future right now [is that there will be] unpredictability

and uncertainty and instability. The psychological consequence of that is anxiety. And zealotry is often, it seems to me—and fundamentalism is just one form of it—an escape from anxiety. If you're really scared, then the simple answer is going to be better than the complicated answer. And so our tolerance for complexity is going to go down.

Interview, Menlo Park, Calif./
The Christian Science Monitor,
6-30:12.

Lou Holtz
Football coach,
University of Notre Dame

4

The greatest power God gave us is the power to choose. We have the opportunity to choose whether we're going to act or procrastinate, believe or doubt, pray or curse, help or heal. We also choose whether we're going to be happy or whether we're going to be sad. We have three simple little rules on our football team. Rule Number 1 is what I refer to as the Do-Right Rule. You know the difference between right and wrong. Do what's right and avoid what's wrong, and if you have any doubt about it, get out the Bible.

At Gonzaga University commencement/
The Christian Science Monitor,
6-12:12.

Erich Honecker
First Secretary,
Communist Party of
East Germany

5

Any attempt by imperialism to destabilize socialist construction or slander its achievements is now and in the future nothing more than Don Quixote's futile running against the steadily turning sails of a windmill.

The New York Times, 10-10:(A)1.

Jiang Zemin
General Secretary,
Communist Party of China

6

The socialist system possesses strong historical vitality and great viability. Those who

(JIANG ZEMIN)

have noticed only some adverse currents and failed to see the irreversible course of history are politically shortsighted observers. Socialism replacing capitalism is the real mainstream of history.

Speech at National Day celebration,
Beijing, Sept. 29/
Los Angeles Times, 9-30:(I)4.

John Paul II
Pope

1

Some people may hesitate to express too much hope or be overly optimistic about the future. Yet many will agree that the world is living through a moment of extraordinary awakening ... It is more like the confluence of many complex global developments in the fields of science and technology, in the economic world, in the growing political maturity of peoples and in the formation of world opinion.

To foreign diplomats,
Copenhagen, June 7/
The New York Times, 6-8:(A)11.

Paul Johnson
Author, Historian

2

In the rise of intellectuals, truth has become a prime casualty. They think that there is only Truth with a capital T, which they feel that they have found and must deliver to others. In that respect, Karl Marx, who thought that he had a direct line to metaphysical truth, is the archtypical intellectual. Intellectuals are simply not inclined to take the scientific approach, to look for evidence that conflicts with their hypothesis just as carefully as they look for evidence that confirms it. But perhaps that matters less than it used to because the literate public is increasingly unlikely to listen to these gurus, in part because there is a pervasive feeling throughout the Western world that utopia is not attainable. One should listen to and read intellectuals but not necessarily take great notice of what they say, particularly when they gang up and produce

manifestoes. Winston Churchill used to say, "Experts should be on tap but never on top." That's very good advice.

Interview, London/
U.S. News & World Report,
3-27:73.

Matjaz Kmecl
President of Yugoslavia

3

Everywhere when a man comes into [political] power, he becomes corrupted, unfortunately. For that reason an elective system in a multi-party state is better from my point of view. There a man must make a greater effort or, at least, learn how to lie well. You know, power is always cynical—a whore, the classics of the world say.

Interview/
The New York Times, 1-23:(A)6.

Helmut Kohl
Chancellor of West Germany

4

We do not wish to force our conceptions upon anyone. Nobody, however, could honestly argue that socialism has proven to be one single failure. It has failed throughout the world, not just in [East Germany]. By contrast, free enterprise means the freedom of decision, personal self-determination and broadly distributed wealth.

Before West German Parliament,
Bonn., Nov. 16/
The New York Times,
11-17:(A)1.

Sherry Lansing
Motion-picture producer

5

I don't want to be defined only by the movies I make. I don't want my obituary to say, "She made these movies." When you lay dying, what it's about is the intimacy you've known, the touch of another human being. Ultimately, what makes your life worthwhile are the other people you've cared about.

Interview/
Cosmopolitan, August:118.

WHAT THEY SAID IN 1989

Jim Lehrer
Co-anchor,
"MacNeil/Lehrer NewsHour,"
PBS-TV

1

It is the lying at the top levels of our society that concerns me the most because morality, like water and unlike money, really does trickle down. I am concerned that some at the top have adopted a concept that lying for the higher good is all right—that dishonesty in the name of righteousness is just fine.

At Southern Methodist University commencement/
The Christian Science Monitor,
6-12:13.

Shirley MacLaine
Actress

2

The most important thing I've learned is that life is like a bottle of syrup. I used to have a bottle with the picture of a girl holding a bottle of the syrup with a picture of her holding a bottle of syrup, and so on. We all need to look at ourselves looking at ourselves. Only when we do that, really look deep inside, can we learn what life is about.

Interview, New York/
Ladies' Home Journal, April:89.

Michael Manley
Prime Minister-elect
of Jamaica

3

There are two kinds of people in the world: people who have the humility to try to learn by experience, and people who suffer from arrogance and are incapable of learning . . . I was trained in the tradition of self-criticism.

Interview/
Newsweek, 2-20:29.

Bette Midler
Actress

4

When you get to a certain position in life, it's very hard to recapture the depth of comfort you had before you made it. You're just different. Or rather, you're *perceived* as different. People are either frightened of you or want something from you. Or their proximity to you makes them feel more successful. They can't really let their hair down unless they're on the same exact footing as you. And then there's a jealousy aspect . . . I know that most of what I have is ephemeral. I also have a mind and want to have a *life* of the mind. This [film] business isn't about acquiring stuff, about wearing fancy clothes or diamonds. Once you realize that it's about perceptions and ideas and the world, you're not interested in the really cheesy trappings of success.

Interview,
Los Angeles/
Ms., March:55,57.

Andrzej Milczanowski
Member, national executive
committee, Solidarity
(banned independent
Polish trade union)

5

It's not enough to be right. That's too little. It's also important to be strong. The history of the world shows that more often people who were right lost than won.

Jan. 23/
The New York Times,
1-28:3.

Devan Nair
Former President of Singapore

6

The unfolding renaissance of the world's most venerable cultures, all emerging in modern technological garbs, does not mean that cultural identities are effaced. No need for that. They are transformed. Confucius in a three-piece suit is still recognizably Confucius, with perhaps a newly acquired taste for golf, Coca-Cola and Vidal Sassoon, and some familiarity with the English language.

Lecture, Susquehanna University,
February/
The Wall Street Journal,
3-28:(A)22.

Sandra Day O'Connor
Associate Justice,
Supreme Court
of the United States

1

Do the best you can, no matter how insignificant it may seem at the time. While you may be a lowly foot soldier . . . no one knows more about solving a problem than the person at the bottom.

At Rockford (Ill.) College
commencement/
USA Today, 5-24:(A)9.

Robert Ornstein
Neurobiologist and
psychologist, University of
California Medical Center,
San Francisco, and
Stanford University

2

When you put a frog in a pan of water and heat the water up slowly, it can't detect the gradual change in temperature and so will remain in the pan until it boils to death. In [mankind's] case, the gradual increase in population, pollution, nuclear weapons, economic growth threaten to "boil" our civilization. But many of us don't register these changes and, in fact, keep working to "turn up the heat" instead of doing something to solve the problem.

Interview/
USA Today, 1-25:(A)9.

Peter O'Toole
Actor

3

There's always a hunger, when you're young, to go from peak to peak and avoid the valleys. I had a pretty hilariously gloomy few years in the '70s. But today I'm quite at home wandering those valleys and occasionally climbing a peak.

Interview, London/
Time, 2-6:63.

Letty Cottin Pogrebin
Writer; Founding editor,
"Ms." magazine

4

An open mind should be more than a catch-all receptacle. It should have a screening mechanism to keep out the trivial, a sorting capacity to organize ideas and reconcile contradictions, and a critical tool to help us decide what we believe. That's the difference between a mind that receives information and a mind that thinks.

The New York Times, 1-16:(A)11.

Dan Rather
Anchorman, CBS News

5

The thing I see happening is the swing back to the nuclear family—home and hearth, kith and kin. More and more, the women who went into the workplace are having children. And parents—which means single parents as well as couples—now must create a home and family environment. When all is said and done, praise and money and fame and glory and career don't matter as much as our children do. As much as our families do. And if that gets me a reputation as a bleeding heart, I don't mind it.

Interview/
Ladies' Home Journal, January:83.

Lawrence S. Ritter
Professor of
finance and economics,
New York University

6

Corruption has a considerable effect on our lives because it is all around us. The emphasis on making money is so great, the emphasis on getting rich, no matter how, is so tremendous that I think it influences virtually every aspect of our society. I think the situation could improve, but I don't think it is likely to. All the emphasis seems to be in the other direction . . . The philosophy that the only things that matter are to win, to get to the top and to make a lot of money is conducive to corruption. I see it everywhere, and I don't think it is in the process of being reversed.

Interview/
Los Angeles Times, 1-29:(IV)3.

Robert A. K. Runcie
Archbishop of Canterbury
(England)

7

We live in a world in which the worst looks as if it is going to happen and the worst often does

(ROBERT A. K. RUNCIE)

happen, and yet out of the anguish and waste, love and trust come in new forms.

At Canterbury Cathedral,
March 26/
Los Angeles Times, 3-27:(I)5.

Tom Selleck
Actor

1

Whenever I get full of myself and think I'm a star, I think about the nice elderly couple who approached me with a camera on a street in Honolulu one day. When I struck a pose for them, the man said, "No, no, we want you to take a picture of *us*." Things like that are very good for me.

Interview/
Ladies' Home Journal, March:42.

Stephen J. Solarz
United States Representative,
D-New York

2

It would be a profound mistake to take the survival and success of democracy for granted. Its durability will depend on the ability of governments to translate the promise of democracy into a better life for their people.

U.S. News & World Report,
5-22:35.

Alexander Solzhenitsyn
Exiled Soviet author

3

In Western civilization—which used to be called Western-Christian but now might better be called Western-Pagan—along with the development of intellectual life and science, there has been a loss of the serious moral basis of society. During these 300 years of Western civilization, there has been a sweeping away of duties and an expansion of rights. But we have two lungs. You can't breathe with just one lung and not with the other. We must avail ourselves of rights and duties in equal measure. And if this is not estab-

lished by the law, if the law does not oblige us to do that, then we have to control ourselves. When Western society was established, it was based on the idea that each individual limited his own behavior. Everyone understood what he could do and what he could not do. The law itself did not restrain people. Since then, the only thing we have been developing is rights, rights, rights, at the expense of duty.

Interview, Cavendish, Vt./
Time, 7-24:60.

Susan Sontag
Author

4

Capitalism is on a roll right now that is just extraordinary. There was the Industrial Revolution and the horrors of all that . . . Then there was some kind of cleaned-up, welfare-state capitalism that emerged in the '30s, that came into its own as a very effective and attractive system called Social Democracy in places like Canada, Holland and the Scandinavian countries. And then there's this new thing, like a third era of capitalism. Call it Thatcherism, call it Reaganism, call it the ascendancy of Japan, the triumph of the multinationals . . . There's a new polycentric, post-nationalist, hyper-capitalist international society being formed. In this world, in which materialism has almost a new dimension, it's so hard to get people to think about questions of injustice. I would use words like "philistinism" and "conformism."

Interview/
Mother Jones, May:13.

Mother Teresa of Calcutta
Indian religious social worker;
Winner, 1979 Nobel Peace Prize

5

Take our congregation: We have very little, so we have nothing to be preoccupied with. The more you have, the more you are occupied, the less you give. But the less you have, the more free you are. Poverty for us is freedom. It is not a mortification, a penance. It is joyful freedom . . . I find the rich much poorer. Sometimes they are more lonely inside. They are never satisfied.

(MOTHER TERESA OF CALCUTTA)

They always need something more. I don't say all of them are like that; everybody is not the same. [But] I find that [kind of] poverty hard to remove. The hunger for love is much more difficult to remove than the hunger for bread.

Interview/Time, 12-4:(B)1.

Donald Trump
Entrepreneur

1

I like thinking big. If you're going to be thinking anyway, you might as well think big.

Time, 1-16:48.

Paul A. Volcker
Former Chairman,
Federal Reserve Board

2

Frankly, I am not very good at planning things way in advance, of doing great studies about what should be done over a period of time, because it all seems very abstract. And I find it very easy to be lazy, unless something compelling comes along and says, look, goddammit, you've got to act. And it's on your desk and that's it. *Then* the adrenaline begins running.

Interview,
New York/
Time, 1-23:50.

Mike Wallace
Co-host, "60 Minutes,"
CBS-TV

3

[Addressing graduating college students]: ... chances are, if you're any good at all, and lucky, you're going to do well—financially. But there is so much more to life than that. Simply put: Do well—but do good, too. Oh, I know, we Americans learned to curl our lips at do-gooders somewhere along the line. Do-gooders, bleeding hearts, people with a conscience went out of style. Pragmatism, selfishness, the free-market euphemism was used. All that took over. Don't

let that happen to you. Don't let time tarnish the ideas you cherish at this moment.

At University of Pennsylvania
commencement/
The Christian Science Monitor,
6-12:12.

Patrick Watson
Canadian journalist

4

Five years ago, the terrific upsurge in world trade and communications began to make it clear to people in non-democratic countries that we who live in the democratic countries have tremendous advantages—economic and intellectual advantages, and advantages that come out of the freer flow of information and technologies and the freer movement of people ... The greatest threat to the health of the modern democracies is the disengagement and the apathy of the citizenry. But once people have tasted the liberty that goes with democracy and the power to run their own lives that goes with democracy, they don't forget that taste. They struggle for democracy again, as they did in Germany at the end of the '30s and in the Philippines with the arrival of the [Ferdinand] Marcos regime.

Interview/
USA Today, 7-11:(A)9.

Eudora Welty
Author

5

I'm one of the people who think best in the morning. I like to wake up ready to go, and to know that during the whole day the phone wouldn't ring, the doorbell wouldn't ring—even with good news—and that nobody would drop in ... At the end of the day, I'd have a drink, watch the evening news ... and then I can do anything I want to.

Interview, Jackson, Miss./
The Writer, January:5.

Joanne Woodward
Actress

6

It's not death I fear, it's reality—which means for me that I will never accomplish or learn or *be*

(JOANNE WOODWARD)

all that I wish I could be before the final curtain . . . Having it all is just not possible. I don't know how any woman can be a corporate officer, or whatever, work all day, and then come home and be a wonderful wife and mother. This '80s notion of having it all, being it all, has placed an enormous burden on women. I'm constantly amazed that some people see me as one of those superwomen. That isn't me at all.

Interview/
Lear's, September:105.

Boris N. Yeltsin
Member, Congress of People's
Deputies of the Soviet Union

1

Communism is just an idea, something you should think about. But don't try to implement it anywhere on earth.

USA Today, 9-15:(A)4.

Clayton K. Yeutter
Secretary of Agriculture
of the United States

2

I've evaluated a lot of folks as they've come up through academia, the business world and government, and my conclusion goes about as follows: that when you look at the very top people in this country or anywhere in the world, there's not a whole lot of difference in ability. There are a lot of smart people in the world, a lot of smart people sitting out in this audience today. There are a lot of people in the world who work hard, really hard. I'm one of them, and I hope many of you will be, too. But that's not the distinguishing characteristic. There are many people who are smart and work hard and who do not reach the top. The distinguishing characteristic at the top in almost all cases is what your faculty here would call "interpersonal skills," or some would call "human relations." Some might simply say it's following the Golden Rule.

At Clemson University commencement/
The Christian Science Monitor, 6-12:12.

Religion

Daniel Bell
Sociologist,
Harvard University

1

From Voltaire to Marx, every Enlightenment thinker thought that religion would disappear in the 20th century because religion was fetishism, animistic superstition. Well, it's not true, because religion is a response, and sometimes a very coherent response, to the existential predicaments faced by all men in all times. Empires have crumbled; political systems have crumbled; economic systems have crumbled. The great historical religions have survived.

Interview, Cambridge, Mass./
The New York Times, 2-7:(B)2.

F. F. Bruce
Religious author;
Former holder of
John Rylands chair of biblical
criticism and exegesis,
Manchester University
(England)

2

Personally, I would not countenance a position which makes a distinction of principle in church service between men and women. My own understanding of Christian priesthood is quite different from the understanding that dominates so much of the current discussion of the subject. If, as evangelical Christians generally believe, Christian priesthood is a privilege in which all believers share, there can be no reason that a Christian woman should not exercise her priesthood on the same terms as a Christian man.

Interview/
Christianity Today, 4-7:24.

George Bush
President of the United States

3

There is no greater peace than that which comes from prayer, and no greater fellowship than to join in prayer with others . . . All of us should not try to fulfill the responsibilities we now have without prayer and a strong faith in God.

Before National Association of
Religious Broadcasters,
Washington/
Los Angeles Times, 2-3:(I)2.

Harvey Cox
Professor of divinity,
Harvard Divinity School

4

[On religion in the Soviet Union in the era of *glasnost,* openness]: There's an enormously increased level of interest in religion, participation in religious services, attendance at churches, and so on. But the real underlying question is whether the churches are going to be given a kind of legal status. The right to own property, the right to publish their own newspapers, and the right to be an actor in public life has still not achieved legal status . . . I think what may be holding it back is a kind of apprehensiveness on the part of the [Soviet] government that this would be indeed a very large step after many, many years of official atheism and kind of a quasi-atheistic religion. I think there's a certain amount of reluctance to take it even under the conditions of *glasnost.*

Interview/
The Christian Science Monitor,
8-18:12.

William Dewart
Clinical psychologist

5

Some go into the clergy believing that "in the end, I answer only to God." That is a very nice arrangement, they suppose, because God is a spiritual entity, after all, and His love is unconditional. They won't have to deal with a foreman or boss, no changes of administration. It's just you and God, who, after all, called you in the first place. At least that's what they believe when they

(WILLIAM DEWART)

begin. But before they know it, they find themselves running up against authority and issues of power everywhere, from the vestry of their own small parish all the way up to the bishop of the diocese. For example, in the Episcopal Church the canons provide for the bishop to make the final decision regarding the very question of one's calling to an ordained priesthood. So the poor individual unconsciously seeking the priesthood in hopes of circumventing issues of authority and power, will certainly find himself walking straight into one of the more authoritative, political organizations in the world.

The Atlantic Monthly, January:42.

Jerry Falwell
Evangelist

1

I feel that I have performed the task to which I was called in 1979. The religious right is solidly in place and, like the galvanizing of the black church as a political force a generation ago, the religious conservatives in America are now in for the duration.

Las Vegas, Nev., June 11/
The New York Times, 6-12:(A)10.

George Gallup, Jr.
Chairman,
Gallup Organization

2

Over the last 54 years of scientific polling, religion in America has been remarkably stable, both in terms of religious beliefs and practices. Essentially, America's religious beliefs have been orthodox, relative to other nations. I would say that the Americans of 1989 are very much like Americans of 1939 in many of their beliefs and values, and even, as a matter of fact, in terms of the percentage of liberals and conservatives. There's much more stability than people realize. It is interesting that as the level of education increased in this country—there are probably now about three times as many people with a college background today as there were in the mid-1930s—religious beliefs did not decline. Marx's and others' prediction that with more

education there would be less attachment to religion simply has not come about. In fact, Americans are unique in that we have a high level of formal education and a high level of attested belief at the same time.

Interview/
Christianity Today, 11-17:23.

John W. Gardner
Professor-designate of public
service, Stanford University;
Former Secretary of Health,
Education and Welfare
of the United States

3

If you're serious about values, then you have to add tolerance very early—*very* early. The more you say, "Values are important," the more you have to say, "There are limits to which you can impose your values on me." And that is *so* hard to sustain! It's one of the toughest things in religion. I've watched many people go through this process of becoming more deeply religious. It's very hard for them to maintain a level of tolerance. In a way, that's almost natural: If you really believe that your immortal soul is in danger if you hold certain beliefs, it's natural for you to pull away from those who hold those dreadful beliefs.

Interview, New York/
The Christian Science Monitor,
10-11:12.

Jozef Cardinal Glemp
Roman Catholic Primate
of Poland

4

Dear Jewish people, do not talk with us from a position of a nation raised beyond all others. Your power lies in the mass media easily at your disposal.

Aug. 26/Time, 9-11:77.

Mikhail S. Gorbachev
General Secretary,
Communist Party
of the Soviet Union;
President of the Soviet Union

5

We [the Soviet leadership] have changed our attitude on some matters, such as religion, which

(MIKHAIL S. GORBACHEV)

admittedly we used to treat in a simplistic manner. Now we not only proceed from the assumption that no one should interfere in matters of the individual's conscience, we also say that the moral values that religion embodied for centuries can help in the work of renewal of our country, too. In fact, this is already happening.

Speech, Rome,
Nov. 30/
Newsweek, 12-1:(A)1.

Ahmad Zaki Hammad
Director, Islamic Society
of North America

1

Islam is a commitment not only to realize the existence of the creator but, more importantly, Islam is a loving adherence to his guidance revealed through the galaxy of prophets and messengers who essentially brought one and the same message, inviting mankind to worship its creator. Mohammed's message is a real affirmation, a confirmation of the heritage of all the prophets. Islam is a completion of the heritage of Moses and Abraham and Jesus, a continuation of the heritage of all the prophets.

Interview/
USA Today,
3-1:(A)9.

Bill Honig
California State Superintendent
of Public Instruction

2

Creationism, by our state board policy, is not science and so should not be taught as part of the science class. The questions of who we are, origins, why we're here, the broader purposes, and those religious ideas should be talked about, not in a doctrinaire or sectarian way, but should be addressed as ethics, morals and religious issues—but not in science.

Interview/
USA Today,
8-9:(A)7.

John Paul II
Pope

3

[On Catholic opposition to a common Eucharist among different Christian churches]: The Catholic position on eucharistic sharing is not meant to offend our partners in dialogue. Rather, it is an expression of our deep conviction, rooted in our doctrine and in accordance with ancient practice, that the Eucharist is only to be shared by those in full communion with one another.

To Lutheran bishops,
Oslo, Norway, June 1/
Los Angeles Times, 6-2:(I)5.

4

Religious life is not threatened merely by vexing restrictions. It can also be threatened by the spread of false values—such as hedonism, power-seeking, greed—which are making headway in various countries and which in practice stifle the spiritual aspirations of large numbers of people.

Speech, Helsinki, Finland, June 5/
Los Angeles Times, 6-6:(I)13.

Gordon Lewis
Chairman, department of the
philosophy of religion,
Denver Seminary

5

I believe the view of Christianity has been censored from the textbooks in our public schools, and there are books documenting that it was done in the name of academic freedom. Society is being defrauded. When the majority of the tax money is coming from people who have to take their kids out of the public schools and send them to a church school in order to have their views fairly represented, that is fraud.

Interview/USA Today, 8-9:(A)7.

David Mains
Religious commentator,
"Chapel of the Air"
radio program

6

Some leaders say we are in a great [religious] revival now. If we are . . . I ask where are the

(DAVID MAINS)

tears? What's happening to the intense spirit of conviction that always marks such things? Why are the converts coming in trickles instead of waves upon waves? . . . How come all the marriage breakups, even among the clergy? We are not in revival, although we may be much closer to its possibility than we realize.

Keynote address at National Association of Evangelicals meeting, Columbus, Ohio/ Christianity Today, 4-7:43.

John L. May
Roman Catholic Archbishop of St. Louis; President, National Conference of Bishops

1

[Saying the American public will not accept an authoritarian church]: [In the U.S.,] there is total freedom of thought in public educational and cultural media, and any form of censorship is abhorred. Authoritarianism is suspect in any area of learning or culture. Individual freedom is prized supremely. Religious doctrine and moral teaching are widely judged by these criteria. To assert that there is a church teaching with authority, binding and loosing for eternity, is truly a sign of contradiction to many Americans who consider the divine right of bishops as outmoded as the divine right of kings.

At meeting of American bishops and the Pope, Vatican City, March 8/ Los Angeles Times, 3-9:(I)14.

John Navone
Theologian, Pontifical Gregorian University

2

The Vatican rejects the pick-and-choose kind of K-mart Catholicism so prevalent in the United States. It is telling the bishops their job is to communicate the real things, not fashionable counterfeits.

At conference with American bishops, Vatican City, March 9/ Los Angeles Times, 3-10:(I)1.

Jacob Neusner
Scholar of Judaism, Brown University

3

The idea of life after death is clearly an embarrassment to modern thinking—most major philosophers have ridiculed it—but it is just as clearly the touchstone of all religion. Religion says that being human has eternal meaning. If religion announces that life is over at the grave, then it is not talking about what people expect religion to discuss.

Newsweek, 3-27:55.

Leo O'Donovan
President-designate, Georgetown University

4

[On why he became a priest]: There was an insistent sense that this was a way in which I could best give and receive. Everything in life is most fundamentally a gift. And you receive it best and you live it best by holding it with very open hands. Every time you try to control it, you really lose control of it.

Interview/ USA Today, 9-21:(A)9.

Madalyn Murray O'Hair
American atheist activist

5

I am completely stunned to find out the U.S.S.R. is absolutely indifferent to atheism. They seemed to think here that if you just leave religion alone, it will go away. But that's ridiculous. The Pope is never going to call me up and say, "Madalyn, I give up." No, he won't do that. You have to fight religion, actively show people why religion is so dangerous.

Interview, Moscow/ Los Angeles Times, 9-16:(I)8.

Luis Palau
Evangelist

6

[On ethical scandals involving evangelists]: Presumably, public preacher types want more

(LUIS PALAU)

attention so they can preach the gospel to more people. One has to constantly examine motives. Money is part of the problem. Sometimes it's greed, but not always. I once accepted a speaking engagement and paid my own way because the organization had no money. This was a big mistake. The Bible says the laborer is worthy of his hire. If we deviate from Scripture in a small way it can open the door to bigger abuses. I have a feeling that today some have a voice on certain platforms in the evangelical world not because of their God-given message, but because of the money they put out.

Interview/
Christianity Today, 2-17:51.

Robert Peel
Christian Science historian

1

[On the growth of dissension in the Christian Science Church]: The logic of Christian Science demands that an ailing church be treated as an ailing patient would be—with total commitment to spiritual ways and means, not human skills and repairs.

U.S. News & World Report,
11-6:76.

Jaroslav Pelikan
Professor of history,
Yale University

2

Christian doctrine right now is chaotic. At no time in recent centuries has the Christian tradition as a force been taken as seriously by as broad a constituency as it now is. But the means of formulating what that tradition implies or what specific issues before us mean can't seem, somehow, to come together. There's also an appalling ignorance of the Christian tradition even within the Christian community. Rudimentary acquaintance with the fundamentals of the Christian doctrine could be taken for granted in another time, even among those who didn't believe it but who nevertheless took it seriously enough to know it. That can no longer be assumed. One of

the prime needs of the moment is simply to address this quite widespread ignorance about the basic data of the Bible and of the major figures of Christian history. Sometimes I get the sense that what will destroy the church is going to be not persecution but boredom.

Interview/
U.S. News & World Report,
6-26:57.

Clarence C. Pope
Episcopal Bishop
of Forth Worth, Texas

3

[Saying there is a breakdown of morals within the Church]: There is growing evidence that strong sentiment exists throughout the Episcopal Church not to trust the Bible when its teaching conflicts with society norms. We now see priests being divorced and remarried in the same way as the laity, and with the blessing of bishops.

Before Episcopal Synod of America,
Fort Worth, Texas, June 1/
The Washington Post, 6-3:(A)6.

Joseph A. Ratzinger
Head of Roman Catholic
Congregation for the
Doctrine of the Faith

4

Today's theologians have an influence not only in the environment of scientific research and university teaching but, through the mass media, bring to the public arena a concert dissonant to the point that their voices drown out that of the bishop evangelist. In many parts of the world, theologians have taken the place of bishops as teachers, engendering a growing insecurity and disorientation.

At conference with American bishops,
Vatican City, March 8/
Los Angeles Times, 3-10:(I)12.

David Seamands
Professor of pastoral ministry,
Asbury Theological Seminary

5

God has allowed the world to arise and judge us [evangelists] . . . The world will not tolerate us

(DAVID SEAMANDS)

making money out of preaching the gospel. We are judged, and so the cost of the house, the place we live—all of that—is being watched . . . And God knows it ought to be watched.

At National Association of
Evangelicals meeting,
Columbus, Ohio/
Christianity Today, 4-7:43.

Alexander S. Shmukler
Organizer, Moscow chapter,
B'nai B'rith

1

[On the new Moscow B'nai B'rith chapter, the first in the Soviet Union]: We hope that our B'nai B'rith chapter will draw together all [Soviet] Jews—those who are planning to emigrate, those who have been refused [permission to emigrate], those who intend to stay and those who are uncertain. What is important is a sense of identity as Jews as well as an opportunity to deepen our understanding of Jewish culture . . . Attention has been focused for a long time on those who are emigrating, and more than half a million have left in the past 15 or 20 years. But well over a million Jews remain, and intend to remain, in the Soviet Union. What of them? To stay, they will need a stable situation, one where they are free to live their lives fully as Jews if they wish, and one where there is none of the past anti-Semitism.

Moscow, Feb. 21/
Los Angeles Times, 2-22:(I)7.

Jacqueline Wexler
President,
National Conference of
Christians and Jews

2

I believe that for the churches, which by their own commitment address the deepest part of the human spirit, to make policies lacking the input of almost half of their membership—women—cries to heaven for change. But the change is very slow in coming. Barriers to ordaining women are being broken down in many denominations: Reconstructionist and Reformed Judaism, for example. There are increasing numbers of female rabbis being ordained and accepted. And barriers have broken down in almost all of mainline Protestantism. Many leading theologians in Protestant denominations and in the Roman Catholic faith are convinced that there are no biblical hindrances to ordination [of women] at all and that it is a proscription which came into the church probably in the fourth century of Christianity. And now it is just so deeply embedded that it is hard to move it administratively.

USA Today, 2-14:(A)9.

Science and Technology

Neil A. Armstrong
Former American astronaut;
First man on the Moon

1

[Supporting continued U.S. manned exploration of space]: We are a nation of explorers. It's a fundamental thing to want to go, to touch, to see, to smell, to learn, and that I think will continue in the future.

The New York Times, 7-17:(A)1.

William Baker
Former chairman,
AT&T Bell Telephone
Laboratories

2

Science and math are the substance of this age, just as exploration and warfare were the substance of other ages. Science is the way to prepare Americans for the 21st century.

Time, 9-11:70.

Bruce Brymer
Lead mission controller for
NASA's "Voyager 2" spacecraft

3

[On the unmanned *Voyager 2* 12-year mission that has taken it past Neptune and will continue further on into space]: It's mind-boggling. We're actually going out to the stars. This spacecraft is going to outlive us. It's going to be out there forever.

Los Angeles Times, 9-24:(I)3.

George Bush
President of the United States

4

Our goal is nothing less than to establish the United States as the pre-eminent spacefaring nation. [A space station is the] critical next step in all our space endeavors. And next, for the next century, back to the Moon, back to the future, and this time back to stay. And then, a journey into tomorrow, a journey to another planet, a manned mission to Mars.

Speech celebrating the 20th
anniversary of the first manned
Moon landing,
Washington, July 20/
The New York Times, 7-21:(A)1.

Michael Collins
Former American astronaut

5

[On his being part of the *Apollo 11* moon-landing mission 20 years ago]: There's so many things that can go wrong on a trip to the moon and back. It's sort of a long and fragile daisy chain of events. And I can remember being in the mobile quarantine facility, the little house trailer aboard the aircraft carrier after we landed in the Pacific, and thinking, "Gee, none of them did [go wrong]. None of those little links broke." And to me, that was the amazing part, that everything worked in sum as well as it did.

Interview,
Washington/
The Christian Science Monitor,
7-20:15.

6

[On criticism that costly space programs should not be undertaken while social problems still exist on Earth]: We cannot launch our planetary probes from a springboard of poverty, discrimination and unrest. But neither can we wait until each and every terrestrial problem has been solved. Such logic 200 years ago would have prevented expansion westward of the Appalachian Mountains, for assuredly the Eastern Seaboard was beset by problems of great urgency then, as it is today.

Speech celebrating the 20th
anniversary of the first manned
Moon landing,
Washington, July 20/
Los Angeles Times, 7-21:(I)1.

Donald Cram
Nobel Prize-winning chemist

1

Research is exciting. It is high-class gambling with my time and my reputation, with the futures of my co-workers and with society's money. We win about 20 per cent of the time and we lose about 80 per cent of the time . . . It's not fun to lose, but it is very instructive. And, believe me, I've had a lot of practice in this art.

At University of Nebraska
commencement/
The Christian Science Monitor,
6-12:13.

Thomas Eisner
Chemist, Cornell University

2

We are destroying species of plants and insects much, much faster than we can study them for chemical activity. With each species that we lose, we lose a notebook of genes—genes that are potentially valuable transferable resources. We should be looking at organisms not previously studied to see if they contain novel chemicals that are biologically active. Insects are the most versatile chemists on earth . . . Every single new idea in chemistry has come not from the minds of chemists but from nature. We've long known about the primary chemicals used for vital functions like metabolism. In addition, we've found that every organism has a shroud of secondary chemicals that are essential to its survival.

Interview, Ithaca, N.Y./
The New York Times 1-10:(B)7.

George Gilder
Author, Economist

3

I believe that the silicon chip is not the product of the evolution of conventional industrial technology. The chip is a radical new machine, and it teaches us radically new truths. For a long time, people imagined that the first computers were just other machines. But there's no relation between the early computers and the assembly of hundreds of transistors on something the size of a tip of a pin.

Interview/
Los Angeles Times, 9-10:(IV)3.

Bill Green
United States Representative,
R-New York

4

Given the Federal budget deficit and earthly demands, I don't see how we can afford expensive manned programs in space in the near future. People also dream of a home in the country or a trip around the world. But like couples with big mortgages and kids in college, this country has bills to pay before taking costly adventures.

July 20/
Los Angeles Times, 7-21:(I)1.

Leroy E. Hood
Professor of molecular biology,
California Institute
of Technology

5

Science is a tough discipline these days, because of the funding and the competition. So the first thing I generally advise students is, "You have to be good, and you have to have a real confidence in yourself. And you have to have a real vision that somehow this is what you want to do." Part of being good is having the drive, part is the intellect, part is the vision—and people have them in different dimensions. I think the most important thing is intellectual curiosity. You have to be fundamentally excited about solving problems.

Interview, Pasadena, Calif./
The Christian Science Monitor,
11-13:14.

Thomas Hughes
Historian of science,
University of Pennsylvania

6

Technology inevitably grows and becomes an interlocking system of many subsystems, especially in a country such as ours where we cherish the large scale, whether it is mass production of arms or of autos. And that is one of the problems we face. Systems are so large and bureaucratized, and there is so much inertia, that it is very difficult for more independent-minded people to get out from under the burden. Still, some do. Wit-

(THOMAS HUGHES)

ness the stories that have come out of Silicon Valley in recent years, where independent inventors, working outside the structure of established institutions, were instrumental in the rise of the computer industry.

Interview/
U.S. News & World Report, 5-8:64.

Shintaro Ishihara
Japanese politician

1

When you look back at history, you'll see that new technologies build new civilizations. Technology determines the quality and quantity of the human economy. The medieval age gave way to the modern age because of the art of navigation, the invention of gunpowder and Gutenberg's art of printing. Now the modern age has come to a close because of nuclear power and electronics.

Interview/Time, 11-20:82.

Donald Kennedy
President,
Stanford University

2

[On public and government support of scientific research, which does not always result in practical or useful advances]: It is not nice to disappoint people, and it is downright dangerous to disappoint your Congressman. The utilitarian argument [also] encourages a pernicious notion, now circulating widely among our policy-makers that, if one appropriates [basic research] money geographically, economic prosperity will distribute itself along with it. That is the way to convert science to another public-works project.

Before American Association for
the Advancement of Science, January/
The Christian Science Monitor, 2-14:13.

Donald Knuth
Professor of computer science,
Stanford University

3

[Saying many scientists don't like working for and being funded by private industry, whose

interest is in bottom-line profits, and would rather do theoretical research]: The scientific community faces a crisis in which a substantial number of the world's best scientists in all fields cannot get financial support for their work unless they subscribe to somebody else's agenda. We need to go back to a system where people . . . are given a chance to set their own priorities . . . Otherwise, we'll face a big slump in our future abilities to tackle new problems.

At World Computer Congress,
San Francisco/
Los Angeles Times, 8-29:(IV)2.

Vladimir Lapygin
Chairman, Defense Committee,
Supreme Soviet of
the Soviet Union

4

[Advocating the continuation of the Soviet space program despite calls for cutbacks in funding due to needs of other domestic programs]: Ignorant people cry for bread and butter. I believe the national space program should be preserved.

The Washington Post, 8-15:(A)12.

Joshua Lederberg
President,
Rockefeller University

5

There has been a penetration of science and technical issues into every area of life. There are more and more dilemmas arising out of the opportunities that technology brings us. Issues have become science-connected in a way we might not have realized previously. There are not many problems that don't have some ingredient that requires scientific input.

The Washington Post, 2-2:(A)23.

Peter Raven
Director,
Missouri Botanical Garden

6

I think biology must be one of the most satisfying careers, because the things you are

WHAT THEY SAID IN 1989

studying are so absolutely and endlessly real and interesting and directly important. You never have to doubt the validity and interest of what you are doing.

Interview, St. Louis/
The Christian Science Monitor,
11-6:14.

Carl Sagan
Professor of astronomy and
space sciences,
and director of the Laboratory
for Planetary Studies,
Cornell University

1

NASA sold the U.S. government a bill of goods, that everything should be launched by NASA's [space] shuttle. NASA thought that would guarantee steady support of its manned spaceflight program. But it delays planetary missions and vital national-security missions to launch reconnaissance satellites. This whole business is due to NASA not having a coherent goal given to it by the President of the United States.

Interview/
USA Today, 5-2:(A)9.

Joseph Sambrook
Chairman of biochemistry,
Health Science Center,
University of Texas

2

It's important to get across to kids the intellectual power of the ideas of modern molecular biology. Genetics is the most intellectually beautiful science—it's like chess.

The Christian Science Monitor,
7-19:12.

Howard Shachman
Professor of molecular biology,
University of California

3

[On criticism of scientific ethics]: We must distinguish between actual fraud or scientific misconduct and errors which may be unavoidable or may result from poor laboratory practices during the course of scientific research. Some workers are sloppy but highly creative and original. Others are more methodical, neat and not very imaginative. Each type can make important contributions, and each warrants support even though we would all like to see the virtues of the two groups merge, with their poor qualities eliminated. Through vigilant actions we may be able to deter falsification and fabrication of data, which must be the target of vigorous action by the scientific community, research institutions and government agencies. But the much-needed remedies designed to eliminate such unacceptable acts are totally inappropriate for resolving scientific errors, careless experimental work, poor record-keeping, multiple publishing of the same findings and honorary authorship.

Congressional testimony,
Washington/
The Washington Post,
7-26:(A)24.

Art Winfree
Biologist,
University of Arizona

4

There's more computers around, and more scientists are bowing and scraping before them and believing what comes out of them as if they were some kind of oracle. You have to remember that 90 per cent of what comes out of a supercomputer is junk. You have to remember it's a tricky business. You have to be careful.

The Washington Post, 9-11:(A)3.

Sports

Sparky Anderson
Baseball manager,
Detroit "Tigers"

1

Losing a baseball game ain't a tragedy. Having a bad year is not a tragedy. Those things are disappointments, not tragedies. What happened to Pete Rose [the Cincinnati manager who was suspended from baseball because of alleged betting on the game] is a tragedy. The [baseball] commissioner [A. Bartlett Giamatti] dying—that was a tragedy. Somebody having cancer, that's a tragedy. But not losing a ball game. Thirteen days from now, every ballplayer in our clubhouse will be fishing, hunting, remodeling the house, playing golf. For the next six months they'll basically do nothing. No, this [his team having the league's worst won-lost record] ain't a tragedy.

Interview,
Baltimore, Sept. 20/
Los Angeles Times, 9-24:(III)14.

Arthur Ashe
Tennis player

2

[On whether blacks may be better at certain sports than whites]: It's an extremely hot topic, but my answer is an unequivocal yes. They may be better at *some* things, and I'm referring here to two physical factors in particular: foot speed and vertical leap. These abilities definitely translate into success in certain sports. Bill Russell revolutionized the position of center in basketball because he blocked shots with his leaping ability. Blacks haven't been beaten by whites in the sprints in quite some time. That's not to say they never will be beaten, but it seems that white America believes they [whites] can't sprint as fast. Today, you find junior-high coaches steering white kids away from even trying.

Interview,
Mt. Kisco, N.Y./
People, 3-6:247.

Buzzie Bavasi
Former baseball manager
and owner

3

[On charges that Cincinnati *Reds* manager, Pete Rose, bet on baseball games, which is prohibited by baseball's rules]: They just can't allow anything like that [betting], and it shouldn't matter that he never bet on his team to lose. I'll give you an example. Let's say he has $50,000 riding on the *Reds* and he is friends with the manager of the other team. He might say to that guy, "Listen, you're 14 games out of first [place], with two weeks to play. I'll split it and give you $25,000 if you just make a wrong decision on the game." Now, as far as I know, Pete never did that. But the public doesn't know that. That's what they might be thinking. It plants that doubt. It puts suspicion in the public's mind, and baseball can't have that. They'll think that about Pete the rest of his [managerial] career.

Interview, La Jolla, Calif., June 26/
Los Angeles Times, 6-27:(III)4.

Tim Belcher
Baseball pitcher,
Los Angeles "Dodgers"

4

That's how I pump myself up. I'll scream at myself; I'll get mad at myself. I give up a hit and I yell the unprintable. I'll curse myself. I call myself stupid. Then I'll get back on the mound, take a deep breath, and go after them. People who don't know, they see me give up a little two-out single and then scream at myself and they think, "He's losing his mind." But that's me. That's how I stay on the beam.

Houston, July 25/
Los Angeles Times, 7-26:(III)1.

Bob Boone
Baseball catcher,
Kansas City "Royals"

5

Catching is much like managing. Managers don't really win games, but they can lose plenty

(BOB BOONE)

of them. Same way with catching. If you're doing a quality job, you should be almost anonymous.

Interview, Haines City, Fla./
Los Angeles Times, 3-19:(III)3.

Bobby Bowden
Football coach,
Florida State University

1

We [college] coaches preach and preach [to student-players]: Get your education, stay in school. But the [pro-football] agents come in and offer fantastic amounts of money. There aren't many kids who can turn that down. It used to be the NFL insisted on them graduating, but not any more. The dike has been broken.

USA Today, 1-13:(C)7.

Pat Bowlen
Owner, Denver "Broncos"
football team

2

[On the NFL's new rule aimed at controlling crowd noise that interferes with the game]: I look at it from two standpoints because the game is two things—sports and entertainment. If you look at it as entertainment, the rule stinks. It really affects the fan we're asking to pay $20 for a ticket. But when you look at the game itself, I think the rule is fair . . . You shouldn't allow fans to affect the outcome of the game to the extent they have.

USA Today, 9-8:(E)4.

Tom Braatz
Executive vice president
for football operations,
Green Bay "Packers"
football team

3

[On college players leaving school early to join NFL teams]: It's damaging our relations with the college coaches. And it encourages agents to tamper with other underclassmen. It's touchy, but I wonder if the courts wouldn't see it as

denying somebody the right to work if we [in the NFL] refused somebody [so they could finish their schooling].

USA Today, 1-13:(C)7.

George Bush
President of the United States

4

Sports figures have a role. It's almost a cliche, but I really do think competitive athletics is a great antidote to some of the bad habits out there. Any involvement. Just watching it. Looking up at the people who excel in it . . . There are some with feet of clay, but there are an awful lot that people look up to. When one falls, it breaks the heart of a lot of young people.

To sportswriters,
Washington, Oct. 2/
The New York Times, 10-3:(B)13.

Brett Butler
Baseball player,
San Francisco "Giants"

5

I don't think bunting will ever die out. It'll come back one day because it's part of the game. It'll come back because there will always be some little guy somewhere who won't take no for an answer and who will be determined to take his gifts to the limit.

Interview/The New York Times,
9-4:(A)31.

Steve Carlton
Former baseball pitcher,
Philadelphia "Phillies"

6

If I were a general manager, I'd assemble a [baseball] club like the old Oakland *Raiders* [football team]. They exemplified what it takes to get the job done in the fashion I like to see it done—total dedication, not afraid to get dirty, whatever it takes to get the job done. It's a foxhole mentality. Who do you want in your foxhole? Who do you want to die with? It's like a war.

Interview, Clearwater, Fla./
USA Today, 7-28:(C)2.

Michael Carter
Football player,
San Francisco "49ers";
Former track-and-field athlete

1

In football, you get close to a lot of guys. You're on the road and the fans and the world are against you, but you have your teammates as your family. In track, you don't have that. You are alone.

Miami/The New York Times,
1-18:(B)12.

Jack Clark
Baseball player,
San Diego "Padres"

2

[On his having been the New York *Yankees* designated hitter in 1988]: When you're a DH, it's hard to justify that you're a real ballplayer.

USA Today, 4-4:(A)6.

Roger Craig
Baseball manager,
San Francisco "Giants"

3

Baseball is changing. The players want to have fun. They want to relax. They want to do it their way. Guys my age, [*Dodger* manager] Tommy [Lasorda], [*Cubs* manager Don] Zimmer, we've got to learn to cope with these things. Every year it gets tougher to manage. It's the human element.

Interview,
San Francisco/
USA Today, 10-3:(E)15.

Randy Cross
Football player,
San Francisco "49ers"

4

Football's as much an escape for the people who play the game as the ones that watch it. That's always been one of the prime criticisms of athletes in general. They're pampered and taken care of for so many years that all of a sudden the big slobs can't handle their lives [when they leave

the sport]. But they haven't been trained to; so they don't know what to do.

News conference, Miami, Jan. 18/
Los Angeles Times, 1-19:(III)10.

Mario M. Cuomo
Governor of New York (D)

5

Baseball, more than any other sport, is a uniquely American tradition that binds generation to generation, unlike any other ritual in society. It's a Little Leaguers' game that major leaguers play extraordinarily well, a game that excites us throughout adulthood. The crack of the bat and the scent of horsehide on leather bring back our memories that have been washed away with the sweat and tears of summers long gone ... even as the setting sun rushes the shadows past home plate.

The New York Times, 7-6:(B)11.

Ron Darling
Baseball pitcher,
New York "Mets"

6

It's not the [employment] contract that makes you secure; it's the performance. The day after I signed my contract this winter, there was a cartoon in the newspaper showing a Brinks truck backing up to my house, and the guy was handing me the money in a bag. But his partner was saying, "And he never even won 20 [games in a season]." That's how they judge you.

Interview, West Palm Beach, Fla./
The New York Times, 3-14:(B)16.

7

The truth is, I do get tired of being a *Met* sometimes. I'm talking about all the soap-opera stuff that comes with being a *Met*. A lot of it is wonderful, don't misunderstand me. But sometimes I wish it were more like San Diego, or someplace else, where all that matters is whether you pitch well or don't pitch well ... If the games were played on Macintosh computers, we'd probably win every season. But they're not played on a Macintosh. They're played on grass and dirt,

437

WHAT THEY SAID IN 1989

(RON DARLING)

with umpires and people in the stands, and human beings on the field. Real live stuff. And in that context, we [*Mets*] haven't been tough enough. Maybe we're too good for our own good. When we play well, we're like Barnum & Bailey's Traveling Baseball Show. We're the best show on earth. But we can also play miserably, like we did in the seventh game of the [1988] playoffs, and I include myself there. Why did we play that way? It comes down to toughness.

Interview/Esquire, April:67,70.

Eddie J. DeBartolo, Jr.
Owner, San Francisco "49ers"
football team

1

We [in the NFL] have an enormous business, not like it was when Pete [Rozelle] became commissioner 29 years ago. I don't find fault or point fingers at the past, but we need input from all the owners, not just a few. We need committees with rotating memberships. We need to restructure the commissioner's office with appropriate deputies. We have enormous problems in player relations, and the new television contract coming up. Everybody has a stake and everybody has something to contribute.

The New York Times, 7-20:(B)12.

Anita DeFrantz
United States Representative
to the International
Olympic Committee

2

Our [IOC] medical commission has stressed rehabilitation of athletes who are using steroids, but I think it's time to send a stronger message. It's not like athletes are taking them because they have a cold. They're taking them to cheat.

July 31/Los Angeles Times,
8-1:(III)2.

Wayne Duke
Commissioner, Big Ten
(college football)

3

I go in the [team's] dressing rooms [after a game] . . . and there's a disappointment in there

after a loss. People who are critical of our bowl record, or even people who are critical of the team's performance that day, don't have to see, first hand, the terrible disappointment that is felt by the players and the coaches who have put so much into the game. The guy up in the stands who has been tailgating all day and who thinks he has all the answers, doesn't have to see what losing does to the players and coaches.

Interview/Los Angeles Times,
1-1:(III)6.

Richard J. Durbin
United States Representative,
D-Illinois

4

I rise to condemn the desecration of a great American symbol. No, I am not referring to flag-burning; I am referring to the baseball bat. Several experts tell us that the wooden bat is doomed to extinction, that major-league baseball players will soon be standing at home plate with aluminum bats in their hands. Baseball fans have been forced to endure countless indignities by those who just cannot leave well enough alone. Designated hitters, plastic grass, uniforms that look like pajamas, chicken clowns dancing on the baselines, and of course the most heinous sacrilege, lights in [Chicago's] Wrigley Field. Are we willing to hear the crack of a bat replaced by the dinky ping? Are we ready to see the Louisville Slugger replaced by the aluminum ping dinger? Is nothing sacred? Please do not tell me that wooden bats are too expensive, when players who cannot hit their weight are being paid more money than the President of the United States. Please do not try to sell me on the notion that these metal clubs will make better hitters. What is next? Teflon baseballs? Radar-enhanced gloves? I ask you. I do not want to hear about saving trees. Any tree in America would gladly give its life for the glory of a day at home plate. I do not know if it will take a Constitutional amendment to keep the baseball traditions alive, but if we forsake the great Americana of broken-bat singles and pine tar, we will have certainly lost our way as a nation.

Before the House,
Washington, July 26/
The Washington Post, 7-27:(A)22.

438

Harry Edwards
Professor of sports sociology,
University of California,
Berkeley

1

[Comparing football with basketball]: In basketball there's a tension, but it's one that's much less severe. It's not a life-and-death type of tension. Football is about as close as you can get to war and still remain civil . . . In war, you have groups of individuals systematically going against each other. All you have to do is stand on the sidelines for a couple of games and see a guy carried off the field with a broken bone coming through the skin . . . There is a great deal more camaraderie in football than in basketball in a lot of ways. They tend to know each other better. In basketball, you get a heck of a lot of respect for what you can do with the ball, not so much for what you do away from the ball. In football, you get a lot of respect for what you do for the team.

Interview/The New York Times,
1-23:(B)10.

2

[On blacks in sports]: Things have changed for the better, but the struggle is not linear. It's dynamic and ever-changing. Jesse Owens and Joe Louis struggled for the legitimacy of black athletic talent. Later, Jackie Robinson, Bill Russell and others struggled for access. In the late '60s, athletes like Muhammad Ali, Tommie Smith, John Carlos, Arthur Ashe and Kareem [Abdul-Jabbar] fought for recognition of the dignity of the black athlete. Now we're in the struggle for power, and that's the most difficult of all. If we can broaden democratic participation in sports, then there is at least the possibility that we can devise credible strategies for approaching the situation in society as a whole.

Interview/Time, 3-6:63

Chris Evert
Tennis player

3

People are always asking when I will retire, so I felt pressured to give them an explanation. When you've been on a pedestal, there is no way to go but down. People don't like to see you fall. But very few athletes retire on top. And if you've been a champion, you'd like to play a little past your prime . . . Knowing me, once I decide to quit, I can't see myself playing again, even exhibitions. If I'm not competing, my heart won't be in it.

Interview/The New York Times,
5-31:(B)9.

4

My whole career, people have been talking about how tough I am. Now that I'm losing some, I can see how tough I was—the killer instinct, the single-mindedness, playing like a machine. Boy, that's what made me a champion.

Time, 9-11:85.

Tom Flores
President and general manager,
Seattle "Seahawks"
football team

5

[Criticizing a new NFL rule barring fans from making too much noise if it interferes with the visiting team's play]: How can you silence the crowd and tell them not to yell at all? It is something the colleges have lived with for years, at games where they have 100,000 people, and the noise problem hasn't hurt their game at all. There are certain home-field advantages in football, and crowd involvement is one of them. You can't take away those advantages.

The Washington Post, 9-6:(G)10.

Red Foley
Baseball official scorer

6

Definitely, there is more pressure being a scorer today because of all the big money tied to personal stats . . . My first judgment is usually the right one. I don't make incorrect calls, I make unpopular ones. These are judgment calls and I don't have to explain judgment calls any more than an umpire does.

Interview/Los Angeles Times,
8-6:(III)2.

WHAT THEY SAID IN 1989

A. J. Foyt
Auto-racing driver

1

Safety—that's the biggest change I've seen in racing, that and speed. But the safety's made the speed a whole lot more comfortable. I'd rather crash one of these cars at 200 m.p.h. than the ones we ran years ago at 150. Even though the speeds are very high, I feel that the cars are five times as safe as they used to be.

Los Angeles Times, 8-6:(III)3.

A. Bartlett Giamatti
Commissioner-designate
of Baseball

2

[Another baseball strike would be] a misfortune for everyone, not just the owners and players. It would damage the people's trust in their institutions and the ability of groups in the public eye to surmount narrow self-interest... My influence [over baseball] will be what I make it, and I can't say for sure what that will be. My charge is to preserve the integrity of the game. That's the basis for the prosperity of all the actors, you know, and if both sides keep it in mind it should help them work things out.

Interview,
Scottsdale, Ariz./
The Wall Street Journal,
3-10:(A)12.

A. Bartlett Giamatti
Commissioner of Baseball

3

[On the moral responsibility of players]: Whether you like it or not, people will see you as a hero. If you really don't want to assume those burdens, you should go and do your best imitation of Mr. Thoreau. It's said that Americans build up their heroes to tear them down. But there's a responsibility to maintain that trust. I'm not sure heroes don't tear themselves down because there's so much pressure on them. You have a burden and glories from having achieved a certain level, and you can't shuck off the burdens.

Interview, April/
Newsweek, 9-11:49.

4

[On baseball fans]: Some people come to watch and cherish the esthetics of the game and to pass it on to the next generation. For some, the occasion is an event to see friends, to smoke and drink and emulate the energy on the field. Then there is a hard core of goons who belong to neither group, and that's the trouble. The street has invaded the garden, and those who seek the sanctuary of the enclosed green space are bringing in all that from which they're trying to get away.

Interview, April/
Newsweek, 9-11:49.

5

[On whether new baseball expansion teams would dilute the quality of play]: Hitting a major-league fastball is perhaps the most difficult act in American sport . . . Major-league baseball players of the kind of quality the American people have had every right to expect since 1876 are scarce items. To expand is not to say that they will degrade the quality. [But] one must be responsible, deliberate and prudent.

Washington, Aug. 2/
The Washington Post, 8-3:(B)3.

6

If we have known freedom, then we love it; if we love freedom, then we fear, at some level— individually or collectively—its loss. And then we cherish sport. As our forebears did, we remind ourselves through sport of what, here on earth, is our noblest hope. Through sport, we re-create our daily portion of freedom, in public.

At University of Michigan Law School/
Newsweek, 11-6:88.

Steven Gillers
Professor,
New York University
Law School

7

[On the scheduled hearing before the baseball commissioner regarding Cincinnati *Reds* manager Pete Rose's alleged betting on games, which is not permitted by baseball's rules]: Baseball

(STEVEN GILLERS)

rules, as I see them, are pre-Magna Carta; even the most elemental due-process rights are not guaranteed. If this were a public matter, it would require a guarantee of due process. But due process is not involved here in a hearing before the commissioner. Due process binds government, not private industry.

June 22/The New York Times,
6-23:(B)14.

Ed Goren
Producer, CBS coverage of
college football's
Heisman Trophy
award ceremony

1

[The Heisman] is the most recognizable trophy in all of sports. If you lined up the Super Bowl trophy, the World Series trophy, all the major trophies, the Heisman is the one. No matter what happens, one thing you can never take away is the tradition. The winners of the Heisman become part of the specialness that is the tradition of the trophy.

Los Angeles Times, 8-29:(III)6.

Dallas Green
Baseball manager,
New York "Yankees"

2

[On pitching]: Throwing strikes is mental. If you get used to throwing them, you'll throw them. If you get used to throwing balls, you'll throw balls.

June 6/The New York Times,
6-7:(B)11.

Dennis Green
Football coach,
Stanford University

3

My idea is to look for the best student who is the best football player. Some places take an easier way, and look for the best student who may not be quite the best player; others look for the best player even if he's not a good student. But I think Stanford, with a whole country to choose from, can find both bests.

News conference,
Stanford, Calif., Jan 3/
The New York Times, 1-4:(B)8.

Ron Heller
Football player,
Philadelphia "Eagles"

4

Training camp is the absolute worst time in your life. You start dreading it a month before. You count the Saturdays you have left before you report. Then you count the days, the hours. It's wake up, eat, practice, eat, practice, eat, go to meetings, go to bed. It gets old real quick. You're sore, your head aches, there's almost no spare time. You come out of a shower and try to shake your head dry, and it hurts, just from hitting all the time. And people think it's just a physical game, but we spend hours in the classroom, too. So we're mentally and physically drained. The good part is that you're with a lot of funny people.

Interview/The Washington Post,
9-1:(F)14.

Orel Hershiser
Baseball pitcher,
Los Angeles "Dodgers"

5

[On criticism of his new contract which will pay him $7.9-million over three years]: I don't feel there's greed involved. I think it's do the best you can. You're only worth as much as they'll pay you. Since we got to where we agreed on a contract, I guess that's what I'm worth. It's supply-and-demand economics. I know the numbers break new ground, but what I did on the field and what the *Dodgers* did broke new ground last year. Even when 7.6 [million dollars] was on the table, it's still "Do the best you can." If you're negotiating at 50 cents and they get to 75 cents and you know they have a dollar in their pocket, are you supposed to stop?

Interview,
Vero Beach, Fla./
The New York Times, 2-21:(B)11.

(OREL HERSHISER)

1

You can't take home your won-loss record, your earned-run average or your innings-pitched numbers. You hope you still have your friends and you are financially secure enough to move on to the next step of life. Otherwise, all you have when you leave the game [retire] is a bunch of people who will pat you on the back and say: "I remember when . . ." That would be sad.

Interview,
Vero Beach, Fla./
The Wall Street Journal,
3-15:(A)10.

Larry Holmes
Former heavyweight boxing
champion of the world

2

I fought Mike Tyson with a broke right hand. I fought "Bonecrusher" Smith with a broke hand. I fought David Bey with a broke hand. Man, I've had so many problems with this thumb, I've asked the doctors to cut it off. But they won't . . . I fought Michael Spinks with a slipped disk in my neck. I fought Kenny Norton with my left biceps pulled off my arm. I fought Muhammad Ali with eight stitches in my eye. I fought Leroy Jones with a twisted ankle. Man, I've fought with fevers, stomachaches, everything. But, you know, you've got to do it. The opportunity to pick yourself up a few million dollars doesn't come often. It's like a once-in-a-lifetime dream.

Interview/
The Washington Post,
2-22:(A)1.

Kelly Hrudey
Hockey player,
Los Angeles "Kings"

3

The hockey world speaks of loyalty, but sooner or later you find out that the only responsibility you have is to get as much money as you can and play the game as well as you can. Loyalty doesn't exist.

Interview/The New York Times,
2-27:(B)11.

Jim Irsay
Vice president and
general manager,
Indianapolis "Colts"
football team

4

[On the use of instant replays for officiating close or controversial plays]: Every poll shows that the football public is overwhelmingly in favor [of the replays]. After a close play on the field, the first thing the fan says is, "Let's check the instant replay . . ." If we [owners] throw out replay officiating now after it's become part of the game, there will be a national uproar if a team misses the Super Bowl on a bad call that could have been corrected.

At National Football League
convention, Palm Desert, Calif.,
March 19/
Los Angeles Times, 3-20:(III)4.

5

[Criticizing a new NFL rule barring fans from making too much noise if it interferes with the visiting team's play]: Our concern is: What is too loud? . . . When you are dealing with the fans, it is difficult to try to calm their enthusiasm. I have received letters from season ticket-holders saying if they can't yell, they would rather sit home and watch the game on TV . . . Even when the crowd is against you on the road and yelling, that's what makes the game great.

The Washington Post, 9-6:(G)10.

Jimmy Johnson
Football coach,
University of Miami

6

We ask our players to be the best, to be intense for 60 minutes of a football game. How can someone criticize me for playing hard? I don't want [the players] to let up [even when they're winning big]. It's not that we want to embarrass [the other team], but we run our offense, we're going to do the best that we can do. When I was at Oklahoma State and Nebraska was putting up 50 and 60 points against me, they still kept running that power sweep. That's their offense. We pass

(JIMMY JOHNSON)

the football. Like it or not, that's how we play, and we'll keep on playing that way.

Interview, Miami/
The Washington Post,
1-4:(C)6.

Tom Kite
Golfer

1

The prize money we [golfers] are playing for is so out of line compared with what the players were playing for just a few years ago. Just go back to 1981 and I was the leading money winner with $376,000. But now I make that in two weeks. It shows you how things can change so much. I have trouble believing the dollar amounts we're playing for right now. I think most players do. We keep knocking on wood, hoping it keeps up, and pinch ourselves every day to make sure we're not dreaming.

Interview/The New York Times,
4-3:(B)16.

Bowie Kuhn
Former Commissioner
of Baseball

2

The Rose matter [the scandal involving Cincinnati manager Pete Rose's alleged gambling on baseball games] just reinforces the need for baseball to always be on guard. Baseball would be naive if it thinks that it's not possible to fix games. But no matter what baseball does, I think we will see the time when some games are fixed. It's unavoidable.

Interview/Los Angeles Times,
7-30:(III)7.

Tony La Russa
Baseball manager,
Oakland "Athletics"

3

You come up to the plate when the season starts. You get to first when you are in contention in September. You get to second and in scoring position when you win the division title. You get to third when you win the pennant. And you get to home, you score, when you win the World Series.

Interview,
Oakland, Calif./
USA Today,
10-3:(E)4.

Tom Lasorda
Baseball manager,
Los Angeles "Dodgers"

4

[On whether his players are trying enough this year to win]: Trying's not important. Truck drivers could try. If I brought truck drivers in, sat them down and told them I was going to pay them $800,000 a year, they'd try from 3 a.m. to midnight. I don't want tryers. I want doers. Try, hell. For $800,000 a year, I'd wrestle piranhas.

Interview/
Los Angeles Times,
8-14:(III)2.

Frank Layden
Former basketball coach,
Utah "Jazz"

5

[On fan abuse of teams during games]: It's bad, and it's getting worse. When it comes to basketball crowds, we're a banana republic. I don't know why that is; maybe it's modern life. A man can't yell at his boss and he can't control his kids, so he comes to a game and takes it out on us. And we can't go after him, so it's safe, like making fun of the animals at the zoo. Hey, if the loudmouths knew the gorillas could get out, they'd treat them with more respect.

The Wall Street Journal,
1-13:(A)9.

Abe Lemons
Basketball coach,
Oklahoma City University

6

Doctors bury their mistakes. Coaches still have theirs on scholarship.

Los Angeles Times, 7-31:(III)2.

Valerie C. Lorenz
Executive director,
National Center for
Pathological Gambling

1

What distresses me really is the way state lotteries have expanded—the tremendous amount of advertising that they do and the new games they're constantly coming up with. For instance, Oregon has now come up with a game on the NFL. It is really encouraging our young people, especially our young males, to gamble on a combination of state lottery and football games. It is making the state a legalized bookmaker.

Interview/
USA Today, 8-28:(A)11.

Dan Marino
Football player,
Miami "Dolphins"

2

[Saying success on the field begins with the mind]: When you have a chance to win the game, you've got to have that takeover attitude. That's the kind of thing that has to grow with a team. I think it has to grow from the beginning, so that's the way everybody has to look at it going into the season. A lot of games last year—we were in a position to win and we didn't. And it might have been because of this attitude thing. The last few years we'd walk on the field for some games and we'd feel maybe we can win, maybe we can't.

Interview/USA Today, 7-31:(C)3.

Gene Mauch
Former baseball manager,
California "Angels"

3

Good offensive bunting changes defenses and can change the momentum of a game . . . In a close game, a bunt can change everything. If you have a lead base runner at second and a guy at the plate who can bunt, you're not just talking about a percentage play but the ability to divide a pitcher's attention and maybe start to wear him down.

The New York Times,
9-4:(A)31.

Tim McCarver
Baseball announcer;
Former player

4

[On baseball commissioner A. Bartlett Giamatti's barring Cincinnati *Reds* manager Pete Rose from baseball for life for Rose's betting on baseball games]: From day one as a player, the danger of betting on baseball is something that's pounded and pounded into your head. If I do it, or anyone does it, you have to be prepared to suffer the consequences. People who portrayed Giamatti as being an ogre in this situation were being absurd. He has to protect the integrity of baseball. He's a very fair man, but he's tough-minded and a traditionalist to the first degree. That's why he was named commissioner in the first place.

Interview, Aug. 24/
The New York Times, 8-25:(B)9.

Joe McIlvaine
Vice president for baseball
operations, New York "Mets"
baseball club

5

When you take players from the amateur rank, whether it's high school or the best major college in the country, the most important thing to do is assume they know nothing. Start from scratch. Because you soon find out that you're going to be right most times. Most of these kids, despite their amateur background, have big gaps in their [baseball] education. They may know how to do one thing, but no one has taught them even how to grip the baseball . . . You have to start from the beginning. You see some of these kids who think they know everything . . . And you get a good instructor there, and five minutes later they're sitting there and they're enthralled because they realize they haven't heard this stuff before.

Interview/The New York Times,
9-21:(B)11.

Art McNally
Supervisor of game officials,
National Football League

6

[On game officiating]: Once the game begins it's a war, and your only true friends are the other

(ART McNALLY)

guys in that seven-man officiating crew. You're in the game, doing a service that you literally love, or else you would not survive. It's natural that, in an emotional game, there are going to be outbursts. If you're working a game and you know you're doing a good job, you shut everything else out. You learn to live with it. If you can't, then I hope I find out real quick.

Interview, New York/
USA Today, 9-8:(E)4.

Jon Miller
Broadcaster,
Baltimore "Orioles"
baseball club

1

[Comparing TV and radio broadcasts of baseball games]: I think you can get a more vivid picture listening to a well-done radio broadcast than watching a telecast. On a telecast, you can only see a few things; on radio, you see the whole field . . . When you're at a game, the first thing that ever hits you as a kid is a guy hits a popup and it goes 3,000 feet in the air. Major-league popups are astounding. You never see that on TV. On radio, you can help somebody visualize the fly ball.

The Washington Post,
3-31:(B)2.

Martina Navratilova
Tennis player

2

[Tennis] is a game and it is to be enjoyed, not endured. If you have to endure it, then you shouldn't be playing. It has become apparent that I have touched people's lives through tennis. Some people are not even tennis players, but I inspire them to do better at what they do, whether it's losing weight or quitting smoking or doing better on their job. I get letters [that tell me] even though I lost that match, I did something good for somebody.

Interview/
Los Angeles Times,
8-6:(III)8.

James B. Noel
Assistant counsel,
National Football League

3

[Criticizing the Oregon Lottery's new plan allowing betting on NFL games]: If Oregonians turn from being fans interested in whether their favorite teams win or lose games into gamblers concerned about whether they win or lose bets, the nature of public interest in our sport changes. As the question, "Who won?" is replaced by, "Did they cover the point spread?" fans become cynical. Close or controversial plays that have always been know as "the breaks of the game" invariably become fuel for suspicion about whether "the fix was in."

July 17/The New York Times,
7-18:(A)1.

Keith Olbermann
Sportscaster, KCBS-TV,
Los Angeles

4

[On his humorous style of sportscasting]: Sports is an aspect of life that is sometimes poignant, sometimes sad, sometimes inspiring and sometimes it's funny. For years growing up watching sportscasters read off the scores, I never saw that. Then I read Jim Bouton's [book] *Ball Four* and it was a revelation. These were human beings, they weren't bubble-gum cards. They were people who did stupid things and played pranks . . .

Interview/
Los Angeles Times,
1-22:(Calendar)3.

Steve Ortmayer
Operations director,
San Diego "Chargers"
football team

5

I sometimes worry about the pressure [the media] put on the entire [NFL] organization. The whole system of the NFL media is that it thrives on strikes, on trades and on contract hassles. That's the thing that bugs me.

USA Today, 1-5:(C)8.

Dave Parker
Baseball player,
Oakland "Athletics";
Former player,
Cincinnati "Reds"

1

[On charges that Cincinnati *Reds* manager Pete Rose bet on baseball games, which is prohibited by baseball's rules]: Rose knew what the ramifications of gambling were. From day one, when you sign your first professional contract, Rule 21 [prohibiting betting on baseball] is preached to you. That's Number 1 in baseball's 10 commandments. Rose had no regard for the rules . . . I don't wish bad things on anybody. I'll just say this about Pete Rose: He's a bad person and things are coming back on him for the way he treated people like myself. This all happened because of all the people who got raw deals from Pete. I think he started believing all that people were writing about him, being larger than life and all.

USA Today, 6-30:(C)6.

Mike Reid
Golfer

2

Sports is like life with the volume up. The friendships are tighter, the laughter is louder and some nights seem a little longer.

Interview, Hawthorn Woods, Ill./
USA Today, 8-14:(C)6.

Jerry Rice
Football player,
San Francisco "49ers"

3

[On playing in the Super Bowl]: Some people say if you're scared, you should take off your uniform. But I feel like there's nothing wrong with being a little bit scared. I think you play your best football when you're scared.

Los Angeles Times, 1-20:(III)8.

Frank Robinson
Baseball manager,
Baltimore "Orioles"

4

I think getting to the World Series as a manager would be more enjoyable than as a player. As a

player, you control what you do and there's not much you can do about anyone else. As a manager, you're the one that pulls a whole team together and molds it into a winner. That's more satisfying than getting there as a player, and it's something I haven't accomplished.

Interview/The Washington Post,
6-21:(B)5.

John Rooney
Professor of geography,
Oklahoma State University

5

[On the growing popularity of golf]: There is evidence to suggest that many of the high-impact exercises—jogging, running, racquetball, handball—are either stagnant or declining. Golf is viewed as an alternative. You can commune with nature, get a decent amount of exercise, have fun and do some business on the side . . . Golf moved toward democratization in the 1960s. That's when more blue-collar and factory workers started to play. The catalyst for the shift was Arnold Palmer. He looked like a blacksmith, played the game with an aggressive flair and was charismatic. Palmer came from a rather spartan background. His success helped take the game out of the exclusive realm of the wealthy.

The New York Times, 9-4:(A)1.

Pete Rose
Baseball manager,
Cincinnati "Reds";
Former player

6

I've dealt with pressure for all of my playing career, and now as a manager. I thrive on pressure. I've never been asked a question I couldn't answer. I mean about baseball. I could talk all day long about baseball and it wouldn't be boring. That's because I know what I'm talking about. Or at least I think I do.

Interview, Cincinnati, April 3/
The New York Times, 4-4:(B)16.

7

[On charges that he bet on baseball games, which is prohibited by baseball's rules]: I've been

(PETE ROSE)

on the cover of *Time*. It took me 4,256 hits to get on the cover of *Time*. It took me 24 years to get on the cover of *Time*. And, all of a sudden, I'm accused of betting on baseball, and I'm on the cover again. The easiest part of my job is coming to the ballpark. It's harder to relax at home watching those TV shows [about him]. I've had friends call me and thought I died because [they were] sitting there watching Tom Brokaw on NBC News, and all of a sudden my picture's up there. They hear him say, "He may have managed his last game." They say, "What happened to him, his plane crash or something?" No, they think he bet on a baseball game.

Interview,
Cincinnati, July 27/
Los Angeles Times, 7-28:(III)1.

1

[On charges that he bet on baseball games, which is prohibited by baseball's rules]: It was a hatchet job, a piece of crap. If people think this is all bad for baseball, I just want them to know: It ain't my fault. I didn't start this thing. I just want a fair hearing. If I get a fair shake, I will prove everybody wrong. Believe me . . . I think everybody in this world, you can find a little bit of dirt on anybody—if you want to dig enough. Whether it's what he does off the field, or the way he has sex—you know, anything. I mean, and there's a lot of people out there, no matter what I did, they wouldn't like it. Because they don't like me.

Interview,
Cincinnati/
The Washington Post, 7-31:(B)6.

Al Rosen
President and general manager,
San Francisco "Giants"
baseball club

2

Any business is interested in turning a profit. But this one is mostly about winning. Trying to do both, you have anxieties and pressures.

Interview, Chicago/
USA Today, 10-3:(E)11.

3

When you stand up at the plate, there are nine guys waiting to get you out; it's the loneliest place in the world. But the thing is, great hitters love that and need that; that's the place they most want to be in the world.

The New York Times, 10-4:(B)14.

Ron Rothstein
Basketball coach,
Miami "Heat"

4

[On losing streaks]: You have to look at the big picture . . . The pressure is natural. You always impose it upon yourself. It's got to be kept in perspective, and that's the toughest thing I've had to do. The hardest thing any coach has to do. In most places, you lose 12 in a row, and you're fired. Here, you lose 12 in a row, and you're building. I lose 12 in a row next year, and I get fired; I don't know.

The Washington Post, 1-12:(B)4.

Darrell Royal
Former football coach,
University of Texas

5

A head [college football] coach is guided by one primary objective—to dig, claw, wheedle, coax that fanatical effort out of his players. He wants his team to play on Saturday as if they were planting the flag on Iwo Jima.

Los Angeles Times, 9-9:(III)2.

Pete Rozelle
Commissioner,
National Football League

6

[On instant replays]: I think we [in football] have the most complex rules in sports, very complicated. And so many of them. And when you have seven men trying to get a perfect angle on seeing what happens on every play involved, it's a very difficult situation . . . If you have a key call made, that was clearly established in instant replay, I'd like to see that corrected.

State of the League address, Miami,
Jan. 20/Los Angeles Times, 1-21:(III)8.

447

(PETE ROZELLE)

1

Obviously our [the NFL's] lack of a black head coach does concern me, but in some ways we have a great track record. We were the first to integrate in sports, the first to have a black game official, and the first to have a minority officer in a key role. We recommend black coaches to teams that have openings and encourage them to interview them. We don't have the hiring we would like to see, but we can't dictate anything.

News conference, Miami, Jan. 20/
The New York Times, 1-21:36.

2

[Calling for unscheduled testing of players throughout the season for steroid use]: Candidly, I cannot guarantee that our [current policy of] testing [only at training camp before the season begins] has detected, or will detect, every steroid-user in the NFL... With any drug there is always a hard core of people who will not stop using. For this hard core, [random] testing and the promise of disciplinary action appear to be the only meaningful answer.

Before Senate Judiciary Committee,
Washington, May 9/
The New York Times,
5-10:(B)11.

Nolan Ryan
Baseball pitcher,
Texas "Rangers"

3

I'm a strikeout pitcher and have always been a strikeout pitcher. But when people say I [go] for strikeouts because they are the most important thing to me, more important even than to win, that's bull. I mean, do you realize how many pitches I've thrown, how many times I would have liked to get the out with one rather than the three or four necessary for a strikeout? It comes down to the fact the people like to categorize pitchers. But I've never started a game thinking I wanted to strike out 10 or 15 batters. Those figures only represent the stuff I had on that particular night.

Interview,
Arlington, Texas/
Los Angeles Times, 8-29:(III)4.

Bo Schembechler
Football coach,
University of Michigan

4

If you win all the time, maybe you don't have as much appreciation for it. The thing that has balanced out my career is the fact that I haven't been as successful in bowls. If I had the same record I had in bowls as I do in the regular season, I'd probably be too cocky and have too big an ego.

Interview/Los Angeles Times,
1-2:(III)11.

Marge Schott
President,
Cincinnati "Reds"
baseball club

5

I don't think fans relate sports with unions and strikes. I wonder how many of them we've turned off [with high player salaries and economic problems]. It's pretty tough for the average individual to relate to a star making $2-million. I just hope we don't get to the point where we lose it in the small towns, because fans in the stands are very important to us. That's all we have. Owners have to use restraint.

USA Today, 1-6:(C)3.

Richard Schultz
Executive director,
National Collegiate
Athletic Association

6

A lot of people want to say that drugs are unique to athletics or that cheating is unique to athletics. Every problem that we have is societal. You can look at society and you can see the same things. In fact, we [in sports] have probably done a heck of a lot better job in solving our drug problem than society has. We've probably done a lot better job of solving most of our problems than society has. I'm not going to say that we don't have problems—we do have—but about 97 per cent of everything that's going on today in intercollegiate athletics is very good and very positive. But because of the tremendous visibility

(RICHARD SCHULTZ)

of athletics, a prominent school goes on probation and the impression is, everybody's doing it and it's widespread. Or if we have one athlete that tests positive for drugs—even though maybe we tested thousands and that the rate is like 1½ per cent, which is unbelievably low in today's society—people will get the impression that everybody's doing it. That's just not the case.

Interview, San Francisco/
Los Angeles Times, 1-17:(III)5.

Tom Seaver
Former baseball pitcher,
New York "Mets"

1

I used to get asked if baseball was still fun for me. Well, that's an over-simplified question. Baseball meant a lot to me beyond just fun. But I viewed going to All-Star games as fun in the purest sense. It's one of the most enjoyable experiences you can have as a player. It's a lighter moment when you can show off your talent and it doesn't go on your permanent record. Basically, it is a show. You have to remember that.

Interview/Los Angeles Times,
7-7:(III)3.

Fred Snowden
Former basketball coach,
University of Arizona

2

When I look back [at being a coach], what I miss most are the associations. The friendships and the great camaraderie that exists between players and coaches, and between a coach and other coaches. And I miss the unique kinds of challenges that coaching presents. As a coach, your report card is marked instantly, that night. You know that night whether you did well or not. They put it up in lights on a scorecard. I miss the immediacy of that, the instant decision-making process that you live with all the time as a coach. Corporate decisions [in the non-sports sector] don't quite work that way. There are meetings and management groups and eventually you

come to a decision, but it doesn't always happen right away. As a coach, you call a timeout and you see the players walking back toward the bench and you know that you had better come up with an idea, and a very good idea, before they get there. That's a lot of pressure. That is very unique in the world.

Interview/Los Angeles Times,
8-9:(III)9.

Willie Stargell
Former baseball player,
Pittsburgh "Pirates"

3

[On being inducted into the Baseball Hall of Fame]: Even as a little boy playing baseball, you know about the Hall of Fame—Ruth, Cobb, Gehrig. It's special, something hard to describe. Everybody thinks about it, but when you stand up on that platform [at the induction ceremony], there is nothing in your career that can equal the feeling.

USA Today, 1-10:(C)2.

George Steinbrenner
Owner,
New York "Yankees"
baseball club

4

[On players who complain about criticism of their performance]: These guys are a bunch of little babies. We've got guys earning $2-million a year, and they don't want criticism. Try telling that to the cab driver, policeman or fireman in New York, and see what he thinks. If they [the players] don't like it, it's too bad. They're in the oven; if they can't stand the heat, then it's time to get out and get into something else.

Interview, Tampa, Fla., May 18/
The New York Times, 5-19:(B)13.

5

When [former Baseball Commissioner] Peter Ueberroth said some time ago baseball was now free of the drug problem, I could not go along with that. Whether we've made more progress than any other sport, I can't say. [But] the problem is

WHAT THEY SAID IN 1989

there. I know we've made progress, but this isn't just a baseball problem. It's the most serious problem facing the entire nation today.

Interview/USA Today, 7-3:(C)3.

Barry Switzer
Football coach,
University of Oklahoma

1

[There is] a public commitment on my part to join with other coaches around the country who are calling for changes in rules to permit universities to provide [their football] players with reasonable [financial] assistance, perhaps based on financial need as proposed by Dick Schultz, executive director of the NCAA. The time has come to change a system where coaches must choose between abiding by certain rules [which prohibit aid above the scholarships limits] or acting like caring individuals. We made the rules and we can change them . . . We have created a system that does not permit me or the program to buy a pair of shoes or a decent coat for a player whose family can't afford these basic necessities.

The Washington Post, 6-21:(B)3.

Syd Thrift
Former director,
Kansas City "Royals"
Baseball Academy

2

Baseball is the only business with no research and development. There have to be better ways to achieve a higher percentage of success in developing high-school and college players. Players at all levels are receptive to things that make sense. I'm talking about the utilization of video for instruction, not normal video but video with overlays. We're on the verge of big breakthroughs on that. I'm talking about time-measured leads, about a knowledge of the aerodynamics of a baseball in flight, how you translate that into everyday common sense to help a pitcher know what the value of a four-seam and two-seam fastball is and to know when to throw them . . . The young players today want to know anything and

everything that will make them better. They get turned off by stories about the past. They are thirsting for knowledge.

Interview/The New York Times,
1-2:31.

Gene Upshaw
Executive director,
National Football League
Players Association

3

We've [the players union] been well led. It's that our situation is difficult. We've been forced to conclude agreements out of weakness rather than conviction. Take average career length. Ours is just over three years, the shortest in sports. That means we risk more by striking— and go into strikes weaker—than any other players' union. Another thing is that NFL teams don't play that often, so our members don't get to know guys on other teams the way people in other sports do. The worst parts for us are that owners share equally in about 90 per cent of league revenues, and that stadiums are full in most cities every football Sunday. We're not only dealing with a monopoly, but one where there's little internal competition.

Interview, Washington/
The Wall Street Journal, 1-17:(A)20.

Jim Walden
Football coach,
Iowa State University

4

[On players' use of steroids to build strength]: There is nothing like football. Football is the only game where you organize vigilance. You need strength, speed and an assassin's type mentality to succeed. So, [University of Colorado] *Buffaloes* cannot be allowed to become larger *Buffaloes* through drugs. Giving them a physical advantage like that is dangerous.

Los Angeles Times, 9-9:(III)10.

Bill Walsh
Former football coach,
San Francisco "49ers"

5

The style of football being played [today] is more of a running, moving, throwing type of

(BILL WALSH)

game. There's less of the pocket passing going on. Many of the universities with the most acceptable programs are not developing their quarterbacks. Certainly, Miami has done that, but there aren't that many others that really utilize our style of football. Fewer and fewer quarterbacks each year are coming out, and fewer we can look to train.

USA Today, 4-21:(C)6.

John Wathan
Baseball player,
Kansas City "Royals"

1

Contrary to what the public probably thinks, most pitchers do not want to call their own game. They like to be led [by the catcher]. They like to be told what to do, by somebody who knows exactly what he's doing. They want the decision-making left up to somebody else, while they just make the deliveries.

Interview, Haines City, Fla./
Los Angeles Times, 3-19:(III)12.

Tom Watson
Golfer

2

[On his current slump]: Some guys think my swing's the same, that I just haven't been making the putts like I did when I was winning. But it's more than that. It's part of being an athlete in any sport. It's losing that touch and feel.

Interview, Harrison, N.Y./
The New York Times, 6-9:(B)15.

Reggie Williams
Football player,
Cincinnati "Bengals";
Cincinnati City Councilman

3

As much as I feel good about the Super Bowl XVI experience [in 1982] . . . it's one that I sometimes wake up in a cold sweat about because we lost. And that losing is one of the worst memories I have in my athletic life . . . the dismal

realization that we had lost, that it was over, that there was no time on the clock, that our great comeback of the second half was still a touchdown short.

Interview, Cincinnati/
USA Today, 1-11:(C)8.

4

I've always felt good about how the popularity of professional football has created a forum for the way an athlete can be a benefit to the community. Every honor I receive creates a mandate for me. The two—[being a member of the City] Council and football—have complemented each other. I have to do well at both, so there will be no skeptics.

Interview, Miami/
The New York Times, 1-21:35.

Mookie Wilson
Baseball player,
Toronto "Blue Jays"

5

It means everything to me [to play every day]. I was always asked in New York [where he played for the *Mets*, but not on an everyday basis] if I'd rather be a platoon player with the *Mets* or an every-day player with [a less prestigious club like] an Atlanta or a Seattle. I always answered the latter, and that amazed people. But I'm not a spectator. And I could never be a *fan* of baseball; I've got to be on the field. And hey, look, I mess up out there, more even than people notice. But that's where I have to be, win, lose or draw. People are wrapped up in winning, and they believe everything should take a back seat to it. If you are talking about individual numbers and statistics, that's probably right. But playing every day is not just a personal statistic. It's much more than that. It's what helped make my life happy.

Interview, Toronto/
The New York Times, 9-20:(B)11.

Charles Yesalis
Professor of health policy and
administration, exercise and sports
science, Pennsylvania State University

6

[On the use of steroids by athletes]: Some members of the sports-medicine community

451

(CHARLES YESALIS)

have, with the best of intentions, adopted a conservative strategy and used strong, but often unfounded, pronouncements emphasizing the adverse, particularly permanent and lethal, health effects of anabolic steroids. Athletes, on the other hand, have simply not witnessed longtime anabolic-steroid users dropping like flies. This aggressive health-education strategy does not seem to have had any major impact on the use of steroids . . . There likely is a concern by some that if, in fact, no deleterious long-term effects are identified, the use of anabolic steroids would increase further, while the moral issue of fair play would remain . . . To move toward a solution to this problem, sacrifices—measured by fewer victories and lost revenues—will probably have to be made by athletes, academic institutions and sports federations. Anabolic steroids work too well to believe otherwise.

At conference at Amateur Athletic Association, July 30/ Los Angeles Times, 7-31:(III)2.

Don Zimmer
Baseball manager, Chicago "Cubs"

1

I do what I want to do. If I get fired [some day], I want it to be because I was doing what I think I should be doing, not because I was doing what my general manager or some writer or some fans think I should be doing.

Interview, Chicago/ USA Today, 10-3:(E)14.

The Indexes

Index to Speakers

A

Abalkin, Leonid I., 263
Abbott, Berenice, 329
Abbott, Diane, 154
Abrahamson, James, 70
Abrams, Elliott, 218
Abramson, Jerry, 180
abu Sharif, Bassam, 309
Adams, Gordon, 70
Adedeji, Adebayo, 210
Adelman, Kenneth L., 70
Advani, Lal Kishanchand, 240
Afanasyev, Yuri, 263
Aganbegyan, Abel, 263
Aguilar Zinser, Adolfo, 218
Ahtisaari, Martti, 210
Akhromeyev, Sergei F., 70, 240, 264
Albee, Edward, 404
Alexander, Lamar, 101
Alexis, Marcus, 22
Alfonsin, Raul, 219
Amaker, Norman, 22
Ameche, Don, 380
Amin, Mustafa, 309
Anderson, Glenn M., 176
Anderson, Sparky, 435
Andrews, Julie, 393
Aoun, Michel, 309
Applegate, Douglas, 14
Aquino, Corazon C., 240
Arafat, Yasir, 309-310
Arbatov, Georgi A., 185, 240, 264
Archer, Jeffrey, 350
Archey, William T., 264
Arens, Moshe, 185, 310
Arias, Oscar, 185, 219
Arias Calderon, Ricardo, 219
Arkin, William M., 128
Arledge, Roone, 342
Armacost, Michael H., 34, 241
Armstrong, Neil A., 431
Aronson, Bernard W., 219-220
Arsht, Leslye, 149
Ashe, Arthur, 435
Asoyan, Boris A., 210
Aspin, Les, 70, 210
Atkins, Chester G., 128, 241
Atwater, Lee, 22, 154

Atwood, Donald J., 128
Atwood, Margaret, 22, 350
AuCoin, Les, 128, 329
Auster, Paul, 350
Awad, Mubarak, 310
Aziz, Tarik, 311

B

Bagdikian, Ben, 34
Bahr, Egon, 264
Bailey, F. Lee, 149
Bailey, Thomas, 84
Bailey, Wilford S., 101
Baka, Wladyslaw, 265
Baker, James A., III, 71, 128, 185-187, 210-211, 220-221, 241-242, 265-266, 311-312
Baker, Pauline, 211
Baker, William, 431
Bakes, Phil, 176
Baliles, Gerald L., 34, 84, 266, 362
Ball, George, 34
Barco Vargas, Virgilio, 55
Barenboim, Daniel, 393
Barko, Jim, 55
Barnes, John, 267
Barnes, Julian, 350
Barnet, Richard, 187
Barnett, A. Doak, 242
Bar-On, Hanan, 312
Barr, Roseanne, 380
Barry, Marion, 55
Barth, John 350
Bartlett, David Conant, 342
Baryshnikov, Mikhail, 404
Batkin, Leonid, 187
Batten, James, 342
Baucus, Max, 34
Bauer, Gary, 128
Bausch, Pina, 404
Bavasi, Buzzie, 435
Bays, Karl D., 35
Beck, Paul Allen, 154
Behan, Neil J., 55
Beilenson, Anthony C., 84, 154
Beilin, Yossi, 312
Belcher, Tim, 435
Bell, Daniel, 413, 425

Index to Subjects

A

Abdul-Jabbar, Kareem, 439:2
Ability, 424:2
Abortion—*see* Women
Abrams, Elliott, 197:2
Accomplishing one's desires, 423:6
Acheson, Dean, 185:5, 198:4
Acquired immune deficiency syndrome (AIDS)—
  see Medicine
Acting/actors:
  characteristics of characters played,
    387:3
  characters/roles, 380:4
    analyzing a character, 390:3
  comedy, 383:3
  doing aspect, 384:1
  exposing yourself, 385:3
  good/bad actor, 388:4
  judging own material, 380:1
  luck aspect, 388:2
  Method School, 383:5
  need love and protection, 385:7
  pretending, 383:5, 384:1
  process of, 391:5
  selfish profession, 383:2
  sex appeal, 388:2
  sponges, actors are, 382:1
  stage/theatre, 404:1, 406:4, 407:2, 407:3,
    407:4, 408:4
  stars/celebrities, 386:5, 387:3, 391:2, 391:4,
    392:3
  studio system, 391:3
  technical aspect, 381:6
  television, 375:5, 378:3
  and writers, 391:1
Advertising—*see* Commerce
Afghanistan:
  Communism, 248:4
  multi-nationality, 255:1
  Najibullah, 259:3
  rebels, 248:4, 254:1, 259:3, 259:4
  foreign relations/policy with:
    Soviet Union, 203:4, 209:1, 240:2, 240:6,
      254:1, 254:6, 258:7, 259:3, 259:4,
      259:5, 259:6, 260:3
    U.S., 240:6, 248:4, 254:1
Africa, pp. 210-217
  education and health, 210:1

Africa *(continued)*
  population, 210:1
  shattered world, 216:4
  foreign relations/policy with:
    Europe, colonization by, 216:4
    Soviet Union, 203:4
  See also specific African countries
Agriculture/farming, 54:1, 54:2
Air transportation—*see* Transportation
Alaska, 118:4
Albanese, Licia, 396:1
Alcohol—*see* Medicine: drug abuse
Ali, Muhammad, 439:2, 442:2
Alvarez, A., 351:4
America/U.S.:
  benevolent, 21:3
  century, American, 18:5
  cooperative aspect, 16:6
  decay, 20:1
  decision-making system, 20:3
  diversity, 14:3
  dominant country, 16:4
  ethics, 20:4
  excellence as goal, 188:4
  flag desecration, 14:1, 14:2, 14:5, 14:6, 15:1,
    15:2, 15:3, 15:4, 16:2, 16:3, 16:5, 16:7,
    17:2, 17:4, 17:5, 18:1, 18:2, 18:3, 21:1
  freedom, 16:1, 21:2
  I/us aspect, 19:3
  ignorance of world, 19:1
  industrious, 21:3
  kinder/gentler, 14:4
  leadership/decline, 17:1, 18:5, 20:2
  liars, nation of, 17:3
  memory, American, 19:2
  moral principle, 14:4
  past, recreation of, 19:4
  patriotism, 19:2
  religious aspect, 20:1, 428:1, 428:2
  resilience, 20:2
  success aspect, 19:4
  system isn't working, 20:3
  unease, 18:4
  unity, 14:3
  utopian society, 21:2
American Airlines—*see* Transportation: air
American Bar Association (ABA), 150:2
American scene, the, pp. 14-21

U

V

W

Wage, minimum—*see* Labor: wages
Walesa, Lech—*see* Poland
Wallace, George C., 25:3
War/peace, 195:5, 225:3, 416:4
  causes, 289:1, 416:3
  nuclear aspect, 185:1
  regional conflicts, 78:2, 82:4, 191:1, 209:1
  World War II, 281:1, 299:1, 304:3
Warming/greenhouse effect—*see* Environment: air
Warren, Earl, 129:5
Warsaw Pact—*see* Europe, Eastern: defense
Washington, D.C.:
  Congressional control of, 135:6
  drugs, 62:4, 63:2, 68:3
  as news center, 342:4
  statehood issue, 135:6
Wealth/rich, 417:2, 421:6, 422:5
Webster, Daniel, 145:1, 145:4
Welles, Orson, 382:5
Western civilization, 422:3
Whitman, Walt, 350:5
Williams, Mary Alice, 343:6
Williams, Tennessee, 406:5, 412:1
Wilson, Edmund, 354:1
Women/women's rights:
  abortion, 23:3, 27:2, 27:3, 29:3, 29:5, 32:2, 32:4, 33:3, 33:5
    Democratic Party (U.S.) aspect, 157:1
    Republican Party (U.S.) aspect, 156:4, 157:1
    Supreme Court, U.S., aspect, 28:1, 31:2, 32:6, 33:4
  conservatism, 157:6
  Democratic Party (U.S.) aspect, 157:1, 161:5
    See also abortion, *this section*
  education:
    college enrollment, 108:5
    learning skills, 111:1
    teachers, 107:6
  having it all, 423:6
  history, 30:4, 31:6
  home, staying at, 25:2
  Iran, 30:3

Women/women's rights: *(continued)*
  leadership, positions of, 28:2
  military aspect, 75:2
  motion pictures, 380:2, 385:5
  movement, women's:
    mainstream, 28:3
    power struggles in, 22:4
  National Women's Hall of Fame, 30:4
  newscasters, 343:6
  politics/voting, 157:6
    Republican Party, 161:5
  potential/role, 30:3
  progress, 32:1
  religion/ordination, 425:2, 430:2
  Republican Party (U.S.) aspect, 156:4, 157:1, 161:5
  on U.S. Supreme Court, 26:4
  working/jobs, 22:5, 25:2, 31:5, 32:3, 108:5, 175:5
  "Yes, you can," 242:5
World awakening, 419:1
World Health Organization (WHO)—*see* Medicine
Worst happens, 421:7
Wright, Jim—*see* Congress, U.S.: House: Speaker
Writing—*see* Journalism: newspapers; Literature; Motion pictures; Stage

X

Xerox Corp., 44:2

Y

Yemen, 200:5
Youth, 421:3
Yugoslavia, 290:3

Z

Zambia, 212:1
Zanuck, Darryl F., 380:1
Zealotry, 418:3
Zhao Ziyang—*see* China
Zimmer, Don, 437:3
Zola, Emile, 350:5